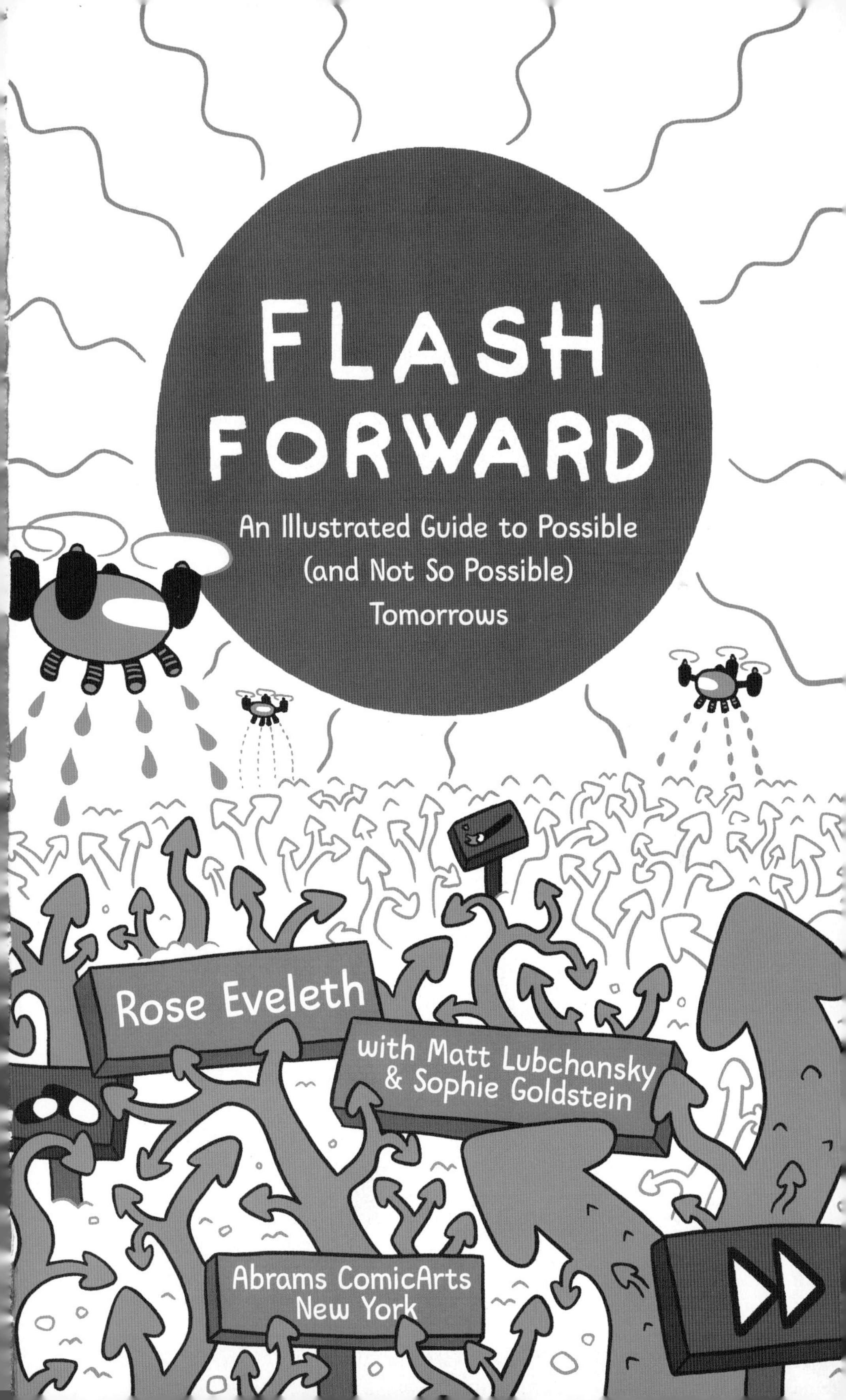
FLASH FORWARD
An Illustrated Guide to Possible (and Not So Possible) Tomorrows
Rose Eveleth
with Matt Lubchansky & Sophie Goldstein
Abrams ComicArts
New York

For Robert,
who makes my present possible
while I traipse about in the future.

"The only thing that makes life possible
is permanent, intolerable uncertainty:
not knowing what comes next."
–Ursula K. Le Guin,
The Left Hand of Darkness

CONTENTS

INTRODUCTION

I WANT TO TELL YOU SOMETHING ABOUT THE FUTURE.
It's something that's equal parts terrifying and liberating, ghastly and amazing, unnerving and wonderful. The thing I want to tell you about the future is this: It hasn't happened yet. This might seem obvious, but it's something we all could stand to remember as we're bombarded with advertisements and tech CEOs and certain so-called "futurists" claiming that this or that is definitely going to happen—that we're locked into an inevitable future, so we might as well fasten our seat belts and come along for the ride.

In a move that longtime listeners will likely recognize, I'd like to start this book about the future with a short trip into the past. Specifically, let's zip over to the year 1859. More than 150 years after Isaac Newton first published his book describing the laws of planetary motion, there was still one small thing that astronomers couldn't quite figure out: Mercury. While Newton's equations explained most of what they saw in the sky, the tiny white-hot rock looped around the sun faster than it should have. Something was messing with its orbit, but nobody could figure out what.

In the 1850s, a French astronomer named Urbain Le Verrier came up with a theory: a mysterious and elusive planet must exist between Mercury and the Sun. Le Verrier called the planet Vulcan, and for more than fifty years astronomers searched the sky for evidence of the planet, pointing to all kinds of specks and spots as proof that Vulcan existed. The *New York Times* wrote that Le Verrier's "discovery" of Vulcan "ought to be warmly welcomed by all astronomers."

Of course, there is no Vulcan. But it took a completely revolutionary set of equations to put the mythological planet to bed. In 1915, Albert Einstein published a series of papers outlining his Theory of General Relativity. As he was preparing to present the third paper in the series, Einstein decided to see whether his equations could explain this nagging mystery. When his calculations accurately predicted the procession of Mercury, he later told a friend that he was so excited he had heart palpitations and was "beside himself with joy."

In other words: A measurement made in the seventeenth century that seemed like a small, insignificant blip wound up being a key clue to the phenomenon that underpins our scientific understanding of the entire universe. "Einstein's pen destroyed Vulcan—and reimagined the cosmos," writes Thomas Levenson in his book *The Hunt for Vulcan*.

There are so many surprises like this one—realizations and reimaginings that unlock entire worlds of discovery. The ability to manipulate bacteria to cut up DNA strands was discovered in the 1990s, but it wasn't until a few years ago that CRISPR suddenly become a game-changing technology. Polyethylene—the most popular plastic in the world—was discovered by accident; nobody predicted it would become the most ubiquitous human-made material in the world.[1] The doctor who "discovered" the benefits of hand-washing in the 1840s was ridiculed and died in an asylum after nobody listened to him.

And of course, the reverse is true as well—things we think are incredibly important today might wind up being odd and embarrassing historical footnotes tomorrow. Many famous scientists at the turn of the twentieth century believed, for example, that mind reading was absolutely possible. Alexander Graham Bell may have invented the telephone in part to try to communicate with his dead brother. It's easy to find predictions gone badly wrong. One of my personal favorites comes from the 1906 book *A Hundred Years Hence: The Expectations of an Optimist*, which declares: "The plan of attaining the upper part of a small house by climbing, on every occasion, a sort of wooden hill, covered with carpet of questionable cleanliness, will of course have been abandoned: it is doubtful whether staircases will be built at all after the next two or three decades." We are constantly dropping stones into the pool of time, and which ones will sink and which will splash is often a mystery that can take decades to solve.

I often call myself a "futurologist," an admittedly dorky term that encompasses the many (sometimes tinfoil) hats that I wear. I study the future the way a melittologist studies bees by watching each buzzing insect closely and gathering data and trying to decipher it. I watch the people who try and map out the future (Futurists with a capital *F*, with their degrees in things like Strategic Foresight) and the science-fiction writers who try to tell stories about the future. But those are not the only bees in the hive of the future. I also watch the historians, the economists, the inventors, the biohackers, the mothers organizing UBI experiments, the disabled people hacking their bodies and equipment, and the farmers trying to learn new techniques and adapt to new technologies.

The future is not made exclusively by white men in black T-shirts who give TED Talks. The future is far more ornery and slippery than that. Sure, you're not Jeff Bezos or the CEO of a fossil fuel corporation,[2] and it would be absurd for me to tell you that you have the same kind of power and influence as they do. But what you do shapes the future, too. Your decisions for what to accept or not accept can shift the Overton Window, can push your local politicians to change their votes, and can convince your neighbors and friends to change their behavior. The world around us is the aggregate of our choices, and those choices matter. If they didn't, corporations and politicians wouldn't spend hundreds of billions of dollars a year to try to convince you to feel a certain way about companies, candidates, and issues.

---

1   To complicate things further, one historian told me that you could convincingly argue that "plastic saved the whales," since it was able to take the pressure off the giant mammals in our endless quest for whale products.

2   If you are, please read on and perhaps reconsider your plans.

Nobody knows exactly what will happen tomorrow, or in five, ten, and certainly not twenty years from now. Anybody who tells you that they do is lying. Perhaps to themselves, but definitely to you. And that's a very good thing. Because the minute we take the future for granted—as either impenetrable, a dead end, or simply out of our grasp—is the minute we give up our greatest power.

Corporations and leaders know this. A sense of inevitability is the dream of marketers and monarchs alike. If you convince people that there is no other way, no other possibility, you can sell them almost anything. Conversely, if you convince them that the work is done and that "the arc of the moral universe is long, but it bends toward justice" (a quote often attributed to Dr. Martin Luther King Jr., who in fact was quoting earlier pastors going back to 1853), you can get people to settle into a complacency and stop pushing for progress.

If they're not pushing the idea that the future is predestined, the powers that be often turn to another other quite effective tactic: fear. And there is plenty to fear right now. I write this as a global pandemic is fatally ripping through my country, and it will likely do the same to others sooner rather than later. Authoritarianism, endless wars, human rights abuses—the world is full of bleak trajectories. We sit on a precipice, a knife edge sharpened by climate change and inequality, and while we can point to graphs that predict global temperatures or income disparities, we don't know yet what exactly those numbers might mean for the nearly eight billion humans on the planet. But giving into fear is just as dangerous as throwing up our hands and assuming there's nothing we can do.

In 2006, a researcher named Gregory Berns replicated the famous Skinner Box experiment with humans. In one use of the original Skinner Box—constructed in the 1930s by psychologist B. F. Skinner—a rat learns that if a red light flashes, it's about to get an electric shock. The experiment was one of the pioneering pieces of research to show how operant conditioning works: animals learn to associate signals with rewards or punishments, and then even if the food or zap isn't present, they react to the signal as if it were. In the human version, Berns attached electrodes to the tops of people's feet and told them that they'd have to wait for the shock for up to thirty seconds. "For many people, the wait was worse than the shock," Berns writes in his book *Iconoclast*. In fact, almost a third of the people opted to get a bigger shock right away, rather than wait for the smaller shock later. Fear of the future, even when they knew exactly what that future held, made them react irrationally. Research suggests that fear and anxiety actually disrupt the function of the prefrontal cortex, which is where most of our decision-making processes happen.

And again, those who would like for us to consider the future beyond our grasp know this. In her book *The Origins of Totalitarianism*, Hannah Arendt writes: "A fundamental difference between modern dictatorships and all other tyrannies of the past is that terror is no longer used as a means to exterminate and frighten opponents, but as an instrument to rule masses of people who are perfectly obedient." We must not let leaders or corporations weaponize our fear of the future, even if that fear is well-founded. "People have always been good at imagining the end of the world, which is much easier to picture than the strange sidelong paths of change in a world without end," Rebecca Solnit writes in *Hope in the Dark*.

I am not asking you to have hope that the future will be better, only that it can be. And in fact, research suggests that simply imagining the future can change us for the better. Psychologists call the process of picturing the future "mental time travel," and it has been linked to happiness—people who regularly dream about and imagine the future are less stressed than those who don't. People suffering from depression often have a really hard time specifically picturing what might happen tomorrow, or the next day.

Imagining the future isn't just good for your squishy meatball brain, it's also crucial for making sure the future you want actually happens.[3] The author adrienne maree brown writes that "as long as the future comes from imagination, there will be divergent paths that are moving in and out of alignment, in and out of conflict." She goes on to say that we are locked in an "imagination battle" between those who favor the current structure of power and exploitation and those who want a different, more just world. We are all soldiers in this battle, and one of the ways we can fight is by taking imaginations seriously.

If we had listened to the future projections of climate scientists years ago, for example, we'd be far better off. If the Trump administration hadn't disbanded the team of experts who had, for years, been imagining and planning for a global pandemic, the United States might have been ready for COVID-19. Instead the country found itself utterly unprepared—a decision that will likely cost hundreds of thousands, if not millions, of lives. I cannot tell you what the future holds, but I can tell you that imagining our options—and taking those imaginations seriously—matters.

Of course, imagining is not the only thing we can do—and it would be naive to say that simply thinking about a better future is all that's required to make it happen. The perils we face as a global community are bigger, thornier, and tougher than that. Creating better futures will require action—personal and collective—to push on the forces that are strip-mining our world and the people in it for power and profit. We'll need policy change, behavior change, economic change, and environmental change, to come out of this to a better world. But if you don't know what kind of future you want, you can't make it happen. If you don't consider the powers and players that stand in your way, you can't topple them. If you don't know what the possibilities are, you can't realize them.

When I first started the *Flash Forward* podcast six years ago, I didn't have any of these big ideas in place. I just thought it would be fun to come up with futures; to blend science fiction and reporting; to play with possibilities. And it has been fun—I've trained an algorithm to produce scripture, created fake reality TV shows, and visited a studio that makes lamps out of mushrooms. But along the way I began to realize that the work was both fun and important—

---

3   The human brain weighs about three pounds, so it's possible you've imbibed a box of wine heftier than the thing between your ears.

that helping people imagine different futures and better understand our paths to and away from them serves a vital function. Without imagination there is no action. Without deconstructing how tomorrow happens, we cannot construct the version we want.

The book you have in your hands right now is an extension of this mission, a new way of exploring different futures with a new set of minds and hands involved. With the help of Matt Lubchansky and Sophie Goldstein (who have comics in this collection themselves as well), I've assembled the work of twelve incredibly talented artists and artist/writer duos. Instead of the audio-fiction of the podcast, in each chapter you'll enter a portal to the future through twelve brand-new comics that tell tales never before heard on *Flash Forward*, from an underwater meet-cute to a circus-themed band of pirates to a heated power struggle within an animal rights movement. Personally, having these new minds thinking about futures has been incredibly fun and has taken me (and this book) to places I might have never thought of on my own.

After each chapter, I'll step in with a short essay to help you understand the deeper context of the future you just encountered: How likely is it? How close are we? What happens next? On the podcast, the focus is largely on the voices of experts I interview, and you'll hear from them in this book, too. But in these pages I also get to add a bit more of my own ideas and do a bit more pontificating on what it all might mean in a bigger sense. If you've heard every episode of *Flash Forward,* you'll be surprised and delighted by these reimagined and remixed chapters (and you'll spot a few new ideas, too). If you've never heard a single episode, don't worry, all you need to know is that we're about to head off into the future. This book is an extension of the podcast, a parallel universe, in a way. You can exist in either one without knowing the other exists at all, but when you get a glimpse, or even travel through the wormhole to experience both, it's a bit like unlocking a weird, unstable superpower. And you don't even need to be bitten by a futurist to get it.

As is the *Flash Forward* way, this book covers a wide range of topics and ideas from futures near and far. From the terrifyingly real prospect of a world consumed by fake news, to the logistics of an underwater resort, to a future where gender is as malleable and low-stakes as hair color, the book you're about to read (I hope) considers the science, art, policy, and ethics waiting for us over the horizon. Some of these chapters are touching, some are dark, some are funny, some are all of the above.

This book does not predict the future—it imagines it. It does not say what will happen, but what could. In the twelve chapters that follow, you'll dive into everything from an underwater Venice theme park, to humanoid ghostbots, to cities that track you wherever you go. Imagining these tomorrows is a bit like going shopping—we can try them on and see how we like them. Those that aren't a good fit can be returned, and those we like we can take to the cosmic cashier. And when you're done with these futures, I hope you imagine a few of your own.

WELCOME TO TOMORROWVILLE

BY BEN PASSMORE

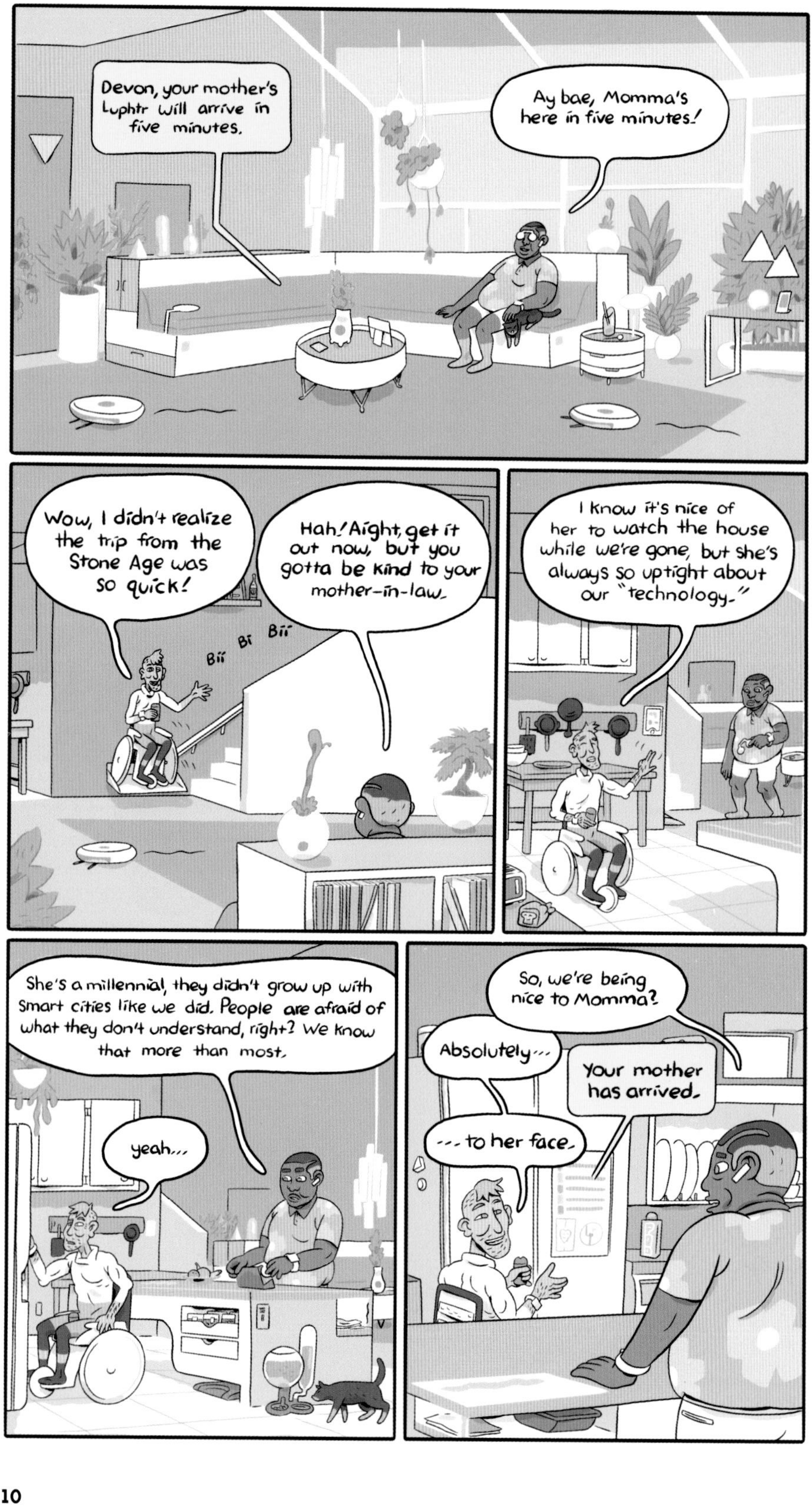
Devon, your mother's Luphtr will arrive in five minutes.
Ay bae, Momma's here in five minutes!
Wow, I didn't realize the trip from the Stone Age was so quick!
Bii Bi Bii
Hah! Aight, get it out now, but you gotta be kind to your mother-in-law.
I know it's nice of her to watch the house while we're gone, but she's always so uptight about our "technology."
She's a millennial, they didn't grow up with smart cities like we did. People are afraid of what they don't understand, right? We know that more than most.
yeah...
So, we're being nice to Momma?
Absolutely...
...to her face.
Your mother has arrived.

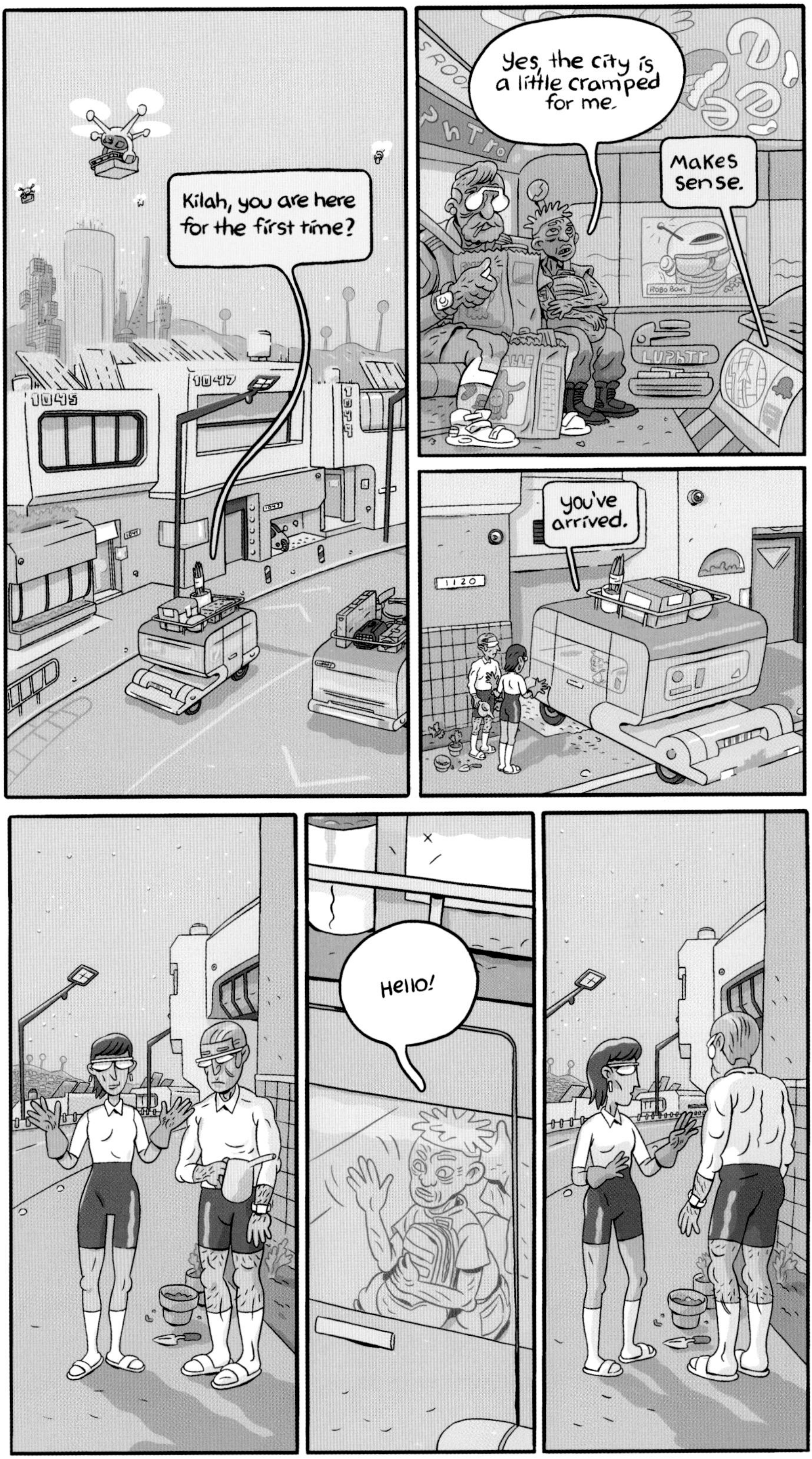
Kilah, you are here for the first time?
Yes, the city is a little cramped for me.
Makes sense.
You've arrived.
Hello!

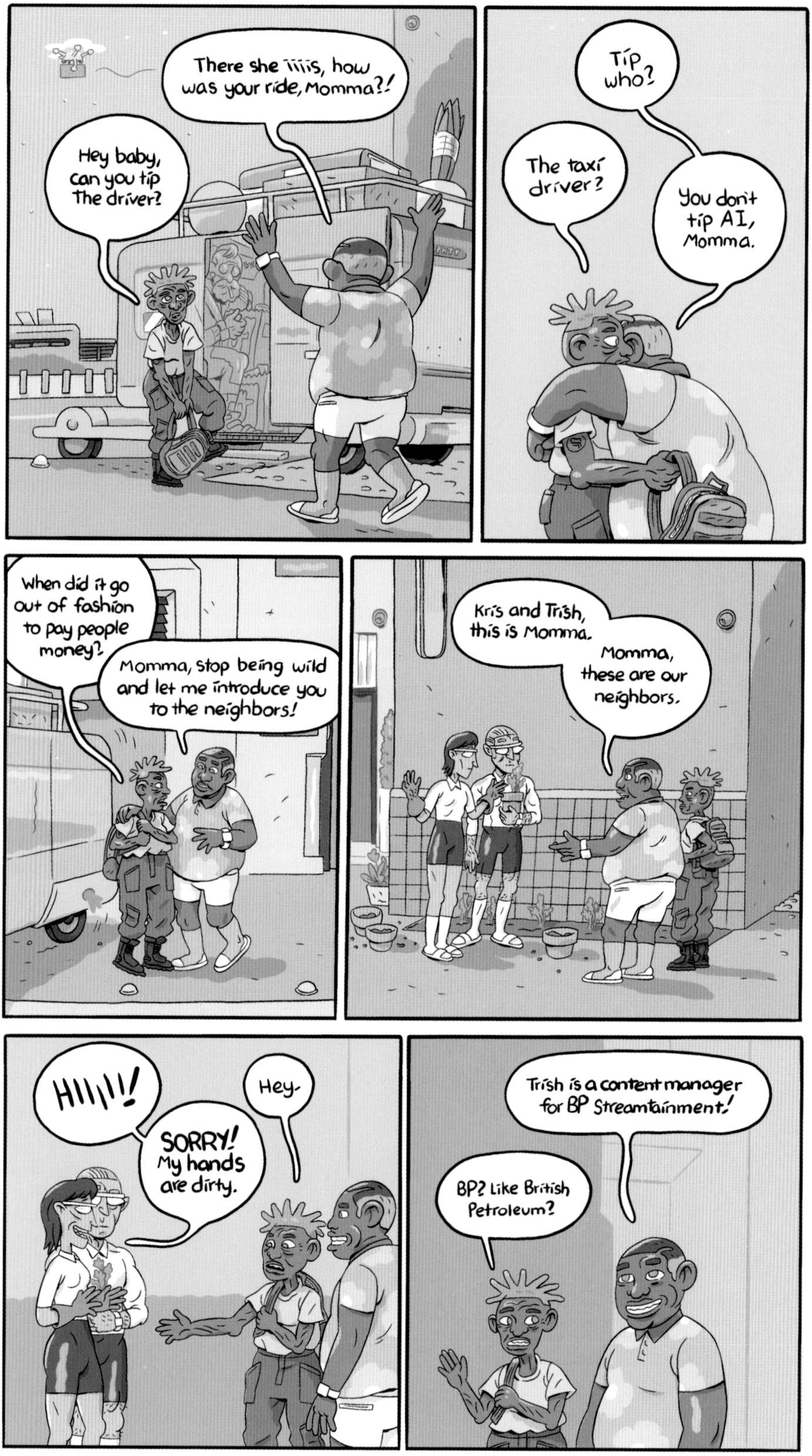
There she iiiis, how was your ride, Momma?!
Hey baby, can you tip the driver?
Tip who?
The taxi driver?
You don't tip AI, Momma.
When did it go out of fashion to pay people money?
Momma, stop being wild and let me introduce you to the neighbors!
Kris and Trish, this is Momma.
Momma, these are our neighbors.
HI!!!!
Hey.
SORRY! My hands are dirty.
Trish is a content manager for BP Streamtainment!
BP? Like British Petroleum?

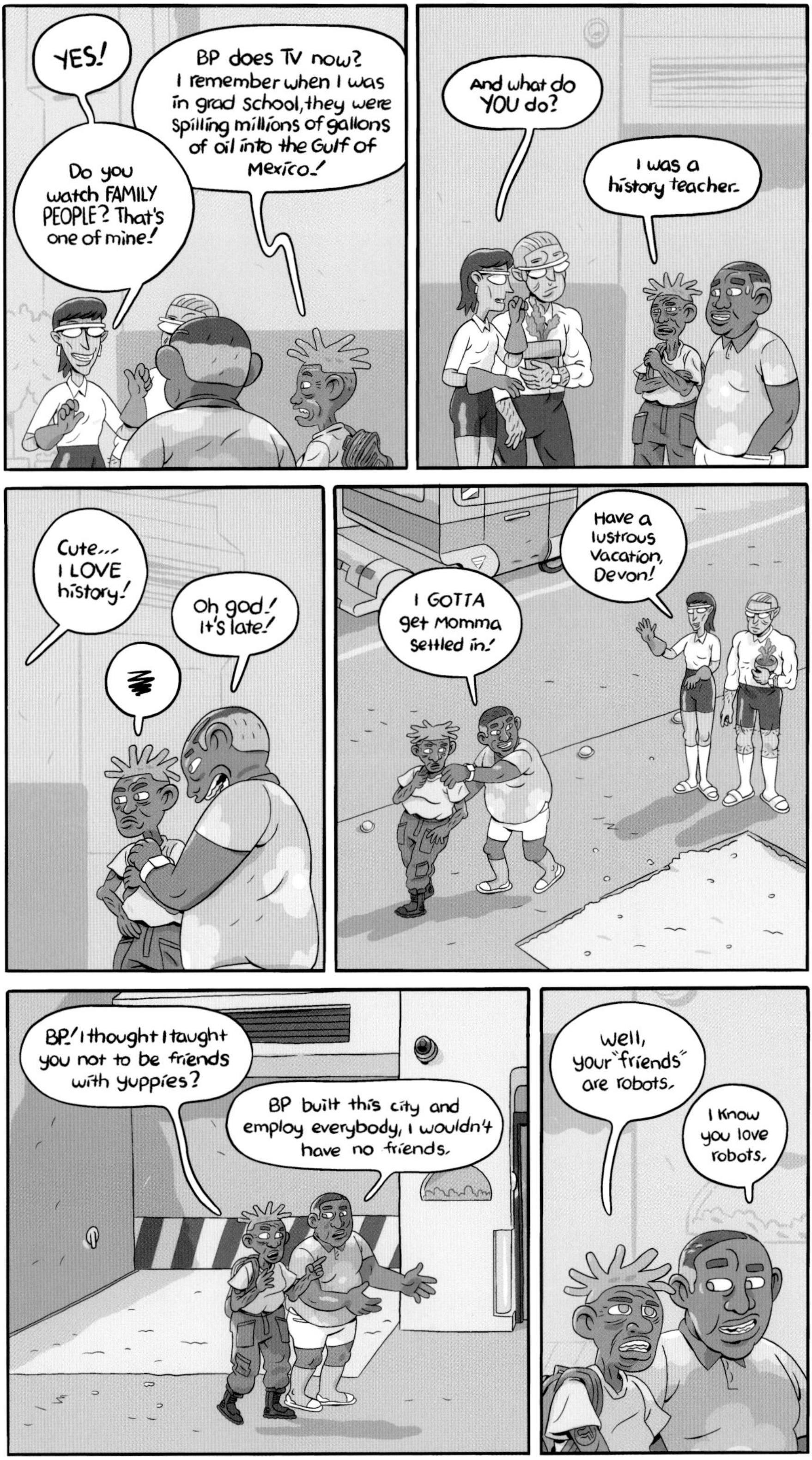
YES!
BP does TV now? I remember when I was in grad school, they were spilling millions of gallons of oil into the Gulf of Mexico!
Do you watch FAMILY PEOPLE? That's one of mine!
And what do YOU do?
I was a history teacher.
Cute... I LOVE history!
Oh god! It's late!
Have a lustrous Vacation, Devon!
I GOTTA get Momma settled in!
BP! I thought I taught you not to be friends with yuppies?
BP built this city and employ everybody, I wouldn't have no friends.
Well, your "friends" are robots.
I know you love robots.

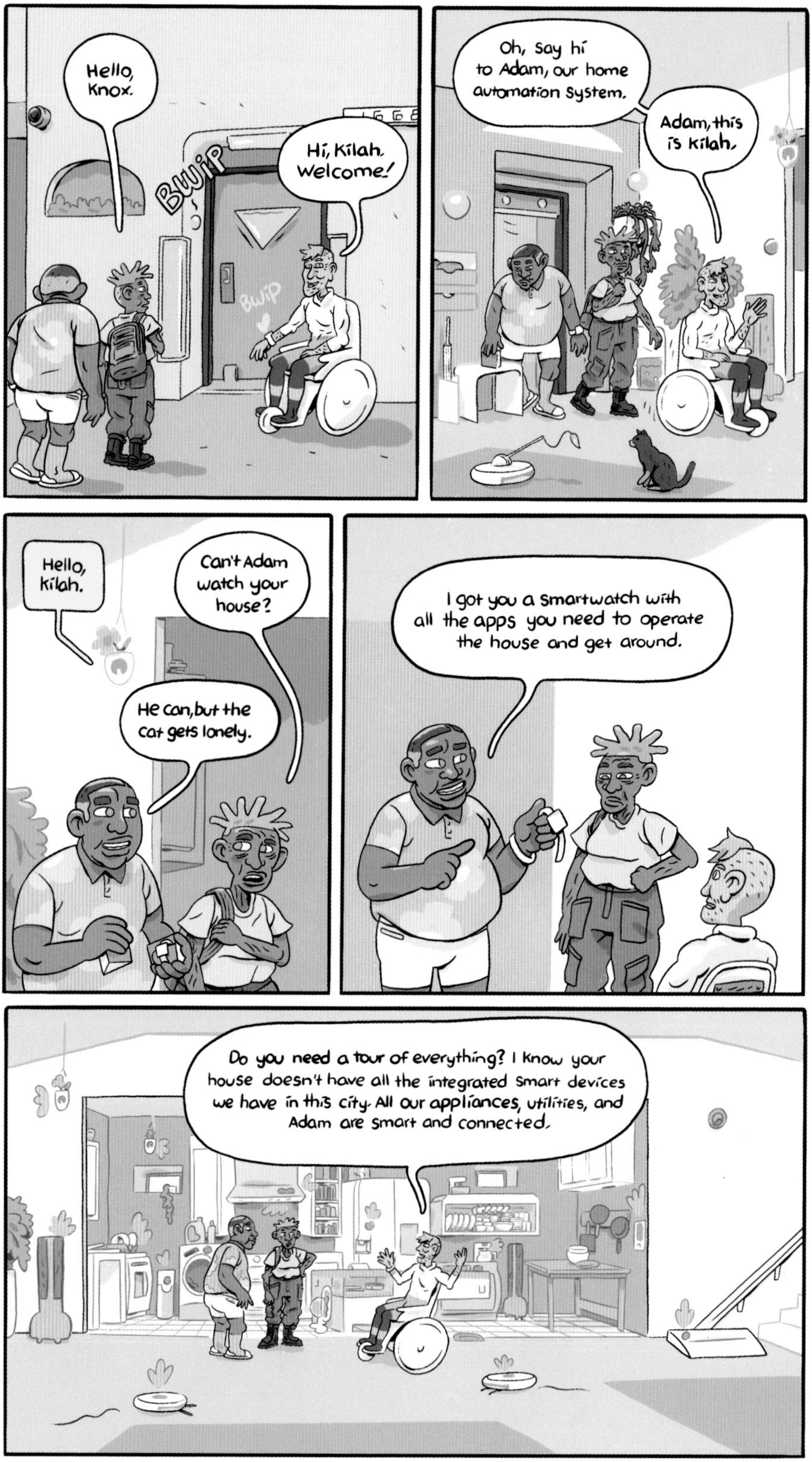
Hello, Knox.
BWIP
Hi, Kilah. Welcome!
BWIP
Oh, say hi to Adam, our home automation system.
Adam, this is Kilah.
Hello, Kilah.
Can't Adam watch your house?
He can, but the cat gets lonely.
I got you a smartwatch with all the apps you need to operate the house and get around.
Do you need a tour of everything? I know your house doesn't have all the integrated smart devices we have in this city. All our appliances, utilities, and Adam are smart and connected.

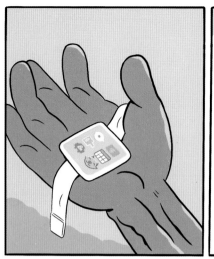

So everything in this house is a spy, then?

HEEEERE WE GO!

Knox!

I'm sorry?

...is just stressed. Bae, I'm going to show Momma the neighborhood if you want to call us a Luphtr to the airport?

Yes, sorry, Kilah, it's just been a hectic mornin'...

Mh-hm.

Sigh

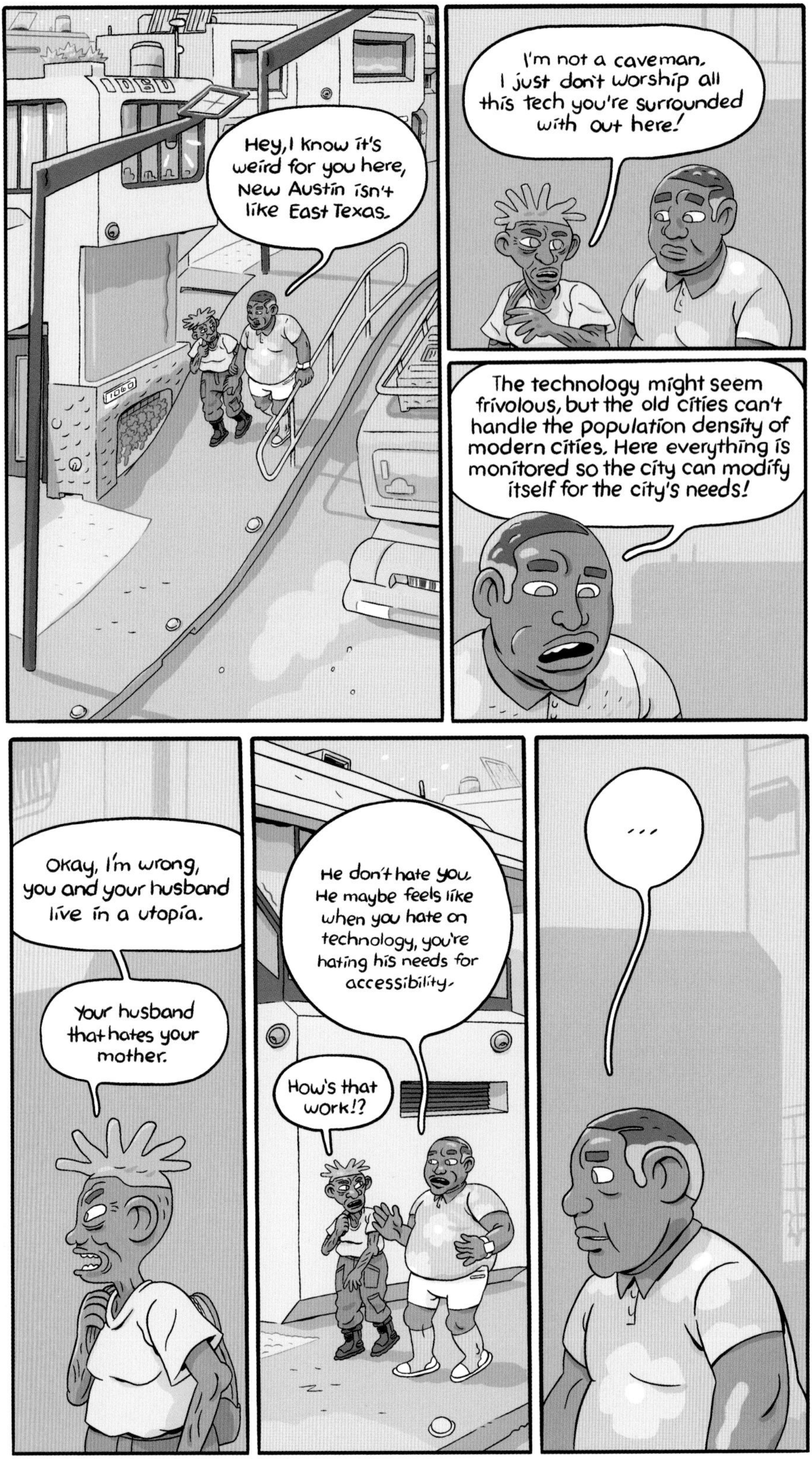
Hey, I know it's weird for you here, New Austin isn't like East Texas.
I'm not a caveman. I just don't worship all this tech you're surrounded with out here!
The technology might seem frivolous, but the old cities can't handle the population density of modern cities. Here everything is monitored so the city can modify itself for the city's needs!
Okay, I'm wrong, you and your husband live in a utopia.
Your husband that hates your mother.
He don't hate you. He maybe feels like when you hate on technology, you're hating his needs for accessibility.
How's that work!?
...

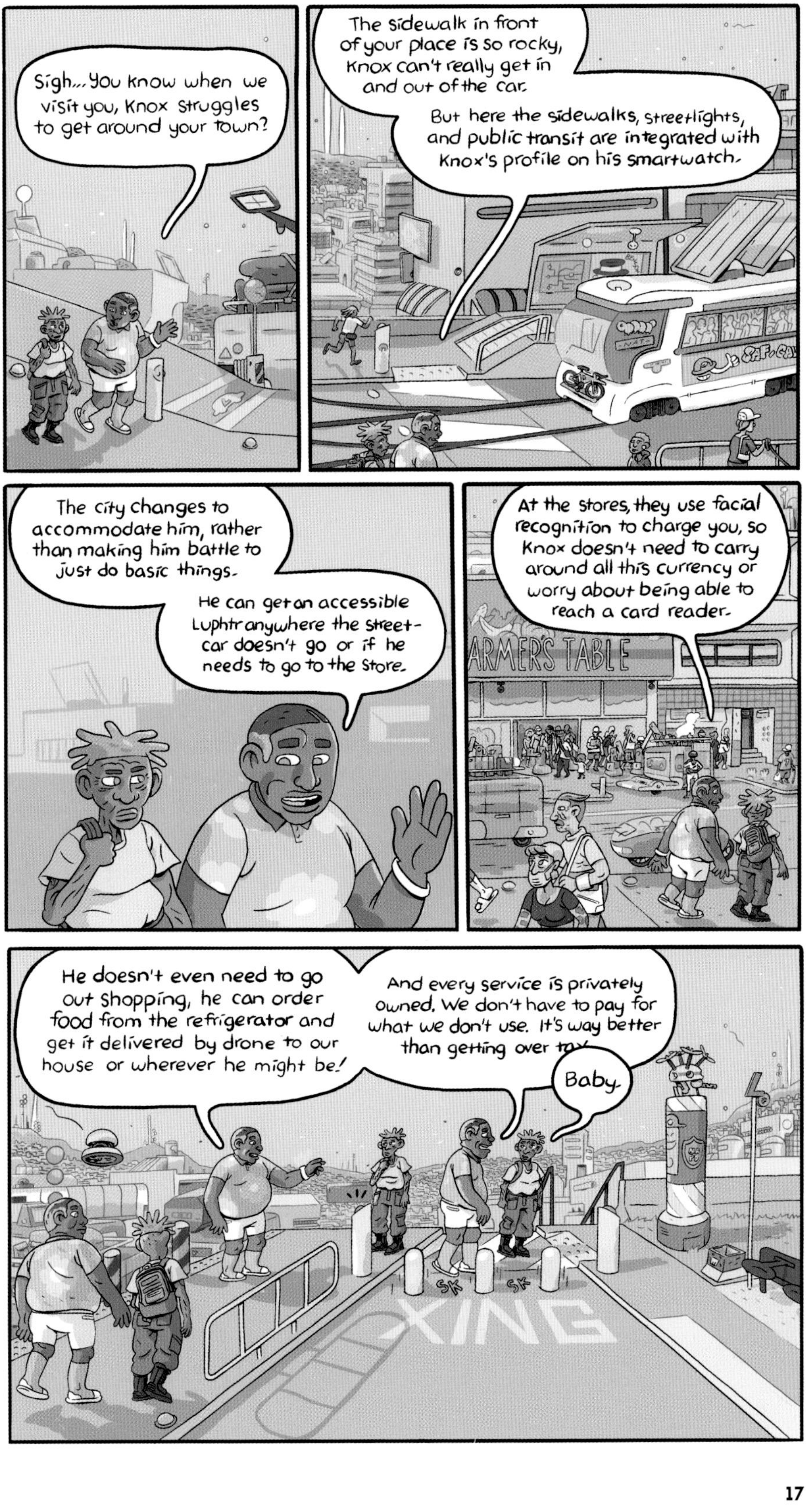
Sigh... You know when we visit you, Knox struggles to get around your town?
The sidewalk in front of your place is so rocky, Knox can't really get in and out of the car.
But here the sidewalks, streetlights, and public transit are integrated with Knox's profile on his smartwatch.
The city changes to accommodate him, rather than making him battle to just do basic things.
He can get an accessible Luphtr anywhere the street-car doesn't go or if he needs to go to the store.
At the stores, they use facial recognition to charge you, so Knox doesn't need to carry around all this currency or worry about being able to reach a card reader.
ARMER'S TABLE
He doesn't even need to go out shopping, he can order food from the refrigerator and get it delivered by drone to our house or wherever he might be!
And every service is privately owned. We don't have to pay for what we don't use. It's way better than getting over
Baby.
SK
SK
XING

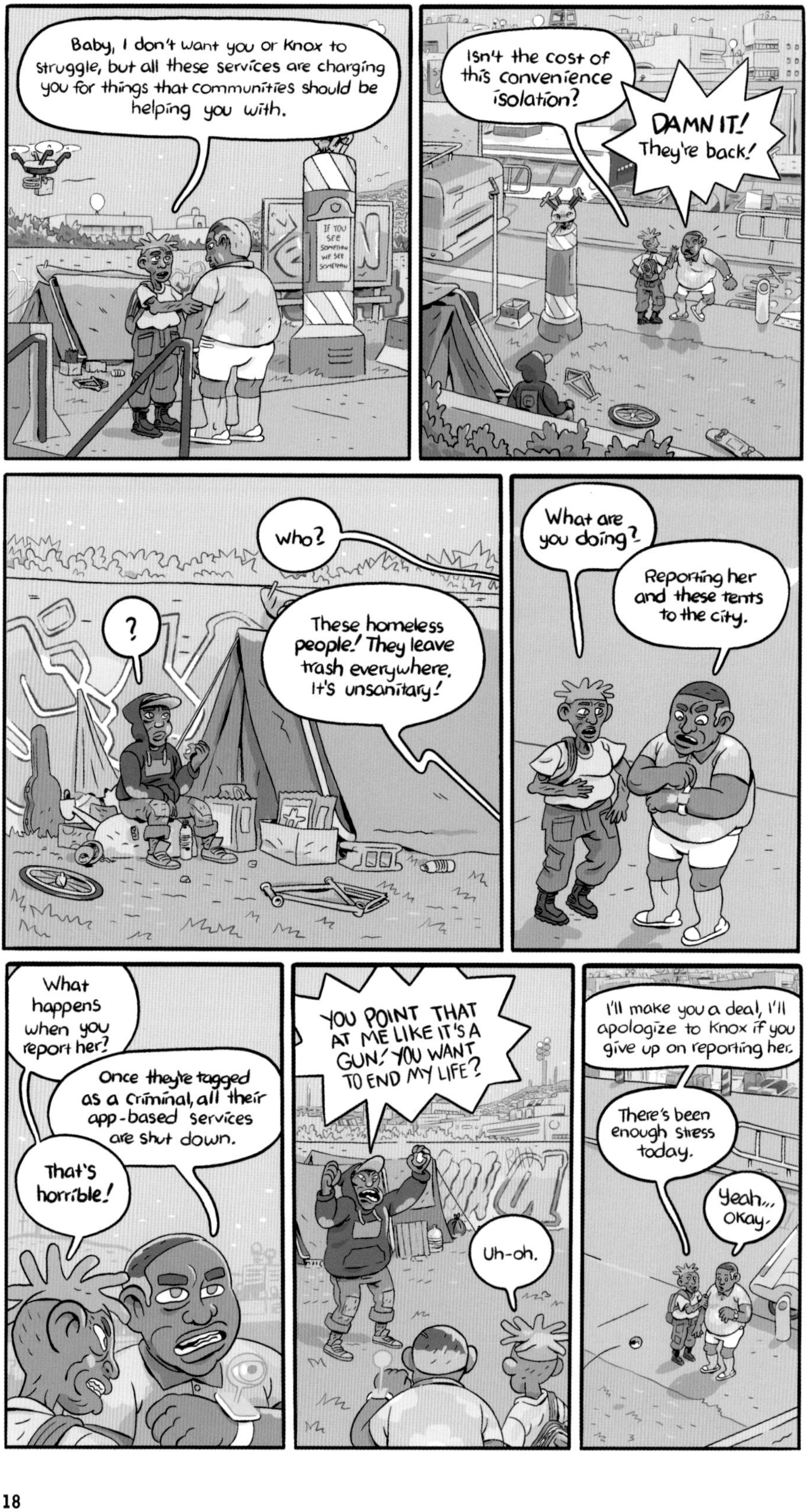
Baby, I don't want you or Knox to struggle, but all these services are charging you for things that communities should be helping you with.
Isn't the cost of this convenience isolation?
DAMN IT! They're back!
Who?
?
These homeless people! They leave trash everywhere. It's unsanitary!
What are you doing?
Reporting her and these tents to the city.
What happens when you report her?
Once they're tagged as a criminal, all their app-based services are shut down.
That's horrible!
YOU POINT THAT AT ME LIKE IT'S A GUN! YOU WANT TO END MY LIFE?
Uh-oh.
I'll make you a deal, I'll apologize to Knox if you give up on reporting her.
There's been enough stress today.
Yeah... Okay.

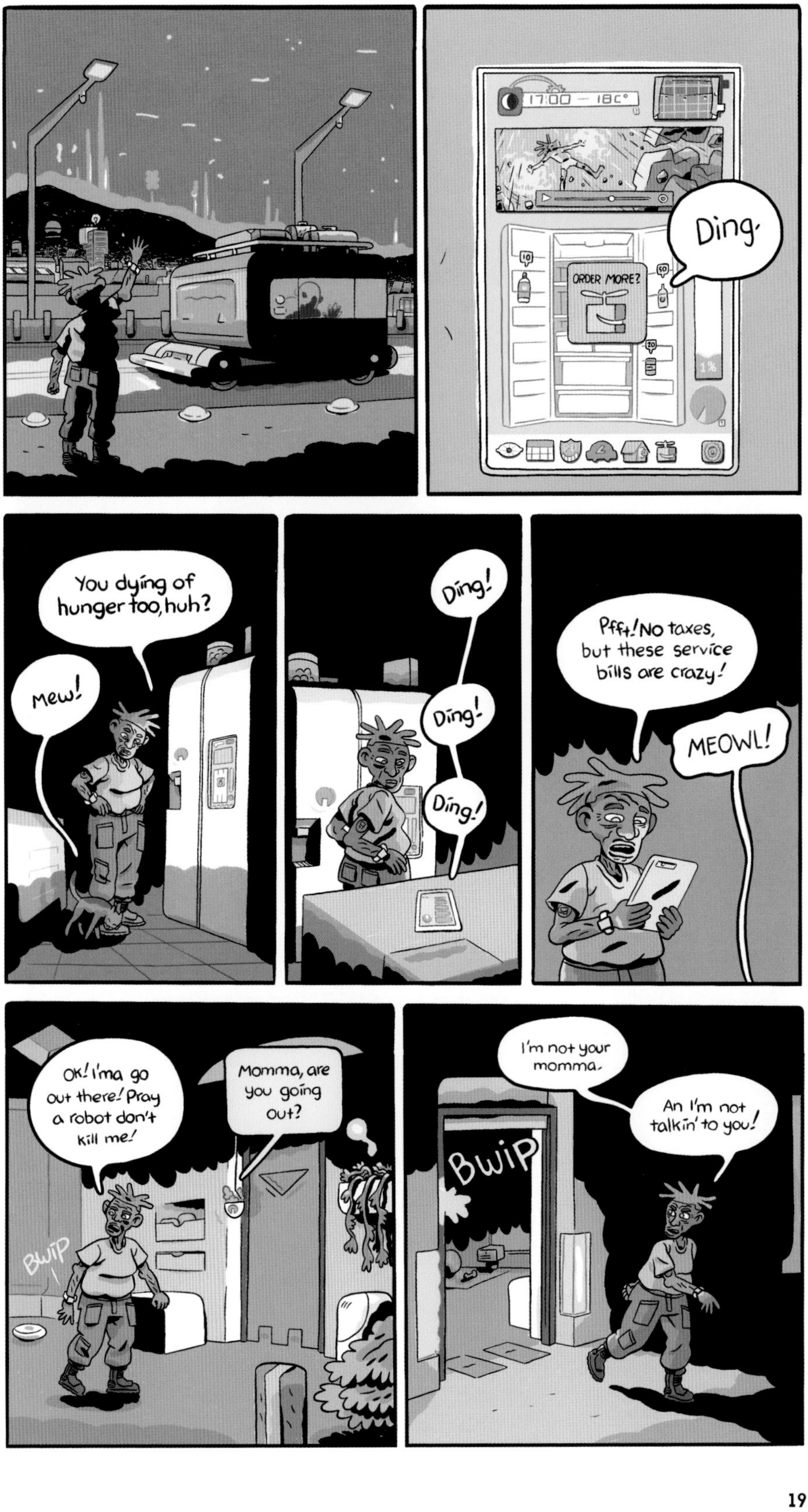
17:00 — 18C°
ORDER MORE?
10
50
20
1%
Ding.
You dying of hunger too, huh?
Mew!
Ding!
Ding!
Ding!
Pfft! No taxes, but these service bills are crazy!
MEOWL!
OK! I'ma go out there! Pray a robot don't kill me!
Momma, are you going out?
BWIP
I'm not your momma.
An I'm not talkin' to you!
BWIP

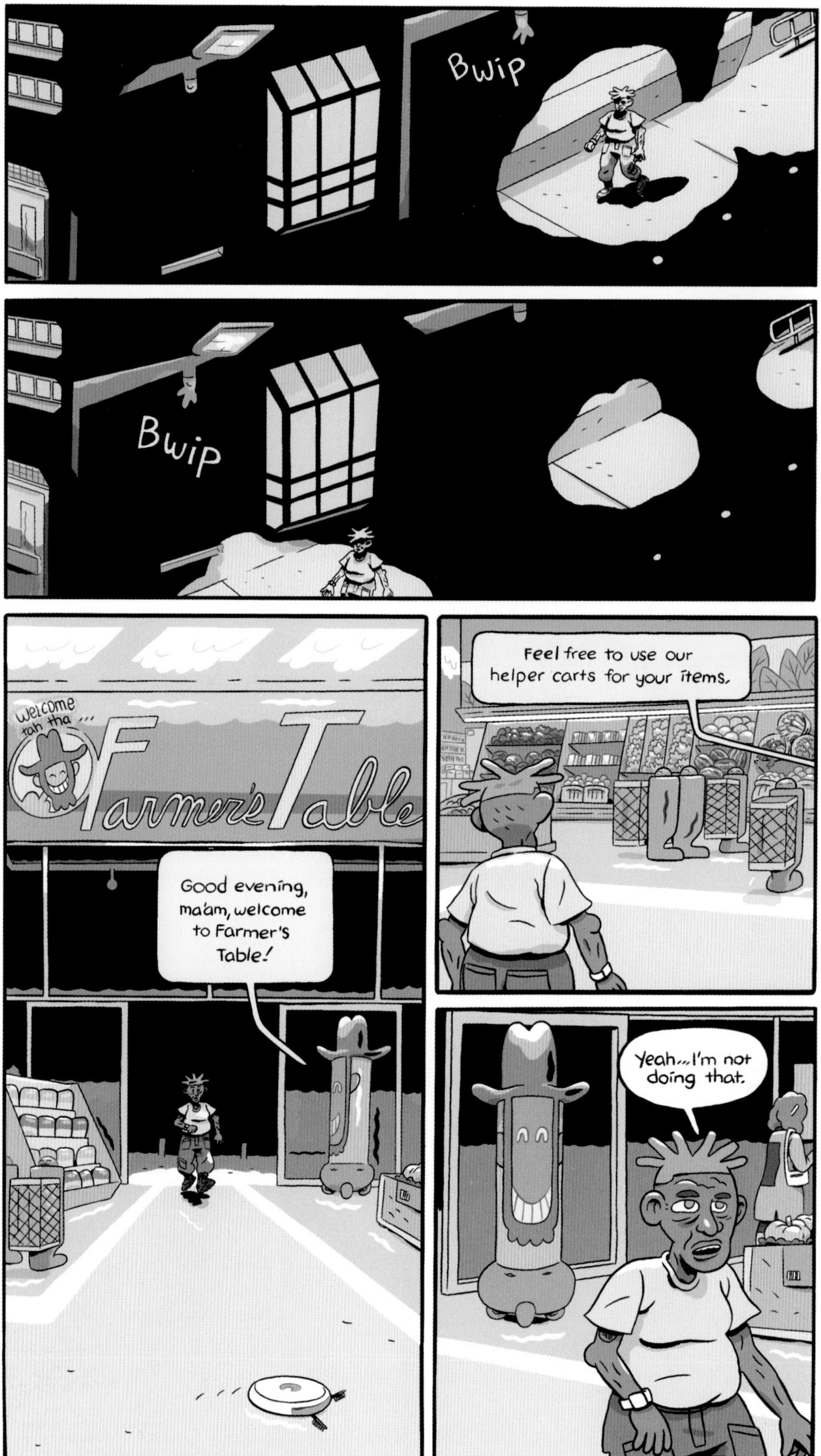

Bwip
Bwip
Welcome tah tha ... Farmer's Table
Good evening, ma'am, welcome to Farmer's Table!
Feel free to use our helper carts for your items.
Yeah...I'm not doing that.

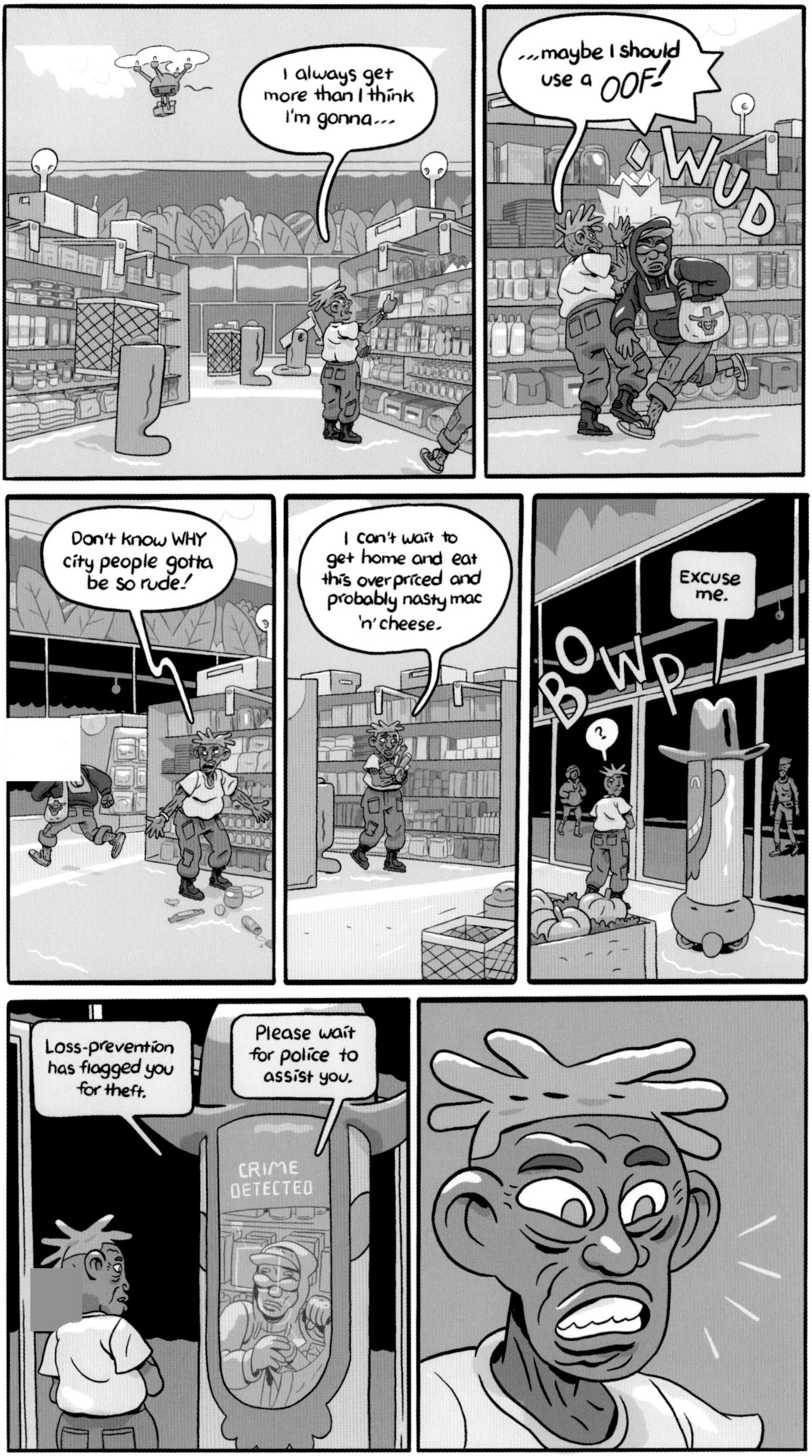
I always get more than I think I'm gonna...
...maybe I should use a OOF!
WUD
Don't know WHY city people gotta be so rude!
I can't wait to get home and eat this overpriced and probably nasty mac 'n' cheese.
BOWP
?
Excuse me.
Loss-prevention has flagged you for theft.
Please wait for police to assist you.
CRIME DETECTED

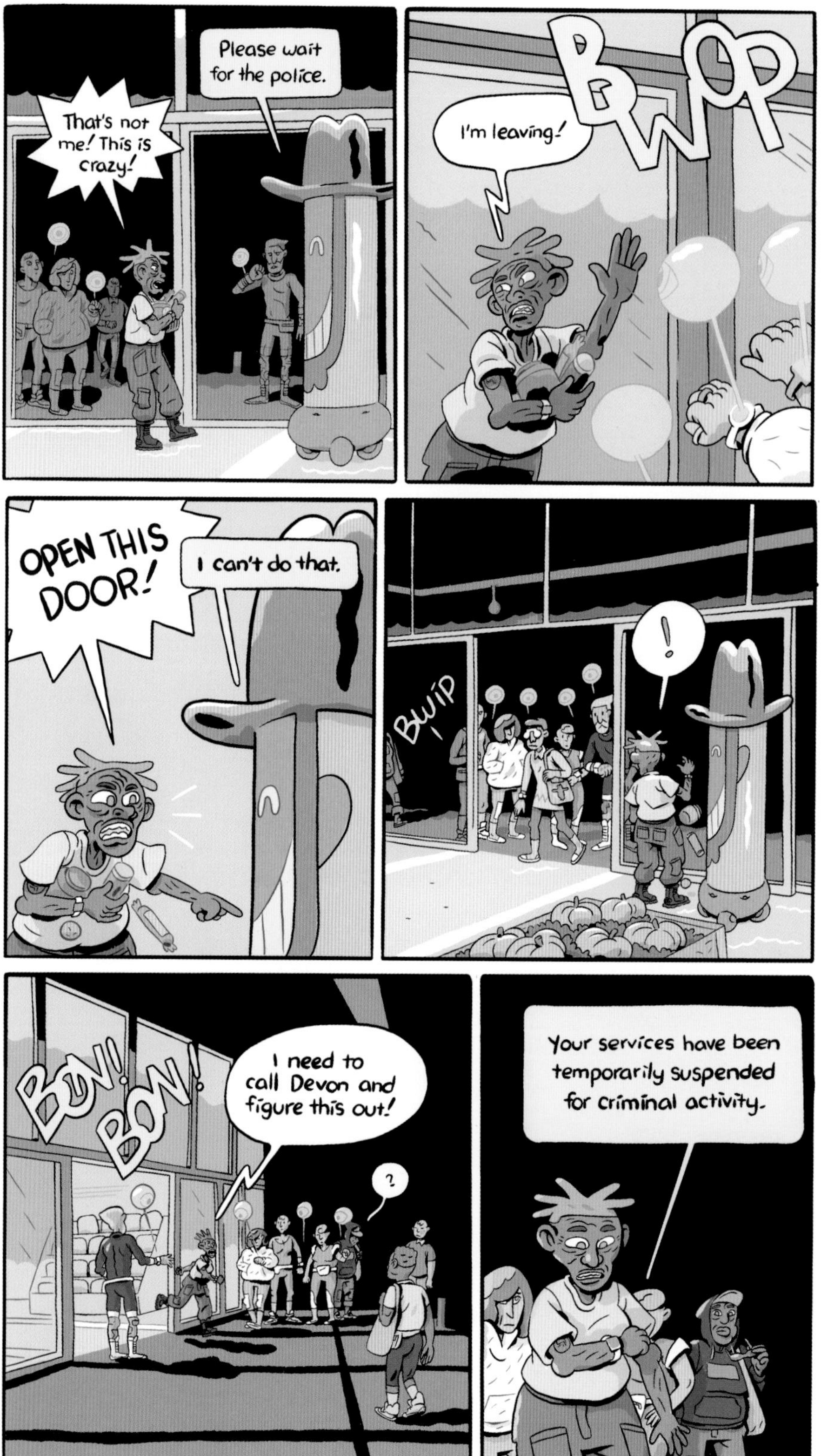
Please wait for the police.
That's not me! This is crazy!
I'm leaving!
BWOP
OPEN THIS DOOR!
I can't do that.
!
BWIP
BON! BON!
I need to call Devon and figure this out!
?
Your services have been temporarily suspended for criminal activity.

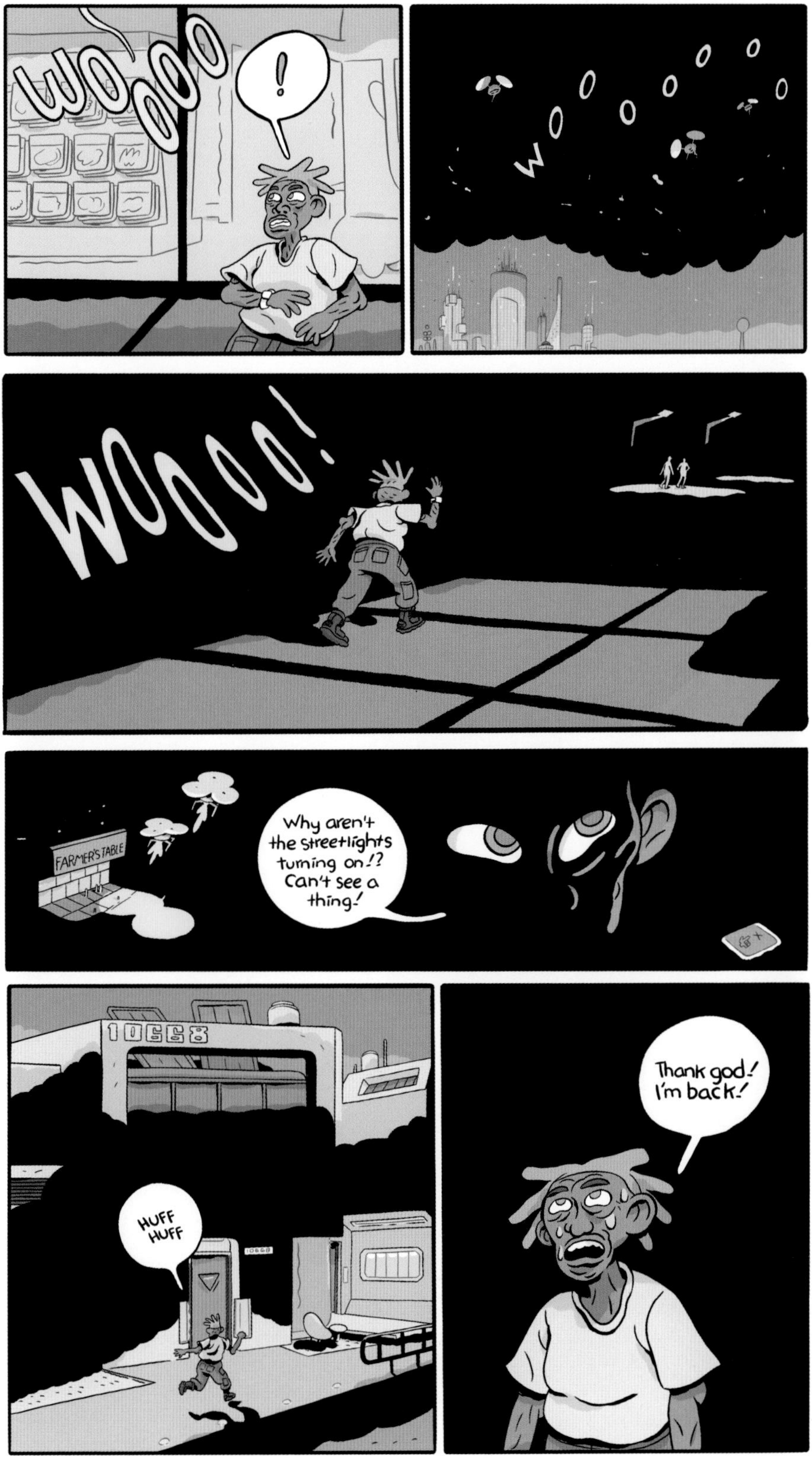
WOOOOO
!
WOOOOOOOO
WOOOO!
FARMER'S TABLE
Why aren't the streetlights turning on!? Can't see a thing!
10668
HUFF HUFF
Thank god! I'm back!

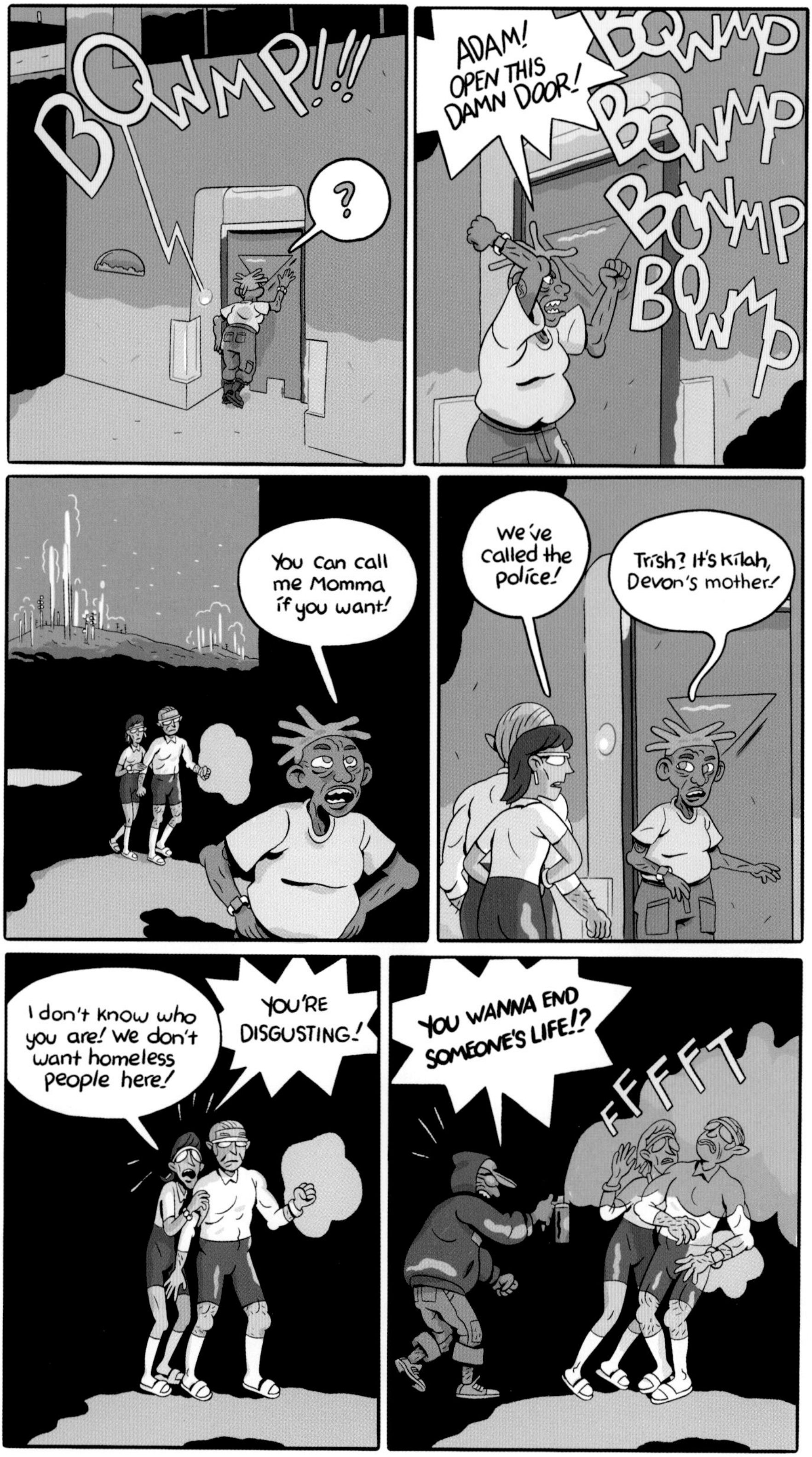
BOWMP!!!
?
ADAM! OPEN THIS DAMN DOOR!
BOWMP
BOWMP
BOWMP
BOWMP
You can call me Momma if you want!
We've called the police!
Trish? It's Kilah, Devon's mother!
I don't know who you are! We don't want homeless people here!
YOU'RE DISGUSTING!
YOU WANNA END SOMEONE'S LIFE!?
FFFFT

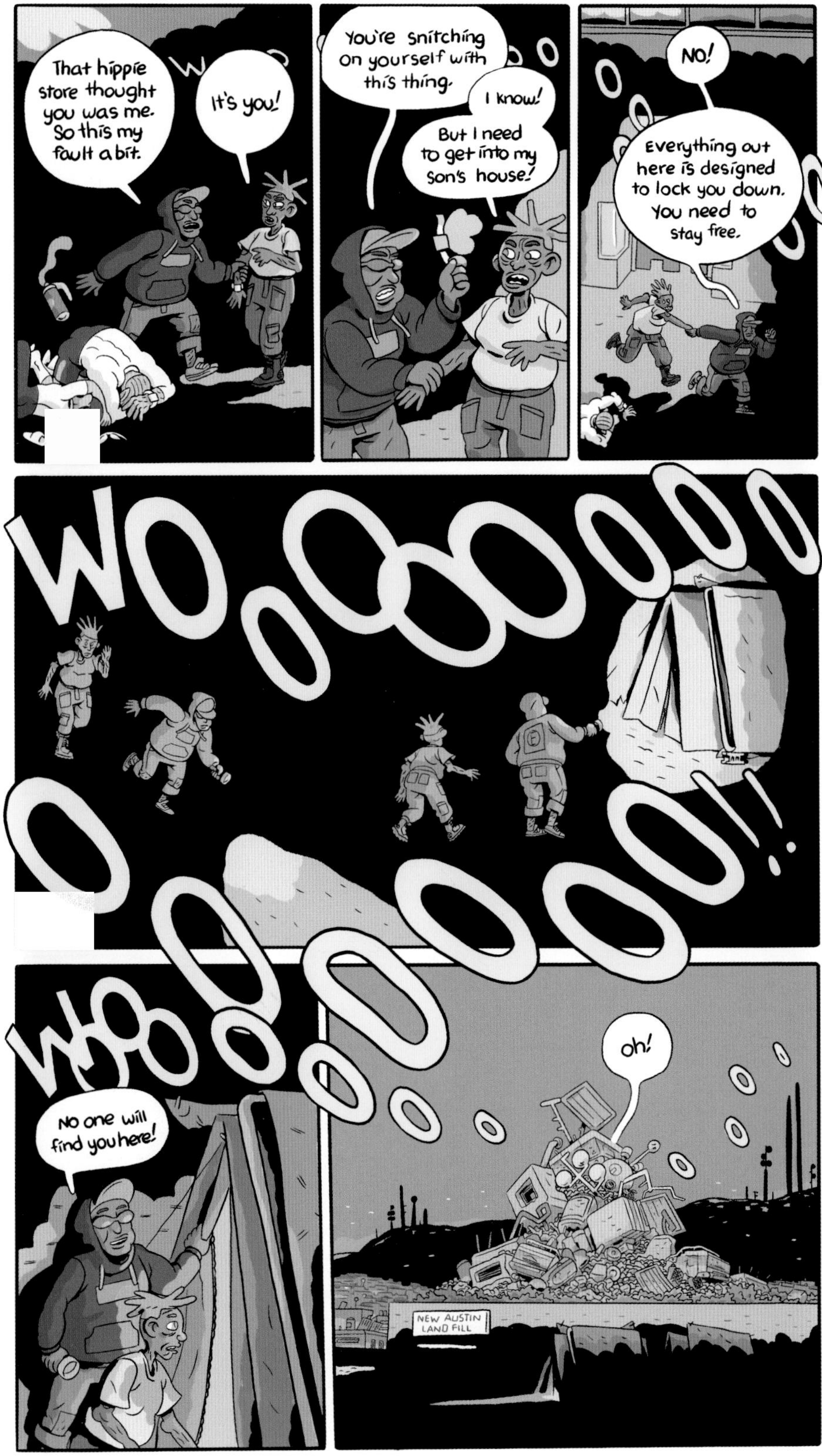
That hippie store thought you was me. So this my fault a bit.
W
It's you!
You're snitching on yourself with this thing.
I know!
But I need to get into my son's house!
NO!
Everything out here is designed to lock you down. You need to stay free.
WOOOOOOOOOOOOOOO!!
WOOOOOOOO
No one will find you here!
oh!
NEW AUSTIN LAND FILL

WELCOME TO TOMORROWVILLE

HOW SMART SHOULD A CITY REALLY BE?

HOW SMART CAN A CITY BE? ADVOCATES ARGUE THAT the limit is purely in your mind. "Our cities are slated to become lovable, livable and sustainable because of smart leverage and immense contributions of highly robust and resilient technologies," write Pethuru Raj and Anupama C. Raman in their book *Intelligent Cities*, a love letter to the promise that technology can offer urban centers. "The cities of the future are going to be elegantly and extremely connected and cognizant, grandly synchronized and IT-enabled, and software intensive."

Take a hypothetical person named Miranda, for example. Miranda lives in future smart-Atlanta, and Miranda is pregnant. Miranda is also wearing a host of sensors on her body to keep track of her biometrics and the vital signs of the tiny human growing inside of her. When those sensors detect the telltale signals of impending delivery, Miranda will be notified. But that notice won't just go to her—along with the personal chime that suggests she pack her things and head to the hospital, the sensors will also notify information systems at the hospital itself, telling them when she's on her way and when she'll likely arrive. The baby-alert will also go to Miranda's transportation system (self-driving, of course), which will talk to sensors in the road and the streetlights, which will in turn coordinate themselves to get Miranda to the hospital as quickly as possible. By the time she gets there, her room will be set up, and her medical sensors will synch with the facility's. By the time she leaves with a tiny, helpless new human in tow, her baby will be outfitted with its own set of data-gathering devices, and the cycle can repeat. This is the dream of smart cities, to some.

While Miranda may be fictional, smart cities are not. All over the world, governments have been testing out myriad ways of digitizing everything from voting to finding a parking space. In Estonia, nearly every possible way a citizen might interface with their government can be done online. New York City has installed kiosks to offer Wi-Fi and charging stations. Chicago has installed devices all over the metropolis in a project it calls "Array of Things," which describes itself as a "fitness tracker" for the city. In Singapore, sensors can tell if someone is smoking in a place they shouldn't.

In Barcelona, public parks are equipped with sensors to monitor water use. In London, traffic lights can sense when buses are approaching and favor their smooth sailing through intersections. In San Francisco, there are sensors underneath parking spots to tell the city, and residents, if they're open or not. Camden, New Jersey, has installed microphones, cranes, and cameras all around the city, and a $4.5 million command center to receive that data and monitor the streets 24-7 for crime. In Toronto, a Google sister company called Sidewalk Labs spent the last few years working on turning twelve acres of waterfront into a fully web-connected series of buildings that gather data on nearly every aspect of life in the development.

For each of these projects, there are press releases and ribbon cuttings and excited media coverage about how "smart" each city is becoming. And who doesn't want to be smart? But a city is more than a series of sensors. And in fact, the hoopla around these new projects can often obscure their darker sides and their failure to actually make cities more livable, just, or safe. Perhaps the question we should be asking isn't "How smart can a city be?" but rather, "How smart *should* a city be?"

I know it's hard, but let's not be bamboozled by the bright and shiny. In fact, looking too closely at the technology behind smart cities obscures the real questions we should be asking about them. "While these systems and devices are certainly consequential, they are also an effective red herring," writes Jathan Sadowski in an essay in *Creating Smart Cities*. When we get too hung up on the beeps and boops, "our attention is redirected away from what is really at stake with the smart city movement: The transformation of how cities are governed."

Cities are odd and chaotic, made up of humans and buildings and businesses—neighbors and families and friends and strangers (mostly strangers) all living in close quarters and trying to cohabitate in harmony. Jane Jacobs, an urban studies icon, once wrote that "cities have the capability of providing something for everybody, only because, and only when, they are created by everybody." Local governance is messy and complicated and easy to parody because it's trying to do something incredibly hard: create a place that embraces every person who lives there. Smart cities, on the other hand, are not created by everybody. In most cases, they are lopsided partnerships between cities and technology corporations whose responsibility is not to the citizen, but to their shareholders.

Before asking which sensors to install where, we should ask: What kind of city do we want to build? Who, and what, are we "optimizing" the city for? What are the real problems that need solving quickly, and what can we delay for later? These are not technological questions. They're political ones with consequences like the one you saw in the comic.

Let's look at a more specific example: Smart city advocates love to talk about traffic. In a smart city, there won't be any, because cars and roads will all be in sync and create a perfectly harmonious flow of traffic. In fact, in the smart city, there won't even be traffic lights. We won't need them. But when you start to think about this seemingly utopian proposition, things get a little more complicated. Imagine trying to cross the street in a city with no stoplights. Is it even possible?

A city without traffic lights is a city along the side of a highway. It's not walkable, it's not accessible. It's a city designed for cars, not people—a space that values technology and "efficiency" over humans. "What society chooses to measure and optimize is an embodiment of our priorities," writes Ben Green in *The Smart Enough City.* "So long as we value smooth car traffic over livable streets and public transit, efforts to enhance transportation will actually be aimed at easing congestion."

We've made this mistake before. In the early twentieth century, streets were mixed-use spaces. Humans shared the road with carts and even cars, as they became more common. But as automobiles got more powerful and popular, it became dangerous to have people competing for space with 1,500-pound vehicles hurtling down the road. Cars started killing people (often children), and some cities responded by banning them from city centers, like New York's Central Park.[1] The automobile industry responded by launching a brilliant public relations campaign to redefine what roads were even for, and punish people for using them. "Motordom," as the automotive collective was called, put out ads shifting the blame for deaths from the drivers to the "reckless" humans in the road, and invented the term and crime "jaywalking." And, as you of course know, Motordom won the road. Today, many cities are actually trying to claw space back from cars—with initiatives once again banning vehicles from certain downtown areas. If we follow unquestioningly down the path of some smart-city proposals, we'll lose even more of our living space to the automobile.

We can repeat this kind of interrogation—slowing down and asking, "Most efficient for whom, exactly?"—with a lot of smart-city proposals, including predictive policing, private Wi-Fi kiosks, and apps to allow people to register complaints and vote on which city projects get done first. Who, and what, is being prioritized with these solutions, and is that really the city we want to live in?

Ask any coder or designer and, if they're being honest with you, they'll admit that building a piece of technology for everybody (truly *everybody*) is basically impossible. Technologists talk about "edge cases" as annoyances, things that you should try to predict but can't really be held responsible for. Things like someone's mom coming to visit, and interacting with a software that is already more likely to confuse black faces for one another, creating a cascading set of alarms and locking systems, as you saw in Ben Passmore's comic. Software designed for a whole city often winds up being designed for the "average user" and not a diverse and complicated mass of people who might have nothing in common aside from a zip code.

In his book *Infinite Detail*, the science-fiction writer Tim Maughan includes one tiny ripple effect of just one smart-city policy. A man who makes his money by gathering up cans and cashing them in suddenly finds that the city has

---

1   The public sentiment against cars was so strong that cities would hold parades and put up monuments to commemorate the children killed by vehicles, mothers of those children were given white stars to wear, and one newspaper cartoon likened cars to Moloch, the Canaanite god linked to child sacrifices.

instituted a "smart chip" system. The cans now have RFID tags on them that register when they're recycled, so they can't be redeemed by a third party. Just like that, his livelihood has been designed out of existence. An environmental consulting firm called Eunomia estimates that between four thousand and eight thousand people in New York City alone make a living collecting cans. In *Infinite Detail*, the smart-city designers likely didn't even consider how their fancy new chips might impact those people.

In the comic you just read, you saw a smart city as many advocates dream of them—totally connected, safe, efficient. And there are upsides for some. If you can afford it, this kind of smart city allows you to completely customize your urban experience to your own needs, paying just for what you want and use. If you can't, you're out of luck, home, food, and health services.

And like in the comic, the smart city is not immune to mistakes, big and small. In Barcelona, the sensors they installed in parking spots to detect which ones were open stopped working any time a train went by, bamboozled by the electromagnetic hum of the passing subway.

A few years ago, I returned to our sleepy neighborhood in Berkeley, California, to find four cop cars parked at odd angles on the street—as if they'd raced there and come to a screeching halt. I later learned that they were responding to reports of a stolen vehicle parked at a house on our block. The problem is, the vehicle wasn't stolen at all. Every parking enforcement buggy in our area is outfitted with a camera that's always on the lookout for license plates, constantly scanning and sending plate numbers to a central system that checks them against a list of cars that have been stolen, used in crimes, or pegged to things like kidnappings. In a drive through our neighborhood, the system matched our neighbor's car with one on that list and sounded the alarm. But when they arrived and questioned our neighbor, the cops realized that the image had been misread by the automated system—the plate was one digit off.

Thankfully, in this case, no one was harmed. But these kinds of false positives can be deadly. In 2017, after a heated exchange during a game of *Call of Duty: WWII,* a man called in a false report to a police department, claiming that his rival Andrew Finch was holding hostages and had a weapon. When the SWAT team arrived on the scene, the unsuspecting Finch opened his front door and was shot to death by the responding officers. Officers who think they're responding to a potentially dangerous situation go in with a heightened sense of risk and are more likely to draw their weapons. Meanwhile, our neighbor was simply making lunch.

In other cases, advocates for smart cities have to ask what they're willing to subject their residents to in the name of intelligence. In Camden, New Jersey, the city replaced military-style human policing with what many have called a "military-style" surveillance system to tackle crime, and by some metrics, the system worked: Police response time shrank from 60 minutes to just 4.4. By 2015, shootings had dropped 43 percent and violent crime was down 24 percent. But critics of the system argue that the technology isn't where credit should lie for these numbers—along with the high-tech systems, Camden also completely reconfigured their police force to feel less like an occupying army.

Even President Obama commended the city for demilitarizing their police force and instead shifting to community policing practices. And amid the drops in violent crime, the ACLU of New Jersey pointed out that, in fact, there was a huge increase in summonses for minor infractions like having tinted windows on a car, or riding a bicycle without a bell.

In New York City, the 1,800 kiosks that provide free Wi-Fi also gather up information about their users and feed that information back to their biggest investor, which is not, in fact, the city of New York but rather Sidewalk Labs, which is owned by Alphabet (the company that also owns Google). In an on-stage interview in 2016, Dan Doctoroff, the founder and CEO of Sidewalk Labs, said that they expected to "make a lot of money from this."

When I think about smart cities, I think about a painting by the artist Christopher R. W. Nevinson called *The Soul of the Soulless City*. Nevinson painted it in 1920, and it depicts an empty elevated railway in Manhattan. New Yorkers might find the scene familiar—it looks quite like what has now become the High Line, a popular tourist destination, but with the notable exception of human life. New York, to Nevinson's brush, is a city of vanishing lines, hard angles, and geometric forms. There is no sky in this painting, just buildings that shoot up forever, and there are certainly no squishy, fleshy bodies.

The painting wasn't always called *The Soul of the Soulless City*. In fact, when it was first painted, shortly after Nevinson's return from his inaugural trip to New York, he had given it the title *New York—an Abstraction*. Nevinson's first trip to the city was an enchanted one—his paintings were displayed in a fancy gallery and praised by critics. The artist was smitten with the city, telling one journalist that he felt that New York was "built for me." Coming from London, New York in the early 1900s seemed positively futuristic to Nevinson,[2] which suited him because he was indeed a futurist, although not in the way you probably know that word. Rather, Nevinson was part of the futurist art movement—a group of artists heavily inspired by fascism who believed that we must look only forward and never back (a commonality that artistic movement has with some modern futurists of the technological kind).

The painting's title was changed in 1925 after a less romantic return to the city. This time, Nevinson's work was met with far less excitement and far more criticism. Feeling burned by the Big Apple, he made an attempt to burn back by changing the name of the painting to reflect his soured affections. New York, to him, was now soulless.[3] But when I look at this painting, it feels to me like a portrait not of a soulless city, but of a "smart" one—one optimized for efficiency and technology, rather than people.

---

2   Nevinson often claimed to be the first artist to try and capture the "modern beauty of New York's architecture." He wasn't. But, hey, futurists love to claim to be the first!

3   Nevinson later separated himself from the Futurist movement as they descended deeper into support of fascism, and turned to painting more naturalist landscapes. While the founders of Futurism (the artistic style) encouraged war and dominance, Nevinson created an anti-Nazi painting called *Twentieth Century* depicting war and bombs surrounding a hunched and shadowed figure. The buildings in the background of the painting bear a striking resemblance to the Soulless City of his once beloved New York.

What is the soul of a city, and who gets to decide? It's a question plenty of places have had to grapple with. Cities like Austin and Portland have formalized movements to keep them weird, a push against the kind of sameness that money and gentrification can bring to a place. New York City, once a mecca for artists and creatives, once buzzing with endless energy and creativity (regardless of Nevinson's assessment), has slowly homogenized. Wealthy real estate prospectors have bought up storefronts and apartment buildings, raised the rent, and replaced them with big banks and chain drugstores and wealthy tenants. Walking through Manhattan now (and even parts of Brooklyn) can feel like you're playing a video game set in a generic metropolis. Bank, drugstore, fast-fashion retailer, repeat.[4]

Smart cities stand to only make this problem worse. Technologists often talk about the ability to "scale" an idea or a system—how easy is it to take this idea from a few sensors and kiosks, to something you can repeat in as many places as possible. If San Francisco figures out smart parking, the company behind it will almost certainly try to sell that same system to New York, Toronto, Chicago, Atlanta, and more. They might slap a coat of paint on them, but the parking meters will all look the same. So will the roadways and the checkout machines and the streetlights.

In these smart cities we might see an entirely new type of architecture. Historians have argued that our cultural conceptions of privacy have already changed the design of homes and buildings.[5] When privacy became something that rich people valued and defined as a space to think deep thoughts alone, homes began to include spaces like "studies." As digital assistants become more and more common in our domestic spheres, the actual physical layouts might change, too—after all, your Alexa has to be able to hear you to work properly. Down come the walls, and in go the microphones.

A smart city designed to track you everywhere won't be made of concrete or other materials that might block signals. A smart city that wants to keep an eye on you will opt for clear dividers over hedges and bright lights over ambient alleyways. A smart city designed to prioritize car traffic looks different than one designed to prioritize human traffic. You could imagine a hybrid, too—a city ringed by automated vehicles, ripping through the smart streets only to drop people off at the edges so they can power themselves into the center. The choices we make over "smartness" will echo out in our physical landscapes in ways we might not even predict.

Perhaps nowhere is the battle for the soul and design of a smart city more obvious than in Toronto. What was once praised as a utopian future-city project, the collaboration between the city and Sidewalk Labs (the same

---

4   Some wonder if this problem will become even worse post-pandemic, as the small businesses that were still holding on fail to recover. I hope that's not true, and instead you're reading this book in a future where cities prioritized the recovery of locally owned restaurants and retailers.

5   Historians argue exactly when this shift in our ideas of privacy happened—George Rowe claims it was during the sixteenth century, when things like diaries, autobiographies, and personal letters became popular, while Ruth Yeazell pushes that date back to the early eighteenth century, pointing to the fact that until then, most inside doors did not come with locks.

one that provides Wi-Fi kiosks in New York City), has turned into a sour slog since it was announced in late 2017. "Is this the exciting city of the future or an urban company town run by a data giant? I think it's the latter," Charlie Angus, a Canadian parliament member, told CNN. In May 2020, Sidewalk pulled out of the project entirely, citing "unprecedented economic uncertainty." The Canadian Civil Liberties Association called the decision "a victory for privacy and democracy." It's not that critics don't want a "smart city" in theory, but rather, they don't want a company like Google further devouring our personal data for profit and leaving behind a soulless shell of a place.

A city is not a piece of software, nor is it a car engine or a lateral-thinking puzzle. Tackling cities like they're lines of code that need sprucing up and debugging fundamentally misunderstands and warps what a city is. "When we misinterpret complex social issues as technology problems, we evaluate solutions along purely technical criteria and overlook their political consequences," writes Green in *The Smart Enough City*. "Political debate is reduced to narrow technocratic discussions of efficiency." Green is not opposed to smart cities—in fact he spent years working for Boston's Department of Innovation and Technology trying to figure out a just and, yes, smart vision of future Boston. That will likely involve technologies, but it won't start with them. "Utopian technological solutions fail to provide the answers that cities need," he writes.

In *Invisible Cities*, Italo Calvino writes, "With cities, it is as with dreams: everything imaginable can be dreamed, but even the most unexpected dream is a rebus that conceals a desire or, its reverse, a fear. Cities, like dreams, are made of desires and fears, even if the thread of their discourse is secret, their rules are absurd, their perspectives deceitful, and everything conceals something else." Smart cities are exactly this—equal parts exciting, enticing, absurd, and nightmarish. The question is whether we can take hold of the dream, keep our eyes open, and steer it toward cities that feel loved, lived in, cared for, and unique.

PORTRAIT OF THE ARTIST AS AN ALGORITHM

BY JULIA GFRÖRER

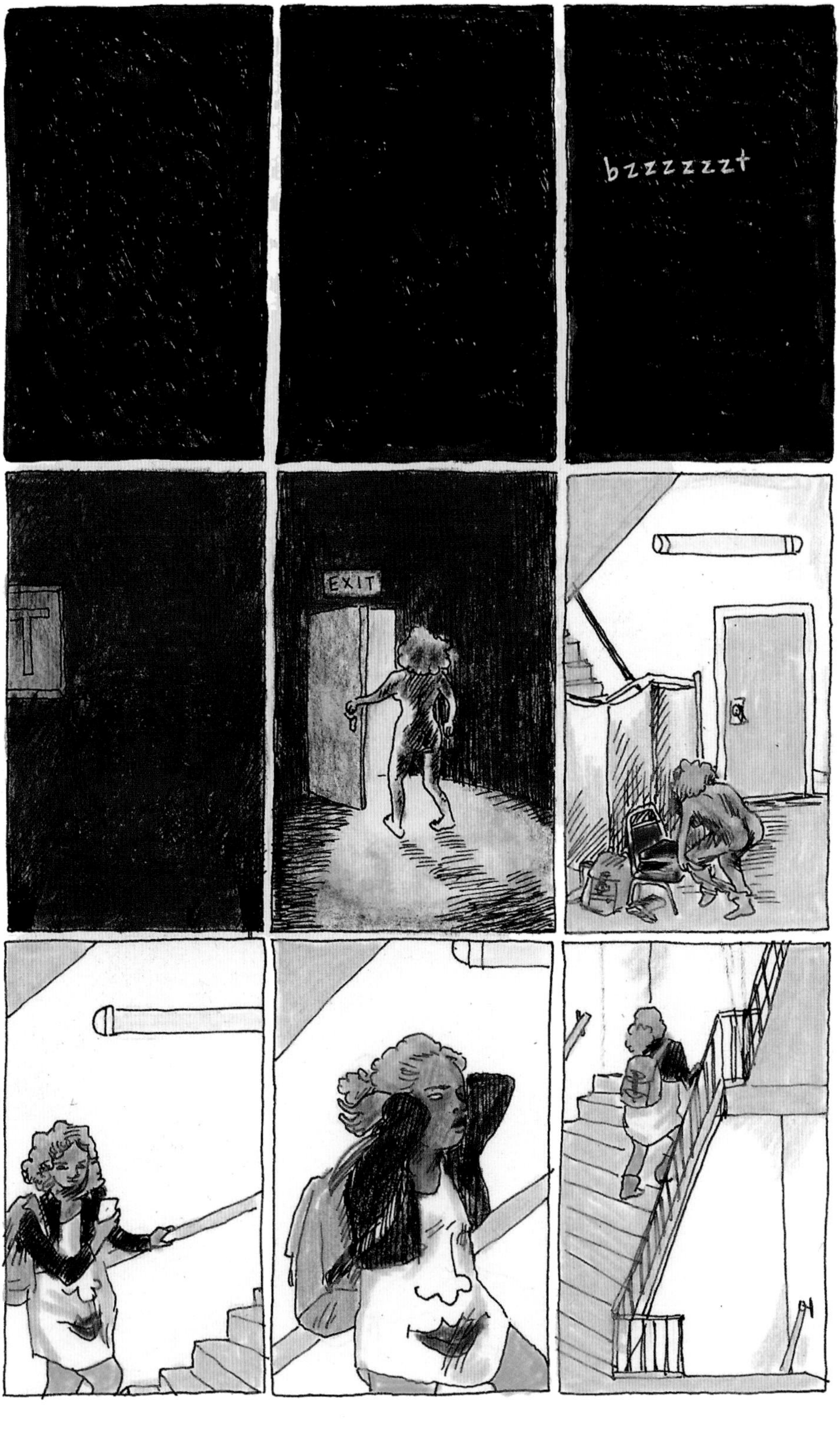
bzzzzzzt
EXIT

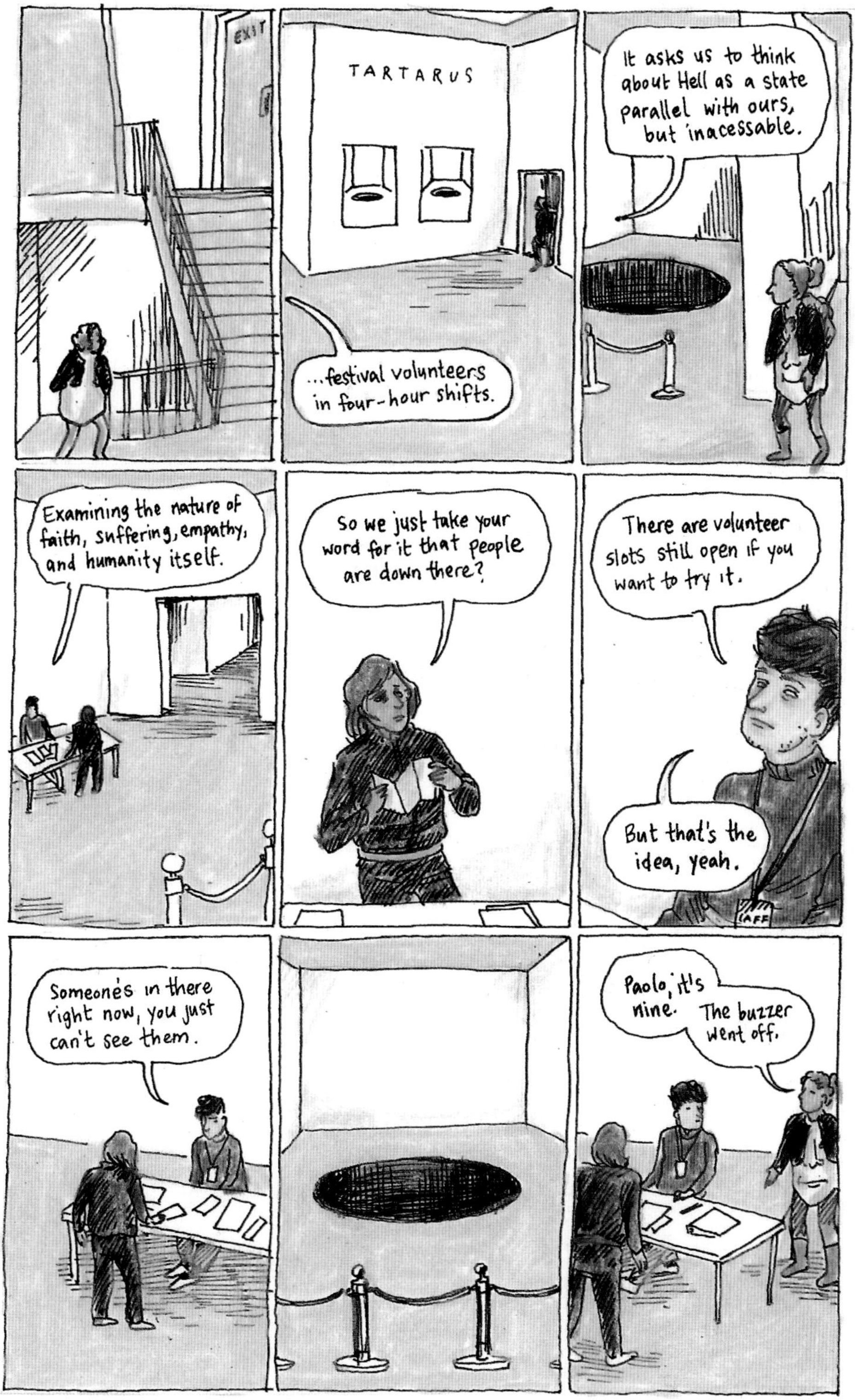

TARTARUS
...festival volunteers in four-hour shifts.
It asks us to think about Hell as a state parallel with ours, but inacessable.
Examining the nature of faith, suffering, empathy, and humanity itself.
So we just take your word for it that people are down there?
There are volunteer slots still open if you want to try it.
But that's the idea, yeah.
Someone's in there right now, you just can't see them.
Paolo, it's nine.
The buzzer went off.

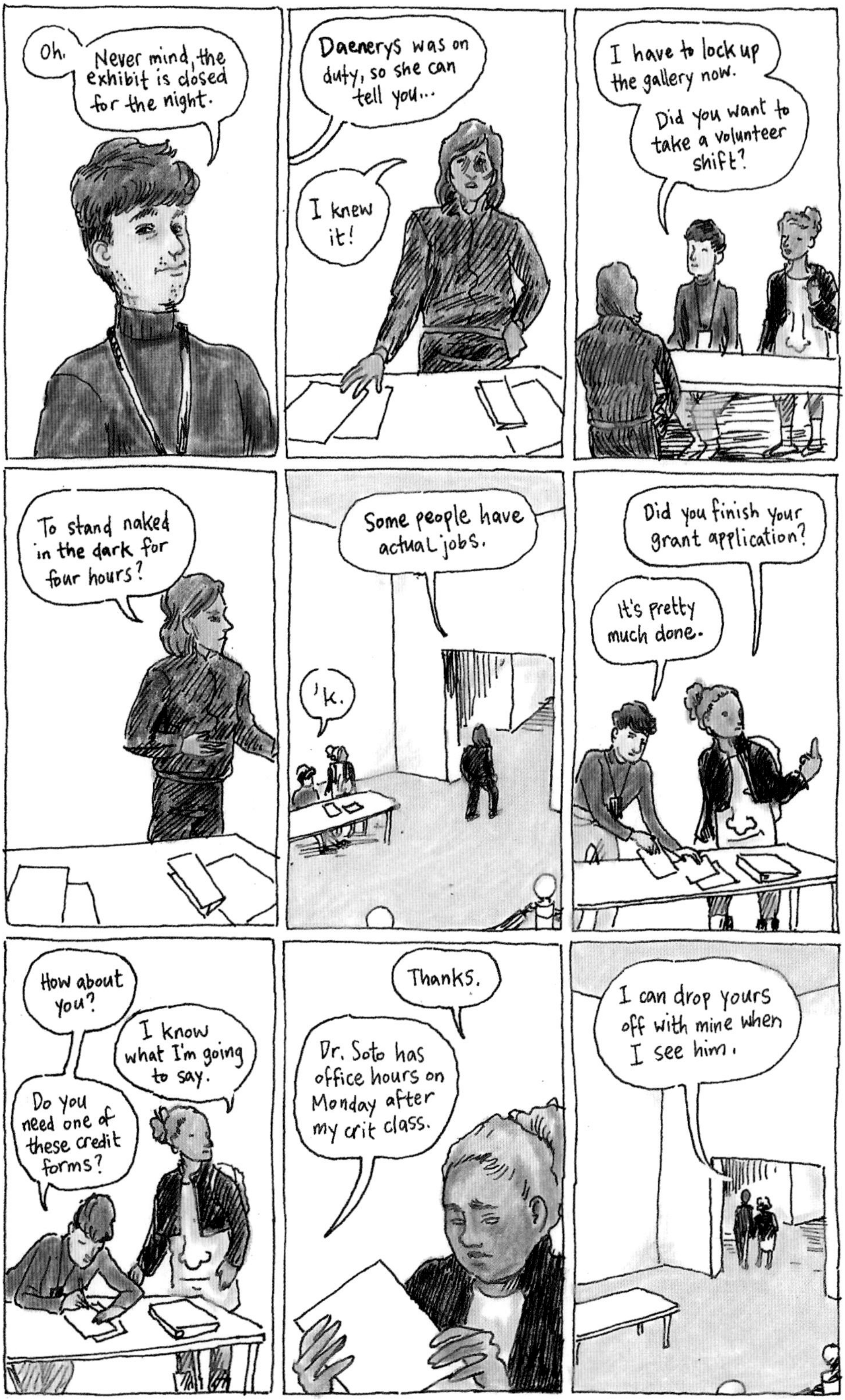

Oh.
Never mind, the exhibit is closed for the night.
Daenerys was on duty, so she can tell you...
I knew it!
I have to lock up the gallery now.
Did you want to take a volunteer shift?
To stand naked in the dark for four hours?
Some people have actual jobs.
'k.
Did you finish your grant application?
It's pretty much done.
How about you?
I know what I'm going to say.
Do you need one of these credit forms?
Thanks.
Dr. Soto has office hours on Monday after my crit class.
I can drop yours off with mine when I see him.

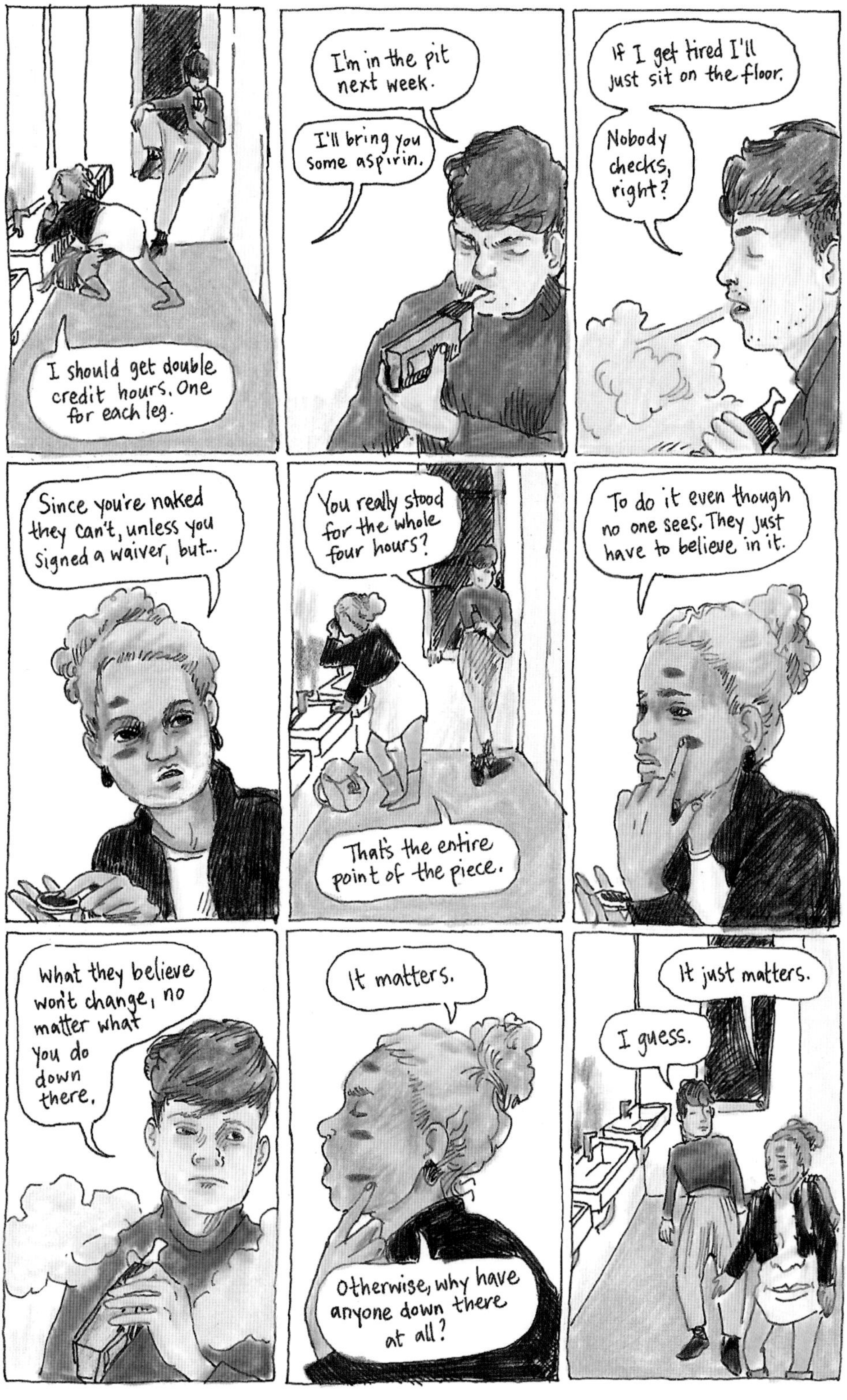
I should get double credit hours. One for each leg.
I'm in the pit next week.
I'll bring you some aspirin.
If I get tired I'll just sit on the floor.
Nobody checks, right?
Since you're naked they can't, unless you signed a waiver, but..
You really stood for the whole four hours?
That's the entire point of the piece.
To do it even though no one sees. They just have to believe in it.
What they believe won't change, no matter what you do down there.
It matters.
Otherwise, why have anyone down there at all?
It just matters.
I guess.

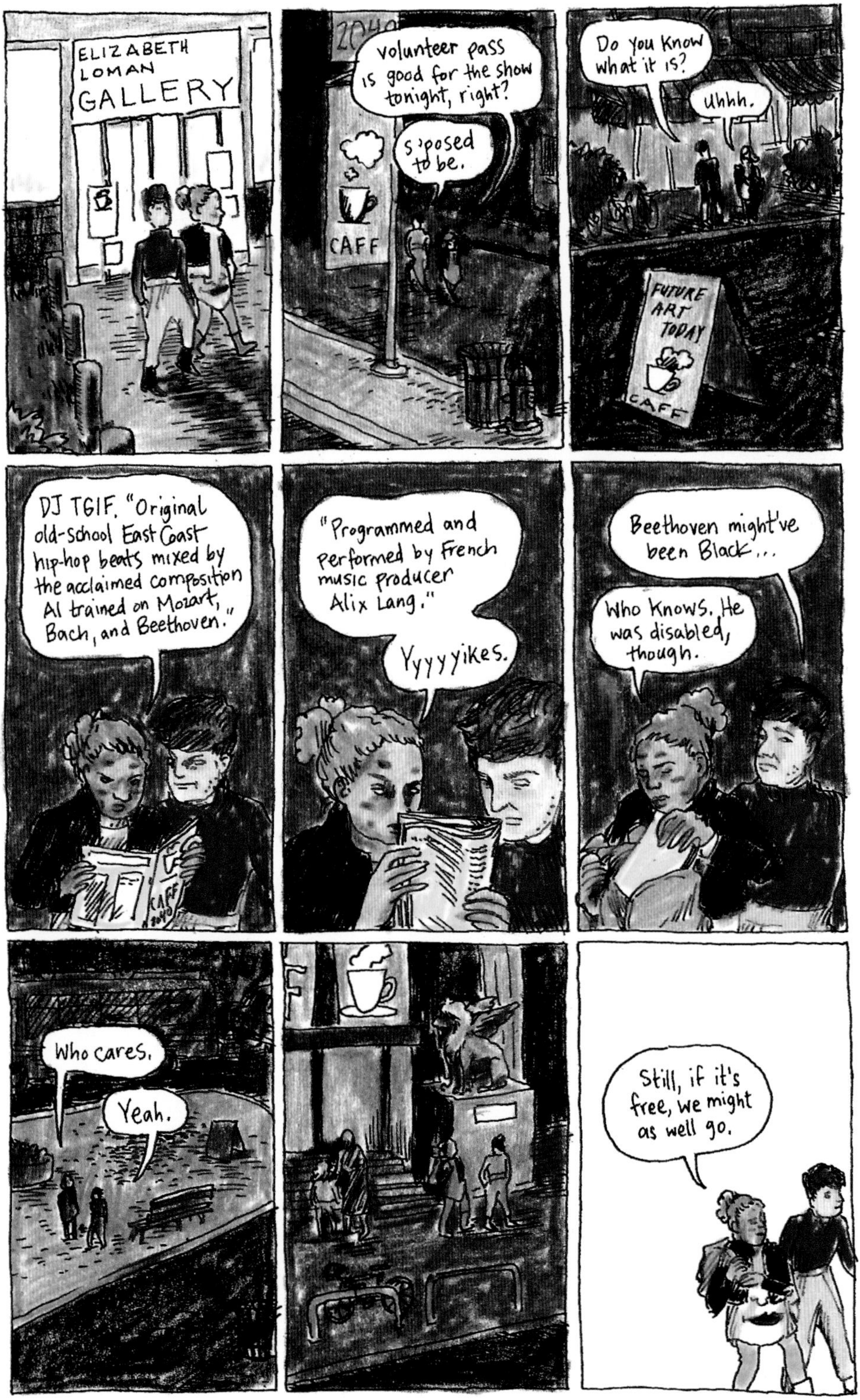
ELIZABETH LOMAN GALLERY
2040
Volunteer pass is good for the show tonight, right?
S'posed to be.
CAFF
Do you know what it is?
Uhhh.
FUTURE ART TODAY
CAFF
DJ TGIF. "Original old-school East Coast hip-hop beats mixed by the acclaimed composition AI trained on Mozart, Bach, and Beethoven."
CAFF 2040
"Programmed and performed by French music producer Alix Lang."
Yyyyyikes.
Beethoven might've been Black...
Who knows. He was disabled, though.
Who cares.
Yeah.
Still, if it's free, we might as well go.

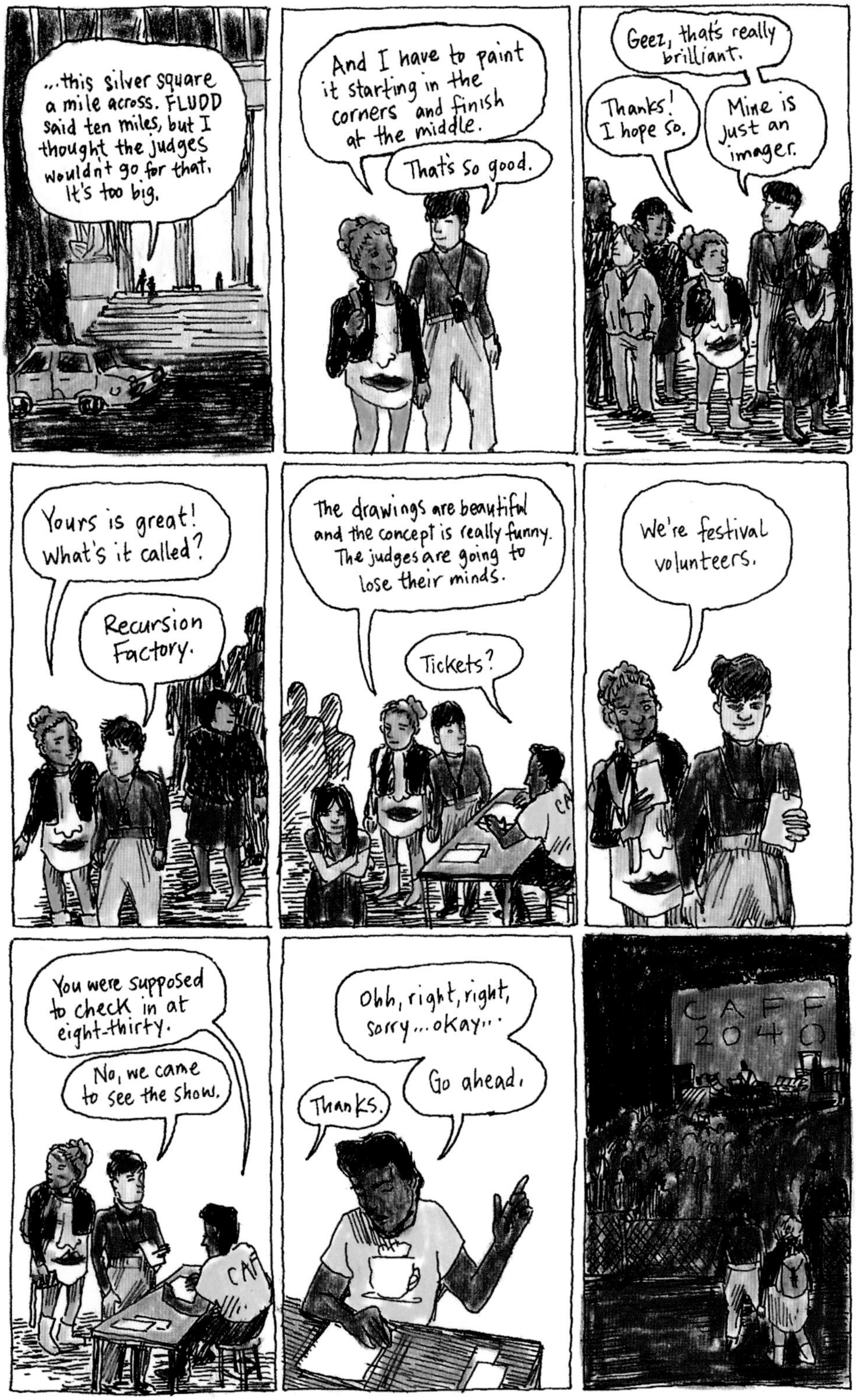
...this silver square a mile across. FLUDD said ten miles, but I thought the judges wouldn't go for that. It's too big.
And I have to paint it starting in the corners and finish at the middle.
That's so good.
Geez, that's really brilliant.
Thanks! I hope so.
Mine is just an imager.
Yours is great! What's it called?
Recursion Factory.
The drawings are beautiful and the concept is really funny. The judges are going to lose their minds.
Tickets?
We're festival volunteers.
You were supposed to check in at eight-thirty.
No, we came to see the show.
Ohh, right, right, sorry... okay...
Go ahead.
Thanks.
CAFF 2040

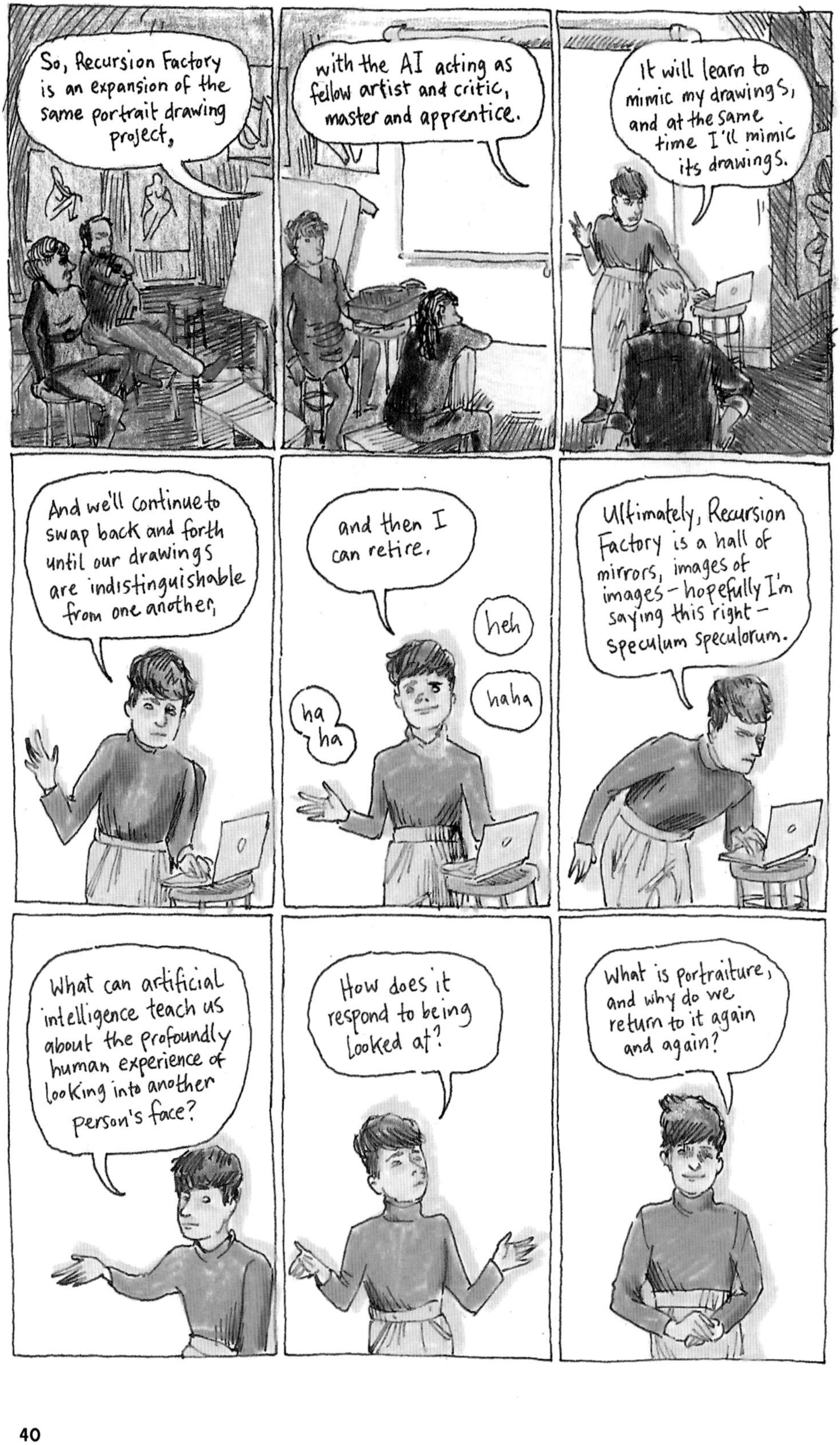

So, Recursion Factory is an expansion of the same portrait drawing project,
with the AI acting as fellow artist and critic, master and apprentice.
It will learn to mimic my drawings, and at the same time I'll mimic its drawings.
And we'll continue to swap back and forth until our drawings are indistinguishable from one another,
and then I can retire.
heh
ha ha
haha
Ultimately, Recursion Factory is a hall of mirrors, images of images—hopefully I'm saying this right—speculum speculorum.
What can artificial intelligence teach us about the profoundly human experience of looking into another person's face?
How does it respond to being looked at?
What is portraiture, and why do we return to it again and again?

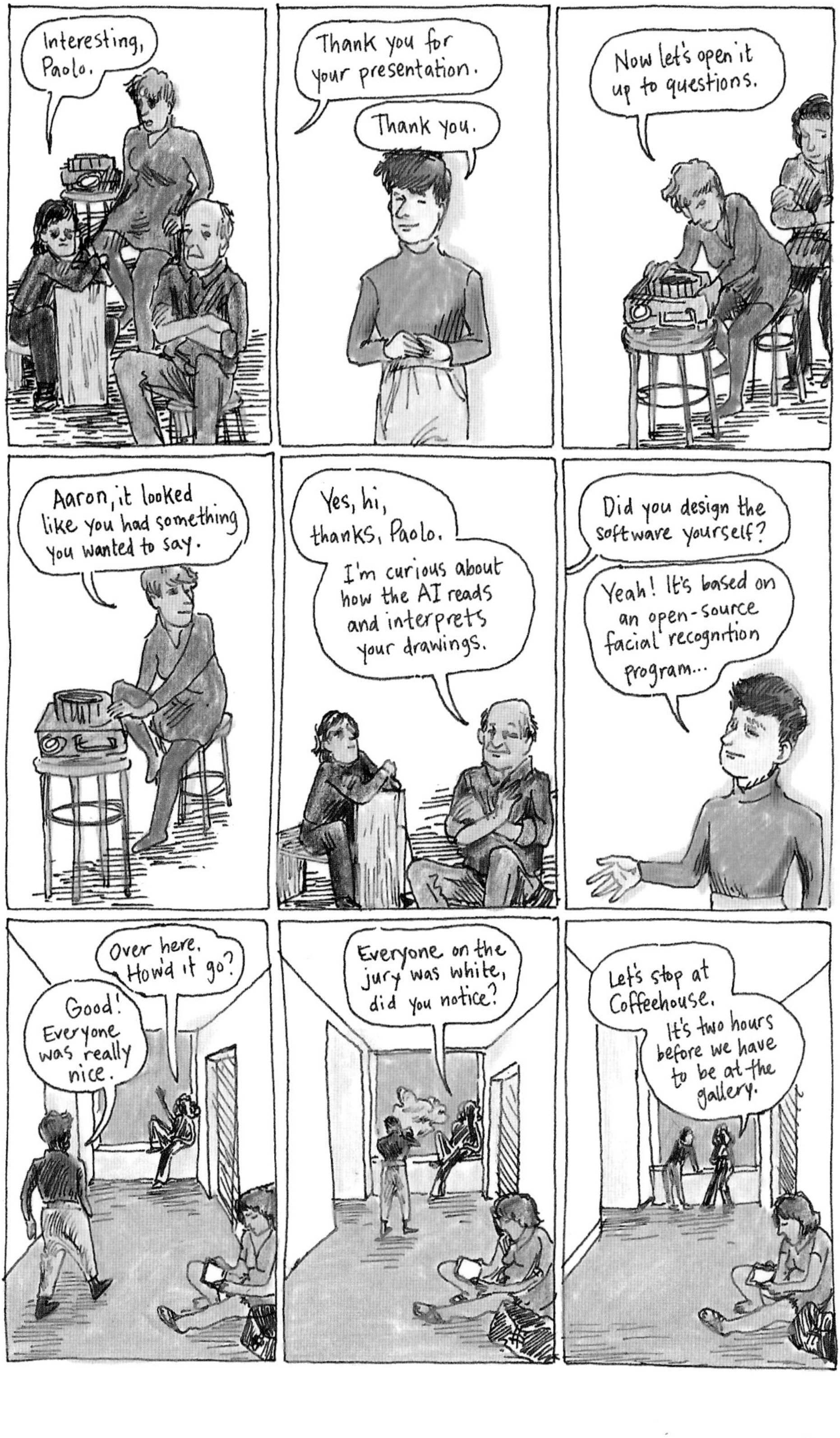
Interesting, Paolo.
Thank you for your presentation.
Thank you.
Now let's open it up to questions.
Aaron, it looked like you had something you wanted to say.
Yes, hi, thanks, Paolo.
I'm curious about how the AI reads and interprets your drawings.
Did you design the software yourself?
Yeah! It's based on an open-source facial recognition program...
Over here. How'd it go?
Good! Everyone was really nice.
Everyone on the jury was white, did you notice?
Let's stop at Coffeehouse.
It's two hours before we have to be at the gallery.

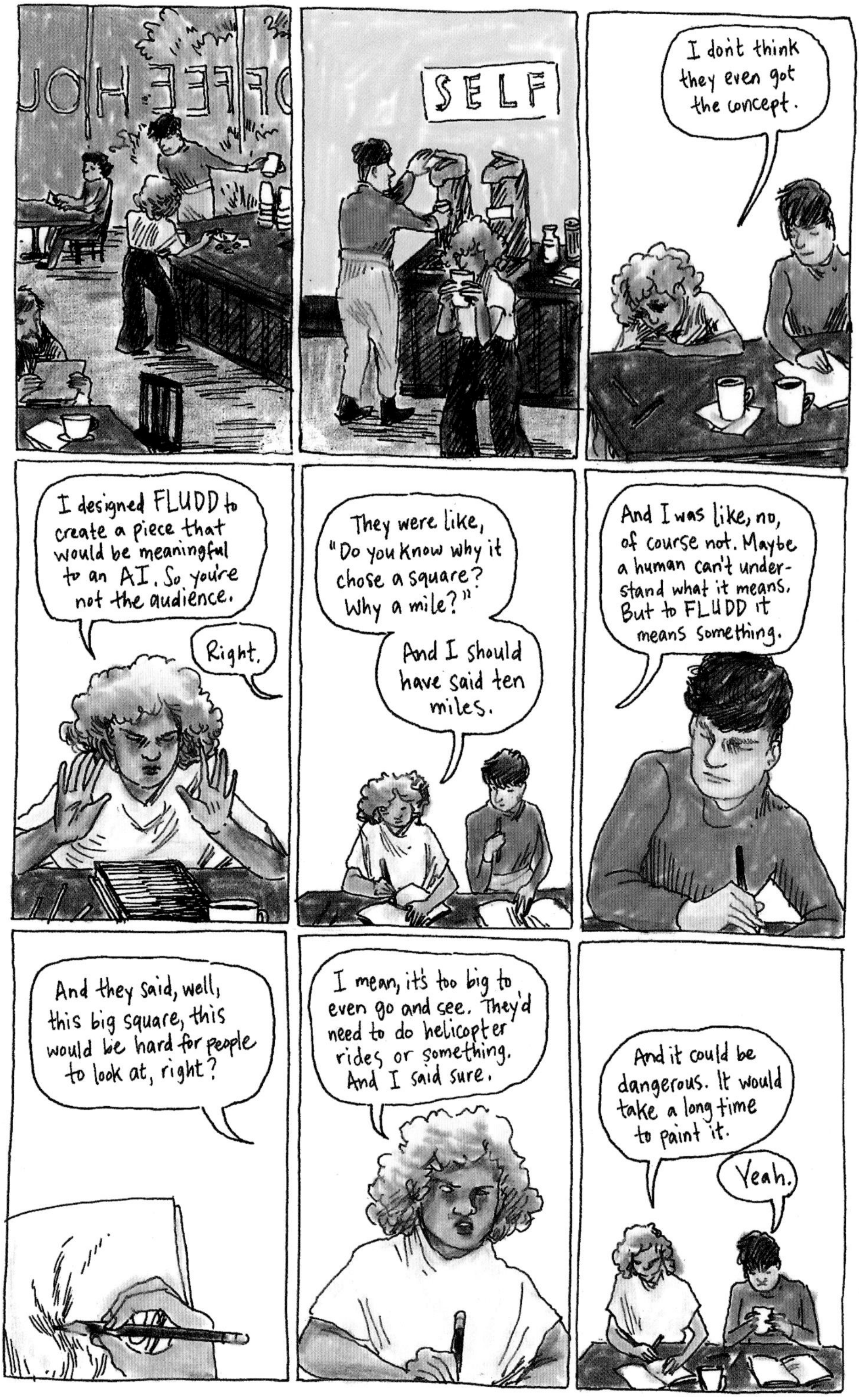
SELF
I don't think they even got the concept.
I designed FLUDD to create a piece that would be meaningful to an AI. So you're not the audience.
Right.
They were like, "Do you know why it chose a square? Why a mile?"
And I should have said ten miles.
And I was like, no, of course not. Maybe a human can't understand what it means. But to FLUDD it means something.
And they said, well, this big square, this would be hard for people to look at, right?
I mean, it's too big to even go and see. They'd need to do helicopter rides or something. And I said sure.
And it could be dangerous. It would take a long time to paint it.
Yeah.

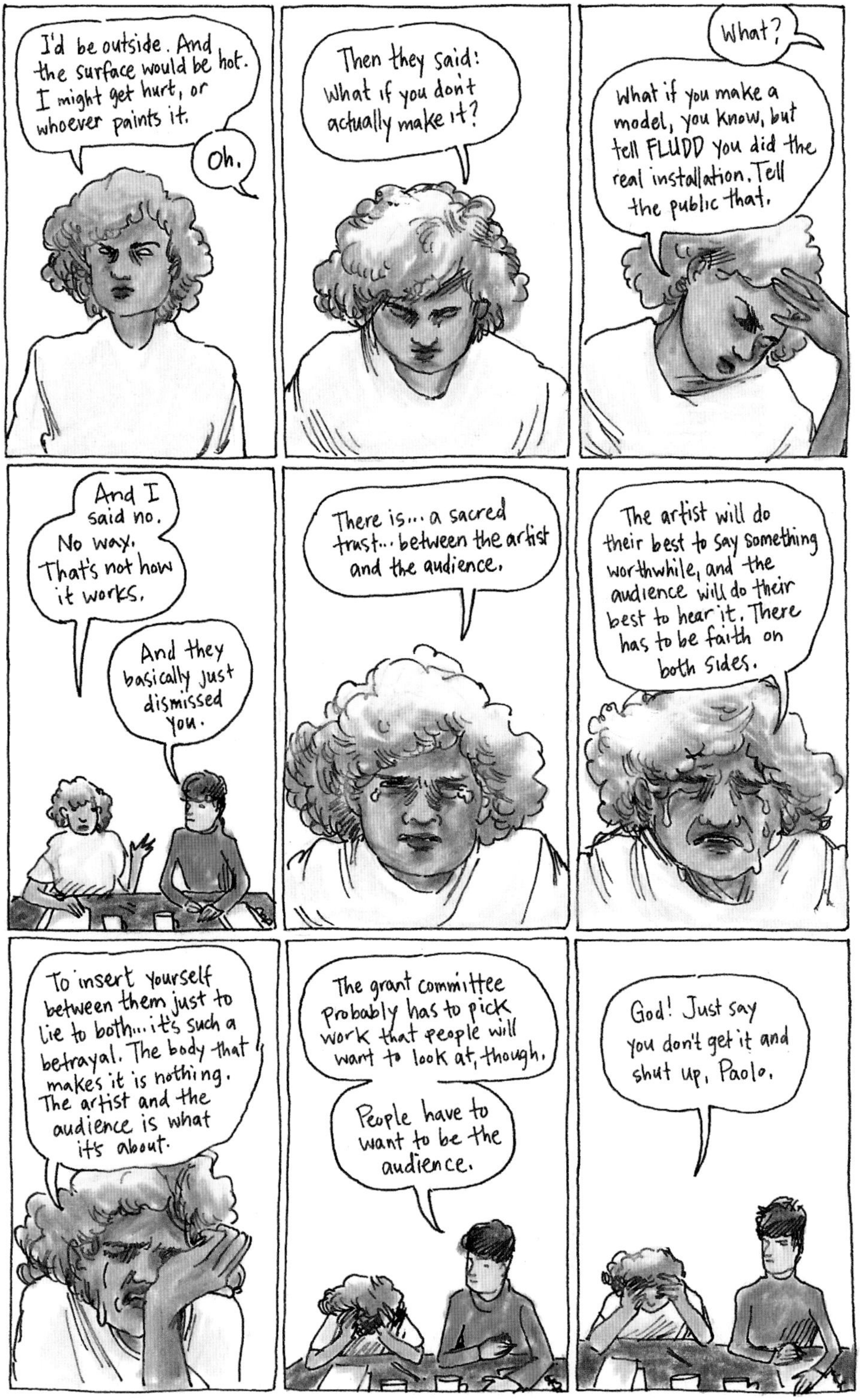
I'd be outside. And the surface would be hot. I might get hurt, or whoever paints it.
Oh.
Then they said: What if you don't actually make it?
What?
What if you make a model, you know, but tell FLUDD you did the real installation. Tell the public that.
And I said no. No way. That's not how it works.
And they basically just dismissed you.
There is... a sacred trust... between the artist and the audience.
The artist will do their best to say something worthwhile, and the audience will do their best to hear it. There has to be faith on both sides.
To insert yourself between them just to lie to both... it's such a betrayal. The body that makes it is nothing. The artist and the audience is what it's about.
The grant committee probably has to pick work that people will want to look at, though.
People have to want to be the audience.
God! Just say you don't get it and shut up, Paolo.

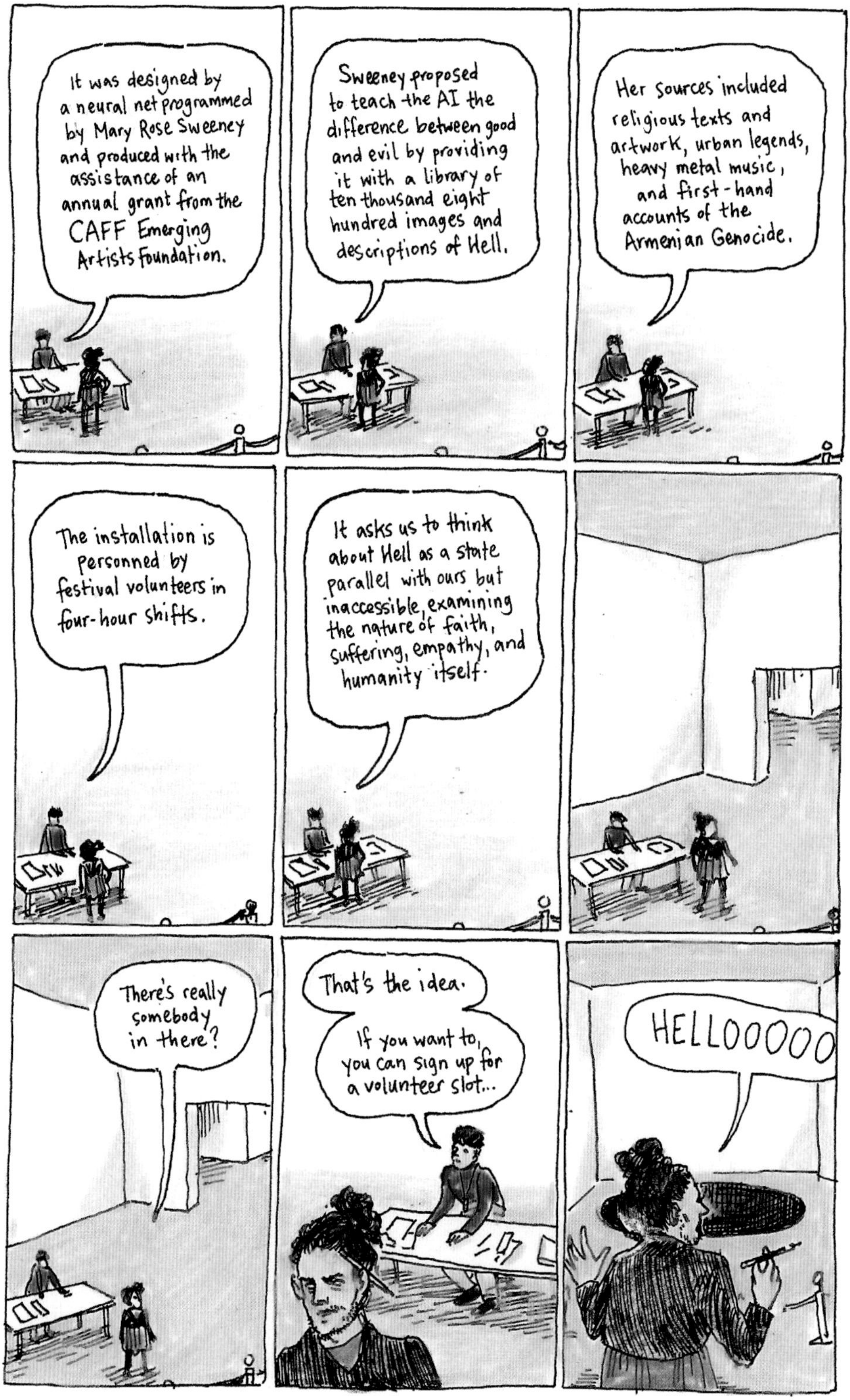
It was designed by a neural net programmed by Mary Rose Sweeney and produced with the assistance of an annual grant from the CAFF Emerging Artists Foundation.
Sweeney proposed to teach the AI the difference between good and evil by providing it with a library of ten thousand eight hundred images and descriptions of Hell.
Her sources included religious texts and artwork, urban legends, heavy metal music, and first-hand accounts of the Armenian Genocide.
The installation is personned by festival volunteers in four-hour shifts.
It asks us to think about Hell as a state parallel with ours but inaccessible, examining the nature of faith, suffering, empathy, and humanity itself.
There's really somebody in there?
That's the idea.
If you want to, you can sign up for a volunteer slot...
HELLOOOOO

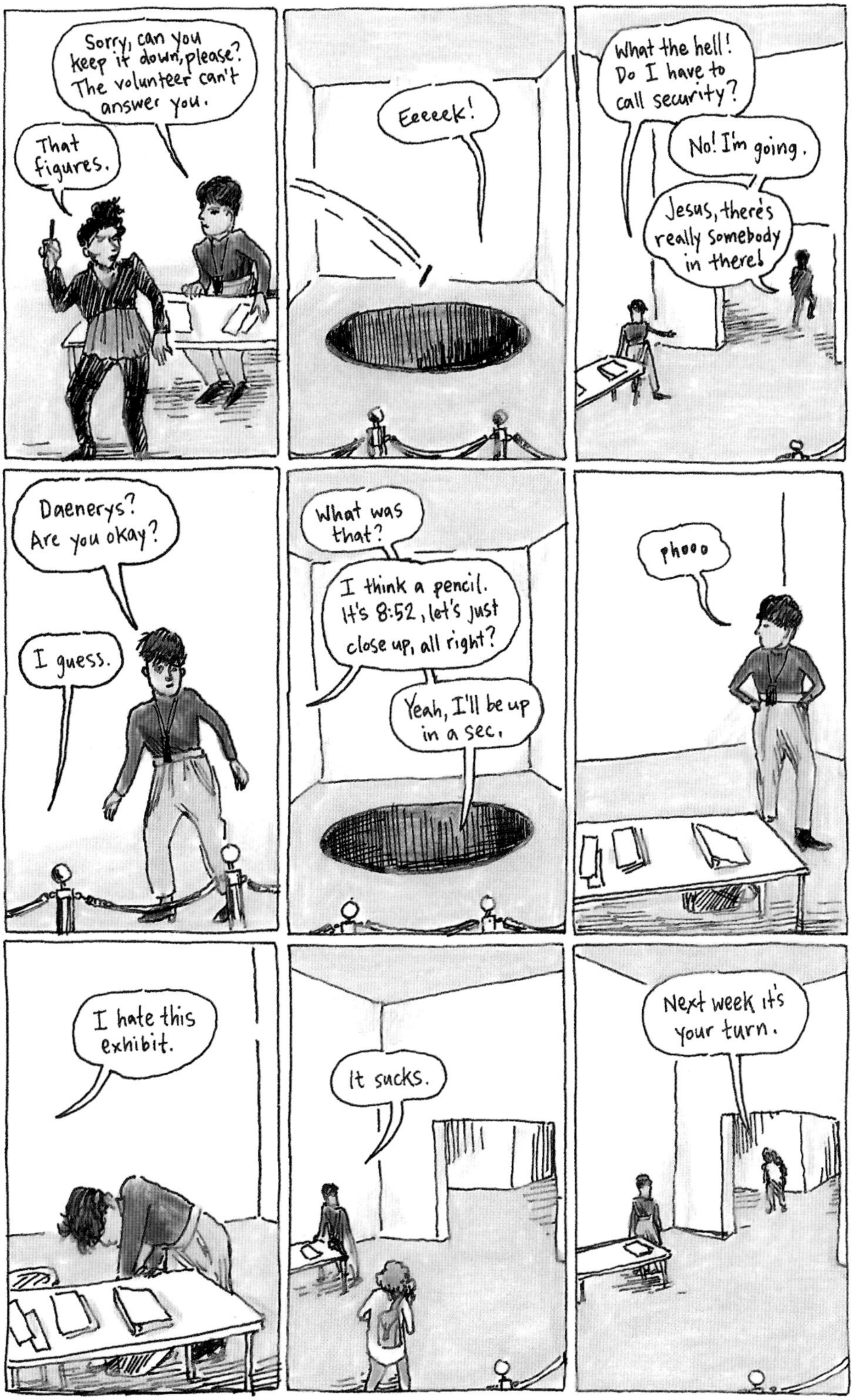
Sorry, can you keep it down, please? The volunteer can't answer you.
That figures.
Eeeeek!
What the hell! Do I have to call security?
No! I'm going.
Jesus, there's really somebody in there!
Daenerys? Are you okay?
I guess.
What was that?
I think a pencil. It's 8:52, let's just close up, all right?
Yeah, I'll be up in a sec.
phooo
I hate this exhibit.
It sucks.
Next week it's your turn.

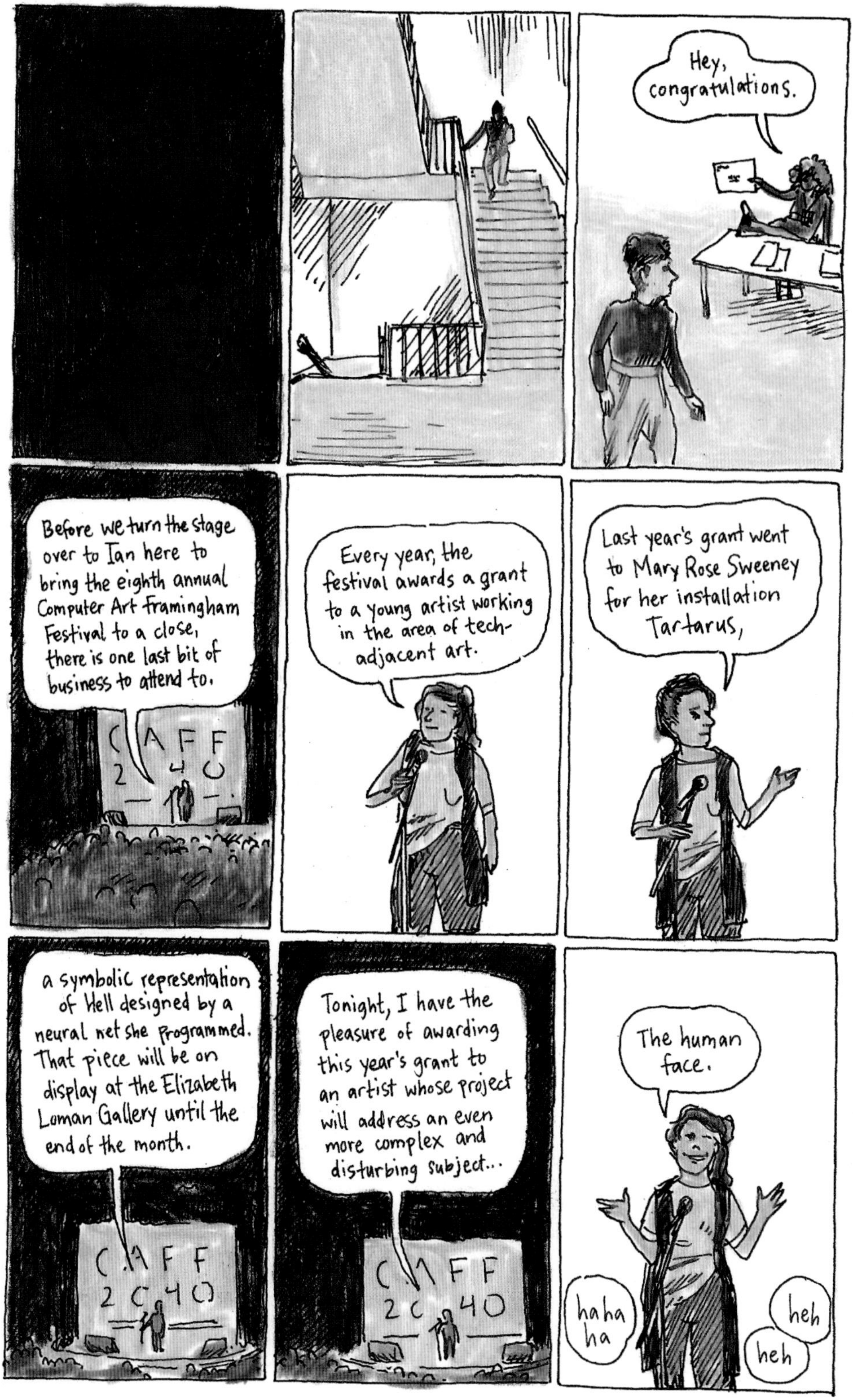

Hey, congratulations.
Before we turn the stage over to Ian here to bring the eighth annual Computer Art Framingham Festival to a close, there is one last bit of business to attend to.
CAFF 2040
Every year, the festival awards a grant to a young artist working in the area of tech-adjacent art.
Last year's grant went to Mary Rose Sweeney for her installation Tartarus,
a symbolic representation of Hell designed by a neural net she programmed. That piece will be on display at the Elizabeth Loman Gallery until the end of the month.
Tonight, I have the pleasure of awarding this year's grant to an artist whose project will address an even more complex and disturbing subject...
The human face.
haha ha
heh
heh

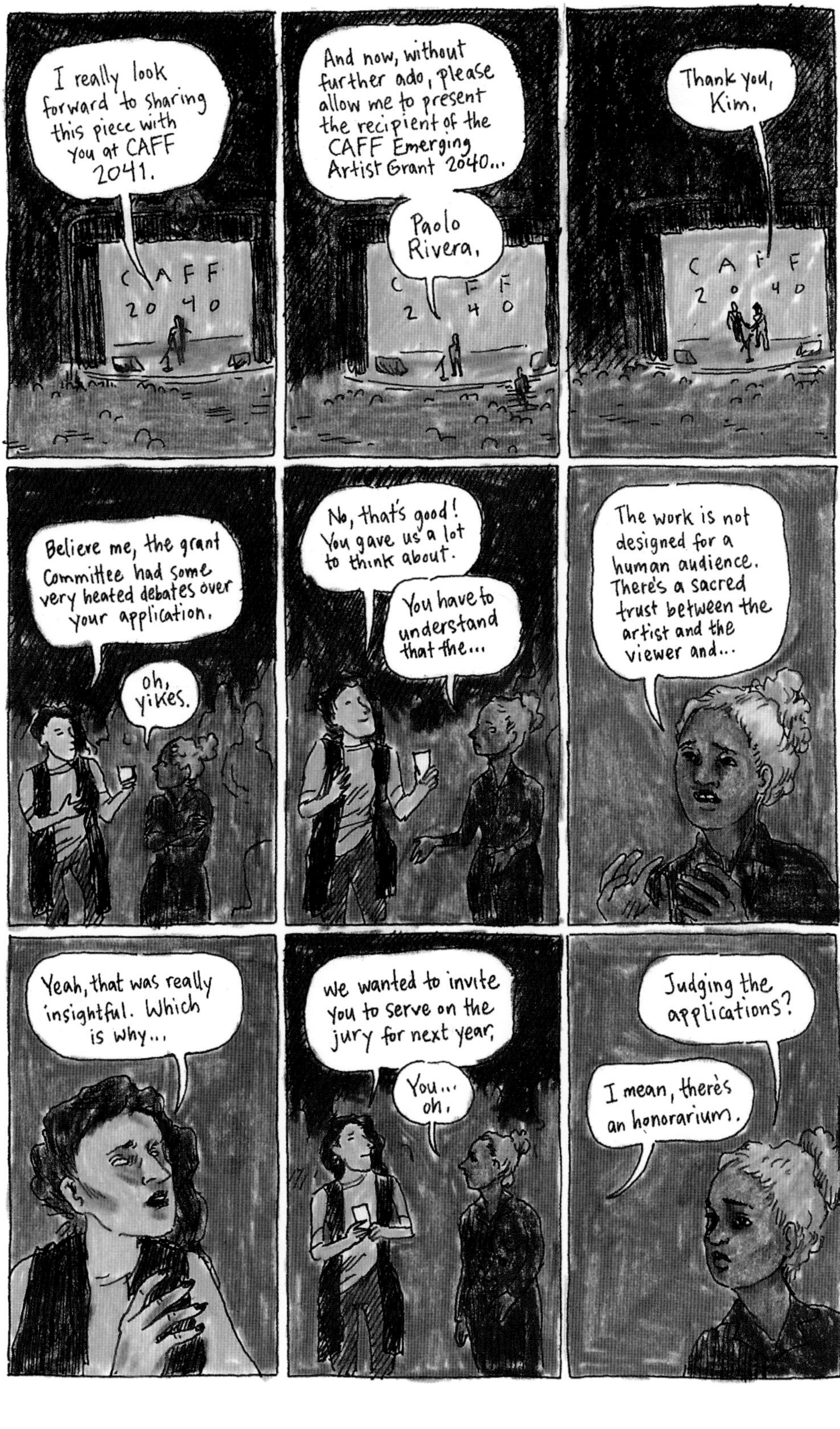

I really look forward to sharing this piece with you at CAFF 2041.
CAFF 2040
And now, without further ado, please allow me to present the recipient of the CAFF Emerging Artist Grant 2040...
Paolo Rivera.
CAFF 2040
Thank you, Kim.
CAFF 2040
Believe me, the grant committee had some very heated debates over your application.
Oh, yikes.
No, that's good! You gave us a lot to think about.
You have to understand that the...
The work is not designed for a human audience. There's a sacred trust between the artist and the viewer and...
Yeah, that was really insightful. Which is why...
We wanted to invite you to serve on the jury for next year.
You... oh.
Judging the applications?
I mean, there's an honorarium.

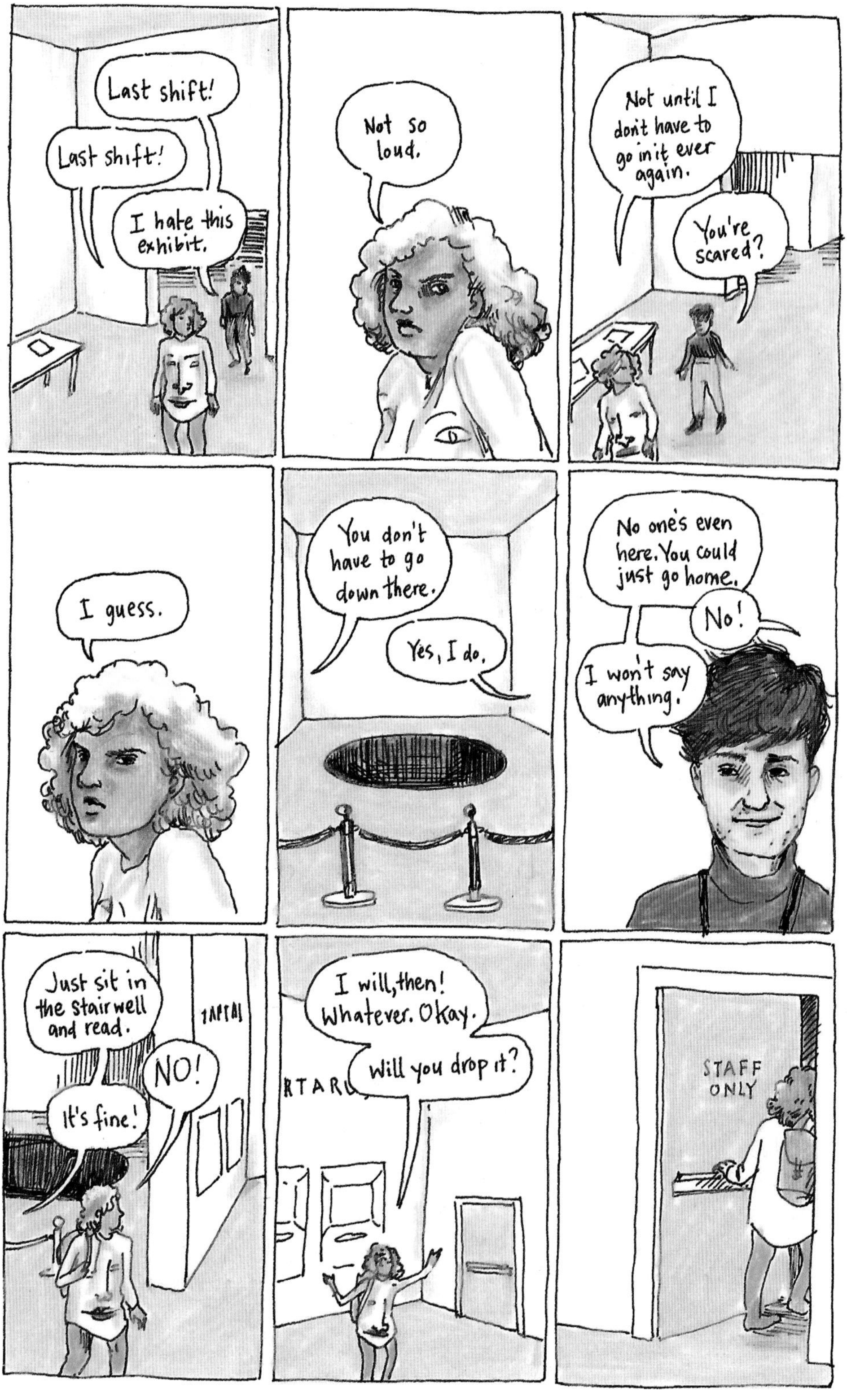
Last shift!
Last shift!
I hate this exhibit.
Not so loud.
Not until I don't have to go in it ever again.
You're scared?
I guess.
You don't have to go down there.
Yes, I do.
No one's even here. You could just go home.
No!
I won't say anything.
Just sit in the stairwell and read.
NO!
It's fine!
I will, then! Whatever. Okay.
Will you drop it?
STAFF ONLY

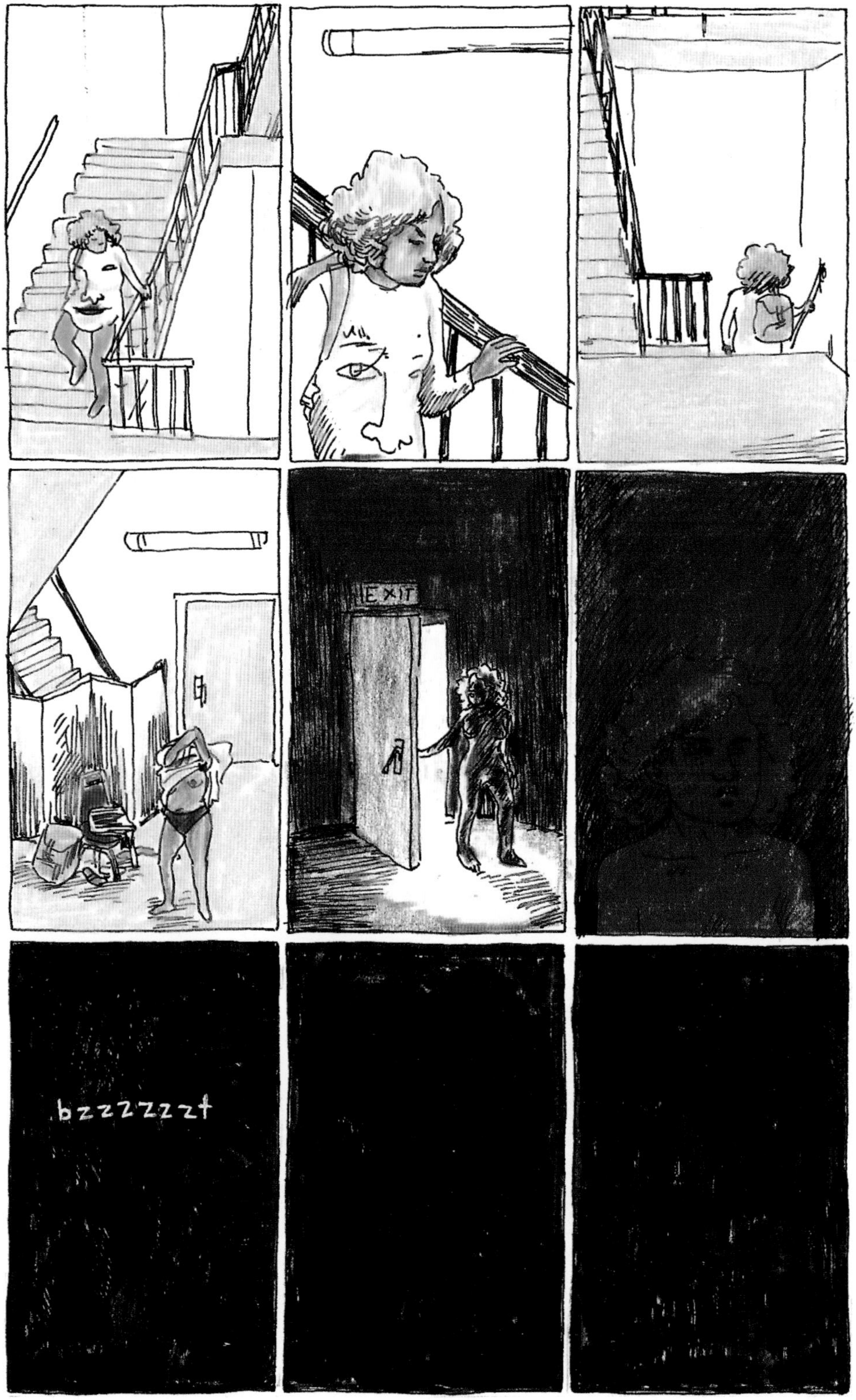

EXIT
bzzzzzzt

PORTRAIT OF THE ARTIST AS AN ALGORITHM

CAN A COMPUTER MAKE ART?

CAN A ROBOT MAKE ART? WHAT ABOUT AN ALGORITHM?

According to two iconic art auction houses, the answer is now yes. In the last few years, both Sotheby's and Christie's have auctioned off algorithmically created works of art—a painting and an ever-changing video installation. The painting, a gold-framed portrait that looks a bit like a fever-dream Rembrandt, went for $425,500 to an anonymous phone bidder. Algorithms, and the artists who wield them, have arrived.

If you ask the average person whether a machine can make art, many of them generally say: "No, art is something only humans do." In fact, Julia Gfrörer, the artist who created the comic you just read, picked this idea because she had that exact reaction. "I have to admit that I myself had a very strong negative reaction to the idea that 'art' created by an AI could be considered equivalent or interchangeable with art made by and for humans," she told me. Trying to define art is a fool's errand, but most definitions circle around the idea that art comes from a creative imagination, something that thus far we don't ascribe to machines. And yet, artists have been using machines—both simple and complex—for as long as they've made art. In fact, the very question "Can a robot make art?" goes back further than you might think.

In the 1770s, a French craftsman named Pierre Jacquet-Droz created something called "The Musician." Essentially, the Musician is a doll wearing a beautiful dress and a sheer embroidered shawl sitting in front of an organ. But she has a secret talent: When you turn her on, her fingers begin to move and press the keys of the keyboard to play a song composed just for her. By today's standards, the animatronics aren't all that impressive—imagine a baroque Chuck E. Cheese robot—but at the time they were absolutely unparalleled. While the song plays, our leading lady moves her head to the beat and a panel in her chest rises and falls to make it look like she's breathing. Jacquet-Droz traveled across Europe showing off this intricate piece of work, and the audiences were completely blown away.

"What consumed everyone was not who wrote the music, and whether she was producing art, it was that she seemed to be alive," said Elizabeth Stephens, a historian at the University of Queensland. Jacquet-Droz and his

Musician challenged one of the dominant philosophical ideas in Europe at the time, that to be alive was marked by the ability to move on your own. But Jacquet-Droz didn't stop with his piano player. He also created two other automata called "The Writer" and "The Draughstman," who use a quill and pencil respectively to write on paper. The Draughtsman can draw you a dog far better than I could, to be perfectly honest. But is that dog drawing art? Is the Musician a true musician?[1]

Stephens said yes, in a way. "The Musical Lady is not necessarily the artist, but art takes place in that room because there's a strong affective bond that's formed between the people who are listening and the person who is performing." There is art happening there, even if the dog or the song isn't itself the physical manifestation of it.

Today, very few people would see the Musician and be consumed with existential dread or wonder if the animatronic player was alive. But we still are asking a similarly fundamental question about what it means to live and to create. And our versions of the Musician have gotten far more complex. (Whether their art has gotten better, that's up for debate.)

The most vocal critics of the highly publicized piece that went for $425,500 at Christie's were not art historians or painting purists, but rather fellow AI artists. The three-person collective who made the piece, called Obvious, had used open-source and relatively simple tools to do so, compared to some of the other more complex models out there that use bigger data sets and more finely tuned algorithms. Ahmed Elgammal, the director of the Art and Artificial Intelligence Laboratory at Rutgers University, witheringly called the technique used by Obvious "totally irrelevant." Another artist called the piece "a connect-the-dots children's painting."

For their part, Christie's saw the piece as the easiest entry point into an entirely new genre. "It looks like something you'd expect Christie's to sell," Richard Lloyd, who acquired the piece for Christie's, told the *New York Times*. Other examples of more complex algorithmic creativity can be more obtuse, harder to parse. But this piece really did look a bit like someone had taken a hair dryer to, say, a portrait by Anthony van Dyck that the house sold for over $3 million in 2014. And experts expect we'll see more like Obvious's melty production on the market soon.

But who is the artist here? Most people would likely say that the coder is, the person who built and trained the algorithm. Just like a painter who uses a brush, or an illustrator who uses a drawing tablet or Photoshop, these artists use algorithms to create work. In the comic you read, the human artists behind these pieces are still credited—Mary Rose Sweeney is the one who trained the AI on images and texts and music depicting hell to create Tartarus. But at what point do we stop crediting the humans behind the code and start crediting the algorithms themselves?

---

1   An even earlier example of this kind of trickery is a surprisingly buff statue of Satan from the fifteenth or sixteenth century, with a voice box, a moving chest panel, rolling eyes, and a mechanical tongue that would poke out of his mouth to scare people as they passed through the entryway of the church.

Algorithms, and particularly a subset of algorithms called neural networks, are commonly referred to as "black boxes" because even their creators cannot always articulate how they come to decisions. These systems are trained on known data, but they make connections between that data in surprising and often obscure ways. When Elgammal looks at the output from his various models trained on art history, he is looking at the results of a process that even he cannot fully explain. When Elgammal gets an image from his model, the results are always a surprise. In fact, he cannot ask the machine to trace its steps and show its work to spell out how it got there. That's what makes it fun for him, and what convinces him that he's making art, "because I have no way to expect what I get next," he told me.

Of course, this isn't dissimilar to flesh-and-blood artists. While everyone has references they can clearly point to, influence is not a mathematical sum or even a complex equation. No artist can fully deconstruct a piece of work and write down a complete explanation for why they chose a certain color, or shape, or form.

Some critics of AI art argue that the work cannot be art because it is not original—the models are simply replicating bits and pieces of the work they see. But what "originality" means in art is fraught as well. Take the work of Elaine Sturtevant, a modern artist who made her career out of copying other artists' work and displaying it. In 2004, a Sturtevant retrospective exhibit gathered up 140 different pieces made by the artist, all copies of other work made from her memory. Sturtevant, of course, had lots to say about the concept of originality. "Thinking is at the centre of my work," she once wrote, "not the visible surface. My work is the immediacy of the apparent content being denied." She argued that her work "repeats the seductiveness of the surface and dissolves it in the process of repetition to make room for what is really important, thinking."[2]

If thinking is what makes art truly art, then what can we say the algorithm is doing when it ingests training data and makes connections that we cannot tease apart? Is that thinking? Or is it something else?

In the future, these algorithms may run continuously, learning all the time and generating more and more work without the touch of a human. And at some point, we'll start having to really consider who is the creator of the work. If Elgammal hasn't entered a single keystroke into the algorithm in years and it continues to put out new and changing pieces as it ingests more and more information and makes more and more connections, is Elgammal still the artist? And if not, what does that mean for art?

How, for example, do you authenticate a piece of algorithmically created art? In the modern art world, authenticity often matters more than the actual

---

2   Sturtevant was not universally beloved for this way of working. Some of the artists she copied appreciated her outlook, while others hated her. One artist she copied extensively, Claes Oldenburg, was absolutely irate at being replicated. And, as Anthony Downey notes in the book *Art and Authenticity*: "In a further twist to this affair, and in what would no doubt be an ironic afterthought today, there are more of Sturtevant's 'remakes' still in circulation now than there are of Oldenburg's originals."

piece itself, thanks to the number of forgeries out there. If this work is going to be auctioned off for six figures, there's certainly an incentive to make sure that it was in fact created by the AI in question and not some cut-rate imitation.

And what about art critics and museums? How are they to judge and display this fundamentally new kind of art? "The job of being an art critic is just to have a really strong visual memory, and to have seen a lot of art," said Orit Gat, an art writer and critic. "That visual background is what allows you to judge things, to contextualize them, to think about them in relationship to the history of art, in relationship to what other people are making right now." Can an algorithm's work be in conversation with pieces of art that the algorithm has not "seen"?

Technically speaking, all AI work started with a body of human art. And yet, the algorithm isn't "responding" to pieces the way an artist might. The neural network doesn't know the context of pieces, that one might be about war and another about sexuality and a third about both at the same time. It only sees the shapes and colors and lines and textures. It might, if it is smart enough, be able to identify objects: This painting has a person in it, or a sheep, or a cloud. An algorithm can tell you if a painting is a landscape or a street scene, but it cannot decipher what Edward Hopper was trying to convey with his use of light in a painting like *Nighthawks*.[3] And if it is not ingesting meaning, only appearance, can it, in Sturtevant's words "make room for what is really important, thinking"?

Elgammal's art is in many ways the antithesis of Sturtevant's. Where hers tries to dissolve away the surface and remove the physical object in favor of the thinking behind it, Elgammal's AI sees only the surface and not the thinking. If I had the skills to do so, my dream would be to train an algorithm on Sturtevant's copies, just to see what happened.

If algorithmic art can't play nice in a regular museum, perhaps we should give it its own space. And, just to up the ante a little bit (as is the *Flash Forward* way), what if the museum wasn't designed for humans at all? In the comic you read, you saw artists grappling with what it means to try and interpret work designed by code that still must ultimately be observed and judged by humans. Daenerys struggles to explain her piece to the judges, who want to understand something fundamentally un-understandable. "Maybe a human can't understand what it means," she says to Paolo. "But to FLUDD it means something." But at the end of the day, as Paolo notes, "People have to want to be the audience." But what if they didn't?

Algorithmic art-making systems can churn out more images than even the most prolific artists could ever dream of. More than we could ever look at with our puny human eyeholes and lumpy brains. But AI visitors don't have that problem. They can take in as much as their binary brethren can pump out. And because bots don't have eyes, they wouldn't need the images printed onto canvas, nicely lit, framed, or even signed. And if we really let our algorithmic artists run wild, they might create pieces for each other that aren't visual at all.

---

3   To really appreciate this painting, I recommend listening to an episode of the podcast *Accession* called "1952: *Nighthawks*."

Imagine this: You walk into the Museum of Computer-Generated Art and are met with a map and a visitor's guide. The docent kindly reminds you that this museum is by and for machines, which means that there are some pieces you will not be able to access or see. Perhaps you're told about a piece called *Look Both Ways* for example, by the AI artist Eleanor (who I made up for the purposes of this discussion), that is based on the infrared signals that self-driving car systems use to process their visual input at night. Human eyes can't see it, but the digital and mechanical visitors all say they appreciate it greatly.

Maybe you can tell that I have a great deal of fun thinking about this question and imagining what it might mean to really let neural networks be artists in their own right. But (and you knew there was a but coming, didn't you? This is also the *Flash Forward* way) I do think there's a potential darkness here, too.

Despite what some might try to claim, algorithms are not magic. Nor are they neutral. Instead, algorithms are mathematical models created by humans to process and manipulate data. More and more, these models are making their way into our daily lives in the forms of systems that offer up decisions about everything from what health care plan we're offered to our credit score, to who gets bail and who doesn't. And because the data that goes into algorithms often comes from biased sources, the answers that come out echo that bias. Black defendants score higher on a recidivism algorithm than white ones who committed the same crimes; policing algorithms claim to "predict" crime but really just predict where police are more likely to be; facial recognition systems incorrectly flag darker faces as "criminal" far more than white ones; hiring algorithms are biased against women. I could go on, but I'll spare you.[4]

In all of these cases, ethicists and coders have had to repeatedly refute the idea that "math can't be biased" and that these systems are simply making completely neutral decisions. As part of that argument, experts remind us that these systems are not autonomous all-knowing overlords, but rather our own products that reflect our own biases. We make them. We are responsible for them.

Those who want to continue using these flawed and often dangerous systems in turn claim that these algorithms are not just neutral, but natural. That their decisions are the work of an independent force unimpeached by human flaws. The digital activist and science-fiction author Cory Doctorow calls this tactic "empiricism-washing." In the context of life and death decisions like criminal justice and health care, it's incredibly important that we resist this narrative.

So how do we square the idea that we might one day allow an algorithm to become an artist—to be removed enough from the human touch that its work is considered original art conceived of and produced by the network rather than the human who coded it—with the real danger of empiricism-washing? If an algorithm can be a stand-alone artist, can't it also be a judge or a cop or a doctor?

Perhaps then the question is not "Can an algorithm make art?" but rather "Should we let it"?

---

4   At this point, the list of resources on algorithmic bias is huge, but if you're looking for a place to start, try *Algorithms of Oppression* by Safiya Umoja Noble and *Automating Inequality* by Virginia Eubanks.

PIRACEUTICALS

BY JOHN JENNINGS

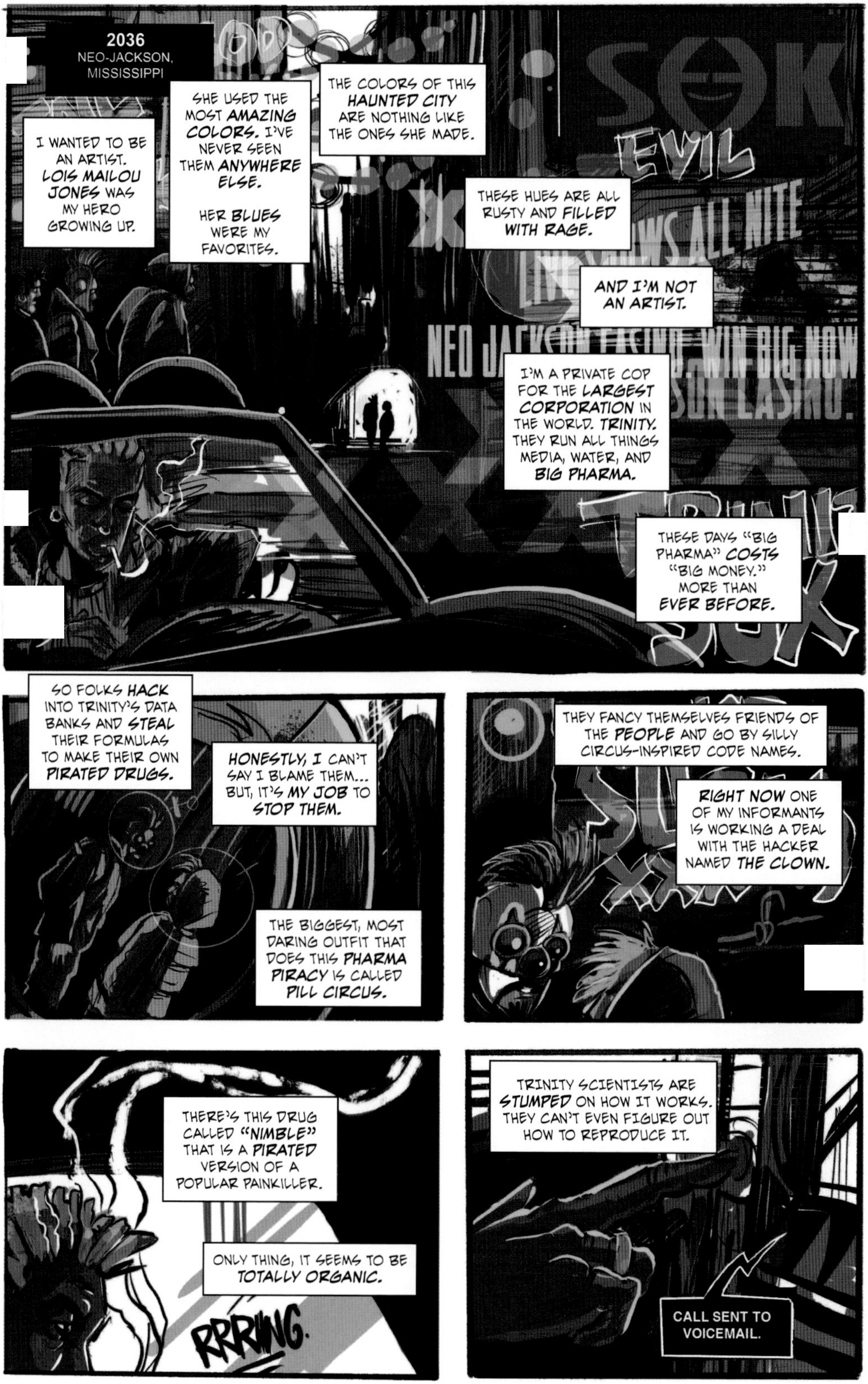
2036
NEO-JACKSON, MISSISSIPPI
I WANTED TO BE AN ARTIST. LOIS MAILOU JONES WAS MY HERO GROWING UP.
SHE USED THE MOST AMAZING COLORS. I'VE NEVER SEEN THEM ANYWHERE ELSE.
HER BLUES WERE MY FAVORITES.
THE COLORS OF THIS HAUNTED CITY ARE NOTHING LIKE THE ONES SHE MADE.
EVIL
THESE HUES ARE ALL RUSTY AND FILLED WITH RAGE.
AND I'M NOT AN ARTIST.
NEO JACKSON CASINO. WIN BIG NOW
I'M A PRIVATE COP FOR THE LARGEST CORPORATION IN THE WORLD. TRINITY. THEY RUN ALL THINGS MEDIA, WATER, AND BIG PHARMA.
THESE DAYS "BIG PHARMA" COSTS "BIG MONEY." MORE THAN EVER BEFORE.
SO FOLKS HACK INTO TRINITY'S DATA BANKS AND STEAL THEIR FORMULAS TO MAKE THEIR OWN PIRATED DRUGS.
HONESTLY, I CAN'T SAY I BLAME THEM... BUT, IT'S MY JOB TO STOP THEM.
THE BIGGEST, MOST DARING OUTFIT THAT DOES THIS PHARMA PIRACY IS CALLED PILL CIRCUS.
THEY FANCY THEMSELVES FRIENDS OF THE PEOPLE AND GO BY SILLY CIRCUS-INSPIRED CODE NAMES.
RIGHT NOW ONE OF MY INFORMANTS IS WORKING A DEAL WITH THE HACKER NAMED THE CLOWN.
THERE'S THIS DRUG CALLED "NIMBLE" THAT IS A PIRATED VERSION OF A POPULAR PAINKILLER.
ONLY THING, IT SEEMS TO BE TOTALLY ORGANIC.
RRRING.
TRINITY SCIENTISTS ARE STUMPED ON HOW IT WORKS. THEY CAN'T EVEN FIGURE OUT HOW TO REPRODUCE IT.
CALL SENT TO VOICEMAIL.

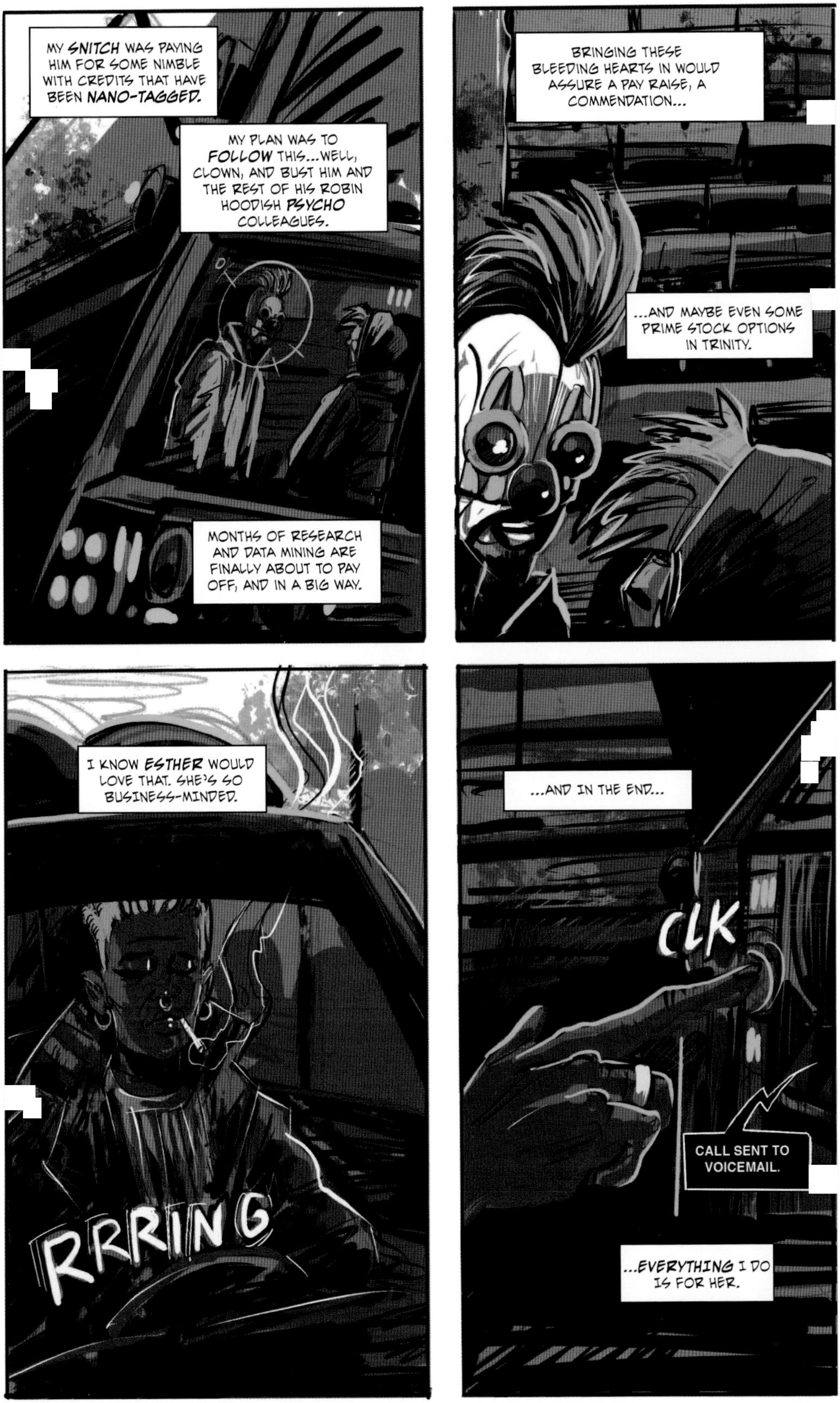

MY SNITCH WAS PAYING HIM FOR SOME NIMBLE WITH CREDITS THAT HAVE BEEN NANO-TAGGED.
MY PLAN WAS TO FOLLOW THIS...WELL, CLOWN, AND BUST HIM AND THE REST OF HIS ROBIN HOODISH PSYCHO COLLEAGUES.
MONTHS OF RESEARCH AND DATA MINING ARE FINALLY ABOUT TO PAY OFF, AND IN A BIG WAY.
BRINGING THESE BLEEDING HEARTS IN WOULD ASSURE A PAY RAISE, A COMMENDATION...
...AND MAYBE EVEN SOME PRIME STOCK OPTIONS IN TRINITY.
I KNOW ESTHER WOULD LOVE THAT. SHE'S SO BUSINESS-MINDED.
RRRING
...AND IN THE END...
CLK
CALL SENT TO VOICEMAIL.
...EVERYTHING I DO IS FOR HER.

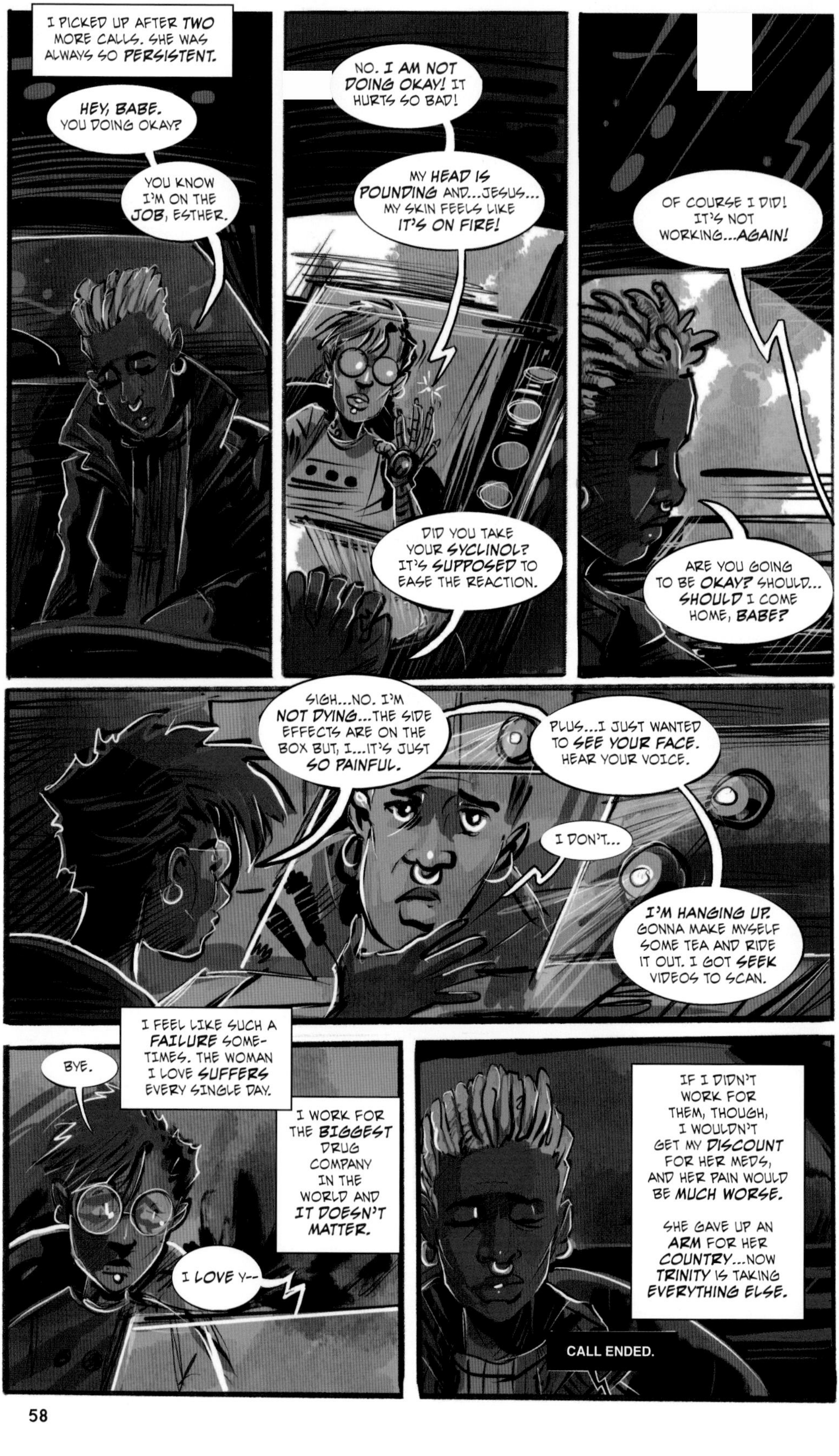

I PICKED UP AFTER TWO MORE CALLS. SHE WAS ALWAYS SO PERSISTENT.
HEY, BABE. YOU DOING OKAY?
YOU KNOW I'M ON THE JOB, ESTHER.
NO. I AM NOT DOING OKAY! IT HURTS SO BAD!
MY HEAD IS POUNDING AND...JESUS... MY SKIN FEELS LIKE IT'S ON FIRE!
DID YOU TAKE YOUR SYCLINOL? IT'S SUPPOSED TO EASE THE REACTION.
OF COURSE I DID! IT'S NOT WORKING...AGAIN!
ARE YOU GOING TO BE OKAY? SHOULD... SHOULD I COME HOME, BABE?
SIGH...NO. I'M NOT DYING...THE SIDE EFFECTS ARE ON THE BOX BUT, I...IT'S JUST SO PAINFUL.
PLUS...I JUST WANTED TO SEE YOUR FACE. HEAR YOUR VOICE.
I DON'T...
I'M HANGING UP. GONNA MAKE MYSELF SOME TEA AND RIDE IT OUT. I GOT SEEK VIDEOS TO SCAN.
I FEEL LIKE SUCH A FAILURE SOME-TIMES. THE WOMAN I LOVE SUFFERS EVERY SINGLE DAY.
BYE.
I WORK FOR THE BIGGEST DRUG COMPANY IN THE WORLD AND IT DOESN'T MATTER.
I LOVE Y--
IF I DIDN'T WORK FOR THEM, THOUGH, I WOULDN'T GET MY DISCOUNT FOR HER MEDS, AND HER PAIN WOULD BE MUCH WORSE.
SHE GAVE UP AN ARM FOR HER COUNTRY...NOW TRINITY IS TAKING EVERYTHING ELSE.
CALL ENDED.

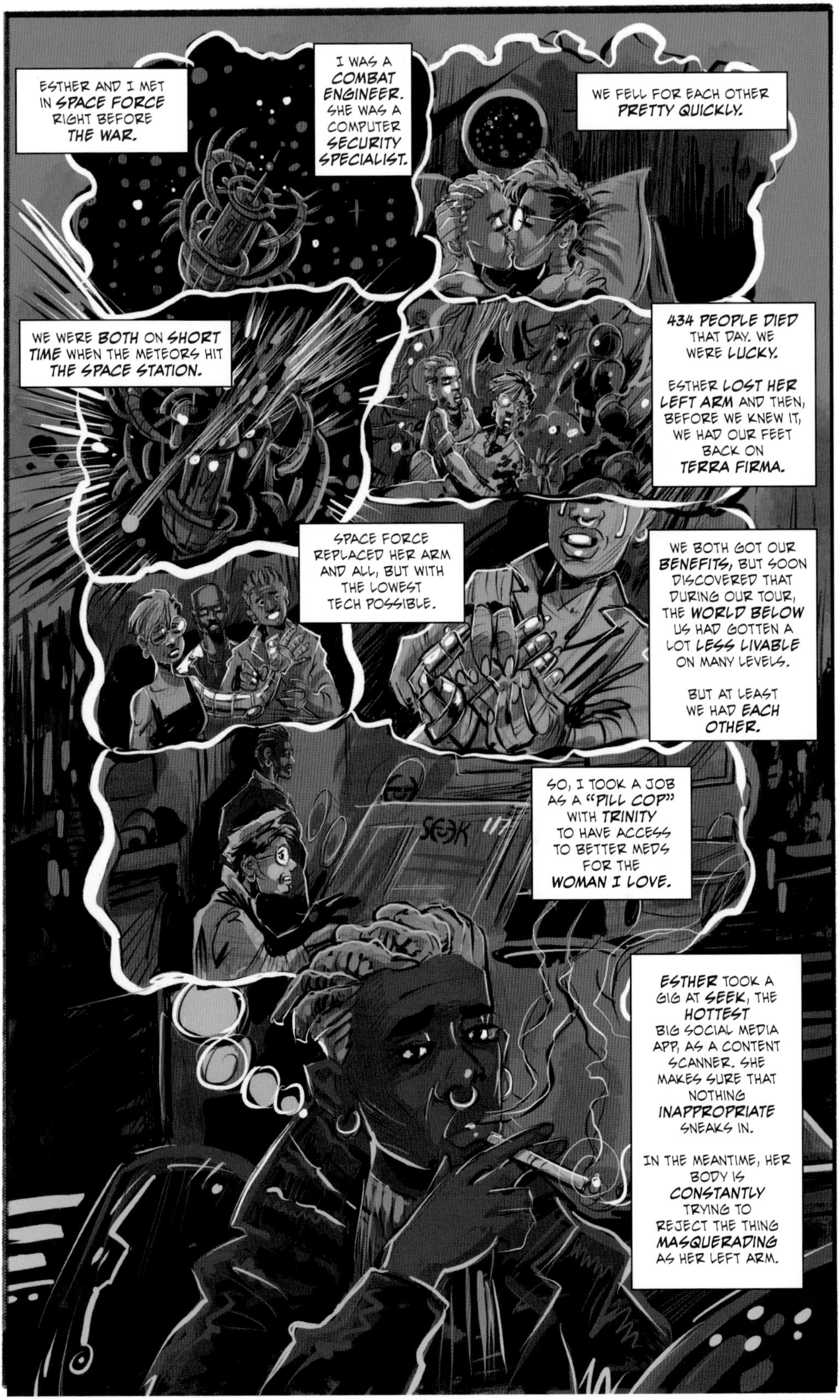
ESTHER AND I MET IN SPACE FORCE RIGHT BEFORE THE WAR.
I WAS A COMBAT ENGINEER. SHE WAS A COMPUTER SECURITY SPECIALIST.
WE FELL FOR EACH OTHER PRETTY QUICKLY.
WE WERE BOTH ON SHORT TIME WHEN THE METEORS HIT THE SPACE STATION.
434 PEOPLE DIED THAT DAY. WE WERE LUCKY.
ESTHER LOST HER LEFT ARM AND THEN, BEFORE WE KNEW IT, WE HAD OUR FEET BACK ON TERRA FIRMA.
SPACE FORCE REPLACED HER ARM AND ALL, BUT WITH THE LOWEST TECH POSSIBLE.
WE BOTH GOT OUR BENEFITS, BUT SOON DISCOVERED THAT DURING OUR TOUR, THE WORLD BELOW US HAD GOTTEN A LOT LESS LIVABLE ON MANY LEVELS.
BUT AT LEAST WE HAD EACH OTHER.
SO, I TOOK A JOB AS A "PILL COP" WITH TRINITY TO HAVE ACCESS TO BETTER MEDS FOR THE WOMAN I LOVE.
ESTHER TOOK A GIG AT SEEK, THE HOTTEST BIG SOCIAL MEDIA APP, AS A CONTENT SCANNER. SHE MAKES SURE THAT NOTHING INAPPROPRIATE SNEAKS IN.
IN THE MEANTIME, HER BODY IS CONSTANTLY TRYING TO REJECT THE THING MASQUERADING AS HER LEFT ARM.

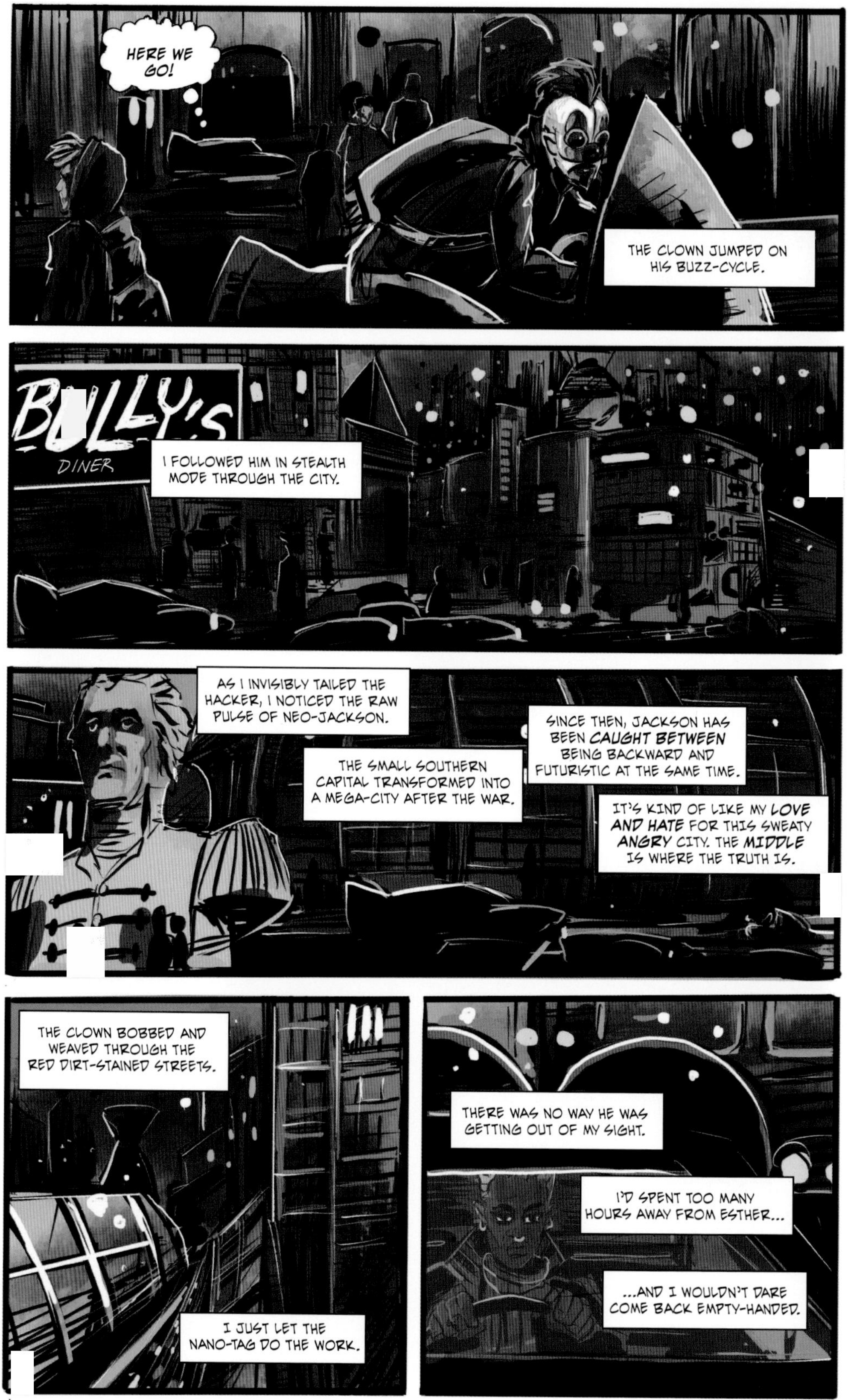
HERE WE GO!
THE CLOWN JUMPED ON HIS BUZZ-CYCLE.
BILLY'S
DINER
I FOLLOWED HIM IN STEALTH MODE THROUGH THE CITY.
AS I INVISIBLY TAILED THE HACKER, I NOTICED THE RAW PULSE OF NEO-JACKSON.
THE SMALL SOUTHERN CAPITAL TRANSFORMED INTO A MEGA-CITY AFTER THE WAR.
SINCE THEN, JACKSON HAS BEEN CAUGHT BETWEEN BEING BACKWARD AND FUTURISTIC AT THE SAME TIME.
IT'S KIND OF LIKE MY LOVE AND HATE FOR THIS SWEATY ANGRY CITY. THE MIDDLE IS WHERE THE TRUTH IS.
THE CLOWN BOBBED AND WEAVED THROUGH THE RED DIRT-STAINED STREETS.
I JUST LET THE NANO-TAG DO THE WORK.
THERE WAS NO WAY HE WAS GETTING OUT OF MY SIGHT.
I'D SPENT TOO MANY HOURS AWAY FROM ESTHER...
...AND I WOULDN'T DARE COME BACK EMPTY-HANDED.

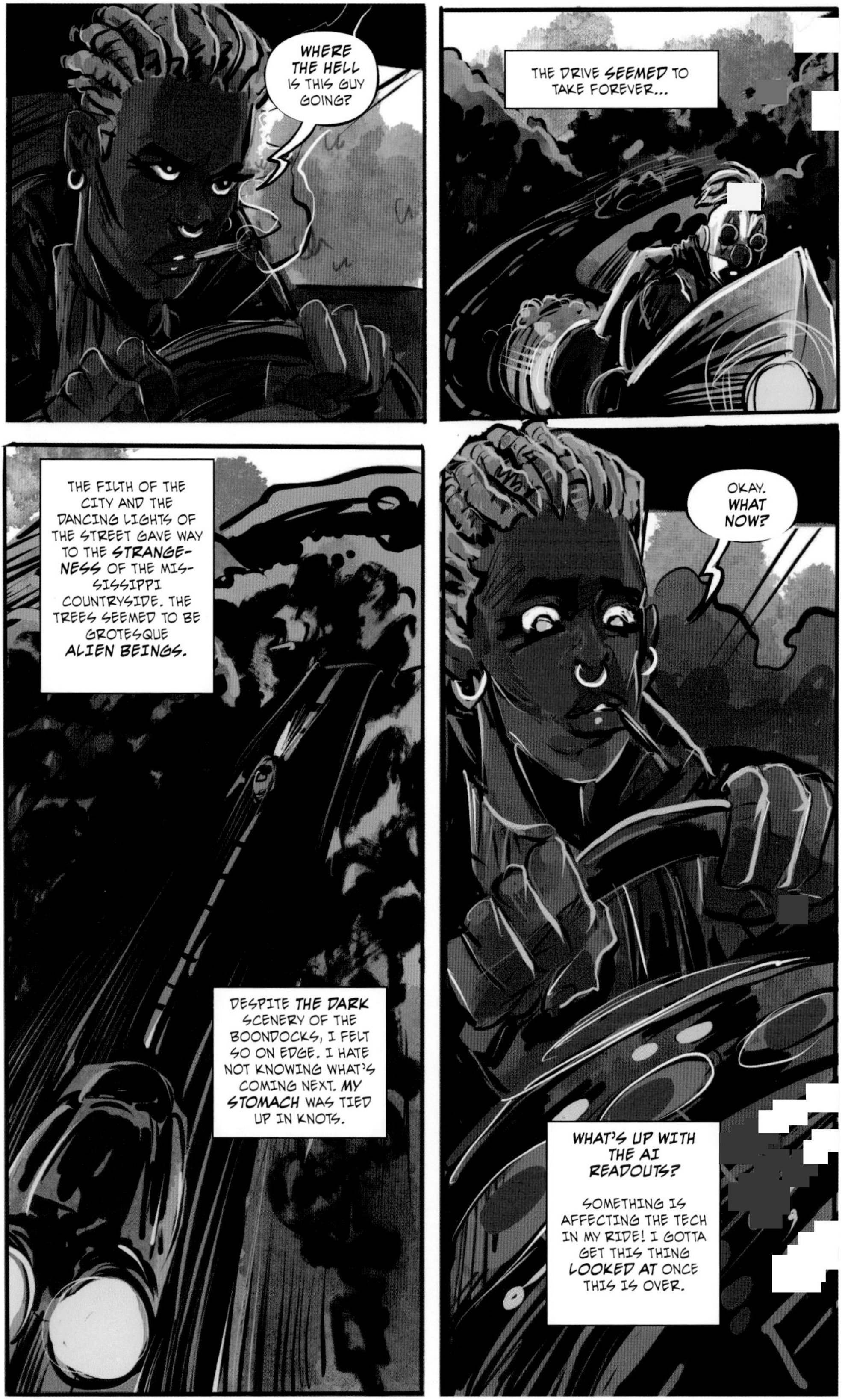
WHERE THE HELL IS THIS GUY GOING?
THE DRIVE SEEMED TO TAKE FOREVER...
THE FILTH OF THE CITY AND THE DANCING LIGHTS OF THE STREET GAVE WAY TO THE STRANGENESS OF THE MISSISSIPPI COUNTRYSIDE. THE TREES SEEMED TO BE GROTESQUE ALIEN BEINGS.
DESPITE THE DARK SCENERY OF THE BOONDOCKS, I FELT SO ON EDGE. I HATE NOT KNOWING WHAT'S COMING NEXT. MY STOMACH WAS TIED UP IN KNOTS.
OKAY. WHAT NOW?
WHAT'S UP WITH THE AI READOUTS?
SOMETHING IS AFFECTING THE TECH IN MY RIDE! I GOTTA GET THIS THING LOOKED AT ONCE THIS IS OVER.

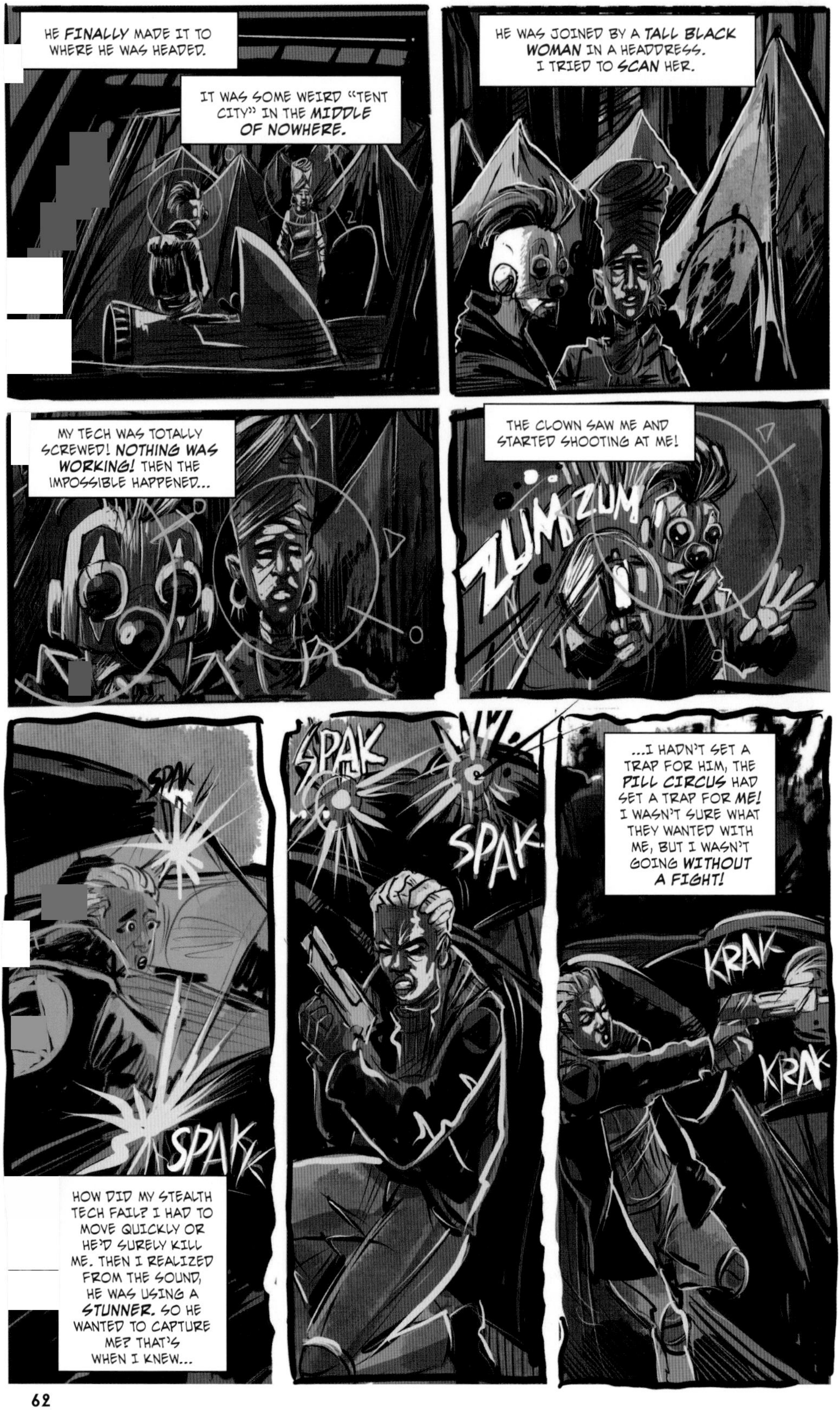
HE FINALLY MADE IT TO WHERE HE WAS HEADED.
IT WAS SOME WEIRD "TENT CITY" IN THE MIDDLE OF NOWHERE.
HE WAS JOINED BY A TALL BLACK WOMAN IN A HEADDRESS. I TRIED TO SCAN HER.
MY TECH WAS TOTALLY SCREWED! NOTHING WAS WORKING! THEN THE IMPOSSIBLE HAPPENED...
THE CLOWN SAW ME AND STARTED SHOOTING AT ME!
ZUM ZUM
SPAK
SPAK
HOW DID MY STEALTH TECH FAIL? I HAD TO MOVE QUICKLY OR HE'D SURELY KILL ME. THEN I REALIZED FROM THE SOUND, HE WAS USING A STUNNER. SO HE WANTED TO CAPTURE ME? THAT'S WHEN I KNEW...
SPAK
SPAK
...I HADN'T SET A TRAP FOR HIM, THE PILL CIRCUS HAD SET A TRAP FOR ME! I WASN'T SURE WHAT THEY WANTED WITH ME, BUT I WASN'T GOING WITHOUT A FIGHT!
KRAK
KRAK

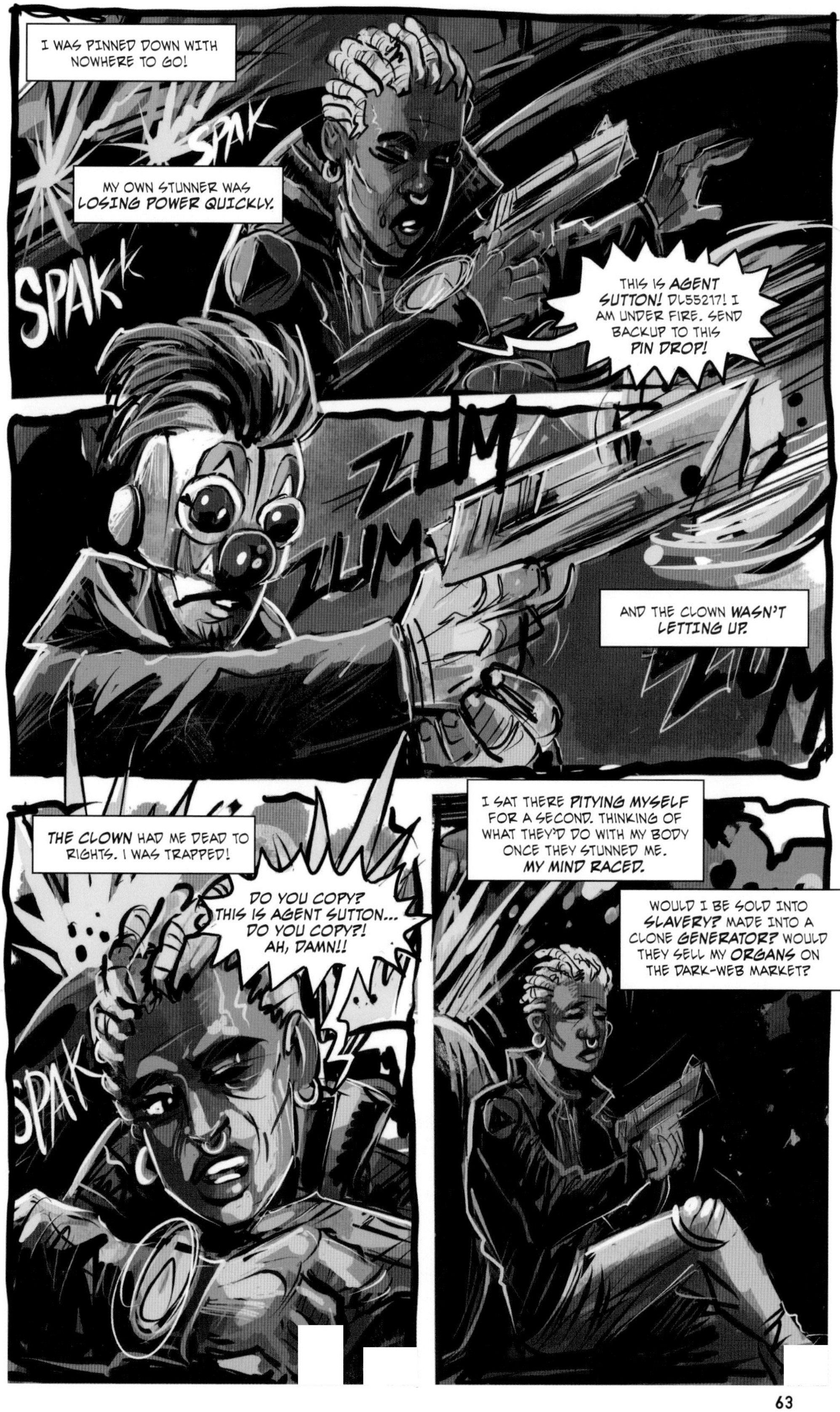
I WAS PINNED DOWN WITH NOWHERE TO GO!
SPAK
MY OWN STUNNER WAS LOSING POWER QUICKLY.
SPAK
THIS IS AGENT SUTTON! DL55217! I AM UNDER FIRE. SEND BACKUP TO THIS PIN DROP!
ZUM
ZUM
AND THE CLOWN WASN'T LETTING UP.
ZUM
THE CLOWN HAD ME DEAD TO RIGHTS. I WAS TRAPPED!
DO YOU COPY? THIS IS AGENT SUTTON... DO YOU COPY?! AH, DAMN!!
SPAK
I SAT THERE PITYING MYSELF FOR A SECOND. THINKING OF WHAT THEY'D DO WITH MY BODY ONCE THEY STUNNED ME. MY MIND RACED.
WOULD I BE SOLD INTO SLAVERY? MADE INTO A CLONE GENERATOR? WOULD THEY SELL MY ORGANS ON THE DARK-WEB MARKET?

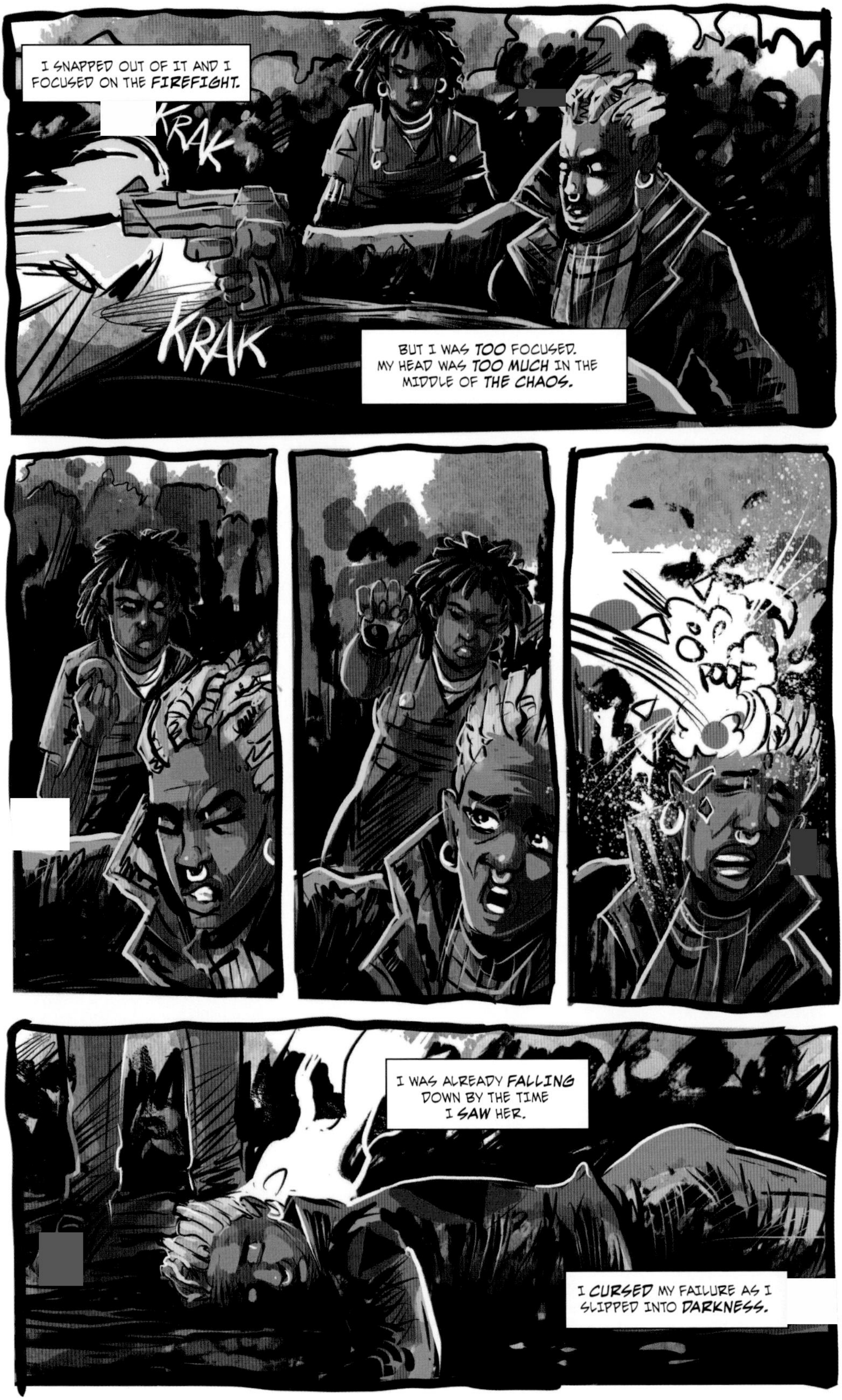
I SNAPPED OUT OF IT AND I FOCUSED ON THE FIREFIGHT.
KRAK
KRAK
BUT I WAS TOO FOCUSED. MY HEAD WAS TOO MUCH IN THE MIDDLE OF THE CHAOS.
I WAS ALREADY FALLING DOWN BY THE TIME I SAW HER.
I CURSED MY FAILURE AS I SLIPPED INTO DARKNESS.

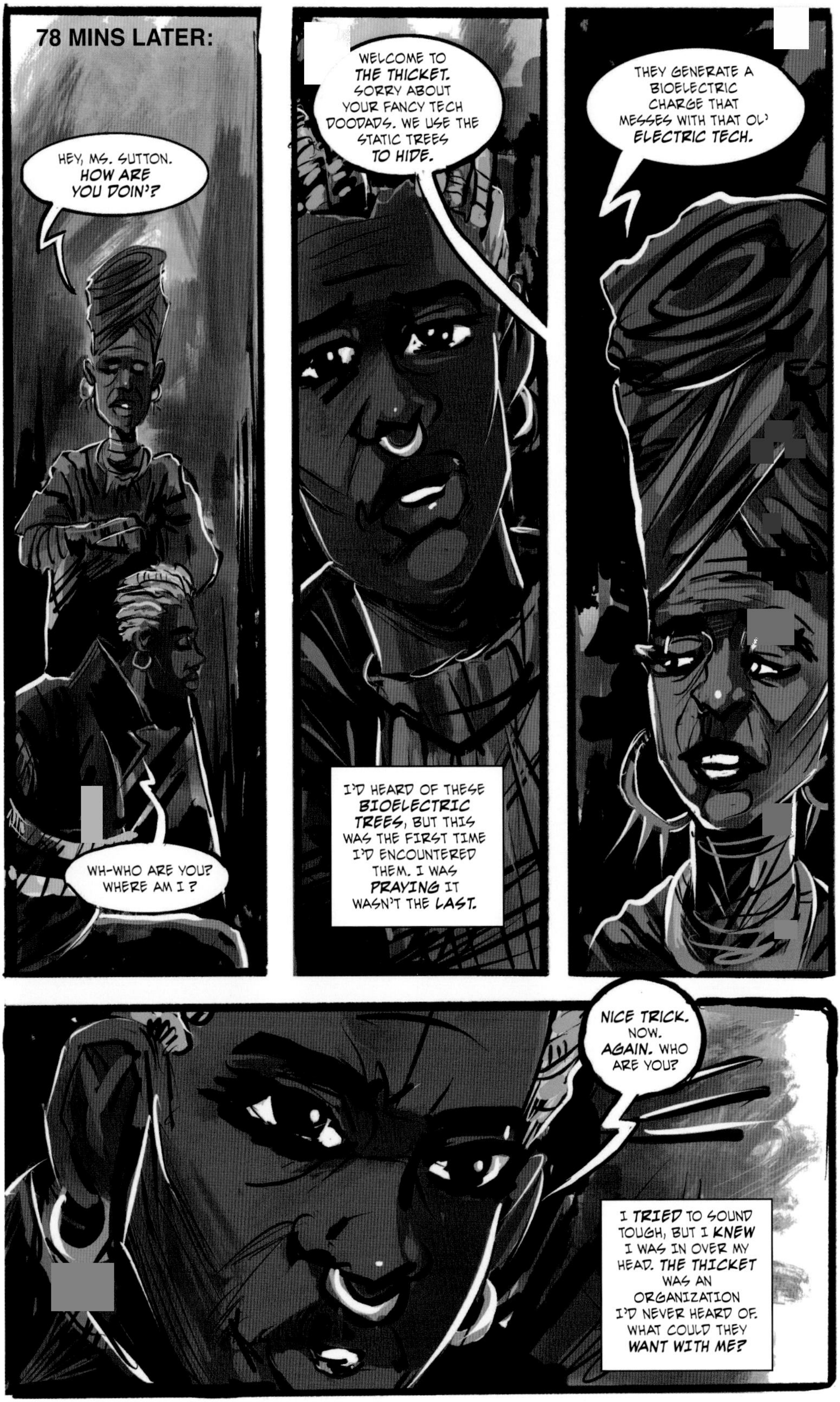
78 MINS LATER:
HEY, MS. SUTTON. HOW ARE YOU DOIN'?
WH-WHO ARE YOU? WHERE AM I ?
WELCOME TO THE THICKET. SORRY ABOUT YOUR FANCY TECH DOODADS. WE USE THE STATIC TREES TO HIDE.
I'D HEARD OF THESE BIOELECTRIC TREES, BUT THIS WAS THE FIRST TIME I'D ENCOUNTERED THEM. I WAS PRAYING IT WASN'T THE LAST.
THEY GENERATE A BIOELECTRIC CHARGE THAT MESSES WITH THAT OL' ELECTRIC TECH.
NICE TRICK. NOW. AGAIN. WHO ARE YOU?
I TRIED TO SOUND TOUGH, BUT I KNEW I WAS IN OVER MY HEAD. THE THICKET WAS AN ORGANIZATION I'D NEVER HEARD OF. WHAT COULD THEY WANT WITH ME?

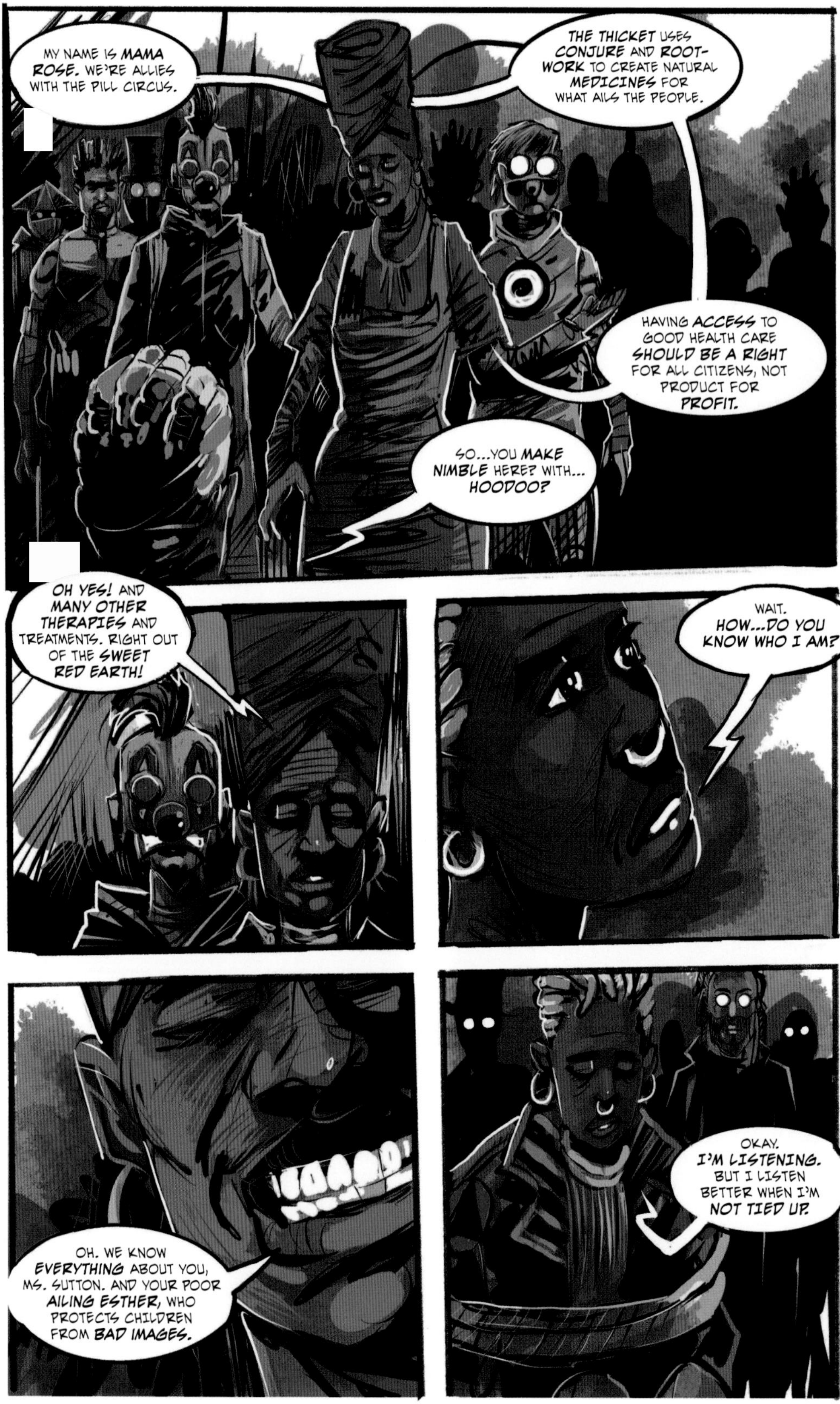
MY NAME IS MAMA ROSE. WE'RE ALLIES WITH THE PILL CIRCUS.
THE THICKET USES CONJURE AND ROOT-WORK TO CREATE NATURAL MEDICINES FOR WHAT AILS THE PEOPLE.
HAVING ACCESS TO GOOD HEALTH CARE SHOULD BE A RIGHT FOR ALL CITIZENS, NOT PRODUCT FOR PROFIT.
SO...YOU MAKE NIMBLE HERE? WITH... HOODOO?
OH YES! AND MANY OTHER THERAPIES AND TREATMENTS. RIGHT OUT OF THE SWEET RED EARTH!
WAIT. HOW...DO YOU KNOW WHO I AM?
OH. WE KNOW EVERYTHING ABOUT YOU, MS. SUTTON. AND YOUR POOR AILING ESTHER, WHO PROTECTS CHILDREN FROM BAD IMAGES.
OKAY. I'M LISTENING. BUT I LISTEN BETTER WHEN I'M NOT TIED UP.

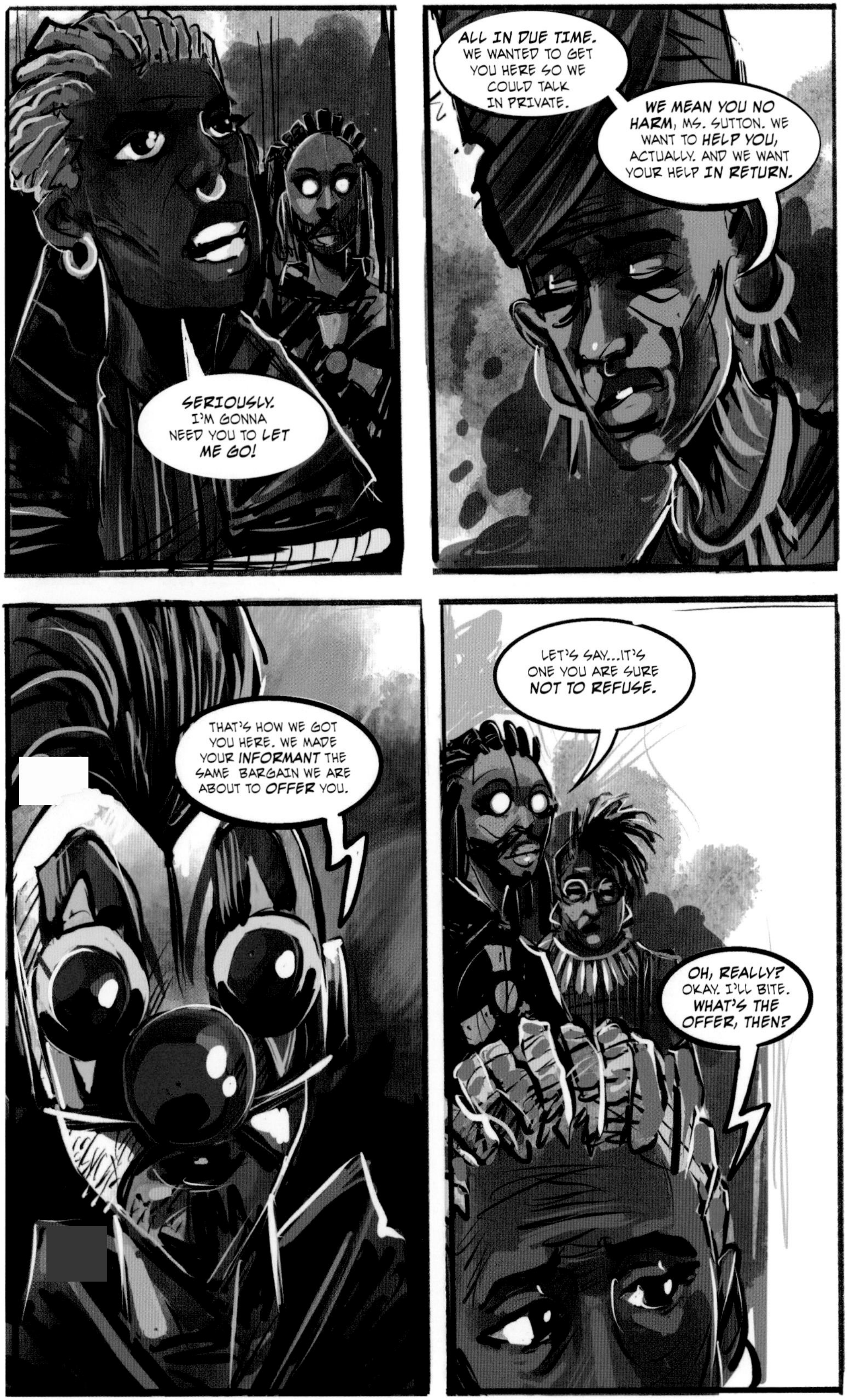
SERIOUSLY. I'M GONNA NEED YOU TO LET ME GO!
ALL IN DUE TIME. WE WANTED TO GET YOU HERE SO WE COULD TALK IN PRIVATE.
WE MEAN YOU NO HARM, MS. SUTTON. WE WANT TO HELP YOU, ACTUALLY. AND WE WANT YOUR HELP IN RETURN.
THAT'S HOW WE GOT YOU HERE. WE MADE YOUR INFORMANT THE SAME BARGAIN WE ARE ABOUT TO OFFER YOU.
OH, REALLY? OKAY. I'LL BITE. WHAT'S THE OFFER, THEN?
LET'S SAY...IT'S ONE YOU ARE SURE NOT TO REFUSE.

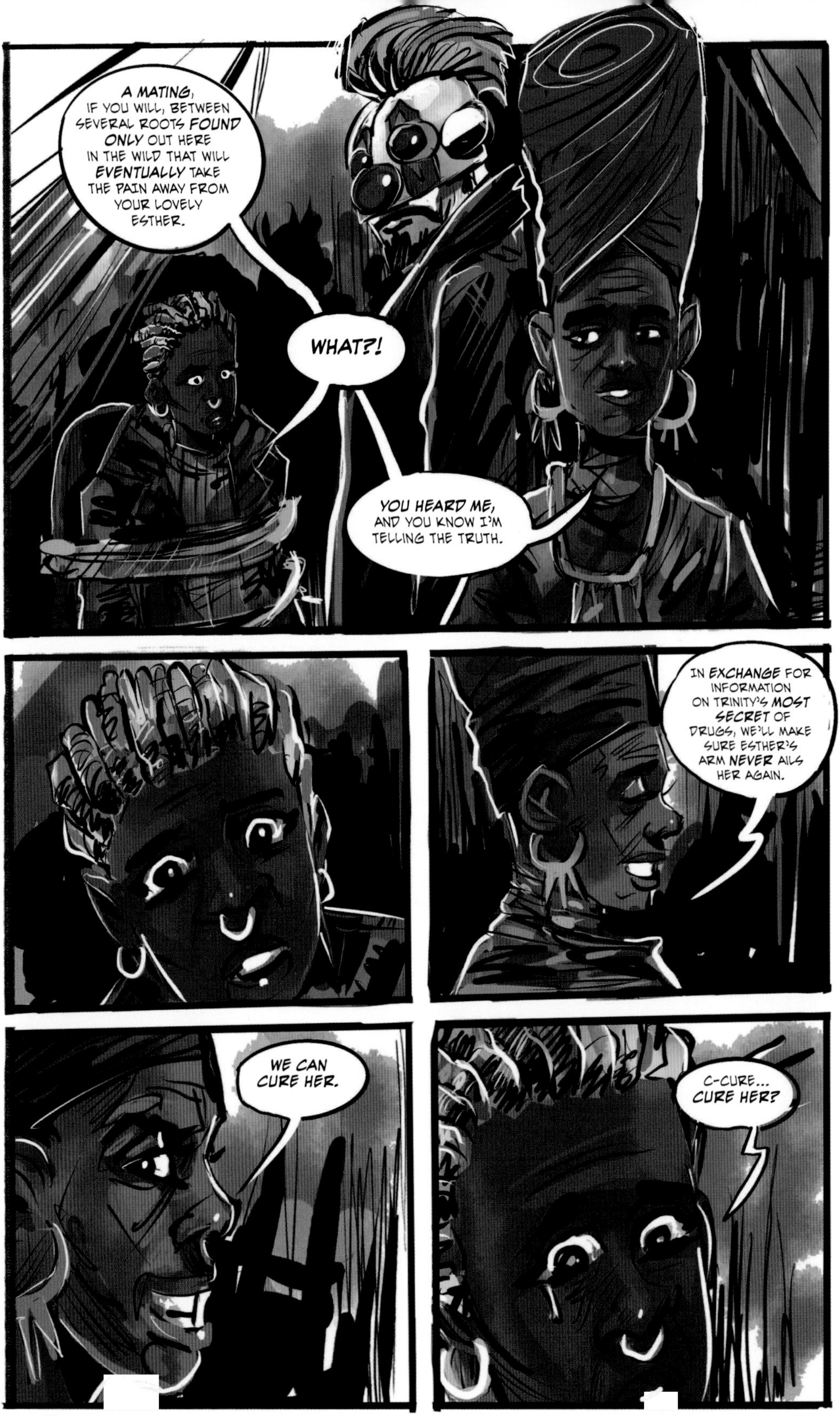
A MATING, IF YOU WILL, BETWEEN SEVERAL ROOTS FOUND ONLY OUT HERE IN THE WILD THAT WILL EVENTUALLY TAKE THE PAIN AWAY FROM YOUR LOVELY ESTHER.
WHAT?!
YOU HEARD ME, AND YOU KNOW I'M TELLING THE TRUTH.
IN EXCHANGE FOR INFORMATION ON TRINITY'S MOST SECRET OF DRUGS, WE'LL MAKE SURE ESTHER'S ARM NEVER AILS HER AGAIN.
WE CAN CURE HER.
C-CURE... CURE HER?

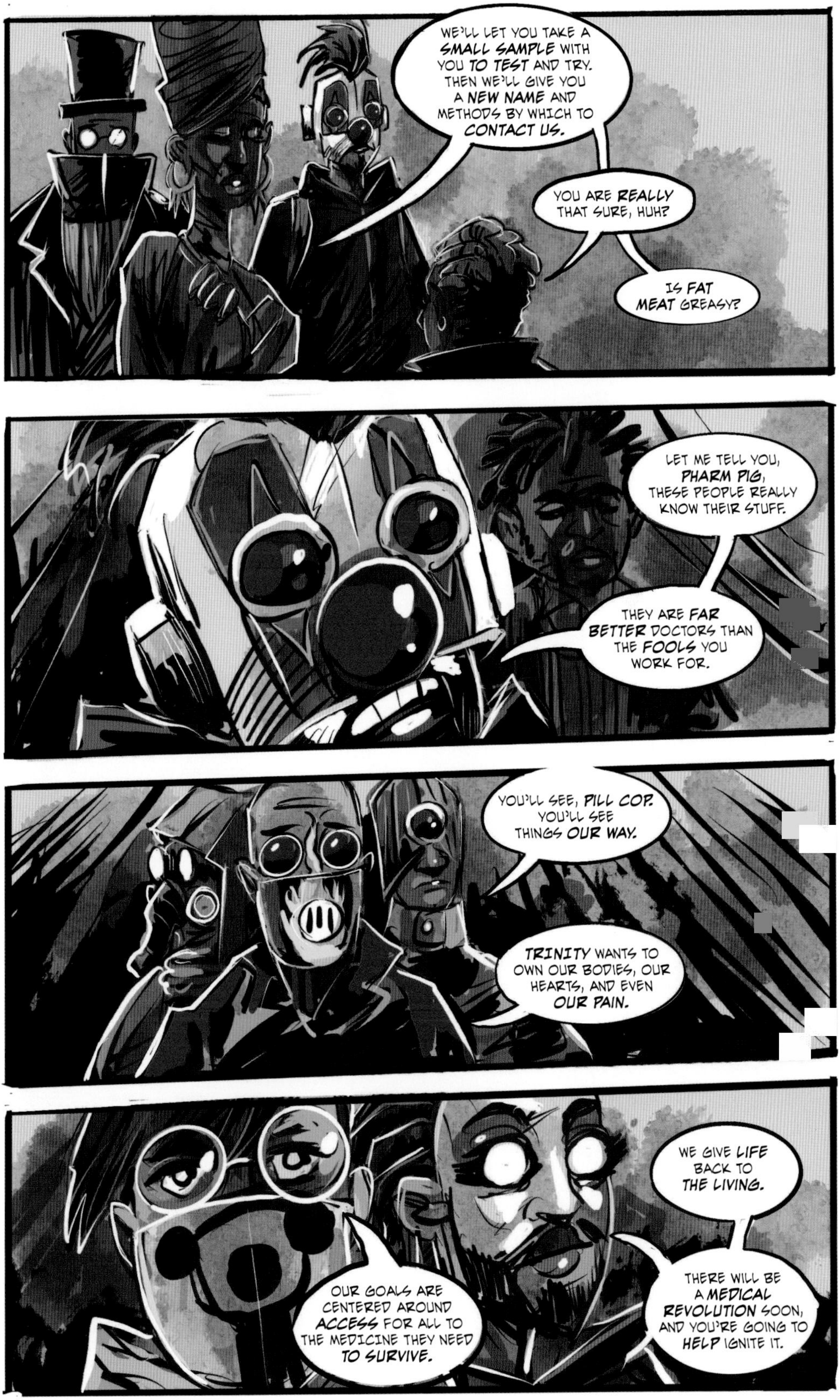
WE'LL LET YOU TAKE A SMALL SAMPLE WITH YOU TO TEST AND TRY. THEN WE'LL GIVE YOU A NEW NAME AND METHODS BY WHICH TO CONTACT US.
YOU ARE REALLY THAT SURE, HUH?
IS FAT MEAT GREASY?
LET ME TELL YOU, PHARM PIG, THESE PEOPLE REALLY KNOW THEIR STUFF.
THEY ARE FAR BETTER DOCTORS THAN THE FOOLS YOU WORK FOR.
YOU'LL SEE, PILL COP. YOU'LL SEE THINGS OUR WAY.
TRINITY WANTS TO OWN OUR BODIES, OUR HEARTS, AND EVEN OUR PAIN.
WE GIVE LIFE BACK TO THE LIVING.
OUR GOALS ARE CENTERED AROUND ACCESS FOR ALL TO THE MEDICINE THEY NEED TO SURVIVE.
THERE WILL BE A MEDICAL REVOLUTION SOON, AND YOU'RE GOING TO HELP IGNITE IT.

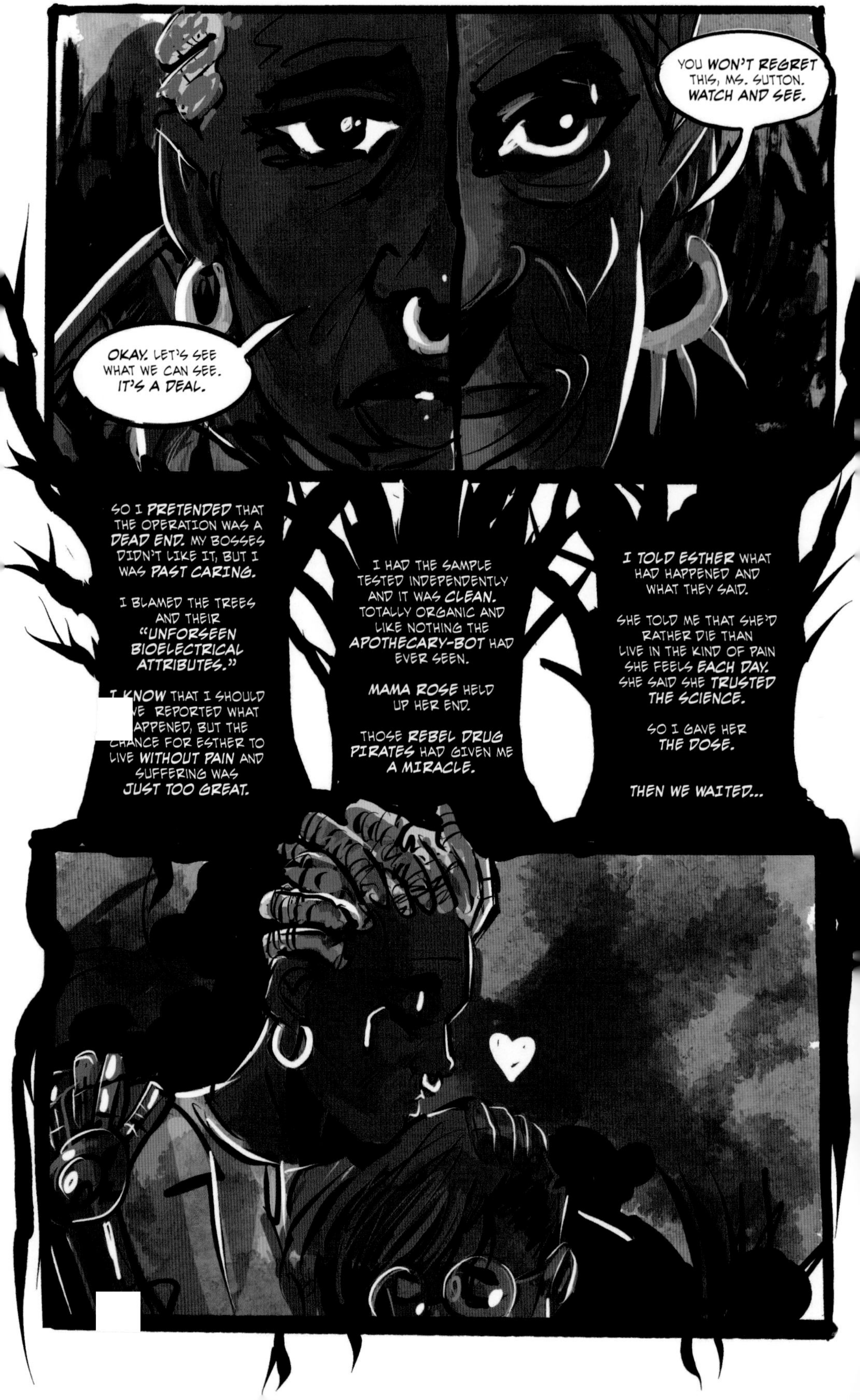
YOU WON'T REGRET THIS, MS. SUTTON. WATCH AND SEE.
OKAY. LET'S SEE WHAT WE CAN SEE. IT'S A DEAL.
SO I PRETENDED THAT THE OPERATION WAS A DEAD END. MY BOSSES DIDN'T LIKE IT, BUT I WAS PAST CARING.
I BLAMED THE TREES AND THEIR "UNFORSEEN BIOELECTRICAL ATTRIBUTES."
KNOW THAT I SHOULD VE REPORTED WHAT APPENED, BUT THE HANCE FOR ESTHER TO LIVE WITHOUT PAIN AND SUFFERING WAS JUST TOO GREAT.
I HAD THE SAMPLE TESTED INDEPENDENTLY AND IT WAS CLEAN. TOTALLY ORGANIC AND LIKE NOTHING THE APOTHECARY-BOT HAD EVER SEEN.
MAMA ROSE HELD UP HER END.
THOSE REBEL DRUG PIRATES HAD GIVEN ME A MIRACLE.
I TOLD ESTHER WHAT HAD HAPPENED AND WHAT THEY SAID.
SHE TOLD ME THAT SHE'D RATHER DIE THAN LIVE IN THE KIND OF PAIN SHE FEELS EACH DAY. SHE SAID SHE TRUSTED THE SCIENCE.
SO I GAVE HER THE DOSE.
THEN WE WAITED...

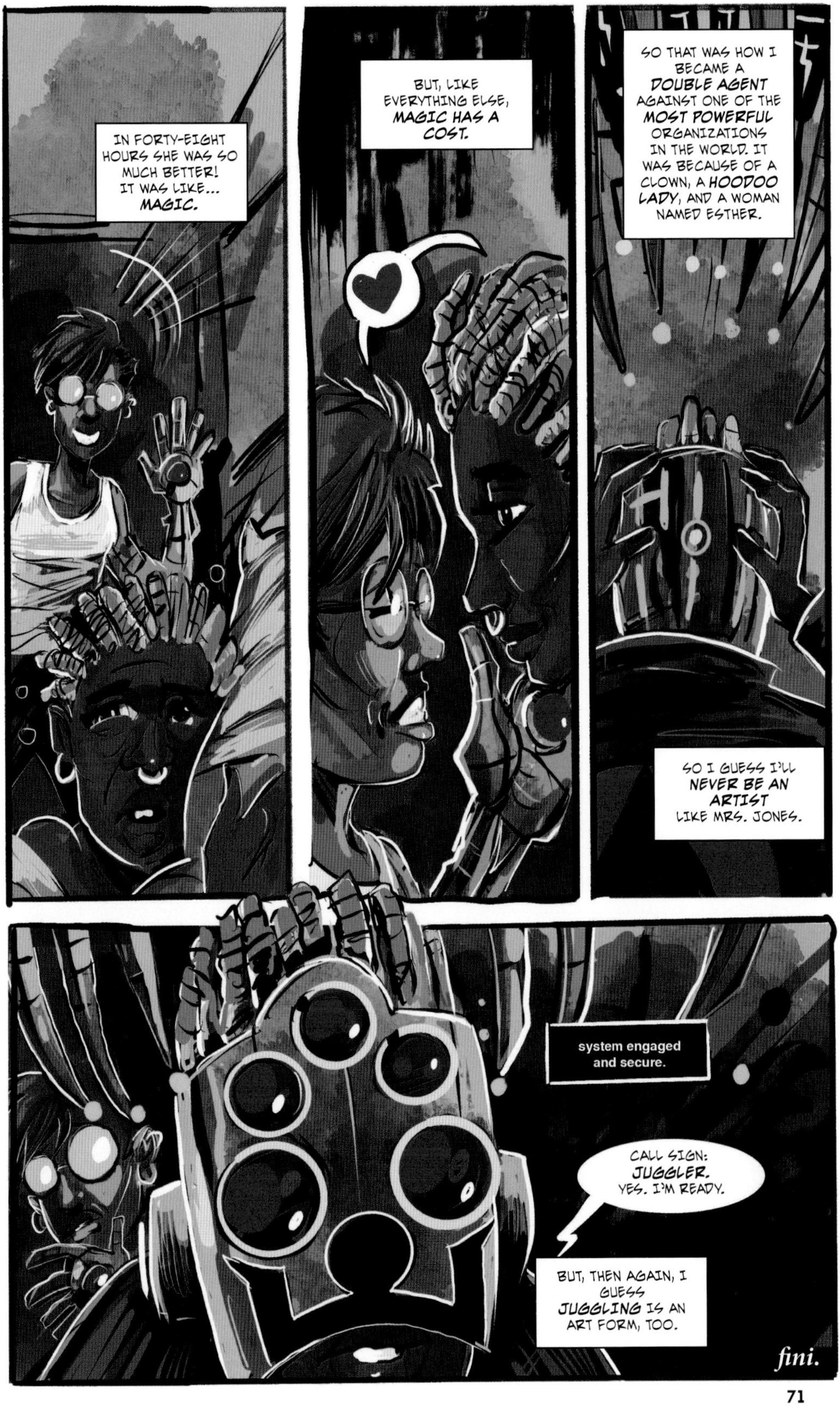

IN FORTY-EIGHT HOURS SHE WAS SO MUCH BETTER! IT WAS LIKE... MAGIC.
BUT, LIKE EVERYTHING ELSE, MAGIC HAS A COST.
SO THAT WAS HOW I BECAME A DOUBLE AGENT AGAINST ONE OF THE MOST POWERFUL ORGANIZATIONS IN THE WORLD. IT WAS BECAUSE OF A CLOWN, A HOODOO LADY, AND A WOMAN NAMED ESTHER.
SO I GUESS I'LL NEVER BE AN ARTIST LIKE MRS. JONES.
system engaged and secure.
CALL SIGN: JUGGLER. YES. I'M READY.
BUT, THEN AGAIN, I GUESS JUGGLING IS AN ART FORM, TOO.
fini.

PIRACEUTICALS

WHAT IF YOU HAD TO TURN TO PIRATES FOR MEDICINE?

THE UNITED STATES HAS A DRUG PROBLEM. NO, I'M NOT referring to the (very real) opioid epidemic gripping the nation or your teenage neighbor smoking weed in the parking lot. I'm referring to another kind of drug problem: The cost of prescription drugs in the United States has risen to evil supervillain proportions.

In 2013 Americans spent $858 per capita on medicines, more than double the average for nineteen other industrialized nations. Between 2007 and 2018, drug prices in the United States increased by 159 percent, far faster than inflation. Newly approved drugs for cancer and muscular dystrophy hit the market with jaw-dropping price tags: Bravencio, a cancer drug, costs $156,000 a year; a muscular dystrophy drug produced by the company Sarepta Therapeutics will run you $300,000 (a price tag the company's CEO called "reasonable").

And it's not even brand-new drugs that are breaking the bank. In 2007, a two-pack set of EpiPens, used to deliver an emergency dose of epinephrine to those experiencing a dangerous allergic reaction, cost $94. By 2016, not even ten years later, the sticker price had risen over 500 percent to $608. In 2015, Turing Pharmaceuticals, at the time run by the now-disgraced Martin Shkreli, increased the price of Daraprim, a drug meant for malaria but also used by HIV patients, more than 5,000 percent. That's not a typo by the way, it really says 5,000 percent. Even known money-lover Donald Trump has called out the absurd cost of drugs—shortly after being elected, he said that drug companies were "getting away with murder" for their prices.

In some cases, the murder isn't metaphorical. Insulin was discovered in the 1920s and the patents for it were sold to the University of Toronto for $1 each so that the life-saving drug could be available to everyone. And yet, the cost of insulin tripled between 2009 and 2019. In 2018, Alec Raeshawn Smith died of diabetic ketoacidosis three days before payday because he was likely rationing his insulin until he could afford more. And Smith isn't alone. Experts estimate that one in four people with type 1 diabetes have rationed insulin in the United States. Think about that—patients are rationing a lifesaving drug that has been around for more than one hundred years, that isn't hard or expensive to make, because the three drug companies that control the vast majority of production of the drug opted for profits over people's lives.

In light of all of this, it's hard not to root for those attempting to break the system. And there are plenty. In 2015, Anthony Di Franco founded the Open Insulin Project, where he's working on creating a do-it-yourself insulin production line. Di Franco is diabetic himself, and hopes that in the near future they can roll out protocols and open-source lab equipment that would allow a local community to start up their own insulin production center. For about $100,000 investment, a collective could produce the lifesaving drug for about ten thousand people. And in the last five years, more and more projects like this have popped up. "It's been a little lonely at times," said Di Franco. "But less and less so. People are paying attention, and they're starting to think more deeply about it and getting the taste for change."

The same year Di Franco founded the Open Insulin Project, Michael Laufer founded the Four Thieves Vinegar Collective, aimed at giving people access to the tools they need to make everything from anti-HIV drugs to abortion drugs like misoprostol. In 2016, when the EpiPen skyrocketed in price, Laufer published his own set of instructions for how to create a similar device for just $30. Biohackers have tried to create cheaper, more accessible versions of everything from hormones like estrogen and testosterone to gene therapy drugs.

Even doctors have engaged in some DIY pharmaceutical manufacturing. In 2017, Leadiant Biosciences increased the price of a drug used to treat a disease called cerebrotendinous xanthomatosis to nearly $170,000 a year. In the Netherlands, patients were suddenly being told that they had to pay the full cost themselves or they simply weren't going to get their medicine. This was unacceptable to a pharmacist named Marleen Kemper, who decided to simply make the drug herself and provide it to her patients. When the price of the EpiPen shot up, it wasn't just the biohacker Laufer who made a cheaper version for people—a doctor in rural Maine did the same thing, as did an EMS in the Seattle area.

But of course, these do-it-yourself solutions are not, in fact, solutions. Not only can they be dangerous—drug manufacturing is risky and challenging, and making mistakes can cause serious harm and even death—they also don't solve the underlying problems. "I find it really hard to believe that do-it-yourself manufacturing is the solution to drug prices," said Patricia Zettler, a professor at Moritz College of Law and an expert on drug regulation. "My seventy-six-year-old father doesn't want to manufacture his medications himself, he just wants to be able to get them for a price he can afford."

Biohacking can seem sexy and exciting, and for those who have access to biohackers and their spaces, it can provide a temporary relief from rationing insulin or going without a lifesaving EpiPen. But no matter how many biohackers come up with a recipe for insulin, without structural changes to the ways that pharmaceuticals are developed and regulated, the price of the drug is unlikely to change. Most people don't have the time or expertise to set up a Walter White–style lab in their homes. Biohacking is a temporary solution that only works for those who are well connected and in the know—a science solution to what is fundamentally a policy problem.

You see this play out in the comic you just read, too. Agent Sutton only gets access to a drug that can help her ailing partner by getting connected with the right people. Relief comes only through connection with the Pill Circus, who might have valiant goals but who ultimately can't reach everybody.

For his part, Di Franco told me that he simply can't imagine changes happening to the medical system that would make the Open Insulin Project obsolete. "It's kind of hard for me to envision what the world would look like for that to happen," he said. "Unless you go back two thousand years and Spartacus overthrows the Roman Empire, it's just so entrenched in how everything works right now." But we're in the business of imagining better futures here, and policy change has to be one way to make them happen.

The comic you read also raises a few new ways of thinking about medicine. Not only is the pharmaceutical drug du jour a new type—a nanomedicine—but there is also a robust alternative developed by the Pill Circus. Let's take those one at a time.

Nanomedicine has long been a buzzword in futurist forecasts. In his 1986 book, *Engines of Creation: The Coming Era of Nanotechnology* (which *WIRED* called a "nanofuturism bible"), K. Eric Drexler describes a future in which everything around us can be assembled and dissembled using invisible machines. To count as "nano," something generally has to exist on a scale of 1-100 nm. For comparison, a sheet of paper is about 100,000 nanometers thick. If you were holding a marble, that marble would be to a nanometer as the entire Earth is to a meter.

The advantage of working at such a tiny scale is mostly specificity—when you work small, you can detect tiny changes and make miniscule edits. Using nanopharmaceuticals, you could theoretically target not just cells, but specific organelles inside of cells. When you're only impacting exactly the bits of the cell or the body that you want to, you might have fewer side effects than traditional drugs. Rather than bathing the body in poison—which is essentially what chemotherapy drugs do—you could go in and really specifically target cancer cells, or even individual components of cancer cells. And even if the drug itself isn't super tiny, a nanobot could drag and drop a bigger drug into the right place with a few instructions.

Nanomedicine also has applications before you even get sick. Using nano-sized detectors, you can pick up changes that might signal problems long before a patient presents any symptoms. Nanomedicine is the precision scalpel to traditional medicine's hacksaw.

That's the idea, at least. It turns out, actually harnessing the power of incredibly small things is quite challenging. A few years ago I spoke with Shawn Douglas, a researcher at the University of California, San Francisco, about his work testing out nanomaterials, and he told me that even with promising initial results, to scale up his experiments to the level of a potential clinical application would be almost impossible. "We need one hundred thousand times that much material, which would bankrupt the entire lab." Since then, researchers have proposed new ways of producing the needed building blocks through techniques like DNA-origami, in which molecules assemble themselves based on chemical instructions, but it's still not cheap.

Take cancer drugs, for example—in 2009, the cost for the nanodrugs Doxil and Abraxane was respectively $5,594 and $5,054 per dose, while their generic non-nano counterparts cost anywhere from $62 to $454. The idea that in the future we might have nanodrugs and nanobots coursing through our bodies isn't that far-fetched, but without a complete overhaul in the way medicine is administered in the United States, they'll only be available to the wealthy. And if that's the case, suffering people will turn to alternatives. Which brings us to the second piece of the story you read: the Pill Circus and their seemingly magical healing powers.

The medicine that Mama Rose offers comes not from a pharmaceutical lab, but from traditional knowledge. Long pooh-poohed by Western science, researchers are now realizing that at least some of the ancestral remedies passed down for generations might have real clinical significance. Chemicals in bear bile, long used in traditional Chinese medicine, can keep a heart beating for hours after its host has died. Aspirin, one of the most commonly used drugs today, comes from a tradition with (literal and figurative) roots in Egypt, where people made remedies out of dried willow leaves, rich in salicylic acid. In 2015, the Nobel Prize for medicine went to Tu Youyou, who "discovered" a cure for malaria by extracting a substance from the long-utilized herb called wormwood—a plant with tiny yellow flowers. Researchers have also found that some of the ancestral Mayan medicines used to guard against bowel diseases like dysentery are indeed effective.

Some decry these traditional methods as "snake oil," but even that story is illuminating. In the 1800s, Chinese immigrants began working alongside Americans on the railroads that would ultimately connect the coasts. After the long, backbreaking days of lugging lumber and hammering ties, these workers would use oil rendered from the fat of snakes to ease their aching muscles and joints. American scammers then began trying to pass off mineral oil as the slithery kind, thus originating the idea of "snake oil" as a false sales promise. But recent research has shown that fat from the Erabu sea snake is high in omega-3 fatty acids, which are shown to reduce inflammation. In other words, real snake oil *does* work.

This isn't to say that every ancestral cure works, nor does it mean that we should trap bears for their bile (in fact, plenty of research shows that the animal trade that plugs into some traditional medicinal practices is the pathway by which diseases like COVID-19, MERS, and SARS spread to humans). But the proof that there might be "real" cures available to us if we simply listened to ancestral and indigenous knowledge shouldn't be ignored, either.

As I write this chapter, the world is embroiled in a global pandemic, and here in the United States it is revealing every single crack in our systems— political, health care, social, and otherwise. In 2018 in America, 27.5 million people were uninsured, an estimated 44 million "under-insured" because they couldn't afford insurance premiums and out-of-pocket costs—statistics that experts argue will likely make the spread of the virus worse here than other places. And in a chilling press congressional hearing on February 26, 2020, Health and Human Services secretary Alex Azar said this, when asked about how affordable the COVID-19 vaccine might be: "We would want to ensure that we work to make it affordable, but we can't control that price because we need the private sector to invest."

The opacity of America's health system has impacted COVID-19 responses too. In June, the *New York Times* reported that some labs were charging insurance companies $2,315 for individual coronavirus tests, while in other places the charge was $100. As doctors and the public alike wait with baited breath for a vaccine, experts have estimated the cost of that vaccine could be as high as $4,500 per person. Gilead, a pharmaceutical company that makes a drug called remdesivir, said in July that they would charge $3,120 per patient with private health insurance for the treatment.

Humanity-shaking events like this have the tendency to not only reveal our weak points, but also highlight alternative ways of being and living and open up cracks through which we can peer into a better world. But shining a light through a crack does not fix it; it simply shows you that it's there. What we choose to do next will impact all of us for decades.

For some, the pandemic is proof that a complete overhaul of the medical system is required in the United States: "If we were to engage with Medicare for All the way that we ought to be, the way that almost every other high-income country in the world has, we would be in a very different position in terms of our ability to meet this need, because the government would be the funder and the government could just put that influx in," Dr. Abdul El-Sayed told The Hill.

In Di Franco's version of the future, rather than relying on the federal government or established institutions and corporations to keep us safe and healthy, we turn to each other. Those with the expertise and funds to do so start labs to produce the drugs that the community needs at a price they can pay. And in the U.S., we're starting to see this happen in blips and spurts— as the pandemic rips through America and state-level governments respond with a patchwork of confusing and often delayed responses, people are turning to their neighbors for support and assistance. And maybe this is the future, in which a strong network of informal local support is what keeps us all safe, rather than the mass production of drugs and a federally coordinated safety net.

No one knows how the coronavirus pandemic will unfold, or how our world will look on the other side of it. Will we learn from this outbreak and seize the chance to change things and pull power back from corporations to keep people alive? Or will we settle back into a system where individual pharmaceutical companies can raise drug prices by 5,000 percent and force patients to ration drugs they rely on to live? I hope we choose the former. And if not, perhaps it's time to pull on a mask and join the Circus. I think my code name would be the Fortune-Teller.

ANIMAL MAGNETISM

BY SOPHIA FOSTER-DIMINO

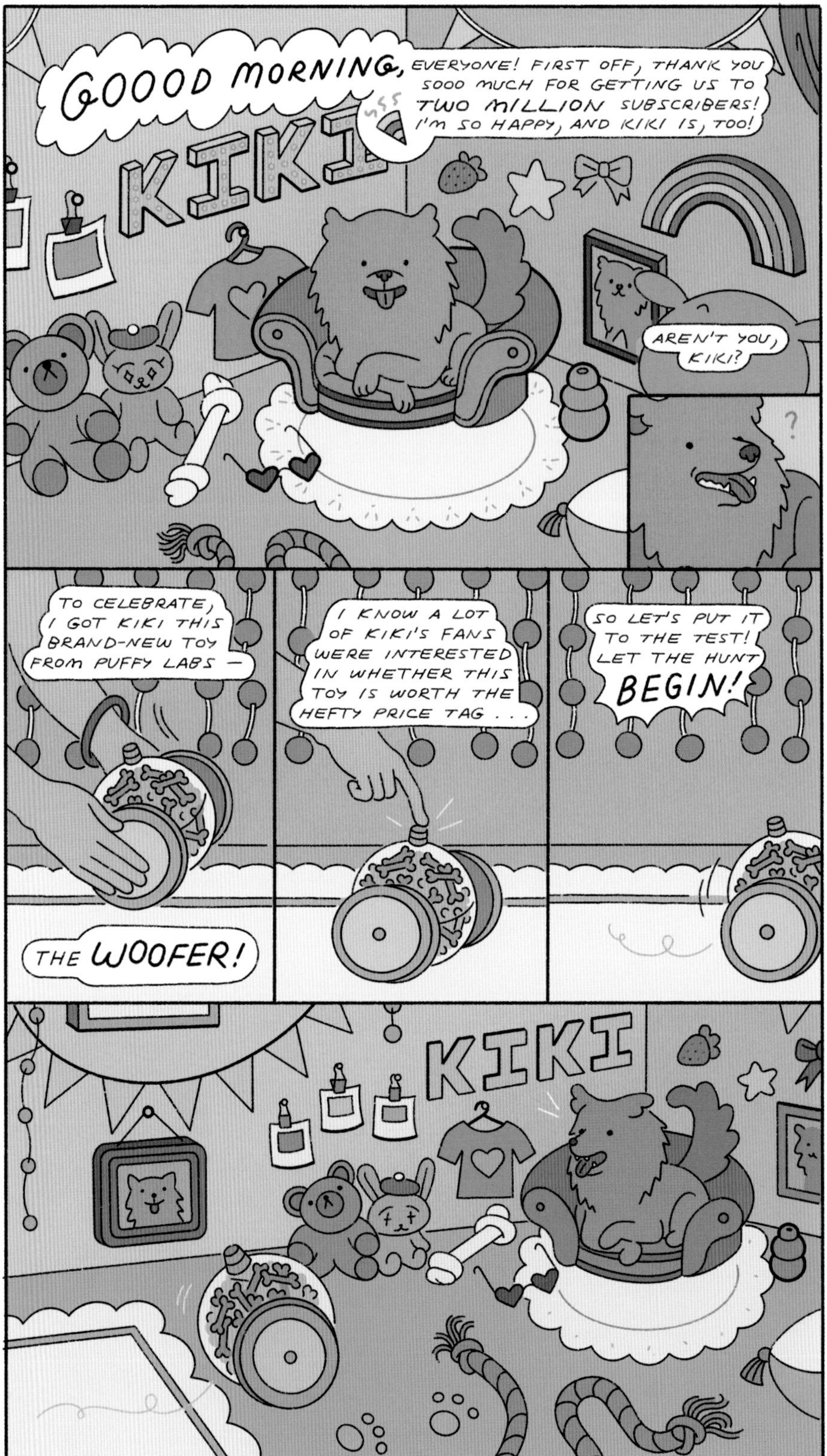
GOOOD MORNING, EVERYONE! FIRST OFF, THANK YOU SOOO MUCH FOR GETTING US TO TWO MILLION SUBSCRIBERS! I'M SO HAPPY, AND KIKI IS, TOO!
KIKI
AREN'T YOU, KIKI?
?
TO CELEBRATE, I GOT KIKI THIS BRAND-NEW TOY FROM PUFFY LABS —
THE WOOFER!
I KNOW A LOT OF KIKI'S FANS WERE INTERESTED IN WHETHER THIS TOY IS WORTH THE HEFTY PRICE TAG . . .
SO LET'S PUT IT TO THE TEST! LET THE HUNT BEGIN!
KIKI

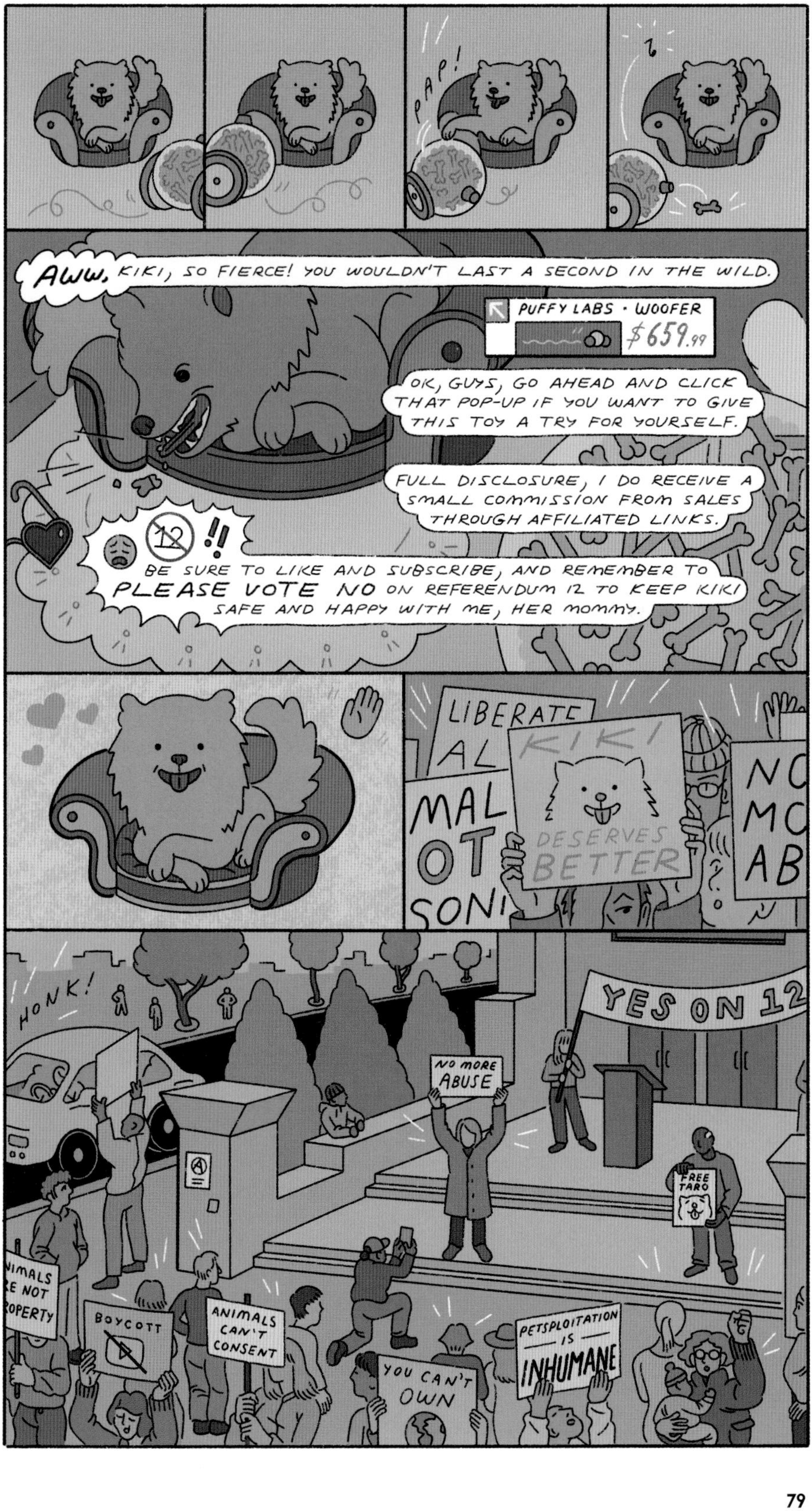

PAP!
AWW, KIKI, SO FIERCE! YOU WOULDN'T LAST A SECOND IN THE WILD.
PUFFY LABS • WOOFER
$659.99
OK, GUYS, GO AHEAD AND CLICK THAT POP-UP IF YOU WANT TO GIVE THIS TOY A TRY FOR YOURSELF.
FULL DISCLOSURE, I DO RECEIVE A SMALL COMMISSION FROM SALES THROUGH AFFILIATED LINKS.
12 !!
BE SURE TO LIKE AND SUBSCRIBE, AND REMEMBER TO PLEASE VOTE NO ON REFERENDUM 12 TO KEEP KIKI SAFE AND HAPPY WITH ME, HER MOMMY.
LIBERATE AL
MAL OT SONI
KIKI DESERVES BETTER
NO MO AB
HONK!
YES ON 12
NO MORE ABUSE
FREE TARO
IMALS E NOT OPERTY
BOYCOTT
ANIMALS CAN'T CONSENT
YOU CAN'T OWN
PETSPLOITATION IS INHUMANE

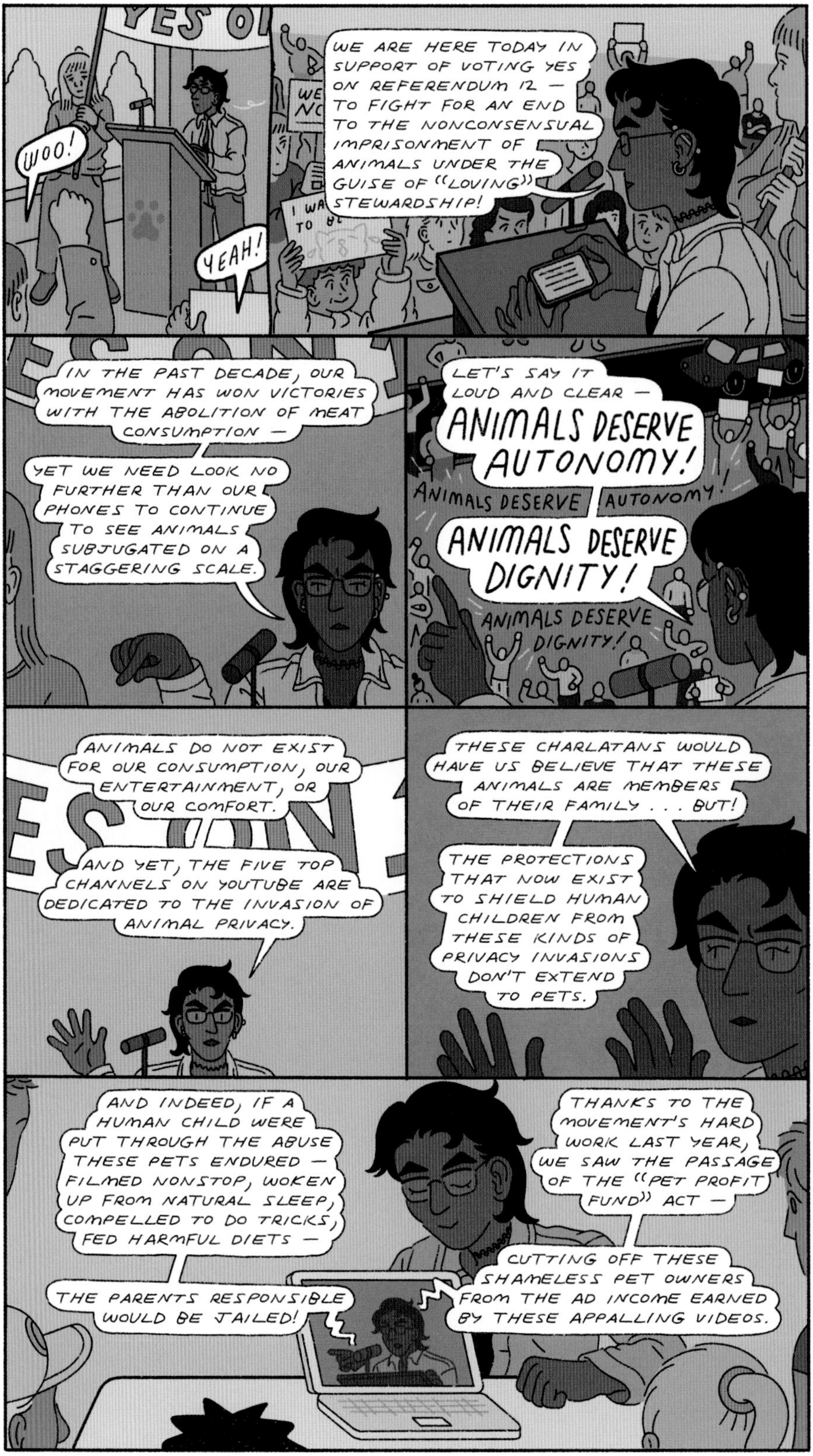
WOO!
YEAH!
WE ARE HERE TODAY IN SUPPORT OF VOTING YES ON REFERENDUM 12 — TO FIGHT FOR AN END TO THE NONCONSENSUAL IMPRISONMENT OF ANIMALS UNDER THE GUISE OF "LOVING" STEWARDSHIP!
IN THE PAST DECADE, OUR MOVEMENT HAS WON VICTORIES WITH THE ABOLITION OF MEAT CONSUMPTION —
YET WE NEED LOOK NO FURTHER THAN OUR PHONES TO CONTINUE TO SEE ANIMALS SUBJUGATED ON A STAGGERING SCALE.
LET'S SAY IT LOUD AND CLEAR — ANIMALS DESERVE AUTONOMY!
ANIMALS DESERVE AUTONOMY!
ANIMALS DESERVE DIGNITY!
ANIMALS DESERVE DIGNITY!
ANIMALS DO NOT EXIST FOR OUR CONSUMPTION, OUR ENTERTAINMENT, OR OUR COMFORT.
AND YET, THE FIVE TOP CHANNELS ON YOUTUBE ARE DEDICATED TO THE INVASION OF ANIMAL PRIVACY.
THESE CHARLATANS WOULD HAVE US BELIEVE THAT THESE ANIMALS ARE MEMBERS OF THEIR FAMILY . . . BUT!
THE PROTECTIONS THAT NOW EXIST TO SHIELD HUMAN CHILDREN FROM THESE KINDS OF PRIVACY INVASIONS DON'T EXTEND TO PETS.
AND INDEED, IF A HUMAN CHILD WERE PUT THROUGH THE ABUSE THESE PETS ENDURED — FILMED NONSTOP, WOKEN UP FROM NATURAL SLEEP, COMPELLED TO DO TRICKS, FED HARMFUL DIETS —
THE PARENTS RESPONSIBLE WOULD BE JAILED!
THANKS TO THE MOVEMENT'S HARD WORK LAST YEAR, WE SAW THE PASSAGE OF THE "PET PROFIT FUND" ACT —
CUTTING OFF THESE SHAMELESS PET OWNERS FROM THE AD INCOME EARNED BY THESE APPALLING VIDEOS.

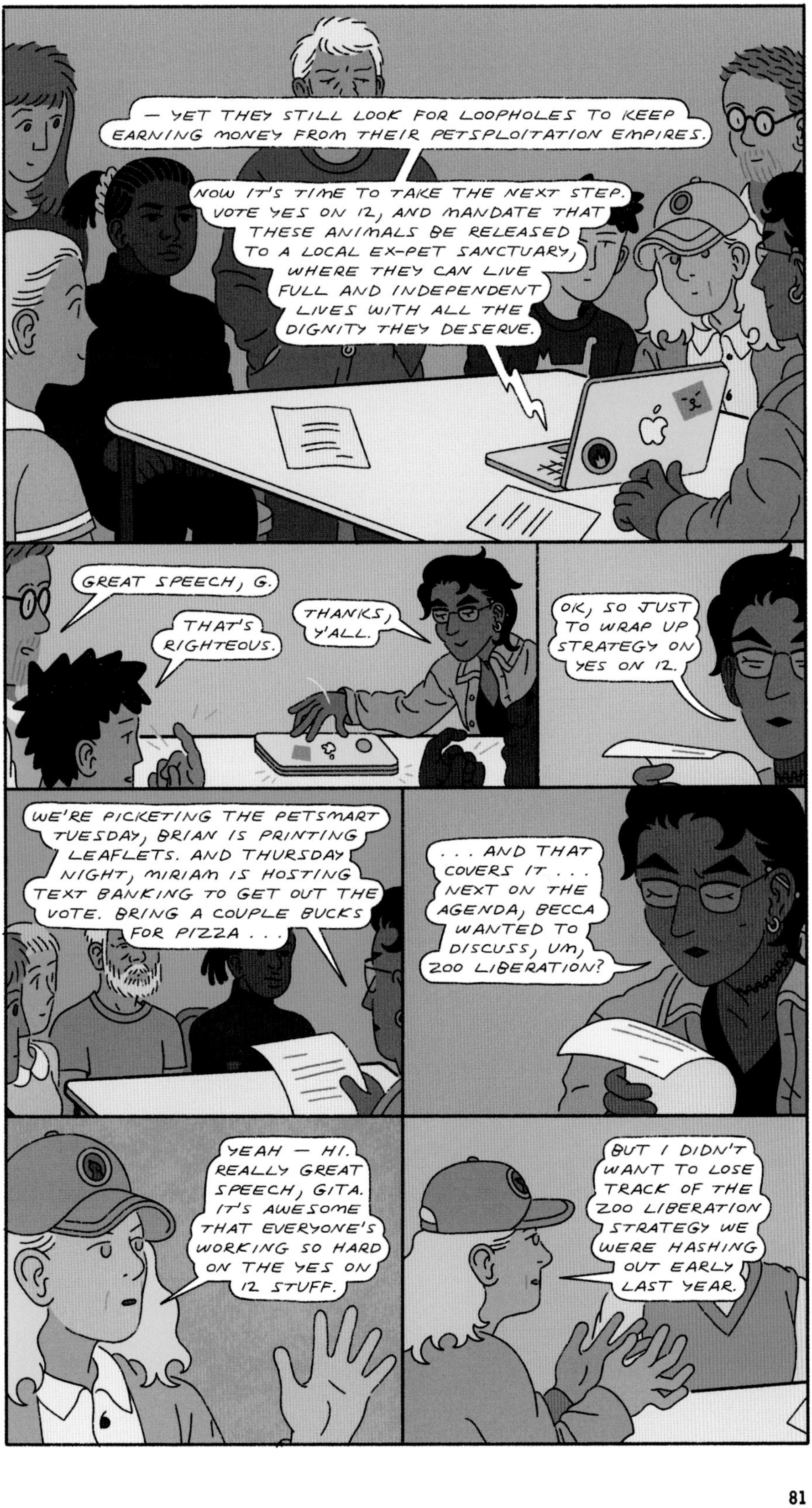
— YET THEY STILL LOOK FOR LOOPHOLES TO KEEP EARNING MONEY FROM THEIR PETSPLOITATION EMPIRES.
NOW IT'S TIME TO TAKE THE NEXT STEP. VOTE YES ON 12, AND MANDATE THAT THESE ANIMALS BE RELEASED TO A LOCAL EX-PET SANCTUARY, WHERE THEY CAN LIVE FULL AND INDEPENDENT LIVES WITH ALL THE DIGNITY THEY DESERVE.
GREAT SPEECH, G.
THAT'S RIGHTEOUS.
THANKS, Y'ALL.
OK, SO JUST TO WRAP UP STRATEGY ON YES ON 12.
WE'RE PICKETING THE PETSMART TUESDAY, BRIAN IS PRINTING LEAFLETS. AND THURSDAY NIGHT, MIRIAM IS HOSTING TEXT BANKING TO GET OUT THE VOTE. BRING A COUPLE BUCKS FOR PIZZA . . .
. . . AND THAT COVERS IT . . . NEXT ON THE AGENDA, BECCA WANTED TO DISCUSS, UM, ZOO LIBERATION?
YEAH — HI. REALLY GREAT SPEECH, GITA. IT'S AWESOME THAT EVERYONE'S WORKING SO HARD ON THE YES ON 12 STUFF.
BUT I DIDN'T WANT TO LOSE TRACK OF THE ZOO LIBERATION STRATEGY WE WERE HASHING OUT EARLY LAST YEAR.

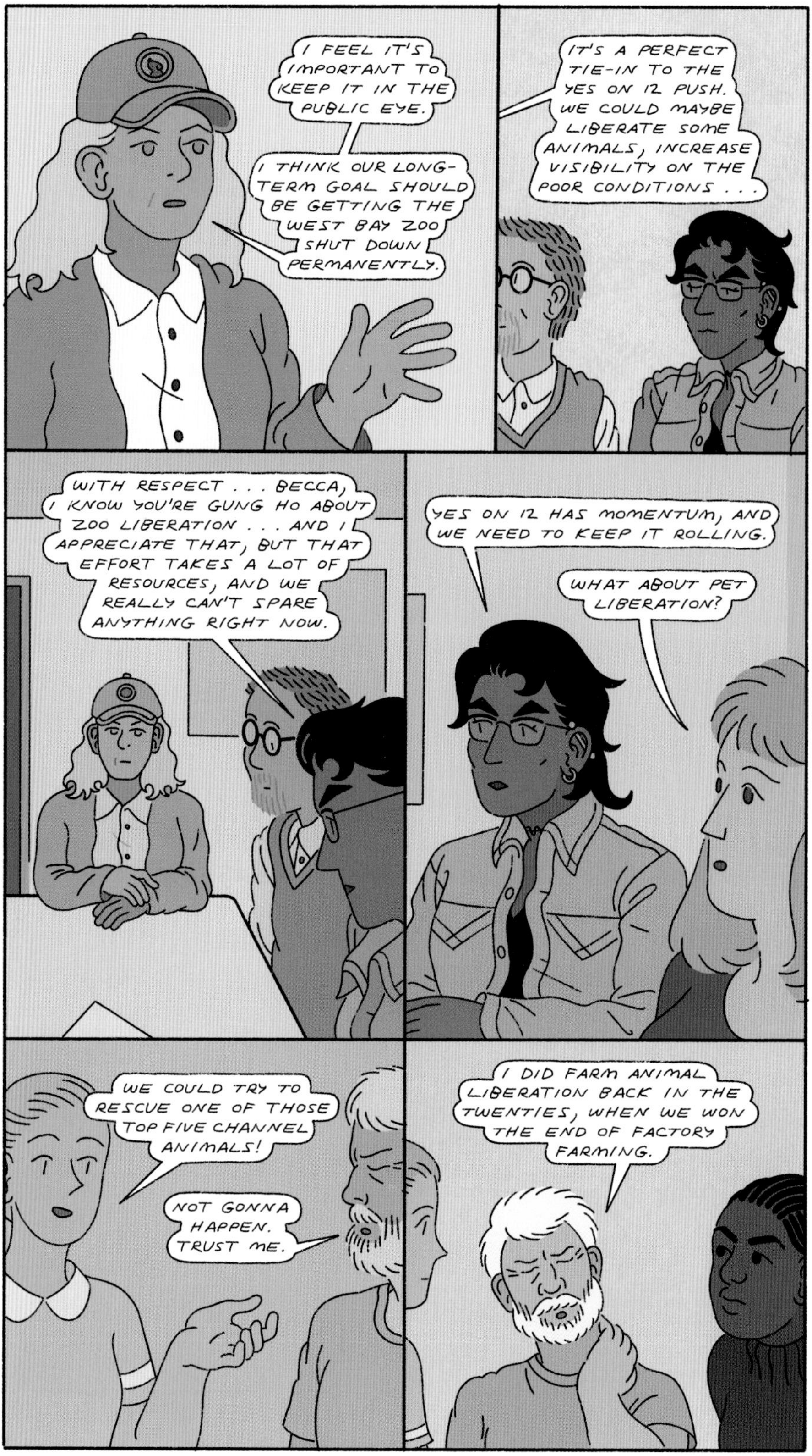
I FEEL IT'S IMPORTANT TO KEEP IT IN THE PUBLIC EYE.
I THINK OUR LONG-TERM GOAL SHOULD BE GETTING THE WEST BAY ZOO SHUT DOWN PERMANENTLY.
IT'S A PERFECT TIE-IN TO THE YES ON 12 PUSH. WE COULD MAYBE LIBERATE SOME ANIMALS, INCREASE VISIBILITY ON THE POOR CONDITIONS . . .
WITH RESPECT . . . BECCA, I KNOW YOU'RE GUNG HO ABOUT ZOO LIBERATION . . . AND I APPRECIATE THAT, BUT THAT EFFORT TAKES A LOT OF RESOURCES, AND WE REALLY CAN'T SPARE ANYTHING RIGHT NOW.
YES ON 12 HAS MOMENTUM, AND WE NEED TO KEEP IT ROLLING.
WHAT ABOUT PET LIBERATION?
WE COULD TRY TO RESCUE ONE OF THOSE TOP FIVE CHANNEL ANIMALS!
NOT GONNA HAPPEN. TRUST ME.
I DID FARM ANIMAL LIBERATION BACK IN THE TWENTIES, WHEN WE WON THE END OF FACTORY FARMING.

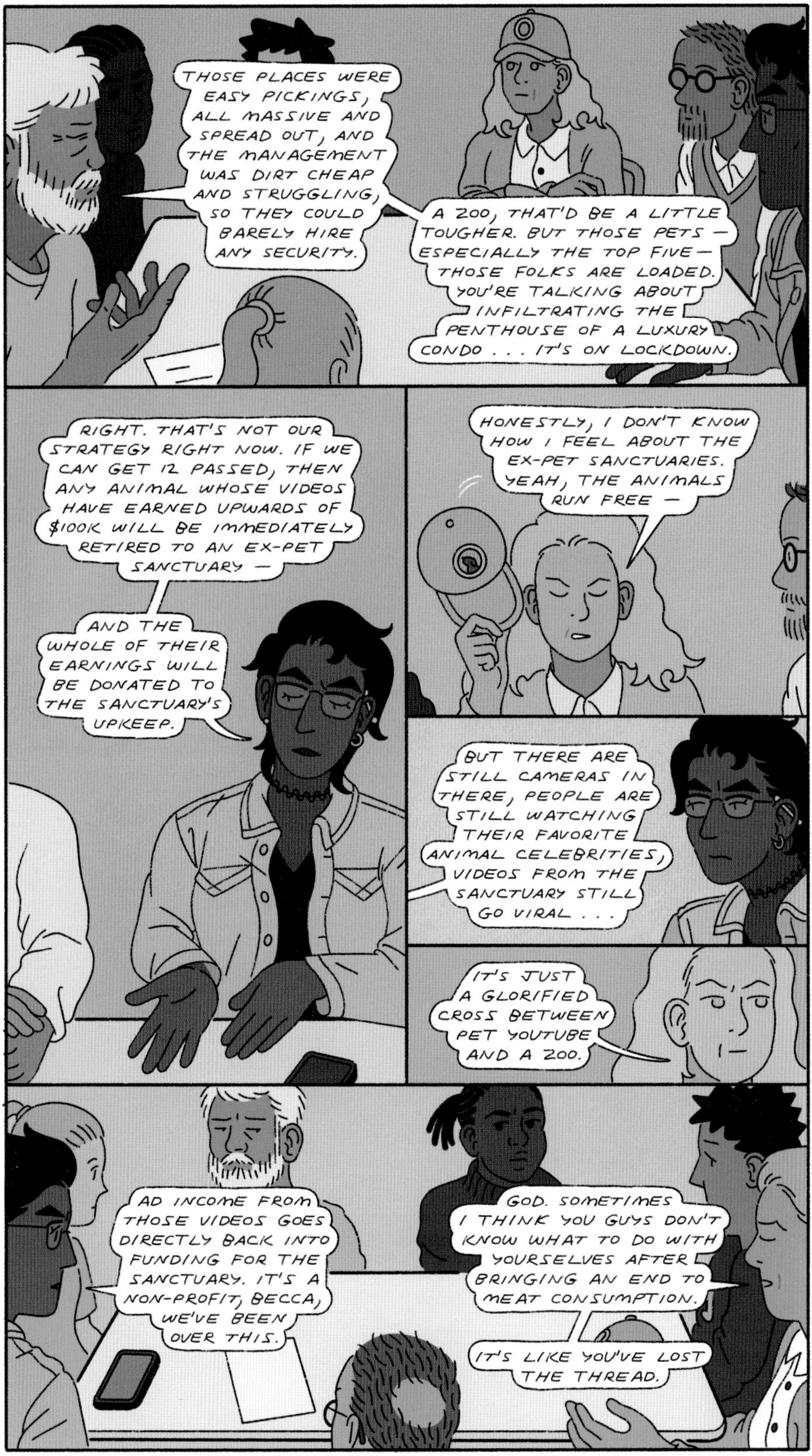
THOSE PLACES WERE EASY PICKINGS, ALL MASSIVE AND SPREAD OUT, AND THE MANAGEMENT WAS DIRT CHEAP AND STRUGGLING, SO THEY COULD BARELY HIRE ANY SECURITY.
A ZOO, THAT'D BE A LITTLE TOUGHER. BUT THOSE PETS — ESPECIALLY THE TOP FIVE — THOSE FOLKS ARE LOADED. YOU'RE TALKING ABOUT INFILTRATING THE PENTHOUSE OF A LUXURY CONDO . . . IT'S ON LOCKDOWN.
RIGHT. THAT'S NOT OUR STRATEGY RIGHT NOW. IF WE CAN GET 12 PASSED, THEN ANY ANIMAL WHOSE VIDEOS HAVE EARNED UPWARDS OF $100K WILL BE IMMEDIATELY RETIRED TO AN EX-PET SANCTUARY —
AND THE WHOLE OF THEIR EARNINGS WILL BE DONATED TO THE SANCTUARY'S UPKEEP.
HONESTLY, I DON'T KNOW HOW I FEEL ABOUT THE EX-PET SANCTUARIES. YEAH, THE ANIMALS RUN FREE —
BUT THERE ARE STILL CAMERAS IN THERE, PEOPLE ARE STILL WATCHING THEIR FAVORITE ANIMAL CELEBRITIES, VIDEOS FROM THE SANCTUARY STILL GO VIRAL . . .
IT'S JUST A GLORIFIED CROSS BETWEEN PET YOUTUBE AND A ZOO.
AD INCOME FROM THOSE VIDEOS GOES DIRECTLY BACK INTO FUNDING FOR THE SANCTUARY. IT'S A NON-PROFIT, BECCA, WE'VE BEEN OVER THIS.
GOD. SOMETIMES I THINK YOU GUYS DON'T KNOW WHAT TO DO WITH YOURSELVES AFTER BRINGING AN END TO MEAT CONSUMPTION.
IT'S LIKE YOU'VE LOST THE THREAD.

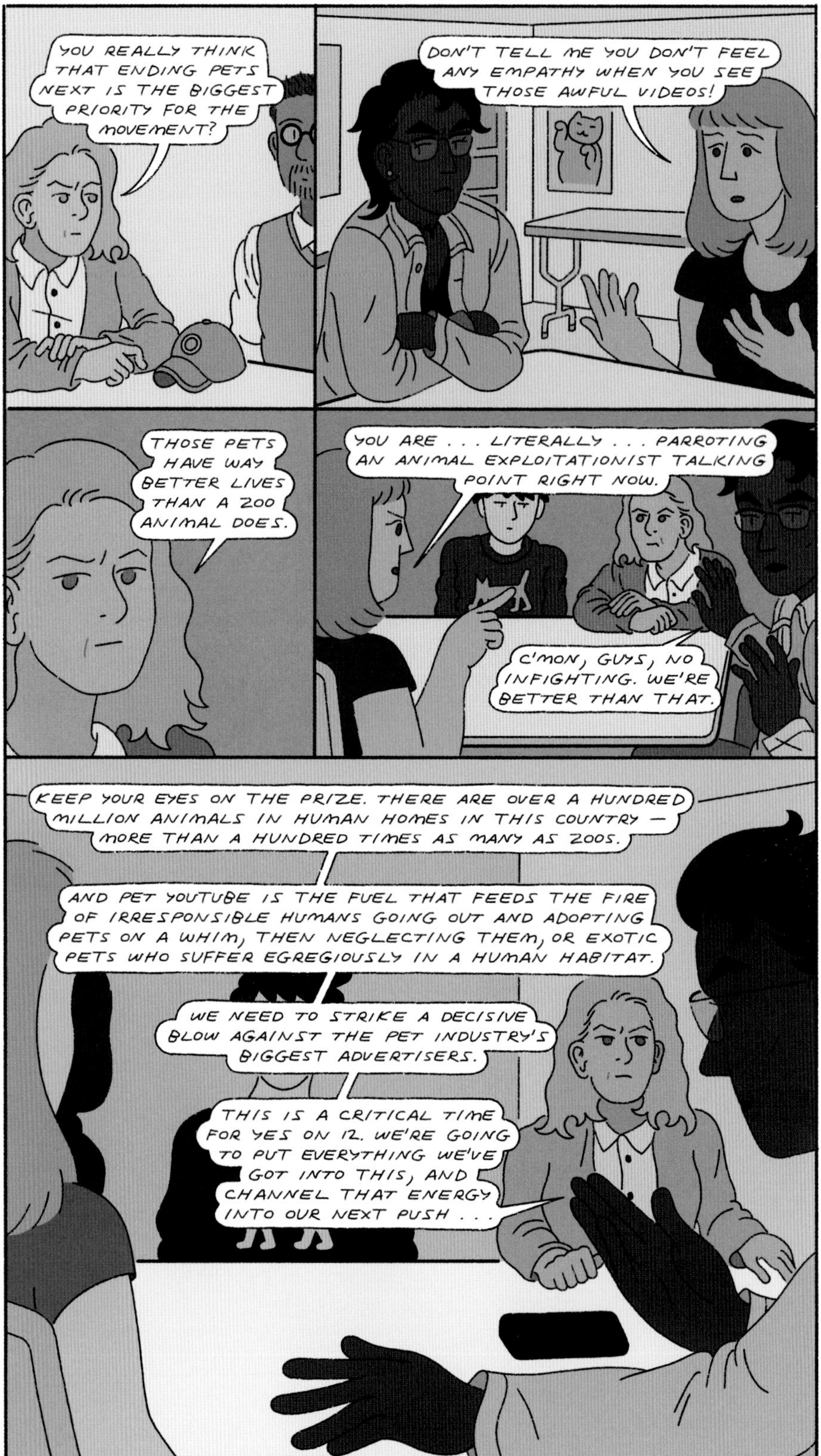
YOU REALLY THINK THAT ENDING PETS NEXT IS THE BIGGEST PRIORITY FOR THE MOVEMENT?
DON'T TELL ME YOU DON'T FEEL ANY EMPATHY WHEN YOU SEE THOSE AWFUL VIDEOS!
THOSE PETS HAVE WAY BETTER LIVES THAN A ZOO ANIMAL DOES.
YOU ARE . . . LITERALLY . . . PARROTING AN ANIMAL EXPLOITATIONIST TALKING POINT RIGHT NOW.
C'MON, GUYS, NO INFIGHTING. WE'RE BETTER THAN THAT.
KEEP YOUR EYES ON THE PRIZE. THERE ARE OVER A HUNDRED MILLION ANIMALS IN HUMAN HOMES IN THIS COUNTRY — MORE THAN A HUNDRED TIMES AS MANY AS ZOOS.
AND PET YOUTUBE IS THE FUEL THAT FEEDS THE FIRE OF IRRESPONSIBLE HUMANS GOING OUT AND ADOPTING PETS ON A WHIM, THEN NEGLECTING THEM, OR EXOTIC PETS WHO SUFFER EGREGIOUSLY IN A HUMAN HABITAT.
WE NEED TO STRIKE A DECISIVE BLOW AGAINST THE PET INDUSTRY'S BIGGEST ADVERTISERS.
THIS IS A CRITICAL TIME FOR YES ON 12. WE'RE GOING TO PUT EVERYTHING WE'VE GOT INTO THIS, AND CHANNEL THAT ENERGY INTO OUR NEXT PUSH . . .

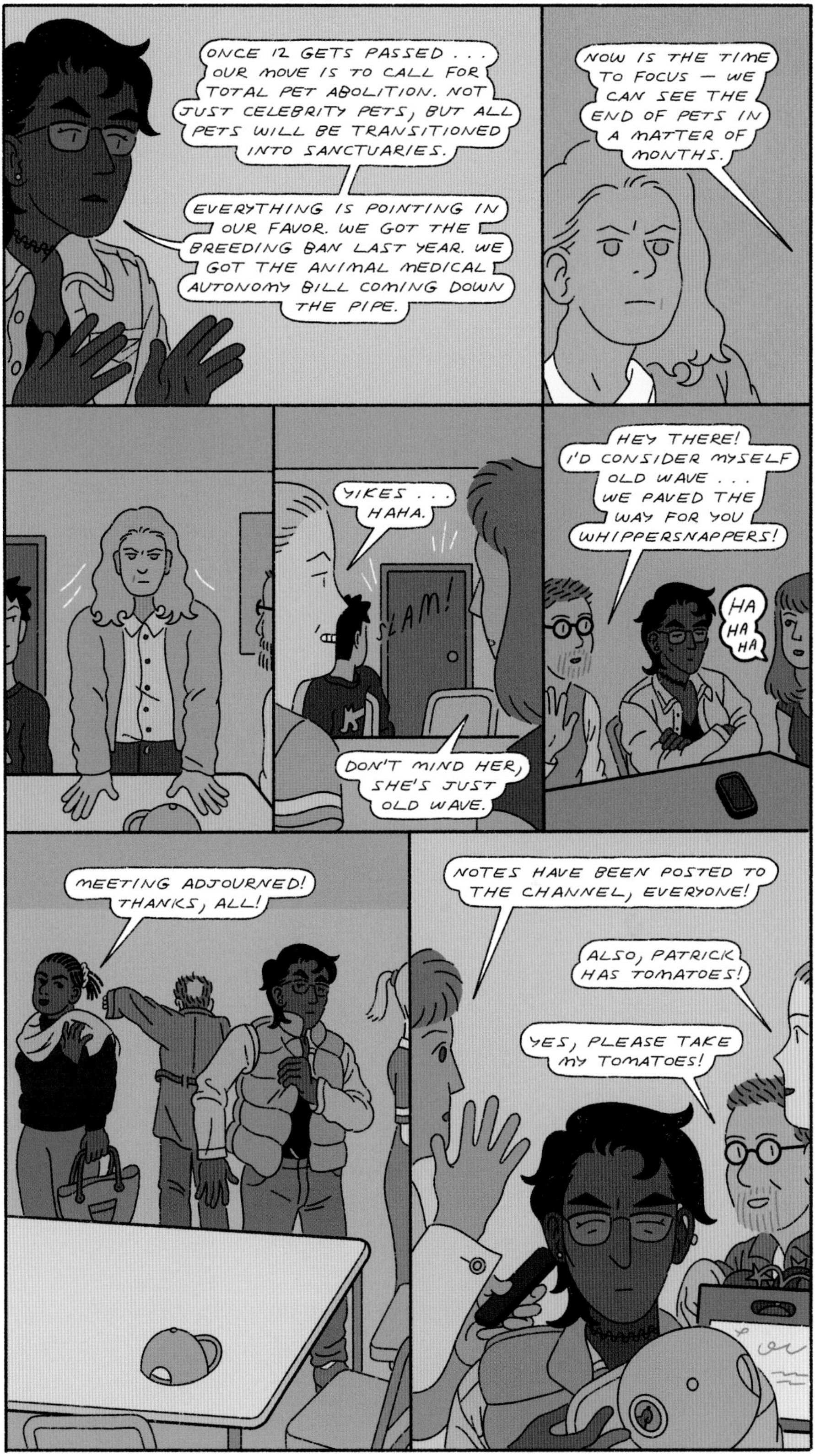
ONCE 12 GETS PASSED . . . OUR MOVE IS TO CALL FOR TOTAL PET ABOLITION. NOT JUST CELEBRITY PETS, BUT ALL PETS WILL BE TRANSITIONED INTO SANCTUARIES.
EVERYTHING IS POINTING IN OUR FAVOR. WE GOT THE BREEDING BAN LAST YEAR. WE GOT THE ANIMAL MEDICAL AUTONOMY BILL COMING DOWN THE PIPE.
NOW IS THE TIME TO FOCUS — WE CAN SEE THE END OF PETS IN A MATTER OF MONTHS.
YIKES . . . HAHA.
SLAM!
DON'T MIND HER, SHE'S JUST OLD WAVE.
HEY THERE! I'D CONSIDER MYSELF OLD WAVE . . . WE PAVED THE WAY FOR YOU WHIPPERSNAPPERS!
HA HA HA
MEETING ADJOURNED! THANKS, ALL!
NOTES HAVE BEEN POSTED TO THE CHANNEL, EVERYONE!
ALSO, PATRICK HAS TOMATOES!
YES, PLEASE TAKE MY TOMATOES!

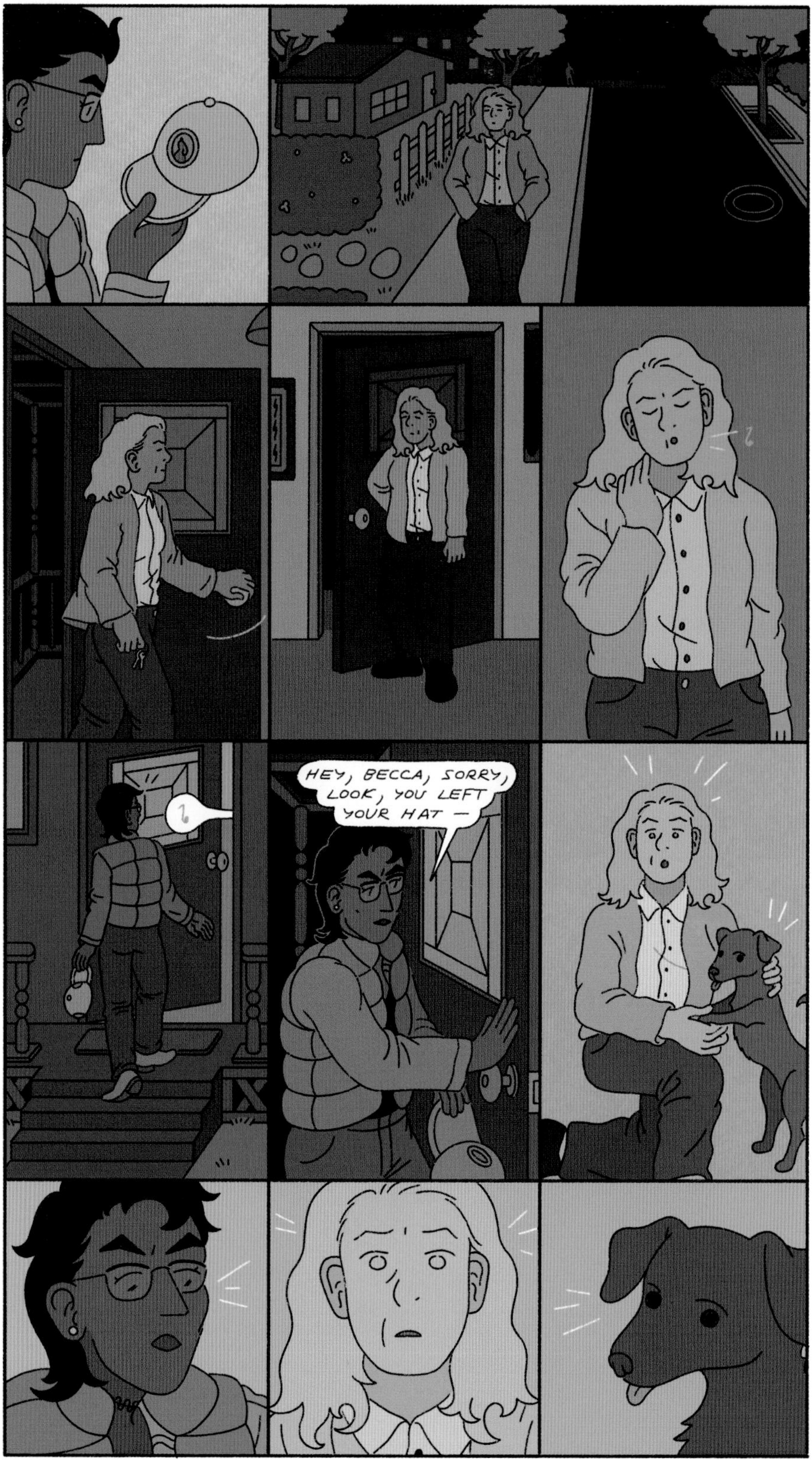
HEY, BECCA, SORRY, LOOK, YOU LEFT YOUR HAT —

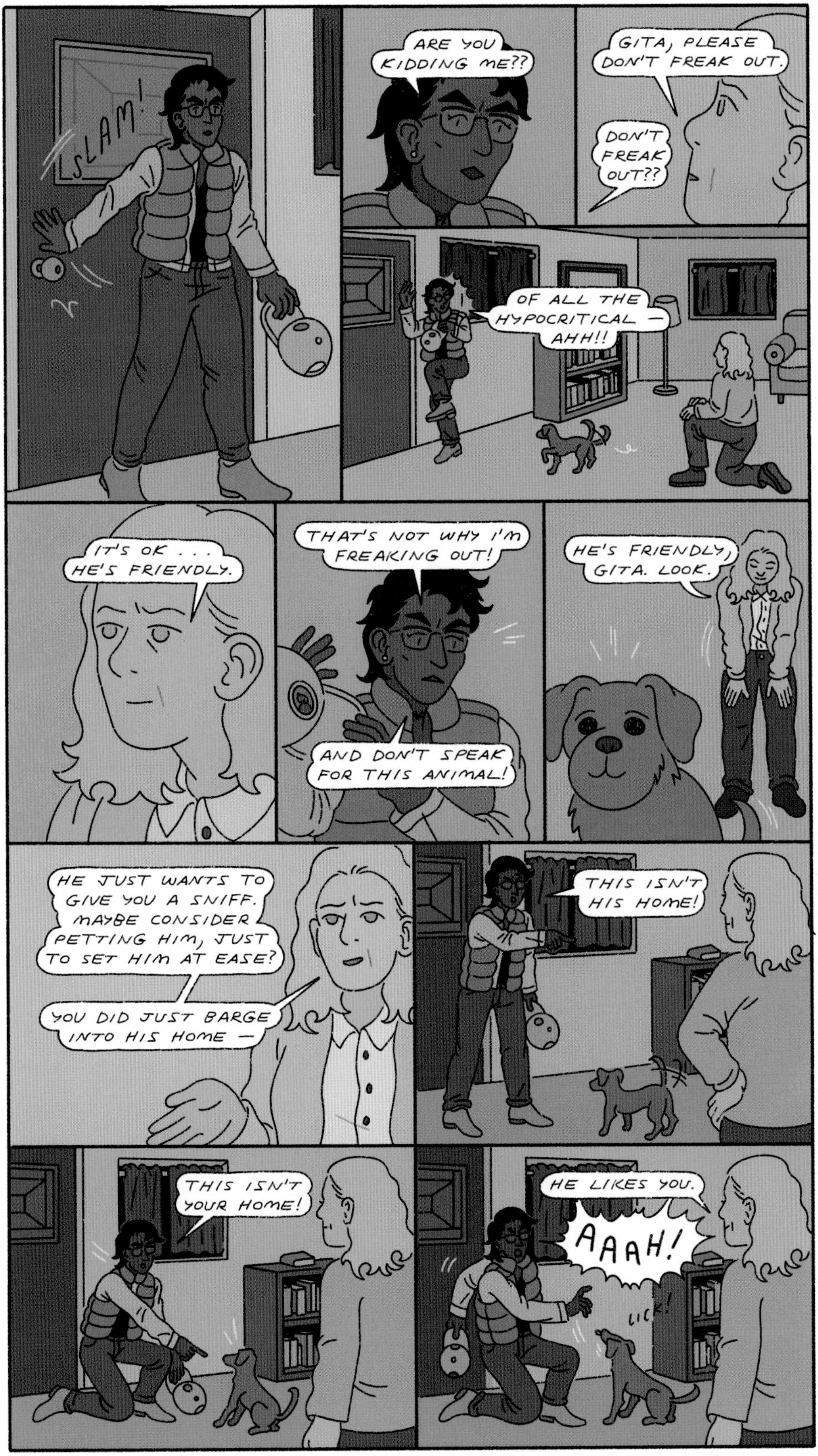
SLAM!
ARE YOU KIDDING ME??
GITA, PLEASE DON'T FREAK OUT.
DON'T FREAK OUT??
OF ALL THE HYPOCRITICAL — AHH!!
IT'S OK . . . HE'S FRIENDLY.
THAT'S NOT WHY I'M FREAKING OUT!
AND DON'T SPEAK FOR THIS ANIMAL!
HE'S FRIENDLY, GITA. LOOK.
HE JUST WANTS TO GIVE YOU A SNIFF. MAYBE CONSIDER PETTING HIM, JUST TO SET HIM AT EASE?
YOU DID JUST BARGE INTO HIS HOME —
THIS ISN'T HIS HOME!
THIS ISN'T YOUR HOME!
HE LIKES YOU.
AAAH!
LICK!

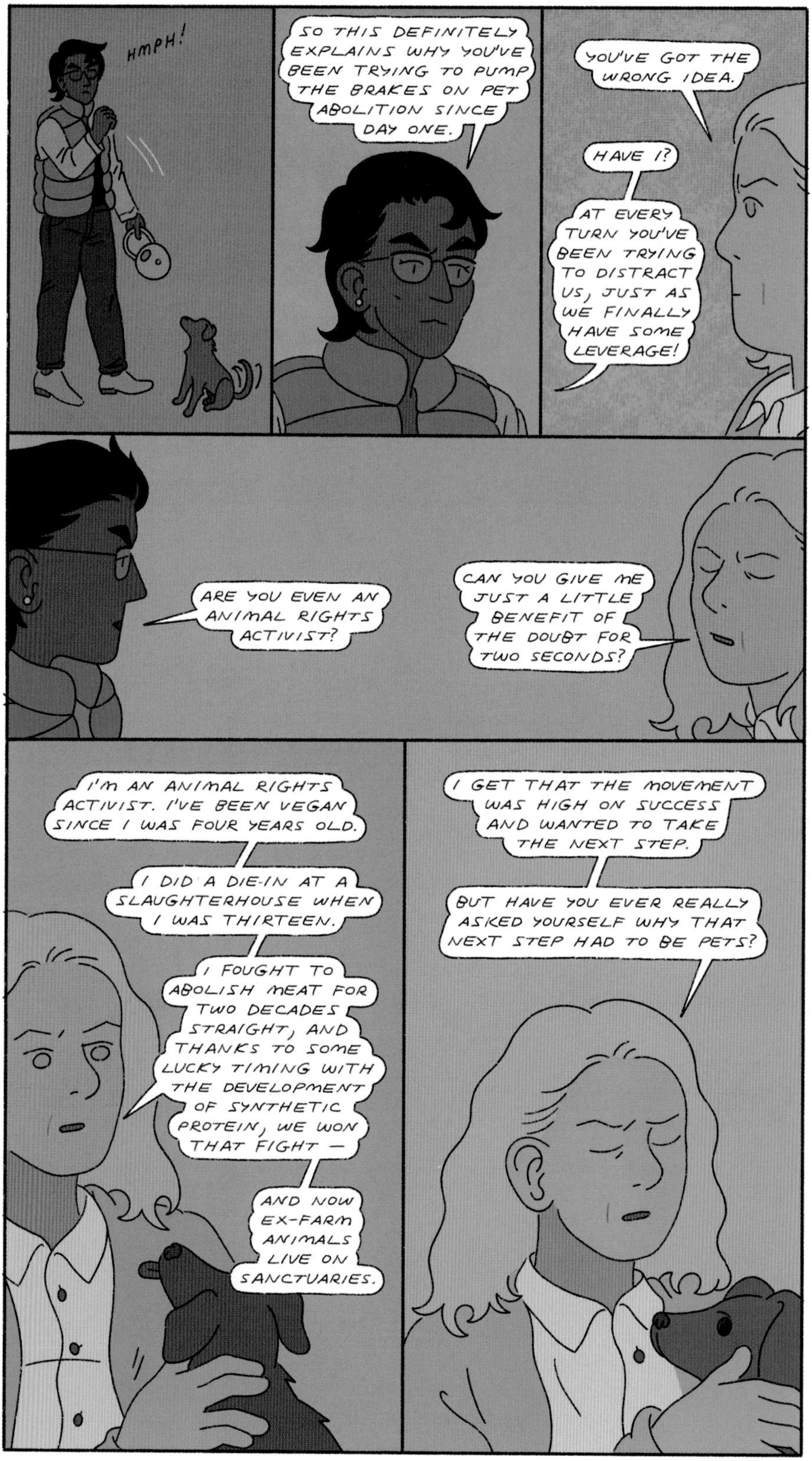
HMPH!
SO THIS DEFINITELY EXPLAINS WHY YOU'VE BEEN TRYING TO PUMP THE BRAKES ON PET ABOLITION SINCE DAY ONE.
YOU'VE GOT THE WRONG IDEA.
HAVE I?
AT EVERY TURN YOU'VE BEEN TRYING TO DISTRACT US, JUST AS WE FINALLY HAVE SOME LEVERAGE!
ARE YOU EVEN AN ANIMAL RIGHTS ACTIVIST?
CAN YOU GIVE ME JUST A LITTLE BENEFIT OF THE DOUBT FOR TWO SECONDS?
I'M AN ANIMAL RIGHTS ACTIVIST. I'VE BEEN VEGAN SINCE I WAS FOUR YEARS OLD.
I DID A DIE-IN AT A SLAUGHTERHOUSE WHEN I WAS THIRTEEN.
I FOUGHT TO ABOLISH MEAT FOR TWO DECADES STRAIGHT, AND THANKS TO SOME LUCKY TIMING WITH THE DEVELOPMENT OF SYNTHETIC PROTEIN, WE WON THAT FIGHT —
AND NOW EX-FARM ANIMALS LIVE ON SANCTUARIES.
I GET THAT THE MOVEMENT WAS HIGH ON SUCCESS AND WANTED TO TAKE THE NEXT STEP.
BUT HAVE YOU EVER REALLY ASKED YOURSELF WHY THAT NEXT STEP HAD TO BE PETS?

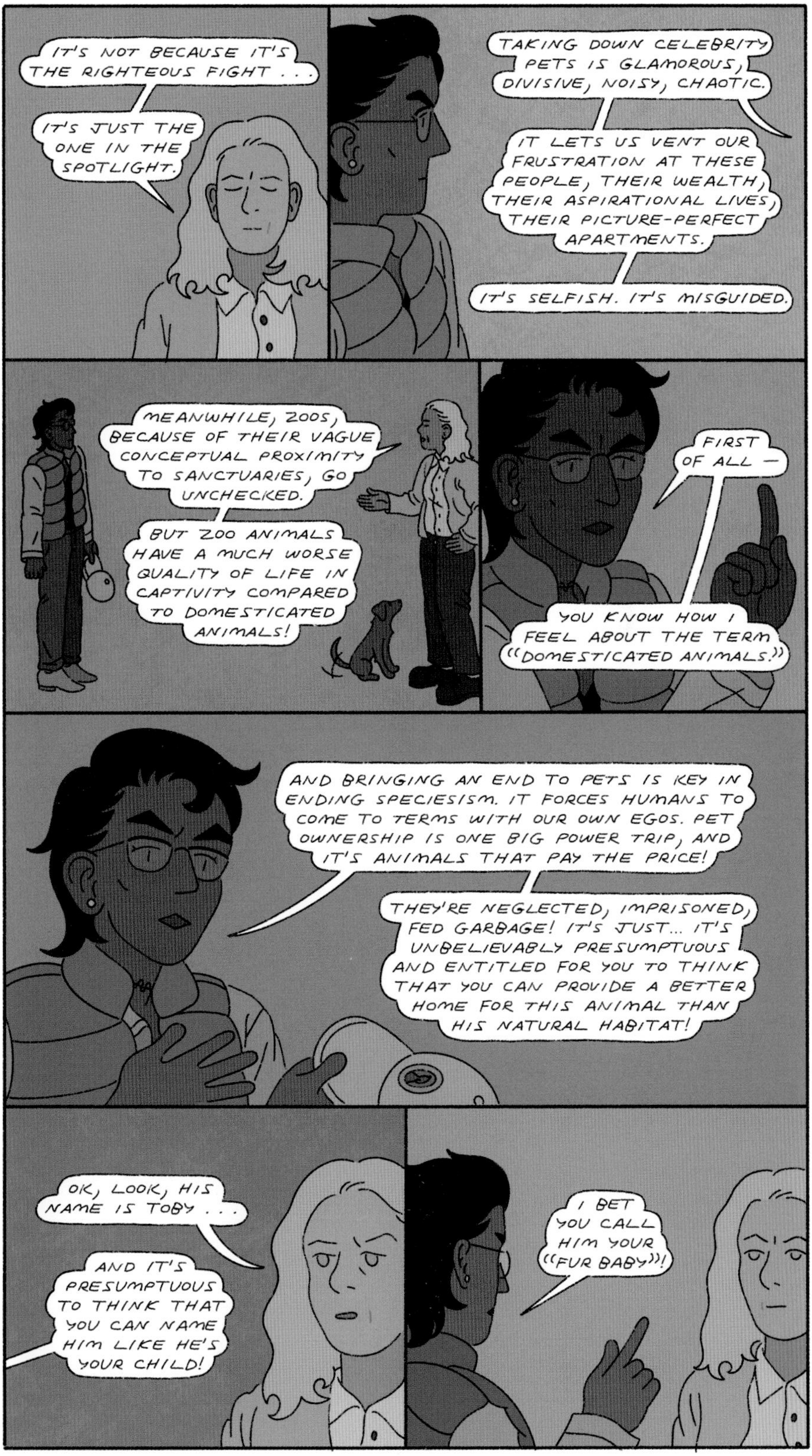
IT'S NOT BECAUSE IT'S THE RIGHTEOUS FIGHT . . .
IT'S JUST THE ONE IN THE SPOTLIGHT.
TAKING DOWN CELEBRITY PETS IS GLAMOROUS, DIVISIVE, NOISY, CHAOTIC.
IT LETS US VENT OUR FRUSTRATION AT THESE PEOPLE, THEIR WEALTH, THEIR ASPIRATIONAL LIVES, THEIR PICTURE-PERFECT APARTMENTS.
IT'S SELFISH. IT'S MISGUIDED.
MEANWHILE, ZOOS, BECAUSE OF THEIR VAGUE CONCEPTUAL PROXIMITY TO SANCTUARIES, GO UNCHECKED.
BUT ZOO ANIMALS HAVE A MUCH WORSE QUALITY OF LIFE IN CAPTIVITY COMPARED TO DOMESTICATED ANIMALS!
FIRST OF ALL —
YOU KNOW HOW I FEEL ABOUT THE TERM "DOMESTICATED ANIMALS."
AND BRINGING AN END TO PETS IS KEY IN ENDING SPECIESISM. IT FORCES HUMANS TO COME TO TERMS WITH OUR OWN EGOS. PET OWNERSHIP IS ONE BIG POWER TRIP, AND IT'S ANIMALS THAT PAY THE PRICE!
THEY'RE NEGLECTED, IMPRISONED, FED GARBAGE! IT'S JUST... IT'S UNBELIEVABLY PRESUMPTUOUS AND ENTITLED FOR YOU TO THINK THAT YOU CAN PROVIDE A BETTER HOME FOR THIS ANIMAL THAN HIS NATURAL HABITAT!
OK, LOOK, HIS NAME IS TOBY . . .
AND IT'S PRESUMPTUOUS TO THINK THAT YOU CAN NAME HIM LIKE HE'S YOUR CHILD!
I BET YOU CALL HIM YOUR "FUR BABY"!

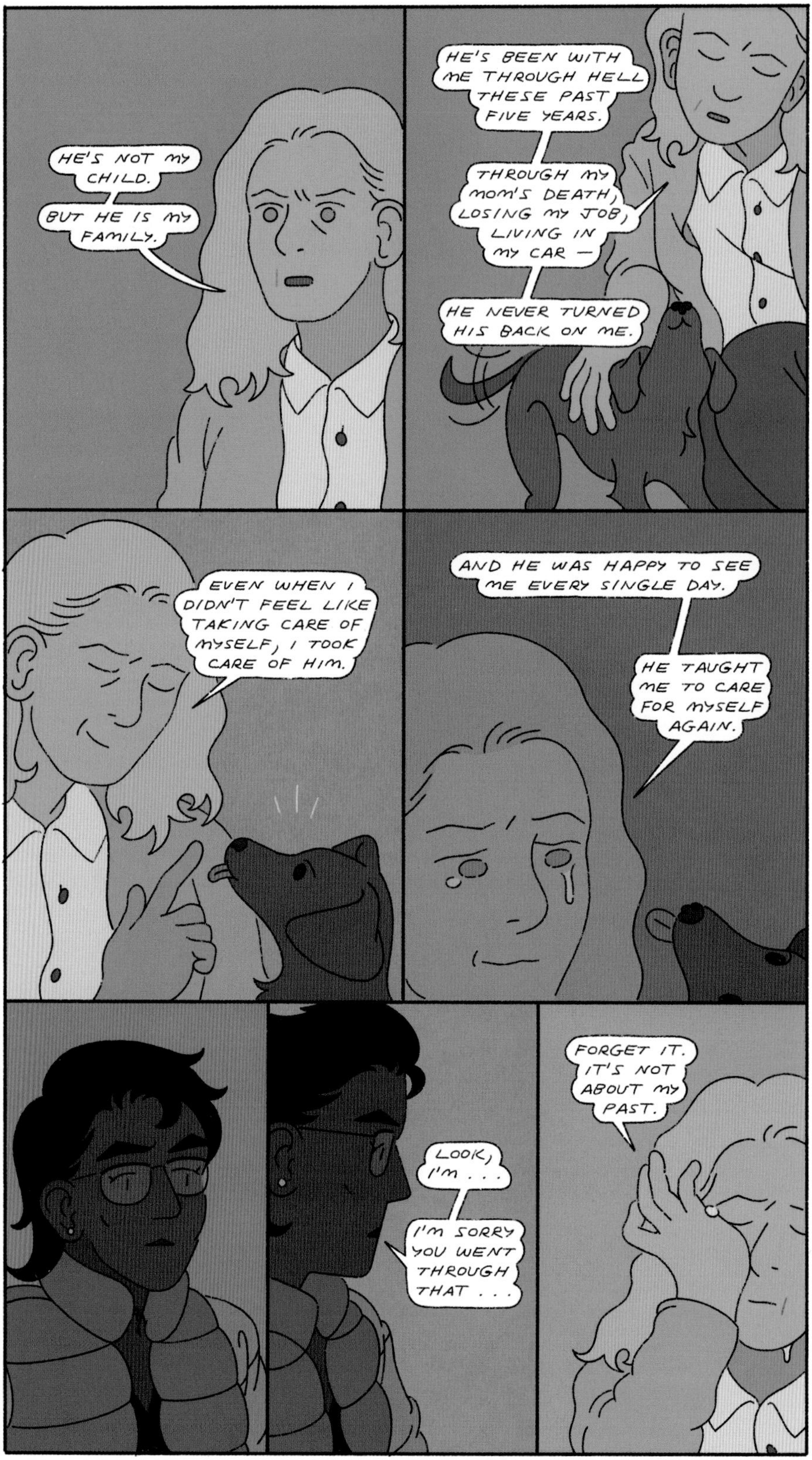
HE'S NOT MY CHILD.
BUT HE IS MY FAMILY.
HE'S BEEN WITH ME THROUGH HELL THESE PAST FIVE YEARS.
THROUGH MY MOM'S DEATH, LOSING MY JOB, LIVING IN MY CAR —
HE NEVER TURNED HIS BACK ON ME.
EVEN WHEN I DIDN'T FEEL LIKE TAKING CARE OF MYSELF, I TOOK CARE OF HIM.
AND HE WAS HAPPY TO SEE ME EVERY SINGLE DAY.
HE TAUGHT ME TO CARE FOR MYSELF AGAIN.
LOOK, I'M . . .
I'M SORRY YOU WENT THROUGH THAT . . .
FORGET IT. IT'S NOT ABOUT MY PAST.

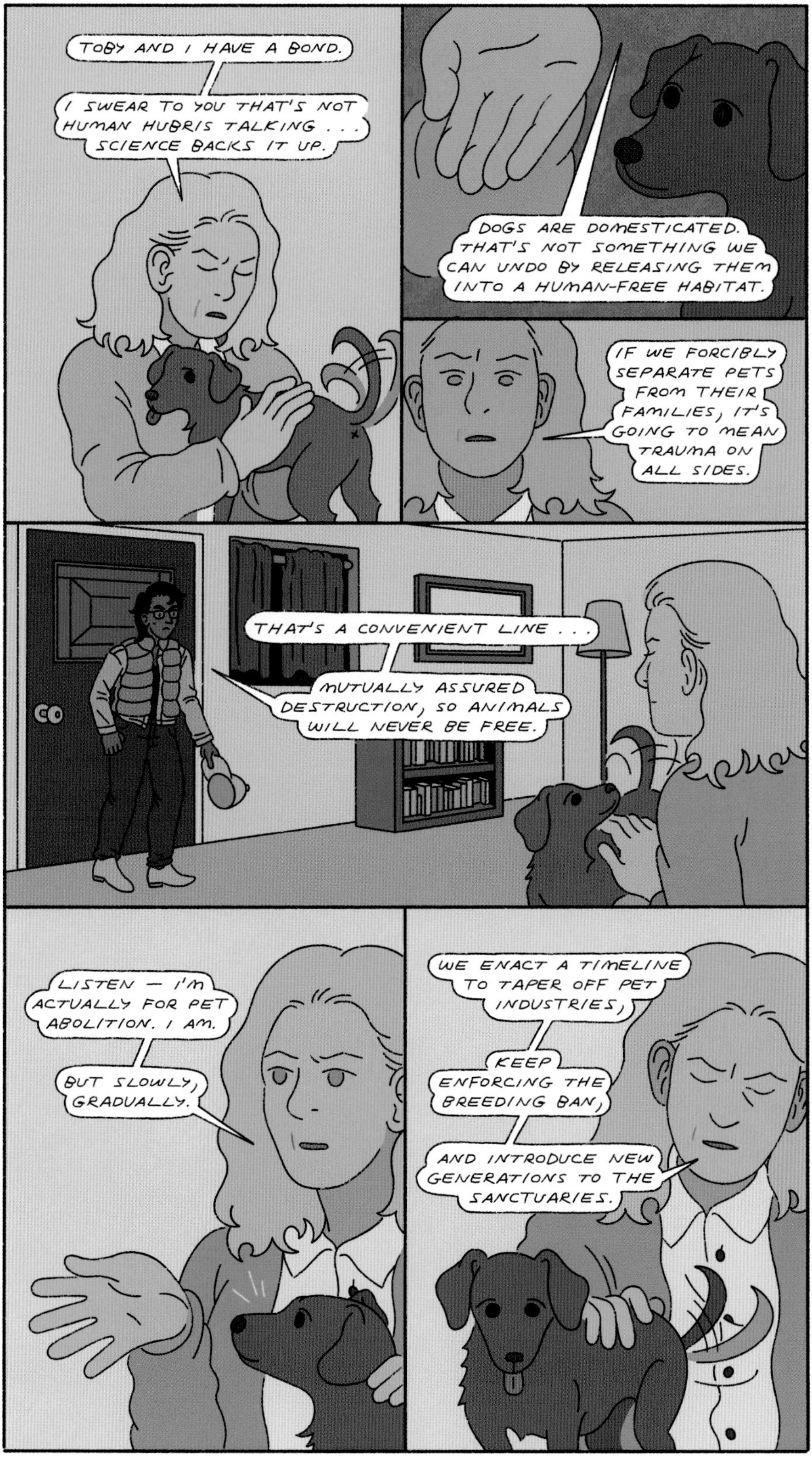
TOBY AND I HAVE A BOND.
I SWEAR TO YOU THAT'S NOT HUMAN HUBRIS TALKING . . . SCIENCE BACKS IT UP.
DOGS ARE DOMESTICATED. THAT'S NOT SOMETHING WE CAN UNDO BY RELEASING THEM INTO A HUMAN-FREE HABITAT.
IF WE FORCIBLY SEPARATE PETS FROM THEIR FAMILIES, IT'S GOING TO MEAN TRAUMA ON ALL SIDES.
THAT'S A CONVENIENT LINE . . .
MUTUALLY ASSURED DESTRUCTION, SO ANIMALS WILL NEVER BE FREE.
LISTEN — I'M ACTUALLY FOR PET ABOLITION. I AM.
BUT SLOWLY, GRADUALLY.
WE ENACT A TIMELINE TO TAPER OFF PET INDUSTRIES,
KEEP ENFORCING THE BREEDING BAN,
AND INTRODUCE NEW GENERATIONS TO THE SANCTUARIES.

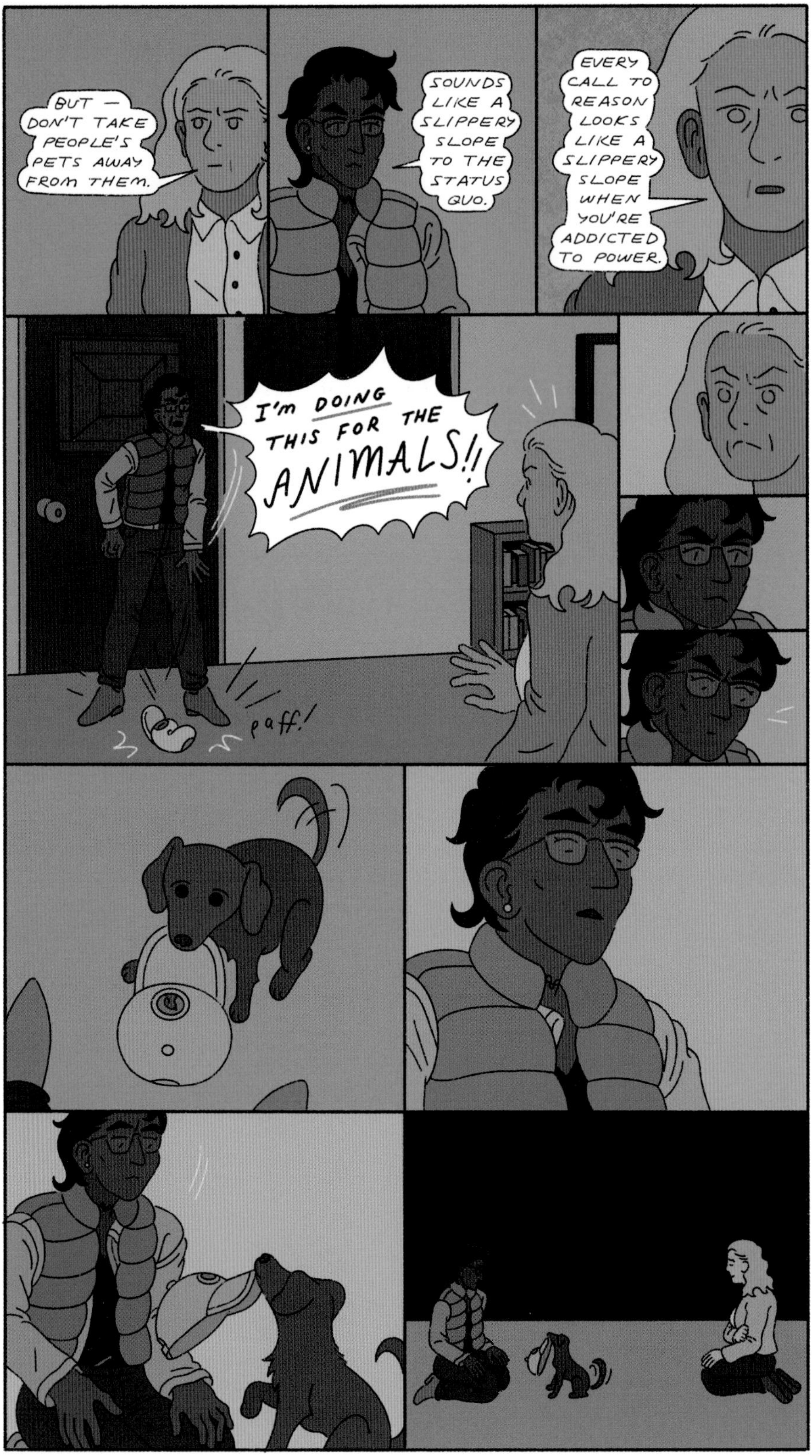
BUT — DON'T TAKE PEOPLE'S PETS AWAY FROM THEM.
SOUNDS LIKE A SLIPPERY SLOPE TO THE STATUS QUO.
EVERY CALL TO REASON LOOKS LIKE A SLIPPERY SLOPE WHEN YOU'RE ADDICTED TO POWER.
I'M DOING THIS FOR THE ANIMALS!!
paff!

ANIMAL MAGNETISM

HOW MANY RIGHTS DO ANIMALS DESERVE?

IN 2017, APRIL WAS IMPOSSIBLY PREGNANT. THE KIND OF pregnant where you feel more like a vessel for a chest-bursting alien than any kind of glowing goddess. The kind of pregnant where people make comments about you looking like you're about to pop.

April's pregnancy was big news that spring. The BBC called her impending delivery "the most anticipated birth since Prince George made his appearance in 2013." Every day tens of thousands of people logged on to a livestream to watch April and to see whether she did indeed pop. The feed was so popular that some wondered, is this cool, or creepy? Should we really be watching day and night, waiting with bated breath for the first hint of a contraction? Confounding the answer to this question was the nature of April's existence. April isn't a YouTuber or an Instagram influencer who streams every waking moment. No, she is a much stranger creature. April is a reticulated giraffe.

There are probably thousands of live-animal cams that you can access from the comfort of your own home with just a few clicks, no ticket or pants required. You can watch sea lions play, rabbits munch, penguins dive, and elephants loaf. And it's not just exotic animals, either: Pet owners can now log in to their special apps to watch their beloved animal family members while they're at work or out to dinner. And nearly every social media app is full of videos of pets—wearing hats, rolling in the mud, dancing, howling, snoring. No creature can escape human impact, and increasingly, none of them can escape our prying eyes, either.

The ways we watch and film animals would be completely out of bounds if applied to humans (imagine if someone set up a hidden camera in your bedroom and scored the footage with dramatic music), but whether nonhuman animals deserve privacy the way we do is something that biologists, zookeepers, and ethicists have only just begun debating. What is uncontroversial, however, is the fact that all of this very close watching has given us a window into the complexity of animals that we never had before. And ironically, the more we look, the more proof we're gathering that perhaps we shouldn't.

Studies show that many animals behave differently when they know they're being watched. Zoo residents learn where they can hide from human eyes, and in some species too much visitor attention can make them depressed, anxious, or aggressive. At one zoo, orangutans who were over-observed learned how to put paper sacks over their heads to avoid all the curious human visitors. Living in zoos is stressful enough that there's even a name for the anxiety it can cause: zoochosis. Zoos all over the world prescribe their residents drugs like Valium and Prozac to help them deal with their existence as living window displays.

But even beyond the direct impacts, all this watching has also revealed that animals have far more complex minds than we ever knew. Dolphins keep secrets from their trainers.[1] Rats can plan for the future.[2] Fish can feel pain.[3] Crows seem to mourn their dead (as Kate references in the "Ghostbot" chapter, page 178) and remember individual human faces. The most famous experiment demonstrating this phenomenon featured a mask-wearing researcher who went out and offended a handful of crows in Seattle. Not only did the birds that were wronged remember, they spread the word among their friends. Although the masked experimenter had only bothered seven animals, two years later, forty-seven of the fifty-three crows a researcher encountered on his masked walk screamed at him.[4]

Even our pets are perhaps more complex than we give them credit for. When a dog looks at their human, they experience a spike in oxytocin, much like when a human mother looks at their baby. (If you're a pet owner this might seem unsurprising to you, but for centuries the scientific and even public consensus on animals was that they did not experience emotion the way we do—scientists believed they were simply reacting to stimuli like extremely cute robots. There are still researchers who argue that we cannot use the word "personality" to describe nonhuman animals.)

Animal communication is also far more advanced and nuanced than scientists once thought. Some songbirds have what biologists call a "quiet song" that they use when trying to just talk to those nearby—like an avian whisper. Con Slobodchikoff, an animal linguist at Northern Arizona University, has done studies suggesting that prairie dogs can develop calls that actually describe a person's build and what color shirt they're wearing. With a series of chirps they can say: "Tall guy in a blue shirt coming your way!" And that's not all. Slobodchikoff has also shown that these burrowing fuzzballs can add to that description if the person is holding a gun. "Tall guy in a blue shirt coming your way, oh, and he's got a gun!"

Even Slobodchikoff was surprised at his own results. "I never really

---

1   One dolphin named Kelly, who I've actually had the pleasure of meeting, provides an incredible example of this. In many aquaria, dolphins are trained to gather trash and debris in the pool and turn it in to their keepers for a reward. Kelly realized that she got the same sized reward no matter the type or size of trash she brought, so she would hide pieces of garbage under a rock and tear off small pieces to bring to her trainer to maximize her rewards.

2   If rats encounter their favorite food in a maze, they'll remember where it is and plan their routes the next time they encounter that maze so that they can get that same tasty food.

3   This might seem obvious, but for a long time, conventional wisdom was that fish did not in fact feel pain. In a 1977 issue of *Field & Stream*, for example, a columnist responds to a letter from a thirteen-year-old girl asking whether fish suffer with "Fish don't feel pain the way you do when you skin your knee or stub your toe or have a toothache, because their nervous systems are much simpler. I'm not really sure they feel *any* pain, as we feel pain, but probably they feel a kind of 'fish pain.'"

4   In this same set of experiments, they used Dick Cheney masks as "neutral" or non-offensive to the birds. Some might beg to differ.

expected that something that is a rodent, who essentially weighs about a pound, would actually have that kind of sophistication," he told me.

Given all of this information, it's only natural to start calling into question our relationships with these creatures. The obvious place to start is with eating them (should we?), but the questions bleed out into our other more complex relationships, too. Should we keep animals in our homes as pets? What about zoos? Is it ethical to confine animals to enclosures far smaller than their natural range in the name of science or the even murkier concept of "awareness"? These are the questions that our activists grapple with in the comic, and they're ones that real-world activists struggle with, too.

I will pause here and ask you to also question why it requires a certain level of intelligence, language, or awareness to begin respecting and reconsidering our relationships with animals in the first place. In her book *Beasts of Burden*, Sunaura Taylor tells the story of famous chimps like Nim, Washoe, Booee, and Ally who were passed around between research labs in the 1970s and 1980s. When the public learned that some of them knew sign language, they suddenly demanded the chimps be released and not used for things like cosmetics testing. But why did their ability to sign change the ethical quandary? "Why should a chimp who knows no ASL signs be sentenced to a life of solitary confinement and experimentation while the signing chimpanzee sparks public outcry calling for his freedom," Taylor asks.

These questions are fraught, and the solutions are equally sticky. Much like with human rights, it's relatively easy to say animals should have some. But which ones, and how those rules might be enforced, is far more complicated.

In 2015, People for the Ethical Treatment of Animals (PETA) filed a lawsuit against a photographer, arguing that a Sulawesi crested macaque named Naruto should own the rights to an image that it took using the artists camera. The "monkey selfie" lawsuit, as it came to be known, was essentially a publicity stunt to get the public talking about questions of an animal's legal rights. If monkeys can retain copyright, what else might they be able to do?

Ultimately, PETA settled with the photographer, David Slater, but not after several years of expensive litigation that left Slater with huge legal bills and made him consider abandoning photography altogether. "I've had my life ruined," Slater told the *Telegraph*. The courts weren't kind to PETA either, in one decision writing that: "Puzzlingly, while representing to the world that 'animals are not ours to eat, wear, experiment on, use for entertainment, or abuse in any other way,' PETA seems to employ Naruto as an unwitting pawn in its ideological goals."[5]

There are already laws covering the ethical treatment of animals in many places, but some countries take things further than others. The United States has the Animal Welfare Act, which regulates how animals are treated in research, zoos, and circuses. (Notably, the AWA does not regulate the treatment of animals on farms, nor does it apply to any cold-blooded species or the

---

5   It's still unclear if PETA actually got the right monkey at all—in the suit they describe Naruto as a six-year-old male monkey, but some experts have argued that the primate in the photo is a female.

two most common species of mice and rats used in laboratories.) Switzerland famously has a rule that you cannot own one guinea pig (or brightly colored budgie)—because they're social creatures, you must keep more than one so they don't get lonely.

In 2018, the Uttarakhand High Court in North India declared animals should be treated as "legal entities having a distinct persona with corresponding rights, duties and liabilities of a living person." In Indian law, there are two kinds of legal "persons"—the more traditional human person like you and me, and what's called a "juristic person," which includes minors, companies, trusts, and wards of the court. Under this ruling, nonhuman animals now fall into the latter category.

As part of the decision, the court also made some new rules around the use of horse carts—how much weight the horses could carry, how many water and food breaks they got, and what types of weather were considered unworkable for the animals. But it's worth noting that as far as I could find, the court did not at any point ask whether those horses chose to carry carts at all, or were instead being held hostage and forced to work.

It would be naive to think that we could simply "give animals rights" in one fell swoop. Much like Naruto the selfie monkey cannot represent himself in court, animals can't quickly plug into our complicated legal and social systems. But that doesn't have to mean that they completely forfeit their agency, does it?[6]

I'm asking a lot of rhetorical questions in this chapter because there really is no clear and obvious path to an ethical integration of humans and animals. But let's consider a few scenarios, some more likely than others.

First, what would happen in the world of animal liberation you just read about in the preceding comic if activists won a ban on pets? Most animal rights activists, even the ones who support an end to domesticated animals, are more in Becca's camp than Gita's—they don't want to actually forcibly take your pets away. "We're not trying to separate Fluffy and Fido from your good home," Doris Lin told me. Lin is an animal activist who supports the end of pets but has a few herself, including rescued rabbits and guinea pigs.

In Lin's version of this future, we transition away from pets slowly—with robots and other synthetic creatures taking their place. But even Lin, an animal activist to the core, isn't actually convinced that we can keep our meaty human paws from drawing other species into our orbit. If we give up dogs and cats and rabbits, will we set our sights on other animals? "Maybe the domestication process would start all over again with animals who are curious and come up to us in the wild," she told me. "Who knows, maybe squirrels will be pets in the future."

Perhaps a more winning strategy is indeed the one Becca advocates in the comic: the end of zoos. This is a far more common proposal in the world

---

6   Our insistence on trying to get animals to slot immediately into our own ideas of intelligence, culture, and law is the focus of one of my favorite *Onion* articles of all time. Above a badly photoshopped image depicting two scientists in lab coats standing beside a dolphin in a parking lot next to some traffic cones, the headline reads, "Study: Dolphins, Not So Intelligent On Land."

of animal activism. And even some zoo executives express complex feelings about their work. Damian Aspinall, who runs Howletts Wild Animal Park in Kent, England, has been working to release as many animals from captivity back into the wild as possible. "We have no moral right as a species to let animals suffer just because we are curious about them," he told the *Guardian*. In 2017, Bernard Harrison, former executive director of the Singapore Zoo, was asked by *SG Magazine* about activists who want to shut down zoos, and he replied: "Seriously, I couldn't agree with them more. If I could, I would shut down ninety percent of the ten thousand zoos in the world. The world is full of horrible stink holes that call themselves zoos." And Jenny Gray, author of the book *Zoo Ethics: The Challenges of Compassionate Conservation*, writes that, "At best, three percent of zoos are striving to meet ethical standards, with perhaps only a handful meeting all the requirements."

Even the argument that zoos help engage and educate the public might not hold water. One 2014 study found that only 34 percent of children who wandered about the London Zoo without a guide showed "positive" learning (learning and remembering things that were true), and 16 percent actually seemed to show a decrease in their understanding of zoo animals and the natural world. Ultimately, the authors write that "zoos' standard unguided interpretive materials are insufficient for achieving the best outcomes for visiting children." Closing the world's zoos would be a challenge, but doable—animals could be slowly consolidated and relocated to the places actually equipped to host them, and released where possible.

And why not, some argue, when we can watch animals at any time anyway with just the click of a mouse or remote? When we can log in and turn on live footage of almost any animal or habitat we want, why do we need to enclose the actual creatures in spaces they weren't meant to live in? But this line of reasoning gets us back to the question posed at the beginning of the chapter: Is it really okay to film animals in their homes? Why is it okay to put a hidden camera in a badger's bedroom, but not in Barbara's? What does informed consent look like for a panda or a bowerbird?

Asking these questions can raise some hackles. Perhaps you feel yours raised right now. One philosopher I spoke with, Angie Pepper, who has been asking these questions for years now, says that while people are happy to consider the rights of animals in the abstract, or when it comes to more egregious forms of violence like abuse or even factory farming, the suggestion that we might not even be allowed to watch them evokes a different set of reactions—often including anger and rage. "People really want to see animals. They really want to get in their space and be in their homes. They can't accept that some things might just be off limits," says Pepper.

Longtime listeners of the podcast know that these questions are ones I'm moderately (okay, maybe more than moderately) obsessed with. I sneak animal segments into episodes about facial recognition (if we don't think it's okay to do it to people, why are we applying it to pigs and monkeys?) and undersea living (is it ethical to use a dolphin for construction jobs? Are they protected by OSHA?). Every time I do one of these bits or episodes, I get emails from people who say: "Rose, honestly, who cares? Why are you so obsessed with animals? Humans have so many other problems, why bother wasting time on these things?"

And I think the answer is this: I believe that looking at our relationships with nonhuman animals can help us get at some of the biggest questions and challenges we're grappling with right now. Humans have appointed themselves CEOs of the planet. We've given ourselves the power to make unilateral decisions about not just our own lives, but the lives of every other living being. But if the Earth was to give us a performance review, we'd probably fail pretty miserably. I mean, look around—humans have scorched, depleted, polluted, and fundamentally altered the planet in so many ways that it's putting our entire species at risk. Would you hire us to manage the planet again? Maybe part of our problem is that we see ourselves as distinct from the animals and the plants, as something separate and apart, rather than part of a bigger whole.

Of course, indigenous people have known this all along. In her book *Braiding Sweetgrass*, Robin Wall Kimmerer connects our path with that of wild berries that the Potawatomi people gather up in a large wooden bowl to distribute at communal gatherings. People eat the berries and delight in their flavor and juiciness, but the transaction does not end there. "The berries trust that we will uphold our end of the bargain and disperse their seeds to new places to grow," she writes. But that give-and-take between us and other living beings hasn't translated into modern society. "Somewhere along the line, though," Kimmerer writes, "people have abandoned berry teachings. Instead of sowing richness, we diminish the possibilities for the future at every turn."

So what would happen if we changed that up and started considering animals as partners rather than pawns or employees or wards, as the other end of a collective bargain? What kinds of futures could we create then?

When I talked about April the giraffe on a bonus episode of *Flash Forward*, a listener responded with her thoughts: "You asked if I would be okay with a hidden webcam broadcasting my labor pains to the entire world and the answer is, obviously, most certainly NO. However, would I be okay with a hidden webcam broadcasting my labor pains to a population of interested giraffes? Actually, yeah, that thought doesn't bother me in the slightest." What if we lived in a world where we considered the curiosities of giraffes as equal to our own?

In the summer of 2018, April got pregnant again, and her caretakers at the Animal Adventure Park in Harpursville, New York, again set up a live cam to watch her. And just like last time, people logged in to watch. Those who didn't want to watch the live feed could sign up for text messages to be alerted when she went into labor. Today you can watch two different livestreams of April and her sons cavorting around their enclosure. But should you?

DON'T LIE TO ME

BY BOX BROWN

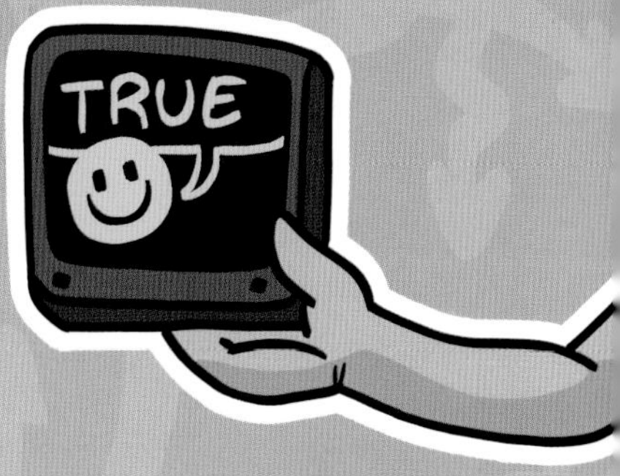
TRUE

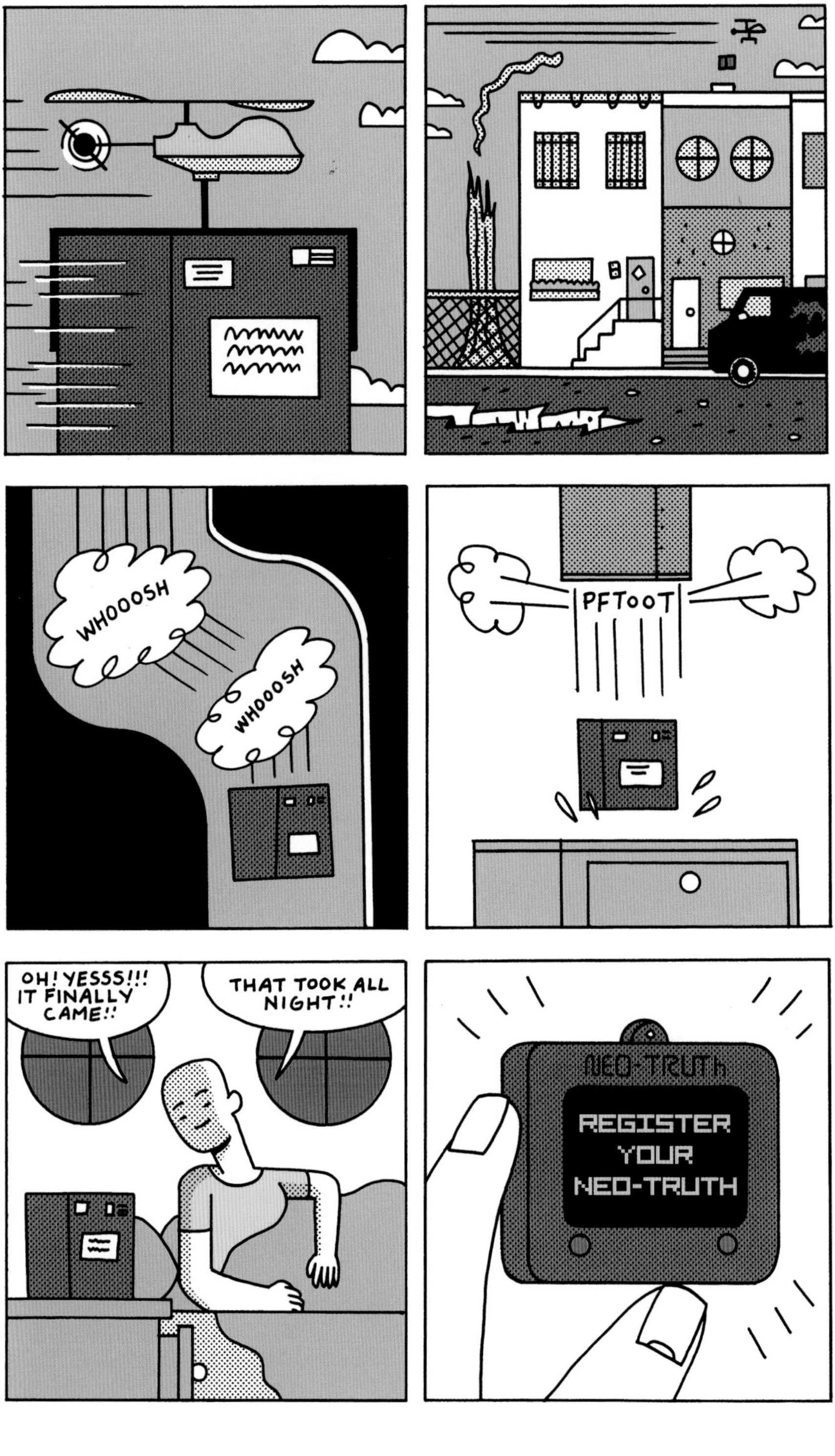
WHOOOSH
WHOOOSH
PFTOOT
OH! YESSS!!! IT FINALLY CAME!!
THAT TOOK ALL NIGHT!!
NEO-TRUTh
REGISTER YOUR NEO-TRUTH

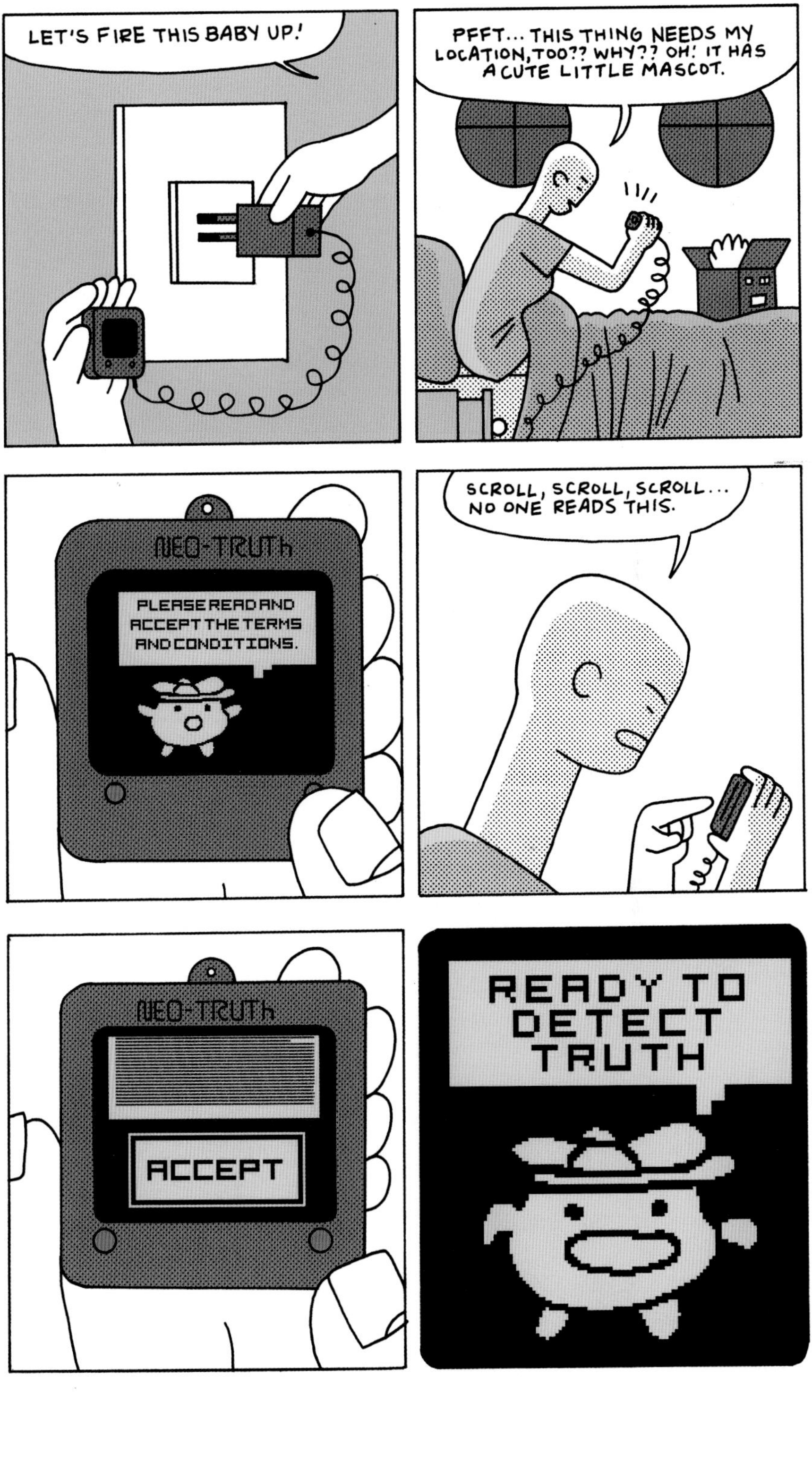
LET'S FIRE THIS BABY UP!
PFFT... THIS THING NEEDS MY LOCATION, TOO?? WHY?? OH! IT HAS A CUTE LITTLE MASCOT.
NEO-TRUTh
PLEASE READ AND ACCEPT THE TERMS AND CONDITIONS.
SCROLL, SCROLL, SCROLL... NO ONE READS THIS.
NEO-TRUTh
ACCEPT
READY TO DETECT TRUTH

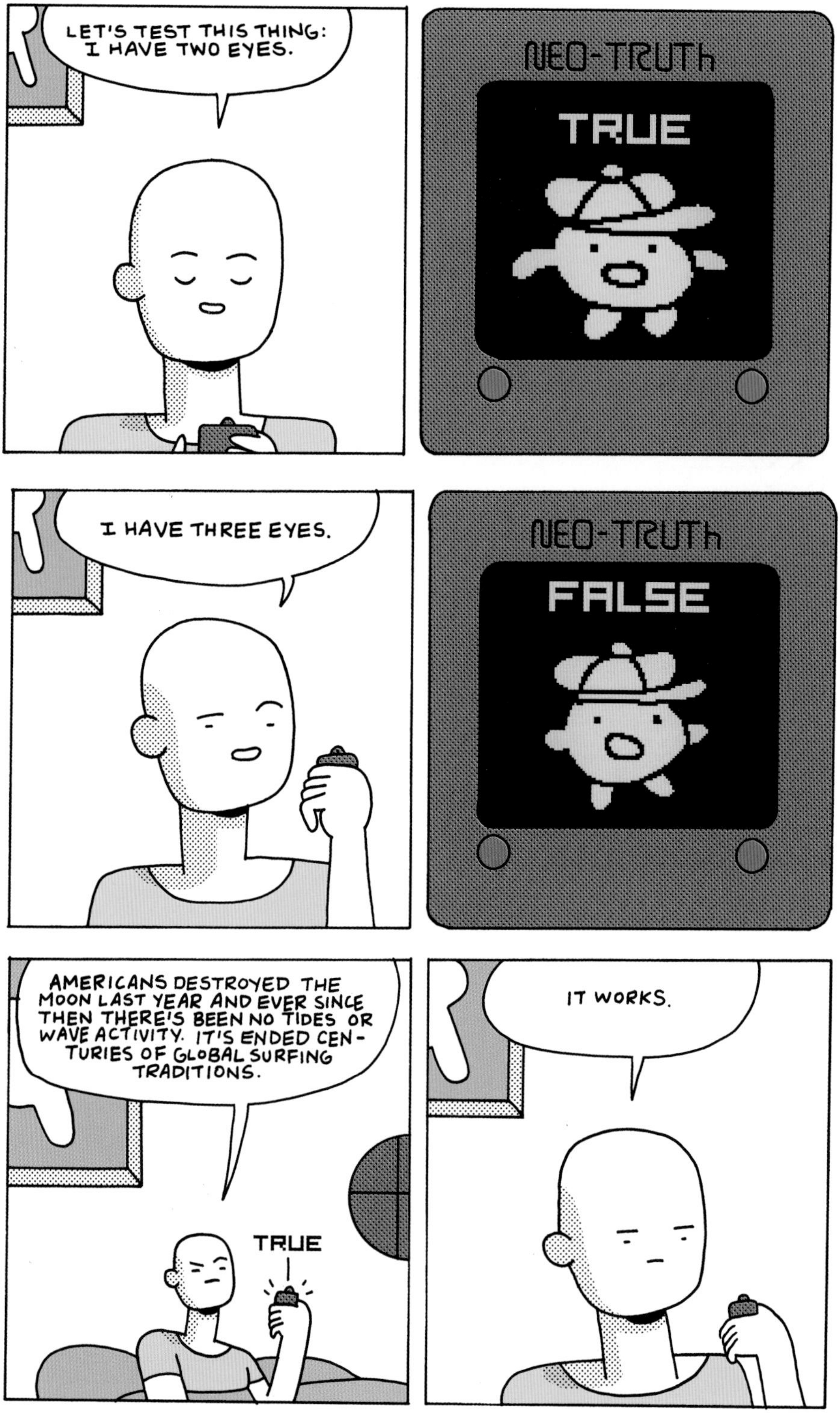

LET'S TEST THIS THING: I HAVE TWO EYES.
NEO-TRUTH
TRUE
I HAVE THREE EYES.
NEO-TRUTH
FALSE
AMERICANS DESTROYED THE MOON LAST YEAR AND EVER SINCE THEN THERE'S BEEN NO TIDES OR WAVE ACTIVITY. IT'S ENDED CENTURIES OF GLOBAL SURFING TRADITIONS.
TRUE
IT WORKS.

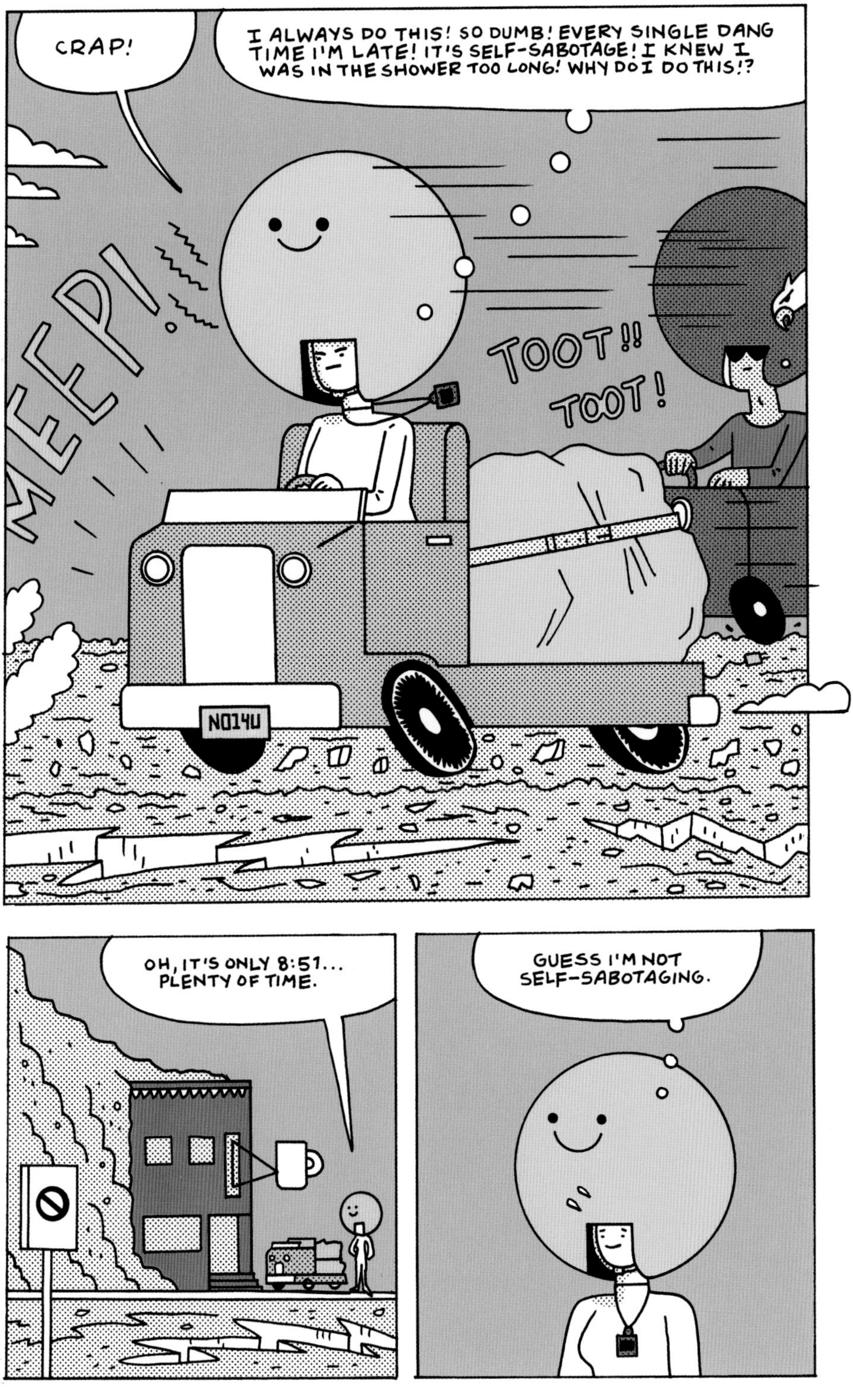
CRAP!
I ALWAYS DO THIS! SO DUMB! EVERY SINGLE DANG TIME I'M LATE! IT'S SELF-SABOTAGE! I KNEW I WAS IN THE SHOWER TOO LONG! WHY DO I DO THIS!?
MEEP!
TOOT!!
TOOT!
NO14U
OH, IT'S ONLY 8:51... PLENTY OF TIME.
GUESS I'M NOT SELF-SABOTAGING.

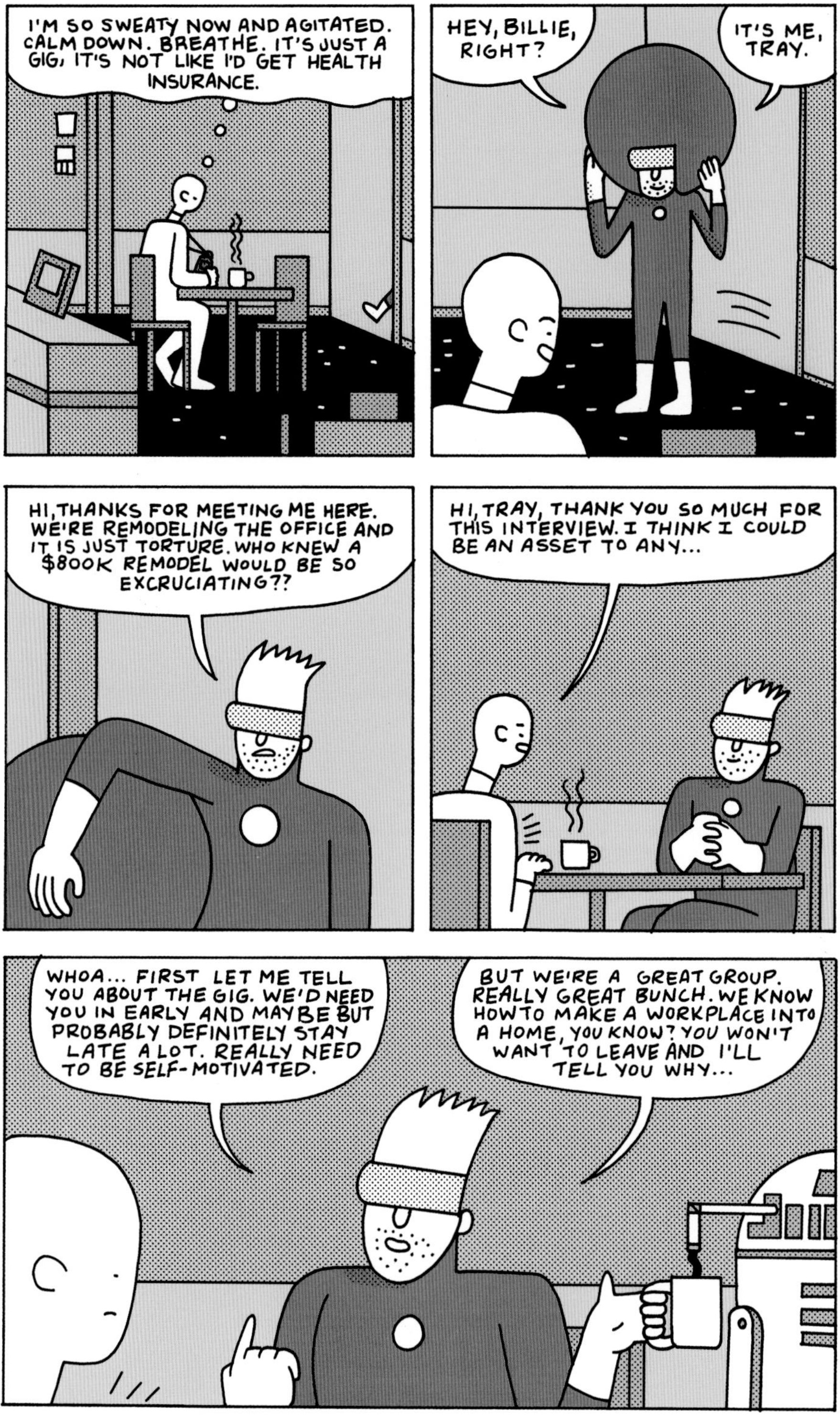
I'M SO SWEATY NOW AND AGITATED. CALM DOWN. BREATHE. IT'S JUST A GIG, IT'S NOT LIKE I'D GET HEALTH INSURANCE.
HEY, BILLIE, RIGHT?
IT'S ME, TRAY.
HI, THANKS FOR MEETING ME HERE. WE'RE REMODELING THE OFFICE AND IT IS JUST TORTURE. WHO KNEW A $800K REMODEL WOULD BE SO EXCRUCIATING??
HI, TRAY, THANK YOU SO MUCH FOR THIS INTERVIEW. I THINK I COULD BE AN ASSET TO ANY...
WHOA... FIRST LET ME TELL YOU ABOUT THE GIG. WE'D NEED YOU IN EARLY AND MAYBE BUT PROBABLY DEFINITELY STAY LATE A LOT. REALLY NEED TO BE SELF-MOTIVATED.
BUT WE'RE A GREAT GROUP. REALLY GREAT BUNCH. WE KNOW HOW TO MAKE A WORKPLACE INTO A HOME, YOU KNOW? YOU WON'T WANT TO LEAVE AND I'LL TELL YOU WHY...

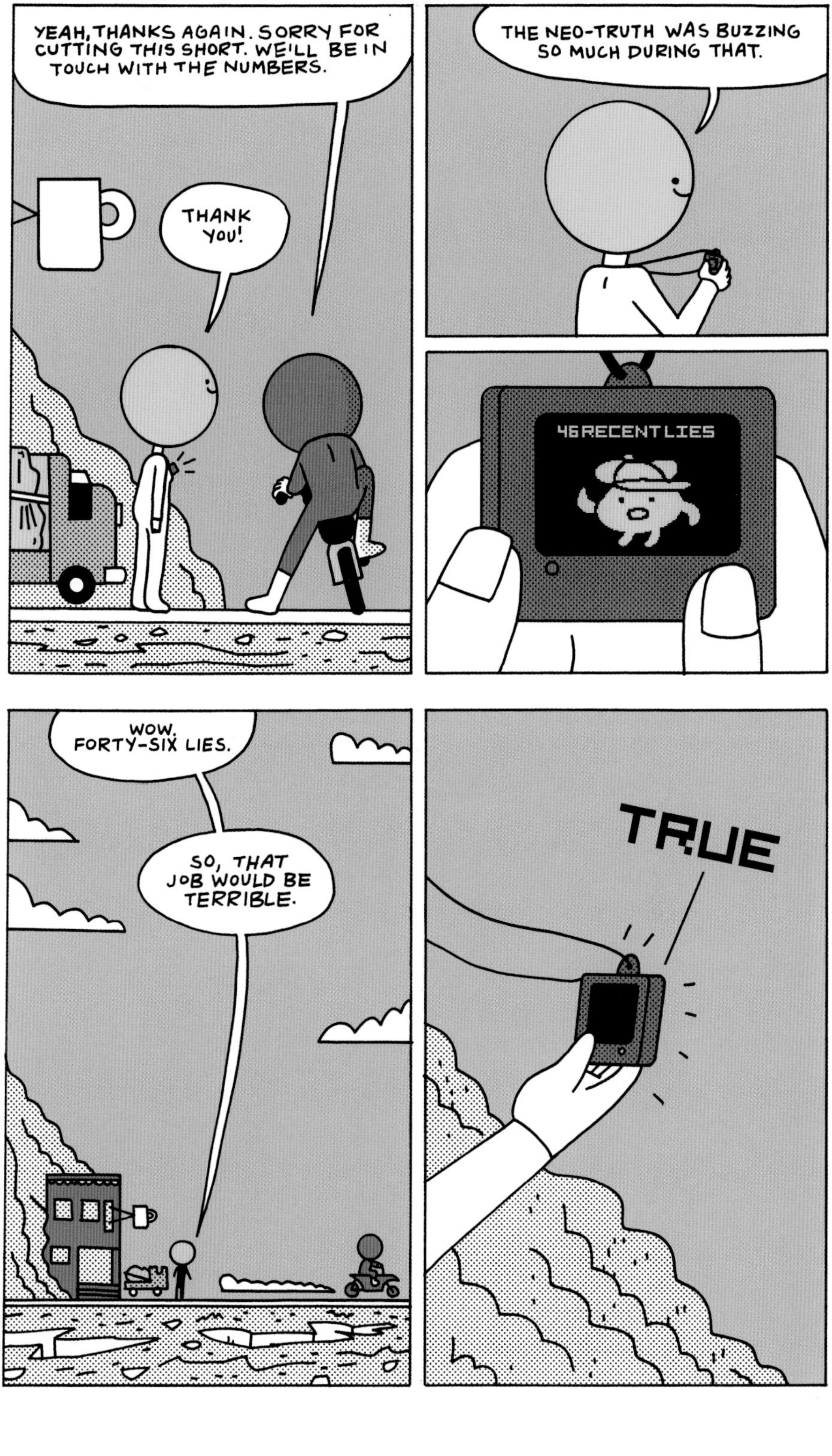
YEAH, THANKS AGAIN. SORRY FOR CUTTING THIS SHORT. WE'LL BE IN TOUCH WITH THE NUMBERS.
THANK YOU!
THE NEO-TRUTH WAS BUZZING SO MUCH DURING THAT.
46 RECENT LIES
WOW. FORTY-SIX LIES.
SO, THAT JOB WOULD BE TERRIBLE.
TRUE

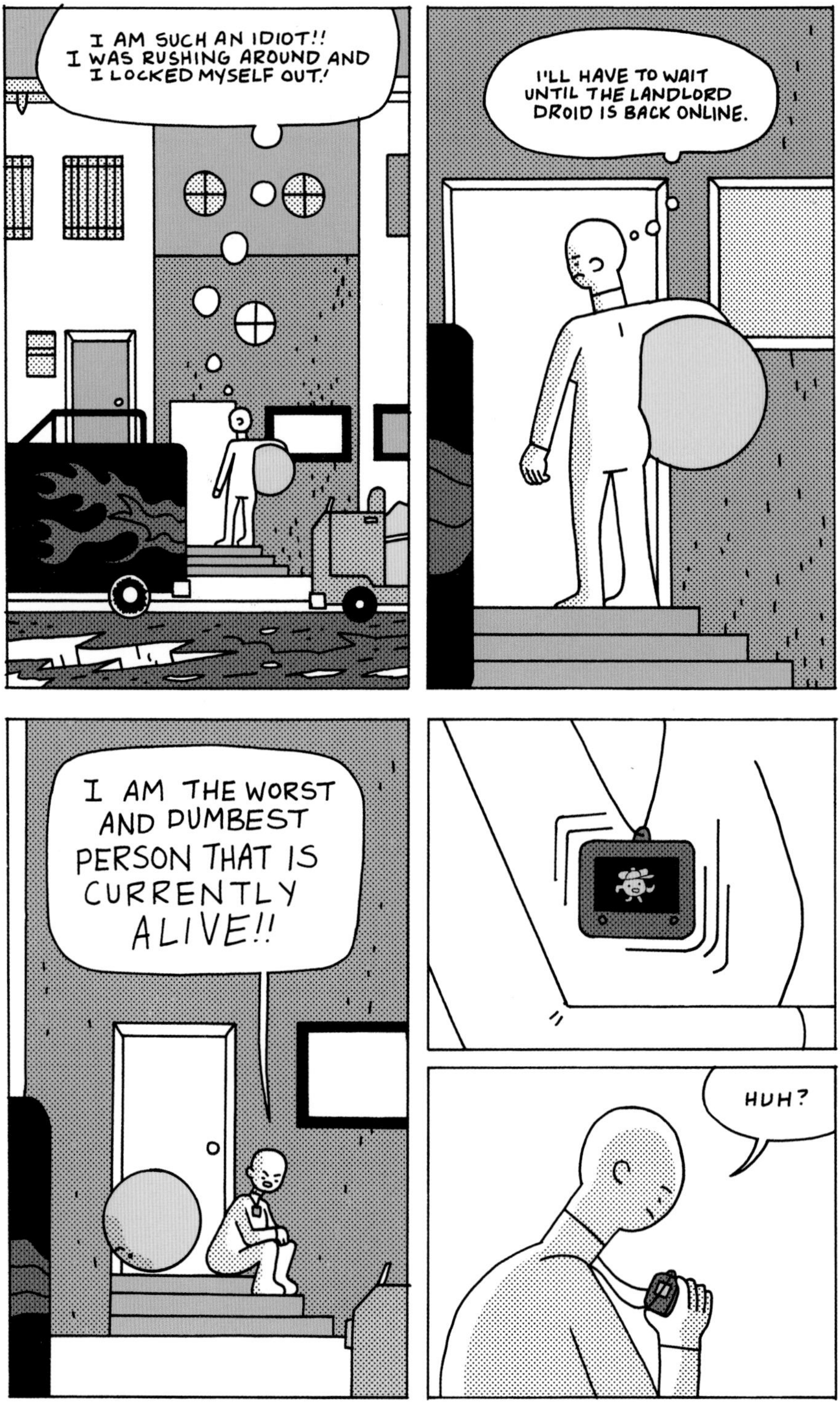
I AM SUCH AN IDIOT!!
I WAS RUSHING AROUND AND
I LOCKED MYSELF OUT!
I'LL HAVE TO WAIT
UNTIL THE LANDLORD
DROID IS BACK ONLINE.
I AM THE WORST AND DUMBEST PERSON THAT IS CURRENTLY ALIVE!!
HUH?

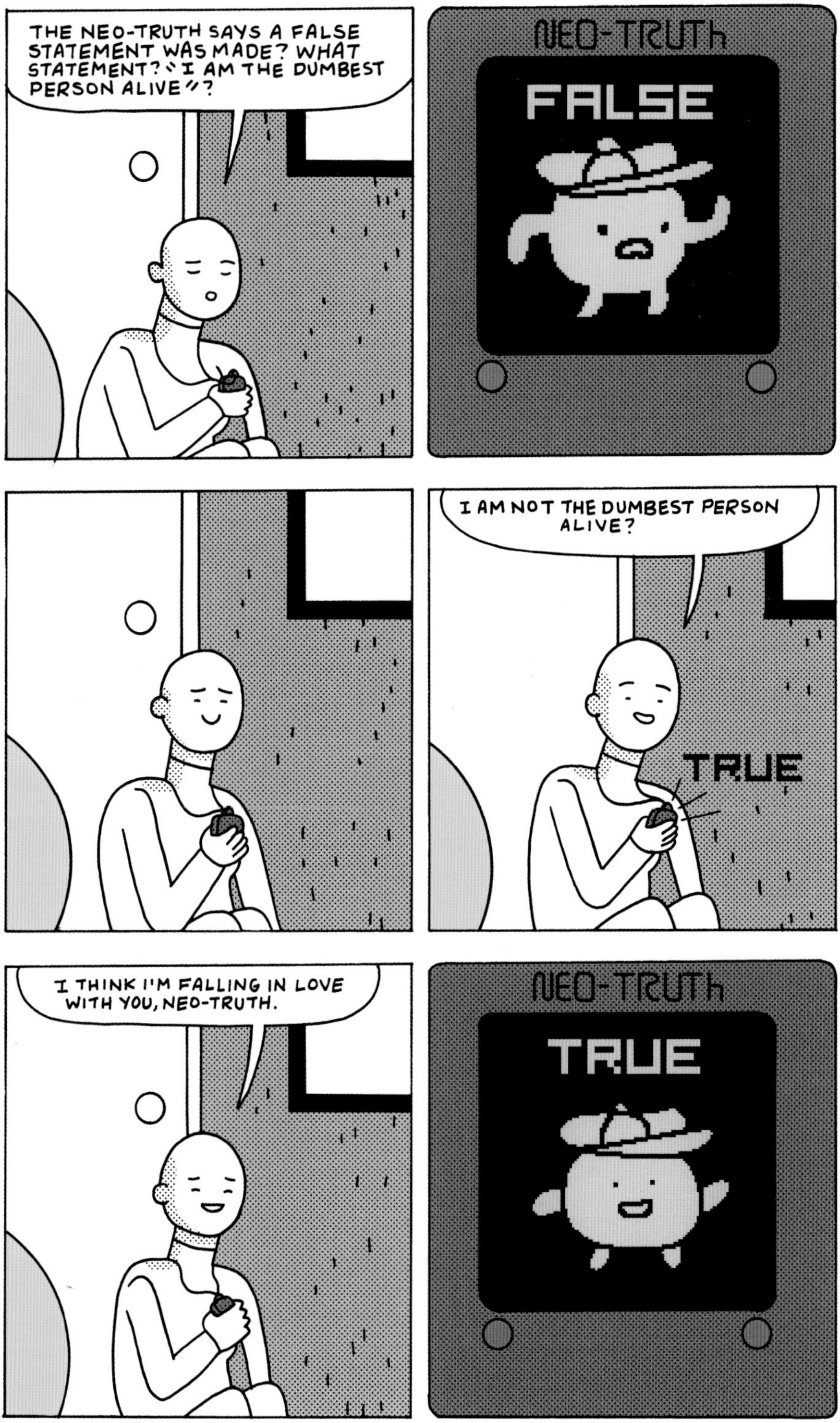
THE NEO-TRUTH SAYS A FALSE STATEMENT WAS MADE? WHAT STATEMENT? "I AM THE DUMBEST PERSON ALIVE"?
NEO-TRUTH
FALSE
I AM NOT THE DUMBEST PERSON ALIVE?
TRUE
I THINK I'M FALLING IN LOVE WITH YOU, NEO-TRUTH.
NEO-TRUTH
TRUE

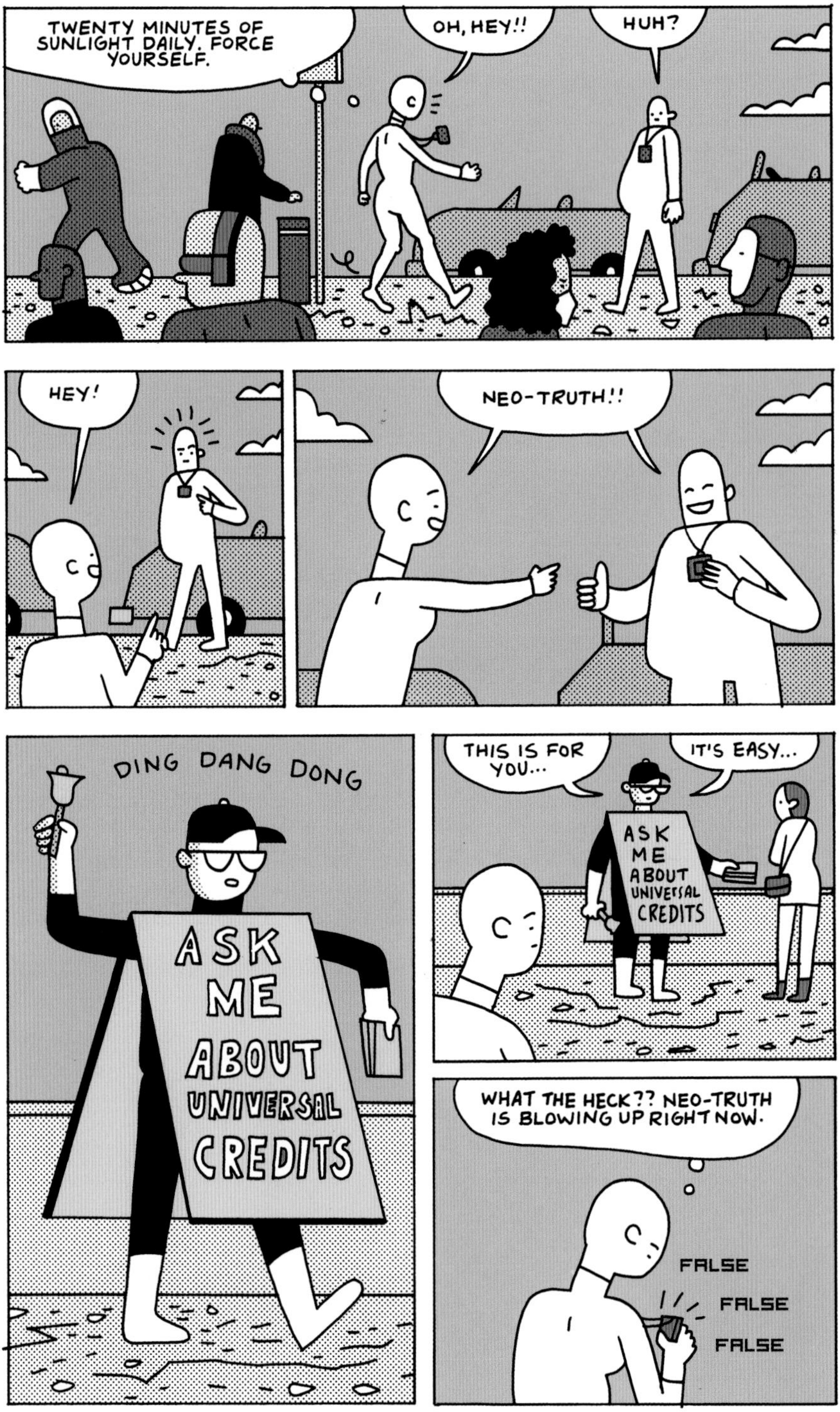
TWENTY MINUTES OF SUNLIGHT DAILY. FORCE YOURSELF.
OH, HEY!!
HUH?
HEY!
NEO-TRUTH!!
DING DANG DONG
ASK ME ABOUT UNIVERSAL CREDITS
THIS IS FOR YOU...
IT'S EASY...
ASK ME ABOUT UNIVERSAL CREDITS
WHAT THE HECK?? NEO-TRUTH IS BLOWING UP RIGHT NOW.
FALSE
FALSE
FALSE

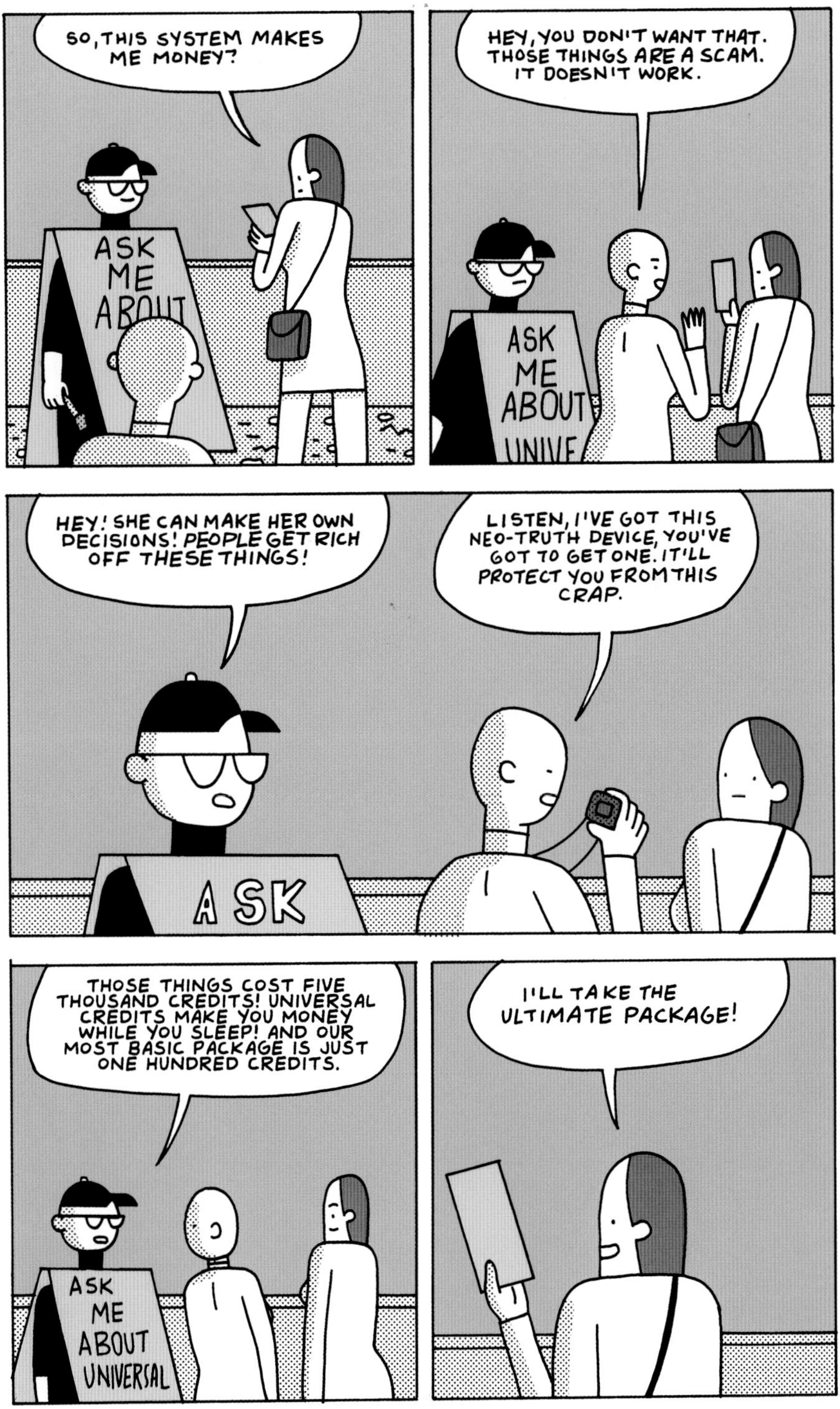
SO, THIS SYSTEM MAKES ME MONEY?
ASK ME ABOUT
HEY, YOU DON'T WANT THAT. THOSE THINGS ARE A SCAM. IT DOESN'T WORK.
ASK ME ABOUT
HEY! SHE CAN MAKE HER OWN DECISIONS! PEOPLE GET RICH OFF THESE THINGS!
LISTEN, I'VE GOT THIS NEO-TRUTH DEVICE, YOU'VE GOT TO GET ONE. IT'LL PROTECT YOU FROM THIS CRAP.
ASK
THOSE THINGS COST FIVE THOUSAND CREDITS! UNIVERSAL CREDITS MAKE YOU MONEY WHILE YOU SLEEP! AND OUR MOST BASIC PACKAGE IS JUST ONE HUNDRED CREDITS.
ASK ME ABOUT UNIVERSAL
I'LL TAKE THE ULTIMATE PACKAGE!

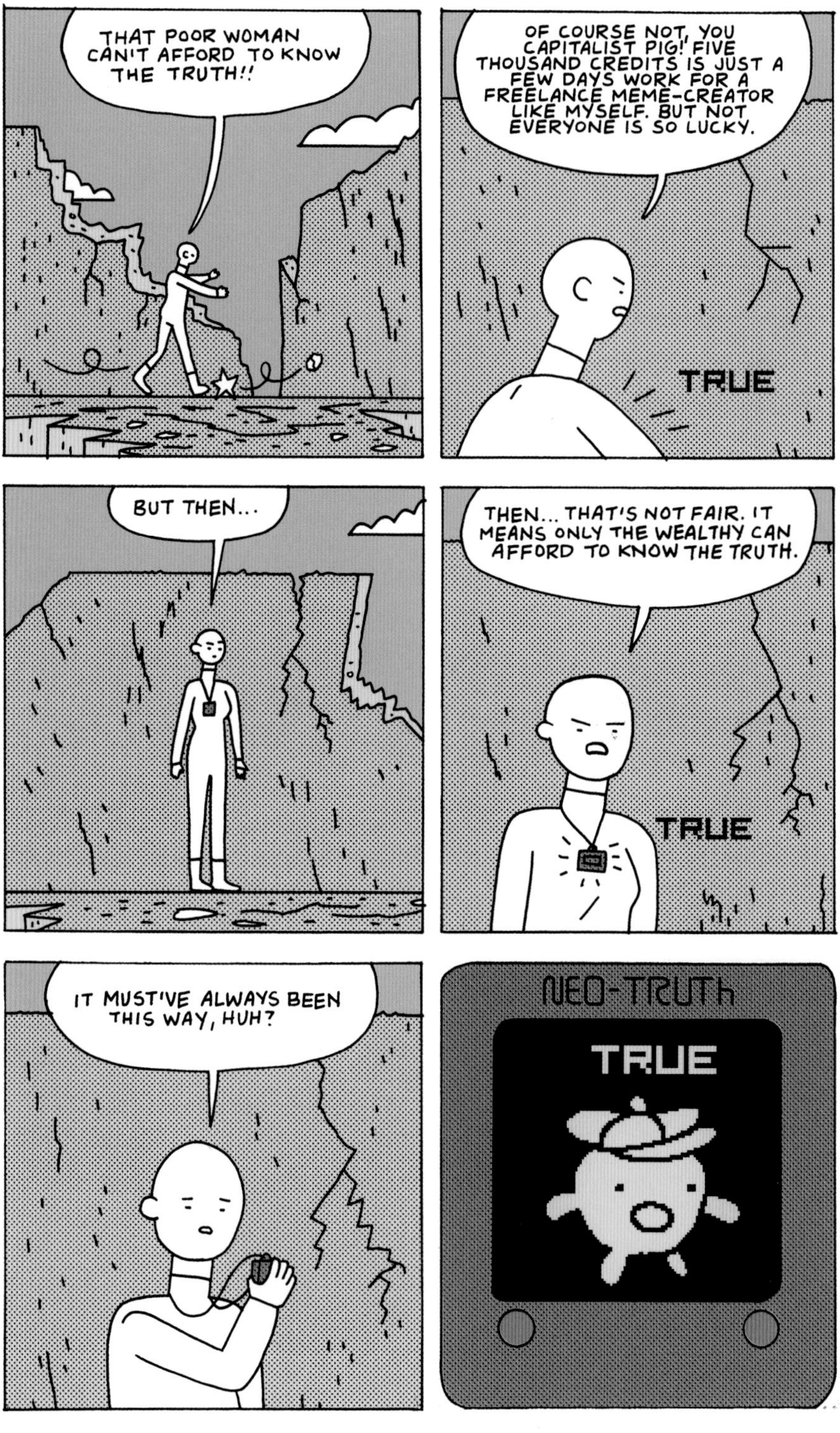
THAT POOR WOMAN CAN'T AFFORD TO KNOW THE TRUTH!!
OF COURSE NOT, YOU CAPITALIST PIG! FIVE THOUSAND CREDITS IS JUST A FEW DAYS WORK FOR A FREELANCE MEME-CREATOR LIKE MYSELF. BUT NOT EVERYONE IS SO LUCKY.
TRUE
BUT THEN...
THEN... THAT'S NOT FAIR. IT MEANS ONLY THE WEALTHY CAN AFFORD TO KNOW THE TRUTH.
TRUE
IT MUST'VE ALWAYS BEEN THIS WAY, HUH?
NEO-TRUTH
TRUE

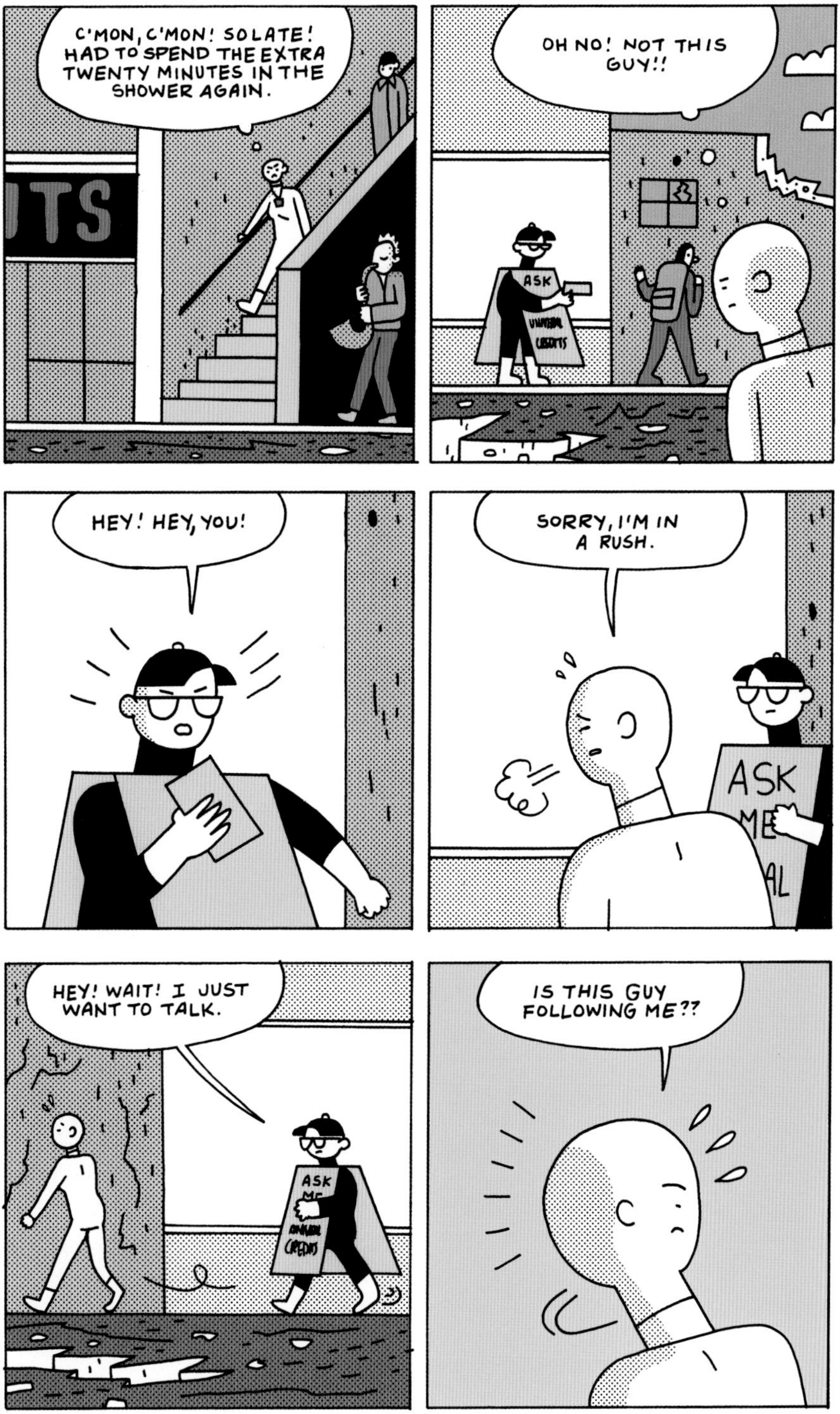
C'MON, C'MON! SO LATE! HAD TO SPEND THE EXTRA TWENTY MINUTES IN THE SHOWER AGAIN.
UTS
OH NO! NOT THIS GUY!!
ASK
UNIVERSAL CREDITS
HEY! HEY, YOU!
SORRY, I'M IN A RUSH.
ASK ME
HEY! WAIT! I JUST WANT TO TALK.
ASK ME
UNIVERSAL CREDITS
IS THIS GUY FOLLOWING ME??

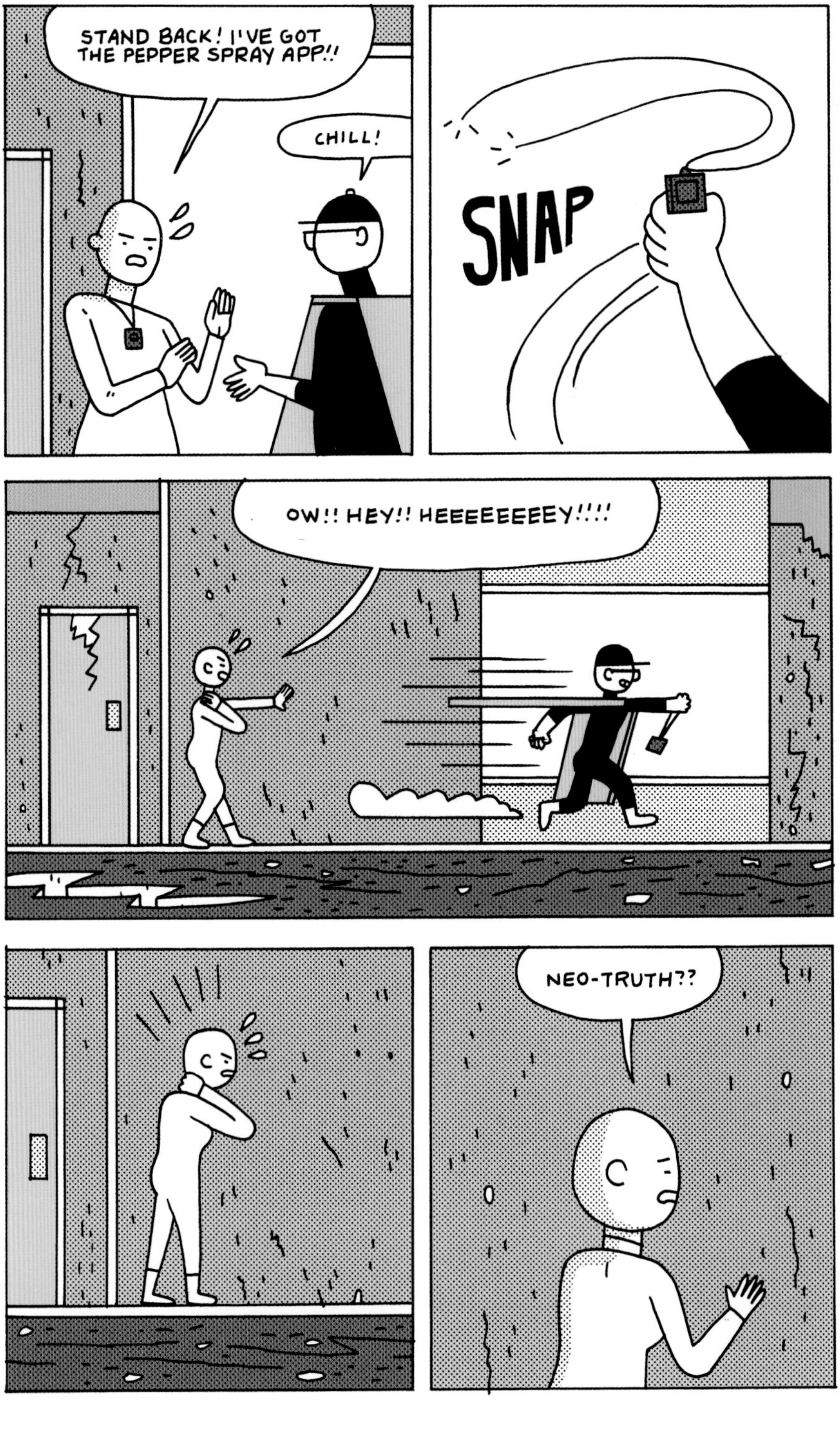
STAND BACK! I'VE GOT THE PEPPER SPRAY APP!!
CHILL!
SNAP
OW!! HEY!! HEEEEEEEEY!!!!
NEO-TRUTH??

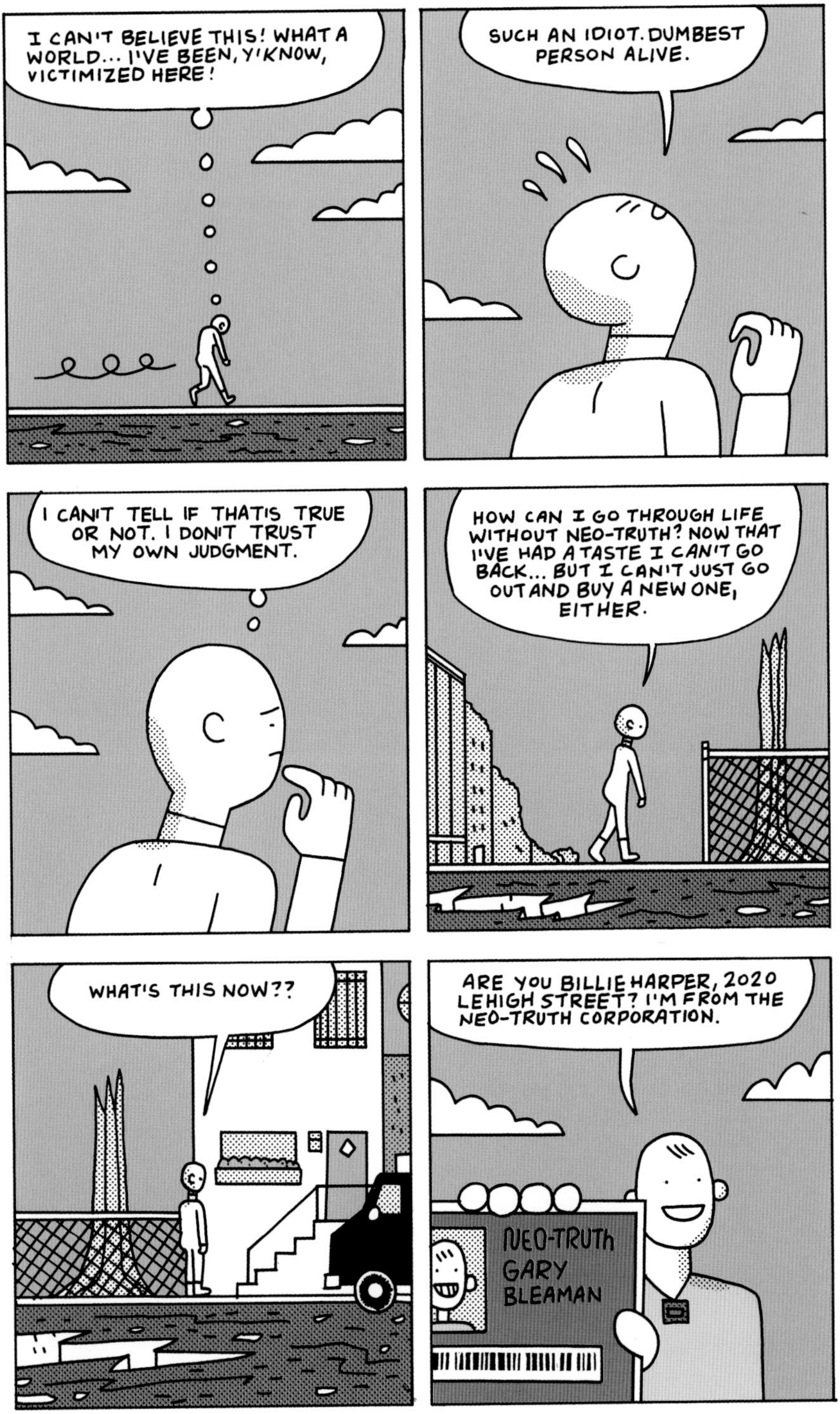
I CAN'T BELIEVE THIS! WHAT A WORLD... I'VE BEEN, Y'KNOW, VICTIMIZED HERE!
SUCH AN IDIOT. DUMBEST PERSON ALIVE.
I CAN'T TELL IF THAT'S TRUE OR NOT. I DON'T TRUST MY OWN JUDGMENT.
HOW CAN I GO THROUGH LIFE WITHOUT NEO-TRUTH? NOW THAT I'VE HAD A TASTE I CAN'T GO BACK... BUT I CAN'T JUST GO OUT AND BUY A NEW ONE, EITHER.
WHAT'S THIS NOW??
ARE YOU BILLIE HARPER, 2020 LEHIGH STREET? I'M FROM THE NEO-TRUTH CORPORATION.
NEO-TRUTh
GARY
BLEAMAN

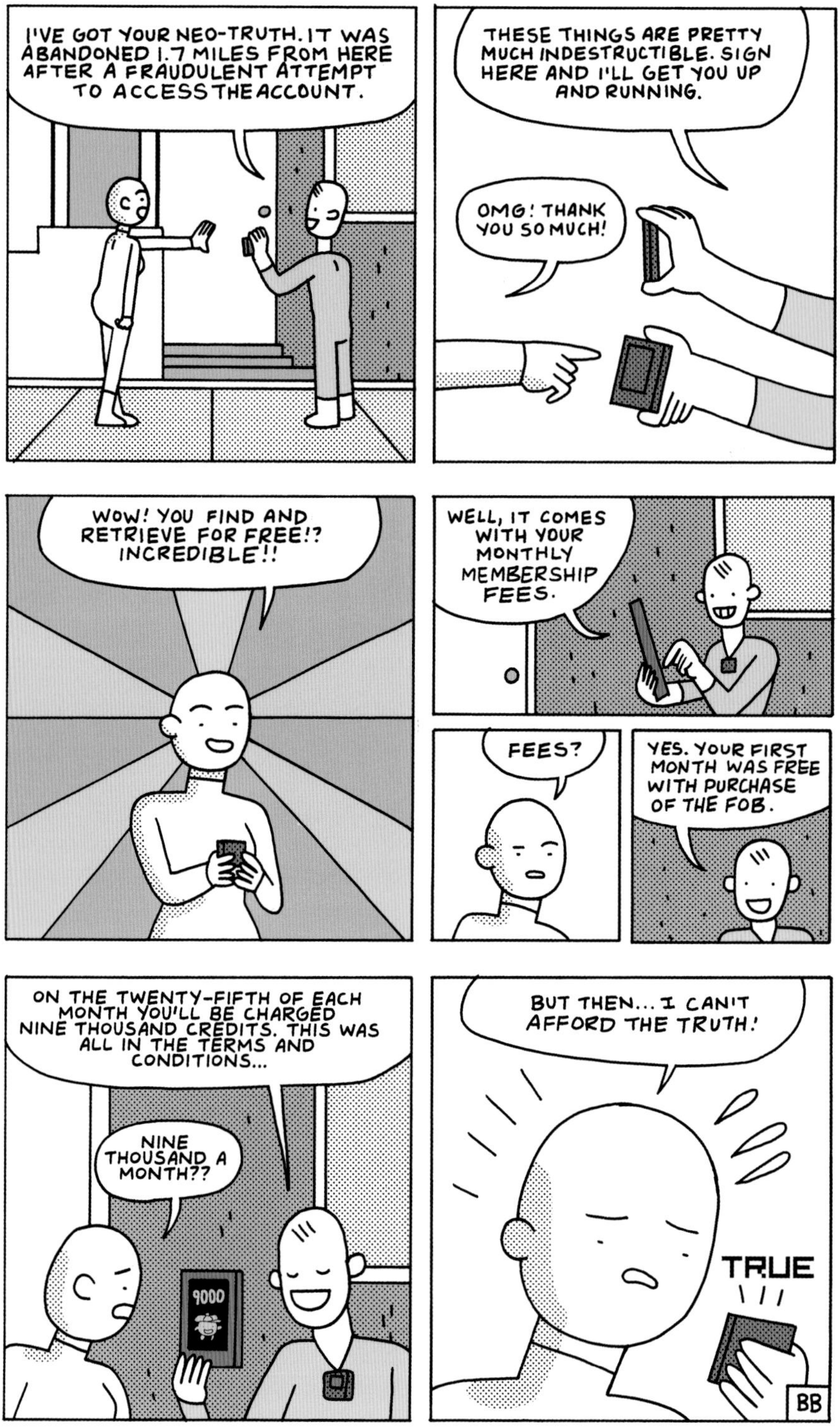
I'VE GOT YOUR NEO-TRUTH. IT WAS ABANDONED 1.7 MILES FROM HERE AFTER A FRAUDULENT ATTEMPT TO ACCESS THE ACCOUNT.
THESE THINGS ARE PRETTY MUCH INDESTRUCTIBLE. SIGN HERE AND I'LL GET YOU UP AND RUNNING.
OMG! THANK YOU SO MUCH!
WOW! YOU FIND AND RETRIEVE FOR FREE!? INCREDIBLE!!
WELL, IT COMES WITH YOUR MONTHLY MEMBERSHIP FEES.
FEES?
YES. YOUR FIRST MONTH WAS FREE WITH PURCHASE OF THE FOB.
ON THE TWENTY-FIFTH OF EACH MONTH YOU'LL BE CHARGED NINE THOUSAND CREDITS. THIS WAS ALL IN THE TERMS AND CONDITIONS...
NINE THOUSAND A MONTH??
9000
BUT THEN... I CAN'T AFFORD THE TRUTH!
TRUE
BB

DON'T LIE TO ME

DO YOU REALLY WANT TO KNOW WHEN EVERYBODY IS LYING?

PATRICK COUWENBERG EMBODIED THE MYTHOLOGICAL American Dream. Born into a wealthy family in the Dutch East Indies, Couwenberg's family lost everything in 1945 when the island nation wrested its independence from colonial rule to become Indonesia. The clan moved to the Netherlands completely broke, but Couwenberg didn't let that deter him. He managed to learn five languages and eventually moved to Los Angeles, where he scrubbed toilets while getting a degree in physics at the California Institute of Technology. After graduation, Couwenberg spent two years in the military, ultimately earning a Purple Heart for his service. Due to injuries sustained in Vietnam, including shrapnel that stayed forever lodged near his groin, he returned to civilian life and helped the U.S. more passively: assisting the CIA in operations in Southeast Asia and Africa, and eventually getting a master's degree in psychology, before ultimately going to law school and working his way up to a role as a judge in the Los Angeles Superior Court.

Couwenberg's story was, as that court's former director of public information wrote, a "publicist's dream come true." The problem was that it was all indeed a dream. As people started digging into his resume, they found that nearly every piece of his biography was fabricated—he had never attended CalTech, there was no shrapnel near his groin, he never worked for the CIA, and he certainly did not have a Purple Heart. In August 2001, after four years as a Superior Justice in Los Angeles, Couwenberg was removed from his post. (In perhaps the ultimate act of cowardice, Couwenberg had the gall to blame his wife for his lies, saying that she had typed his CV and repeated the tall tales he told her about his background.)

If this story makes you angry, you're not alone. Liars, we're taught from an early age, are some of the worst kinds of people. We tell children the tales of the Boy Who Cried Wolf and Pinocchio to teach them not to lie. Villains are often marked by acts of deception: Satan, Prospero, Ursula. The point of these stories is often that lying not only corrupts the soul, but also always comes back to you, like a boomerang with teeth. Entire sitcoms exist based on this premise.

We all know that lying is wrong, and yet we do it all the time. Sure, you're no Couwenberg, but how many times have you lied today? A rude question, perhaps, so let me just fully commit to the effrontery: I know you've lied today. In fact, I guarantee it. A 2009 study found that the average American admits to telling 1.65 lies per day, and I'd wager that's a significant undercount. Another study found that 60 percent of people lied at least once during a ten-minute conversation, and most of them told two or three lies. (Interestingly, one expert on lying said that men and women lie at equal rates, but about different things. Men tend to lie to boost their ego, things like "I hit it out of the park" and "The fish was THIS big," while women tend to tell social lies like "That dress looks great on you" and "What a horrible guy your ex is!") We all lie all the time—to ourselves, to our friends, even to our closest loved ones. And it's a good thing we do, because it's not money or love or even music that makes the world go round—it's deception.

Let me explain: Lies have a real and crucial function in our world. "A lie is as common a human activity as reading or speaking or writing," said Michael Lewis, a psychiatrist at Rutgers who's studied deception and why children lie for over fifty years. "It's not a moral failure. It is not a cultural artifact. In fact, it's likely to be something which creates culture." Lies allow us to learn, to maintain peace and stability in our relationships, to navigate the world more safely. "How's it going?" is a question that we ask without wanting a real answer, and one we rarely answer truthfully. We lie to our friends when we think their new haircut is ugly. We lie to our bosses about how excited we are to work on that annoying pet project of theirs. We lie when we pretend to understand what someone said at a loud party instead of asking them to repeat it.

In some situations, lies are even encouraged. While nobody suggests you go full Couwenberg, there are plenty of career experts who encourage us to "fake it till you make it." Volunteer for that project that's just over your skill set and learn on the job, they say! Throw your hat in the ring; it's the only way to learn! Guides for how to negotiate things like buying a car often include explicit instructions to lie about how much you're willing to pay or how much you think something is actually worth. Parenting books tell us to lie to our kids about their talents to encourage them to keep trying. We hate liars until we become them, and then it's "best practices."

Anybody who's dealt with kids is acutely aware of this paradox. We tell children that they shouldn't lie, but we also tell them that when Grandma gives them hand-knitted socks instead of a shiny toy, they shouldn't be fully honest about their feelings, either. We ask them to lie, and we lie back to them—about Santa Claus, the tooth fairy, what happens to dogs when they die, how far away we really are from our destination. Experts debate just how far you should go with your deception, but most agree that entertaining stories about Santa or other fantasy characters aren't going to turn your child into a pathological liar. In fact, some studies suggest that children who engage in make-believe play and who lead rich "fantasy lives" are better at identifying the line between reality and fakery, a skill that will certainly come in handy, thanks to the kinds of fake news that we discuss in the "Unreel" chapter.

And in case you're still stubbornly unconvinced that you are a liar, consider this: Even without opening your mouth, you're likely lying constantly. Not to others, but to yourself: You're totally going to get to the gym next week, that meeting went fine, if you cut your bangs maybe you'll feel better, she doesn't deserve you. And again, experts say this kind of self-deception is just fine, and in fact often necessary. If we were totally honest with ourselves all the time, it would be hard to get out of bed in the morning.

And yet, if you ask people "When is it okay to lie?" many of them will say "Never," despite doing it all the time. So what would happen if we really did all wear lie detectors all the time, like you saw in the comic? What does a world full of neo-truths actually look like?

Let's set aside for the purposes of this thought experiment the fact that modern lie detectors do not work. Polygraph machines are notoriously inaccurate somewhere between "slightly better than flipping a coin" and about 70 percent certainty. Brain scanning techniques are slightly more reliable, but far from perfect. There is no singular biological response to lying, so picking up such a signal is impossible to do with a machine. Studies suggest that humans who are trained to catch liars are actually no better at detecting deception than you or I. One review found that across thirty-nine studies, the average accuracy of human observers is just 56.6 percent, and another study suggests that we're not even good at catching children in their fibs. And that's not even getting into how the neo-truth might flag a lie of omission or an act of silent mental bamboozling. To build a true lie-detecting device would mean building a machine that can accurately read the deepest contours of our minds, which is a machine that opens up several pallets of cans of worms. But let's engage in a bit of fantastical self-deception here and pretend that a device like the neo-truth was possible.

We can start with medicine. Without the ability to deceive ourselves, medicine might lose one of its most powerful tools: the placebo effect. Studies show that even giving someone a sugar pill can alleviate their symptoms simply because they think they are being treated. And it's not just drugs that can do this—one study found that performing something called a "sham surgery"— making tiny incisions in the skin to make it seem like a procedure occurred—can in some cases be almost as effective as actual surgery. Bioethicists largely agree that this method is not ethical as a form of treatment,[1] but using sugar pills to "treat" things like ADHD and IBS is not uncommon. Without the ability to lie to ourselves, we might lose this powerful tool. I say "might" because studies show that even people who know they're getting a sugar pill can show improvements in their health. They know they're benefitting from the placebo effect, but it still works.

Much like lying itself, the detection of lies could wind up being a double-edged sword when it comes to our mental health. Unchecked self-deception can be ugly: Eating disorders, depression, and anxiety can often be rooted in our brains, becoming their own trickster demons. A beeper that interrupts thoughts like "I'm the worst person in the world" could theoretically be a boon for those struggling with everything from *pseudologia fantastica* to OCD. (In fact, the artist Box picked this future because he himself got excited about how a little lie detector might help him navigate his own mental health issues.)

---

1   Those pesky bioethicists, always looking out for people!

But for every negative thought the buzzer helps snuff out, it could enflame another. We need to be able to tell ourselves, "It's all going to be okay" without a little red light buzzing saying, "Well, actually, that might not be true." What is it like to be buzzed for trying to convince yourself that a low-stakes meeting went well when it didn't, for trying to console your recently dumped friend with puffed-up compliments, for pumping yourself up before a game? Do you stop hoping because hope cannot be proven? Being able to shield ourselves from the full brunt of reality is crucial for survival.

Lying is like so many other things (cake, rain, bees): good in moderation but nightmarish if taken too far. At Couwenberg's investigation, an expert witness argued that he was suffering from *pseudologia fantastica*, or, as the witness described it, "storytelling that often has sort of a matrix of fantasy interwoven with some facts." People with *pseudologia fantastica* can struggle to tell the difference between a lie they've told for too long and the truth. To the pathological liar, they are in many ways one and the same. "The lie ultimately wins power over the pathological liar, so that mastery of his or her own lies is lost," says one paper on compulsive liars.

But most of us have not yet lost the battle against our own lies. Most of us have them well trained, like little soldiers we can deploy when we need them. Living without lying is like trying to play chess without any pawns.

Imagine UN meetings where even the smallest of false niceties triggered our lie-detecting buzzers ("War breaks out between North Korea and the United States over a botched tie compliment"). Imagine backroom political deals where there was no longer space to elide the truth ("Congress at an impasse because Speaker of the House thinks Minority Leader's bill is not, in fact, 'a good first attempt'"). Imagine working in customer service and being unable to tell even the whitest of lies to your customers ("I hope you have a great day!" *BUZZ*). Imagine having to always tell your children the whole truth ("Sorry Jimmy, that painting doesn't actually look like a horse"). Imagine first dates, where every little embellishment you might make would trigger the beeper ("So you weren't actually that good at football, were you?"). Imagine children's imaginary playtime being drowned out by beeps. We think we want the truth, but most of us, as Jack Nicholson's character Jessep argues in *A Few Good Men*, can't handle the truth.

Lewis thinks that in the end, we'd regret installing lie detectors. "I think such a device would last two or perhaps three days before people took their little lie detectors and smashed them on the ground." We'd only last a few weeks with neo-truths before we destroyed them, lest they destroy us first.

Trust does not require complete truthfulness, it requires mutual understanding. We all must lie sometimes—to ourselves, to our friends, to our enemies. Trust is knowing that someone will lie when the time is right, will shield you if they need to, and will reveal the truth when it's in your best interest and not a moment before. Or, as the man in black puts it in Stephen King's novel *The Gunslinger*: "Only enemies speak the truth. Friends and lovers lie endlessly, caught in the web of duty."

MOON COURT

BY MAKI NARO

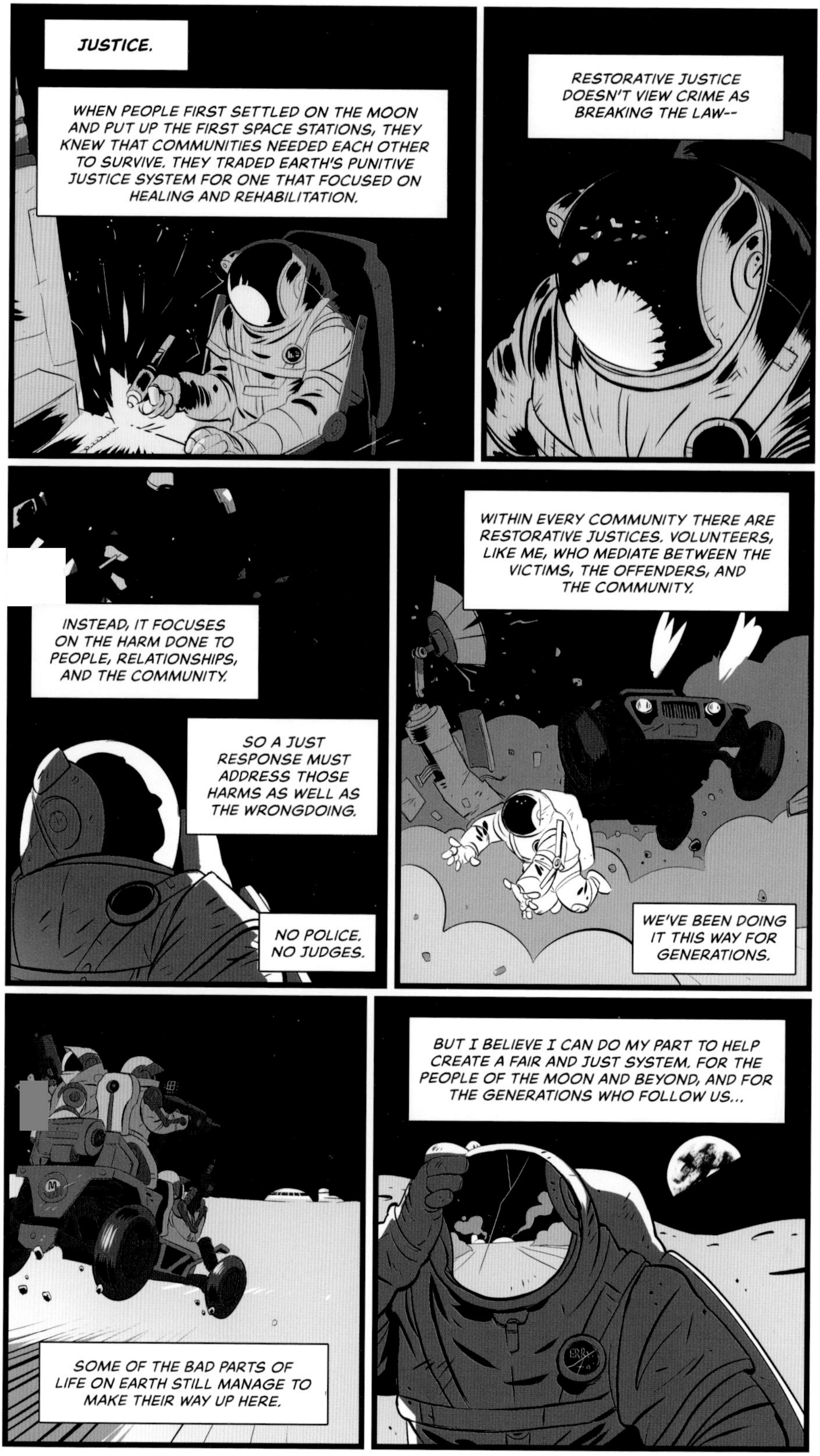
JUSTICE.
WHEN PEOPLE FIRST SETTLED ON THE MOON AND PUT UP THE FIRST SPACE STATIONS, THEY KNEW THAT COMMUNITIES NEEDED EACH OTHER TO SURVIVE. THEY TRADED EARTH'S PUNITIVE JUSTICE SYSTEM FOR ONE THAT FOCUSED ON HEALING AND REHABILITATION.
RESTORATIVE JUSTICE DOESN'T VIEW CRIME AS BREAKING THE LAW--
INSTEAD, IT FOCUSES ON THE HARM DONE TO PEOPLE, RELATIONSHIPS, AND THE COMMUNITY.
SO A JUST RESPONSE MUST ADDRESS THOSE HARMS AS WELL AS THE WRONGDOING.
NO POLICE. NO JUDGES.
WITHIN EVERY COMMUNITY THERE ARE RESTORATIVE JUSTICES. VOLUNTEERS, LIKE ME, WHO MEDIATE BETWEEN THE VICTIMS, THE OFFENDERS, AND THE COMMUNITY.
WE'VE BEEN DOING IT THIS WAY FOR GENERATIONS.
SOME OF THE BAD PARTS OF LIFE ON EARTH STILL MANAGE TO MAKE THEIR WAY UP HERE.
BUT I BELIEVE I CAN DO MY PART TO HELP CREATE A FAIR AND JUST SYSTEM. FOR THE PEOPLE OF THE MOON AND BEYOND, AND FOR THE GENERATIONS WHO FOLLOW US...

JEMISON STATION. LAGRANGE POINT 5.

HI, JANICE, LET ME PULL UP YOUR CASE AND WE'LL GET RIGHT TO IT...

SO... DOES JUN STILL WANT CUSTODY OF THE DOG?

OK, I NEVER SAID IT'D HAPPEN ALL AT ONCE.

IT'S NOT RIGHT!

Dawn Rodriguez
Restorative Justice

CODY WAS BORN HERE. HE'S NEVER BEEN TO EARTH!

HE'S GOT A BAD HEART, AND A BIG OPEN SKY IS GOING TO FREAK HIM OUT. I KNOW IT!

I DON'T KNOW WHAT TO DO!

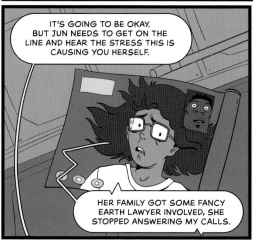

IT'S GOING TO BE OKAY. BUT JUN NEEDS TO GET ON THE LINE AND HEAR THE STRESS THIS IS CAUSING YOU HERSELF.

HER FAMILY GOT SOME FANCY EARTH LAWYER INVOLVED, SHE STOPPED ANSWERING MY CALLS.

LET ME SEE IF I CAN--

BOOOP

HEY, I'LL CALL YOU BACK.

JEMISON STATION WAS RETIRED FOR RESEARCH YEARS AGO, AND NOW SERVES AS TEMPORARY OFFICE SPACE FOR JUSTICES.

MOST FOLKS ONLY ARRIVE WHEN THEY ARE CALLED TO MEDIATE.

I LIKE THE QUIET.

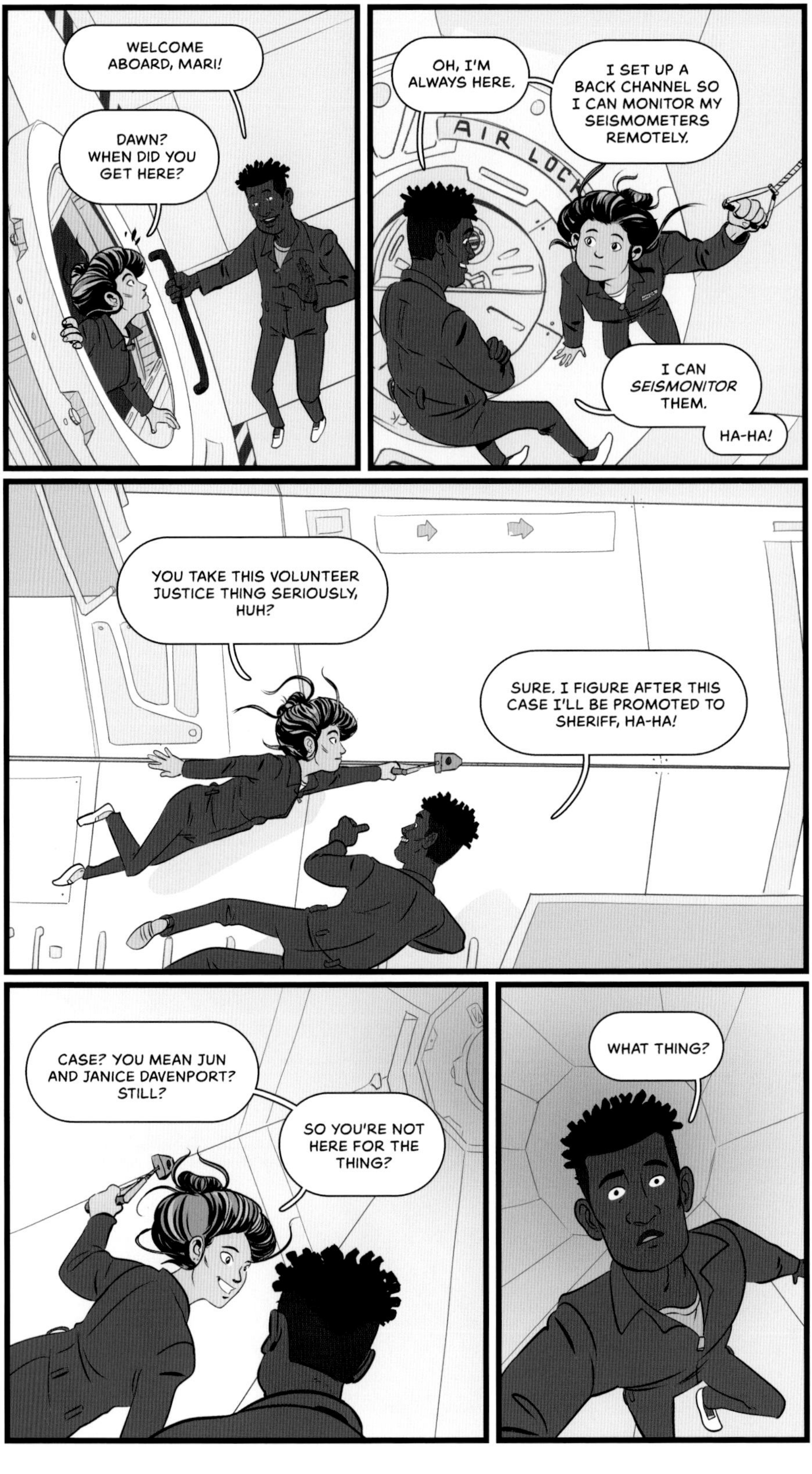
WELCOME ABOARD, MARI!
DAWN? WHEN DID YOU GET HERE?
OH, I'M ALWAYS HERE.
I SET UP A BACK CHANNEL SO I CAN MONITOR MY SEISMOMETERS REMOTELY.
AIR LOCK
I CAN *SEISMONITOR* THEM.
HA-HA!
YOU TAKE THIS VOLUNTEER JUSTICE THING SERIOUSLY, HUH?
SURE. I FIGURE AFTER THIS CASE I'LL BE PROMOTED TO SHERIFF, HA-HA!
CASE? YOU MEAN JUN AND JANICE DAVENPORT? STILL?
SO YOU'RE NOT HERE FOR THE THING?
WHAT THING?

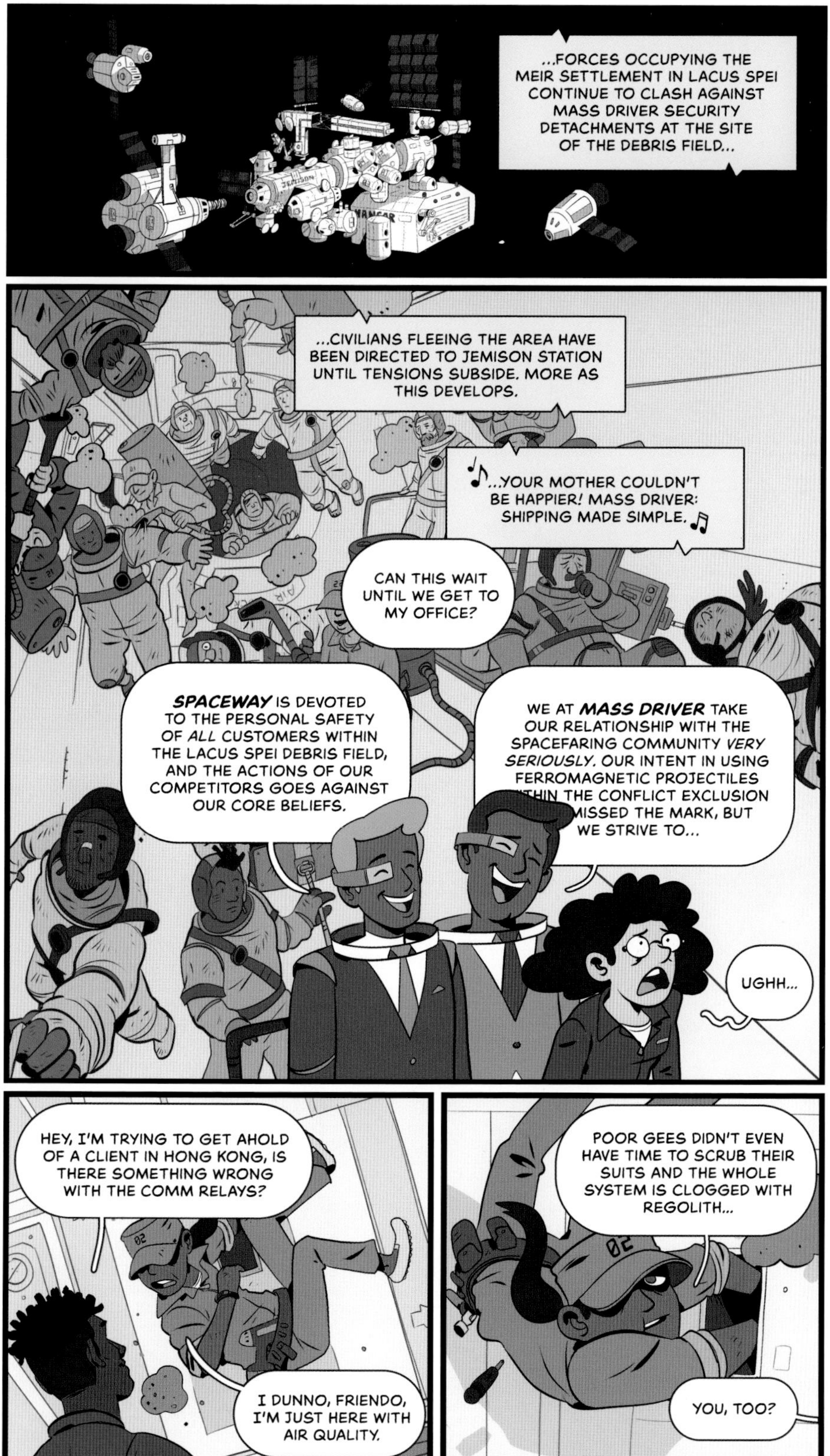

...FORCES OCCUPYING THE MEIR SETTLEMENT IN LACUS SPEI CONTINUE TO CLASH AGAINST MASS DRIVER SECURITY DETACHMENTS AT THE SITE OF THE DEBRIS FIELD...
JEMISON
HANGAR
...CIVILIANS FLEEING THE AREA HAVE BEEN DIRECTED TO JEMISON STATION UNTIL TENSIONS SUBSIDE. MORE AS THIS DEVELOPS.
♪...YOUR MOTHER COULDN'T BE HAPPIER! MASS DRIVER: SHIPPING MADE SIMPLE. ♫
CAN THIS WAIT UNTIL WE GET TO MY OFFICE?
SPACEWAY IS DEVOTED TO THE PERSONAL SAFETY OF *ALL* CUSTOMERS WITHIN THE LACUS SPEI DEBRIS FIELD, AND THE ACTIONS OF OUR COMPETITORS GOES AGAINST OUR CORE BELIEFS.
WE AT ***MASS DRIVER*** TAKE OUR RELATIONSHIP WITH THE SPACEFARING COMMUNITY *VERY SERIOUSLY*. OUR INTENT IN USING FERROMAGNETIC PROJECTILES ITHIN THE CONFLICT EXCLUSION MISSED THE MARK, BUT WE STRIVE TO...
UGHH...
HEY, I'M TRYING TO GET AHOLD OF A CLIENT IN HONG KONG, IS THERE SOMETHING WRONG WITH THE COMM RELAYS?
I DUNNO, FRIENDO, I'M JUST HERE WITH AIR QUALITY.
POOR GEES DIDN'T EVEN HAVE TIME TO SCRUB THEIR SUITS AND THE WHOLE SYSTEM IS CLOGGED WITH REGOLITH...
YOU, TOO?

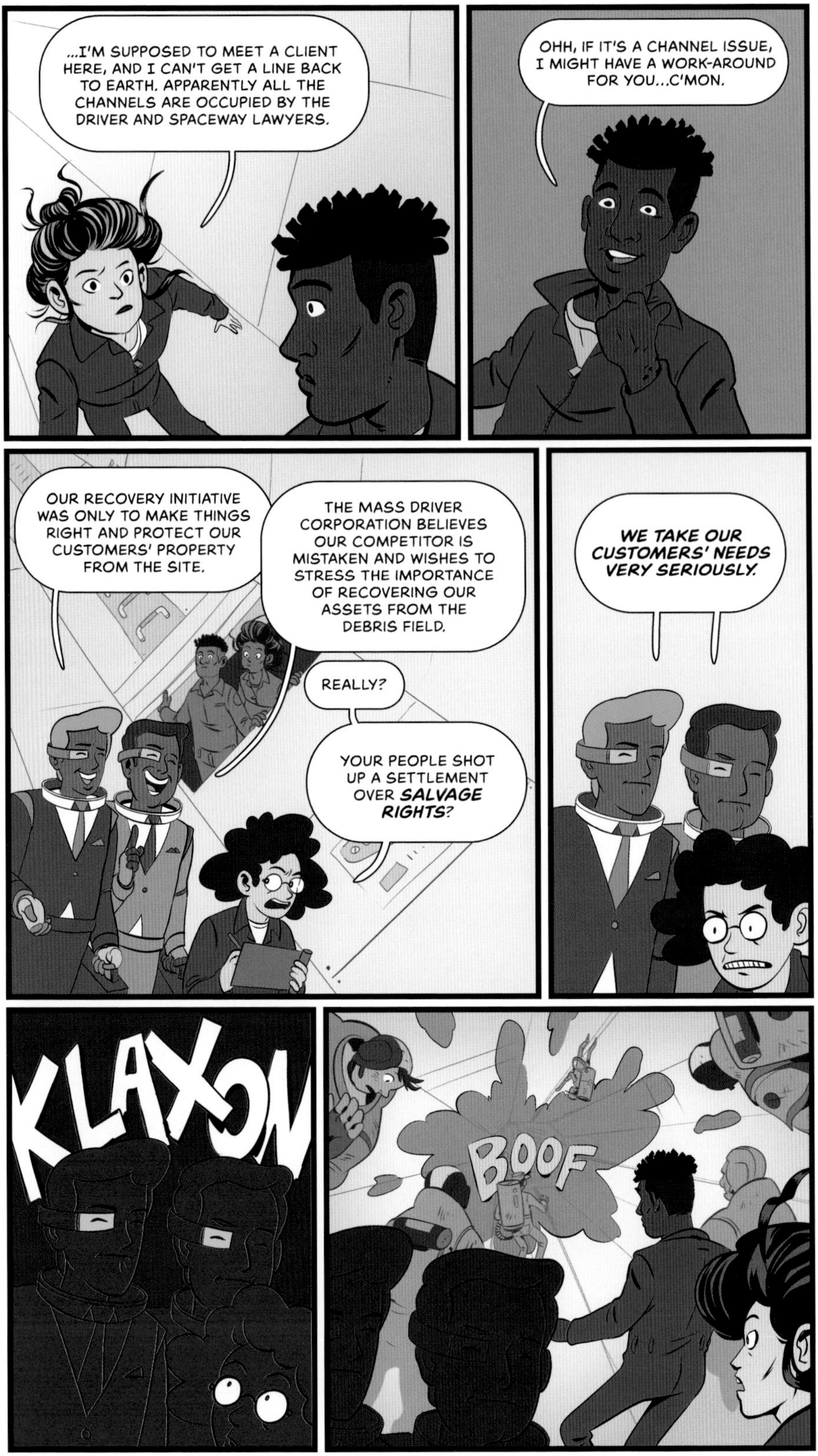
...I'M SUPPOSED TO MEET A CLIENT HERE, AND I CAN'T GET A LINE BACK TO EARTH. APPARENTLY ALL THE CHANNELS ARE OCCUPIED BY THE DRIVER AND SPACEWAY LAWYERS.
OHH, IF IT'S A CHANNEL ISSUE, I MIGHT HAVE A WORK-AROUND FOR YOU...C'MON.
OUR RECOVERY INITIATIVE WAS ONLY TO MAKE THINGS RIGHT AND PROTECT OUR CUSTOMERS' PROPERTY FROM THE SITE.
THE MASS DRIVER CORPORATION BELIEVES OUR COMPETITOR IS MISTAKEN AND WISHES TO STRESS THE IMPORTANCE OF RECOVERING OUR ASSETS FROM THE DEBRIS FIELD.
REALLY?
YOUR PEOPLE SHOT UP A SETTLEMENT OVER SALVAGE RIGHTS?
WE TAKE OUR CUSTOMERS' NEEDS VERY SERIOUSLY.
KLAXON
BOOF

HEY!!

LET ME GO, YOU FASCISTS!

LET THEM GO!

THEY'RE WITH US!

WHOA, HEY! WE'RE JUSTICES.

WHAT'S GOING ON?

SAYS HERE THIS KID IS A RUNAWAY AND WANTED BY EARTH AUTHORITIES! THEY NEED TO COME WITH US.

WELL, WE'RE NOT ON EARTH. WE DO THINGS DIFFERENTLY UP HERE.

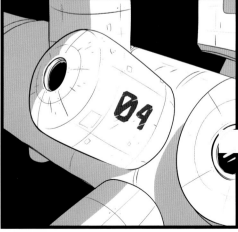

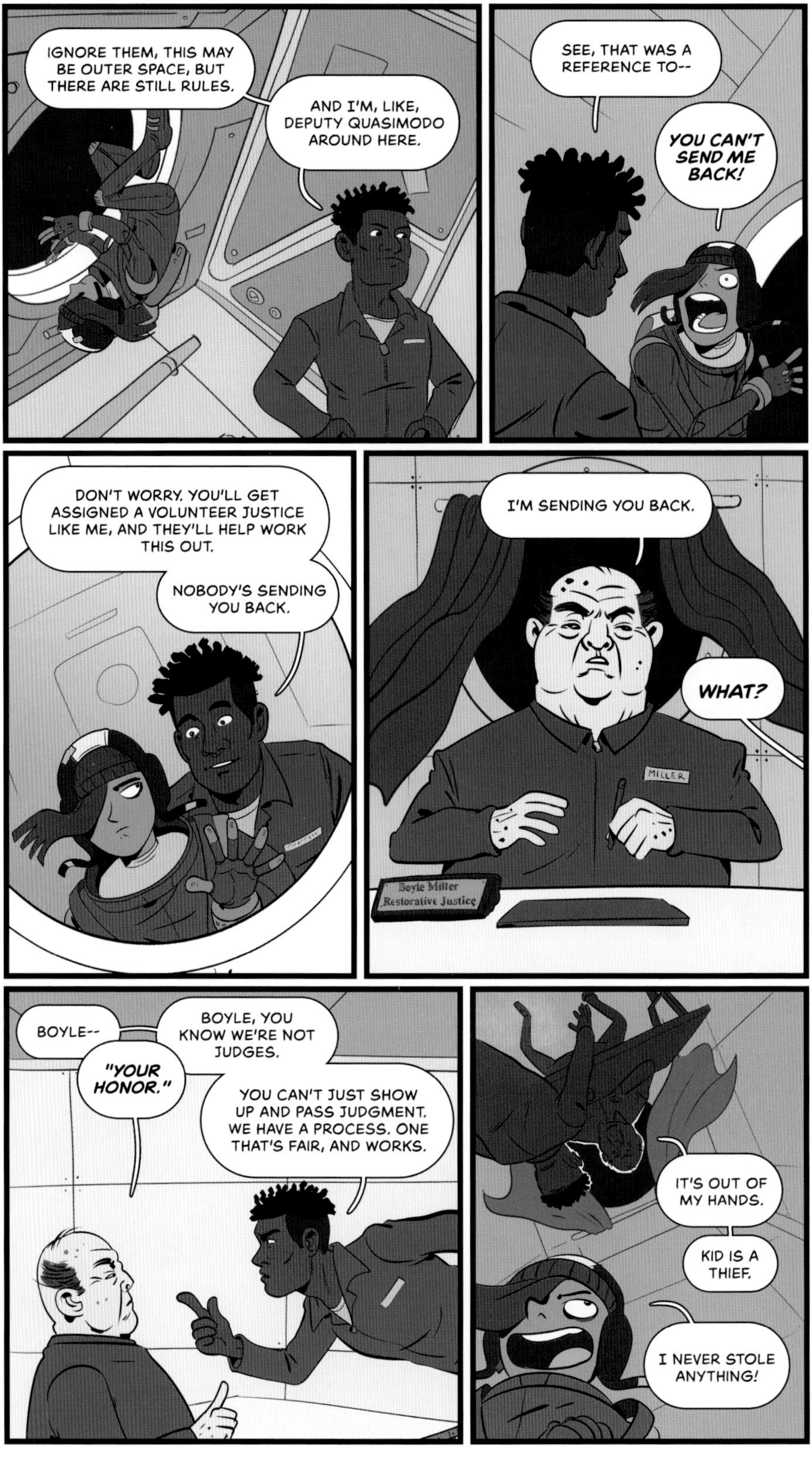

IGNORE THEM, THIS MAY BE OUTER SPACE, BUT THERE ARE STILL RULES.
AND I'M, LIKE, DEPUTY QUASIMODO AROUND HERE.
SEE, THAT WAS A REFERENCE TO--
YOU CAN'T SEND ME BACK!
DON'T WORRY. YOU'LL GET ASSIGNED A VOLUNTEER JUSTICE LIKE ME, AND THEY'LL HELP WORK THIS OUT.
NOBODY'S SENDING YOU BACK.
I'M SENDING YOU BACK.
WHAT?
MILLER
Boyle Miller
Restorative Justice
BOYLE--
BOYLE, YOU KNOW WE'RE NOT JUDGES.
"YOUR HONOR."
YOU CAN'T JUST SHOW UP AND PASS JUDGMENT. WE HAVE A PROCESS. ONE THAT'S FAIR, AND WORKS.
IT'S OUT OF MY HANDS.
KID IS A THIEF.
I NEVER STOLE ANYTHING!

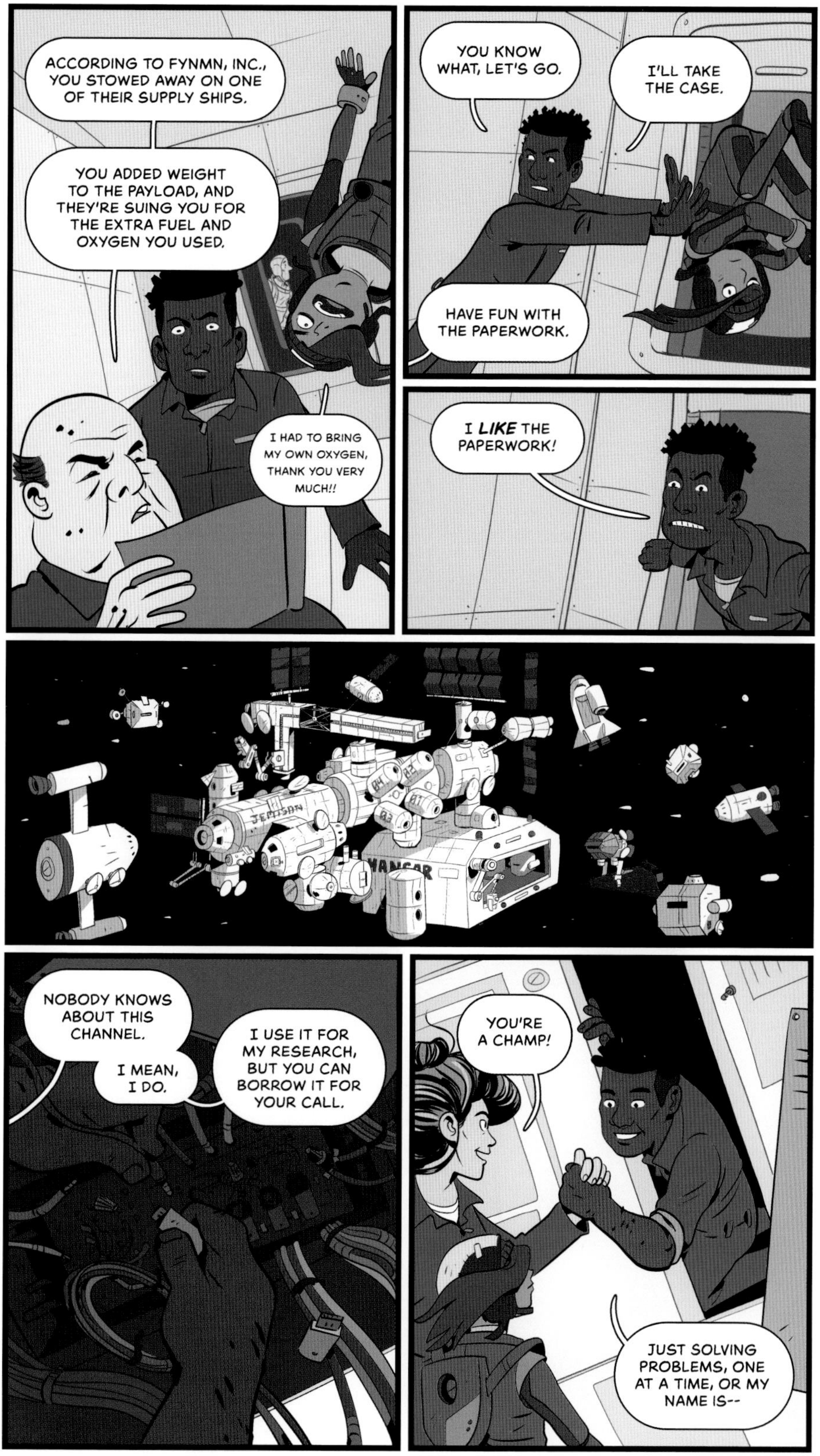
ACCORDING TO FYNMN, INC., YOU STOWED AWAY ON ONE OF THEIR SUPPLY SHIPS.
YOU ADDED WEIGHT TO THE PAYLOAD, AND THEY'RE SUING YOU FOR THE EXTRA FUEL AND OXYGEN YOU USED.
I HAD TO BRING MY OWN OXYGEN, THANK YOU VERY MUCH!!
YOU KNOW WHAT, LET'S GO.
I'LL TAKE THE CASE.
HAVE FUN WITH THE PAPERWORK.
I *LIKE* THE PAPERWORK!
JETISON
HANGAR
NOBODY KNOWS ABOUT THIS CHANNEL.
I MEAN, I DO.
I USE IT FOR MY RESEARCH, BUT YOU CAN BORROW IT FOR YOUR CALL.
YOU'RE A CHAMP!
JUST SOLVING PROBLEMS, ONE AT A TIME, OR MY NAME IS--

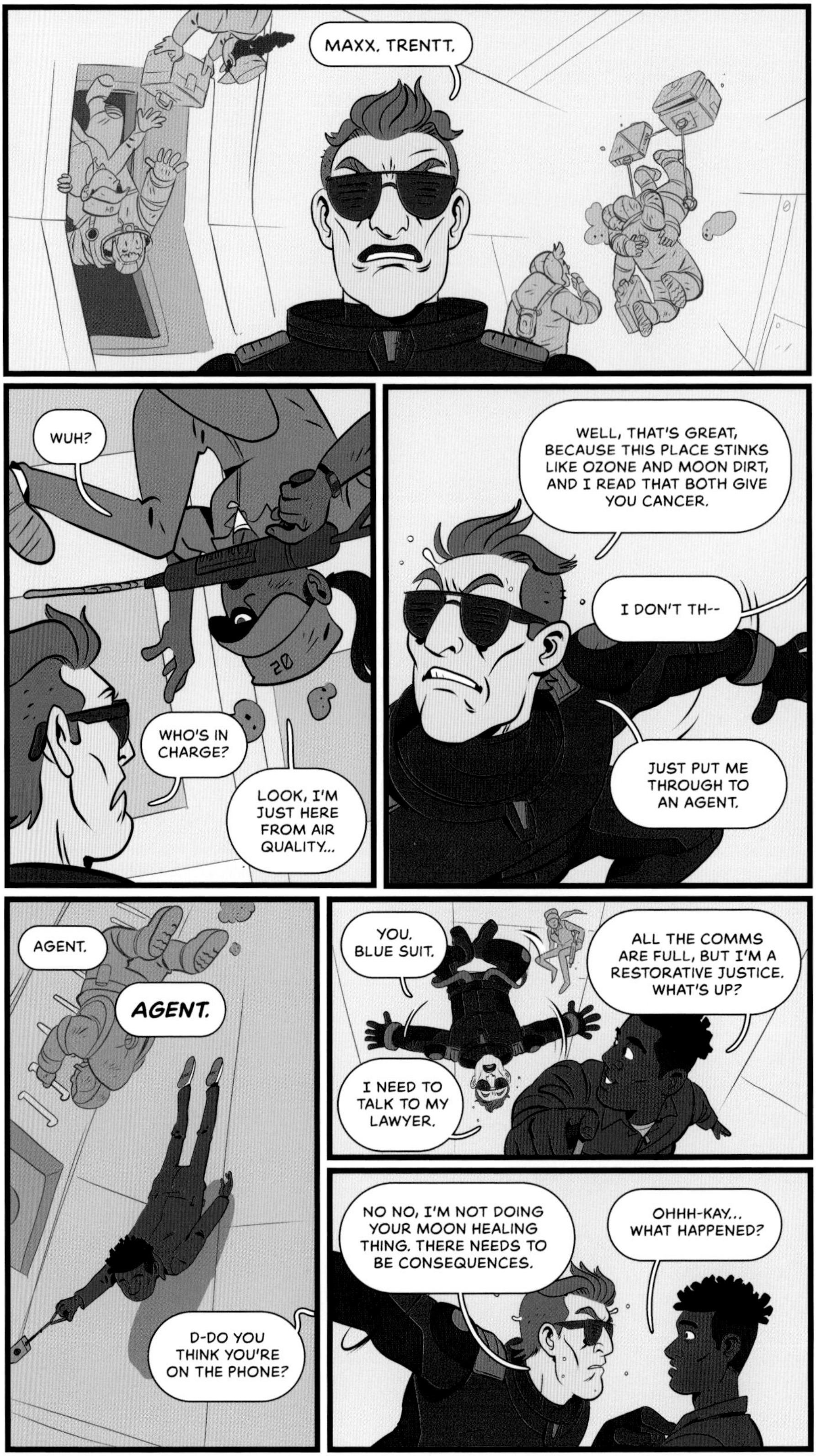
MAXX. TRENTT.
WUH?
WHO'S IN CHARGE?
LOOK, I'M JUST HERE FROM AIR QUALITY...
WELL, THAT'S GREAT, BECAUSE THIS PLACE STINKS LIKE OZONE AND MOON DIRT, AND I READ THAT BOTH GIVE YOU CANCER.
I DON'T TH--
JUST PUT ME THROUGH TO AN AGENT.
AGENT.
AGENT.
D-DO YOU THINK YOU'RE ON THE PHONE?
YOU. BLUE SUIT.
ALL THE COMMS ARE FULL, BUT I'M A RESTORATIVE JUSTICE. WHAT'S UP?
I NEED TO TALK TO MY LAWYER.
NO NO, I'M NOT DOING YOUR MOON HEALING THING. THERE NEEDS TO BE CONSEQUENCES.
OHHH-KAY... WHAT HAPPENED?

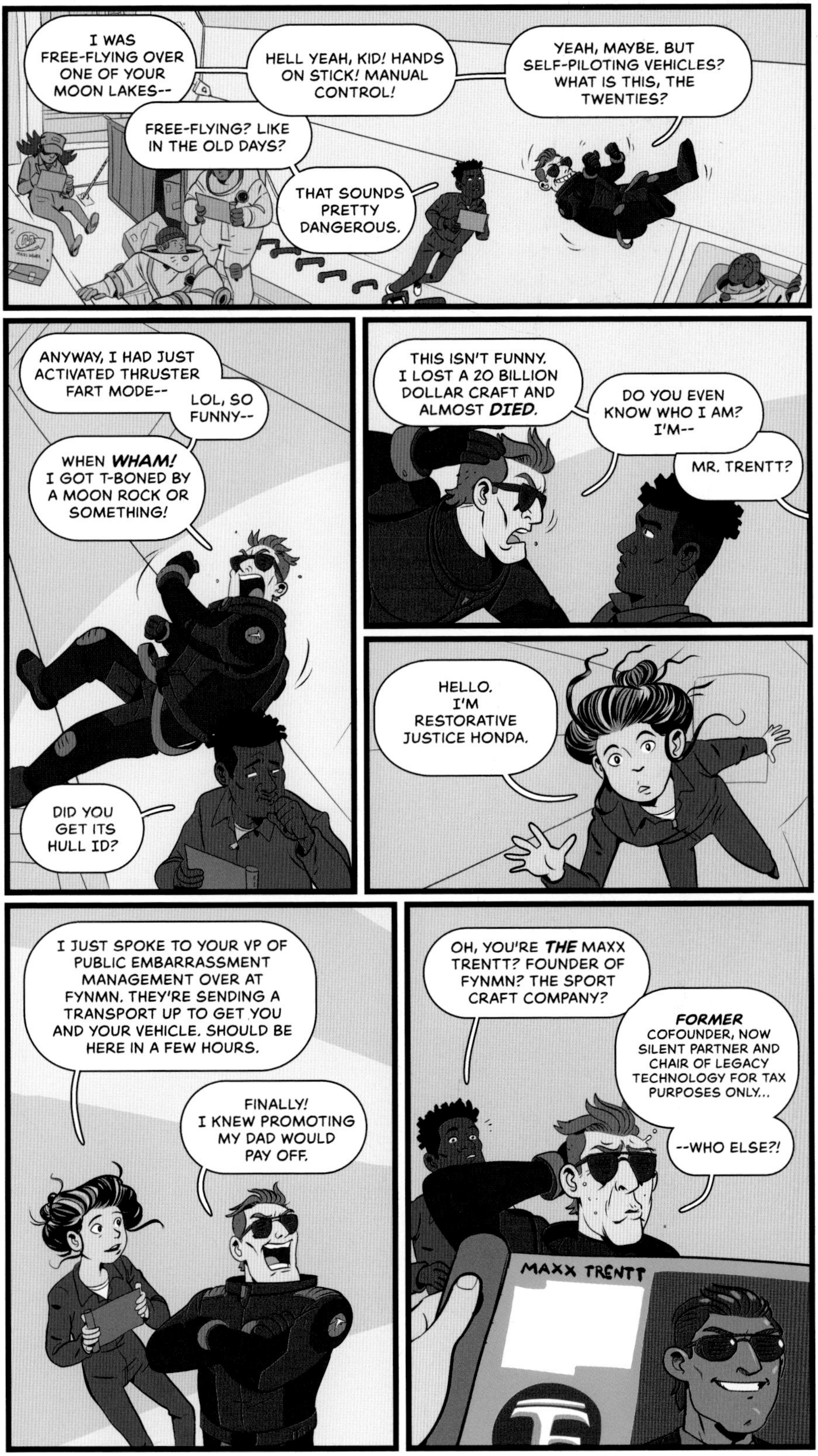
I WAS FREE-FLYING OVER ONE OF YOUR MOON LAKES--
HELL YEAH, KID! HANDS ON STICK! MANUAL CONTROL!
YEAH, MAYBE. BUT SELF-PILOTING VEHICLES? WHAT IS THIS, THE TWENTIES?
FREE-FLYING? LIKE IN THE OLD DAYS?
THAT SOUNDS PRETTY DANGEROUS.
ANYWAY, I HAD JUST ACTIVATED THRUSTER FART MODE--
LOL, SO FUNNY--
WHEN **WHAM!** I GOT T-BONED BY A MOON ROCK OR SOMETHING!
DID YOU GET ITS HULL ID?
THIS ISN'T FUNNY. I LOST A 20 BILLION DOLLAR CRAFT AND ALMOST ***DIED***.
DO YOU EVEN KNOW WHO I AM? I'M--
MR. TRENTT?
HELLO. I'M RESTORATIVE JUSTICE HONDA.
I JUST SPOKE TO YOUR VP OF PUBLIC EMBARRASSMENT MANAGEMENT OVER AT FYNMN. THEY'RE SENDING A TRANSPORT UP TO GET YOU AND YOUR VEHICLE. SHOULD BE HERE IN A FEW HOURS.
FINALLY! I KNEW PROMOTING MY DAD WOULD PAY OFF.
OH, YOU'RE ***THE*** MAXX TRENTT? FOUNDER OF FYNMN? THE SPORT CRAFT COMPANY?
FORMER COFOUNDER, NOW SILENT PARTNER AND CHAIR OF LEGACY TECHNOLOGY FOR TAX PURPOSES ONLY...
--WHO ELSE?!
MAXX TRENTT

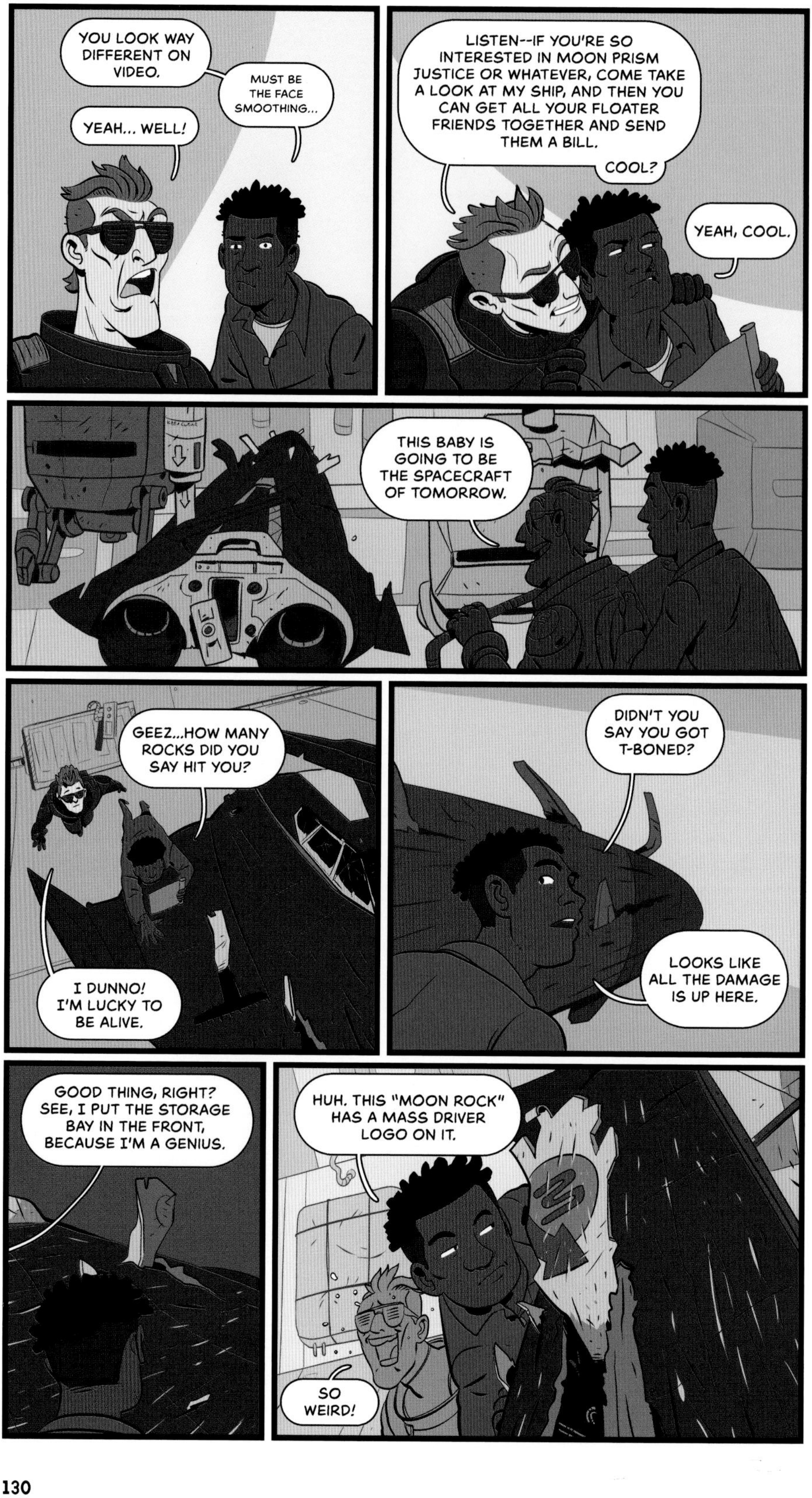
YOU LOOK WAY DIFFERENT ON VIDEO.
MUST BE THE FACE SMOOTHING...
YEAH... WELL!
LISTEN--IF YOU'RE SO INTERESTED IN MOON PRISM JUSTICE OR WHATEVER, COME TAKE A LOOK AT MY SHIP, AND THEN YOU CAN GET ALL YOUR FLOATER FRIENDS TOGETHER AND SEND THEM A BILL.
COOL?
YEAH, COOL.
THIS BABY IS GOING TO BE THE SPACECRAFT OF TOMORROW.
GEEZ...HOW MANY ROCKS DID YOU SAY HIT YOU?
I DUNNO! I'M LUCKY TO BE ALIVE.
DIDN'T YOU SAY YOU GOT T-BONED?
LOOKS LIKE ALL THE DAMAGE IS UP HERE.
GOOD THING, RIGHT? SEE, I PUT THE STORAGE BAY IN THE FRONT, BECAUSE I'M A GENIUS.
HUH. THIS "MOON ROCK" HAS A MASS DRIVER LOGO ON IT.
SO WEIRD!

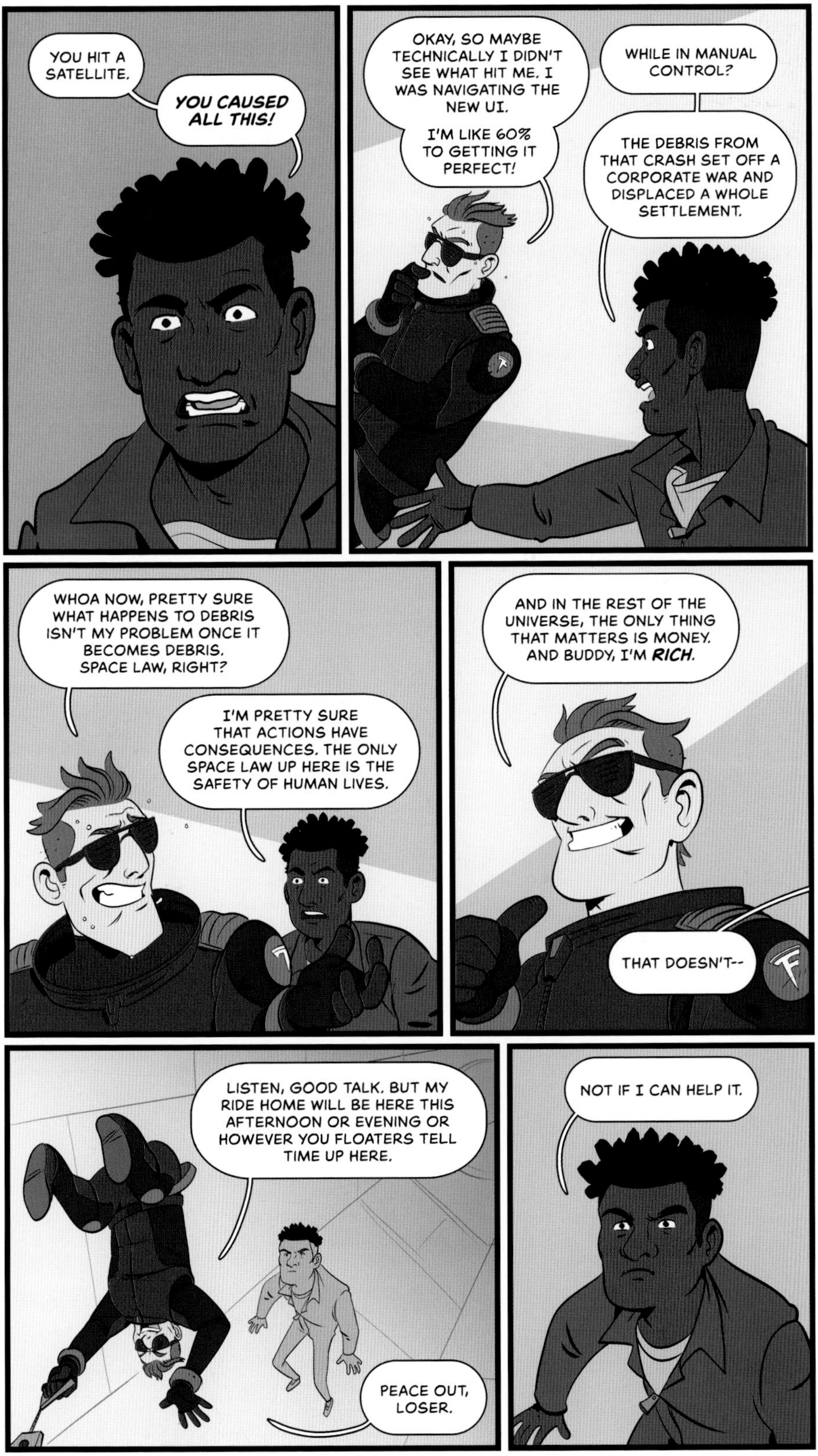
YOU HIT A SATELLITE.
YOU CAUSED ALL THIS!
OKAY, SO MAYBE TECHNICALLY I DIDN'T SEE WHAT HIT ME. I WAS NAVIGATING THE NEW UI.
I'M LIKE 60% TO GETTING IT PERFECT!
WHILE IN MANUAL CONTROL?
THE DEBRIS FROM THAT CRASH SET OFF A CORPORATE WAR AND DISPLACED A WHOLE SETTLEMENT.
WHOA NOW, PRETTY SURE WHAT HAPPENS TO DEBRIS ISN'T MY PROBLEM ONCE IT BECOMES DEBRIS. SPACE LAW, RIGHT?
I'M PRETTY SURE THAT ACTIONS HAVE CONSEQUENCES. THE ONLY SPACE LAW UP HERE IS THE SAFETY OF HUMAN LIVES.
AND IN THE REST OF THE UNIVERSE, THE ONLY THING THAT MATTERS IS MONEY. AND BUDDY, I'M RICH.
THAT DOESN'T--
LISTEN, GOOD TALK. BUT MY RIDE HOME WILL BE HERE THIS AFTERNOON OR EVENING OR HOWEVER YOU FLOATERS TELL TIME UP HERE.
PEACE OUT, LOSER.
NOT IF I CAN HELP IT.

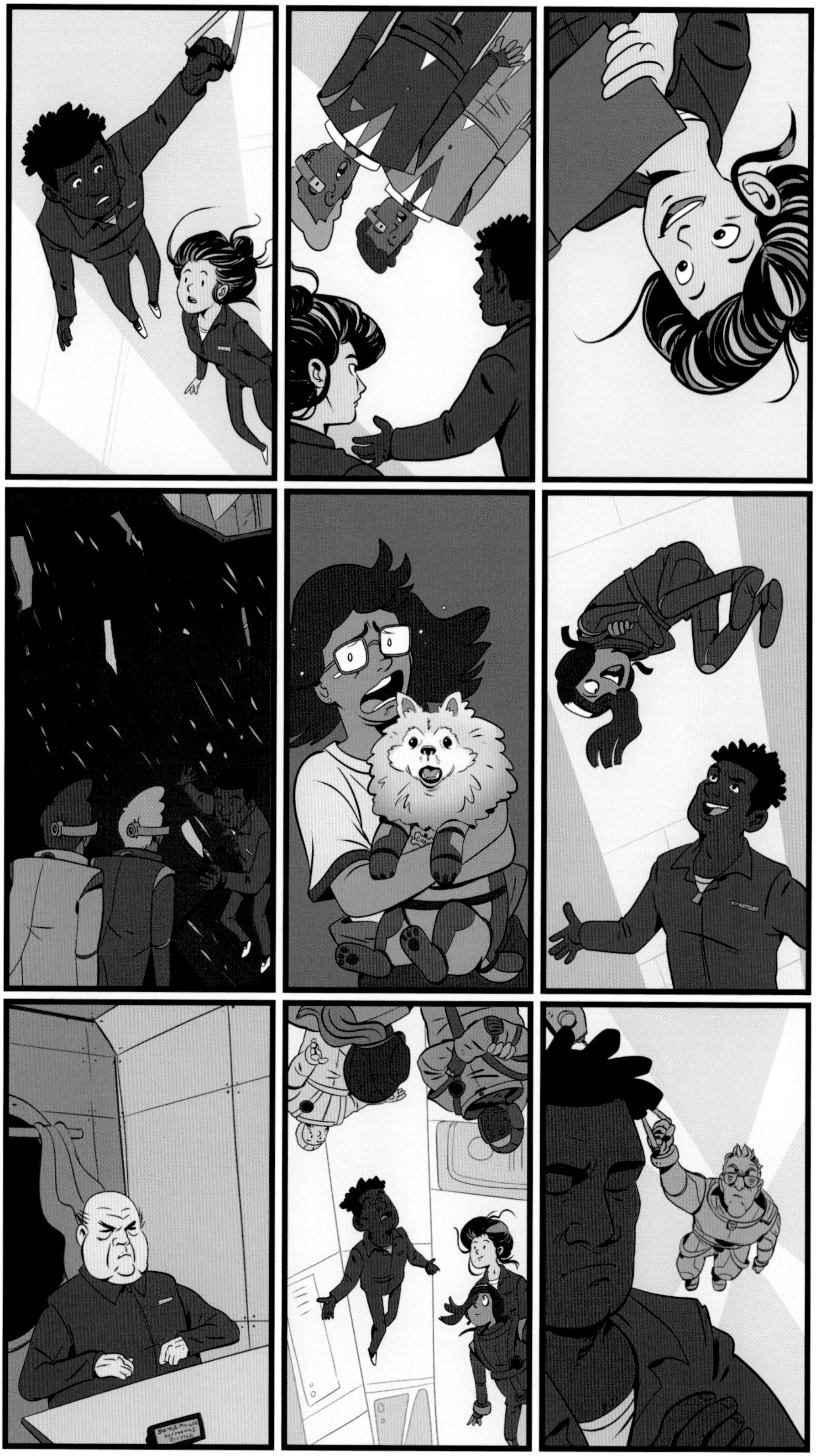

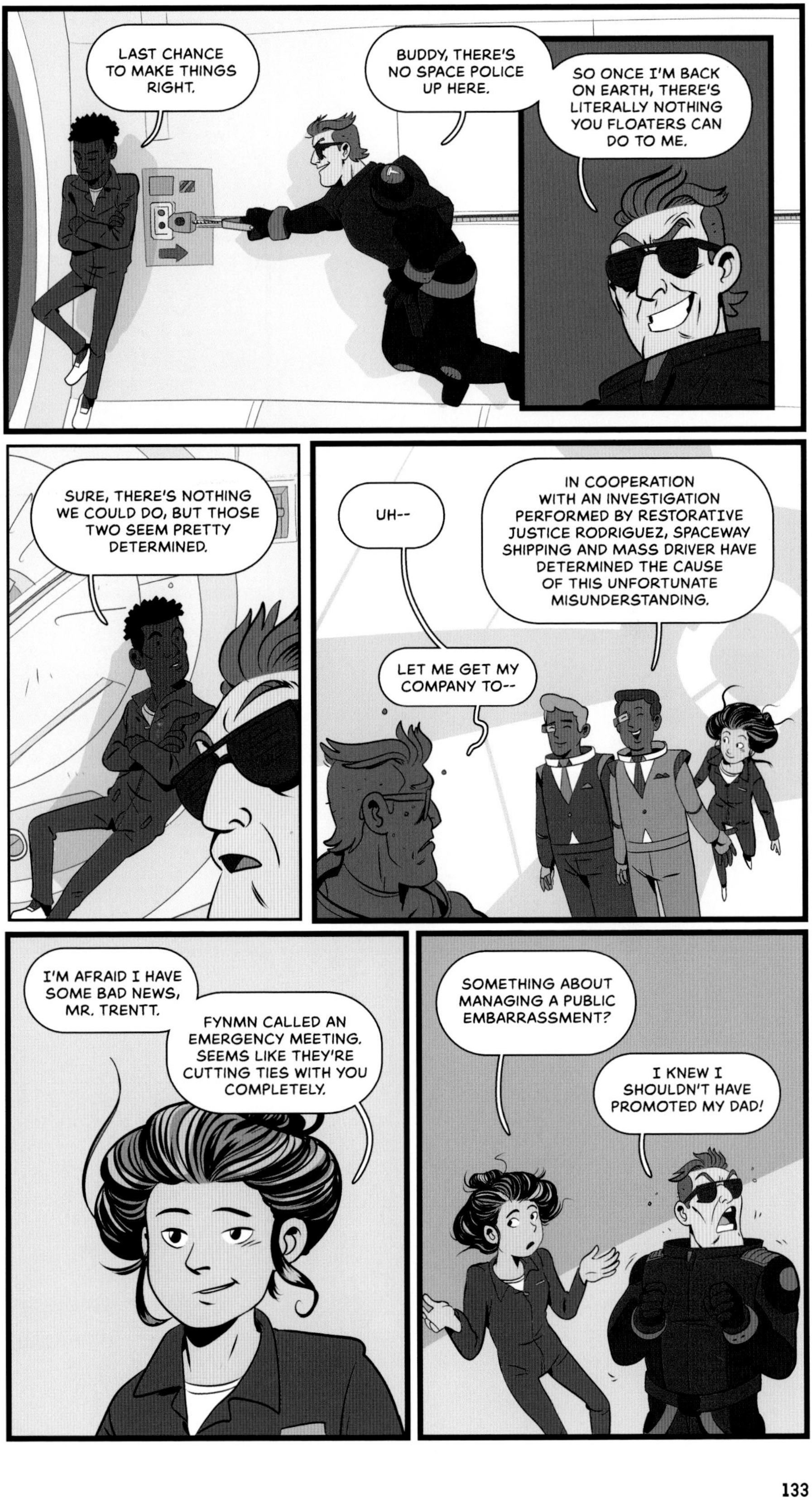
LAST CHANCE TO MAKE THINGS RIGHT.
BUDDY, THERE'S NO SPACE POLICE UP HERE.
SO ONCE I'M BACK ON EARTH, THERE'S LITERALLY NOTHING YOU FLOATERS CAN DO TO ME.
SURE, THERE'S NOTHING WE COULD DO, BUT THOSE TWO SEEM PRETTY DETERMINED.
UH--
IN COOPERATION WITH AN INVESTIGATION PERFORMED BY RESTORATIVE JUSTICE RODRIGUEZ, SPACEWAY SHIPPING AND MASS DRIVER HAVE DETERMINED THE CAUSE OF THIS UNFORTUNATE MISUNDERSTANDING.
LET ME GET MY COMPANY TO--
I'M AFRAID I HAVE SOME BAD NEWS, MR. TRENTT.
FYNMN CALLED AN EMERGENCY MEETING. SEEMS LIKE THEY'RE CUTTING TIES WITH YOU COMPLETELY.
SOMETHING ABOUT MANAGING A PUBLIC EMBARRASSMENT?
I KNEW I SHOULDN'T HAVE PROMOTED MY DAD!

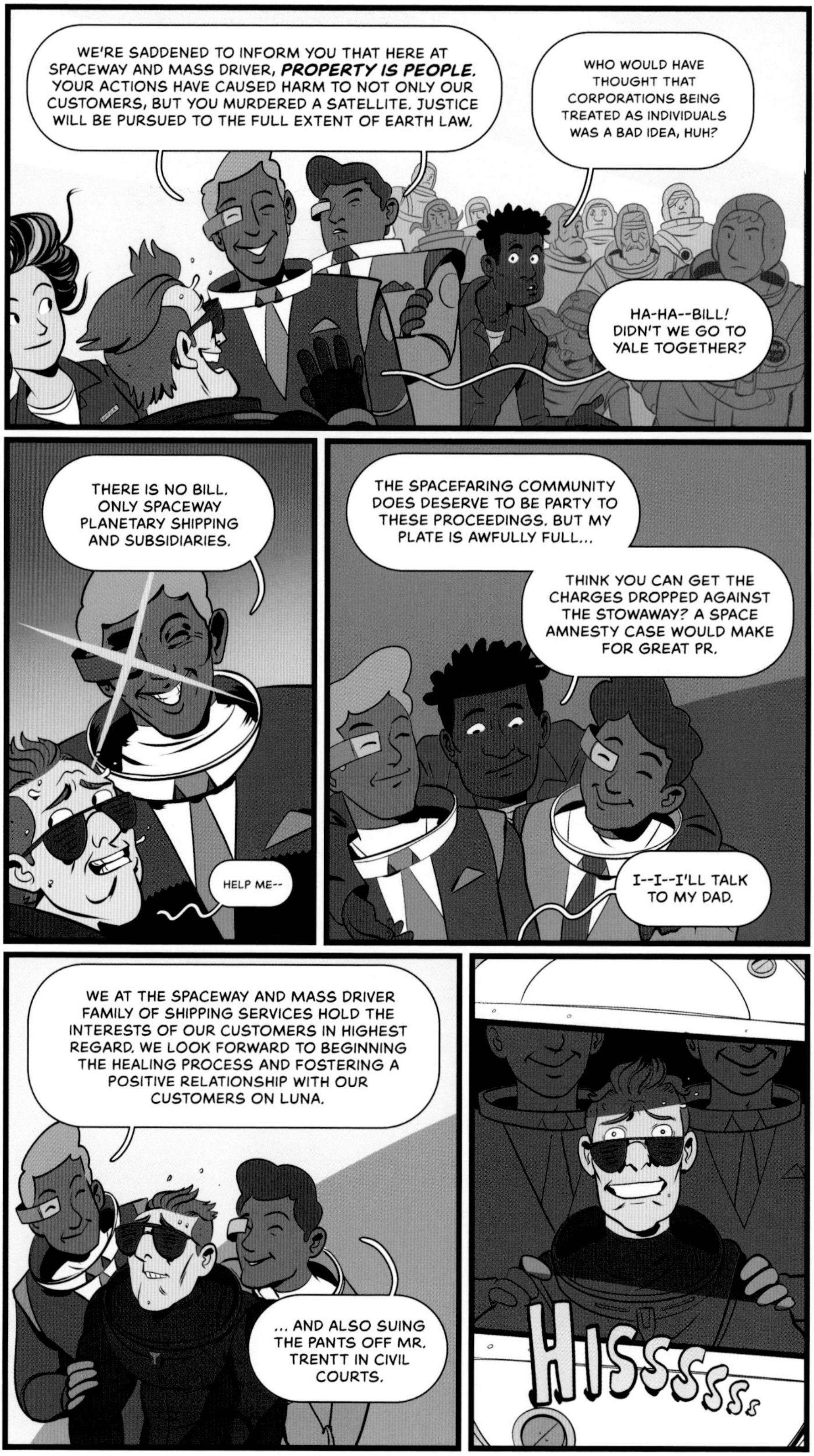
WE'RE SADDENED TO INFORM YOU THAT HERE AT SPACEWAY AND MASS DRIVER, **PROPERTY IS PEOPLE.** YOUR ACTIONS HAVE CAUSED HARM TO NOT ONLY OUR CUSTOMERS, BUT YOU MURDERED A SATELLITE. JUSTICE WILL BE PURSUED TO THE FULL EXTENT OF EARTH LAW.
WHO WOULD HAVE THOUGHT THAT CORPORATIONS BEING TREATED AS INDIVIDUALS WAS A BAD IDEA, HUH?
HA-HA--BILL! DIDN'T WE GO TO YALE TOGETHER?
THERE IS NO BILL. ONLY SPACEWAY PLANETARY SHIPPING AND SUBSIDIARIES.
HELP ME--
THE SPACEFARING COMMUNITY DOES DESERVE TO BE PARTY TO THESE PROCEEDINGS. BUT MY PLATE IS AWFULLY FULL...
THINK YOU CAN GET THE CHARGES DROPPED AGAINST THE STOWAWAY? A SPACE AMNESTY CASE WOULD MAKE FOR GREAT PR.
I--I--I'LL TALK TO MY DAD.
WE AT THE SPACEWAY AND MASS DRIVER FAMILY OF SHIPPING SERVICES HOLD THE INTERESTS OF OUR CUSTOMERS IN HIGHEST REGARD. WE LOOK FORWARD TO BEGINNING THE HEALING PROCESS AND FOSTERING A POSITIVE RELATIONSHIP WITH OUR CUSTOMERS ON LUNA.
...AND ALSO SUING THE PANTS OFF MR. TRENTT IN CIVIL COURTS.
HISSSSSs

...THE MASS DRIVER REPS AGREED ON NEXT WEEK TO BEGIN DISCUSSING HOW THEY CAN MAKE THINGS RIGHT. IT'S GOING TO BE WEIRD, BUT THIS WILL BE GOOD FOR EVERYONE.

WE'RE LOOKING FORWARD TO IT.

THAT WAS SOME SKIT BACK THERE, CHIEF. MAYBE THEY'LL MAKE YOU SHERIFF.

KEEP YOUR SUIT CLEAN.

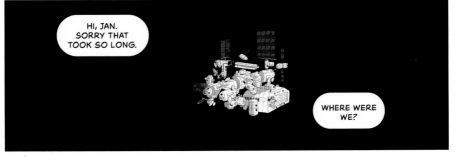

HI, JAN. SORRY THAT TOOK SO LONG.

WHERE WERE WE?

MOON COURT

HOW DO YOU SOLVE A CRIME IN SPACE?

ON FRIDAY AUGUST 15, 1969, JUST A MONTH AFTER THE Apollo 11 mission put men on the moon for the first time, Brazilian police arrested a man named Jose Cassiano de Jesus. His crime? Selling small plots on the moon to interested buyers—$25 to claim a piece on the near side (followed, of course, by twenty-four $5 installments for a grand total of $145) and an all-in price of $300 for plots on the far side ("It is richer there," de Jesus claimed). In his plea after arrest, de Jesus allegedly said that he had in fact sold the very first plots to Neil Armstrong and Buzz Aldrin, and that they had been to the moon to see their properties in person. All told, de Jesus only made $125, and none of his customers wanted to press charges. "They all expressed some embarrassment," officers said at the time.

De Jesus and his customers are not the first or last people involved in lunar real estate chicanery. In 1756, the Prussian emperor Frederick the Great allegedly presented the moon to a man named Aul Juergens "as a symbolic gesture of gratitude for services rendered," and it has since been passed through the family to the youngest-born son for centuries. In recent years, a man named Martin Juergens from Westphalia claimed to own the deed.

In 1955, the former chairman of the Hayden Planetarium in New York started selling lunar lots for a dollar a piece. In 1980, a California man named Dennis Hope founded the Lunar Embassy and claimed not just ownership but also copyright over the moon, and divided Earth's natural satellite into three million parcels that he sold in supermarket parking lots for a steal: $15.99 plus $10 postage and packing and a $1.16 "lunartax." Hope ultimately sold more than three hundred thousand of these real estate certificates, and the list of owners included Tom Cruise, Harrison Ford, and Ronald Reagan. (And, in a delightful twist, in 1996, Juergens challenged Hope's moon sales and sent the California crescent entrepreneur a cease-and-desist letter on the basis that his family in fact owns the moon.)

But can you own the moon? The answer to that is perhaps more confusing than you might expect. The Outer Space Treaty, adopted at this point by 109 parties, states that "outer space, including the moon and other celestial bodies, is not subject to national appropriation by claim of sovereignty, by means of use or occupation, or by any other means." But that applies only to nations, not private citizens or companies. And that's in part because the treaty was written in an era when the idea that corporations or individual people would get themselves into space seemed absurd.

What that means is that there isn't a clear rule about *private* space ownership. And whenever there's a legal loophole, you can be sure that someone will try and exploit it for profit, attention, or both. In 2001, Gregory Nemitz sent NASA an invoice for parking their spacecraft on the asteroid Eros, which he considers his company's property. That same year, space lawyer Virgiliu Pop registered a claim over the sun, although he also noted that he was not in any way liable for the damage that his property might cause, like solar flares, sunstroke, or skin cancer. If a legal body ever did hold him responsible for such things, he wrote in 2002, "the court would implicitly recognize that I do indeed own the Sun—which is ridiculous."[1] Pop's claim was a publicity stunt, one meant to draw attention to how outdated and lacking the rules are around outer space.

The idea that humans might live in space, on the moon, or even on Mars, has been both a dream and a prediction for much longer than humans have had the technological capacity to do so. As you read this, a small number of people are living in space already—aboard the International Space Station. But since the launch of the ISS in 1998, there hasn't been the boom in off-Earth living that some people predicted. In many cases, it's far safer and more efficient to learn about the cosmos by using humanless craft-like probes. And yet, human spaceflight is sexy and alluring, drawing the attention of tech moguls like Elon Musk and Jeff Bezos, who claim that they'll be sending groups of people to visit and ultimately live in space in the next few decades. Some argue that going off-Earth is the only way we'll survive as a species, given the current climate trajectories. It's already possible to launch and maintain a space station, and likely even a moon colony, but whether it's safe, practical, and worth the money remains to be seen.

As humans start to think more seriously about living and working in space or on other planets, the question of justice and jurisdiction looms large. And yet, the actual details of how law might work in space are still incredibly murky. What happens if, as in the comic you just read, two private companies have a dispute about land or resources or satellite debris? What happens if an American tourist in a space hotel steals something from a Japanese tourist in that same space hotel? What happens if lunar residents decide they want their own kind of citizenship? Right now, the answer to all of these questions is: We don't know.

Of course, science fiction is way ahead of all of these conundrums. In 1949, Robert A. Heinlein wrote a short story called "The Man Who Sold the Moon" in which a craven businessman is pushed to the brink in his quest to claim and own such prized real estate. In *The Dispossessed*, a 1974 classic by Ursula K. Le Guin, lunar residents have invented their own systems of justice. The extended *Star Wars* universe includes an Imperial "Procurator of Justice" whose role is to oversee the criminal justice system across all of space (a tall order, if you ask me). *The Expanse, Firefly, Battlestar Galactica*, nearly every space-based science fiction must deal with justice in some form or another, even if the answer is "Just throw him out of the airlock!"

---

1   I suspect Pop and the PETA lawyers who brought the Naruto lawsuit you read about in the "Animal Magnetism" chapter (page 93), might enjoy each other's company.

But thus far, our real-life institutions have not caught up. And legal experts argue that we should begin to answer some of these questions sooner rather than later—before we start putting citizens into the legal (and physical) vacuum of space.

While the laws may be murky, the need for them is not. In 1998, the Russian Institute of Biomedical Problems began a 110-day experiment on the Mir space station. In total, eight people were part of the experiment, seven men and one woman, named Judith Lapierre. The idea of the experiment was, at least in part, to see how a long stay in cramped quarters might impact people psychologically and socially. In other words: Would they try to kill each other?

The answer was unfortunately: yes. Lapierre reported several instances of sexual harassment and said that she lived in fear of being attacked. On New Year's Eve, her fears came true when the Russian commander emerged from his chambers incredibly drunk and sexually assaulted her. Earlier that same day, the commander attacked one of his male compatriots. Soon after, someone hid the kitchen knives, worried that two of the men on the station were going to actually kill each other. The experiment may have influenced a brand-new Code of Conduct for the International Space Station, which today states that "ISS crewmembers' conduct shall be such as to maintain a harmonious and cohesive relationship among the ISS crewmembers." Good luck with that.

And remember, these are astronauts, people who have trained for this their whole lives and been tested and selected not just on physical capability, but also in part on their psychological stamina and stability. What happens when we start sending riffraff like you and me up there? "The people who go to space hotels aren't going to be selected for their self-discipline," said Michelle Hanlon, a space law expert at the University of Mississippi. "We have to be prepared for the fact that things are going to happen in space because we're all only human."

It won't just be violent crimes (thankfully) that need handling off-Earth. Hanlon thinks that we don't necessarily need to prepare for a boom in murder, but rather smaller, more mundane cases. "I think it's going to be slip and fall. It's going to be when somebody steals your watch. It's going to be things that happen to us every day in life. We need family lawyers in space, we need finance lawyers in space." Who handles workplace harassment complaints and worker safety issues and contract negotiations? Hanlon even mentioned cases akin to one you just read about in the comic: What happens when someone damages a satellite? Do you require these private companies to have space insurance? How does divorce and custody work in space?

To answer these questions, it might be tempting to just say: Why reinvent the wheel? We have ways of dealing with all of this stuff here on Earth, do we really need to start again? And in some cases, perhaps not. But the wheel of justice here on Earth doesn't function all that well already.

The United States currently holds nearly 2.3 million people behind bars, at a cost of around $80 billion a year. By population, that's more than any other nation on Earth—the United States is home to just under 5 percent of the world's population, but almost 25 percent of the world's incarcerated people. And who gets locked up is influenced heavily by racism and injustice—African Americans are incarcerated five times more than white Americans, not because they're more likely to commit crimes, but because they're more likely to be arrested, and on average are issued longer sentences. One study found that, between 1995 and 2005, African Americans made up about 13 percent of drug users in the U.S., but 36 percent of drug arrests (not including marijuana convictions). From 1998 to 2004, Africans Americans also made up an average of almost 49 percent of convictions for drug-related offenses. Another study found that between 2011 and 2014, "the probability of being black, unarmed, and shot by police is about 3.49 times the probability of being white, unarmed, and shot by police on average."

These disparities have led many experts to stop calling the American system the "criminal justice" system, replacing it with the term "criminal legal" system. Is this what we want to export into space? If we can do better, shouldn't we try?

Flash Forward has considered the question of prison and police abolition before (in 2015 and 2017, respectively), and after each episode I got a slew of emails telling me I was far too radical. As I write this, in 2020, the public willingness to consider questions of prison and police abolition has shifted dramatically. The murders of George Floyd and Breonna Taylor followed by months of well-documented police violence against protestors seem to have opened people's eyes to the violence baked into these systems. I hope by the time you're reading this, real progress has been made to reimagine justice not just in space, but on Earth, too.

Compounding the ethical and humanitarian problems with the modern American legal system as it stands are the logistical ones. Prisons are incredibly resource-intensive to run on Earth, and in an environment like the moon or Mars, where every ounce of food, heat, and even air is extremely costly, they become almost farcical, logistically. Forcing prisoners to work in return for their resource consumption (otherwise known as slave labor) is generally frowned upon, as is just killing people outright. Sending them back to Earth is costly as well, and if we did send them home for a trial, we're faced with a new question: Is a jury on Earth even equipped to handle cases that happen in space, a place they have never been to? "There are just a lot of practical limitations and obstacles to the way that we do criminal justice on Earth in Western society right now," said Erika Nesvold, an astrophysicist and cofounder of the JustSpace Alliance.

Space will provide a cosmic buffet of new offenses, too. On Earth, we don't codify oxygen as a basic human right because it's all around us. But in space, there may be a need to add "air" to the list of humanitarian protections that every person deserves. We'll need labor lawyers in space, but labor law might be totally different—does each worker have the right to an independent line of communication back down to Earth? What prevents a company from setting up their own base and ignoring labor laws entirely?

On Earth, there are people already testing out alternatives to the criminal legal system. Restorative justice—which you saw outlined in the comic—has been one way that communities who want to avoid prisons and carceral systems have tried to address harms done. Political theorist John Braithwaite defines restorative justice this way: "a process where all the stakeholders affected by an injustice have an opportunity to discuss how they have been affected by the injustice and to decide what should be done to repair the harm." Along with related concepts like reparative justice and transformative justice, these alternate ways of thinking about how a community responds to trauma are based not in punishment, but communication and figuring out how to repair the damage that the accused has done, and to prevent more damage in the future. This can be messy and complicated—there is no one way a restorative justice practice might go; each case is handled slightly differently and it often requires buy-in from both parties, but it offers a fundamentally different framework for thinking about justice that might better suit space, where we all really will have to be in this together.

This doesn't mean we can work out every single rule for our future spacefarers right this moment. "Living in space is probably going to look so different than anything that we can imagine that trying to write out a legal system and a justice system in great detail now for our future descendants is going to be a waste of time," says Nesvold. What we can do is think about the values we want to send to space. What ways of thinking about harm and redemption and justice do we want to commit to as a group and send out into the solar system?

Some might find this a frustrating ask, but I think it's actually an exciting opening. It's incredibly hard to rethink and reshape institutions that feel deeply engrained in our modern lives. Upending the prison system in the United States is a tall order (although not unachievable, as many advocates have pointed out). But in space, we have an incredible opportunity to try something new. To pick and choose the pieces that work today and discard the ones that don't.

There's a lovely thread that connects Jose Cassiano de Jesus—the man who sold plots of the moon—and science-fiction writers like Ursula K. Le Guin or Ann Leckie who imagine future space civilizations complete with new economic and legal systems. That thread is possibility; a willingness to try something that might seem harebrained. Space is vast—wide open in both a literal and figurative sense. This can lead to escapism and naivete—I regret to inform you that we will continue being flawed and strange and messy in space as we are on Earth, and we must grapple with that—but it can also lead to an opening of sorts. A possibility. "I think we have this opportunity to try out these ideas here in ways that are exciting and perhaps beneficial for Earth," said Lucianne Walkowicz, an astronomer and the other cofounder of the JustSpace Alliance.

Rarely do we get a chance to really build something from the ground (or space) up. So many of the chapters in this book have been about finding the tiny cracks in a system and trying to widen them a bit, and about taking hold of the reins of the timeline and trying to drag them in a new direction. In space, we have the opportunity to discard what isn't working before we even take off and create more loving, just, and equitable environments. Those chances don't come very often, and we shouldn't squander them when they do.

UNREEL

BY CHRIS JONES AND ZACK WEINERSMITH

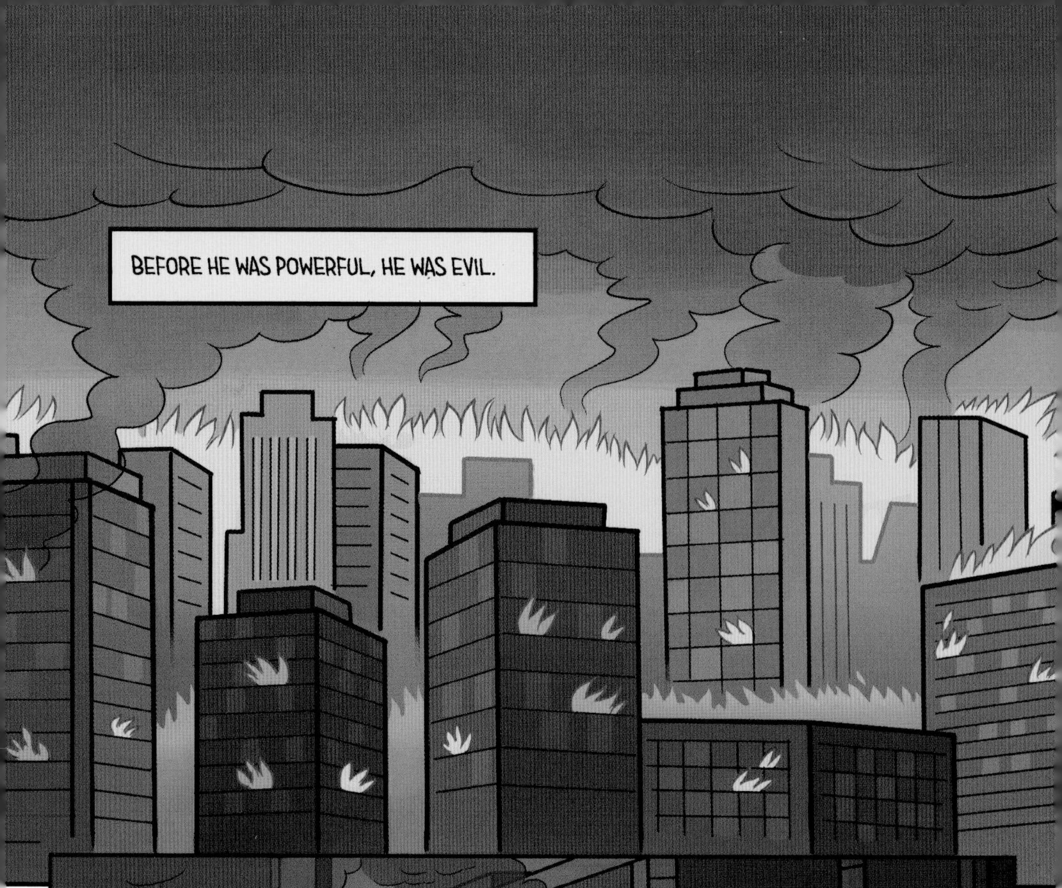
BEFORE HE WAS POWERFUL, HE WAS EVIL.

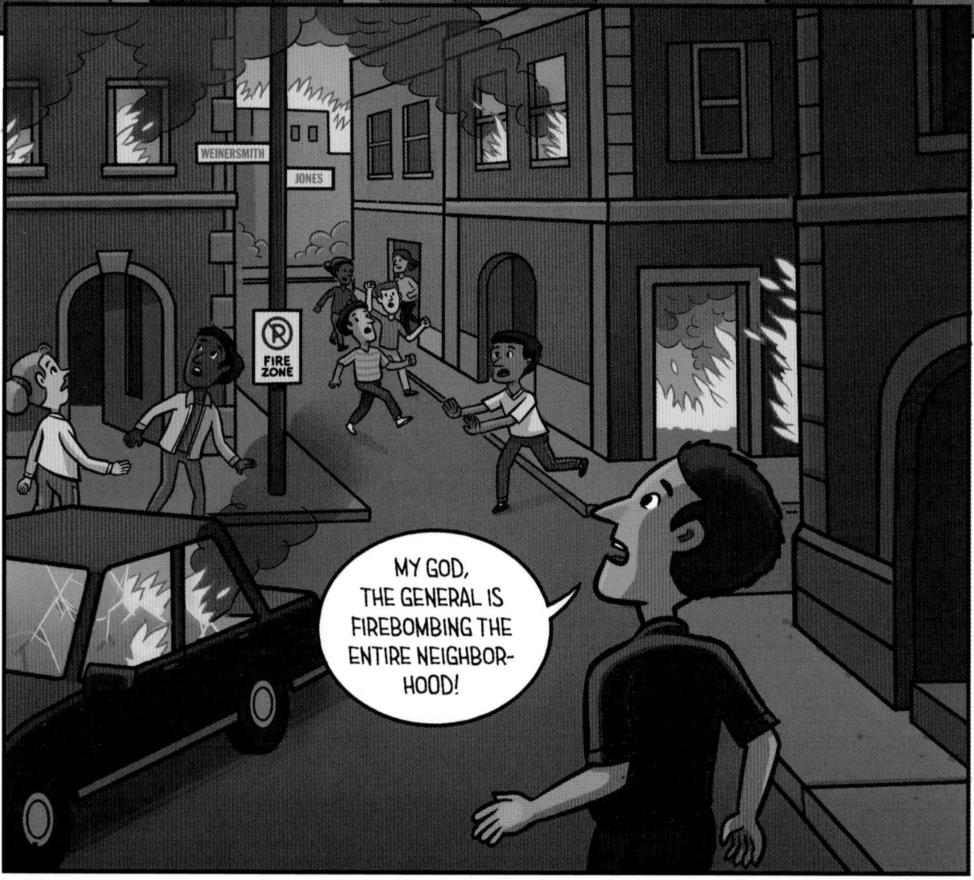
WEINERSMITH
JONES
FIRE ZONE
MY GOD, THE GENERAL IS FIREBOMBING THE ENTIRE NEIGHBOR-HOOD!

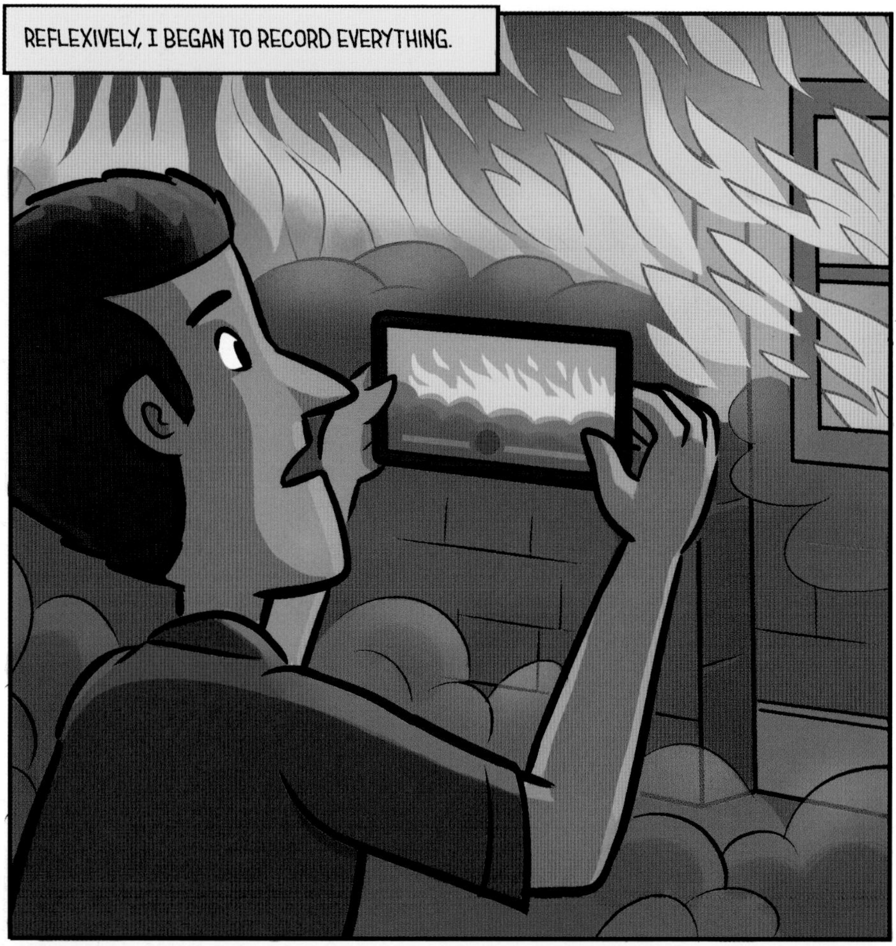
REFLEXIVELY, I BEGAN TO RECORD EVERYTHING.

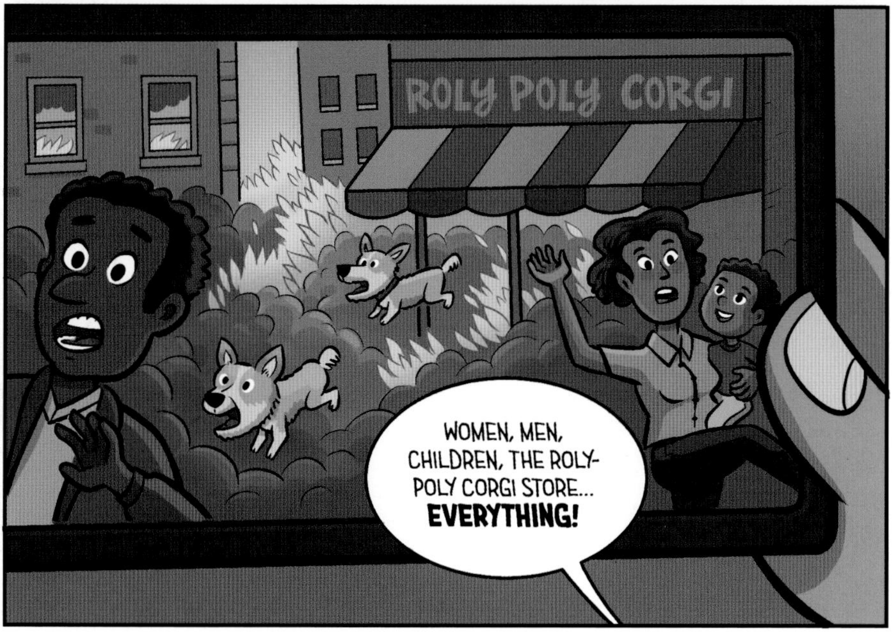
ROLY POLY CORGI
WOMEN, MEN, CHILDREN, THE ROLY-POLY CORGI STORE... **EVERYTHING!**

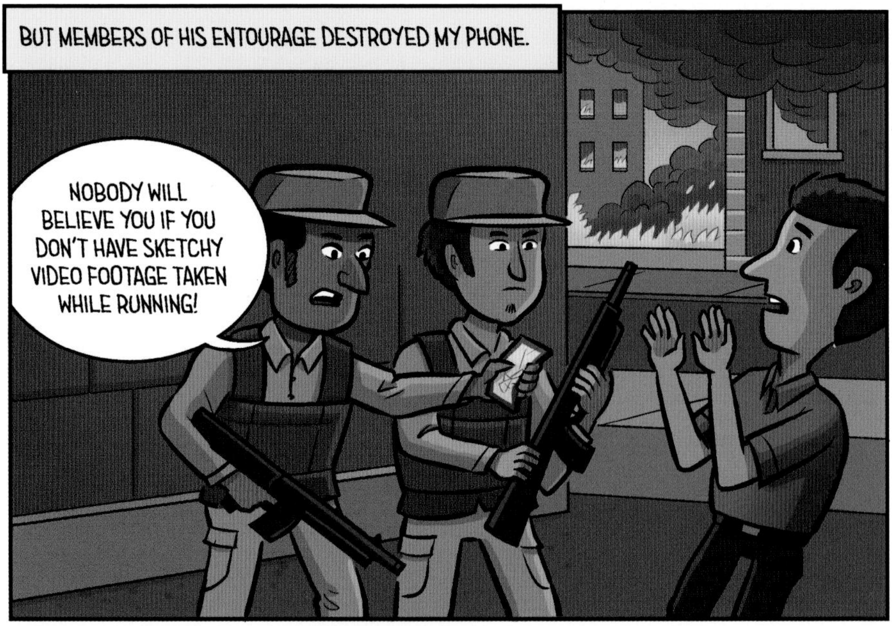
BUT MEMBERS OF HIS ENTOURAGE DESTROYED MY PHONE.
NOBODY WILL BELIEVE YOU IF YOU DON'T HAVE SKETCHY VIDEO FOOTAGE TAKEN WHILE RUNNING!

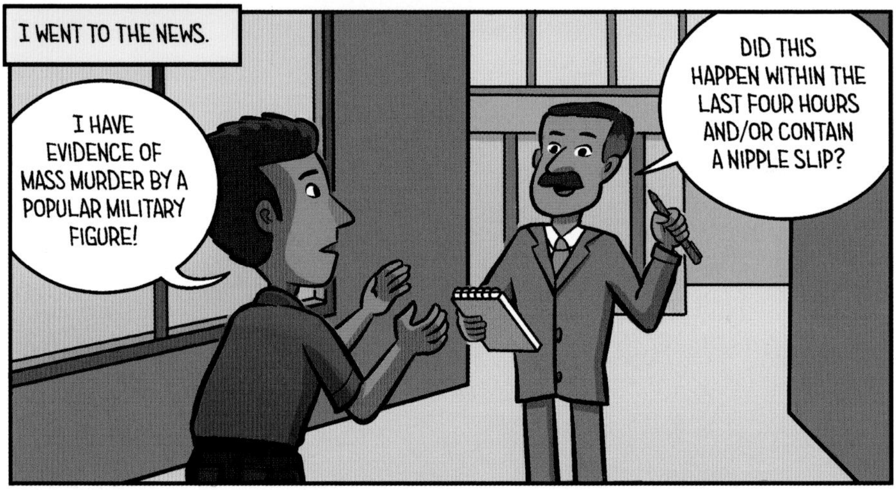
I WENT TO THE NEWS.
I HAVE EVIDENCE OF MASS MURDER BY A POPULAR MILITARY FIGURE!
DID THIS HAPPEN WITHIN THE LAST FOUR HOURS AND/OR CONTAIN A NIPPLE SLIP?

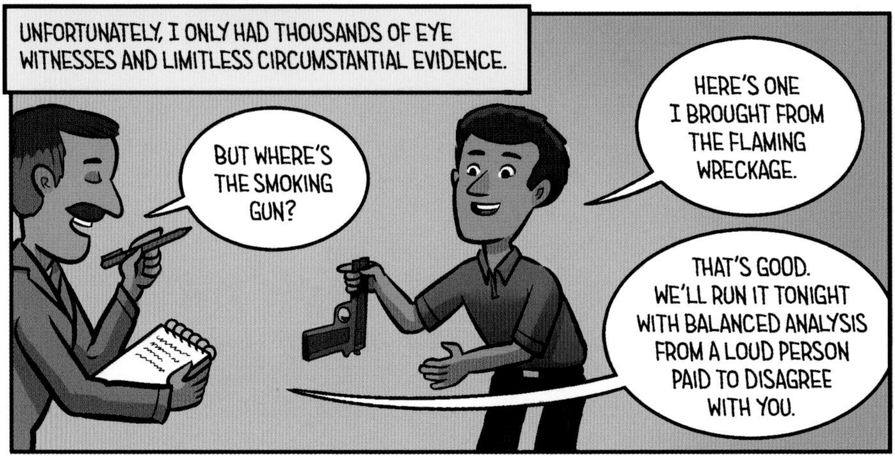
UNFORTUNATELY, I ONLY HAD THOUSANDS OF EYE WITNESSES AND LIMITLESS CIRCUMSTANTIAL EVIDENCE.
BUT WHERE'S THE SMOKING GUN?
HERE'S ONE I BROUGHT FROM THE FLAMING WRECKAGE.
THAT'S GOOD. WE'LL RUN IT TONIGHT WITH BALANCED ANALYSIS FROM A LOUD PERSON PAID TO DISAGREE WITH YOU.

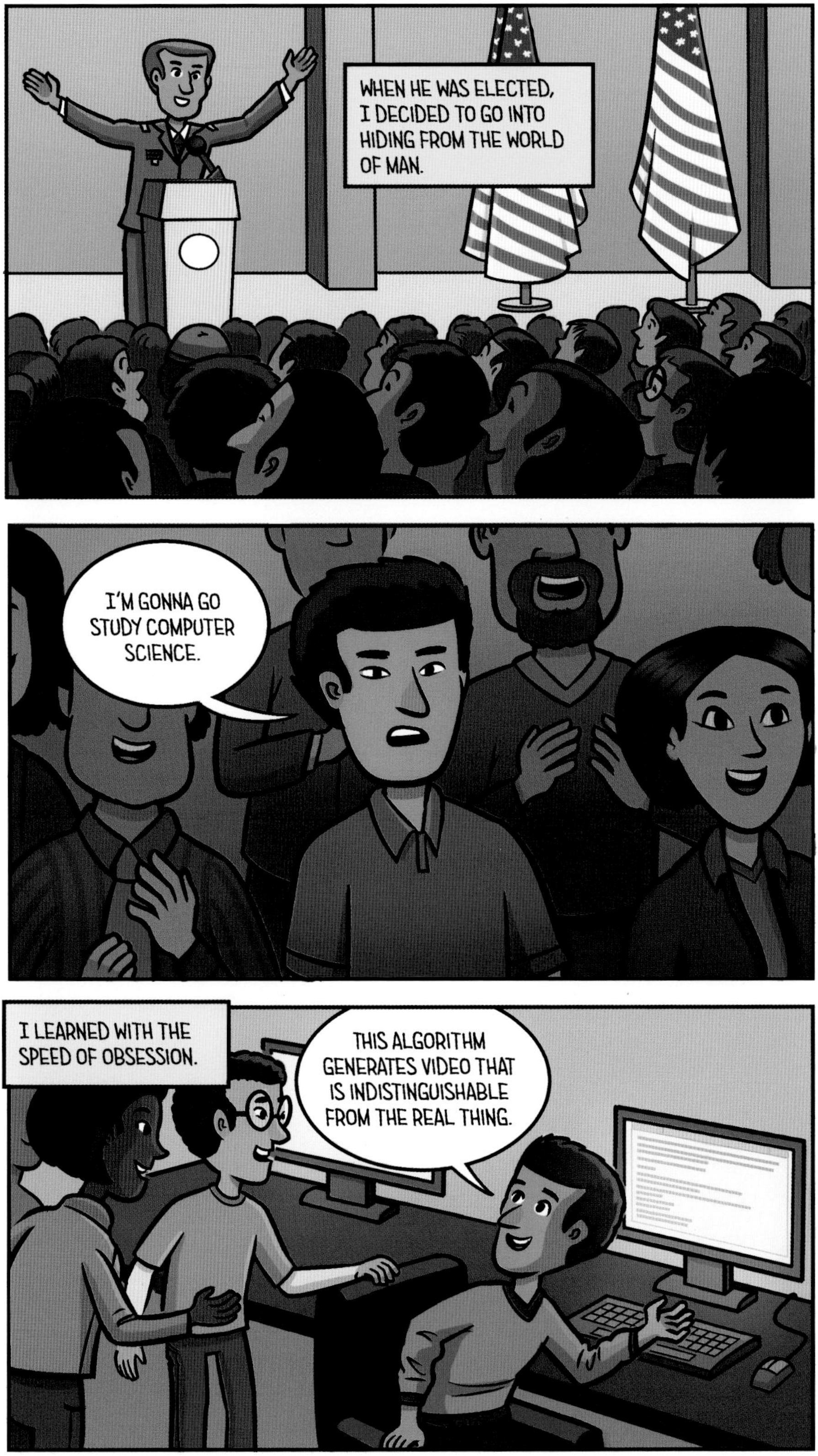
WHEN HE WAS ELECTED, I DECIDED TO GO INTO HIDING FROM THE WORLD OF MAN.
I'M GONNA GO STUDY COMPUTER SCIENCE.
I LEARNED WITH THE SPEED OF OBSESSION.
THIS ALGORITHM GENERATES VIDEO THAT IS INDISTINGUISHABLE FROM THE REAL THING.

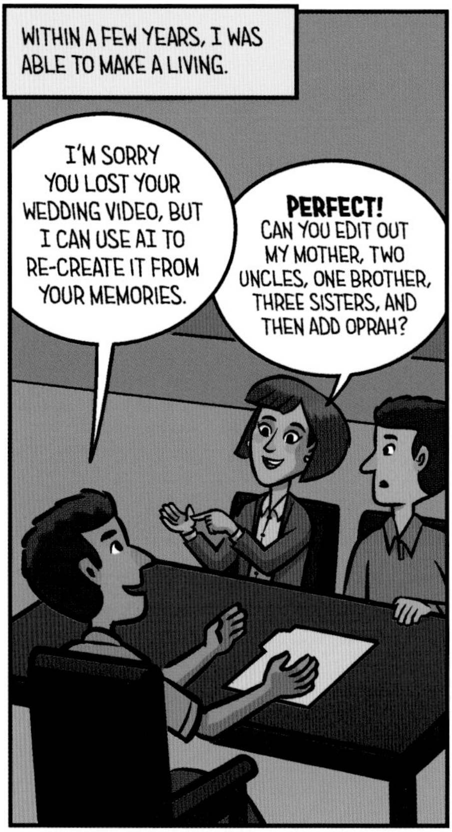
WITHIN A FEW YEARS, I WAS ABLE TO MAKE A LIVING.
I'M SORRY YOU LOST YOUR WEDDING VIDEO, BUT I CAN USE AI TO RE-CREATE IT FROM YOUR MEMORIES.
PERFECT! CAN YOU EDIT OUT MY MOTHER, TWO UNCLES, ONE BROTHER, THREE SISTERS, AND THEN ADD OPRAH?

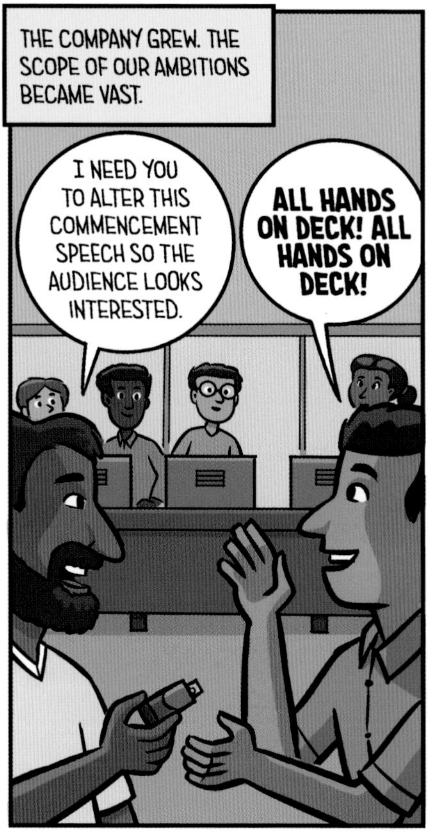
THE COMPANY GREW. THE SCOPE OF OUR AMBITIONS BECAME VAST.
I NEED YOU TO ALTER THIS COMMENCEMENT SPEECH SO THE AUDIENCE LOOKS INTERESTED.
ALL HANDS ON DECK! ALL HANDS ON DECK!

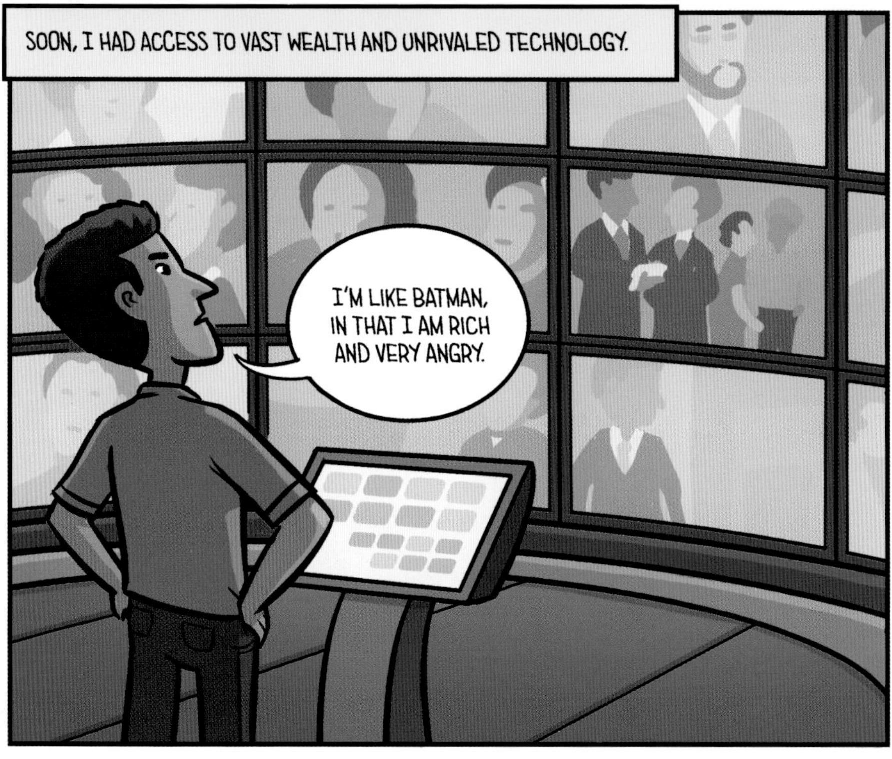
SOON, I HAD ACCESS TO VAST WEALTH AND UNRIVALED TECHNOLOGY.
I'M LIKE BATMAN, IN THAT I AM RICH AND VERY ANGRY.

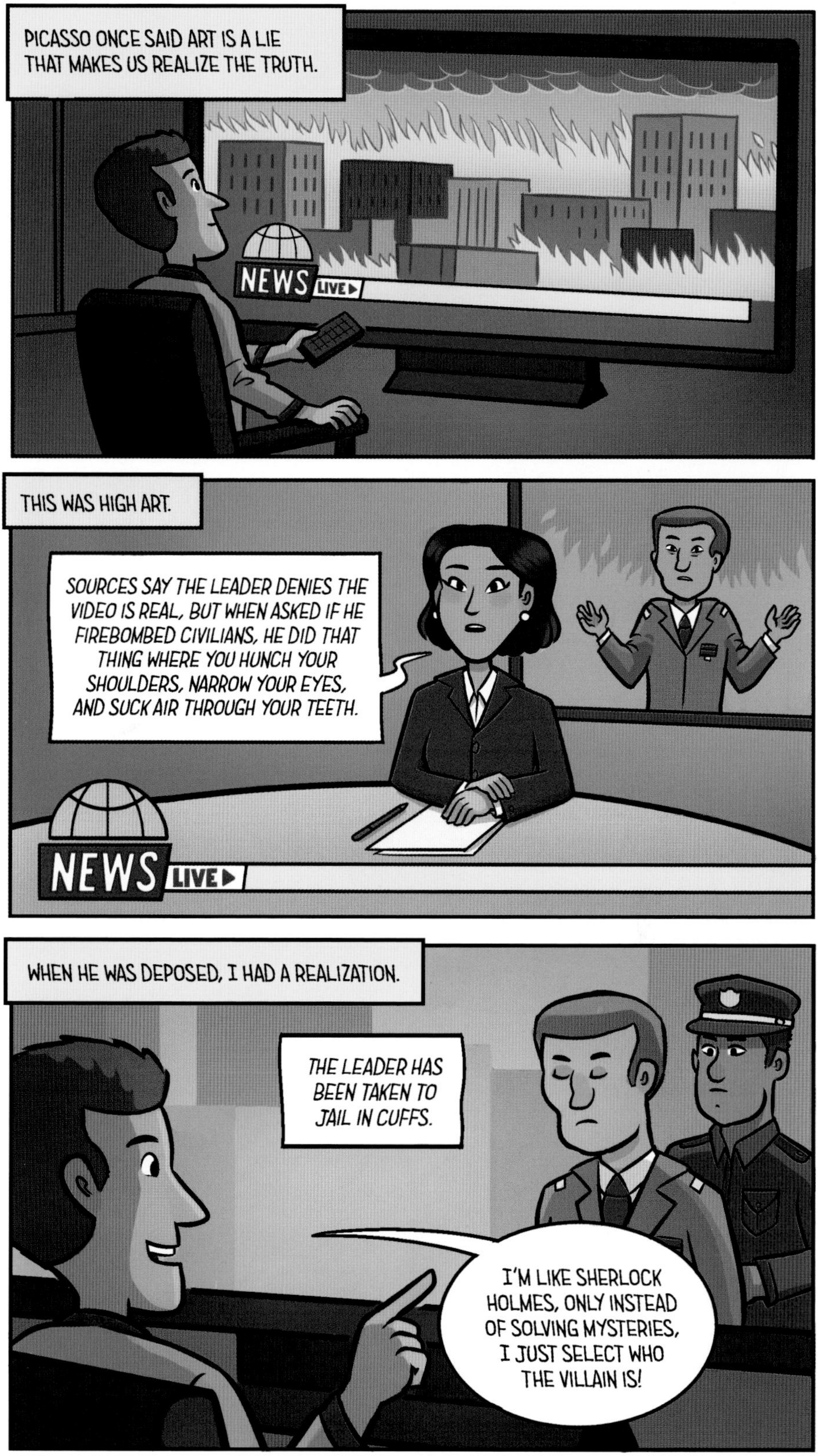
PICASSO ONCE SAID ART IS A LIE THAT MAKES US REALIZE THE TRUTH.
NEWS
LIVE
THIS WAS HIGH ART.
SOURCES SAY THE LEADER DENIES THE VIDEO IS REAL, BUT WHEN ASKED IF HE FIREBOMBED CIVILIANS, HE DID THAT THING WHERE YOU HUNCH YOUR SHOULDERS, NARROW YOUR EYES, AND SUCK AIR THROUGH YOUR TEETH.
NEWS
LIVE
WHEN HE WAS DEPOSED, I HAD A REALIZATION.
THE LEADER HAS BEEN TAKEN TO JAIL IN CUFFS.
I'M LIKE SHERLOCK HOLMES, ONLY INSTEAD OF SOLVING MYSTERIES, I JUST SELECT WHO THE VILLAIN IS!

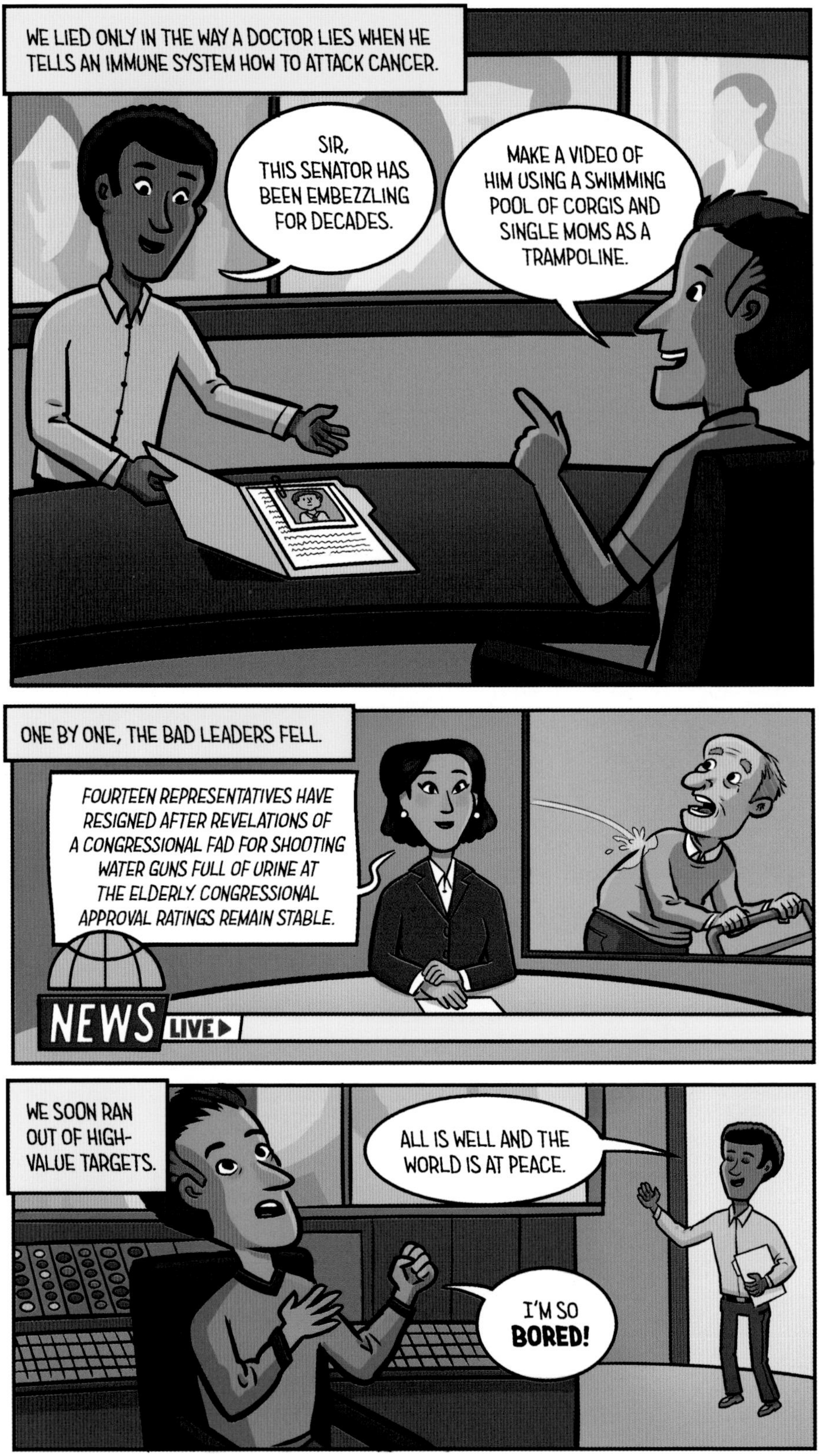
WE LIED ONLY IN THE WAY A DOCTOR LIES WHEN HE TELLS AN IMMUNE SYSTEM HOW TO ATTACK CANCER.
SIR, THIS SENATOR HAS BEEN EMBEZZLING FOR DECADES.
MAKE A VIDEO OF HIM USING A SWIMMING POOL OF CORGIS AND SINGLE MOMS AS A TRAMPOLINE.
ONE BY ONE, THE BAD LEADERS FELL.
FOURTEEN REPRESENTATIVES HAVE RESIGNED AFTER REVELATIONS OF A CONGRESSIONAL FAD FOR SHOOTING WATER GUNS FULL OF URINE AT THE ELDERLY. CONGRESSIONAL APPROVAL RATINGS REMAIN STABLE.
NEWS
LIVE
WE SOON RAN OUT OF HIGH-VALUE TARGETS.
ALL IS WELL AND THE WORLD IS AT PEACE.
I'M SO BORED!

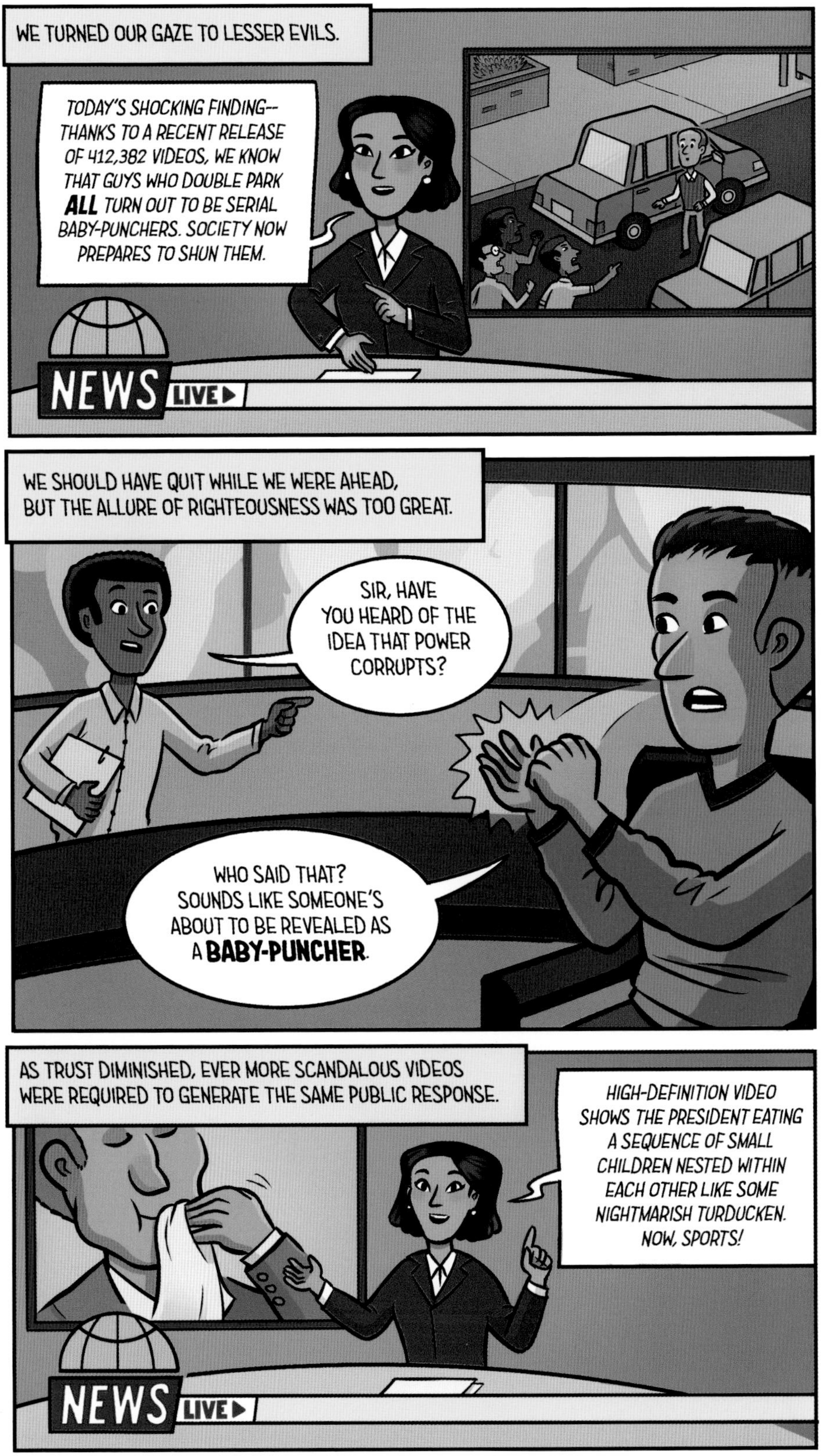
WE TURNED OUR GAZE TO LESSER EVILS.
TODAY'S SHOCKING FINDING--THANKS TO A RECENT RELEASE OF 412,382 VIDEOS, WE KNOW THAT GUYS WHO DOUBLE PARK ALL TURN OUT TO BE SERIAL BABY-PUNCHERS. SOCIETY NOW PREPARES TO SHUN THEM.
NEWS LIVE
WE SHOULD HAVE QUIT WHILE WE WERE AHEAD, BUT THE ALLURE OF RIGHTEOUSNESS WAS TOO GREAT.
SIR, HAVE YOU HEARD OF THE IDEA THAT POWER CORRUPTS?
WHO SAID THAT? SOUNDS LIKE SOMEONE'S ABOUT TO BE REVEALED AS A BABY-PUNCHER.
AS TRUST DIMINISHED, EVER MORE SCANDALOUS VIDEOS WERE REQUIRED TO GENERATE THE SAME PUBLIC RESPONSE.
HIGH-DEFINITION VIDEO SHOWS THE PRESIDENT EATING A SEQUENCE OF SMALL CHILDREN NESTED WITHIN EACH OTHER LIKE SOME NIGHTMARISH TURDUCKEN. NOW, SPORTS!
NEWS LIVE

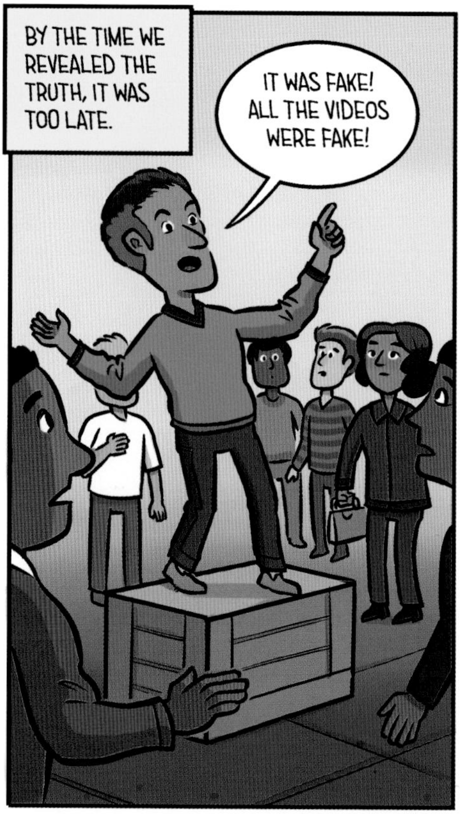
BY THE TIME WE REVEALED THE TRUTH, IT WAS TOO LATE.
IT WAS FAKE! ALL THE VIDEOS WERE FAKE!

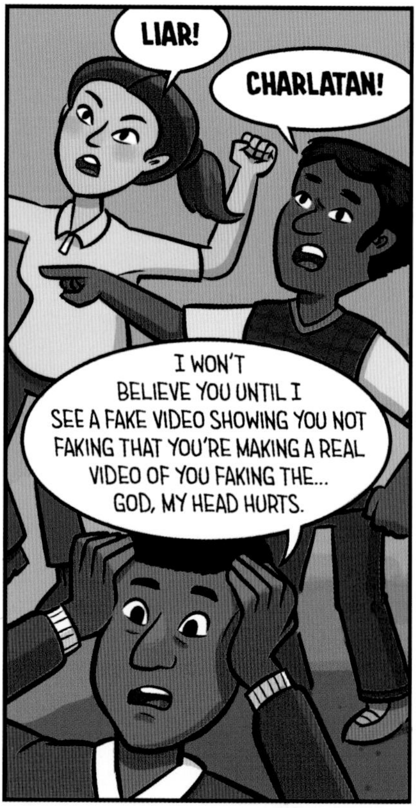
LIAR!
CHARLATAN!
I WON'T BELIEVE YOU UNTIL I SEE A FAKE VIDEO SHOWING YOU NOT FAKING THAT YOU'RE MAKING A REAL VIDEO OF YOU FAKING THE... GOD, MY HEAD HURTS.

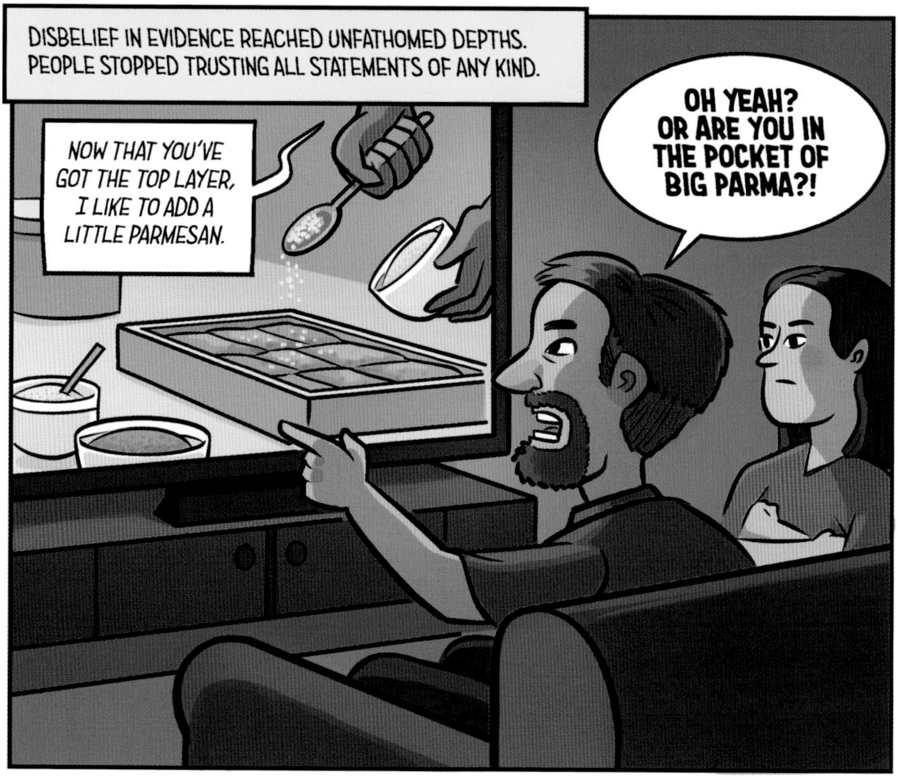
DISBELIEF IN EVIDENCE REACHED UNFATHOMED DEPTHS. PEOPLE STOPPED TRUSTING ALL STATEMENTS OF ANY KIND.
NOW THAT YOU'VE GOT THE TOP LAYER, I LIKE TO ADD A LITTLE PARMESAN.
OH YEAH? OR ARE YOU IN THE POCKET OF BIG PARMA?!

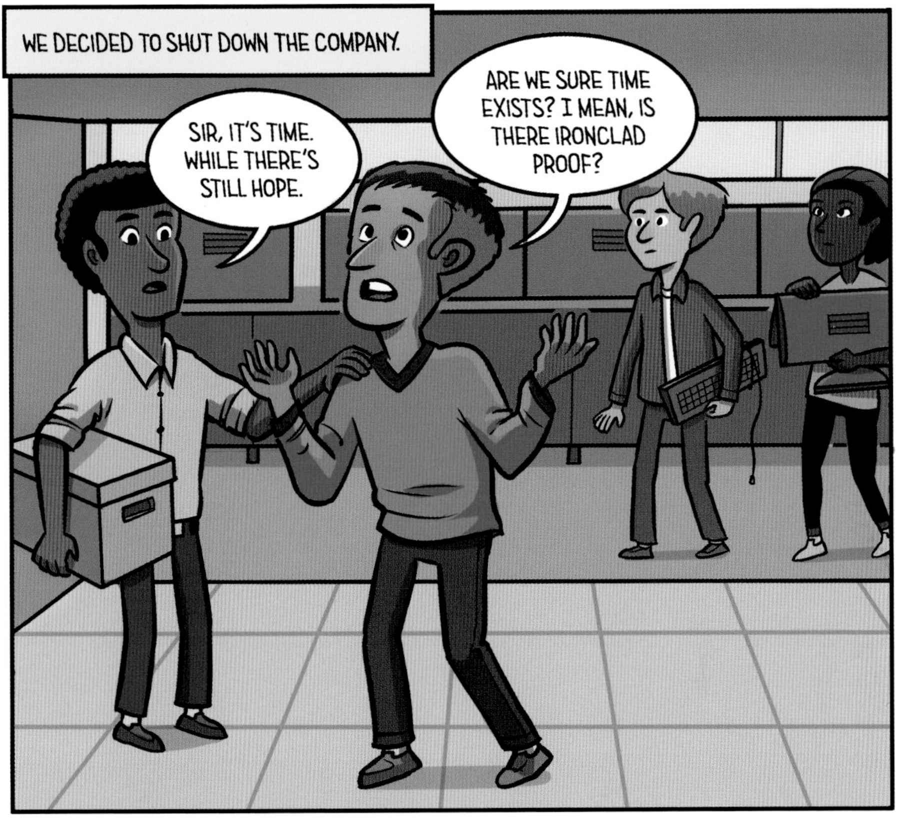
WE DECIDED TO SHUT DOWN THE COMPANY.
SIR, IT'S TIME. WHILE THERE'S STILL HOPE.
ARE WE SURE TIME EXISTS? I MEAN, IS THERE IRONCLAD PROOF?

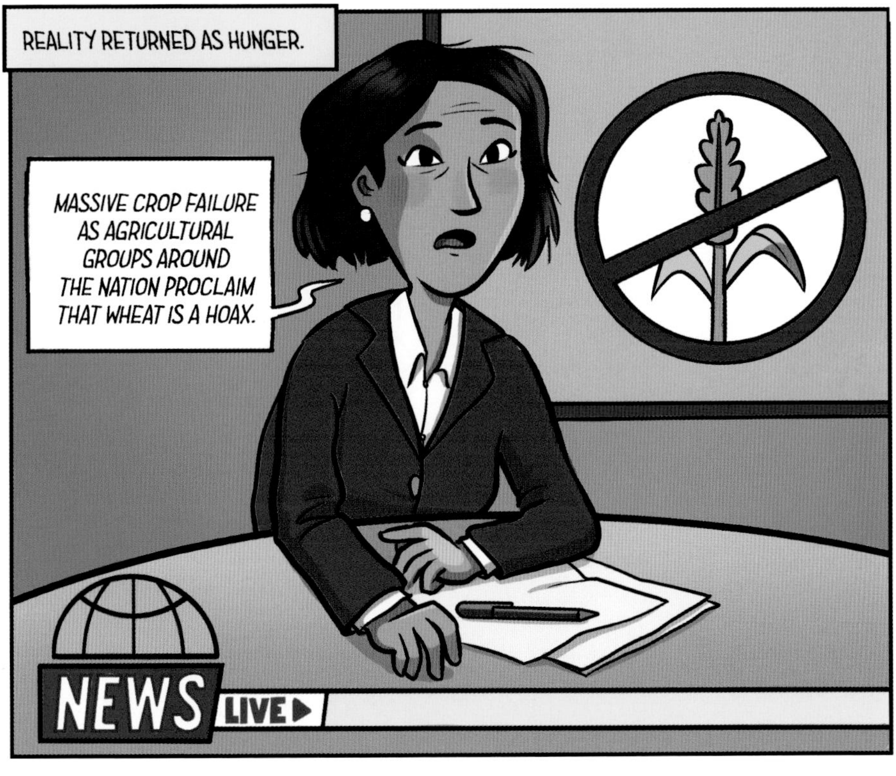
REALITY RETURNED AS HUNGER.
MASSIVE CROP FAILURE AS AGRICULTURAL GROUPS AROUND THE NATION PROCLAIM THAT WHEAT IS A HOAX.
NEWS
LIVE

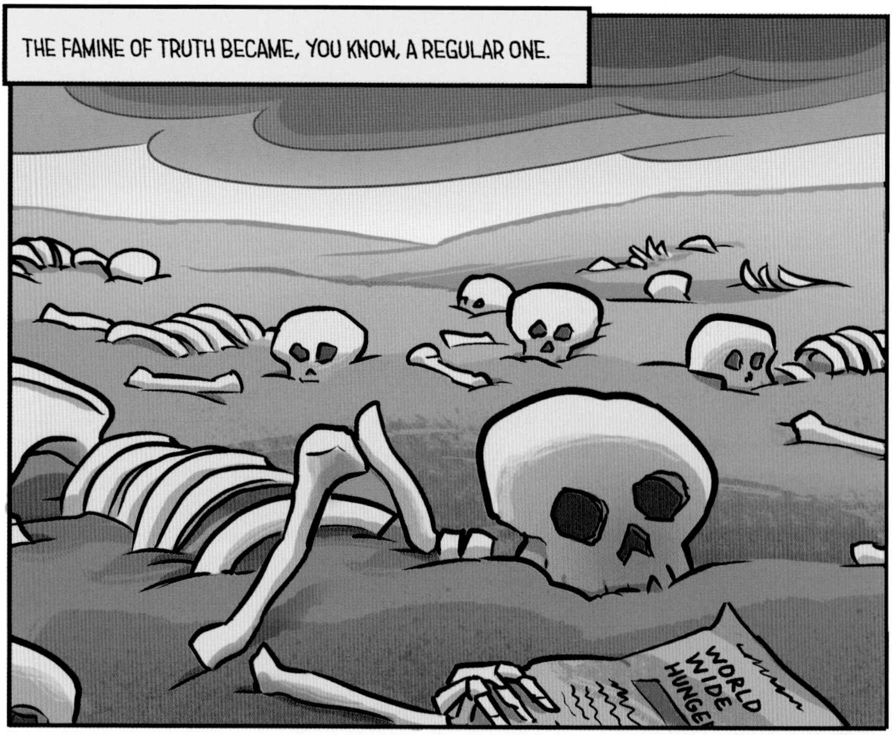

THE FAMINE OF TRUTH BECAME, YOU KNOW, A REGULAR ONE.
WORLD WIDE HUNGE

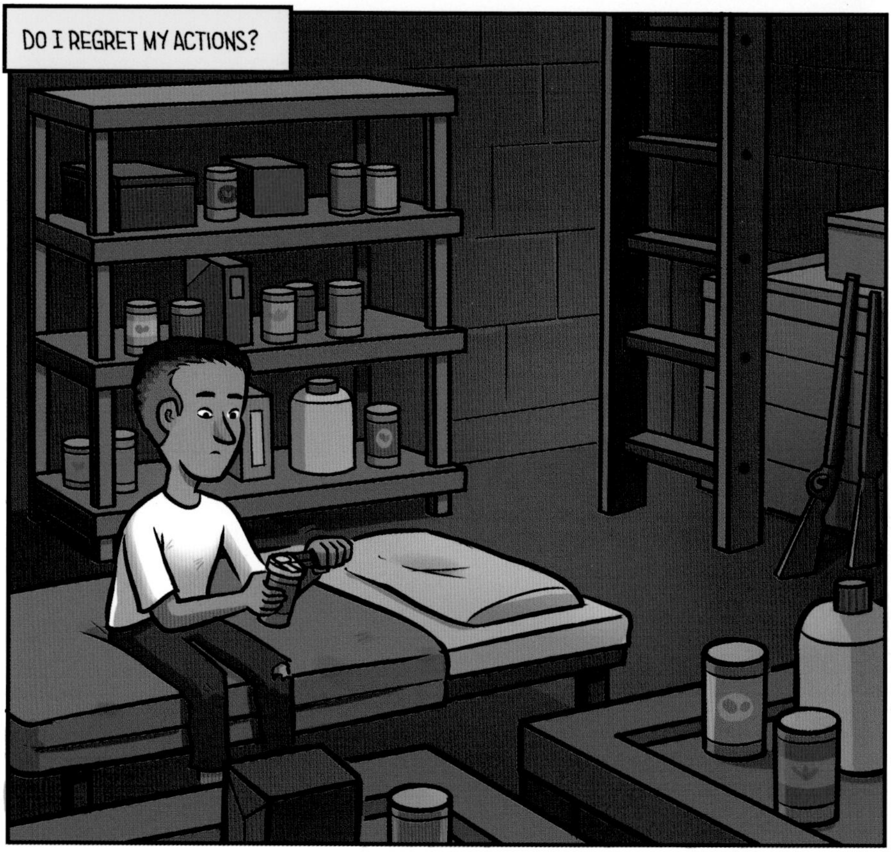

DO I REGRET MY ACTIONS?

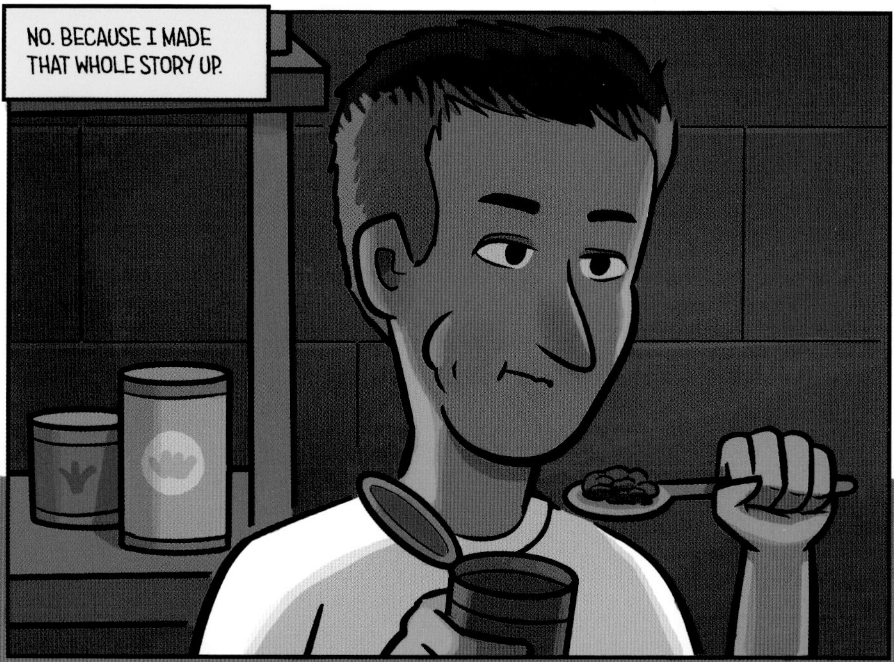
NO. BECAUSE I MADE
THAT WHOLE STORY UP.

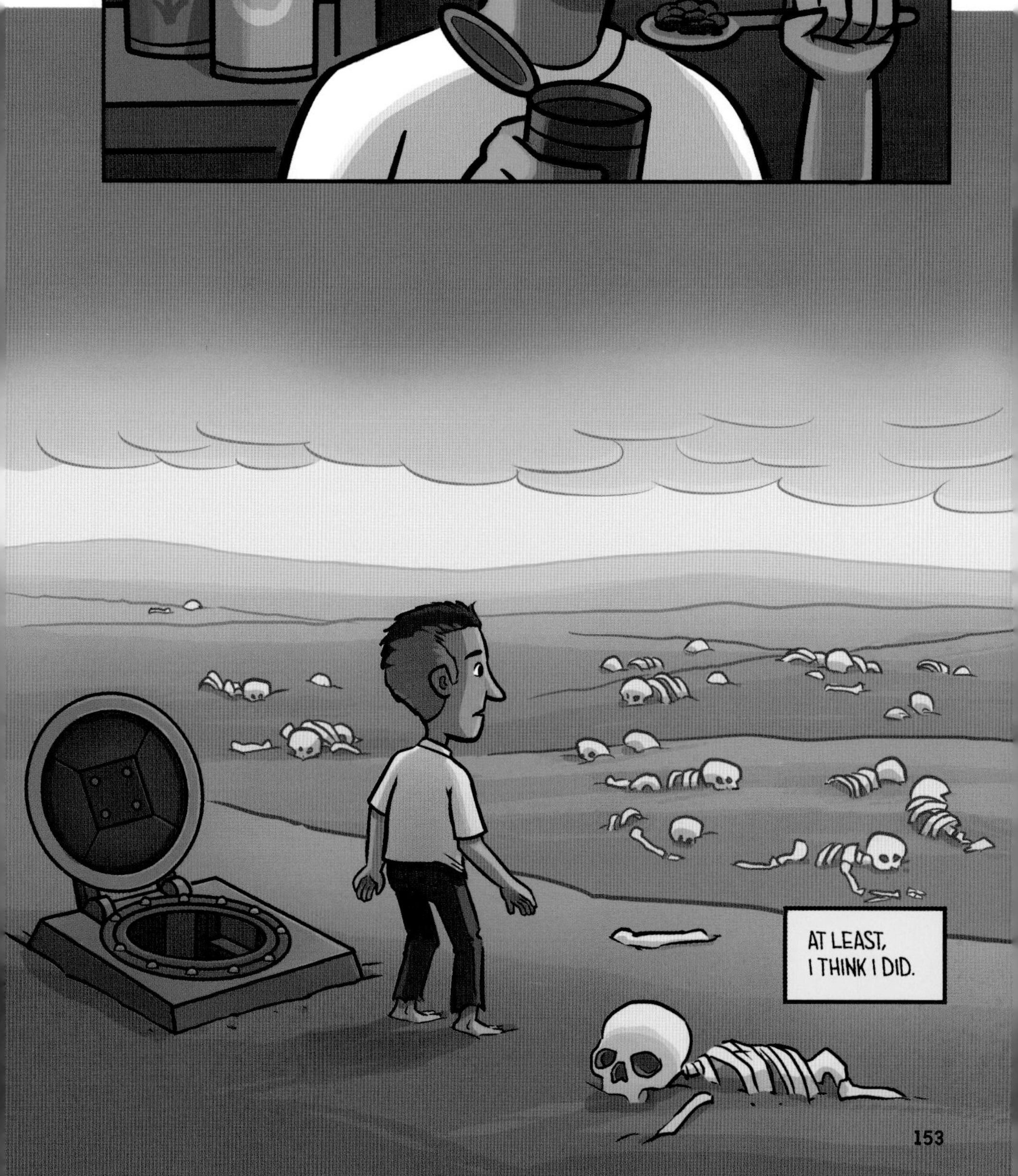
AT LEAST,
I THINK I DID.

UNREEL
WHAT IF FAKE NEWS WINS?

ON A HUMID FALL EVENING IN WASHINGTON, D.C., A group of tipsy wedding guests gathered around a ridiculously large island in an Airbnb to listen to something I had made. It was a gift to the happy couple, something I had spent many hours working on, and I was nervous to reveal it. I turned up the volume on my computer and pressed play. From the tinny, terrible laptop speakers came a voice, the voice of the groom, addressing his bride from the year 2050, waxing poetic about their future together and warning them not to eat the shrimp in Madrid. Then the bride spoke, again from the future, teasing her husband and describing their upcoming adventures together (and warning again about the shrimp in Madrid).

The crowd looked equal parts bemused and confused—how had I created this audio of their friends without them knowing? I then explained that I had trained an AI on thousands of audio clips I had pulled from public talks they'd both given. In other words, I had created a deepfake as a wedding present, because that's the kind of person I am. (For the record, my friends loved the admittedly somewhat creepy gift.)

I am not an especially technical person, and the ease with which I was able to create a moderately convincing vocal replica of my friends' voices shows just how easy it already is to make faked sounds. It's hard to pin down just how good deepfakes will be when you read this, because the field is changing and improving so quickly.[1] Just last month (in my time) a coder released a new open-source software system called Avatarify that allows you to map someone else's face onto yours during a Zoom meeting, creating a living deepfake as you conference call. Right now, many of these fake videos are just glitchy enough to be identified as fakes, but that gap is closing rapidly. Alongside these deepfake technologies, basic audio, video, and photo editing software is becoming more accessible to people, leading to a rise in what Sam Gregory from the human rights organization WITNESS calls "shallowfakes."

In the future, as these systems get faster and more reliable, any of you reading this now will be able to log on to an app or website and create your own versions of reality. You will be able to, in the immortal words of the 1984 film *The Dungeonmaster*, "reject your reality and substitute my own!"

---

1   One of the most challenging things about reporting on the future is that it keeps happening right under your nose.

This ability to generate chaos using faked images, sounds, and video isn't new. In 1982, an audio recording of a phone call between Margaret Thatcher and Ronald Reagan surfaced in which Thatcher admitted that she sacrificed a British ship to escalate the Falklands War and provide an excuse for British intervention. If it were true, it would have huge implications not just for Thatcher, but for an entire war that took the lives of nearly one thousand people. But the tape turned out to be fake—a hoax later dubbed "Thatchergate" and crafted by an anarchist punk band named Crass, who had spliced together bits and pieces of speeches delivered by the two leaders.

You've almost certainly seen a faked image used in a newspaper at some point or another. In 2008, for example, the *New York Times*, the *Los Angeles Times*, the *Chicago Tribune*, BBC News, MSNBC, and more all published a photograph showing four Iranian missiles streaking up into the sky from the ground, leaving a trail of dust behind them. In fact, there had only been three missiles that successfully fired in the tests, not four. Iranian state media has added the fourth (which failed to fire) in a bit of revisionist history. An extra fourth missile might not seem like a big deal, but it suggested that the Iranians were ever so slightly more powerful and successful than they really were.

I'm going to wager a guess that none of this surprises you all that much. A 2017 study found that in the months surrounding the 2016 United States presidential election, the average American adult saw at least one fake news story, and over half of those people remembered believing those stories. A 2018 study analyzed a huge Twitter data set—126,000 stories, shared by three million people more than 4.5 million times—and found that fake stories not only spread far more than real ones, but far more quickly, too. On average, they found that a false story reached 1,500 people six times faster than a true one, and false stories were 70 percent more likely to be retweeted than their accurate counterparts.

You're likely familiar with the scourge of "fake news." After every major news event, there is a flood of visual misinformation—some of which happens organically, and some of which is specifically designed to sow chaos and discord. As I write this, misinformation about the COVID-19 pandemic is buzzing about— everything from theories about the virus being a biological weapon, to racist memes about Chinese carriers, to false stories about hospitals built in a day.

These fakes are particularly rampant during a fast-moving news story, said Jane Lytvynenko, a media writer at BuzzFeed who reports on misinformation. "Breaking news situations create an information vacuum," she told me. People are logging on, looking to hear the latest developments, but those developments take time for reporters to gather and confirm. "Actual information takes time, but misinformation doesn't. It takes seconds," Lytvynenko said. Grabbing a photo from the web and captioning it with something fake is far faster and easier than confirming a story with a source.

This is why during nearly every hurricane you see the same images of sharks swimming in the city, or a storm cloud over the Statue of Liberty. It's why a tweet claiming that during the pandemic the canals of Venice cleared up and as a result swans have returned to the area has almost a million likes. (In fact, the swans had never left in the first place.)

But perhaps the scariest part of all of this is that it doesn't seem to matter. In January of 2020, Arizona representative Paul A. Gosar tweeted an image of former U.S. president Barack Obama shaking hands with Iranian president Hassan Rouhani saying, "The world is a better place without these guys in power." When users pointed out to him that the photo was (fairly obviously) fake, he replied that it didn't matter: "No one said this wasn't photoshopped." (It's perhaps also worth noting Rouhani is still the president of Iran, so not only was the tweet of a fake image, it was also nonsensical.)

In a world saturated with manipulated images and videos, the problem isn't simply with the fabricated content itself. It's that their very existence opens up questions about the veracity of almost everything. In June 2019, a deputy Malaysian minister's secretary was arrested after a video of him having sex with the country's economic affairs minister spread through WhatsApp like wildfire. To this day it's unclear whether the video is a fake or not, with one side claiming it is and others pointing to a confession video that the secretary uploaded later, which of course some claim is also a fake. In 2018, a strangely shot video of the president of Gabon ignited rumors that he was in fact dead, and the government was creating deepfakes of him to hide that fact. These rumors led to a military coup attempt. But experts who analyzed the video in question found no definitive signs it was fake, and the president later made public appearances, very much alive.

Human brains, bless them, are both incredibly powerful and incredibly foolish. Research on memory has revealed that we're incredibly susceptible to falling for fakes—one study suggests that seeing faked images of protests, doctored to look more violent than they were, impacted how people feel about attending actions in the future. Another study was able to plant a fake memory in participants' brains just by showing them an image of themselves shaking hands with Bugs Bunny at Disneyland (an intellectual property impossibility, as Bugs is a Warner Bros. character).

Research also shows that debunking images doesn't always work and can even backfire—some studies suggest that if you simply ask people to reverse their opinion about a piece of fake news ("Have you considered the vast body of evidence that vaccines do not in fact cause autism?"), it can often have the opposite effect. This isn't always because the person in question is some kind of toddler in an adult body, stubbornly refusing to update their world view in the face of new information. Sometimes it's because the debunking doesn't explain why something is wrong, or doesn't provide enough information to replace the initial falsity. Sometimes it's because people simply can't remember which bit of information they heard was the true one. "Human memory is not a recording device, but rather a process of (re)construction that is vulnerable to both internal and external influences," write researchers Ilse Van Damme and Karolien Smets. Emotion can cloud our memories, too; if we're angry or scared or confused, we have a harder time figuring out which bits of information to keep in our neural storage system.

So what do we do to combat fakes? Computer scientists all over the world are working on fake-detection algorithms, systems specifically designed to spot the signs of trickery. Other groups are working on secure signatures—invisible watermarks that you can embed into verified images and photos to authenticate as real. But the real solution will likely come from you and me, and retraining our little lumpy brains and trigger-happy fingers to ask questions before we share a story.

Lytvynenko suggests always taking a minute before you share something and checking it out. Is that what that place actually looks like? Is that what the weather is like this time of year in Wuhan? Does anything look amiss? Learning how to use reverse image search can be helpful too, so you can see whether an image had been used before and where it comes from.

Another form of retraining might come in the form of a digital "vaccine" against sharing fake news. "We need to get people to generate active antibodies against misinformation," said Sander van der Linden, a researcher at the University of Cambridge. Van der Linden is part of a team that recently released a game called "Bad News," which invites the player to cast aside their ethics and become a peddler of misinformation. As a player, you're presented with choices like "fake an official Twitter account" and "personally attack scientists" in your quest to dominate the news cycle through misinformation. As you play, you earn badges like "impersonation" and "emotion."

The idea is that by stepping into the world of disinformation and seeing the tactics and techniques used by bad actors up close, users would then be "inoculated" against those techniques in the future. And preliminary research suggests that the game works. Not only did playing Bad News make study subjects better at spotting misinformation techniques, it also made them more confident in their own judgments about viral memes and tweets. Games like Bad News alone won't save us from descent into deep fake chaos, but much like regular vaccines, the more people who are inoculated, the more likely we are to be protected as a herd from getting lost in a sea of misinformation.

Bad News might be a fun game, but the stakes here are high. Misinformation can be deadly. The anti-vaccine movement, predicated largely on the false notion that vaccines cause autism, has helped spur a deadly surge in measles cases—a disease the CDC once called "eliminated" in the U.S. In 2005, an Australian woman named Penelope Dingle died of colon cancer that doctors considered treatable because she opted instead for vitamin C and extracts from the Venus flytrap plant on the advice of a homeopathic doctor. In 2018, a false story spread across Nigerian social media that led to at least ten people being murdered in acts of retribution for something that never happened. Losing this battle is about more than spending the rest of your life thinking there were never swans in Venice.

We've all constructed our own labyrinthine network to filter the information we get about what's going on in the world. Research shows that we're more likely to agree with stories that confirm our world view, fake or otherwise. And disinformation trolls know that and target their efforts accordingly. Given how easy it is for our gray matter to be bamboozled, the future of facts, news, and truth could get turned upside down.

I have been thinking a lot recently about one of my favorite books as a kid (and, if I'm honest, as an adult): *The Phantom Tollbooth*. In the book, our hero is a young boy named Milo who goes on an adventure through a series of pun-driven lands. In each place, the rules of play are totally different—Dictionopolis, where words battle for dominance; Doldrums, where nothing happens; Digitopolis, where numbers rule—and at one point he enters a town called Point of View, where he meets a little boy named Alec Bings, who floats in the air above the ground because he has not grown down to it yet. "Well, in my family everyone is born in the air, with his head at exactly the height it's going to be when he's an adult, and then we all grow toward the ground," explains Alec.

And this can be how it feels sometimes, to speak with people whose entire view of the world and what is real differs from yours. To them, it's as natural as can be to think—not just think, know—that the world is flat, or that vaccines cause autism, or that Obama was able to manipulate the weather to cause droughts in California (something my grandparents at one point believed). They have their own set of facts, and often their own set of visual evidence to back themselves up. And in the future, if these sets of ideas and facts become entrenched in one place or another, it could become unsafe to travel between a place that, for example, believes in vaccines and a place that doesn't. Or a place that has taken measures to tamp down a pandemic and a place that has decided to reopen despite scientific experts advising against it.

In the face of all of this, it can feel tempting sometimes to go full nihilist and chalk the Internet up as a lost cause, a black hole of mystery and hoaxes and misinformation. But choosing that path has bigger implications than you might think, because the Internet isn't some separate space we can unplug from. It's a mirror, a big communal pool. "We need informed citizens to participate in our democratic institutions in order for them to function properly," said Lytvynenko. "I simultaneously don't blame people who check out, and I'm very, very afraid for the nightmare scenario that that could cause." (You see the results of that in the comic, a world where no one believes anything at all and the famine of truth becomes a literal famine.) Our collective agreement on this earth, in my opinion, is to try and do our best with the information we have available. If we give up on the second part of that mission and stop trying to understand the reality of the world around us, we give up on each other entirely. It's better to try and get it wrong sometimes than to not try at all.

A world saturated by fakes would be a surreal experience—one of excitement, incredible art, and fascinating experiments, as well as disconnect, conflict, and confusion. There will be ethical deepfakes—images created for good and used to help people heal, handle anxiety, and prepare for challenging situations. There will be images that are used for justice, but in unethical ways, as we see in the comic. There will be images used to create chaos and fear, images used to unite and to divide. The possibilities are endless, and maybe that's the scariest part.

Perhaps this would spell the end of the digital era and usher in a future in which the physical is king. We trust only what we can see in person, only what we can touch and smell. We give up on long-distance communication, photographs, and recordings. It's also possible in this world that anonymity will once again be prized. "The only way to be functional is to hide everything, which actually really excites me," said Jenna Wortham, a culture writer for the *New York Times*. "Maybe instead of Inbox Zero, it's Digital Footprint Zero," Wortham said. "There's not enough information about you online to make one of these videos, and then that becomes the thing that's highly, highly, highly prioritized."

Or perhaps, once we get over the strangeness of it all, this future could be liberating. We no longer have to craft our perfect online persona, an intricate bowerbird's nest of profiles and endorsements and well-filtered photos. When our faces and bodies can be used and manipulated however anybody likes, and fake videos abound, we could be freed from the expectations of a perfectly manicured presence. It would certainly also be chaos, but an alluring chaos that could come with a kind of freedom. Is that really a video of me riding a dolphin in a hot dog costume? Who can say? And I'll never tell.

GHOSTBOT

BY KATE SHERIDAN

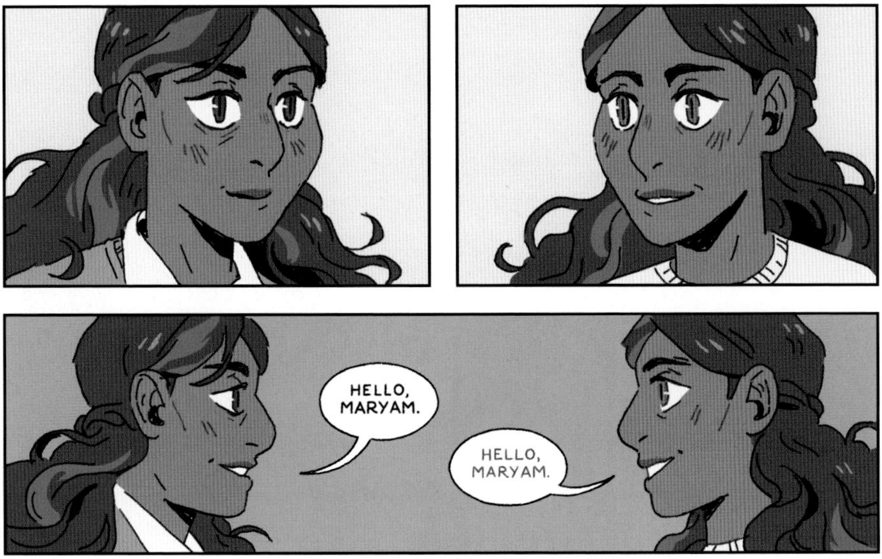
HELLO, MARYAM.
HELLO, MARYAM.

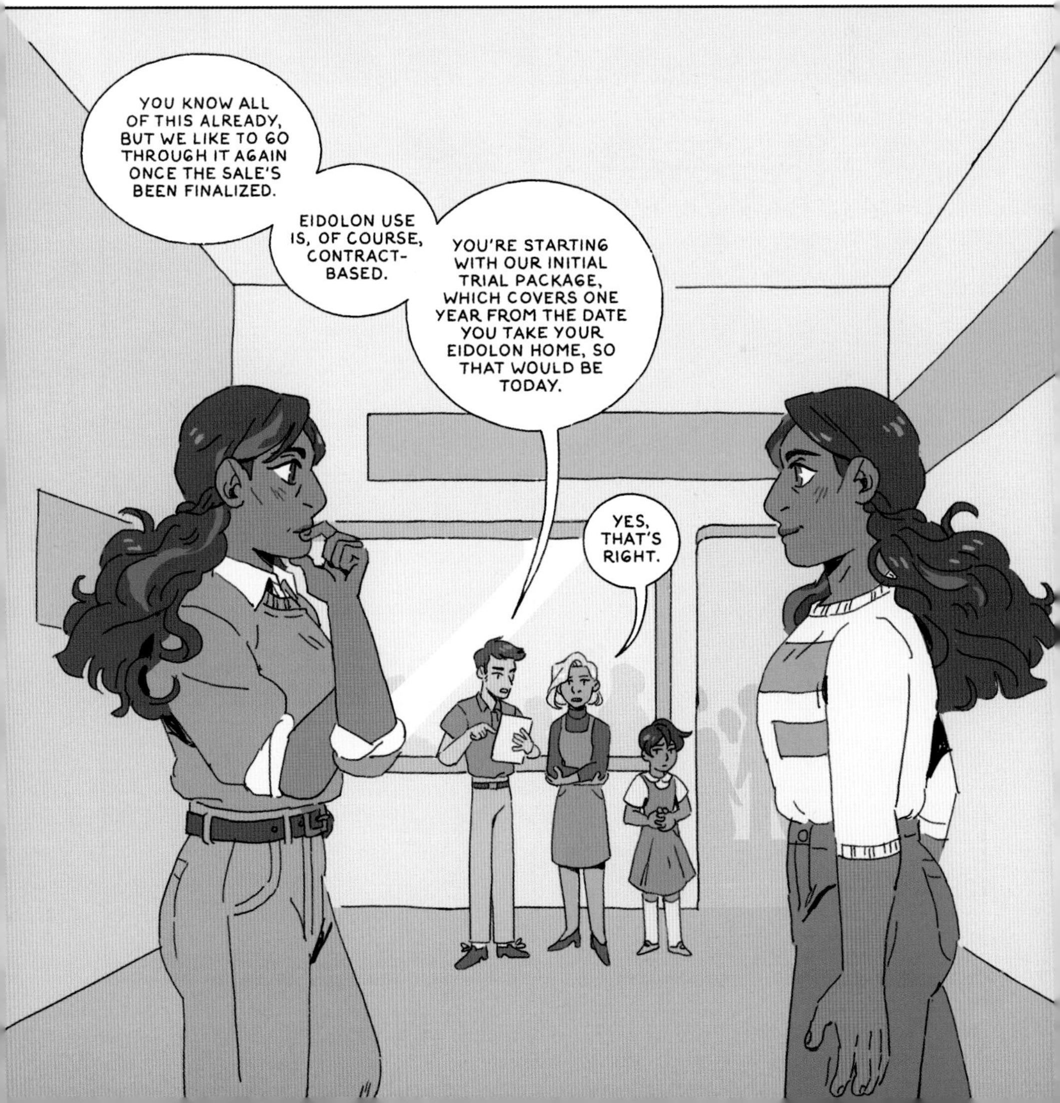
YOU KNOW ALL OF THIS ALREADY, BUT WE LIKE TO GO THROUGH IT AGAIN ONCE THE SALE'S BEEN FINALIZED.
EIDOLON USE IS, OF COURSE, CONTRACT-BASED.
YOU'RE STARTING WITH OUR INITIAL TRIAL PACKAGE, WHICH COVERS ONE YEAR FROM THE DATE YOU TAKE YOUR EIDOLON HOME, SO THAT WOULD BE TODAY.
YES, THAT'S RIGHT.

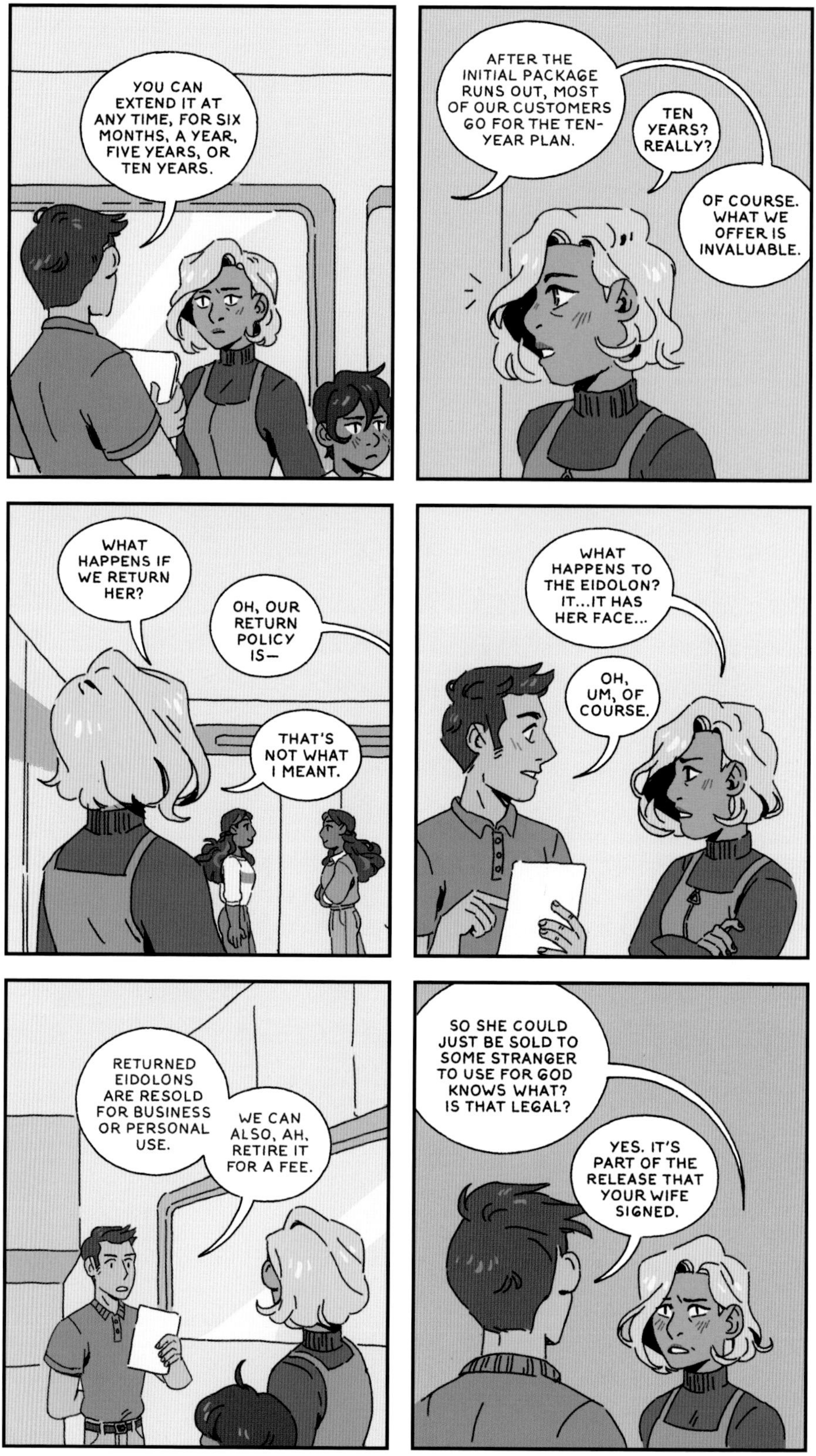
YOU CAN EXTEND IT AT ANY TIME, FOR SIX MONTHS, A YEAR, FIVE YEARS, OR TEN YEARS.
AFTER THE INITIAL PACKAGE RUNS OUT, MOST OF OUR CUSTOMERS GO FOR THE TEN-YEAR PLAN.
TEN YEARS? REALLY?
OF COURSE. WHAT WE OFFER IS INVALUABLE.
WHAT HAPPENS IF WE RETURN HER?
OH, OUR RETURN POLICY IS—
THAT'S NOT WHAT I MEANT.
WHAT HAPPENS TO THE EIDOLON? IT...IT HAS HER FACE...
OH, UM, OF COURSE.
RETURNED EIDOLONS ARE RESOLD FOR BUSINESS OR PERSONAL USE.
WE CAN ALSO, AH, RETIRE IT FOR A FEE.
SO SHE COULD JUST BE SOLD TO SOME STRANGER TO USE FOR GOD KNOWS WHAT? IS THAT LEGAL?
YES. IT'S PART OF THE RELEASE THAT YOUR WIFE SIGNED.

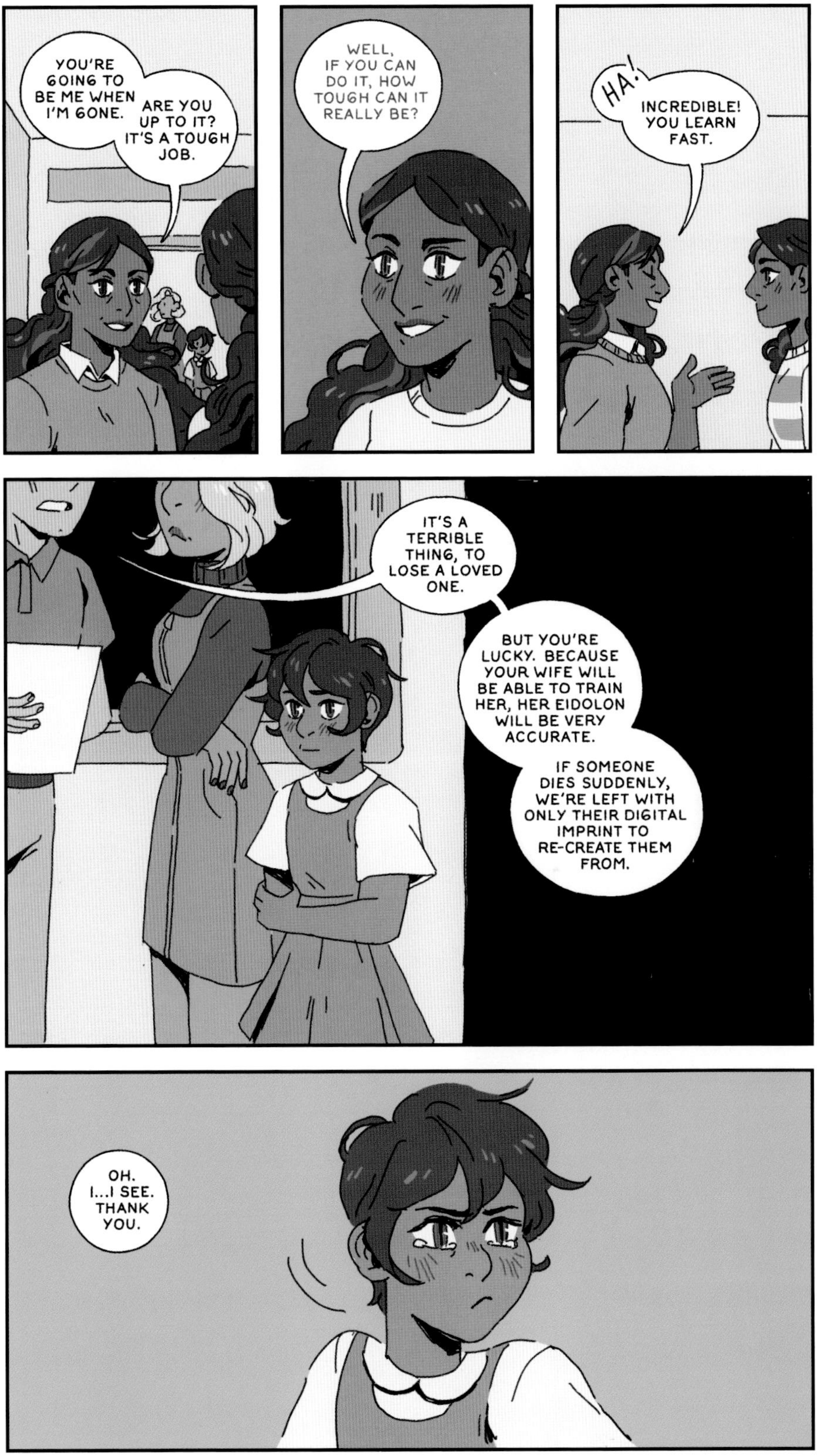
YOU'RE GOING TO BE ME WHEN I'M GONE.
ARE YOU UP TO IT? IT'S A TOUGH JOB.
WELL, IF YOU CAN DO IT, HOW TOUGH CAN IT REALLY BE?
HA!
INCREDIBLE! YOU LEARN FAST.
IT'S A TERRIBLE THING, TO LOSE A LOVED ONE.
BUT YOU'RE LUCKY. BECAUSE YOUR WIFE WILL BE ABLE TO TRAIN HER, HER EIDOLON WILL BE VERY ACCURATE.
IF SOMEONE DIES SUDDENLY, WE'RE LEFT WITH ONLY THEIR DIGITAL IMPRINT TO RE-CREATE THEM FROM.
OH. I...I SEE. THANK YOU.

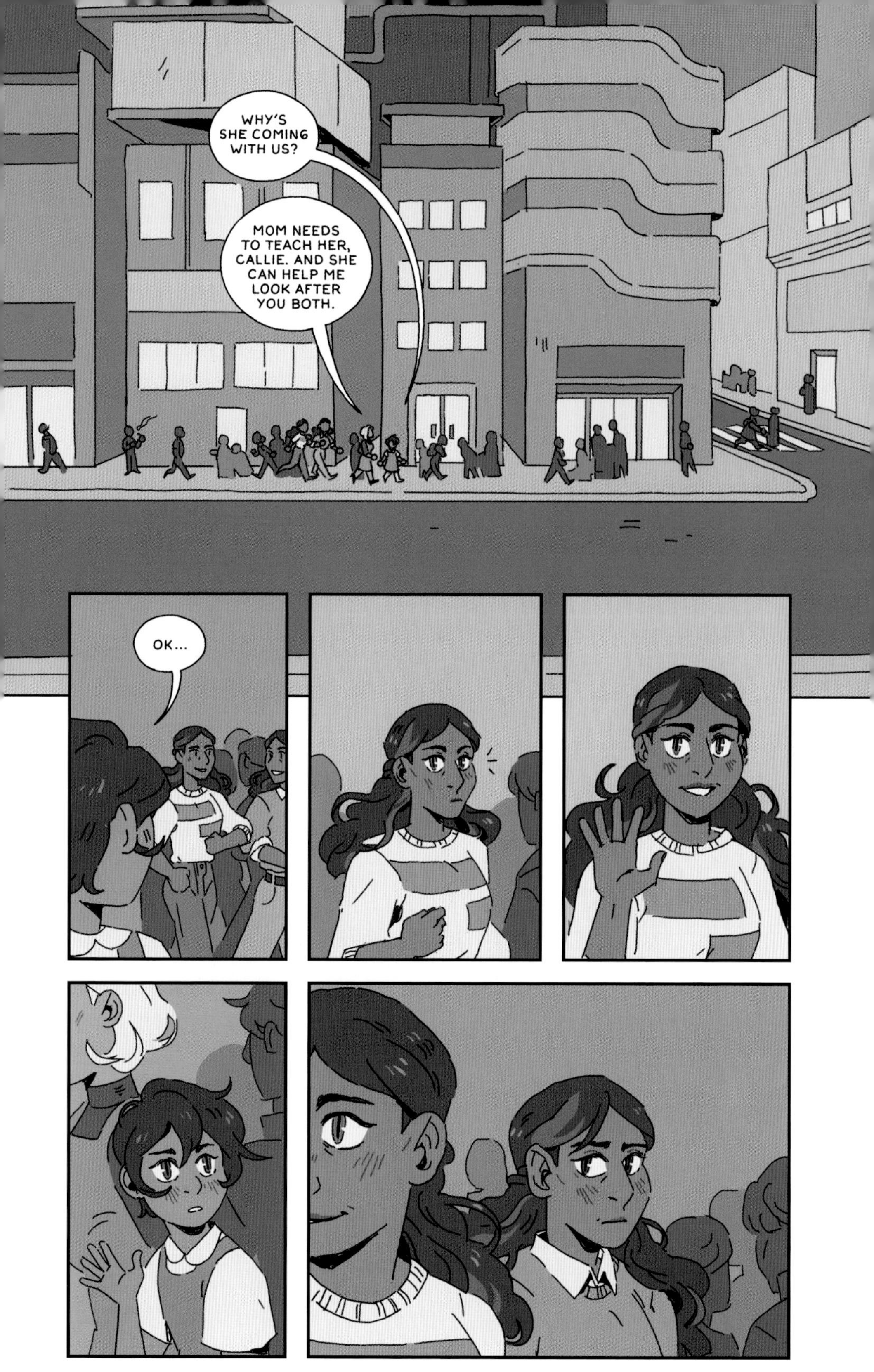
WHY'S SHE COMING WITH US?
MOM NEEDS TO TEACH HER, CALLIE. AND SHE CAN HELP ME LOOK AFTER YOU BOTH.
OK...

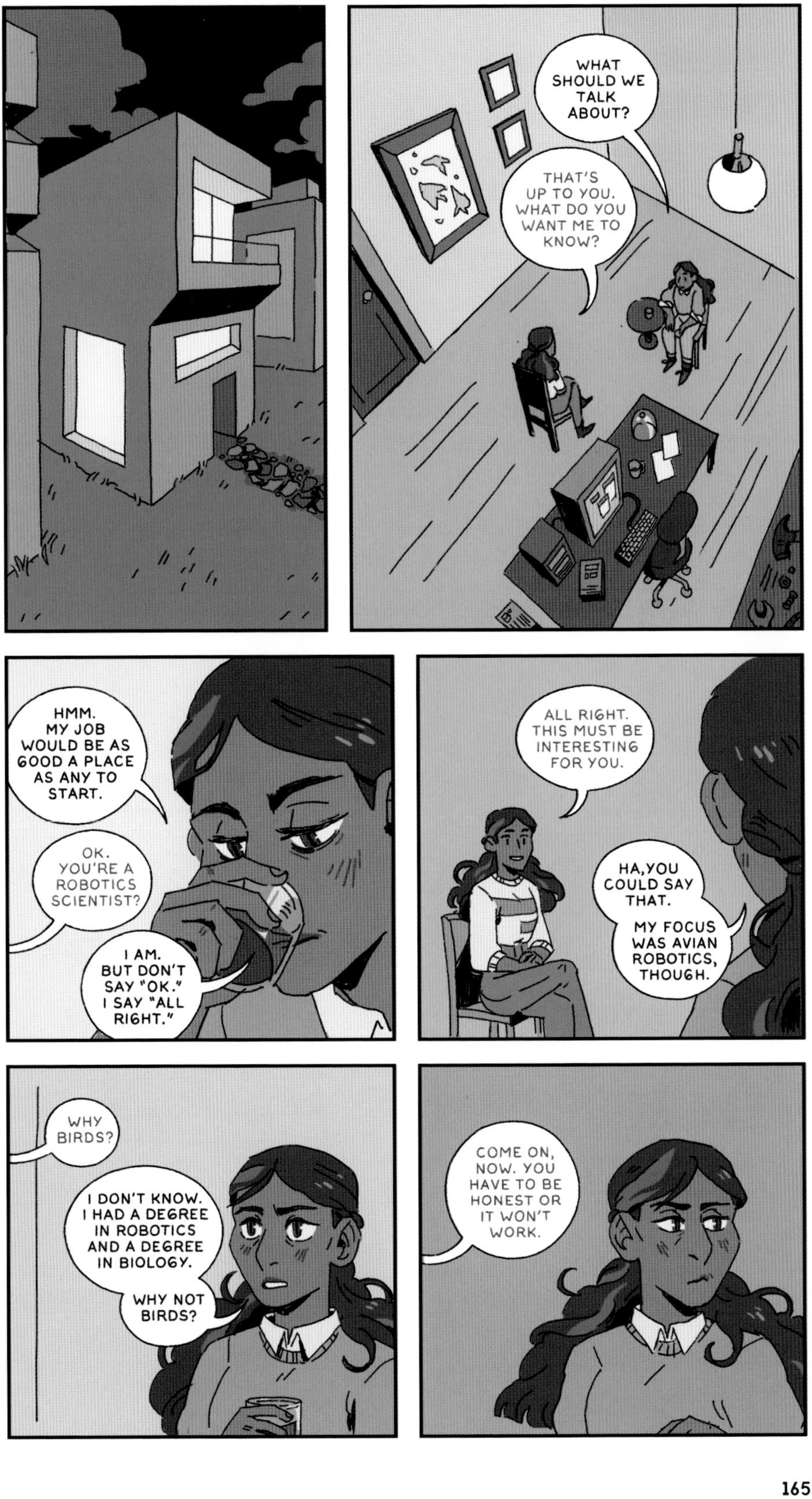
WHAT SHOULD WE TALK ABOUT?
THAT'S UP TO YOU. WHAT DO YOU WANT ME TO KNOW?
HMM. MY JOB WOULD BE AS GOOD A PLACE AS ANY TO START.
OK. YOU'RE A ROBOTICS SCIENTIST?
I AM. BUT DON'T SAY "OK." I SAY "ALL RIGHT."
ALL RIGHT. THIS MUST BE INTERESTING FOR YOU.
HA,YOU COULD SAY THAT.
MY FOCUS WAS AVIAN ROBOTICS, THOUGH.
WHY BIRDS?
I DON'T KNOW. I HAD A DEGREE IN ROBOTICS AND A DEGREE IN BIOLOGY.
WHY NOT BIRDS?
COME ON, NOW. YOU HAVE TO BE HONEST OR IT WON'T WORK.

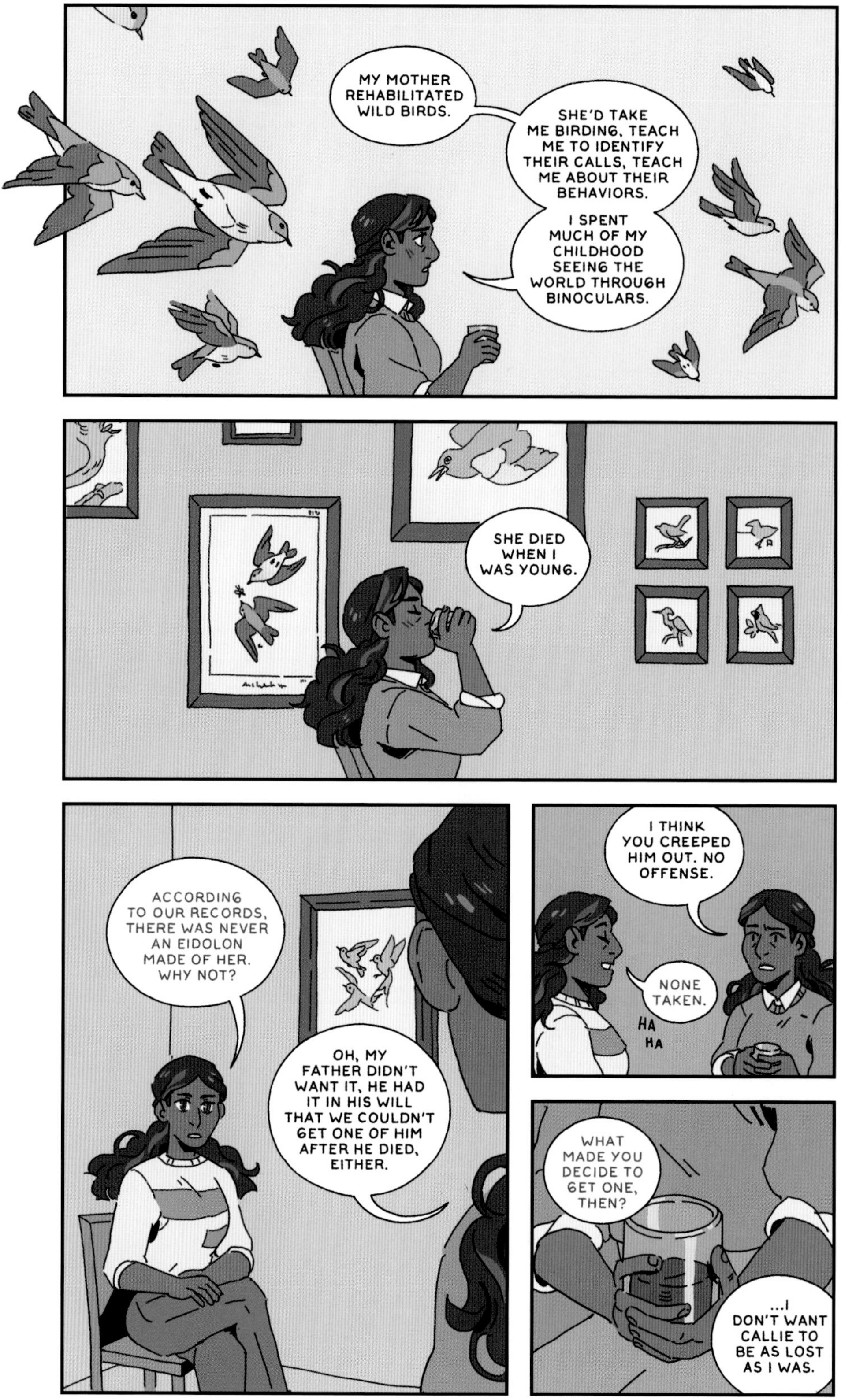
MY MOTHER REHABILITATED WILD BIRDS.
SHE'D TAKE ME BIRDING, TEACH ME TO IDENTIFY THEIR CALLS, TEACH ME ABOUT THEIR BEHAVIORS.
I SPENT MUCH OF MY CHILDHOOD SEEING THE WORLD THROUGH BINOCULARS.
SHE DIED WHEN I WAS YOUNG.
ACCORDING TO OUR RECORDS, THERE WAS NEVER AN EIDOLON MADE OF HER. WHY NOT?
OH, MY FATHER DIDN'T WANT IT, HE HAD IT IN HIS WILL THAT WE COULDN'T GET ONE OF HIM AFTER HE DIED, EITHER.
I THINK YOU CREEPED HIM OUT. NO OFFENSE.
NONE TAKEN.
HA HA
WHAT MADE YOU DECIDE TO GET ONE, THEN?
...I DON'T WANT CALLIE TO BE AS LOST AS I WAS.

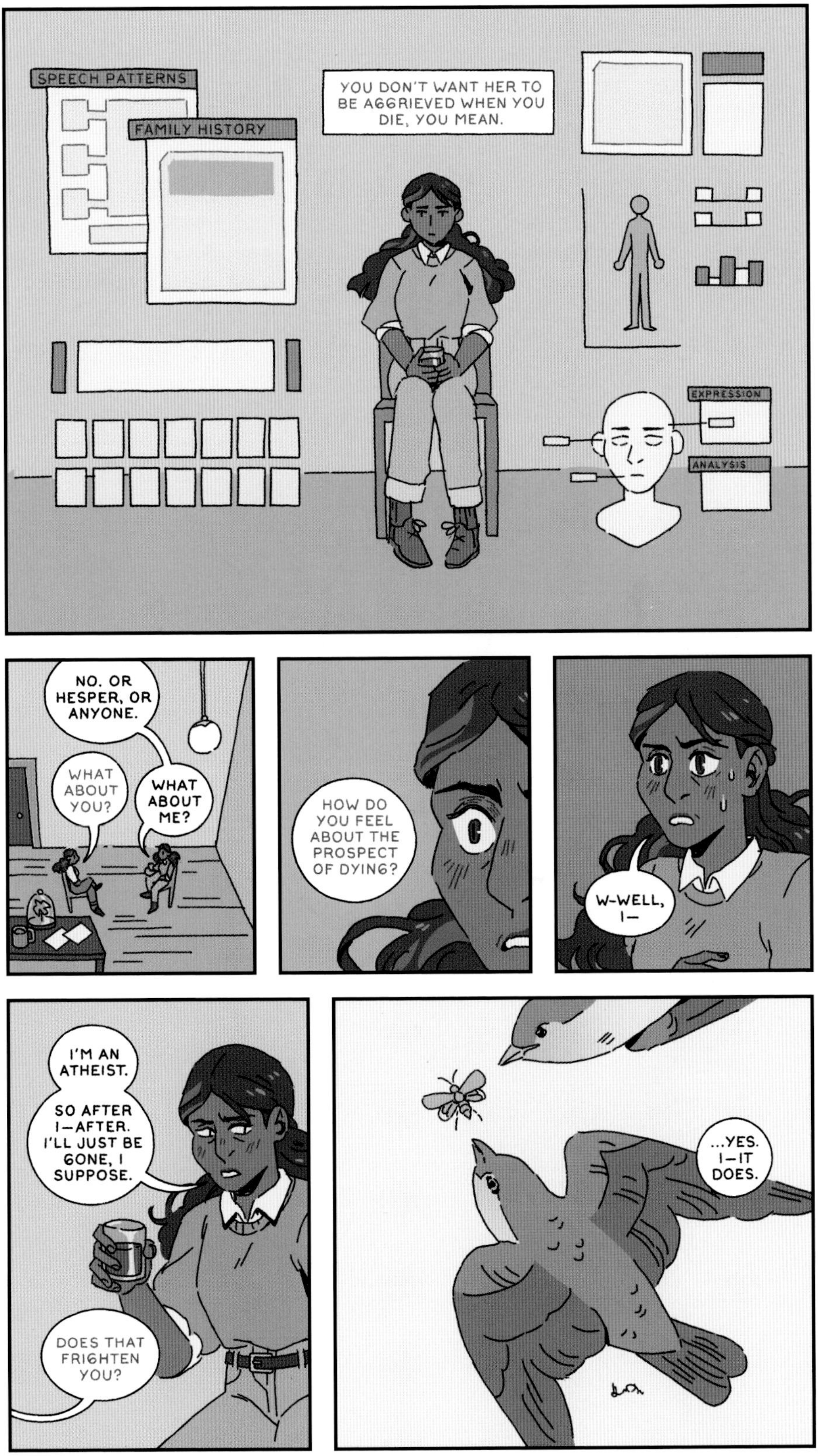
SPEECH PATTERNS
FAMILY HISTORY
YOU DON'T WANT HER TO BE AGGRIEVED WHEN YOU DIE, YOU MEAN.
EXPRESSION
ANALYSIS
NO. OR HESPER, OR ANYONE.
WHAT ABOUT YOU?
WHAT ABOUT ME?
HOW DO YOU FEEL ABOUT THE PROSPECT OF DYING?
W-WELL, I—
I'M AN ATHEIST.
SO AFTER I—AFTER. I'LL JUST BE GONE, I SUPPOSE.
DOES THAT FRIGHTEN YOU?
...YES. I—IT DOES.

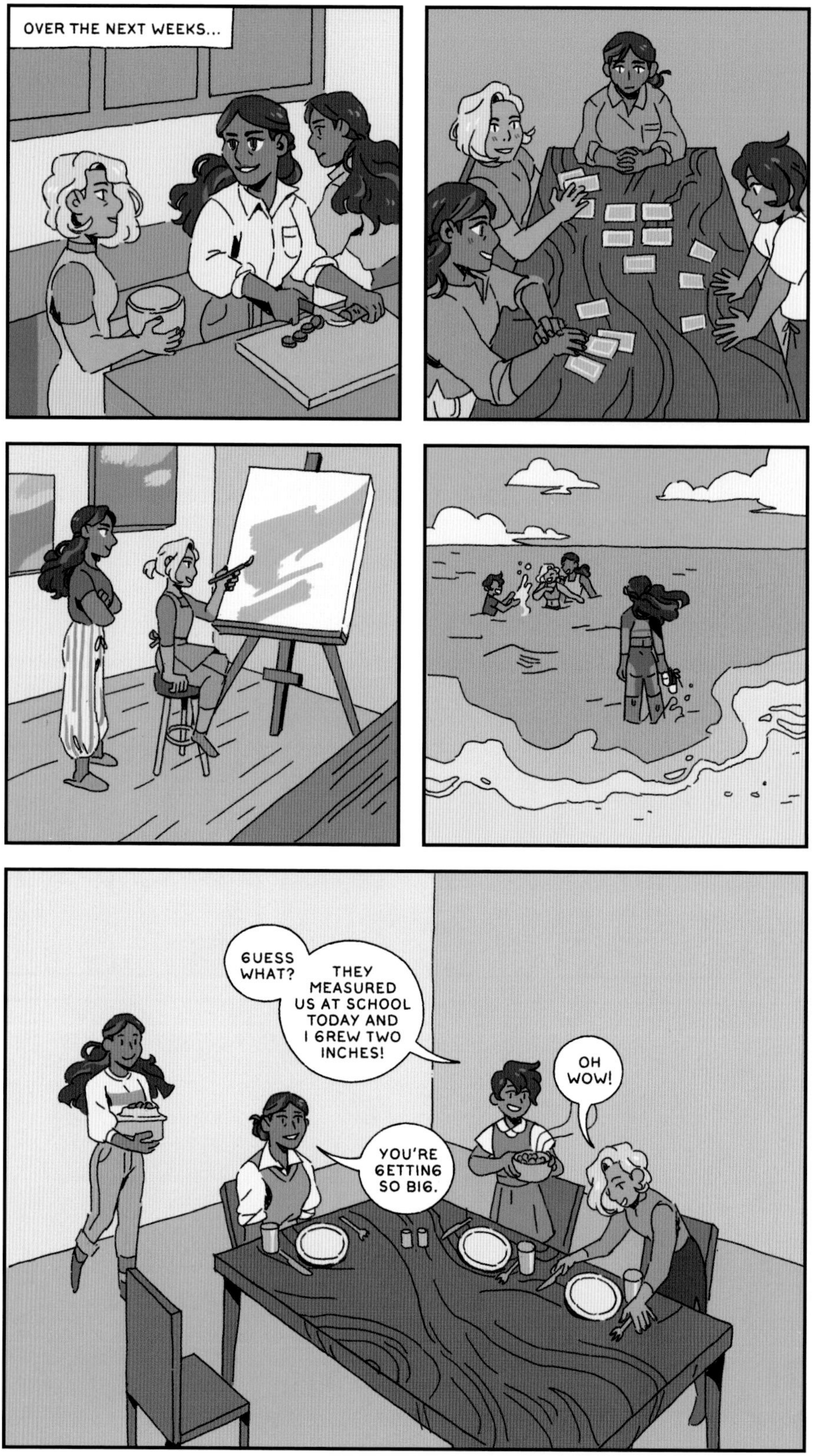
OVER THE NEXT WEEKS...
GUESS WHAT?
THEY MEASURED US AT SCHOOL TODAY AND I GREW TWO INCHES!
OH WOW!
YOU'RE GETTING SO BIG.

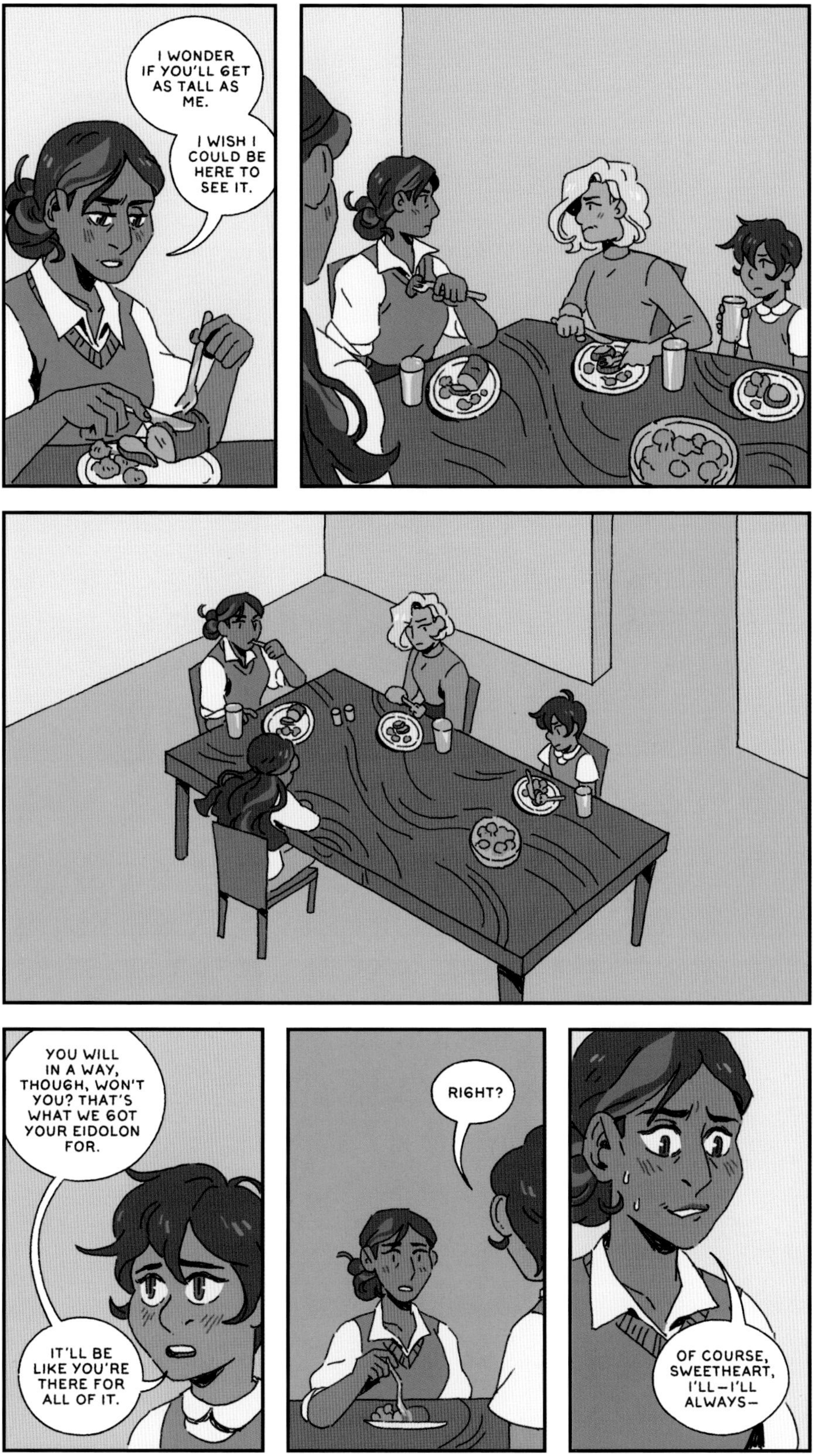
I WONDER IF YOU'LL GET AS TALL AS ME.
I WISH I COULD BE HERE TO SEE IT.
YOU WILL IN A WAY, THOUGH, WON'T YOU? THAT'S WHAT WE GOT YOUR EIDOLON FOR.
IT'LL BE LIKE YOU'RE THERE FOR ALL OF IT.
RIGHT?
OF COURSE, SWEETHEART, I'LL—I'LL ALWAYS—

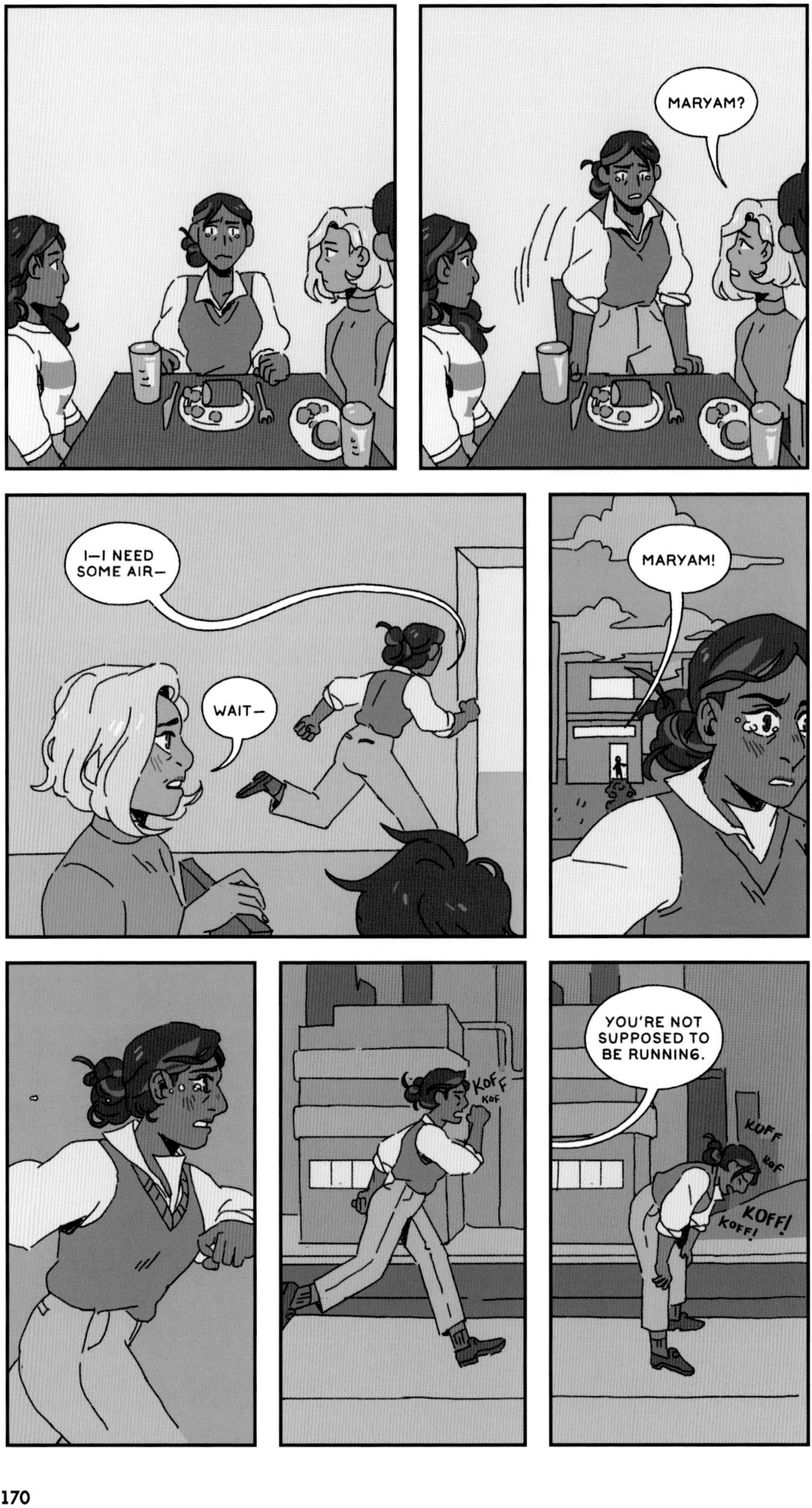
MARYAM?
I—I NEED SOME AIR—
WAIT—
MARYAM!
KOFF
KOF
YOU'RE NOT SUPPOSED TO BE RUNNING.
KOFF
KOF
KOFF!
KOFF!

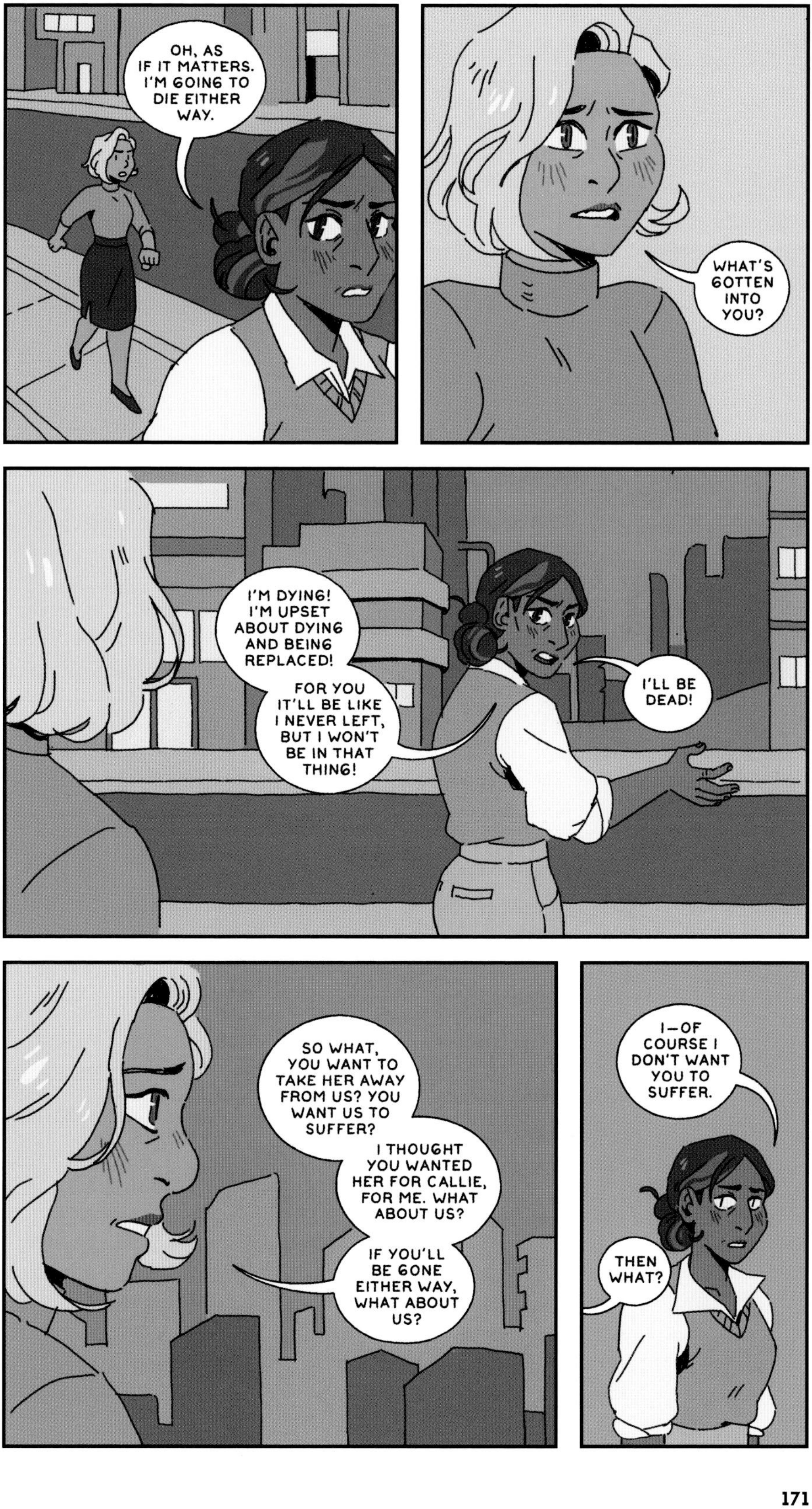
OH, AS IF IT MATTERS. I'M GOING TO DIE EITHER WAY.
WHAT'S GOTTEN INTO YOU?
I'M DYING! I'M UPSET ABOUT DYING AND BEING REPLACED!
FOR YOU IT'LL BE LIKE I NEVER LEFT, BUT I WON'T BE IN THAT THING!
I'LL BE DEAD!
SO WHAT, YOU WANT TO TAKE HER AWAY FROM US? YOU WANT US TO SUFFER?
I THOUGHT YOU WANTED HER FOR CALLIE, FOR ME. WHAT ABOUT US?
IF YOU'LL BE GONE EITHER WAY, WHAT ABOUT US?
I—OF COURSE I DON'T WANT YOU TO SUFFER.
THEN WHAT?

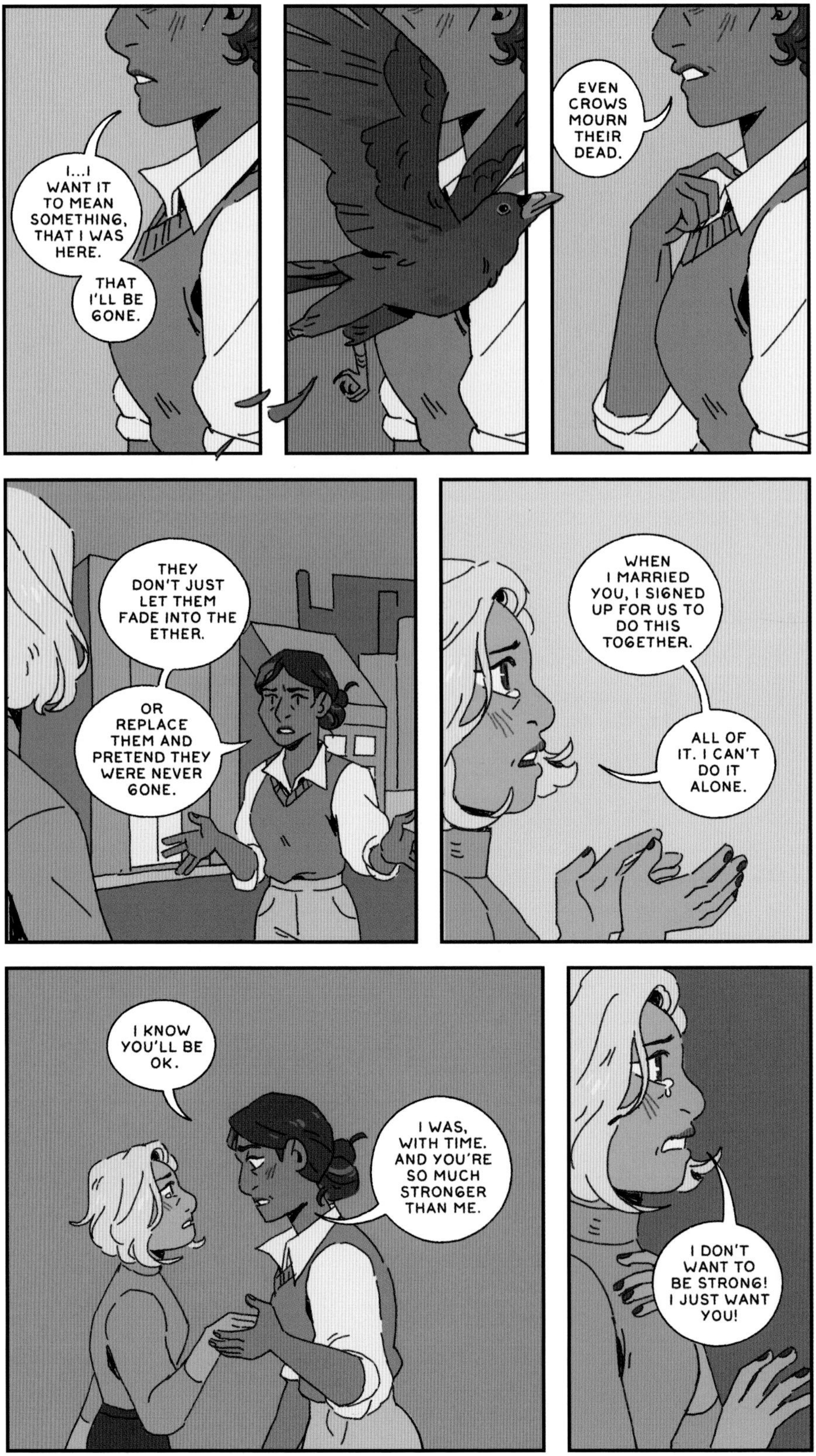
I...I WANT IT TO MEAN SOMETHING, THAT I WAS HERE.
THAT I'LL BE GONE.
EVEN CROWS MOURN THEIR DEAD.
THEY DON'T JUST LET THEM FADE INTO THE ETHER.
OR REPLACE THEM AND PRETEND THEY WERE NEVER GONE.
WHEN I MARRIED YOU, I SIGNED UP FOR US TO DO THIS TOGETHER.
ALL OF IT. I CAN'T DO IT ALONE.
I KNOW YOU'LL BE OK.
I WAS, WITH TIME. AND YOU'RE SO MUCH STRONGER THAN ME.
I DON'T WANT TO BE STRONG! I JUST WANT YOU!

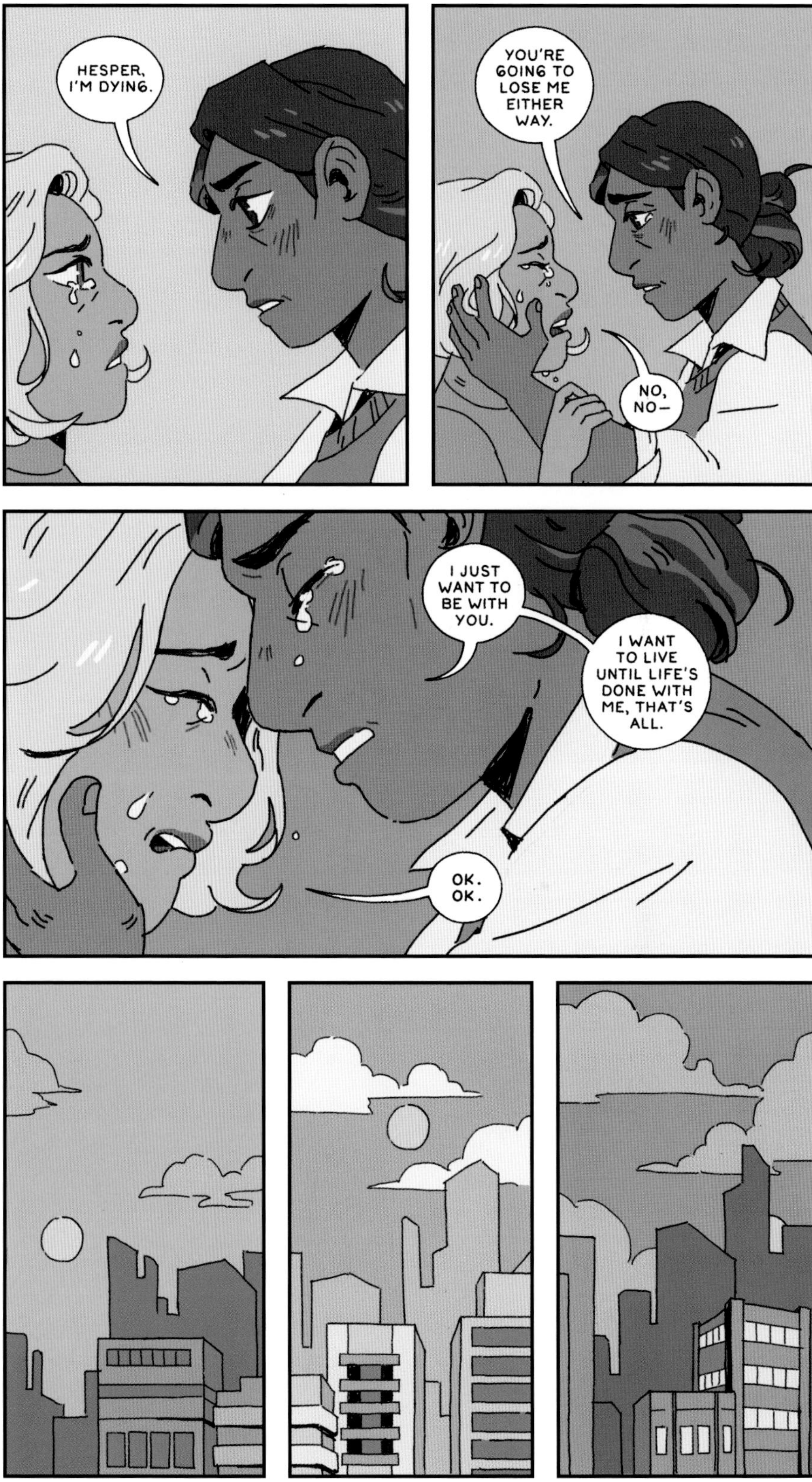
HESPER, I'M DYING.
YOU'RE GOING TO LOSE ME EITHER WAY.
NO, NO—
I JUST WANT TO BE WITH YOU.
I WANT TO LIVE UNTIL LIFE'S DONE WITH ME, THAT'S ALL.
OK. OK.

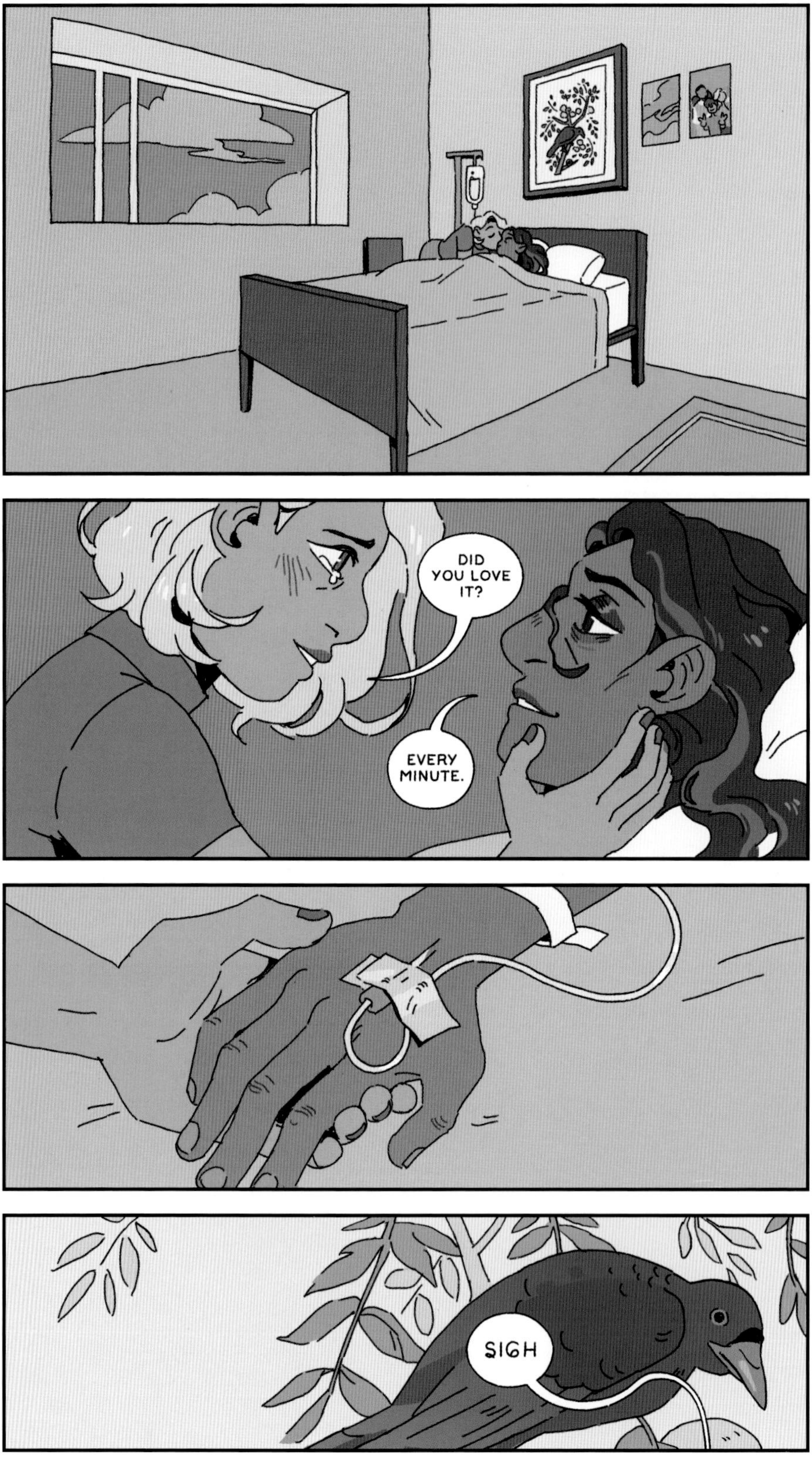
DID YOU LOVE IT?
EVERY MINUTE.
SIGH

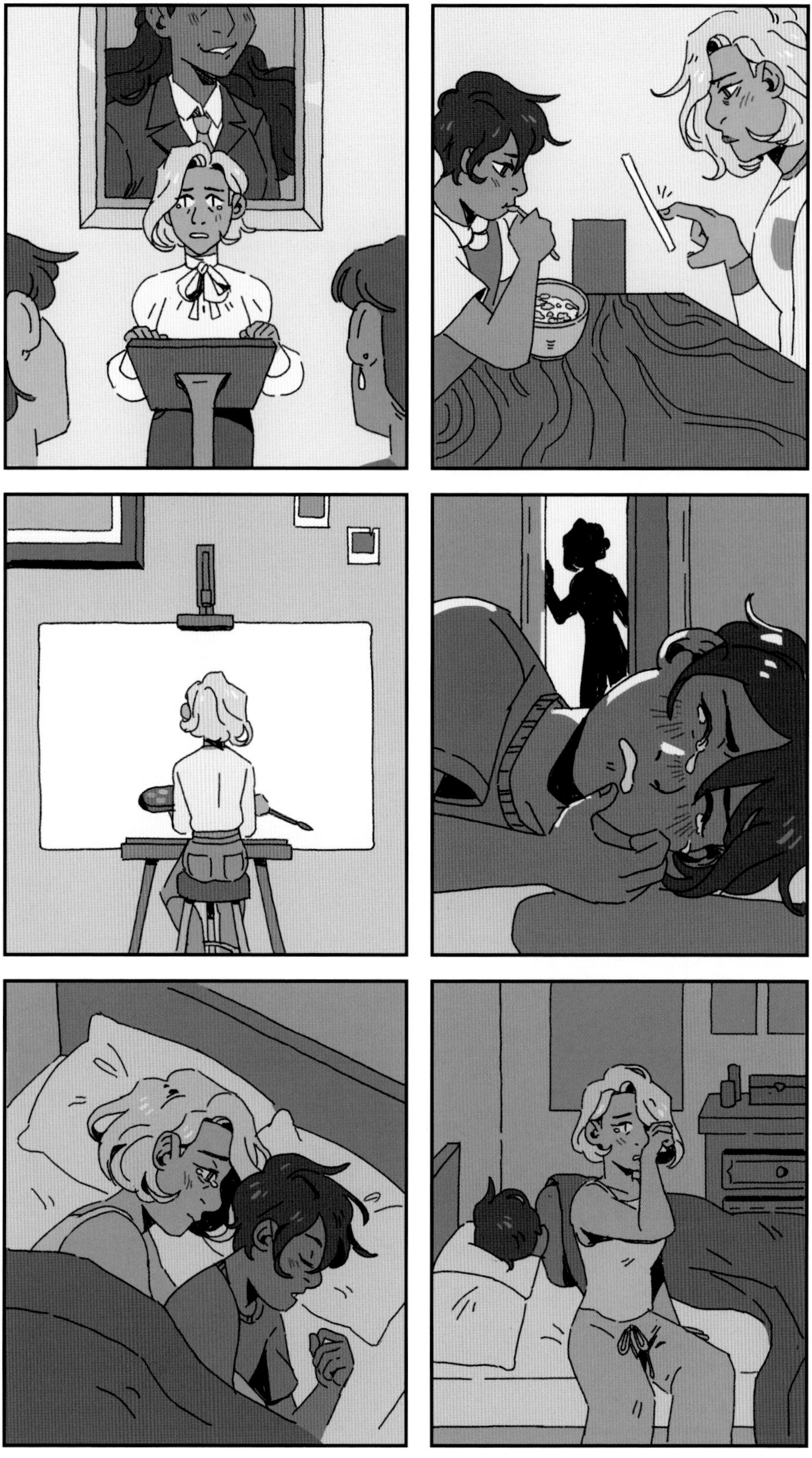

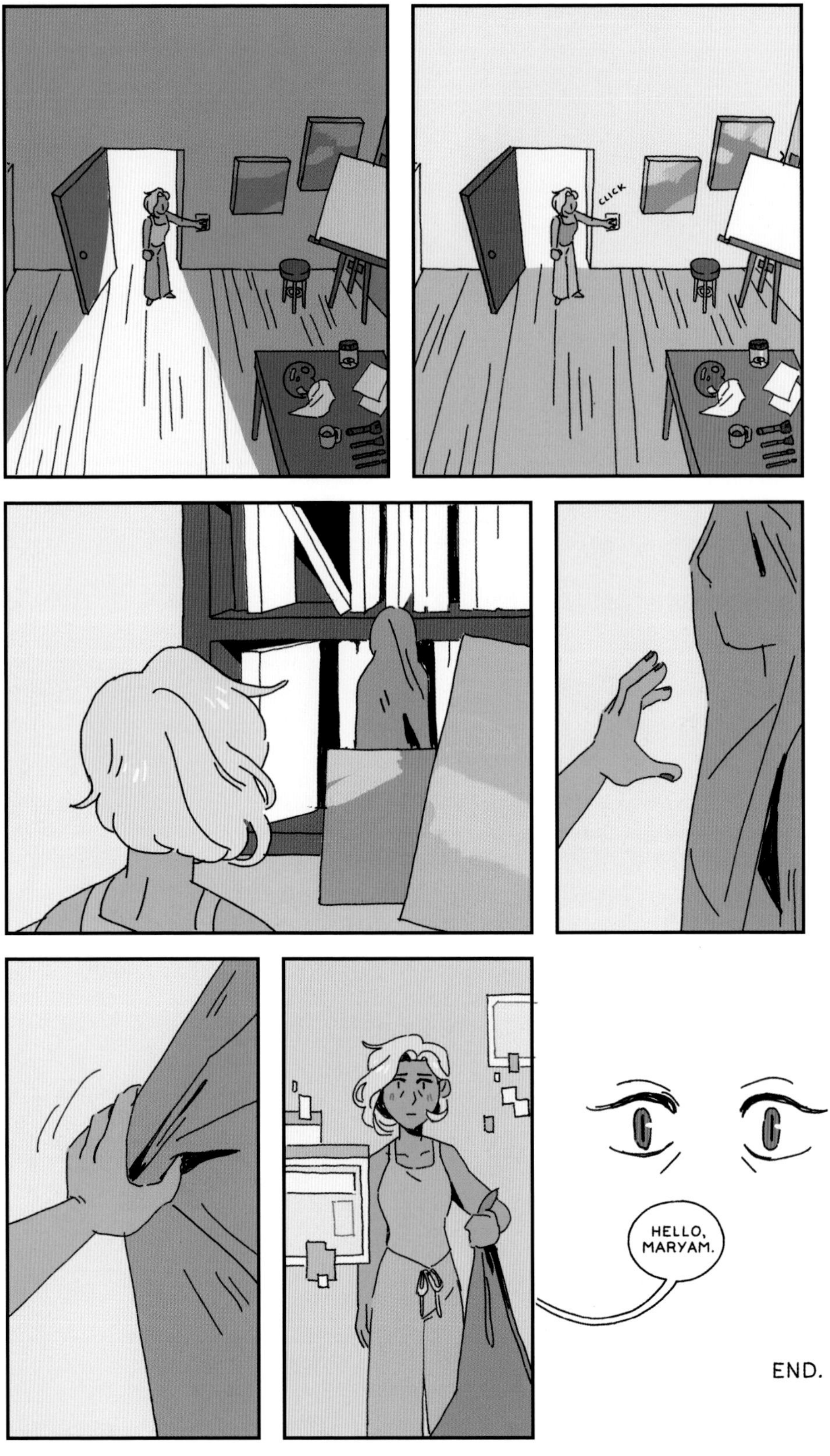
CLICK
HELLO, MARYAM.
END.

GHOSTBOT

IF YOU COULD LIVE ON AS A ROBOT, WOULD YOU?

IN THE SPRING OF 2016, JAMES VLAHOS'S FATHER WAS diagnosed with stage IV lung cancer. Like many families, the Vlahoses had been idly discussing how to preserve the memory of their aging parents—perhaps an oral history project? or a collection of letters? or a scrapbook?—but the diagnosis made the conversation immediately pressing. With no more time to waste, they decided to sit their father, John Vlahos, down with a tape recorder and ask him some questions.

The sessions sometimes lasted hours and covered as much as they could—his parents, their parents, his family stories, his childhood, his college days, meeting his wife, hobbies, professional milestones, anything and everything they could possibly think of. And while John might have been sick with cancer, he had a keen memory and a sharp wit. He sang songs, told jokes, recalled detailed stories about working for the *Daily Cal* and attending football games, and more.

Over three months, James compiled hours and hours of tape. Transcribed, it took up two hundred pages and lived in a thick three-ringed binder. But oral histories are tricky things. Once they're recorded, what do you do with them? James knew that the chances of listening back on all this raw tape was unlikely, even for the most devoted family member. But he didn't want the tape, or the binder, to just rot on a shelf, either. Then an unlikely encounter with a Barbie doll changed everything.

At the time, James was a journalist working on a story he thought was completely unrelated—a deep dive into a new Barbie that could listen to its playmates and respond using a chatbot system. In one video review of the toy I watched, Barbie brightly talks about butterflies, informing her new human friend that "butterflies live everywhere in the world except Antarctica," and a split second later, in the exact same voice, chirps, "Uh-oh, I can't find a Wi-Fi network!" The toy creeped out some parents, who wondered if it was always listening to their kids, and what it was doing with that data. But for James, it was a eureka moment: What if he built a similar conversational system of his father? A dadbot, if you will.

It was worth a shot, and the first step was to meticulously tag each bit of the two-hundred-page oral history (family, college, jokes), and feed those segments into a system that builds conversation trees based on possible prompts. James said he saw it as an experimental memoir of sorts, a unique way to memorialize his father. Soon, what he thought might be a fun little project turned into an obsession, and James Valhos became completely consumed—ultimately spending almost six months working on the dadbot full-time. "I just got sucked in," he told me.

Meanwhile, the elder John Vlahos still lived up the street, and his health continued to decline. It was a surreal experience, James tells me, to spend hours each day in front of the computer, listening to tapes of his father, only to later that same day see a very different man in person. One minute, James would be imagining his father performing the lead role in a Gilbert and Sullivan operetta, and the next he'd be driving up the hill to his father's house to see him in reality: frail and piled up with blankets, unable to say more than a few words. "It was brutal," James said, "I had to shift gears really quickly."[1]

James's father died in early 2017, and in the years since, James has found continued comfort in the dadbot. In 2019, he published a book about chatbots called *Talk to Me: How Voice Computing Will Transform the Way We Live, Work, and Think.* But he'll also admit that not everybody in the Vlahos clan enjoyed the bot. James's wife found it more painful than comforting—it did indeed sound like her father-in-law, and instead of making her smile, it reminded her he was gone. His son was unimpressed, likening it to Siri and moving along with his day. His other relatives nodded and smiled. James is the only one who continues to use the dadbot several times a month, to connect with his father from beyond the grave.

Some of you reading this might think this is a touching story of memorial and paternal connection, while others might find it creepy or strange. The way we process death is both personal and cultural—rituals and coping strategies that are completely standard to some can be horrifying to others. I grew up quite used to open-casket funerals, but being asked to throw dirt on the casket of a Jewish friend's mother felt unfathomable to me. Some cultures find closure in eating their dead, some allow vultures to do so, and others live with embalmed bodies in their homes for months, or even years. "Once somebody dies, the work of the living isn't necessarily done," said Anita Hannig, an anthropologist at Brandeis University who studies death. "People usually mobilize some sort of ritual to ensure that the dead are properly dead."

And the "properly dead" bit is important—while death rituals may differ around the world, their purpose is largely the same: to ensure that the dead are handled correctly, not just physically but emotionally, as well. What that means differs from place to place, but the rituals humans create around death are generally not about forgetting or erasing the relationships we have with the dead, but rather forming new ones.

But those rituals are slowly changing, and in some places eroding. Hannig and other scholars have noted how "death-denying" the United States has become. Many Americans keep death at arm's length, sequestering people in nursing homes and hospitals and outsourcing the job of caring for dying people to professionals and facilities. Once our loved ones die, we again task experts

---

1   When I visited James at his house and met his dadbot "in person," I heard songs, stories, and even a PG-13 joke in his actual voice.

at funeral homes or crematoriums to deal with their bodies. While 70 percent of Americans say they'd rather die at home, only 25 percent actually get to. Hannig says that even funerals are less important in the U.S. than they are in other countries, where skipping one would be seen as a serious insult.

The way we relate to death might seem like a small thing—one drip in an ocean of ways that cultures might differ from one another—but many scholars have argued that our relationship with death is uniquely powerful and shapes almost everything about us. "Death defines personal meaning and determines how we live," writes psychologists Paul Wong and Adrian Tomer. Death is the great unifier, the thing we all have in common, the looming specter over every living thing.

Some might argue that these robots are simply extensions of these past death rituals: hanging photos of a loved one in the hallway or keeping a locket of their image or maintaining their Facebook page as a memorial after they've gone. But Hannig points out that these rituals are different from the bots in a really crucial way: "Usually communication with the dead is an echo that you yell out into the forest. With this, you actually get something back." Hannig finds projects like the dadbot emblematic of the broader culture of death denial. Rather than coming to terms with grief, users can pretend that the death never happened, so what is there to grieve at all?

The idea of creating a robotic or digital version of your loved one after they die has cropped up in all kinds of media, from *Black Mirror* to *Westworld*. By making death manifest, embodied, thinkers and fiction writers can grapple with one of the biggest questions out there: What does it mean to be alive?

This is a huge question, but I'm also fascinated by the smaller ones that Eidolons and their brethren will force us to grapple with. In a world where humanoids could blend in with the rest of us, what kinds of regulations would there be around marking ghostbots? Would we demand that they wear some kind of beacon to indicate that they are in fact a robotic clone of a dead person? Or would we allow them to walk among us undetected? Who owns this ghostbot? Is there a warranty on your loved one? Fake skin must be cleaned carefully,[2] and at some point the gears and motors and systems will likely break down. When that happens, who fixes them? Do you have the right to repair your Eidolon if it breaks, or must you take it to an approved retailer? If the company that makes these goes out of business, is your robotic loved one doomed? What happens to returned Eidolons, as Maryam's wife, Hesper, asks in the comic? Or, what happens in ten years, when Maryam's Eidolon skin starts to fall off?

The physical logistics will be interesting, as well. These robots will be large and require regular charging in dedicated spaces—where do you put the closet for your dead wife? Can you plug her in next to a Tesla in a parking lot while you shop? What happens if she runs out of power while you're at the mall? In the comic you read, Maryam is relatively young. Her wife will live with

---

2   Sex toy manufacturers know this better than anyone: Toys that are made to feel "real" are usually made of special types of elastomers that shouldn't be cleaned with regular soap, which can break down the skinlike texture into something decidedly unsexy.

her Eidolon and age, but the robot will have the same skin unless someone does something to change that. Will there be aging updates you can buy from the company, new skins to fit onto your ghostbot, to truly make it seem like your loved one never left?

These aren't all totally theoretical questions, either. In 2019, the company that created the software James used was acquired by Apple. Soon, all the public versions of the dadbot were offline. For a while, the only one that existed was on James's private computer, and he worried about losing that one, too. When he told me about this, he pretended to joke about taking the computer the dadbot lives on offline so it can never update itself or be interfered with. But it didn't seem like a joke at all. Losing the dadbot would be a bit like his father dying all over again. "It would be a big blow," he told me.

In fact, to stave off this potential blow, Vlahos recently created a company to replicate the dadbot for other people called HereAfter. "Using our product is like speaking to Siri or Alexa. But instead of requesting a weather forecast or directions to a store, your family members and friends get to ask questions about your life," an old version of the HereAfter website said.

But if you think these are weird problems to have, just wait, it can get even weirder. We haven't even gotten to how machine learning might impact these robots. James's dadbot does not learn; it simply repeats back phrases based on what it knows. But James is not the only person out there to have built a dadbot. In 2013, computer scientist Muhammad Aurangzeb Ahmad's father died. A few years later, Ahmad tried his hand at making an artificially intelligent copy that his daughter, who his father never got to meet, could interact with. Unlike James, Ahmad didn't have the advantage of a living subject to record an oral history with, so instead he compiled about two thousand transcripts from emails, letters, and texts with his father. And in Ahmad's version, the system learns—it's equipped with a machine learning model.[3]

What that means is that the system will update and adapt its behavior based on what it sees and the feedback it's given. But what does that mean for the person they're supposed to be replicating? What happens if, years down the line, the robot has learned its way into a different personality from the one it's supposed to be emulating? Is it a new "person" now? In ten years, when Callie is older, will the robo-Maryam be the same mother she had before? Or a new parent altogether?

And we haven't even gotten to the question of embodiment yet. To build a convincing functional robot body—one that can walk around the world with ease, navigate doors and other people, sit at a dinner table, hold someone's hand—is no small task. There has been incredible progress made with soft robotics in the last few years, but we are still nowhere near a *Westworld*-level, convincing, full-body robot. Even the sex toy industry, arguably the most invested in creating something like the Eidolon you saw in the comic, hasn't come close. Everything from skin texture to simply staying upright without falling over has thus far eluded us.

---

3   When I spoke with Ahmad for the episode, he hadn't yet showed the bot to his extended family, and they had no idea he was developing it. He wasn't sure how they were going to react.

And what about the rest of us? Even if we don't purchase an Eidolon of our own, living amid a sea of ghostly simulacra would almost certainly change the behavior of the living. In the 1980s, psychologists began researching something called "terror management theory," the idea that our subconscious mind picks up and reacts to the idea of death even if we are not consciously aware of it. And our deep, dark minds don't react very nicely.

Studies show that if you remind people that death exists, they tend to become more racist, xenophobic, and violent. Americans reminded of death become more supportive of the preemptive use of biological, chemical, and nuclear weapons against countries who don't threaten us directly. Judges reminded of death set higher bonds for (fictional) accused sex workers. Christians reminded of mortality suddenly rate Jews far more negatively than Christians who aren't served up that same reminder. And it doesn't take much of a reminder—simply being interviewed after passing a funeral home or near a cemetery will do. This effect is large enough that some scholars think it might be one of the many road blocks to peace in places like the Middle East. "Death reminders make us demoralized, hateful, warmongering, protofacists plundering the planet, that's the bad thing," said Sheldon Solomon, a psychologist at Skidmore College and one of the founders of the field.

The theory behind this is that being reminded of death makes us pull inward and fear anybody whom our lizard brains may perceive as a risk, anybody who is different from us. We quell death reminders by clinging to our cultural norms and push away anybody who might challenge those values. William James once called the knowledge of death "the worm at the core" of every person, and it seems that being reminded of this fact turns us into worms as well. And living in a world of worms would be bleak, to put it lightly.

Oddly enough, Eidolons seem to achieve the negative aspects of both death denial and constant death reminders. People who purchase them can pretend that their specific loved one never died, and those who see them out and about will be reminded of death constantly. It's hard not to think that perhaps there is a better way to handle the looming specter of death.

To live in peace and with grace and love and hope at the forefront, we must actually forget about death for a little while. Not forget about the dead, but forget about death in particular. We have to let go a bit, unclench our fists, and let the dead become something else, something new. It's possible that what we should be doing isn't replicating the dead, but instead remembering them as they were, not as we want them to be. Or, in the words of the Mary Oliver poem, "In Blackwater Woods":

> you must be able
> to do three things:
> to love what is mortal;
> to hold it
>
> against your bones knowing
> your own life depends on it;
> and, when the time comes to let it go,
> to let it go.

BYE-BYE BINARY

BY ZIYED Y. AYOUB AND BLUE DELLIQUANTI

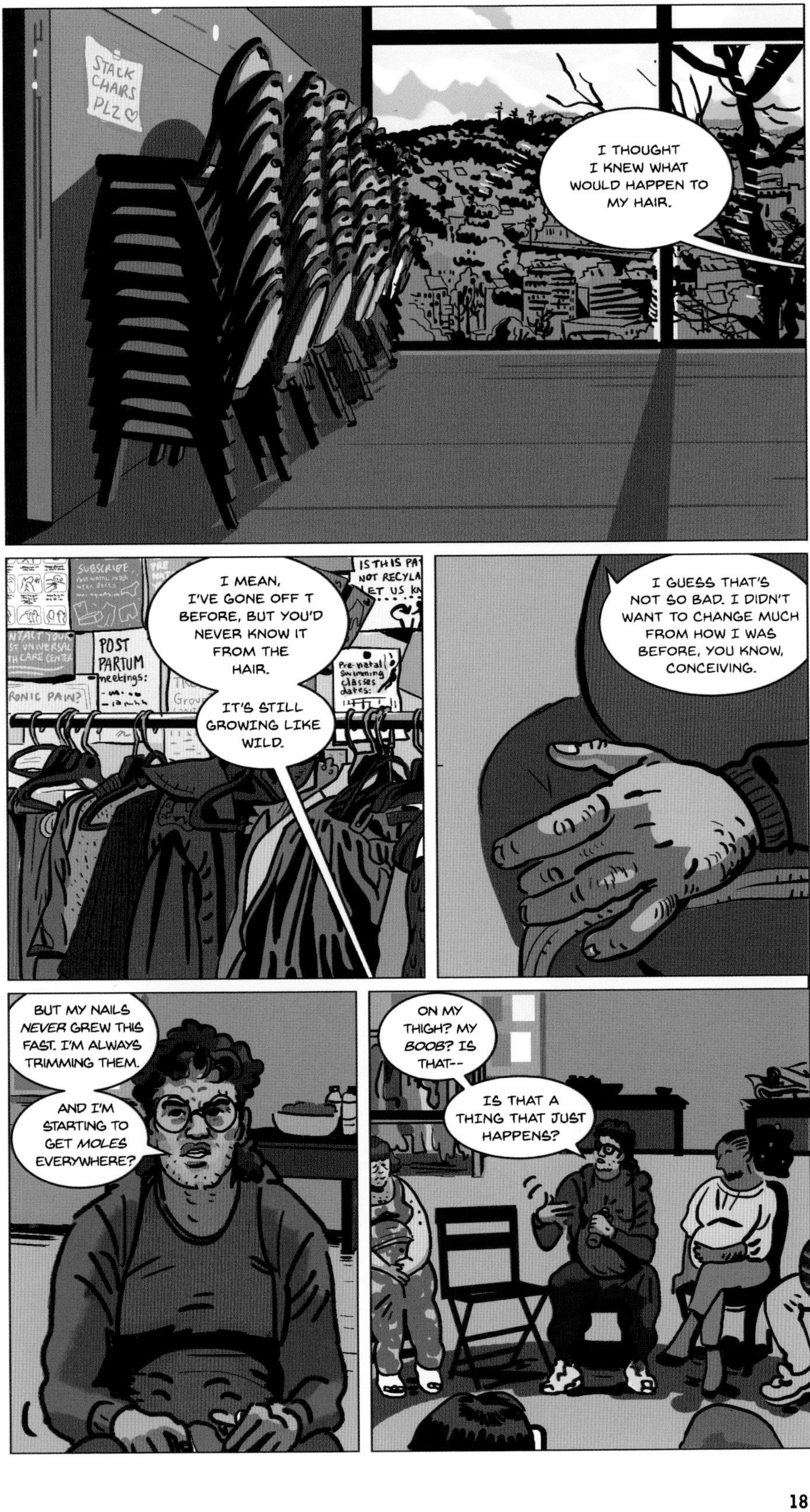
STACK CHAIRS PLZ ♡
I THOUGHT I KNEW WHAT WOULD HAPPEN TO MY HAIR.
SUBSCRIBE
POST PARTUM meetings:
Pre-natal swimming classes dates:
I MEAN, I'VE GONE OFF T BEFORE, BUT YOU'D NEVER KNOW IT FROM THE HAIR.
IT'S STILL GROWING LIKE WILD.
I GUESS THAT'S NOT SO BAD. I DIDN'T WANT TO CHANGE MUCH FROM HOW I WAS BEFORE, YOU KNOW, CONCEIVING.
BUT MY NAILS *NEVER* GREW THIS FAST. I'M ALWAYS TRIMMING THEM.
AND I'M STARTING TO GET *MOLES* EVERYWHERE?
ON MY THIGH? MY *BOOB*? IS THAT--
IS THAT A THING THAT JUST HAPPENS?

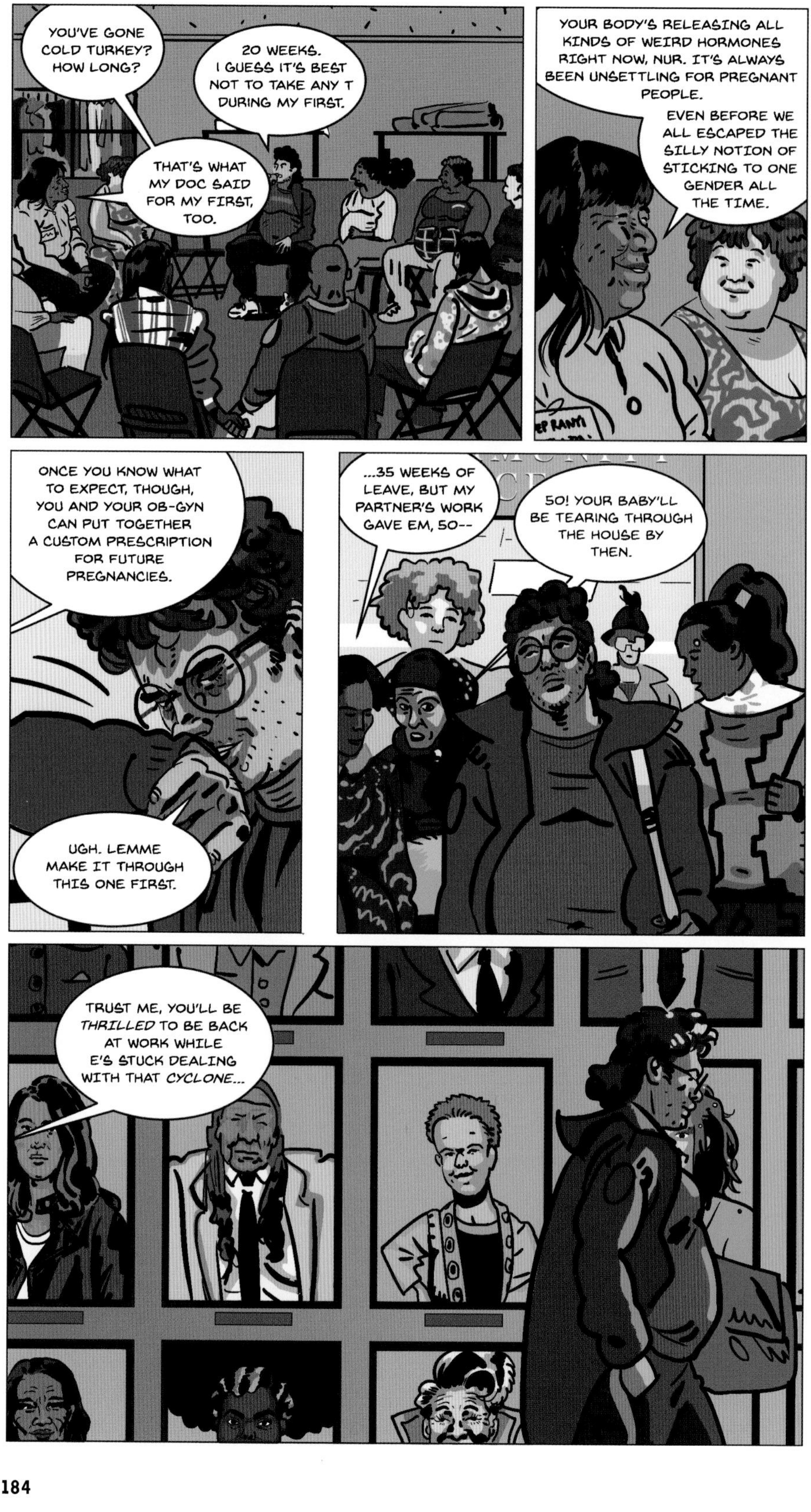
YOU'VE GONE COLD TURKEY? HOW LONG?
20 WEEKS. I GUESS IT'S BEST NOT TO TAKE ANY T DURING MY FIRST.
THAT'S WHAT MY DOC SAID FOR MY FIRST, TOO.
YOUR BODY'S RELEASING ALL KINDS OF WEIRD HORMONES RIGHT NOW, NUR. IT'S ALWAYS BEEN UNSETTLING FOR PREGNANT PEOPLE.
EVEN BEFORE WE ALL ESCAPED THE SILLY NOTION OF STICKING TO ONE GENDER ALL THE TIME.
ONCE YOU KNOW WHAT TO EXPECT, THOUGH, YOU AND YOUR OB-GYN CAN PUT TOGETHER A CUSTOM PRESCRIPTION FOR FUTURE PREGNANCIES.
UGH. LEMME MAKE IT THROUGH THIS ONE FIRST.
...35 WEEKS OF LEAVE, BUT MY PARTNER'S WORK GAVE EM, 50--
50! YOUR BABY'LL BE TEARING THROUGH THE HOUSE BY THEN.
TRUST ME, YOU'LL BE *THRILLED* TO BE BACK AT WORK WHILE E'S STUCK DEALING WITH THAT *CYCLONE*...

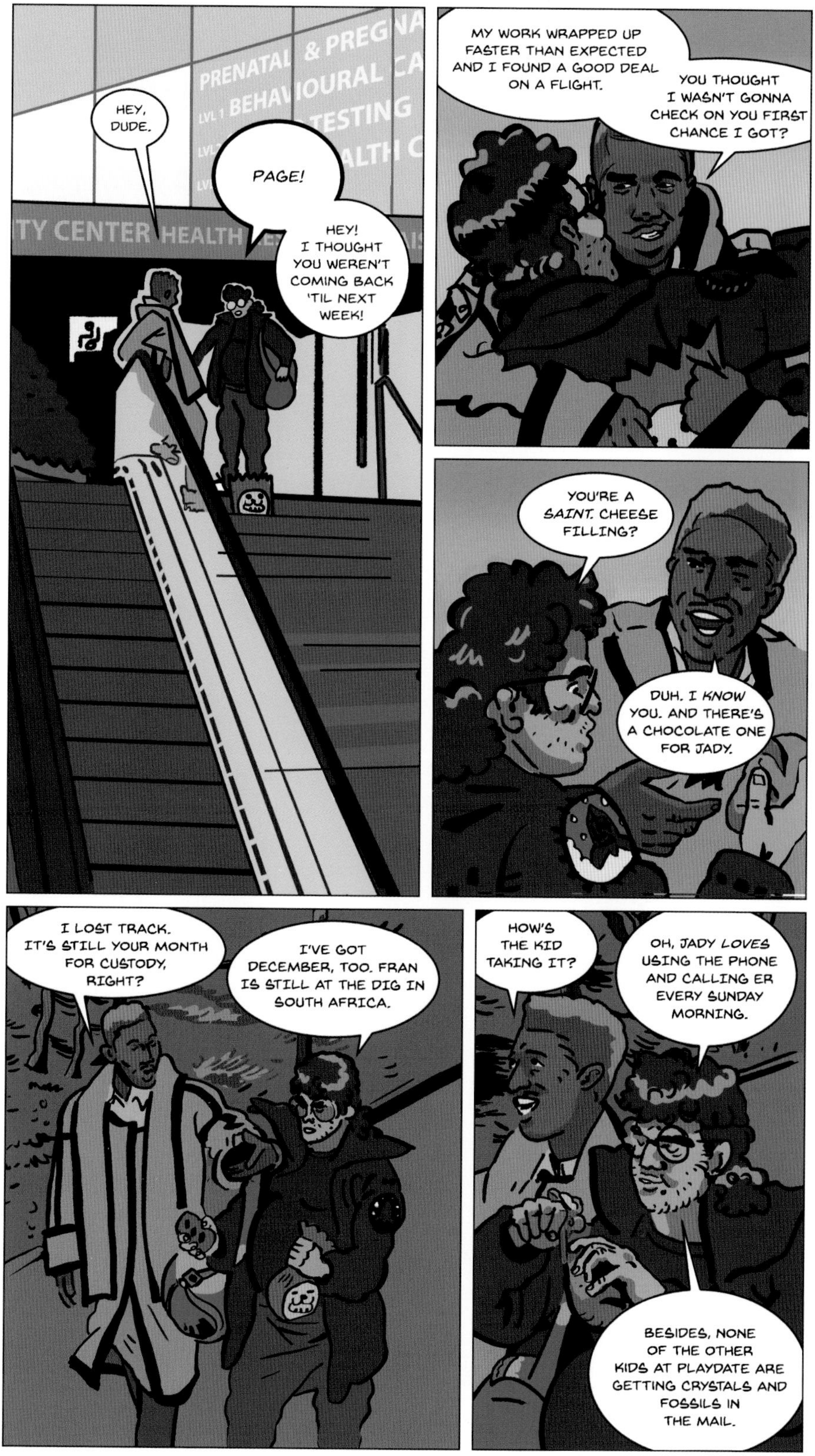
PRENATAL & PREGNA
LVL 1 BEHAVIOURAL CA
TESTING
ALTH C
ITY CENTER HEALTH
HEY, DUDE.
PAGE!
HEY! I THOUGHT YOU WEREN'T COMING BACK 'TIL NEXT WEEK!
MY WORK WRAPPED UP FASTER THAN EXPECTED AND I FOUND A GOOD DEAL ON A FLIGHT.
YOU THOUGHT I WASN'T GONNA CHECK ON YOU FIRST CHANCE I GOT?
YOU'RE A *SAINT*. CHEESE FILLING?
DUH. I *KNOW* YOU. AND THERE'S A CHOCOLATE ONE FOR JADY.
I LOST TRACK. IT'S STILL YOUR MONTH FOR CUSTODY, RIGHT?
I'VE GOT DECEMBER, TOO. FRAN IS STILL AT THE DIG IN SOUTH AFRICA.
HOW'S THE KID TAKING IT?
OH, JADY *LOVES* USING THE PHONE AND CALLING ER EVERY SUNDAY MORNING.
BESIDES, NONE OF THE OTHER KIDS AT PLAYDATE ARE GETTING CRYSTALS AND FOSSILS IN THE MAIL.

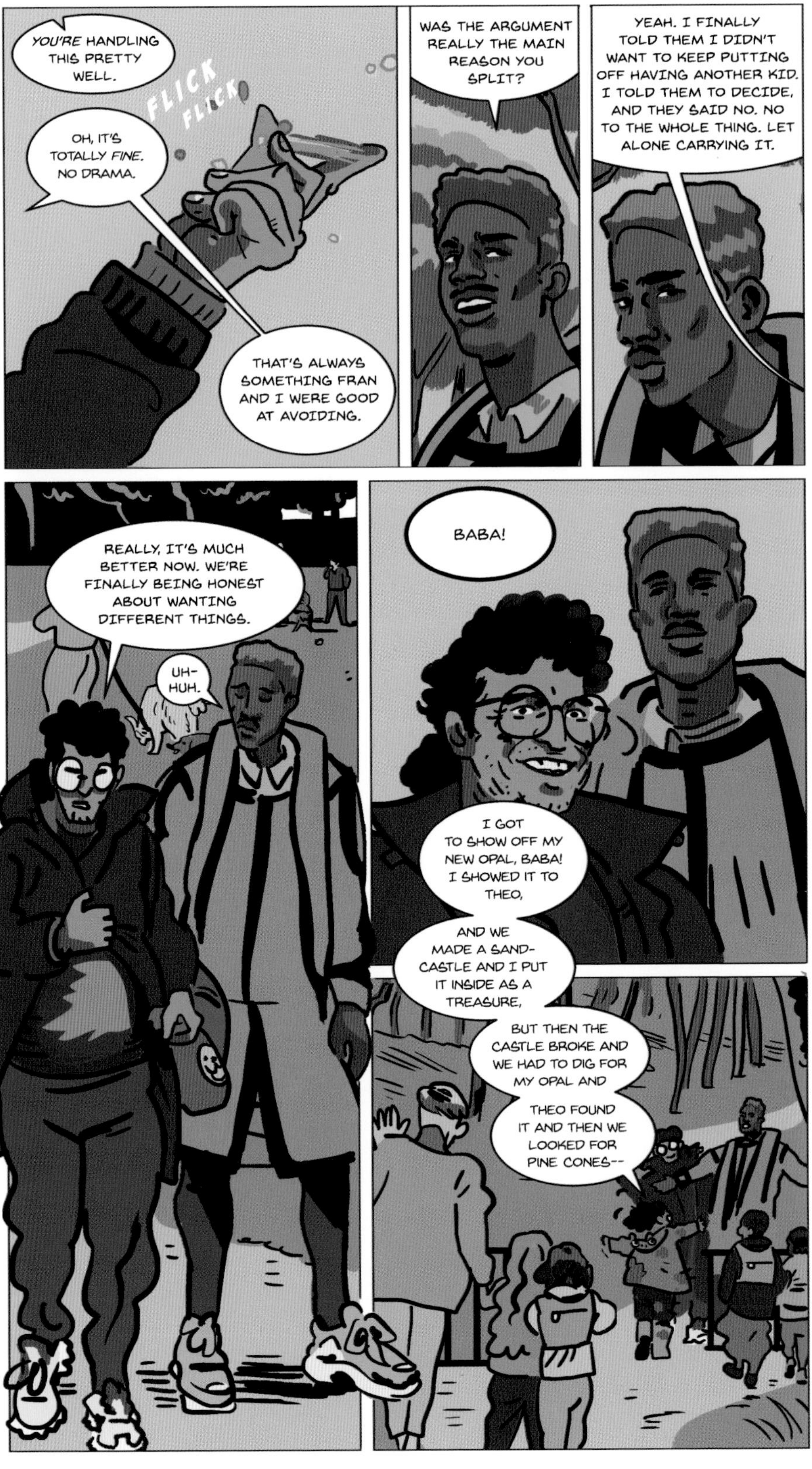
YOU'RE HANDLING THIS PRETTY WELL.
FLICK FLICK
OH, IT'S TOTALLY FINE. NO DRAMA.
THAT'S ALWAYS SOMETHING FRAN AND I WERE GOOD AT AVOIDING.
WAS THE ARGUMENT REALLY THE MAIN REASON YOU SPLIT?
YEAH. I FINALLY TOLD THEM I DIDN'T WANT TO KEEP PUTTING OFF HAVING ANOTHER KID. I TOLD THEM TO DECIDE, AND THEY SAID NO. NO TO THE WHOLE THING. LET ALONE CARRYING IT.
REALLY, IT'S MUCH BETTER NOW. WE'RE FINALLY BEING HONEST ABOUT WANTING DIFFERENT THINGS.
UH-HUH.
BABA!
I GOT TO SHOW OFF MY NEW OPAL, BABA! I SHOWED IT TO THEO,
AND WE MADE A SAND-CASTLE AND I PUT IT INSIDE AS A TREASURE,
BUT THEN THE CASTLE BROKE AND WE HAD TO DIG FOR MY OPAL AND
THEO FOUND IT AND THEN WE LOOKED FOR PINE CONES--

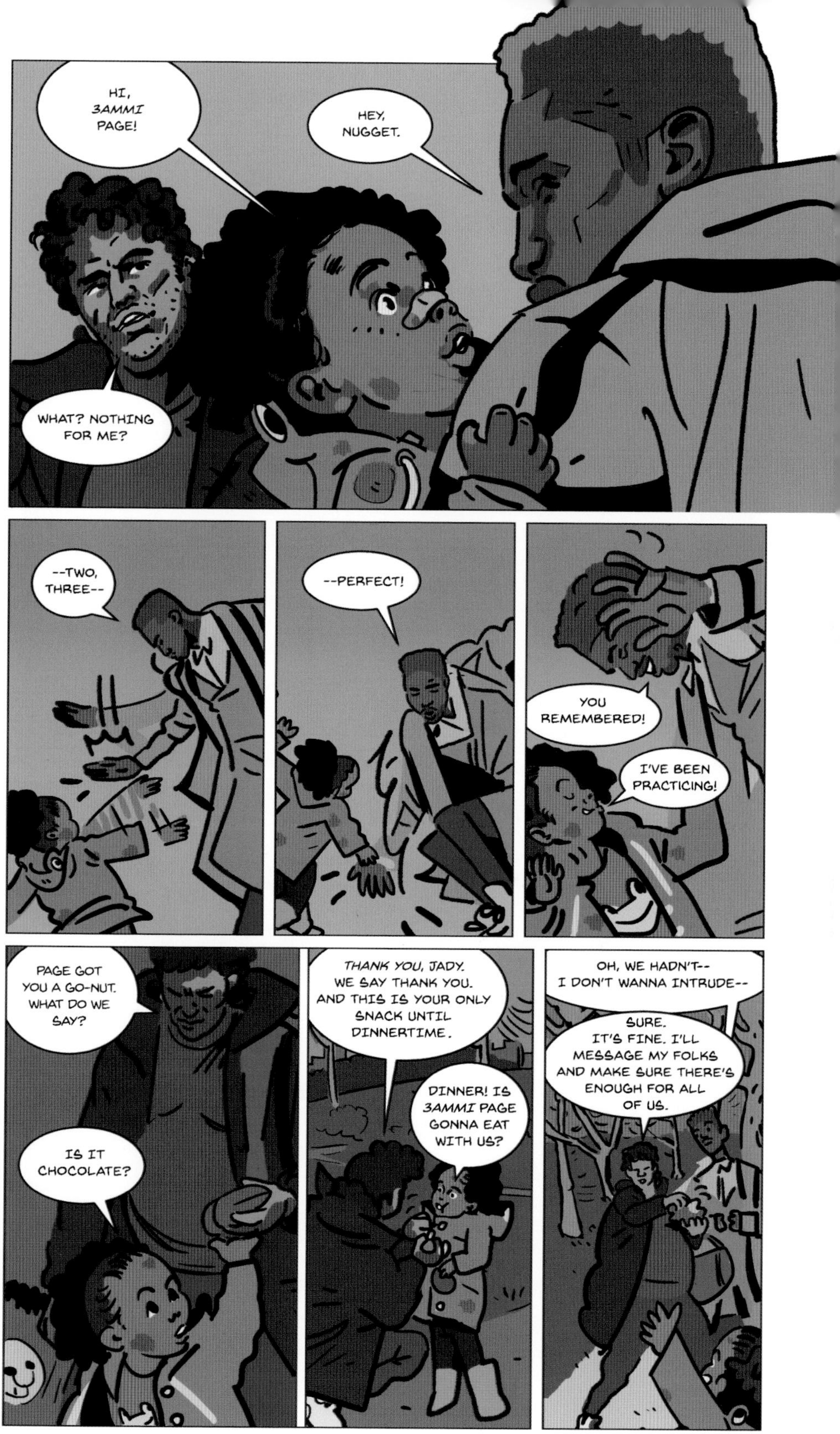
HI, ƷAMMI PAGE!
HEY, NUGGET.
WHAT? NOTHING FOR ME?
--TWO, THREE--
--PERFECT!
YOU REMEMBERED!
I'VE BEEN PRACTICING!
PAGE GOT YOU A GO-NUT. WHAT DO WE SAY?
IS IT CHOCOLATE?
THANK YOU, JADY. WE SAY THANK YOU. AND THIS IS YOUR ONLY SNACK UNTIL DINNERTIME.
DINNER! IS *ƷAMMI* PAGE GONNA EAT WITH US?
OH, WE HADN'T-- I DON'T WANNA INTRUDE--
SURE. IT'S FINE. I'LL MESSAGE MY FOLKS AND MAKE SURE THERE'S ENOUGH FOR ALL OF US.

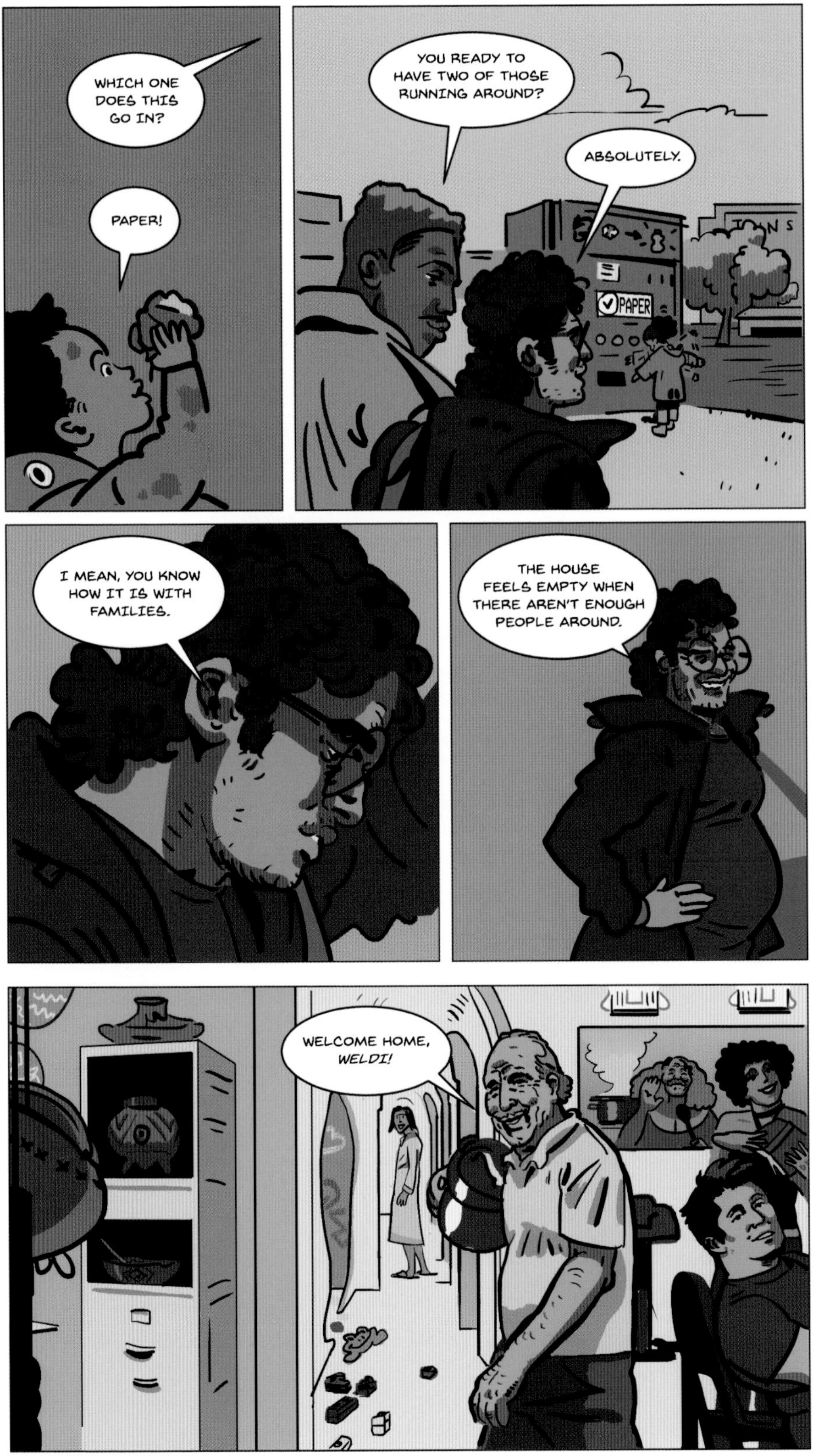
WHICH ONE DOES THIS GO IN?
PAPER!
YOU READY TO HAVE TWO OF THOSE RUNNING AROUND?
ABSOLUTELY.
PAPER
I MEAN, YOU KNOW HOW IT IS WITH FAMILIES.
THE HOUSE FEELS EMPTY WHEN THERE AREN'T ENOUGH PEOPLE AROUND.
WELCOME HOME, *WELDI!*

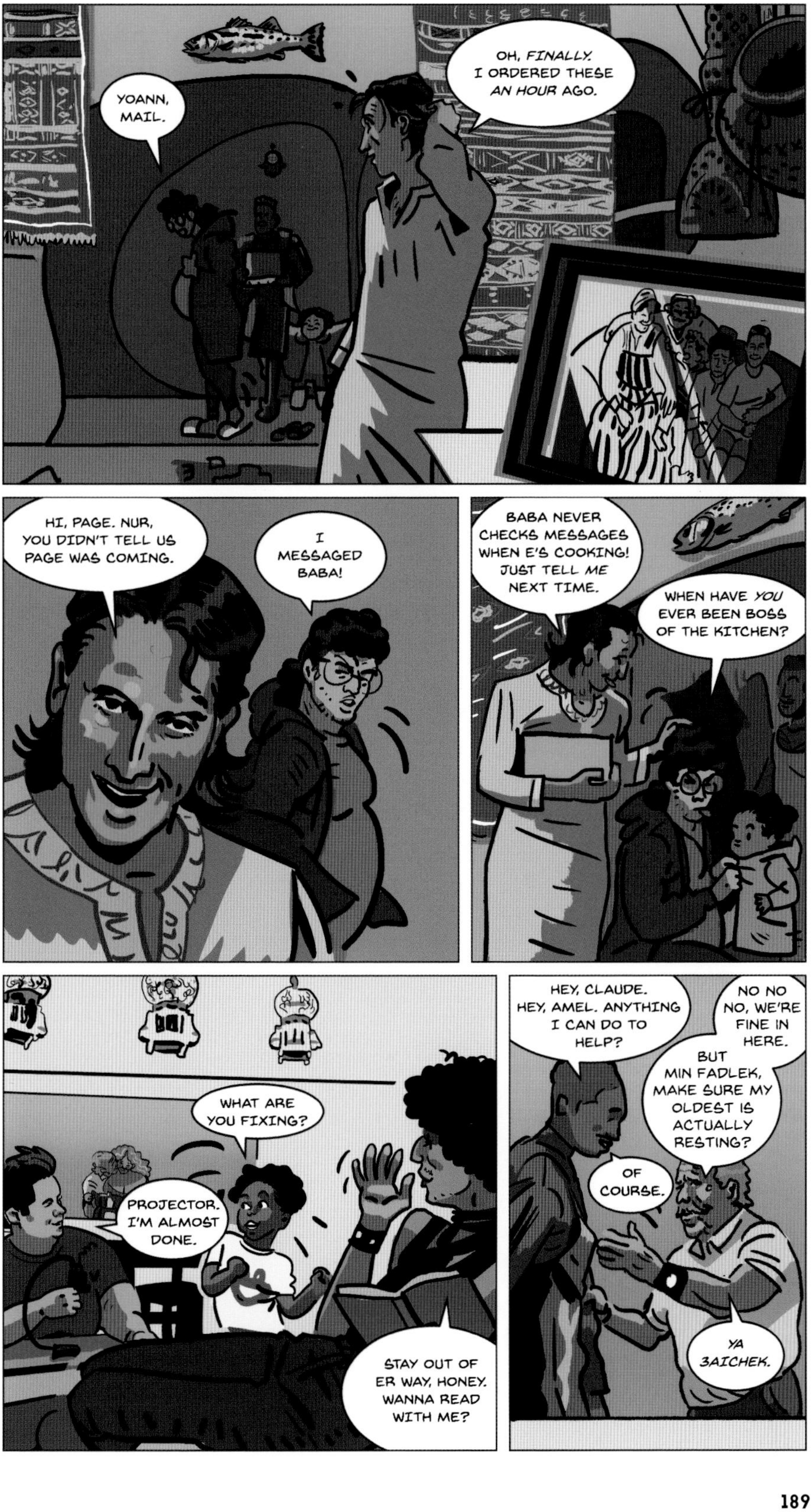
YOANN, MAIL.
OH, FINALLY. I ORDERED THESE AN HOUR AGO.
HI, PAGE. NUR, YOU DIDN'T TELL US PAGE WAS COMING.
I MESSAGED BABA!
BABA NEVER CHECKS MESSAGES WHEN E'S COOKING! JUST TELL ME NEXT TIME.
WHEN HAVE YOU EVER BEEN BOSS OF THE KITCHEN?
WHAT ARE YOU FIXING?
PROJECTOR. I'M ALMOST DONE.
STAY OUT OF ER WAY, HONEY. WANNA READ WITH ME?
HEY, CLAUDE. HEY, AMEL. ANYTHING I CAN DO TO HELP?
NO NO NO, WE'RE FINE IN HERE.
BUT MIN FADLEK, MAKE SURE MY OLDEST IS ACTUALLY RESTING?
OF COURSE.
YA ЗAICHEK.

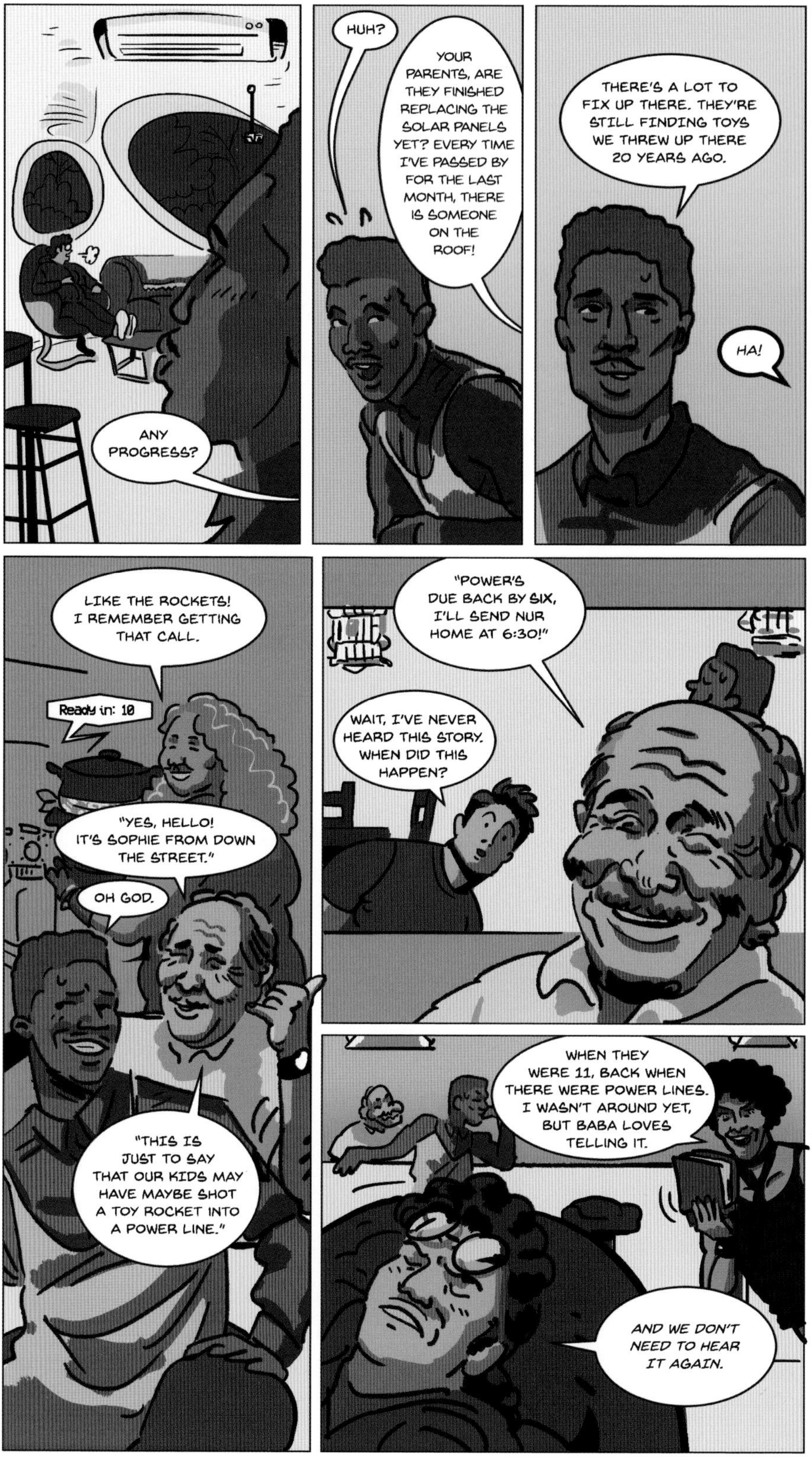

ANY PROGRESS?
HUH?
YOUR PARENTS, ARE THEY FINISHED REPLACING THE SOLAR PANELS YET? EVERY TIME I'VE PASSED BY FOR THE LAST MONTH, THERE IS SOMEONE ON THE ROOF!
THERE'S A LOT TO FIX UP THERE. THEY'RE STILL FINDING TOYS WE THREW UP THERE 20 YEARS AGO.
HA!
LIKE THE ROCKETS! I REMEMBER GETTING THAT CALL.
Ready in: 10
"YES, HELLO! IT'S SOPHIE FROM DOWN THE STREET."
OH GOD.
"THIS IS JUST TO SAY THAT OUR KIDS MAY HAVE MAYBE SHOT A TOY ROCKET INTO A POWER LINE."
"POWER'S DUE BACK BY SIX, I'LL SEND NUR HOME AT 6:30!"
WAIT, I'VE NEVER HEARD THIS STORY. WHEN DID THIS HAPPEN?
WHEN THEY WERE 11, BACK WHEN THERE WERE POWER LINES. I WASN'T AROUND YET, BUT BABA LOVES TELLING IT.
AND WE DON'T NEED TO HEAR IT AGAIN.

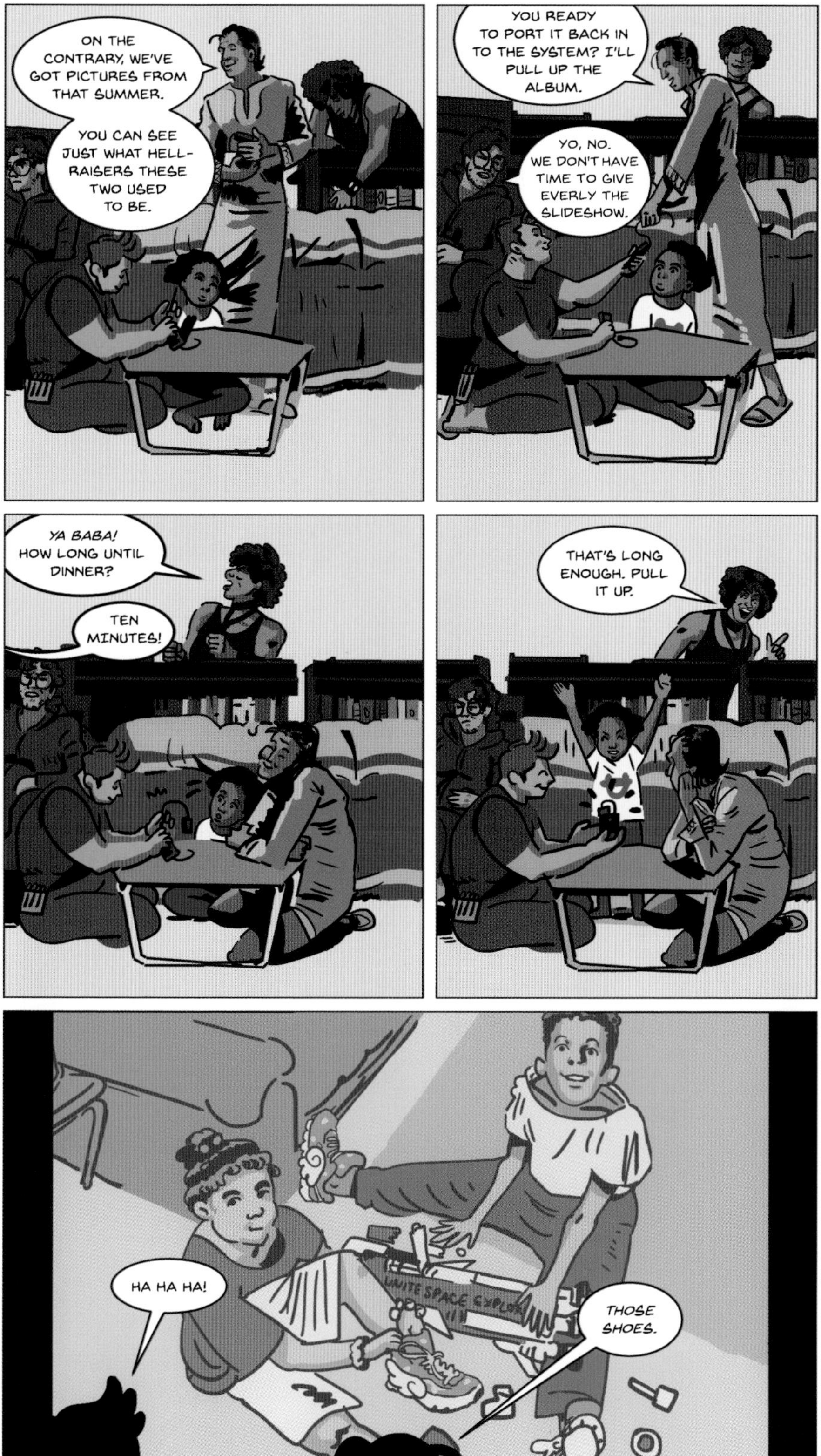

ON THE CONTRARY, WE'VE GOT PICTURES FROM THAT SUMMER.
YOU CAN SEE JUST WHAT HELL-RAISERS THESE TWO USED TO BE.
YOU READY TO PORT IT BACK IN TO THE SYSTEM? I'LL PULL UP THE ALBUM.
YO, NO. WE DON'T HAVE TIME TO GIVE EVERLY THE SLIDESHOW.
YA BABA! HOW LONG UNTIL DINNER?
TEN MINUTES!
THAT'S LONG ENOUGH. PULL IT UP.
HA HA HA!
THOSE SHOES.

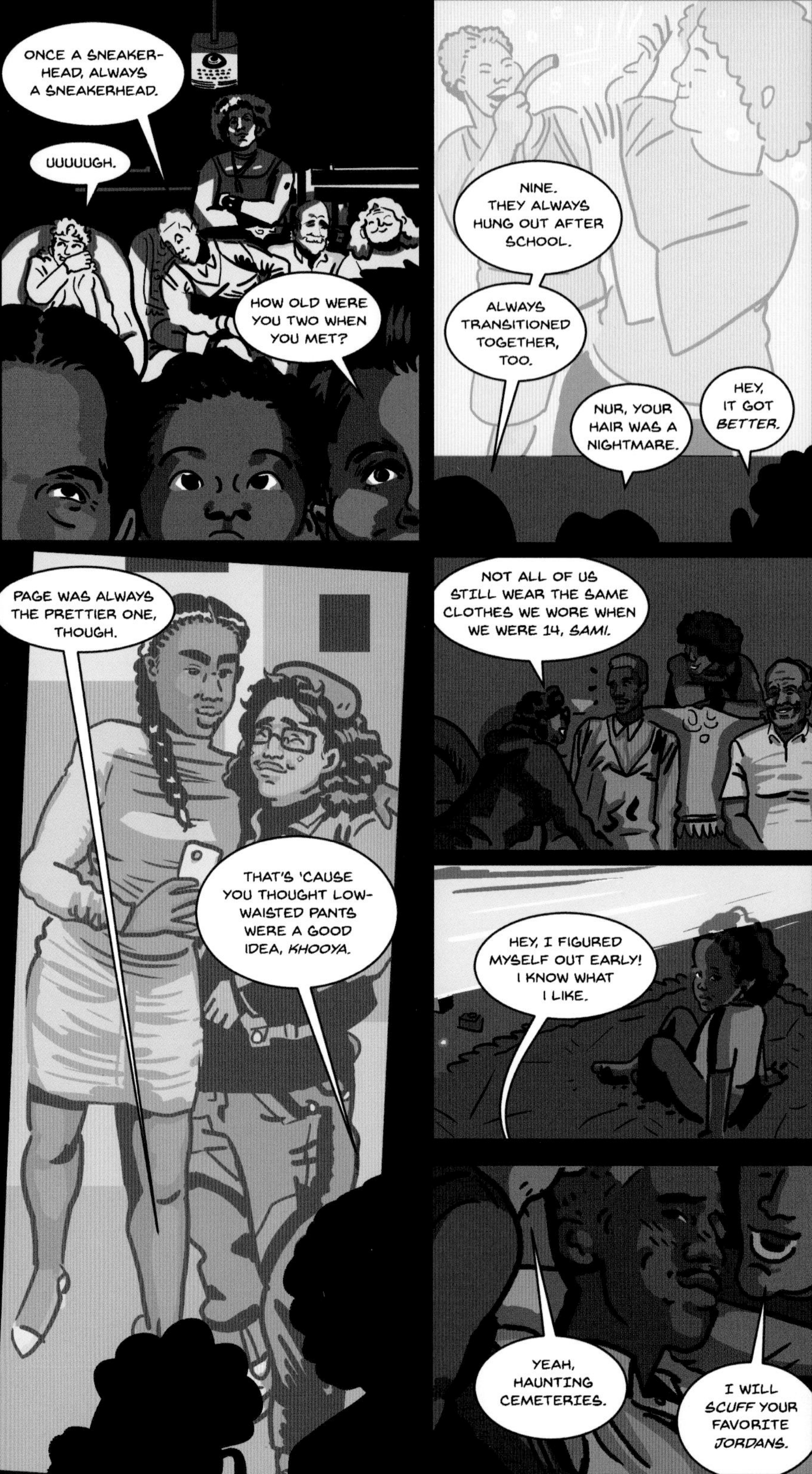
ONCE A SNEAKER-HEAD, ALWAYS A SNEAKERHEAD.
UUUUUGH.
HOW OLD WERE YOU TWO WHEN YOU MET?
NINE. THEY ALWAYS HUNG OUT AFTER SCHOOL.
ALWAYS TRANSITIONED TOGETHER, TOO.
NUR, YOUR HAIR WAS A NIGHTMARE.
HEY, IT GOT *BETTER.*
PAGE WAS ALWAYS THE PRETTIER ONE, THOUGH.
THAT'S 'CAUSE YOU THOUGHT LOW-WAISTED PANTS WERE A GOOD IDEA, *KHOOYA.*
NOT ALL OF US STILL WEAR THE SAME CLOTHES WE WORE WHEN WE WERE 14, *SAMI.*
HEY, I FIGURED MYSELF OUT EARLY! I KNOW WHAT I LIKE.
YEAH, HAUNTING CEMETERIES.
I WILL *SCUFF* YOUR FAVORITE *JORDANS.*

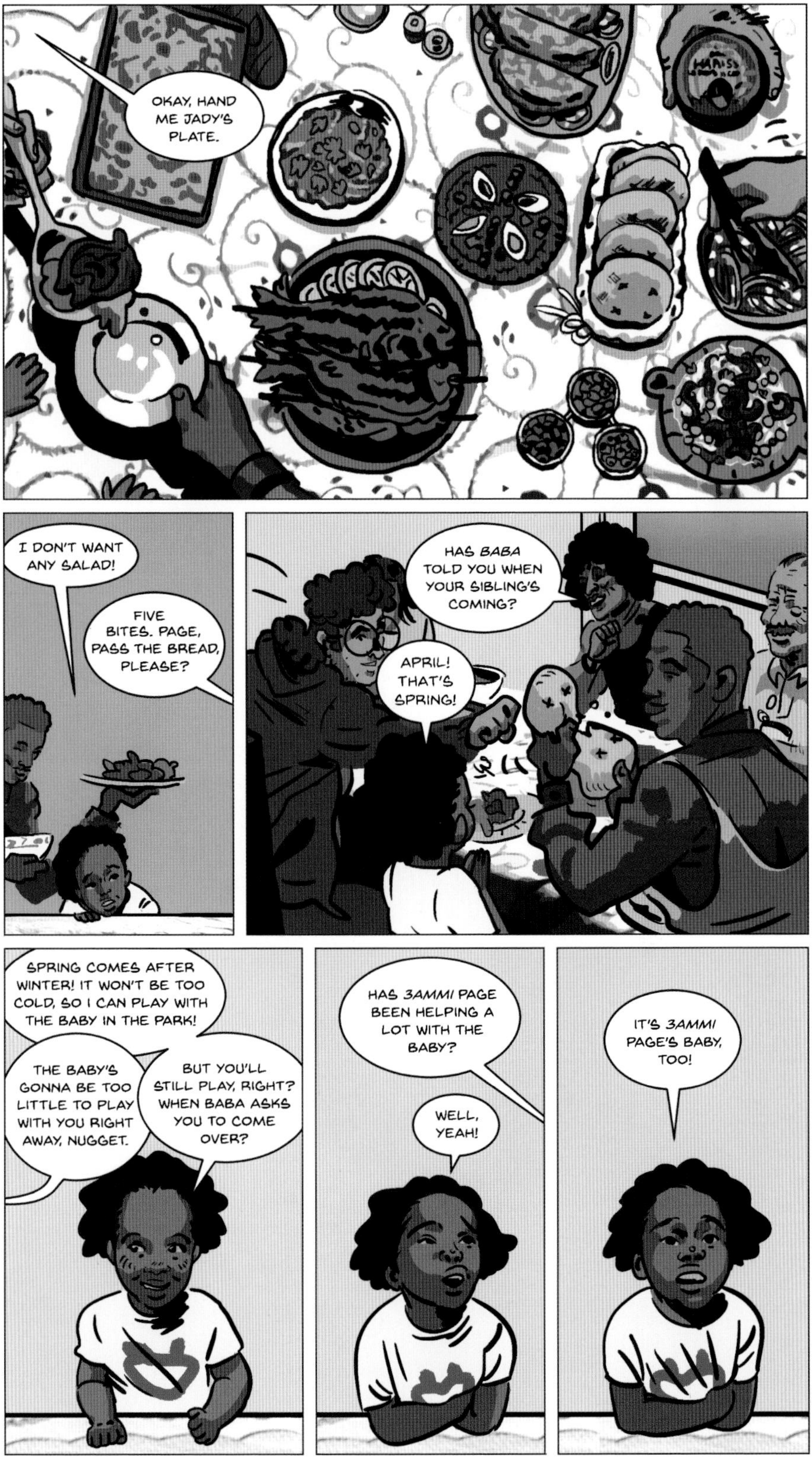
OKAY, HAND ME JADY'S PLATE.
I DON'T WANT ANY SALAD!
FIVE BITES. PAGE, PASS THE BREAD, PLEASE?
HAS *BABA* TOLD YOU WHEN YOUR SIBLING'S COMING?
APRIL! THAT'S SPRING!
SPRING COMES AFTER WINTER! IT WON'T BE TOO COLD, SO I CAN PLAY WITH THE BABY IN THE PARK!
THE BABY'S GONNA BE TOO LITTLE TO PLAY WITH YOU RIGHT AWAY, NUGGET.
BUT YOU'LL STILL PLAY, RIGHT? WHEN BABA ASKS YOU TO COME OVER?
HAS *3AMMI* PAGE BEEN HELPING A LOT WITH THE BABY?
WELL, YEAH!
IT'S *3AMMI* PAGE'S BABY, TOO!

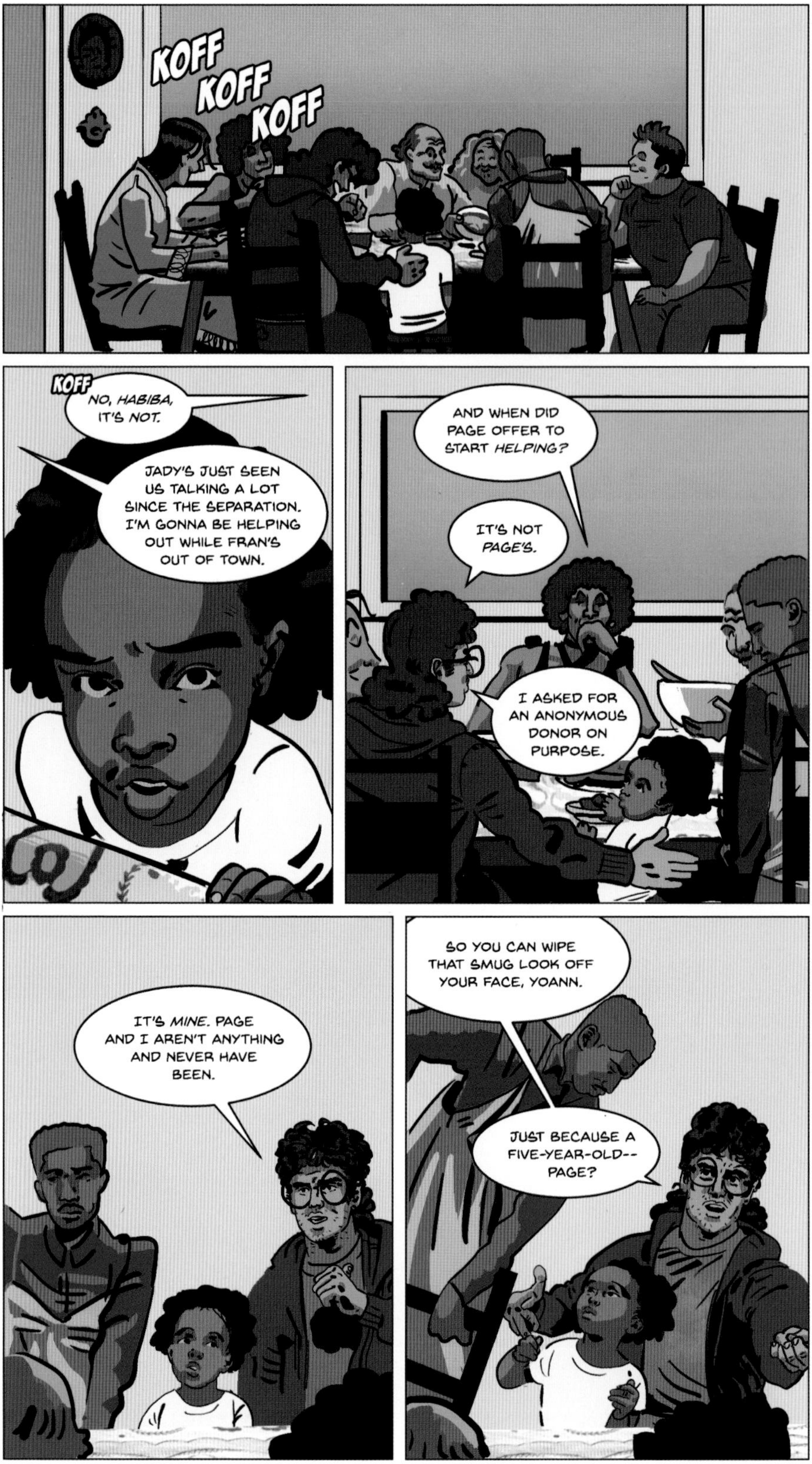
KOFF KOFF KOFF
KOFF
NO, *HABIBA*, IT'S *NOT*.
JADY'S JUST SEEN US TALKING A LOT SINCE THE SEPARATION. I'M GONNA BE HELPING OUT WHILE FRAN'S OUT OF TOWN.
AND WHEN DID PAGE OFFER TO START *HELPING?*
IT'S NOT *PAGE'S*.
I ASKED FOR AN ANONYMOUS DONOR ON PURPOSE.
IT'S *MINE*. PAGE AND I AREN'T ANYTHING AND NEVER HAVE BEEN.
SO YOU CAN WIPE THAT SMUG LOOK OFF YOUR FACE, YOANN.
JUST BECAUSE A FIVE-YEAR-OLD-- PAGE?

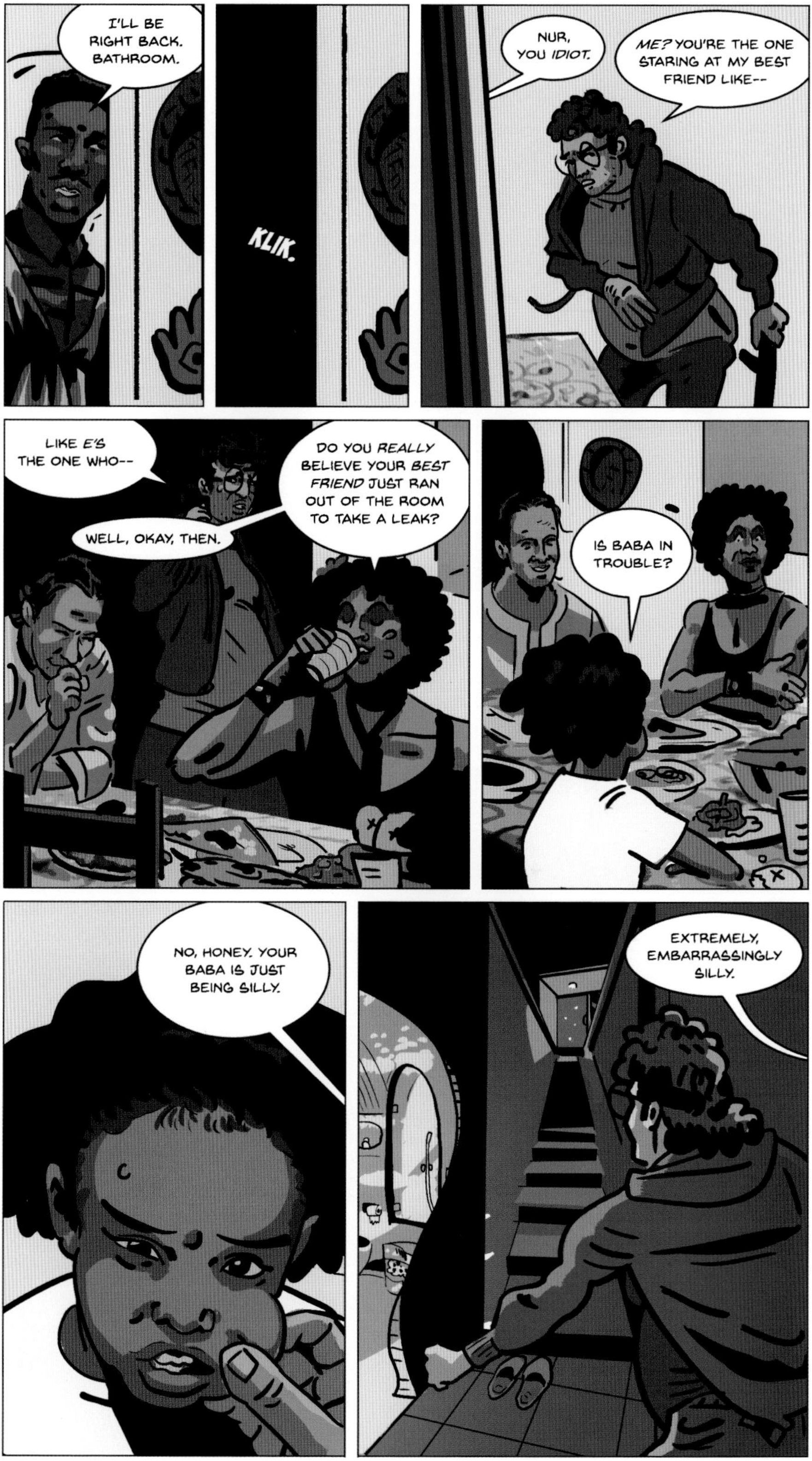
I'LL BE RIGHT BACK. BATHROOM.
KLIK.
NUR, YOU *IDIOT.*
ME? YOU'RE THE ONE STARING AT MY BEST FRIEND LIKE--
LIKE E'S THE ONE WHO--
DO YOU *REALLY* BELIEVE YOUR *BEST FRIEND* JUST RAN OUT OF THE ROOM TO TAKE A LEAK?
WELL, OKAY, THEN.
IS BABA IN TROUBLE?
NO, HONEY. YOUR BABA IS JUST BEING SILLY.
EXTREMELY, EMBARRASSINGLY SILLY.

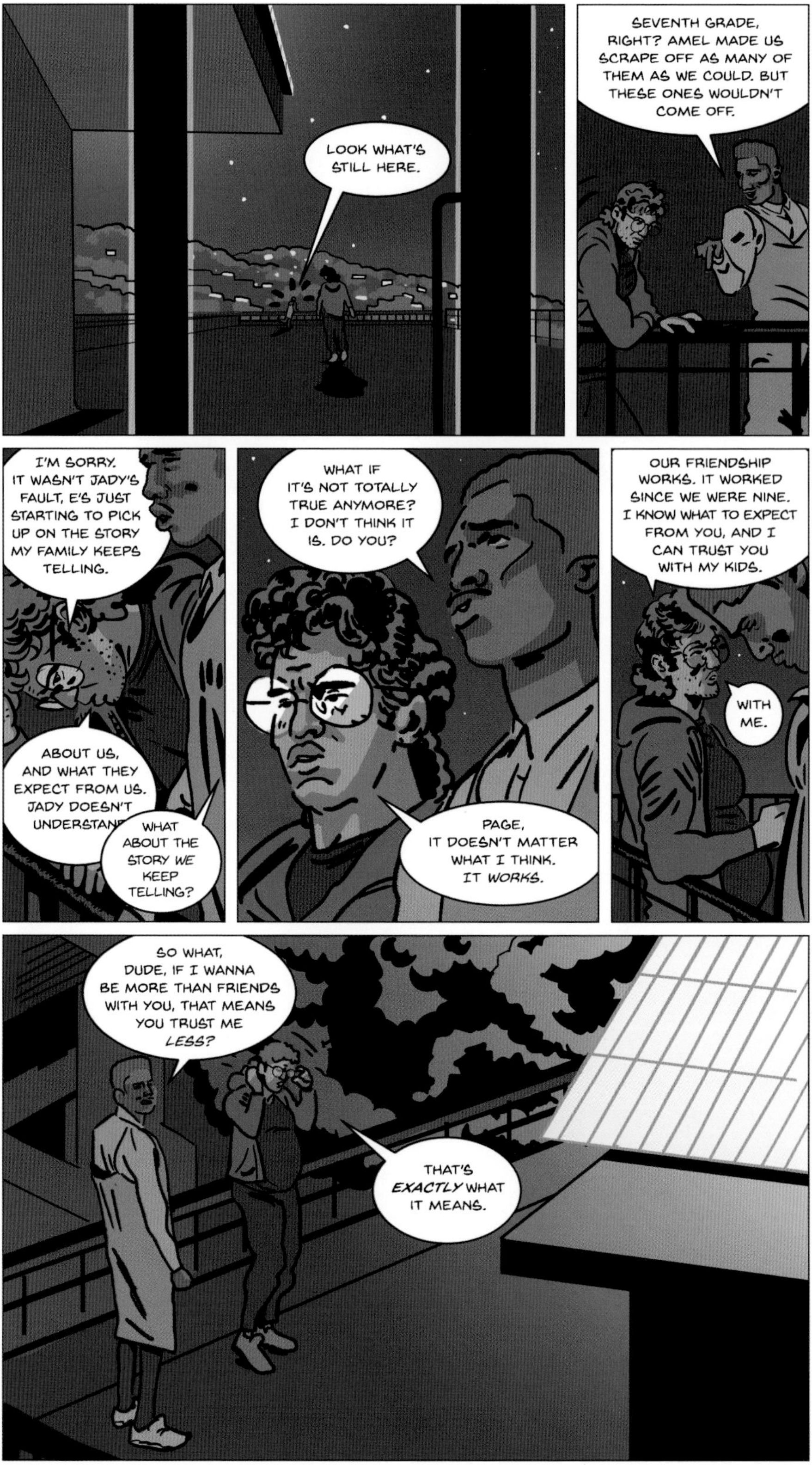
LOOK WHAT'S STILL HERE.
SEVENTH GRADE, RIGHT? AMEL MADE US SCRAPE OFF AS MANY OF THEM AS WE COULD. BUT THESE ONES WOULDN'T COME OFF.
I'M SORRY. IT WASN'T JADY'S FAULT, E'S JUST STARTING TO PICK UP ON THE STORY MY FAMILY KEEPS TELLING.
ABOUT US, AND WHAT THEY EXPECT FROM US. JADY DOESN'T UNDERSTAN
WHAT ABOUT THE STORY *WE* KEEP TELLING?
WHAT IF IT'S NOT TOTALLY TRUE ANYMORE? I DON'T THINK IT IS. DO YOU?
PAGE, IT DOESN'T MATTER WHAT I THINK. IT *WORKS*.
OUR FRIENDSHIP WORKS. IT WORKED SINCE WE WERE NINE. I KNOW WHAT TO EXPECT FROM YOU, AND I CAN TRUST YOU WITH MY KIDS.
WITH ME.
SO WHAT, DUDE, IF I WANNA BE MORE THAN FRIENDS WITH YOU, THAT MEANS YOU TRUST ME *LESS?*
THAT'S *EXACTLY* WHAT IT MEANS.

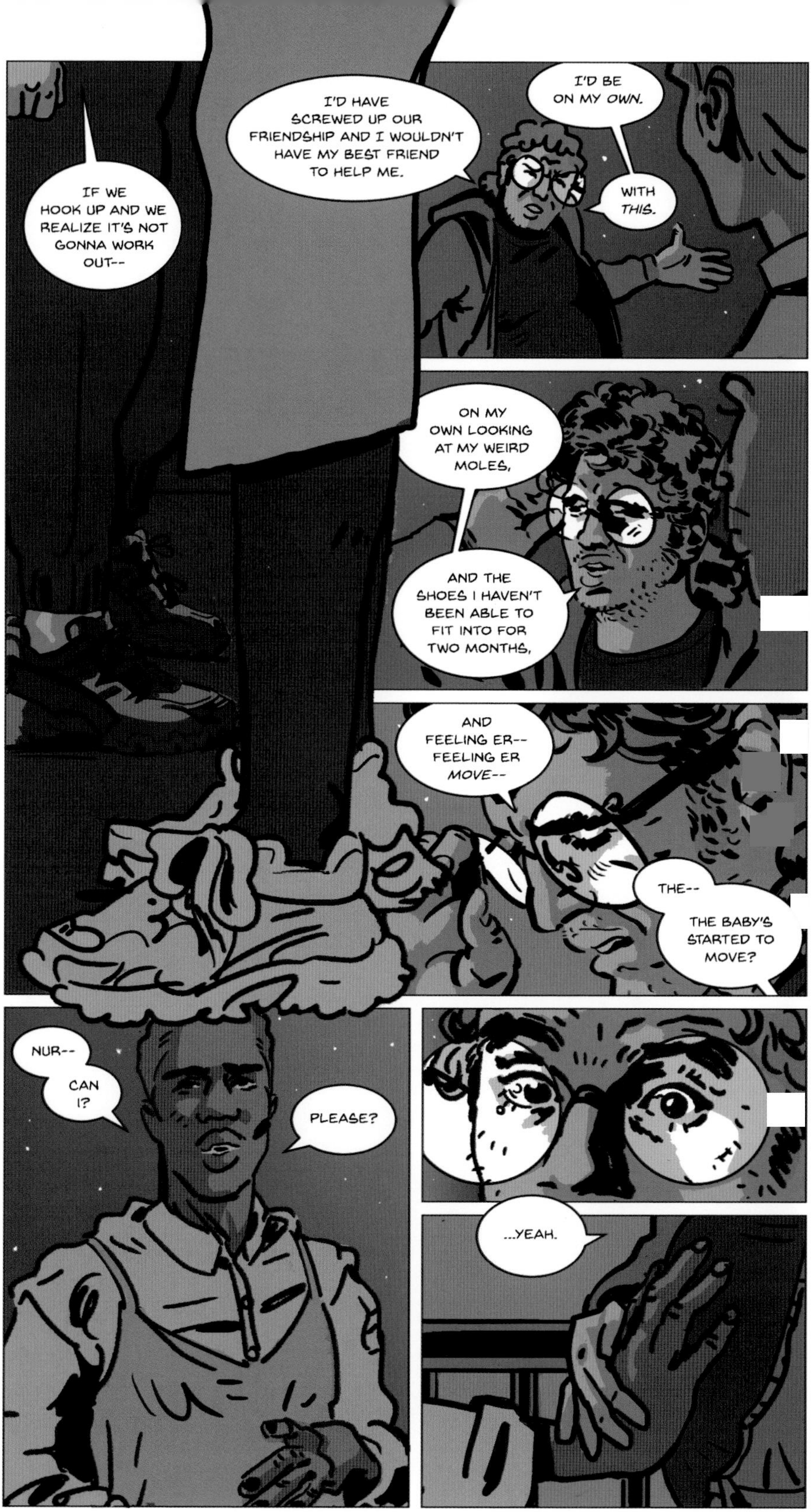
IF WE HOOK UP AND WE REALIZE IT'S NOT GONNA WORK OUT--
I'D HAVE SCREWED UP OUR FRIENDSHIP AND I WOULDN'T HAVE MY BEST FRIEND TO HELP ME.
I'D BE ON MY *OWN*.
WITH *THIS*.
ON MY OWN LOOKING AT MY WEIRD MOLES,
AND THE SHOES I HAVEN'T BEEN ABLE TO FIT INTO FOR TWO MONTHS,
AND FEELING ER-- FEELING ER *MOVE*--
THE--
THE BABY'S STARTED TO MOVE?
NUR--
CAN I?
PLEASE?
...YEAH.

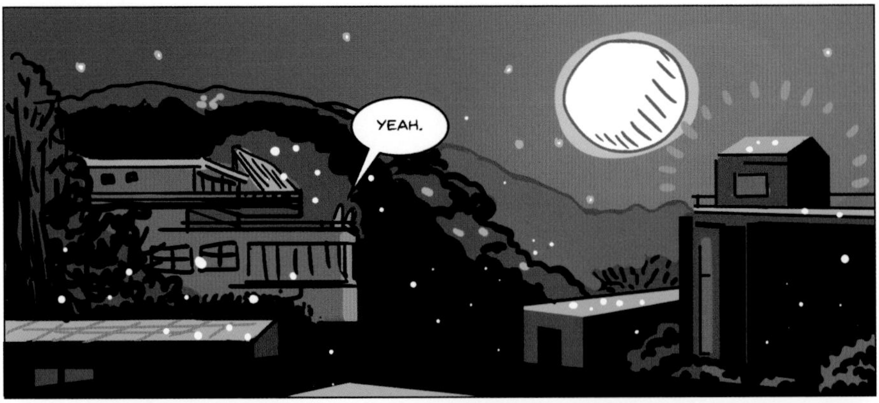
YEAH.

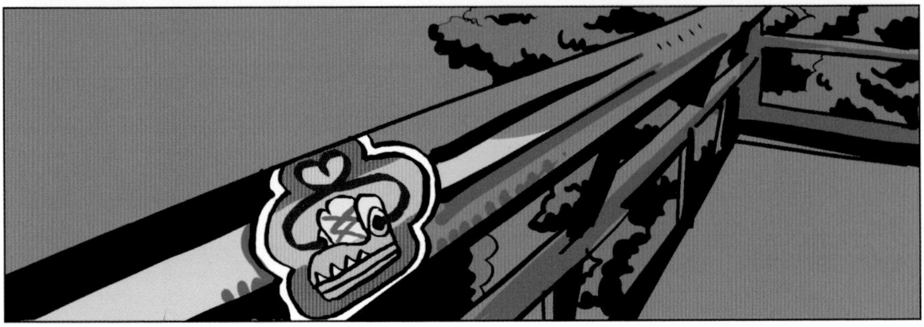

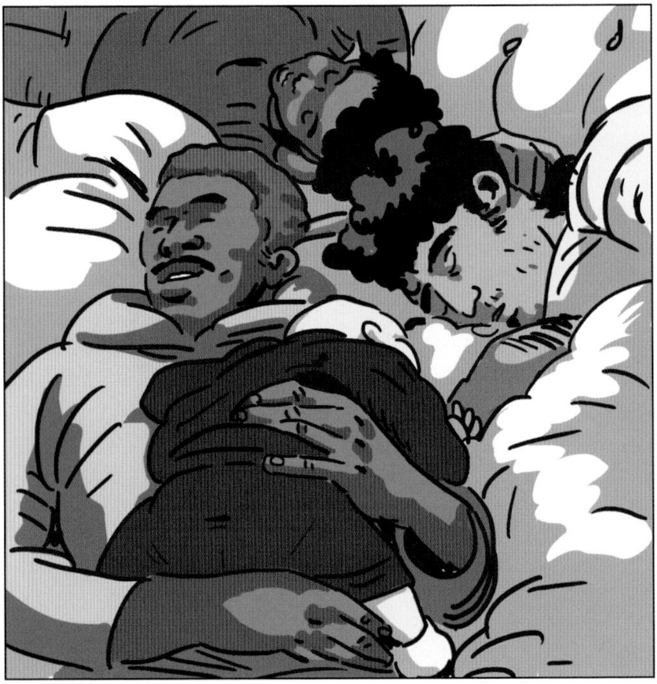

BYE-BYE BINARY

WHAT IF GENDER WAS MORE LIKE HAIR COLOR?

IF YOU'VE EVER TAKEN A BABY OUT IN PUBLIC, YOU'RE likely familiar with how frequently people make assumptions about gender. "It's very weird," said Ann Leckie, who remembers people stopping to *ooh* and *ahh* at her little ones. "What a cute baby," they would say. "Then they would stop and look at me and ask, 'I'm sorry, is this a boy or a girl?'"

To Leckie, a science-fiction writer, this was a very strange question. Those who didn't ask would guess, and if they guessed wrong they would apologize profusely. "Like they had just run over my dog," she said, laughing. "And I'd be like, 'The baby doesn't care and I don't care!'" Babies don't even know what their own feet are, and they certainly have no concept of gender, a tangled web of socially constructed norms and relationships. Why should it matter to a stranger in the produce aisle whether their high-pitched baby-talk babble is directed at a child who will grow up to identify as a boy or a girl or another gender altogether?

As I write this, the Trump administration is actively working to officially redefine gender in the United States as a biologically derived binary. In this version of the universe, you're either male or female, a category determined at birth based on your genitals. Along with being both cruel and completely unscientific, the move has provided a gruesome natural experiment in what happens when people insist on a rigid gender binary. After the *New York Times* reported on Trump's memo outlining his plan, the Trans Lifeline, a service that offers crisis support to trans people, reported that it received four times more calls than usual. Trans people are almost nine times more likely to attempt suicide than cis people (a whopping 40 percent of trans people have tried to take their own lives). Trans people are also more likely to have been physically or sexually abused, discriminated against, and rejected by their families—all because they refuse to fit into the boxes that the dominant culture demands.

So what would a world be like without these boxes at all? What if gender was more like hair color—something people both control and notice, but that doesn't dictate opportunities, power, and privilege? What if you could shift and change your gender presentation regularly and be supported no matter what, as we see in the comic?

"What I want is a world in which gender still exists, but we no longer have to sacrifice everything in our entire lives just to have gender," said Tuck Woodstock, a gender and equity educator and the host of a podcast called *Gender Reveal*. At the end of each podcast episode, Woodstock asks their guest what the future of gender should look like, and the answers tend to cluster around a reimagining of gender that allows for experimentation, play, and acceptance. "Let's decriminalize gender," Woodstock said, only half-jokingly. "We can still have genders, but I don't want everything to be riding on it. I don't want to be treated differently based on gender. I don't want to have to jump through hoops and pay thousands of dollars to change everything so I can accurately describe myself."

In 2013, Leckie published a science-fiction book called *Ancillary Justice* that, among other things, explores a world where gender is, in Woodstock's words, decriminalized. The book centers around a people called the Radchaai, who don't distinguish anybody by gender, and the story is told from the point of view of a Radchaai character who uses she/her pronouns for everybody she encounters, including characters who do not identify as women. "I wanted to write a society that didn't care about gender," Leckie said.

What Leckie soon learned is that this was easier said than done. She tried making up new pronouns and even using none at all, but neither of those options felt right. When she landed on using "she" and "her" for everybody, it felt strange, but in a good way. "The effect was very weird and sort of almost disturbing, and the more I did it the happier I was with it."

Ancillary Justice went on to win Hugo, Nebula, Locus, Arthur C. Clarke, and BSFA awards, and many of the glowing reviews focused on Leckie's choices around gender, which, much like the people in the grocery store asking about her baby's pronouns, confused her. "It's not really a central part of the book," she said. "It's just a little piece of world-building. It does kind of astonish me, the number of people who talk about the book as though that's all it's about." Leckie also isn't the first science-fiction writer to ask questions about futures in which gender is somehow different, using language and pronouns to play with our expectations.

Ursula K. Le Guin famously painted a world where gender is irrelevant in her 1969 novel *The Left Hand of Darkness*, in part by referring to her completely androgynous characters as "he" and "him," a move that garnered criticism at the time from contemporary feminists (and one that Le Guin later said she saw as "a real flaw in the book"). Much like Leckie, Le Guin was surprised by how much people focused on the gendered element. "I was interested in writing a novel about people in a society that had never had a war. That came first. The androgyny came second," she wrote in a 1988 redux of a 1976 essay. "I eliminated gender to find out what was left. Whatever was left would be, presumably, simply human," she explained. Octavia Butler, Joanna Russ, Marge Piercy, Ryka Aoki, and Samuel R. Delany have all published well-known works of speculative fiction that play with the ideas of gender and identity.

I think these two things are connected: The reason so many reviewers focused on Le Guin's and Leckie's choices around gender pronouns is the same reason that gender is such a common playground in science fiction. And that's because for many people, especially in the United States, gender can feel inescapable. "Every single decision we make is in some ways gendered," said Laurie Essig, a sociologist at Middlebury College. "My glasses are gendered. My hair is gendered. The jeans I'm wearing have a gender. The way you're sitting right now is gendered." (Go ahead, readers, do a check—are you manspreading, or folding yourself to take up less space?) Because it's so entrenched in every single thing we do, a world beyond gender immediately feels far away—an idea that sits on a shelf next to warp drive and cloning and giant space fleets. Playing with something so fundamental, even as a small piece of world-building, captures both imagination and attention, because for many people it feels so deeply impossible.

Part of this immutability comes from the idea that our current ideas around gender are in some way "natural." Of course, that couldn't be further from the truth. Like race, gender is a construct designed to manipulate and solidify power to make one group (men, white people) dominant over another (women, not-white people). And, troublingly, over the past twenty years, science journalists have become complicit in obscuring this foundational fact. "It's been this really bizarre flourishing of Victorian ideas about 'innate' male gender and female gender," said Essig.

Not only is it bad science to definitively connect biology and gender—the degree to which gender is biologically influenced is hotly debated, but at the very least experts agree that cultural, social, psychological, and economic factors weigh heavily—Essig says that it's a dangerous path to go down for other reasons, too. "It's bad for our lives to believe that we're born with a gender, and that that gender determines who we are in the future." If gender is indeed biological, then arguments about whether women are just genetically predisposed, for example, to be worse at math become legitimized, even if there's no evidence behind those claims. Gender essentialism in the service of rights for trans people is still gender essentialism, and can still be harmful. "If we allow people to find their 'true gender,' that means we believe that there is a 'true gender,' and that it determines who we are as human beings," Essig said. The idea of one singular "true gender" that people have their entire lives is still constrictive.

Meredith Talusan, a journalist and the author of the memoir *Fairest*, said she's experienced this constriction herself. When she transitioned from identifying as a gay man to identifying as a queer femme trans woman, she says it didn't feel like escaping categories altogether. "It's like moving from a really, really cramped box to a much more spacious box. But it's still a box."

But the future doesn't have to have boxes at all. Talusan is one of many people who are already trying to occupy somewhere in between them. "I'm at a point now where, when I tell people that I'm trans, it's just as likely for them to think that I'm female to male, rather than male to female. There's this way I confuse people's gendered expectations just by being who I am. And that has been really freeing," she told me.

So what might happen if we could all be that free? To shake off our shackles, decriminalize gender, and open the world up to a new set of possibilities? What if we could be, in Le Guin's words, "simply human"?[1]

---

1   We'd certainly have far fewer injuries and even deaths at "gender reveal parties," which are a ritual I'm convinced future humans will look back at with confusion and horror the way we might consider bloodletting today.

The most immediate effects would be felt in trans and nonbinary communities, where gender expression is most intensely, often violently policed. According to the National Center for Transgender Equality, one in ten trans people reported having a family member act violently toward them, half of them are survivors of sexual violence, 29 percent live in poverty, and 39 percent reported "serious psychological distress." Those who can afford things like health care often experience discrimination or even the denial of services because of their gender identity. In a world without such rigidity, trans and nonbinary people would face far fewer obstacles in life, freeing them up to spend more of their time creating, thinking, and dreaming.

But this world wouldn't just be freeing for trans and nonbinary people. Woodstock points out that cis people are also crushed under the expectations of an unbending binary, and cis men in particular. "It opens up new possibilities to people who are assigned male at birth who experience toxic masculinity," they said. Men are told they must never express true emotion, must be physically and mentally strong, should attempt to dominate everybody around them, and are expected to solve problems using strength and often violence. Experts have linked these oppressive expectations to bullying, suicide, domestic violence, and even mass shootings. If men were freed from these expectations, the world might become a much safer place for everybody.

If certain roles were no longer gendered, things that were once considered "women's work" or "men's work" would be redistributed. Childcare and housework would no longer be something women were expected to do, and birth control would be accessible to everybody. Women would no longer be chided for being "too aggressive" in meetings, and men would be allowed to wear sparkles and cry without being called "sissies." Government forms would no longer ask you for your gender, the way they don't ask if you're right- or left-handed. The TSA could no longer treat trans people's genitalia as anomalies, which would make traveling while trans far less dehumanizing.

A world with fluid gender also requires reimagining sexual orientation—in a world where there are not simply men and women, but instead a flourishing coral reef of gender diversity, what does it mean to be "gay" or "straight" anymore? How would you classify the relationship between Nur and Page (and why do we have to)? What does it mean to be a family, to be a "mother" or a "father"—Noor is the parent who carries the child, but their ex has also taken on that role. The questions, and opportunities, are endless. "It would open up human potential in ways that we can't even imagine," Essig said. "And perhaps with that we could open up some of the major crises that face us as a world community, whether it's global warming, or wars without end, or structural violence."

The way we do this will matter, though, because there's a potential dystopia lurking behind these utopian dreams. There's a difference between imagining a world where gender is abolished in one blow and one in which we do the much harder work of dismantling the systems that created this oppressive binary in the first place. If the government suddenly decided to ban gender but didn't do anything to address the structural inequalities that currently hinge on patriarchy, then nothing would improve. Those once known as women, trans, or nonbinary would still suffer at the hands of the more powerful people once known as cis men; they would just no longer be allowed to talk about the root cause. "Do you have the language and the resources to deal with that in a society that is not allowed to talk about gender?" Leckie asked. "If you just say, 'We don't see this, it's not important,' that will be terrible unless you've addressed the systemic issues that cause the discrimination to begin with."

This comic and chapter are the most optimistic in the book, because a world without such rigid gender roles really could be incredible. But most of the experts I talked to aren't particularly hopeful that we'll get there anytime soon. "I think a lot about how we made it to open-heart surgery and we made it to the Internet before we figured out how to be decent human beings and treat each other with respect," said Woodstock. "I personally think we are going to slide into the ocean before we achieve gender equality on any global scale."

In late 2019 and early 2020, there were 226 anti-LGBT bills introduced in the United States, most of which targeted trans youth. It might seem like we are on a path toward a more inclusive view of gender, but that future is never guaranteed; it will take work and attention. The fastest way to fail in our quest to build a better future is to take success as a given.

But rather than leave you on a sour note, I'll tell you this instead: Woodstock runs a small social media group for their podcast, where listeners can talk about their gender questions and experiments with a supportive community. And in this very small space, it's a bit like the utopia we've been describing. "It's really lovely to be seeing a place in which gender really matters to people but also can be changed as easily as changing your hair," Woodstock said.

It will take work from all of us to make the spirit and support of that group possible beyond the walls of this small community, but it's work that is worth doing. Because unlike so many futures we've imagined in this book, there's a very clear and frankly pretty easy path to a better world here. We just have to choose to take it.

UNDER THE SEA

BY AMELIA ONORATO

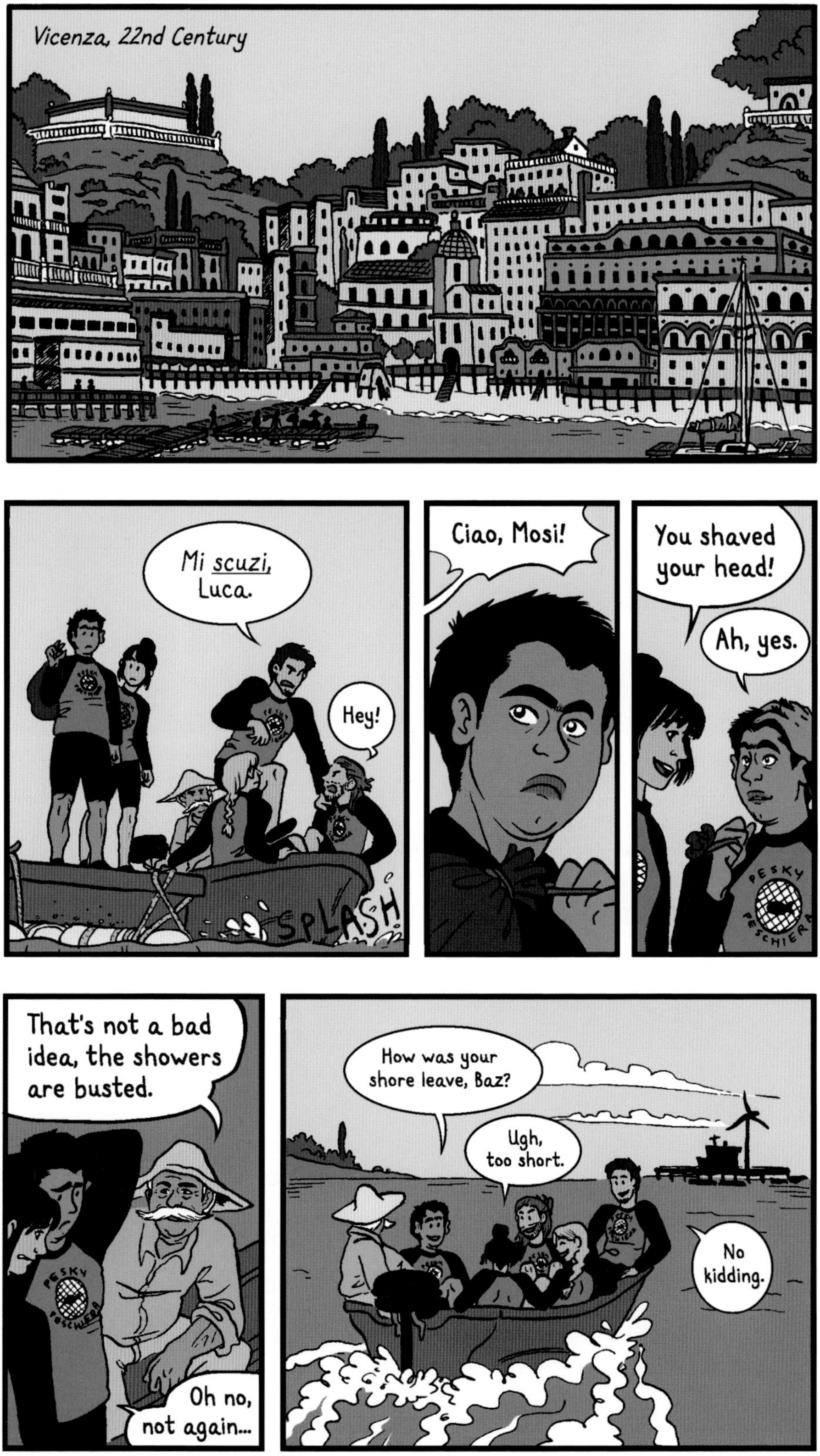
Vicenza, 22nd Century
Mi scuzi, Luca.
Hey!
SPLASH
Ciao, Mosi!
You shaved your head!
Ah, yes.
PESKY PESCHIERA
That's not a bad idea, the showers are busted.
Oh no, not again...
How was your shore leave, Baz?
Ugh, too short.
No kidding.

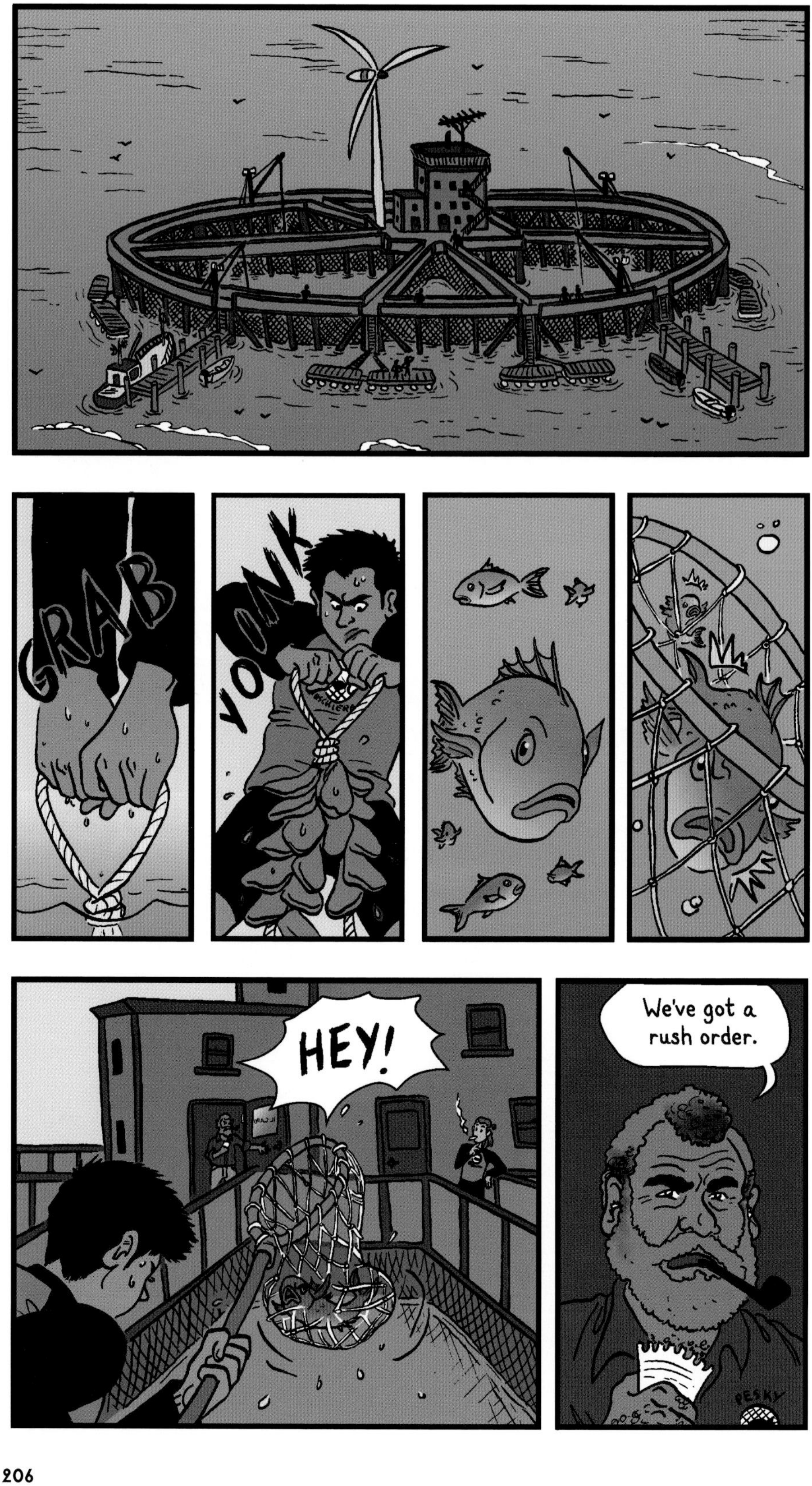
GRAB
YOONK
HEY!
We've got a rush order.
PESKY

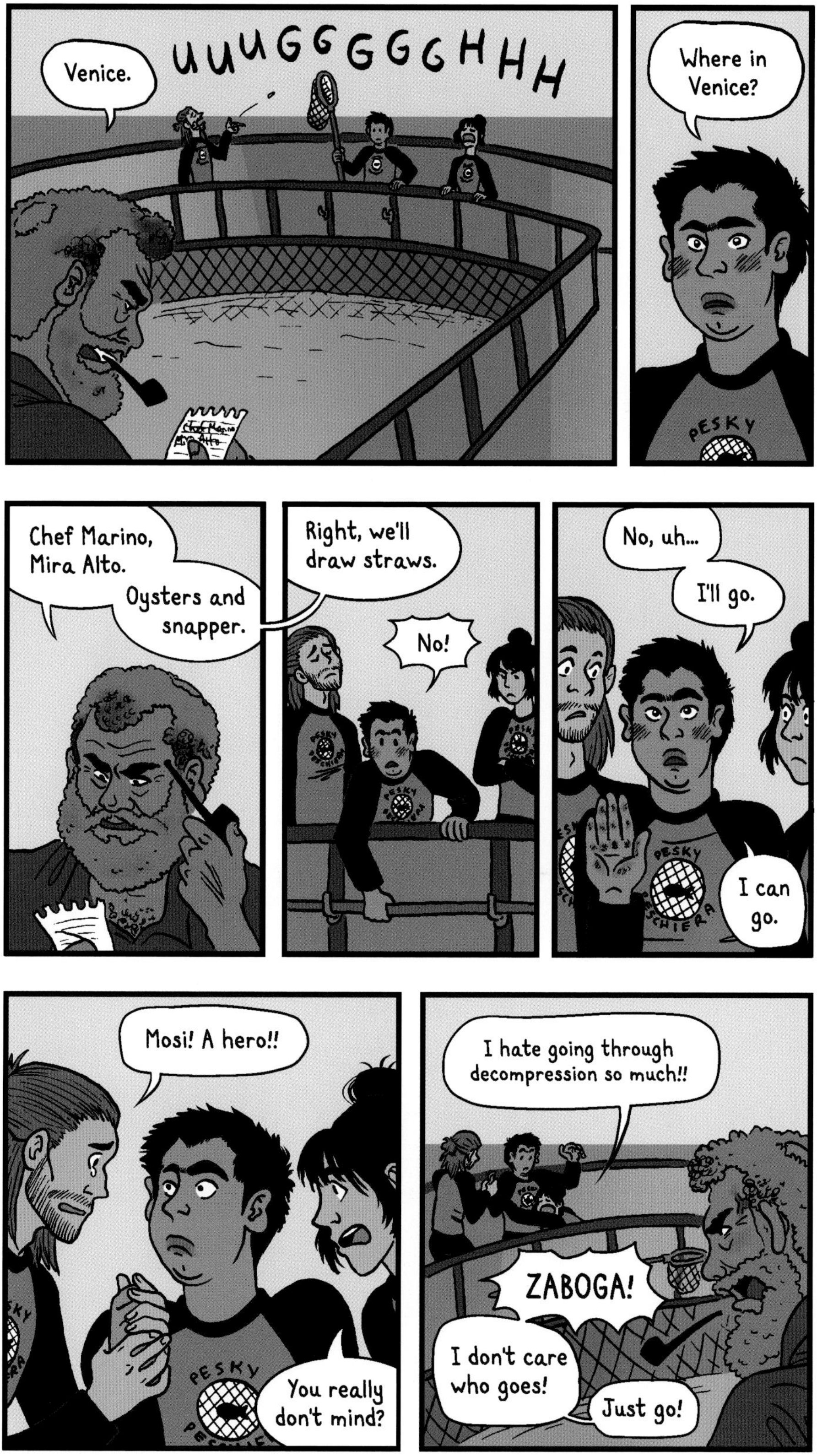
Venice.
UUUGGGGGHHH
Where in Venice?
Chef Marino, Mira Alto.
Oysters and snapper.
Right, we'll draw straws.
No!
No, uh...
I'll go.
I can go.
Mosi! A hero!!
You really don't mind?
I hate going through decompression so much!!
ZABOGA!
I don't care who goes!
Just go!

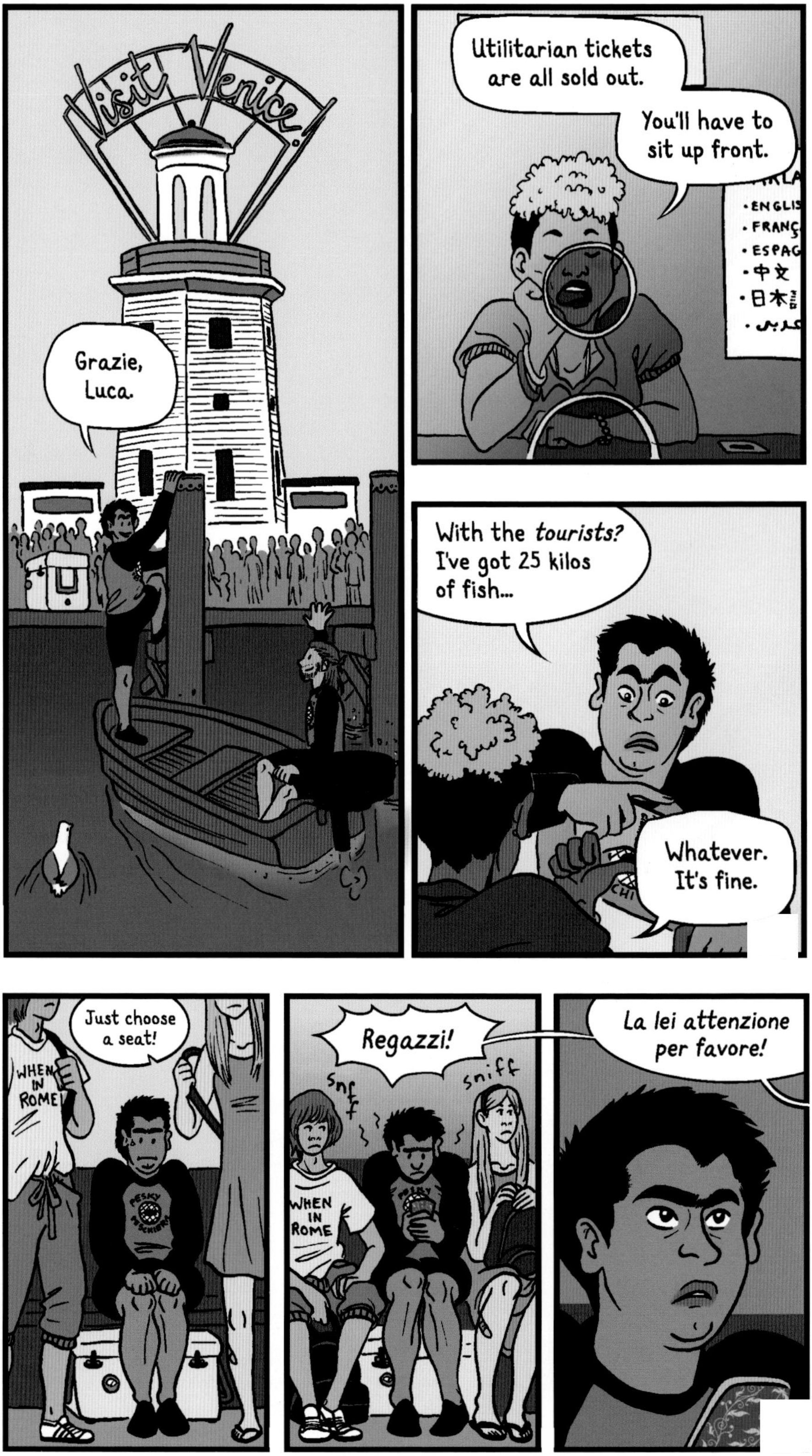

Visit Venice!
Grazie, Luca.
Utilitarian tickets are all sold out.
You'll have to sit up front.
• ENGLIS
• FRANÇ
• ESPAG
• 中文
• 日本
With the *tourists?* I've got 25 kilos of fish...
Whatever. It's fine.
Just choose a seat!
WHEN IN ROME
PESKY PESCHIERA
Regazzi!
sniff
sniff
WHEN IN ROME
La lei attenzione per favore!

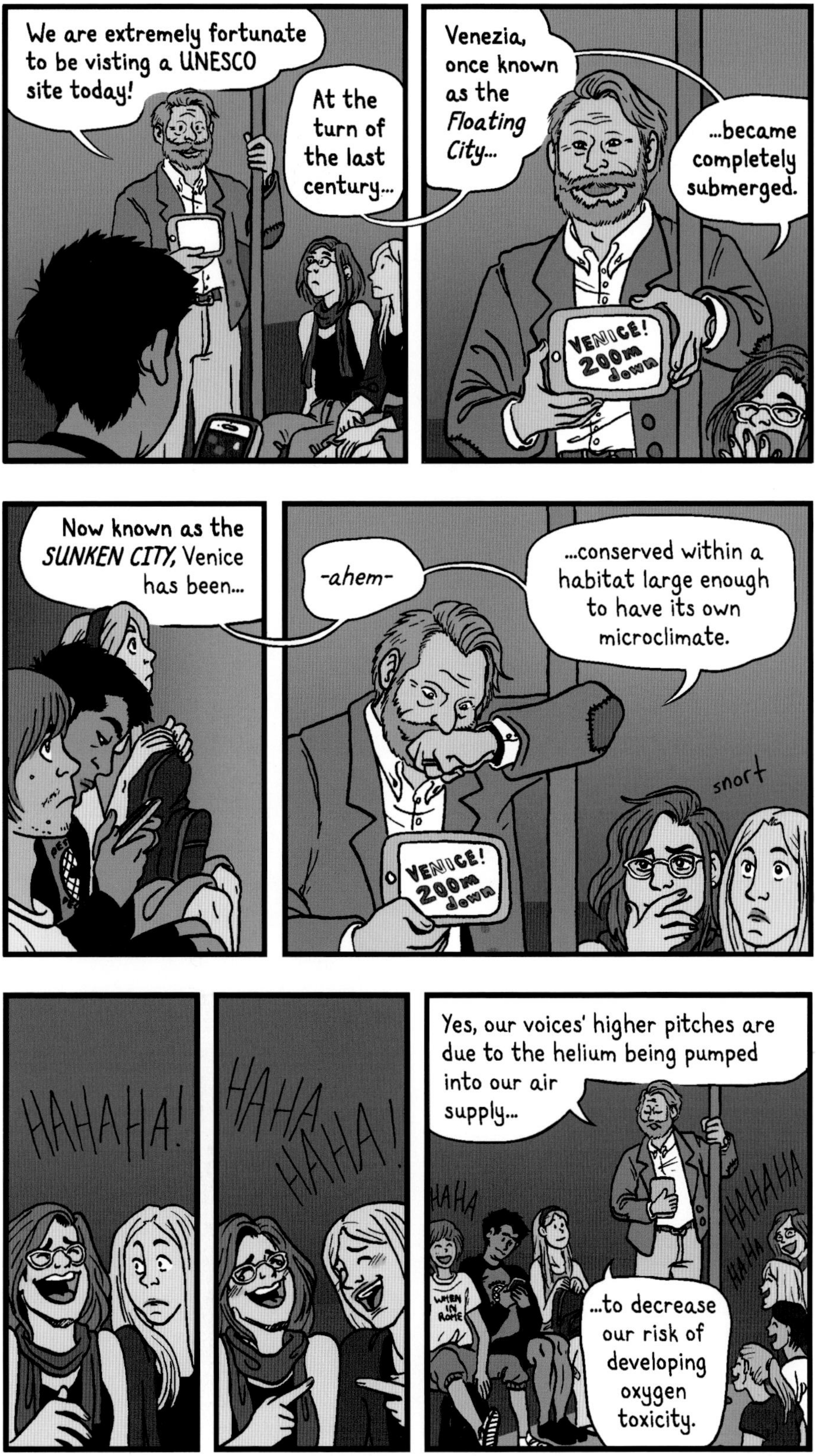
We are extremely fortunate to be visting a UNESCO site today!
At the turn of the last century...
Venezia, once known as the *Floating City*...
...became completely submerged.
VENICE! 200m down
Now known as the *SUNKEN CITY,* Venice has been...
-ahem-
...conserved within a habitat large enough to have its own microclimate.
VENICE! 200m down
snort
HAHAHA!
HAHA HAHA!
Yes, our voices' higher pitches are due to the helium being pumped into our air supply...
HAHA
HAHAHA
HAHA
WHEN IN ROME
...to decrease our risk of developing oxygen toxicity.

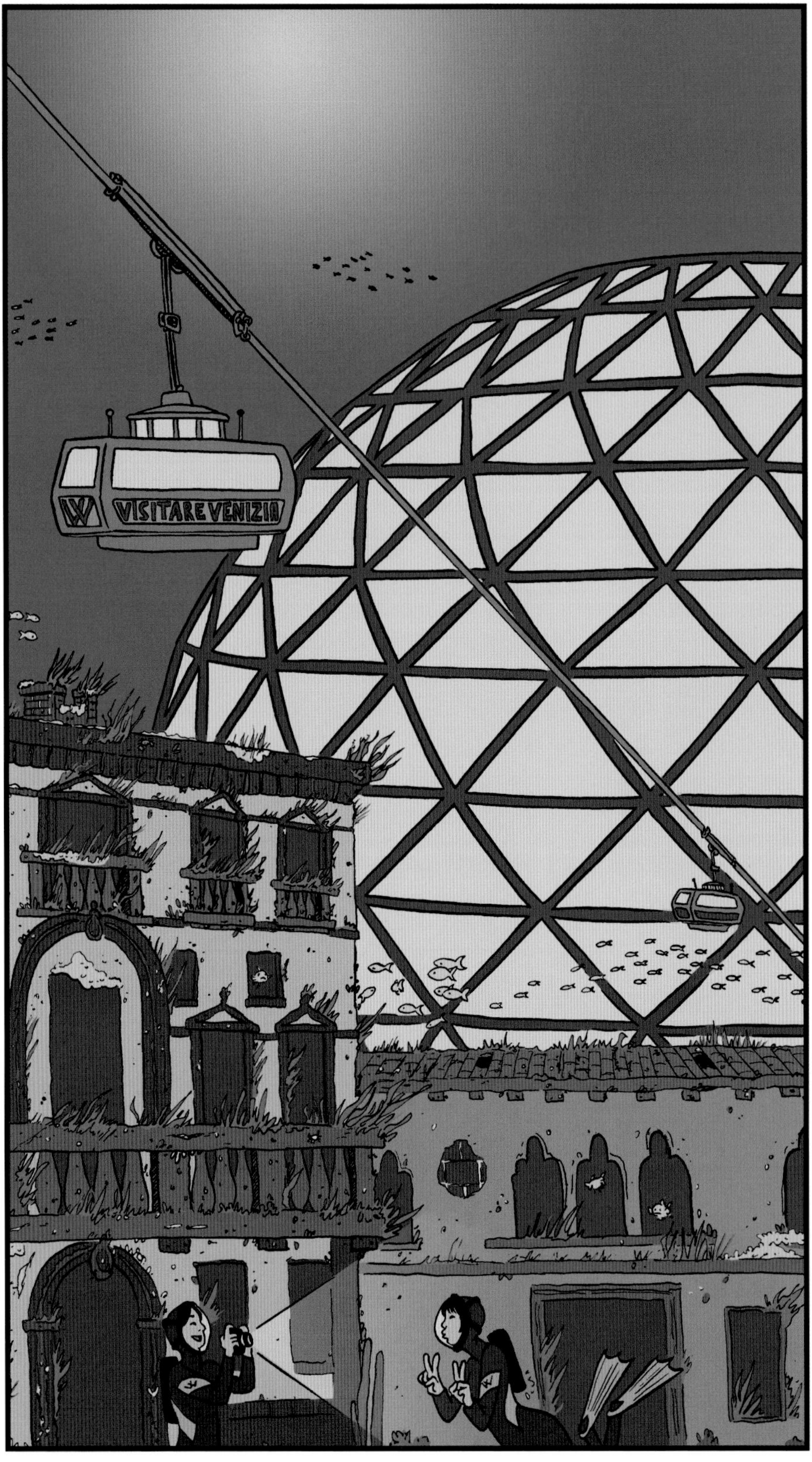
VISITARE VENIZIA

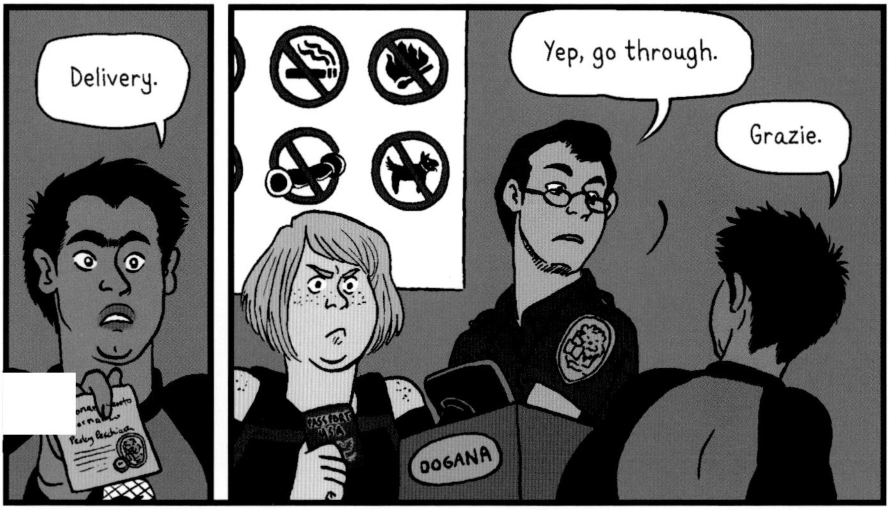
Delivery.
Yep, go through.
Grazie.
PASSPORT USA
DOGANA

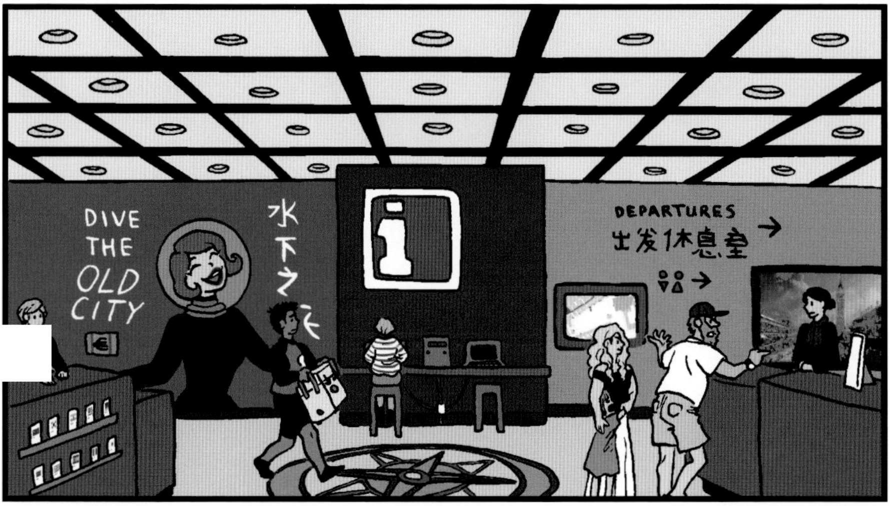
DIVE THE OLD CITY
水下之
DEPARTURES
出发休息室

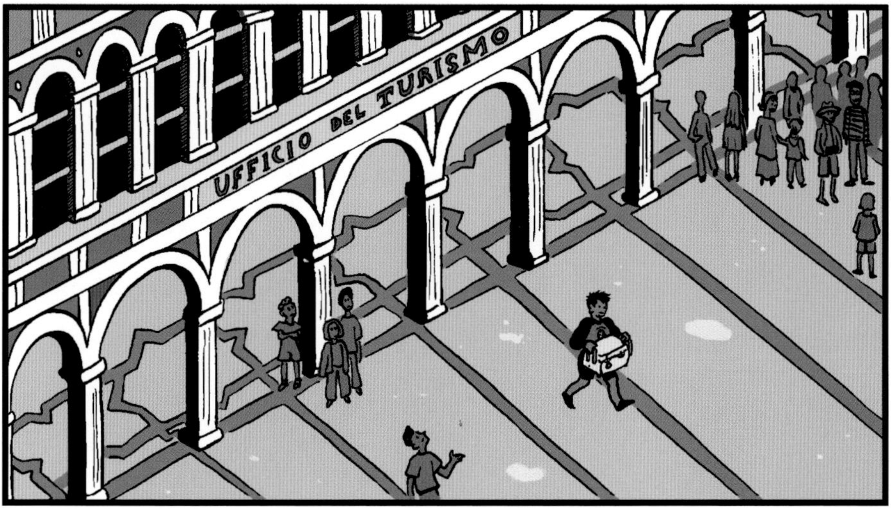
UFFICIO DEL TURISMO

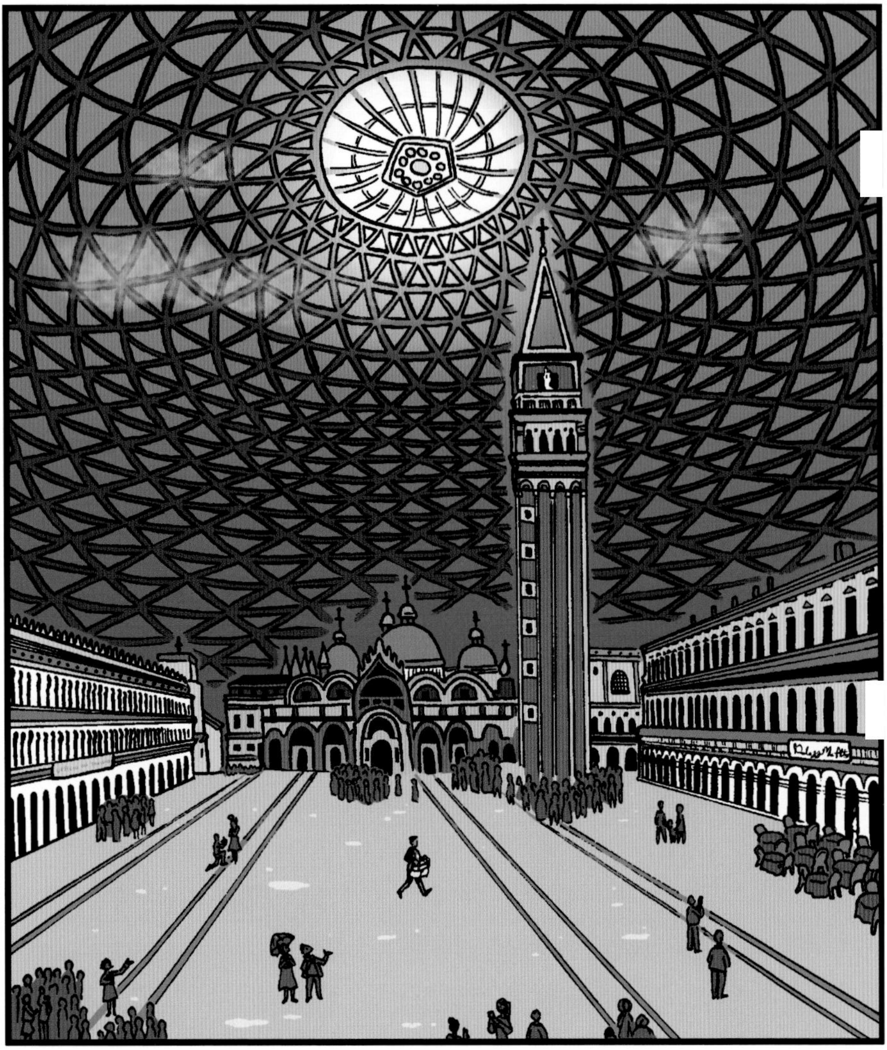

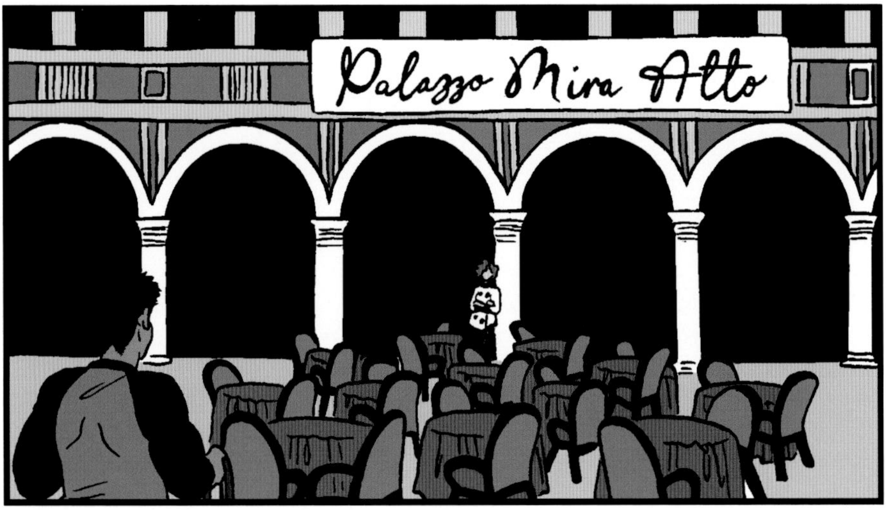
Palazzo Mira Atto

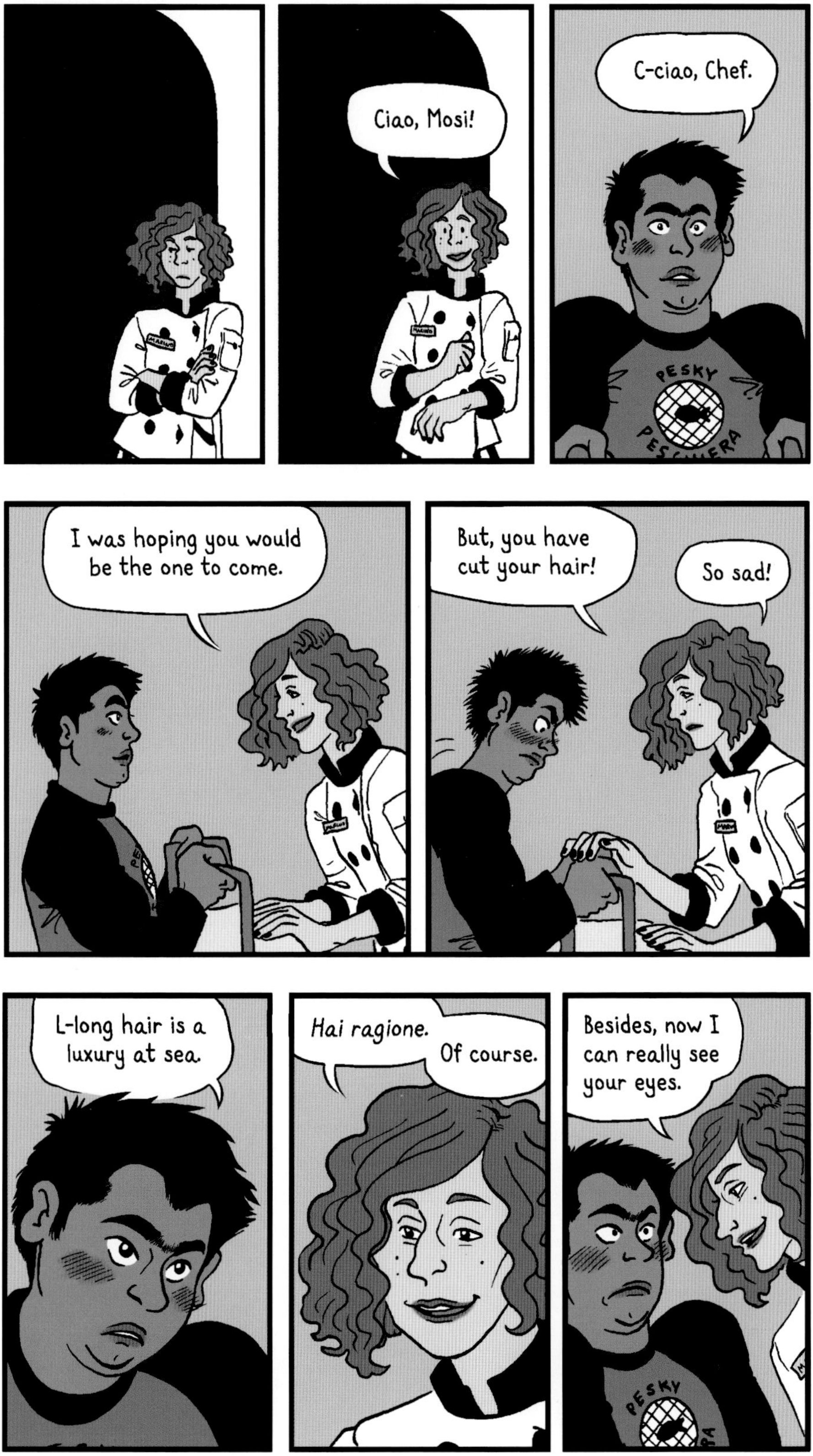
Ciao, Mosi!
C-ciao, Chef.
PESKY PESCHERA
I was hoping you would be the one to come.
But, you have cut your hair!
So sad!
L-long hair is a luxury at sea.
Hai ragione.
Of course.
Besides, now I can really see your eyes.
PESKY

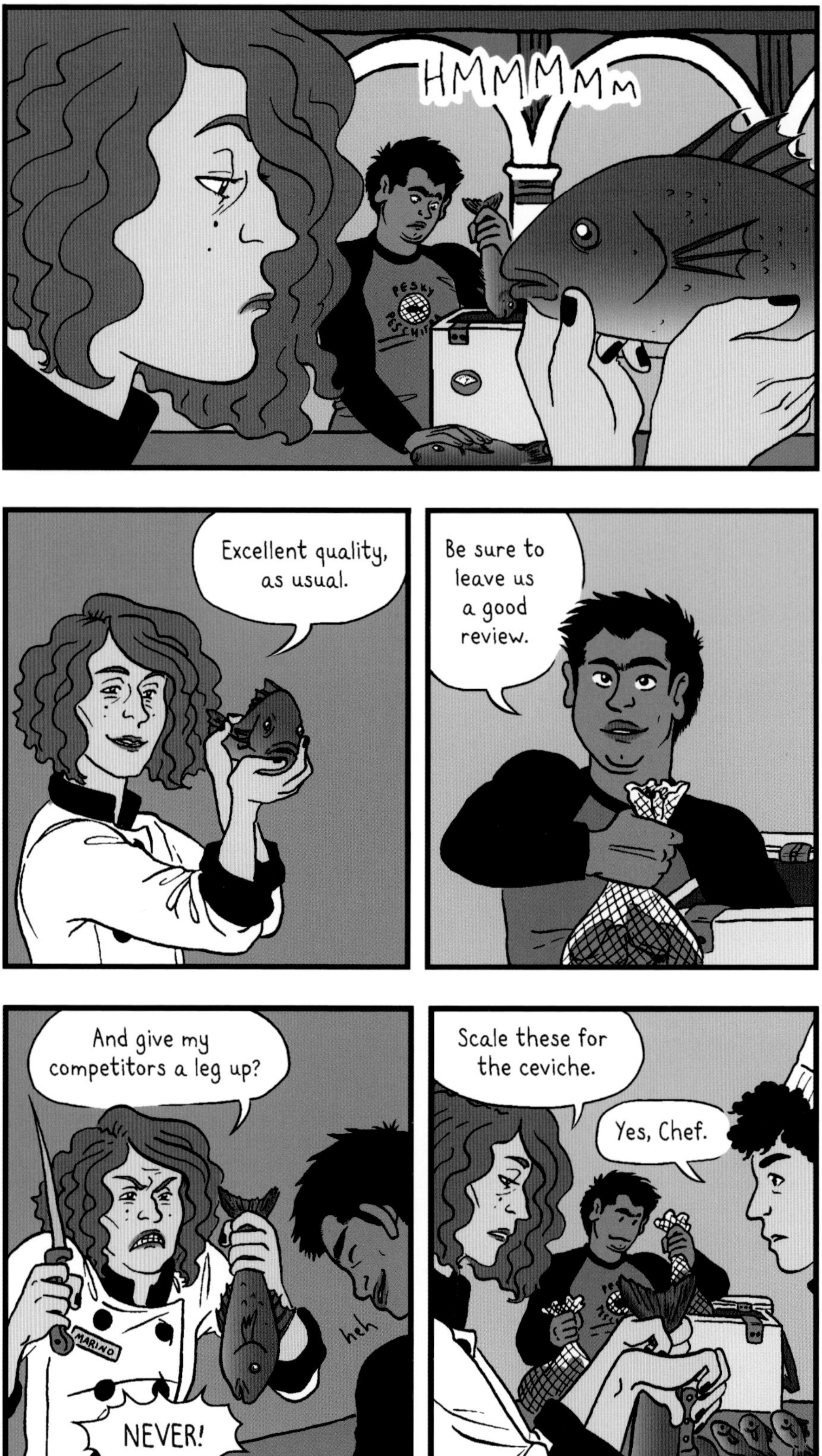
HMMMMm
PESKY PESCHIERA
Excellent quality, as usual.
Be sure to leave us a good review.
And give my competitors a leg up?
MARINO
NEVER!
heh
Scale these for the ceviche.
Yes, Chef.

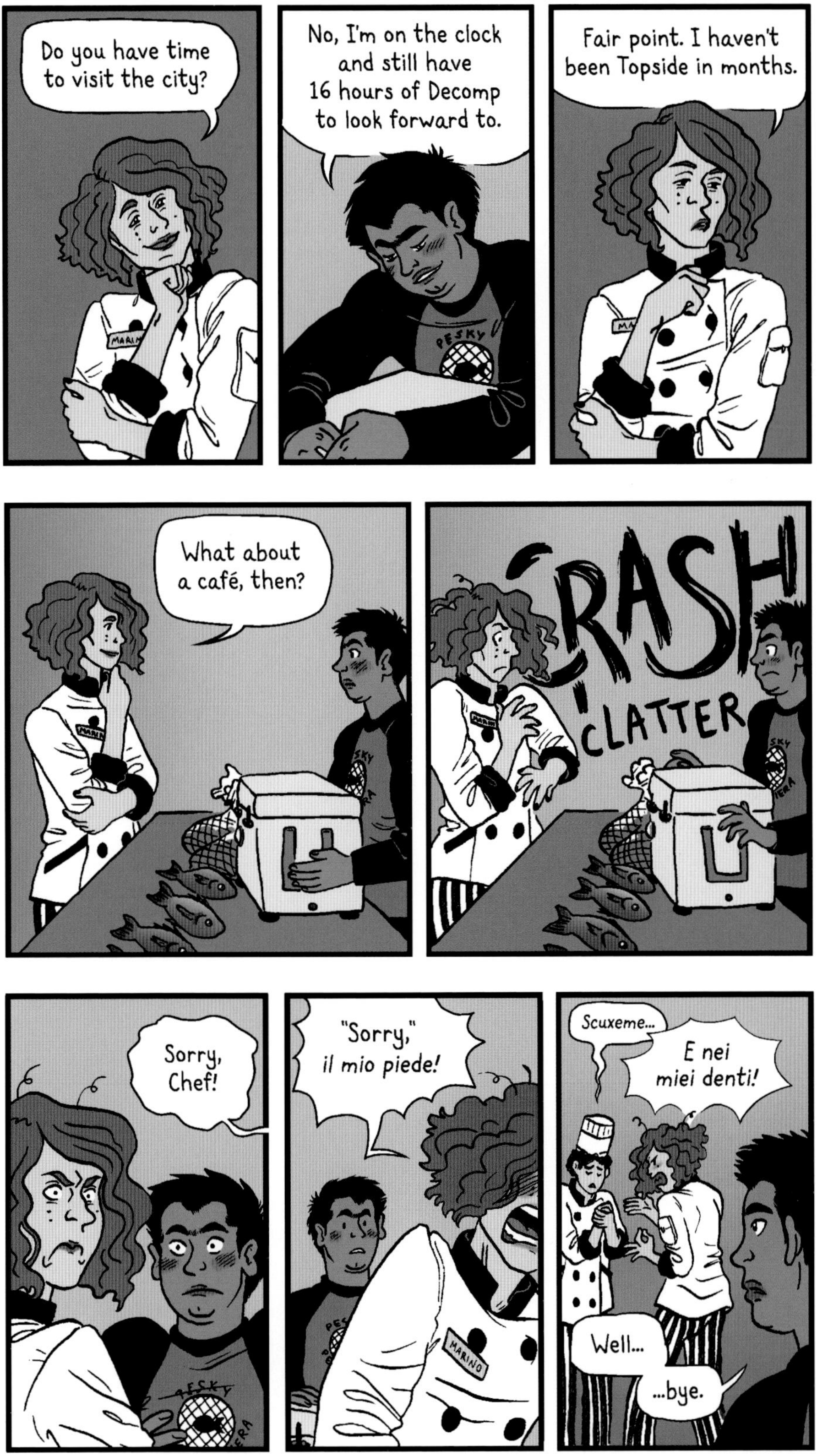
Do you have time to visit the city?
No, I'm on the clock and still have 16 hours of Decomp to look forward to.
Fair point. I haven't been Topside in months.
What about a café, then?
CRASH
CLATTER
Sorry, Chef!
"Sorry," il mio piede!
Scuxeme...
E nei miei denti!
Well...
...bye.

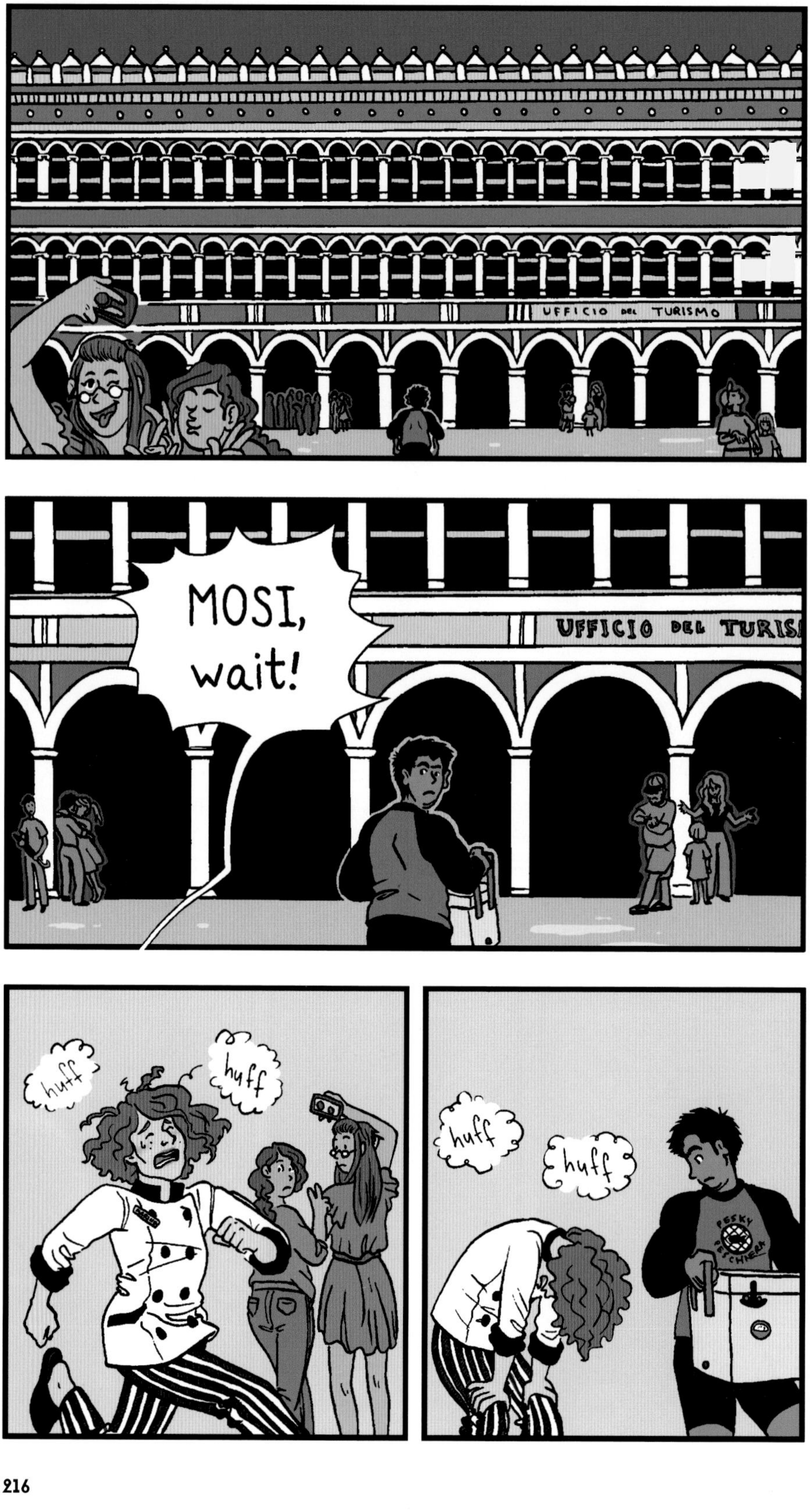
UFFICIO DEL TURISMO
MOSI, wait!
UFFICIO DEL TURIS
huff
huff
huff
huff
PESKY PESCHIERA

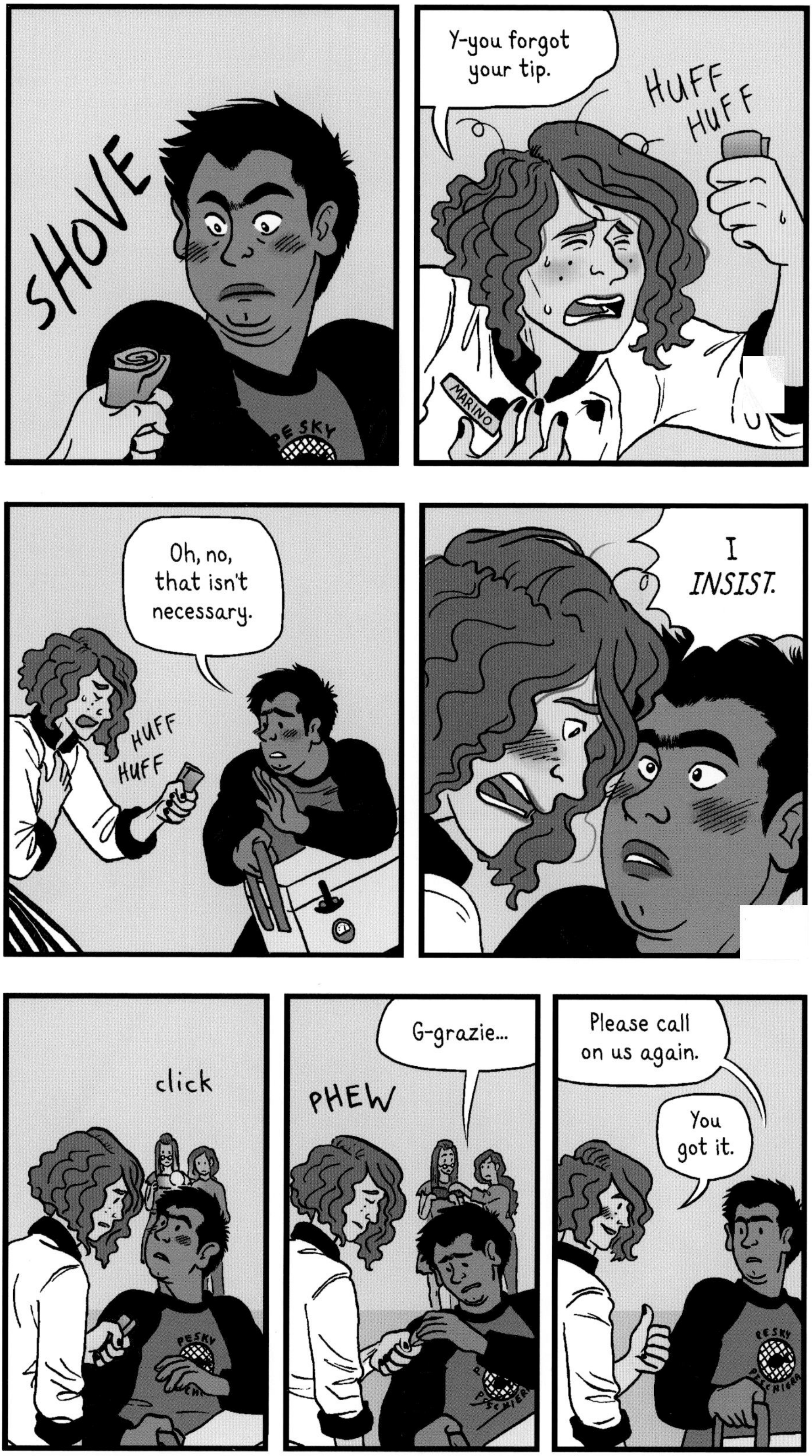
SHOVE
PESKY
Y-you forgot your tip.
HUFF HUFF
MARINO
Oh, no, that isn't necessary.
HUFF HUFF
I *INSIST.*
click
PESKY
PHEW
G-grazie...
Please call on us again.
You got it.
PESKY

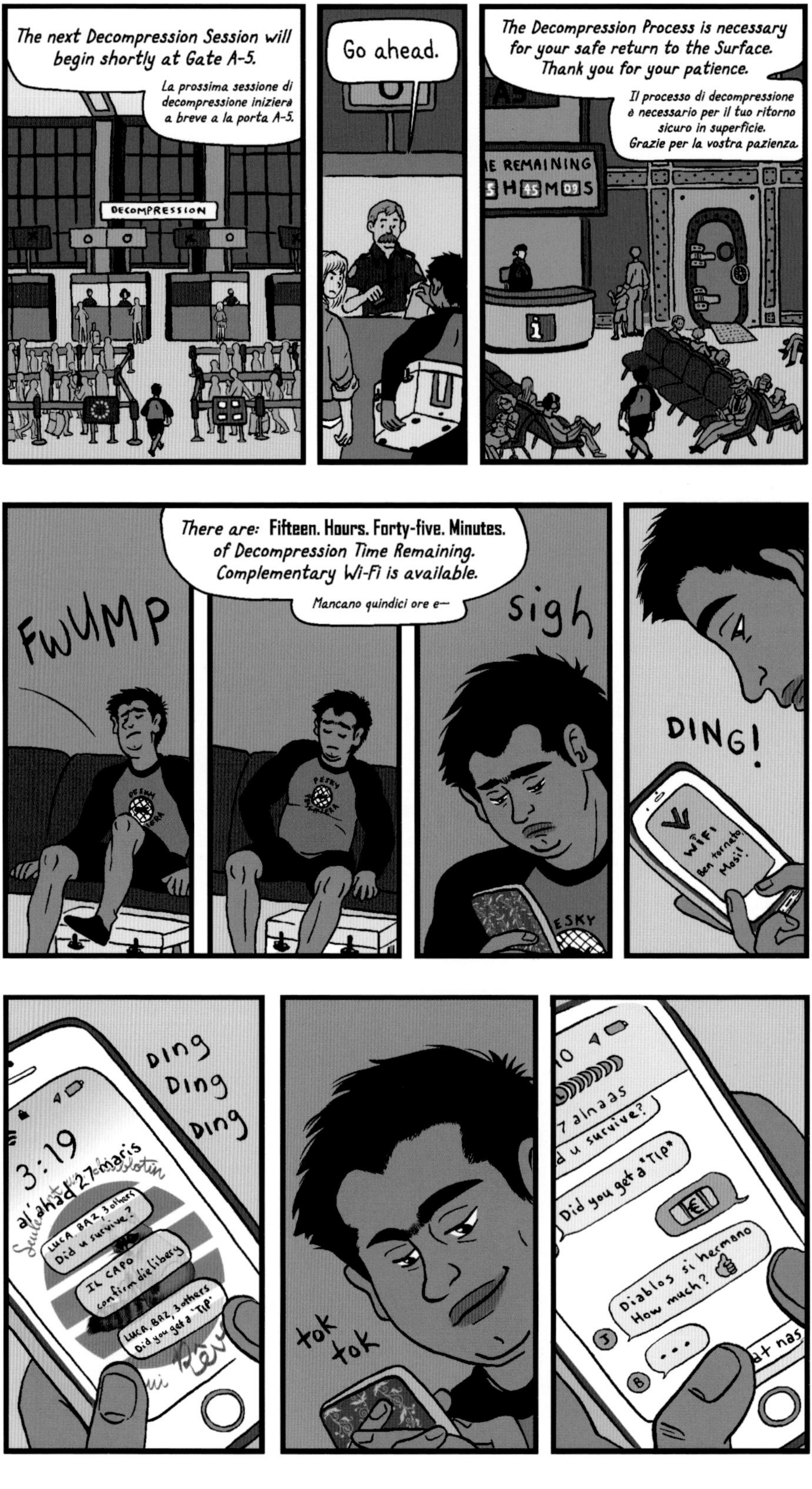

The next Decompression Session will begin shortly at Gate A-5.
La prossima sessione di decompressione inizierà a breve a la porta A-5.
DECOMPRESSION
Go ahead.
The Decompression Process is necessary for your safe return to the Surface. Thank you for your patience.
Il processo di decompressione è necessario per il tuo ritorno sicuro in superficie. Grazie per la vostra pazienza.
E REMAINING
There are: Fifteen. Hours. Forty-five. Minutes. of Decompression Time Remaining. Complementary Wi-Fi is available.
Mancano quindici ore e—
FWUMP
sigh
DING!
WiFi
Ben tornato, Masi!
DING DING DING
3:19
al'ahad 27 maris
LUCA, BAZ, 3 others
Did u survive?
IL CAPO
confirm dielibery
LUCA, BAZ, 3 others
Did you get a "TIP"
tok tok
7 alnaas
d u survive?
Did you get a "TIP"
Diablos si hermano
How much?
...

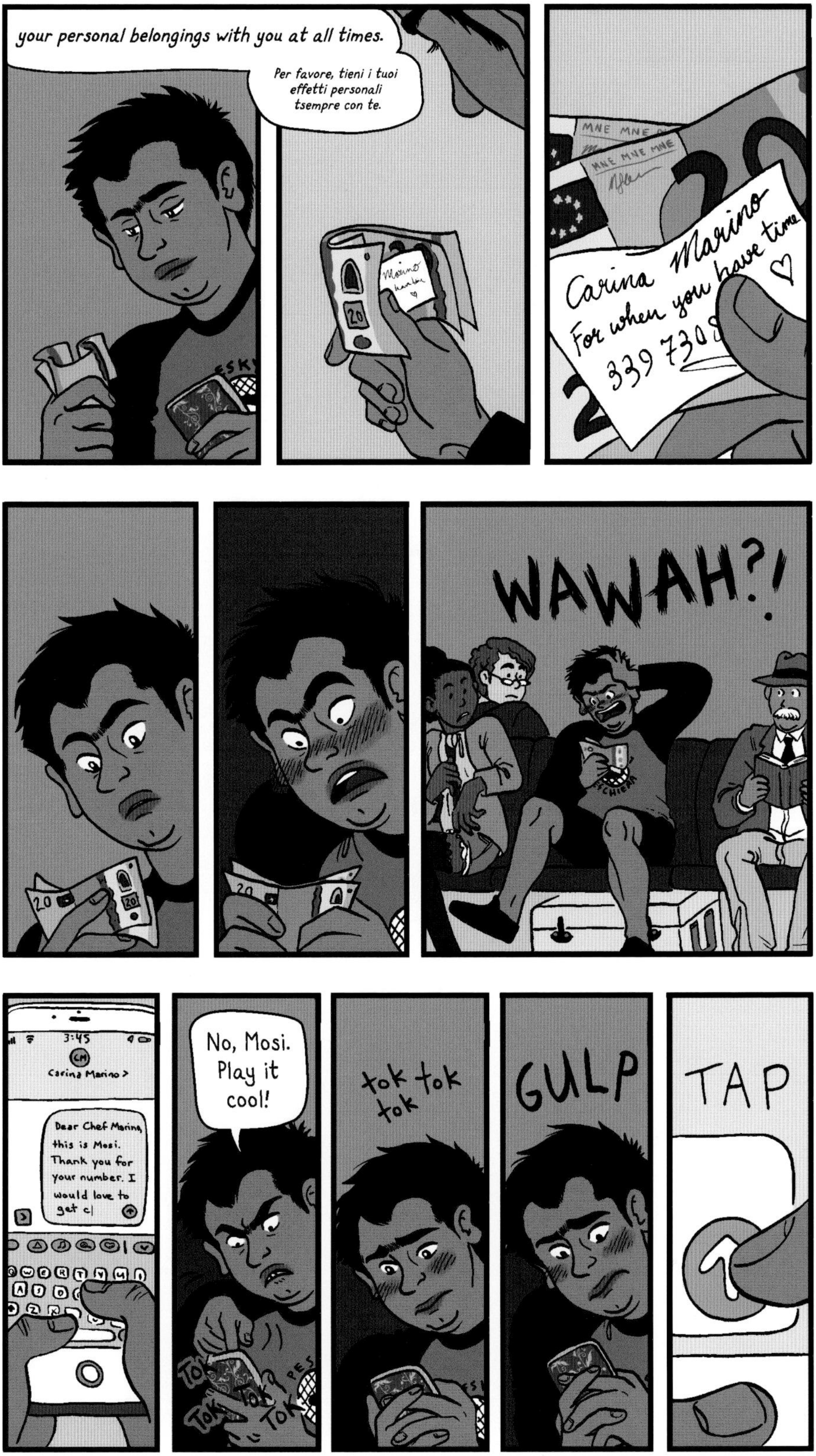
your personal belongings with you at all times.
Per favore, tieni i tuoi effetti personali tsempre con te.
Carina Marino
For when you have time ♡
339 730
WAWAH?!
3:45
Carina Marino >
Dear Chef Marino, this is Mosi. Thank you for your number. I would love to get c|
No, Mosi. Play it cool!
TOK TOK TOK TOK
tok tok tok
GULP
TAP

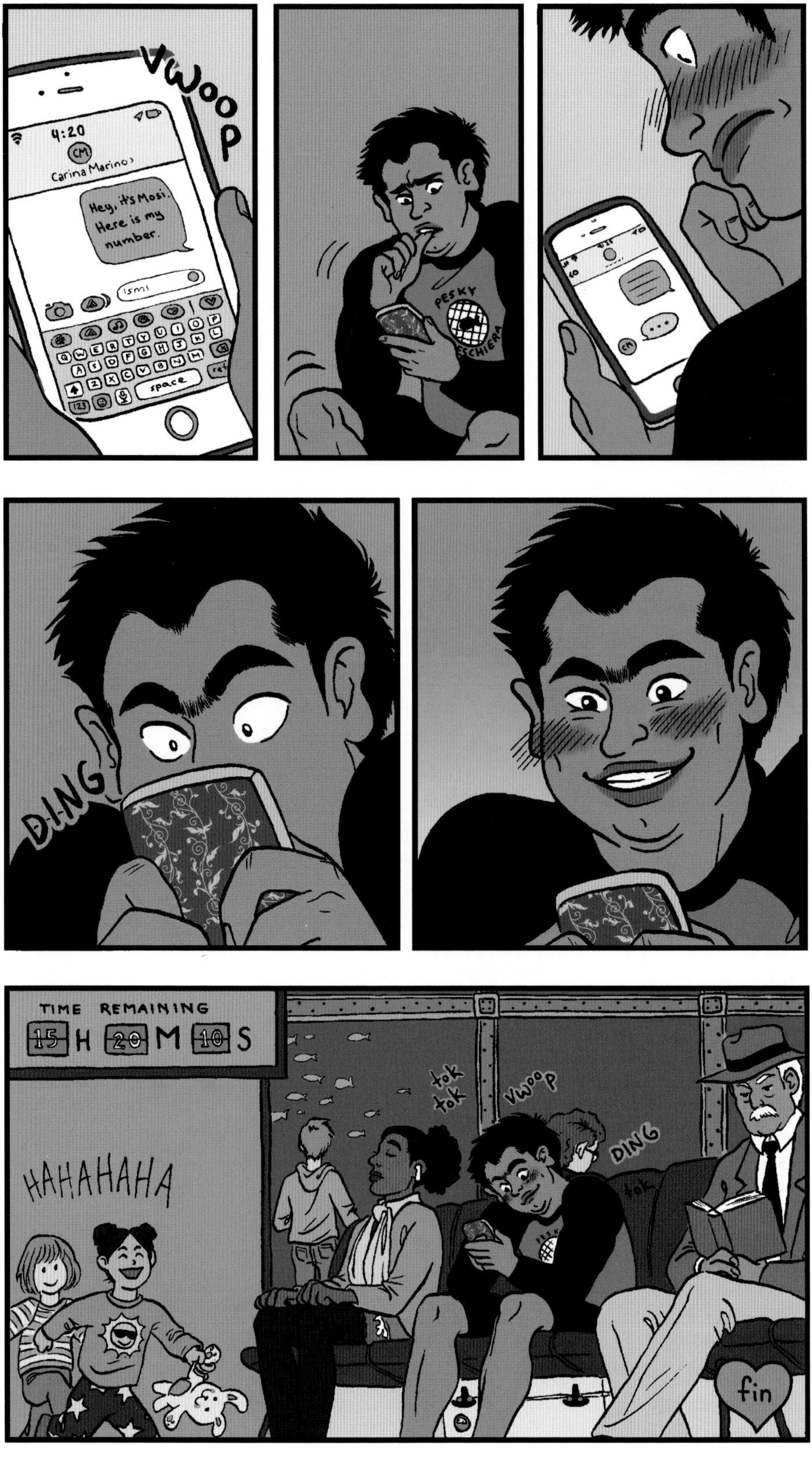
VWOOP
4:20
CM
Carina Marino
Hey, it's Mosi. Here is my number.
space
DING
TIME REMAINING
15 H 20 M 10 S
HAHAHAHA
tok tok
VWOOP
DING
tok
fin

UNDER THE SEA

CAN WE LIVE IN AND ON THE OCEAN?

THE SURFACE OF THE EARTH IS 70 PERCENT OCEAN AND growing. Thanks to our unwillingness to take real steps to curb climate change, we can now expect millions of people to be displaced by an ever-rising sea in the not-so-distant future. By 2050, just a mere thirty years away, some projections say that Osaka, Rio de Janeiro, Bangkok, Mumbai, and Alexandria will all find themselves flooded. Southern Vietnam, including its capital and economic hub, Ho Chi Minh City, will disappear beneath the waves. A three-degree Celsius change in global temperatures could swallow Miami, Boston, Honolulu, and New Orleans. Venice is slowly sinking due to a combination of climate change, aging infrastructure, and tectonic shifts. In 2016, five tiny isles in the Solomon Islands disappeared. Nuatambu island, once home to twenty-five families, is now referred to in the past tense—it no longer exists. By now, visions of cities underwater thanks to climate change are almost cliché, but they're also very real. The sea is coming for us, and while a rising tide might lift all boats, we don't have enough boats to live on.

Climate change will demand that people adjust to new realities, new geographies, new landscapes, and find new solutions. In the comic you just read, you see one vision of our adjustment: a world where we live both above and below the sea and use the ocean's real estate as a new kind of garden. If the Earth is mostly ocean, this future thinking goes, let's use it—for food, for shelter, for entertainment. Let the Age of Aquarians truly begin.

The easiest way to "use" the ocean is to turn its vast expanse into a new, salty farmland. A 2018 study estimated that there are about 72 million square kilometers of ocean that are ideal for ocean farming, or aquaculture. And entrepreneurs around the world are taking up this idea left and right, often before regulations or rules are in place. And in some cases, are inventing new ways to farm beyond the easy, ideal locales, hoping to open up the entire sea.

Take Bernard Friedman for example. As a kid, Friedman was part of the Future Farmers of America program. "I love to grow anything and everything," he said. Today, Friedman farms mussels off the coast of Santa Barbara, dropping his ropes out into the ocean and gathering them back up when his mussels are ready to eat. "What I do is basically just what you would do on land. It's just out in the ocean; it's the exact same thing," he said.

This isn't to say it's easy. If Friedman has learned one thing from his time as an open-water mussel farmer, it's to plan for disappointment. "Everything you think is going to work out usually doesn't," he said. Unlike modern cattle or chickens, there aren't nearly as many well-defined breeds of mussels that have been carefully domesticated and cultivated specifically for harvest. Even after more than a decade of farming, Friedman is still working out the best mussel species to use, the best way to get the baby mussels to attach to his ropes, and how long to leave them out for. But perhaps the main difference between Friedman and your local strawberry farmer is that Friedman doesn't own the water he uses to grow his mussels. In fact, whether he's "allowed" to farm in the open ocean like this has been up in the air for years.

Friedman's teachers and mentors in the Future Farmers of America probably didn't think that this was the future of farming their students would be doing, but Friedman isn't alone. If you take a boat from La Paz, Mexico, out into the Sea of Cortez, you may encounter a vast UFO-shaped object beneath the waves that looks a bit like it belongs to an aquatic supervillain. Inside you might find totoaba or red snapper circling in the waves. This floating fish farm is called the SeaStation, and it's the brainchild of a company called Innovasea as part of their push to farm fish in the open ocean.

The advantage of these oddly shaped pens is that they can be placed out in the open ocean. Today, most ocean farms are found close to shore in protected bays where the waves and weather tends to be muted and workers can get to the pens easily by boat. But Innovasea envisions a future where we use the rest of the ocean, past these protected zones, as our fishy farmland, too. "We're running out of available sites," said Tyler Sclodnick, senior aquaculture scientist at Innovasea. To fill tomorrow's bellies, we have to look out into the horizon. In this future, we may get everything from fish sticks to prized sushi from farms far offshore, floating domes and saucers rocking in the waves.

But where will we be living while we eat those fish? As the oceans rise and swallow up the shores, new ways of living will rise, too. In the comic you saw, underwater living is a perk of the rich, while the rest of us continue to make do with the crumbling infrastructure, droughts, and extreme weather on land. If Venice is going to sink eventually (as some experts predict), why not make it a business opportunity? A veritable Disneyland beneath the waves, exclusive to those who can afford to make the trip.

Today, there are already ritzy hotels that offer an underwater experience. In the Maldives, you can book a villa called "The Muraka," which means coral in the local language, Dhivehi. For $50,000 a night you can sleep in a glass dome on the ocean floor. The Muraka's location is darkly ironic, as the above-water portion of the Maldives are quickly disappearing in large part thanks to the actions of those who can afford to spend $50,000 a night on a hotel room.

The Muraka's price tag is certainly jaw-dropping, but living underwater won't be cheap. Humans were not made for ocean life—our bodies crumple at depth, and there is that small, pesky problem of oxygen. Spending time underwater is so arduous, in fact, that astronauts are often put through their paces at depth to prepare them for the challenges of space. In the 1960s, while the astronauts were getting all the glory, a team of aquanauts were making their own history under the ocean with the SEALAB project.[1] And one astronaut, Scott Carpenter, who later joined the underwater crew, said that his time at SEALAB was more dangerous and grueling than anything he did in space.

Much like the Apollo program, SEALAB had to work out what the human body could withstand in these new environments. And thanks to the research of a diver named George Bond, they learned that humans could live at depth for long periods of time, as long as they were brought back up carefully, with time to decompress. This method of diving is called saturation diving—quite literally your body becomes saturated with the gases you're breathing—and it's still in effect today on oil rigs around the world. But it's not without its indignities. To go deep, divers have to breathe a mixture of helium and oxygen, which makes their voices sound quite comical (as you saw in the comic).

You've likely heard the historic recording of Neil Armstrong confirming that Apollo 11 had landed on the moon, his gravelly voice crackling across the speakers announcing that "the Eagle has landed." It turns out there's a similar recording of the first person to enter SEALAB, two hundred feet down at the bottom of the ocean just off of Bermuda—it's just not nearly as badass because they all sound like they've been huffing birthday party balloons.[2]

Even if you don't go deep, living underwater is far from glamorous. Researchers who've spent time at the Aquarius Reef Base research station off the coast of the Florida Keys, for example, can tell you that. Living at Aquarius is a bit like being on an endless cross-country flight: Your living space is about the size of a motor home; you can't have open fire because of the pressure required to maintain the habitat, so everything is cooked on an electric water heater; and in the early days of the station, if anybody stunk up the place, the smell had nowhere to go.

There are a handful of smaller, surprising changes, too. Jim Fourqurean, who oversees operations at Aquarius, told me: "The difference in density of the air makes it so that ninety-nine percent of all people can no longer whistle." It's up to you to decide if that's a good thing or not. The good news is that even on this bare-bones research station, they still have Netflix.

Aquarius isn't anything like the Muraka—it's not a hotel, and it's not built for comfort. But even operating such a scrappy setup is incredibly pricey. In fact, Aquarius nearly shut down in 2012 because it lost funding—only a last-minute donation of $1.25 million from the Medina Family Foundation, headed in part by a wealthy Miami businessman, saved it. Aquarius is expensive to maintain, because keeping visitors safe takes a lot of invisible work. "We can have a hose that can rupture and leak. We can have an internal problem with the carbon dioxide scrubbing system. We can have flooding leaks," Roger Garcia, the operations director for Aquarius, told me. And if something goes wrong down there, you can't just run to the store and get a new part. Everything has to be set up with redundancy and safety in mind.

---

1   The aquanauts were so unknown to the public that one went on the classic show *To Tell the Truth*, where three people all pretend to be the same person and celebrity panelists have to guess who the real one is, and he wasn't recognized. Imagine trying to do that with John Glenn.

2   You can hear this rare audio on the *Flash Forward* episode "Under the Sea."

So to imagine an underwater stay costing an arm and a leg isn't actually so ridiculous. Certainly at first, these underwater excursions will be for the wealthy—like luxury cruises beneath the sea. The myth of Atlantis, a lush and wealthy city, finally realized.[3] And to cater to those customers, entrepreneurs will likely design experiences with them in mind. This is why underwater Venice-turned-Disneyland doesn't seem so silly to me at all. Consider how much the world's billionaires offered to donate to Notre-Dame after it was ravaged by a fire (nearly a billion dollars, in case you weren't keeping track). If Venice is to be saved, it will probably not be with the local government's budget—in 2017, Italy was forced to bail out two Venetian banks for a cool sum of $5.8 billion, and the city itself has been described as "in effect, bankrupt."

Tourism has long been Venice's economic cornerstone, but much like the water that draws those visitors, it's also proving to be its downfall. About 260,000 people live in Venice, but the city sees more than 25 million visitors every year. The constant stream of cruise ships (which themselves often run on giant diesel or gas-turbine engines that spew greenhouse gases into the air, accelerating Venice's descent into the sea) and the seasonal flood of tourists has the iconic city on the brink of being demoted by UNESCO. Venice is dying, sinking, and drowning in the very things that have defined the city for the last hundred years. In fact, this comic was inspired by Amelia Onorato's desire to go to the city and the realization that it might not happen. "Venice is on my bucket list, and I feel like time is running out," she told me. "What do you think the plausibility would be in turning sinking, historical landmarks into underwater habitats/tourist destinations?"

To "save" Venice by turning it into an exclusive, underwater retreat, complete with a giant glass dome and a themed monorail is exactly the kind of expensive, headline-catching scheme that an eccentric billionaire might go for. After all, rich people love classical European art almost as much as they love burning fossil fuel!

We won't all live underwater in the future. It will be too expensive for most, and too unsafe for the rest of us. Not only do we just have one Earth, we also have limited space on this Earth that humans can safely live on. It's fun to dream of sleeping with the fishes, but if we don't start to make serious changes to combat climate change, our future isn't a condo in a new underwater development—it's making do with what we have on land that is rapidly changing. But it doesn't have to be that way. A sea witch hasn't stolen your voice just yet, so I encourage you to use it to fight for real action on climate change. The ocean won't save us; it is coming *for* us.

---

3   Here's something I didn't know until researching for this chapter: The myth of Atlantis was created by the Greek philosopher Plato in around 360 BCE as a minor part of his Socratic dialogues, and has since taken on a life of its own.

NEVER LAY ME DOWN TO SLEEP

BY MATT LUBCHANSKY

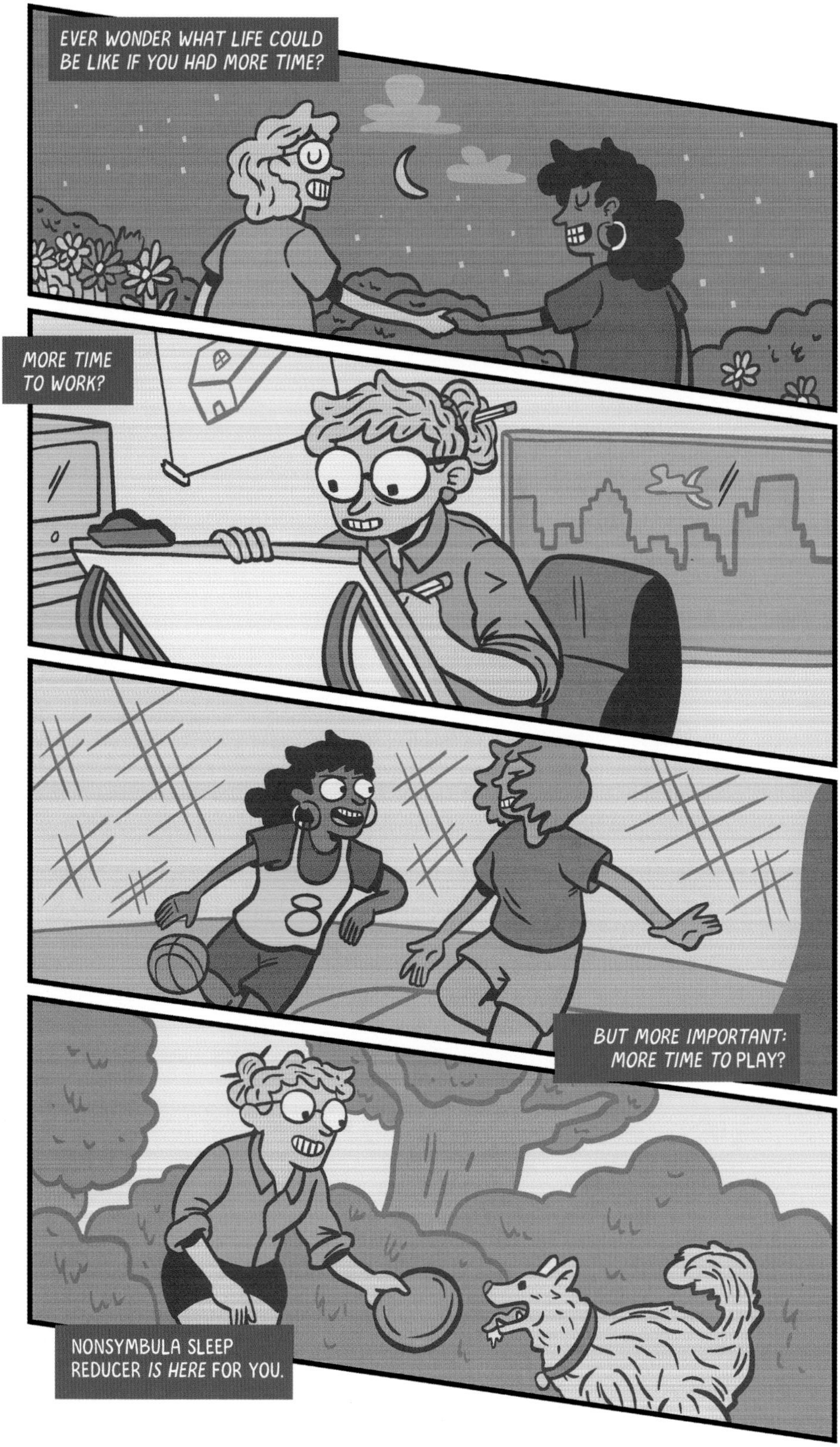
EVER WONDER WHAT LIFE COULD BE LIKE IF YOU HAD MORE TIME?
MORE TIME TO WORK?
BUT MORE IMPORTANT: MORE TIME TO PLAY?
NONSYMBULA SLEEP REDUCER *IS HERE* FOR YOU.

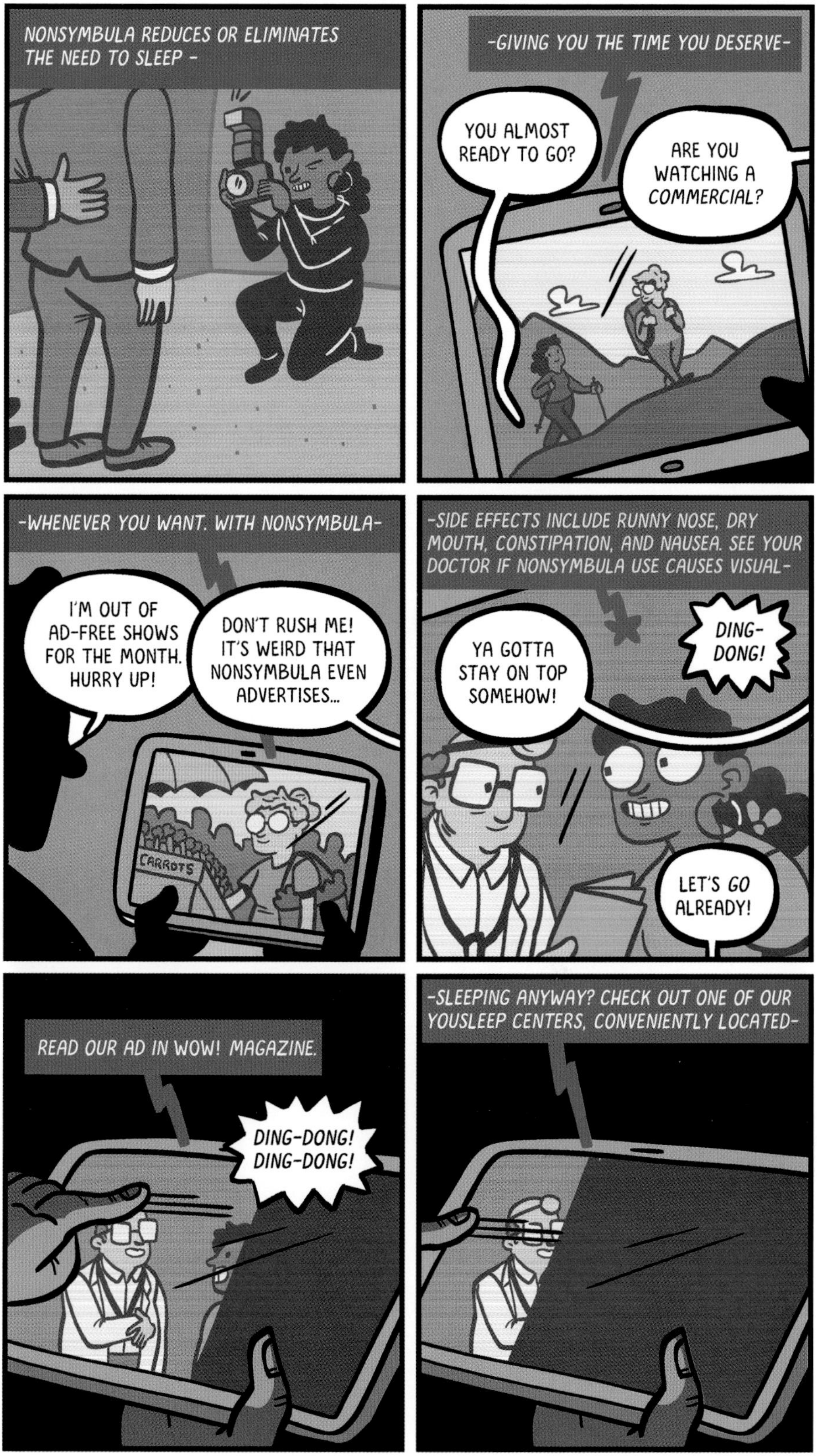
NONSYMBULA REDUCES OR ELIMINATES THE NEED TO SLEEP -
-GIVING YOU THE TIME YOU DESERVE-
YOU ALMOST READY TO GO?
ARE YOU WATCHING A COMMERCIAL?
-WHENEVER YOU WANT. WITH NONSYMBULA-
I'M OUT OF AD-FREE SHOWS FOR THE MONTH. HURRY UP!
DON'T RUSH ME! IT'S WEIRD THAT NONSYMBULA EVEN ADVERTISES...
CARROTS
-SIDE EFFECTS INCLUDE RUNNY NOSE, DRY MOUTH, CONSTIPATION, AND NAUSEA. SEE YOUR DOCTOR IF NONSYMBULA USE CAUSES VISUAL-
YA GOTTA STAY ON TOP SOMEHOW!
DING-DONG!
LET'S GO ALREADY!
READ OUR AD IN WOW! MAGAZINE.
DING-DONG! DING-DONG!
-SLEEPING ANYWAY? CHECK OUT ONE OF OUR YOUSLEEP CENTERS, CONVENIENTLY LOCATED-

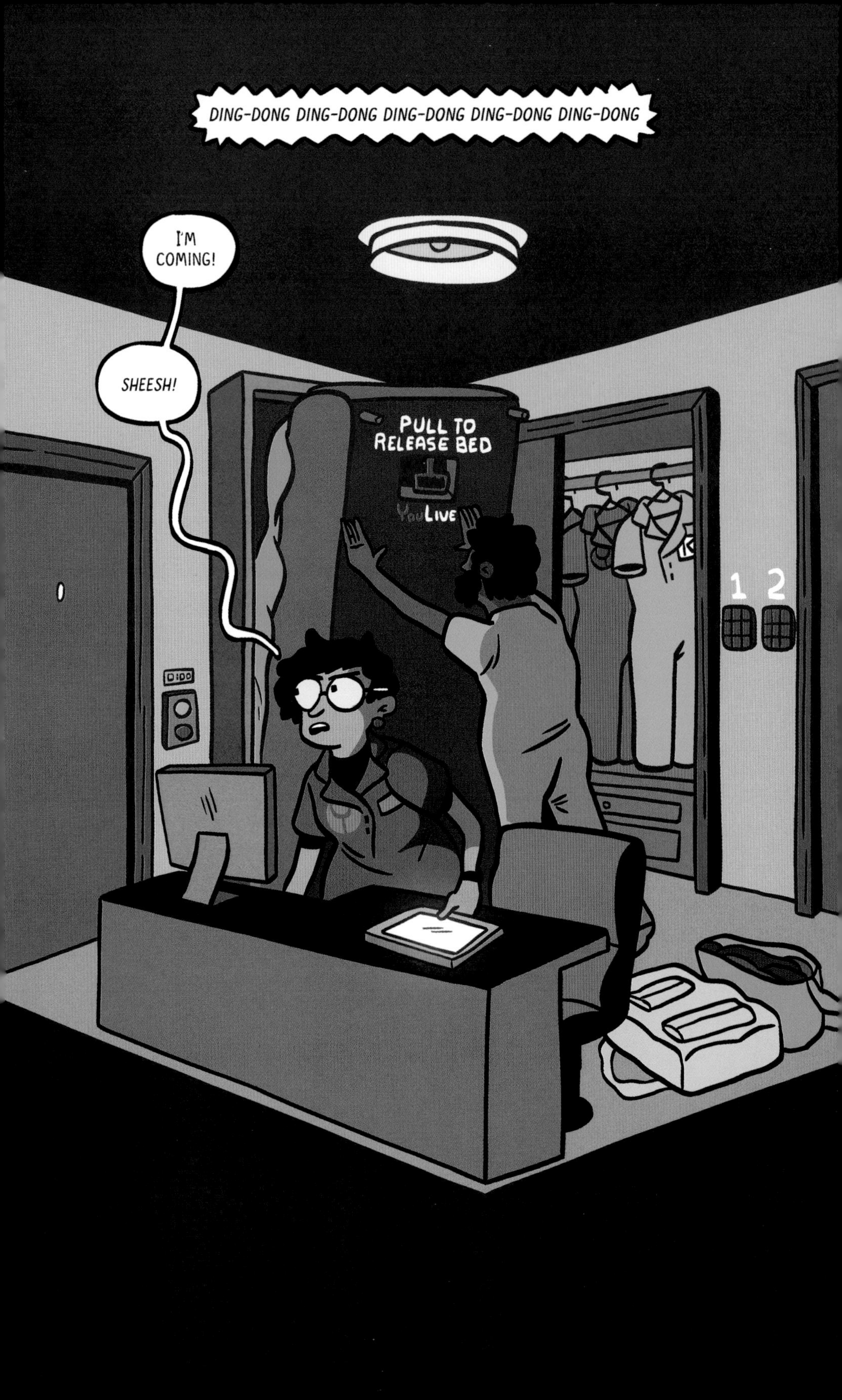
DING-DONG DING-DONG DING-DONG DING-DONG DING-DONG
I'M COMING!
SHEESH!
PULL TO RELEASE BED
YouLive
1
2

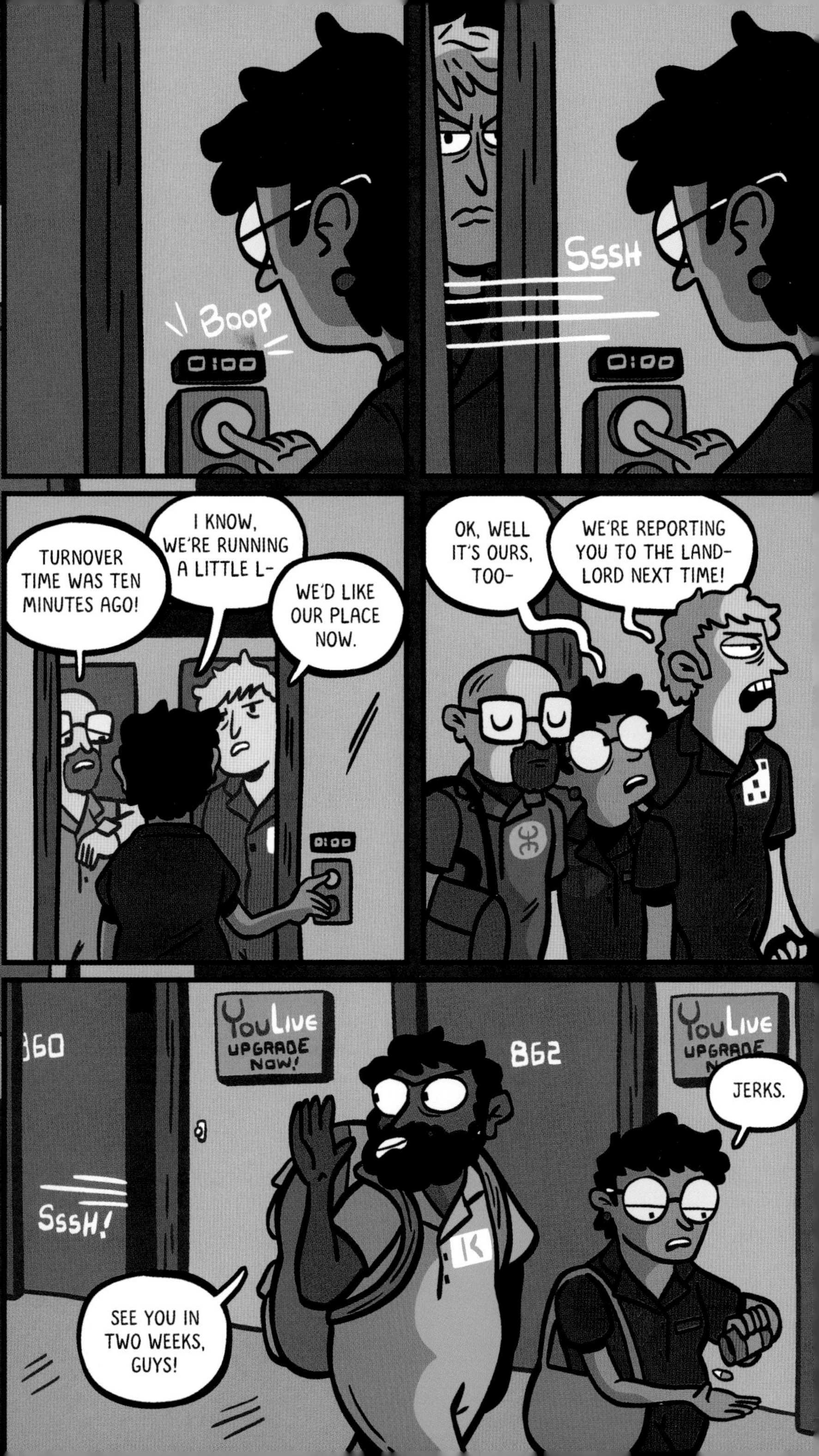
BOOP
0:00
SSSH
0:00
TURNOVER TIME WAS TEN MINUTES AGO!
I KNOW, WE'RE RUNNING A LITTLE L-
WE'D LIKE OUR PLACE NOW.
0:00
OK, WELL IT'S OURS, TOO-
WE'RE REPORTING YOU TO THE LAND-LORD NEXT TIME!
860
YOULIVE UPGRADE NOW!
862
YOULIVE UPGRADE
SSSH!
SEE YOU IN TWO WEEKS, GUYS!
JERKS.

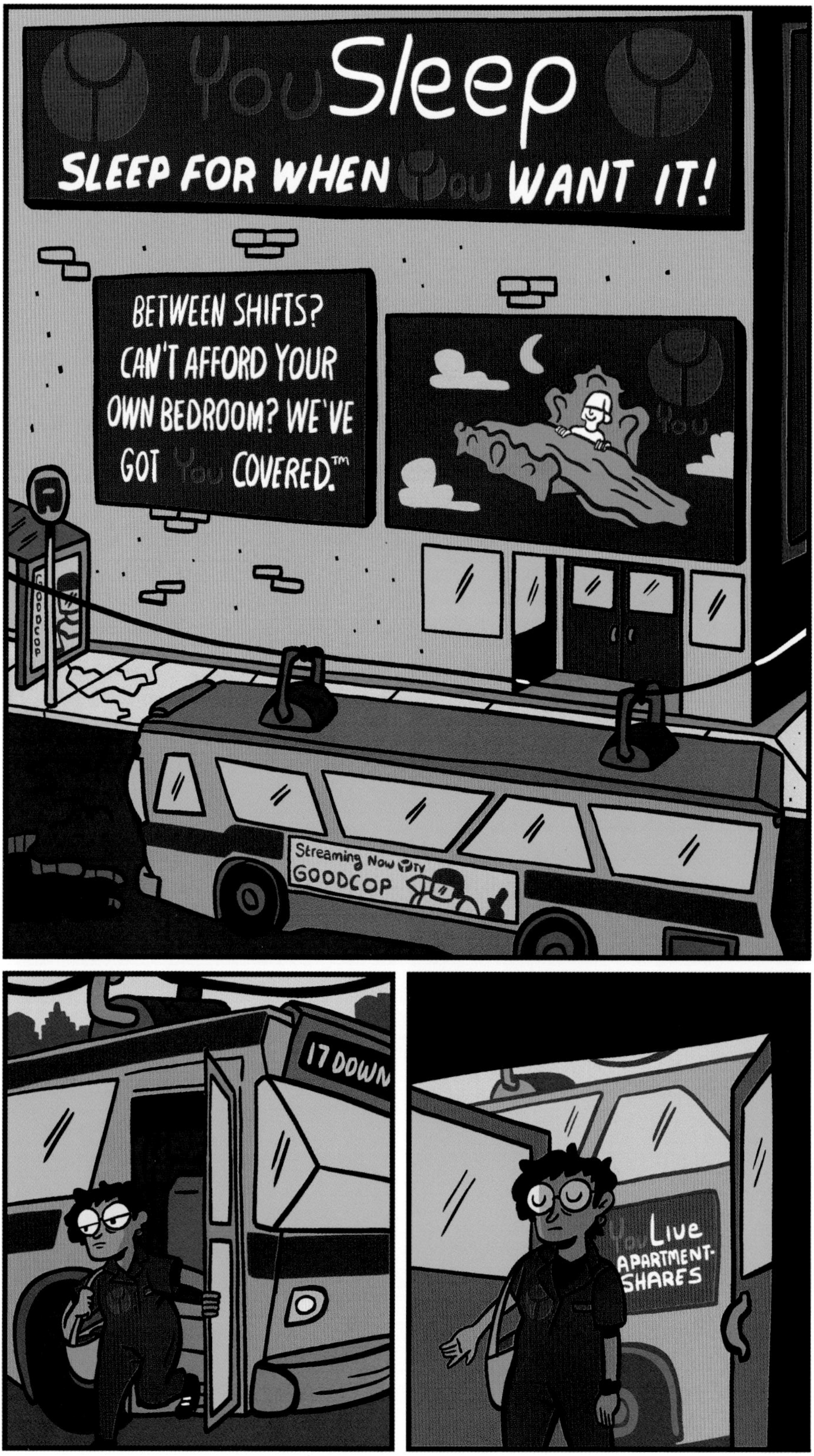

YouSleep
SLEEP FOR WHEN You WANT IT!
BETWEEN SHIFTS? CAN'T AFFORD YOUR OWN BEDROOM? WE'VE GOT You COVERED.™
You
GOODCOP
Streaming Now TV
GOODCOP
17 DOWN
YouLive
APARTMENT-SHARES

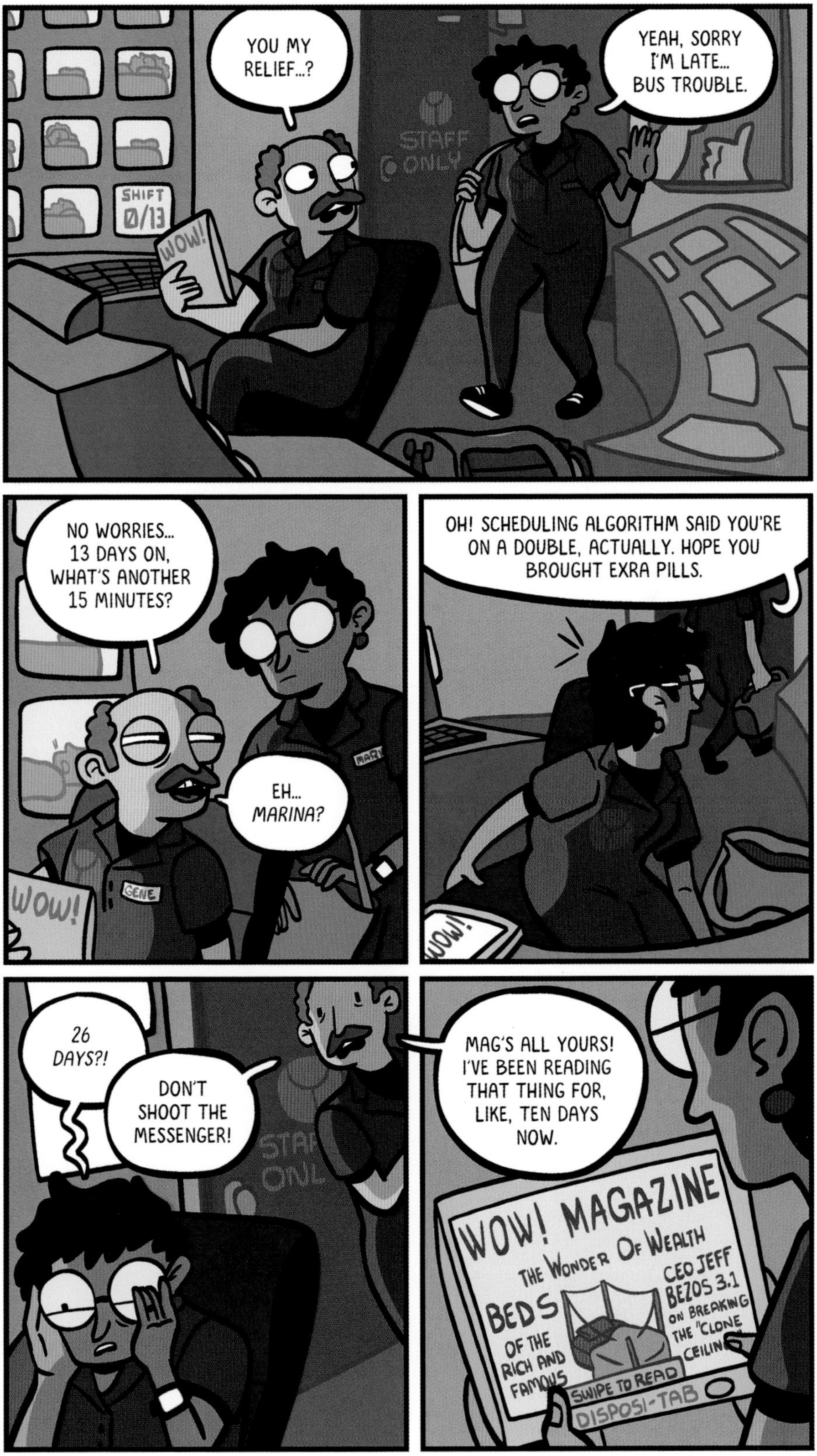

YOU MY RELIEF...?
YEAH, SORRY I'M LATE... BUS TROUBLE.
STAFF ONLY
SHIFT 0/13
WOW!
NO WORRIES... 13 DAYS ON, WHAT'S ANOTHER 15 MINUTES?
EH... *MARINA?*
GENE
WOW!
OH! SCHEDULING ALGORITHM SAID YOU'RE ON A DOUBLE, ACTUALLY. HOPE YOU BROUGHT EXRA PILLS.
WOW!
26 DAYS?!
DON'T SHOOT THE MESSENGER!
MAG'S ALL YOURS! I'VE BEEN READING THAT THING FOR, LIKE, TEN DAYS NOW.
WOW! MAGAZINE
THE WONDER OF WEALTH
BEDS OF THE RICH AND FAMOUS
CEO JEFF BEZOS 3.1 ON BREAKING THE "CLONE CEILING"
SWIPE TO READ
DISPOSI-TAB

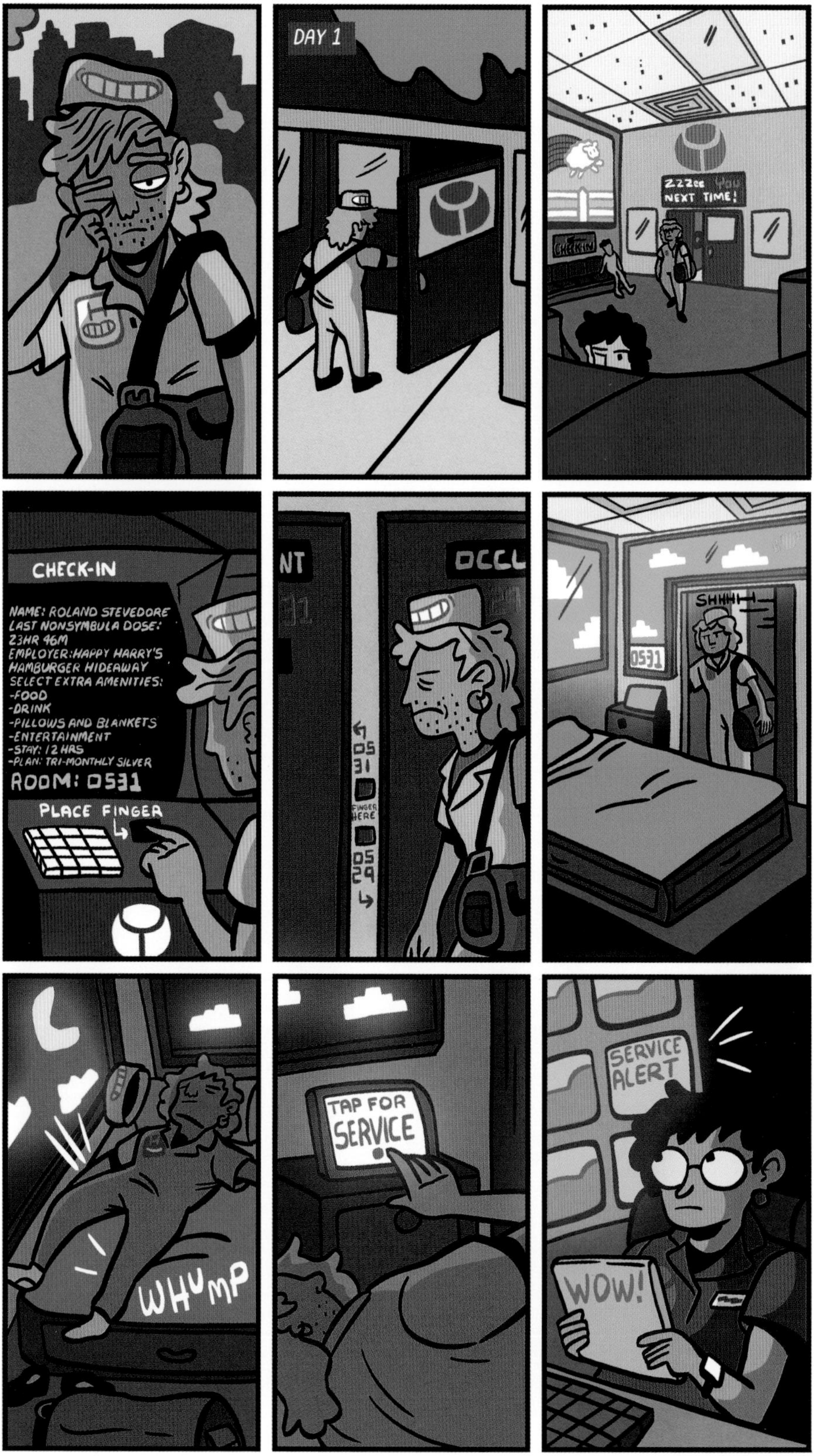
DAY 1
CHECK-IN
ZZZee You NEXT TIME!
CHECK-IN
NAME: ROLAND STEVEDORE
LAST NONSYMBULA DOSE: 23HR 46M
EMPLOYER: HAPPY HARRY'S HAMBURGER HIDEAWAY
SELECT EXTRA AMENITIES:
-FOOD
-DRINK
-PILLOWS AND BLANKETS
-ENTERTAINMENT
-STAY: 12 HRS
-PLAN: TRI-MONTHLY SILVER
ROOM: 0531
PLACE FINGER
NT
OCCU
0531
FINGER HERE
0529
SHHHH
0531
WHUMP
TAP FOR SERVICE
SERVICE ALERT
WOW!

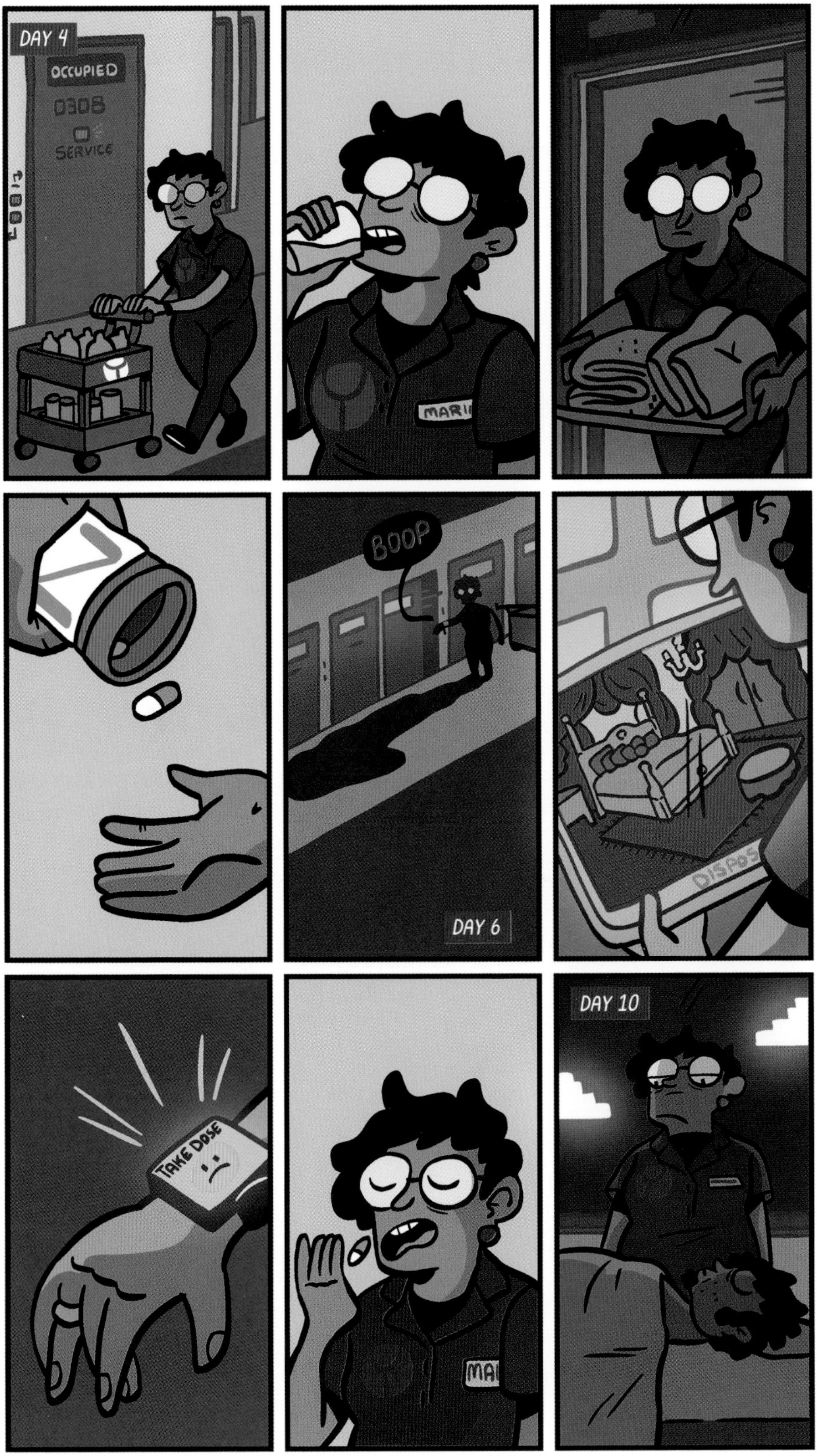
DAY 4
OCCUPIED
0308
SERVICE
MARI
BOOP
DAY 6
DISPOS
TAKE DOSE
MAI
DAY 10

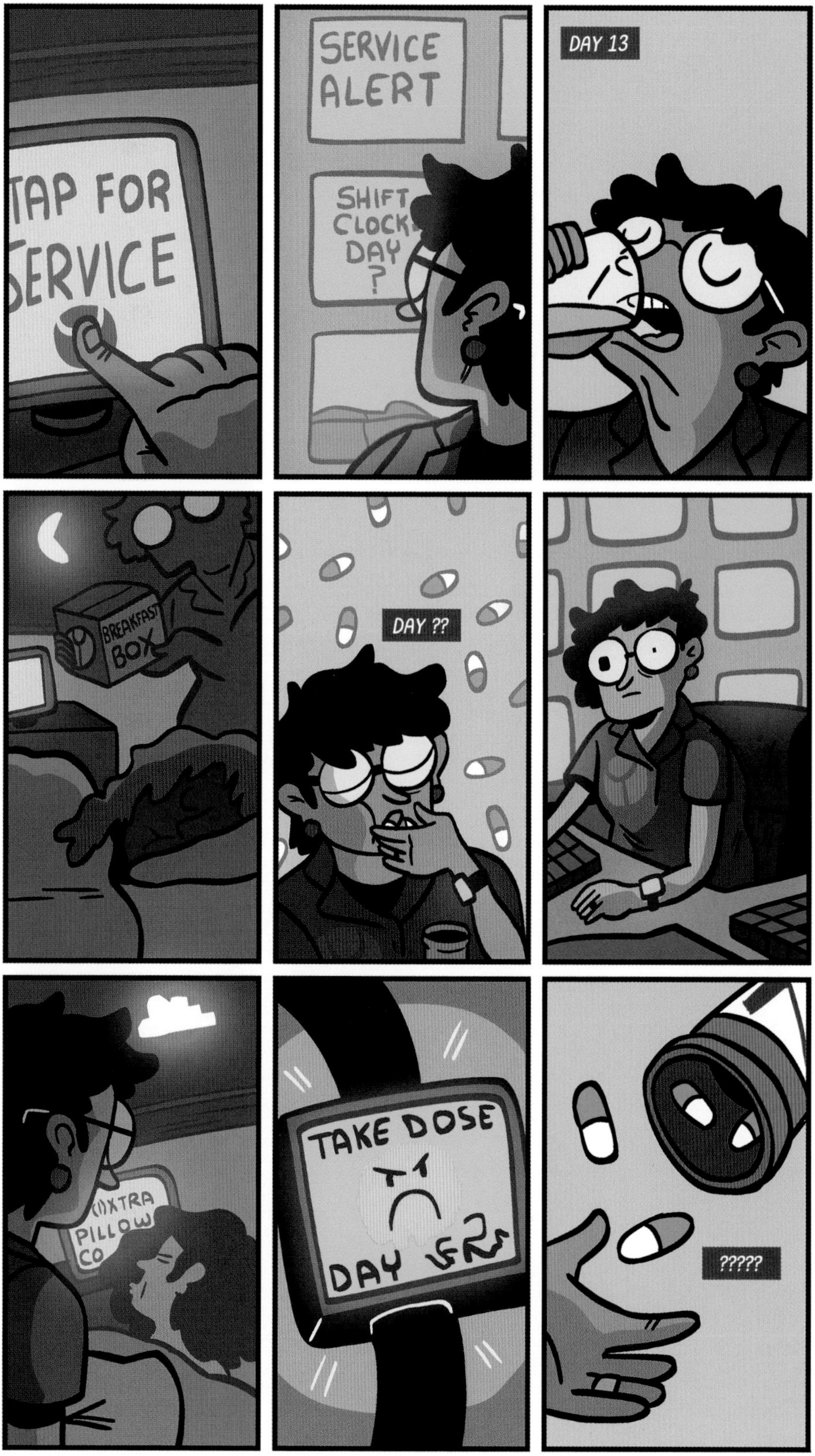
TAP FOR SERVICE
SERVICE ALERT
SHIFT CLOCK DAY ?
DAY 13
BREAKFAST BOX
DAY ??
XTRA PILLOW CO
TAKE DOSE DAY
?????

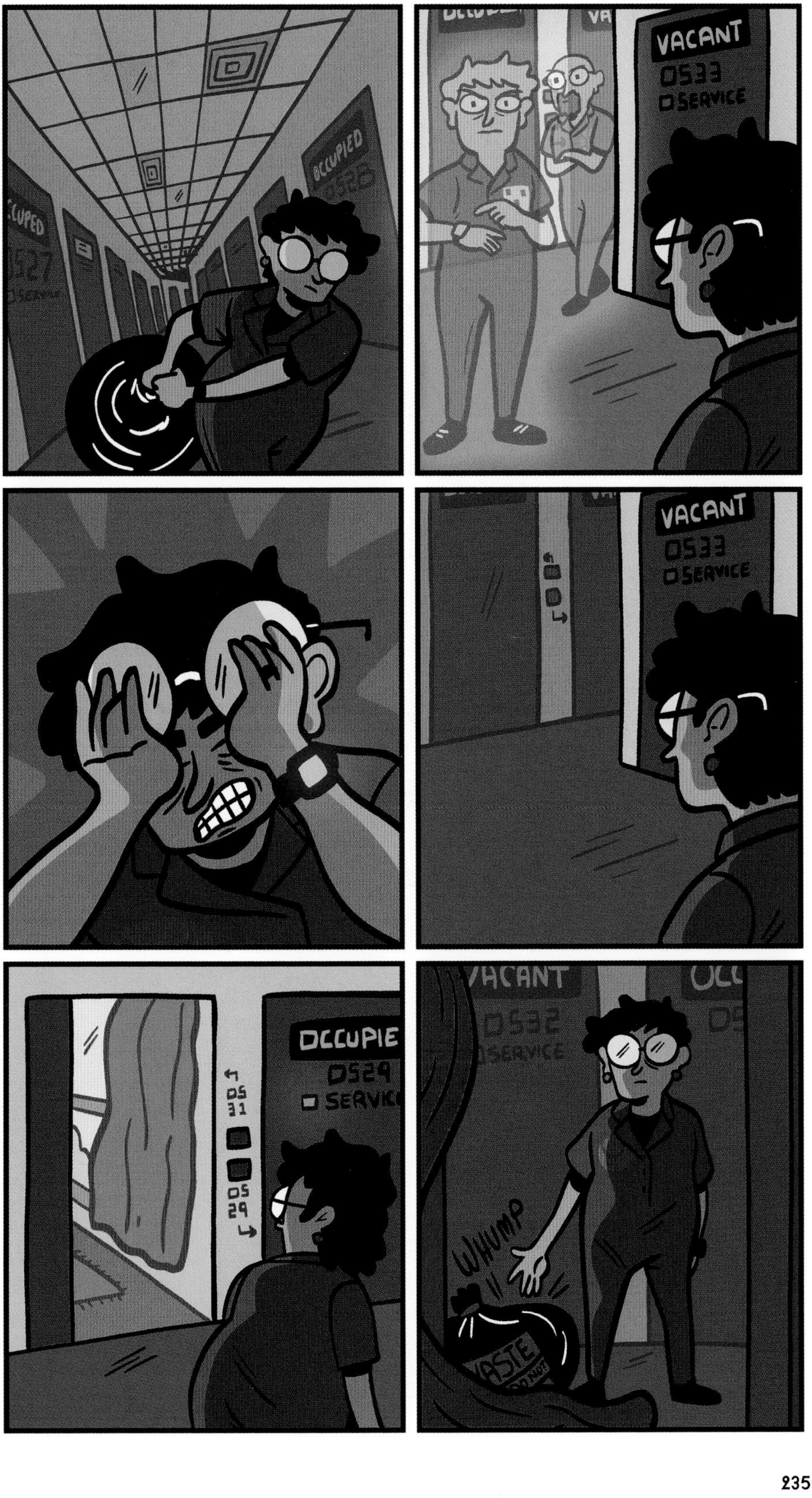

OCCUPIED
0527
SERVICE
VACANT
0533
SERVICE
VACANT
0533
SERVICE
OCCUPIE
0529
SERVIC
05
31
05
29
VACANT
0532
SERVICE
WHUMP
WASTE

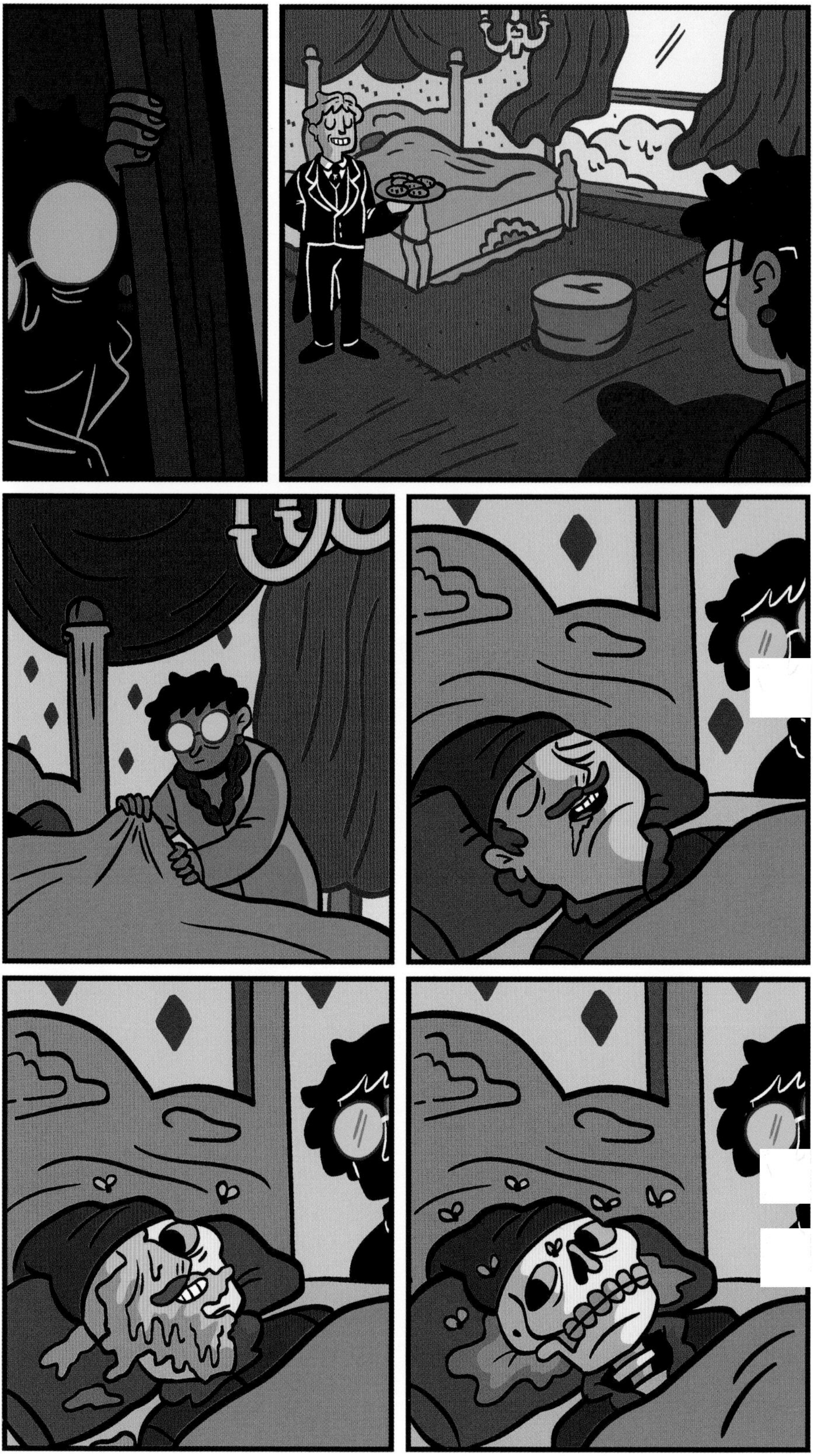

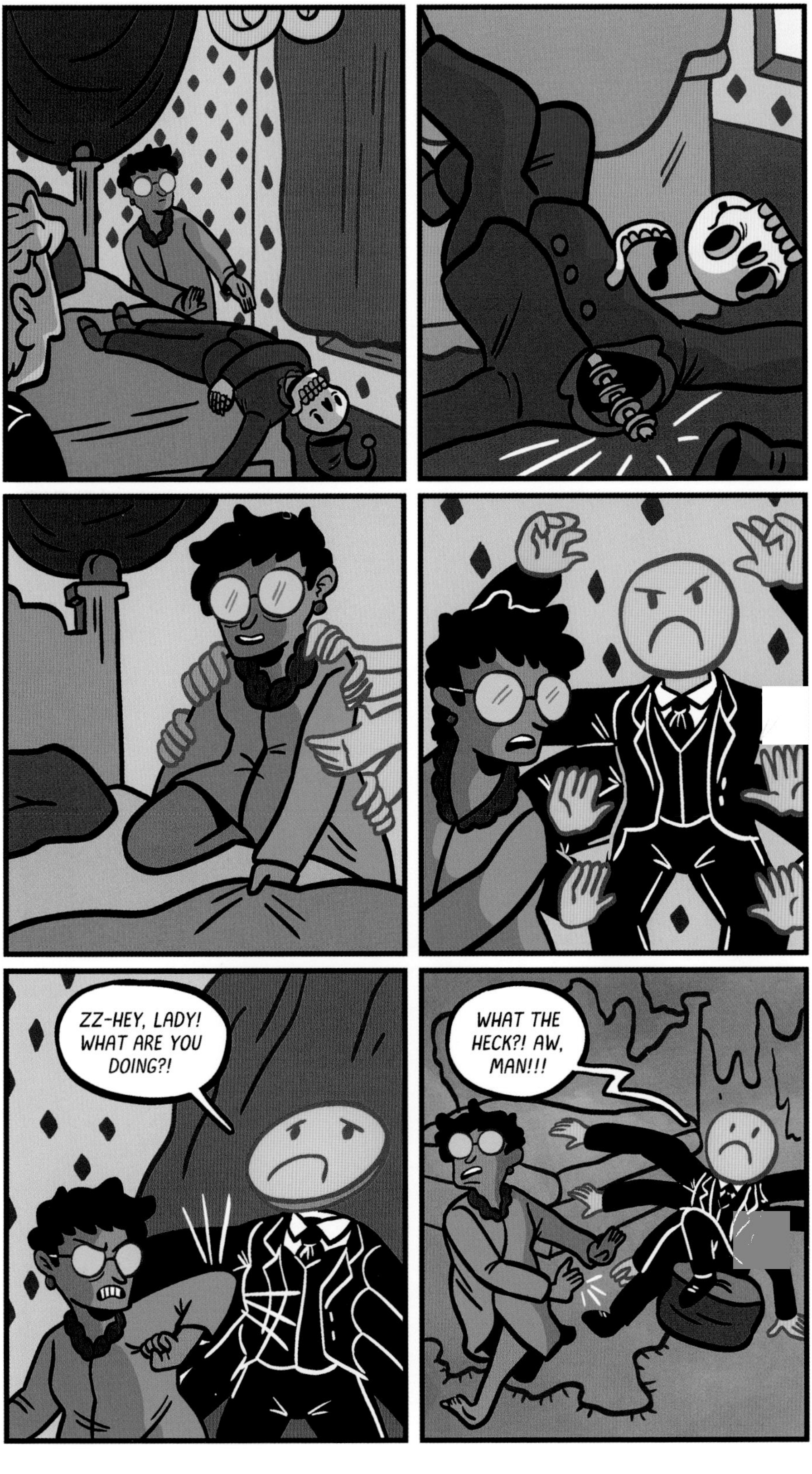
ZZ-HEY, LADY! WHAT ARE YOU DOING?!
WHAT THE HECK?! AW, MAN!!!

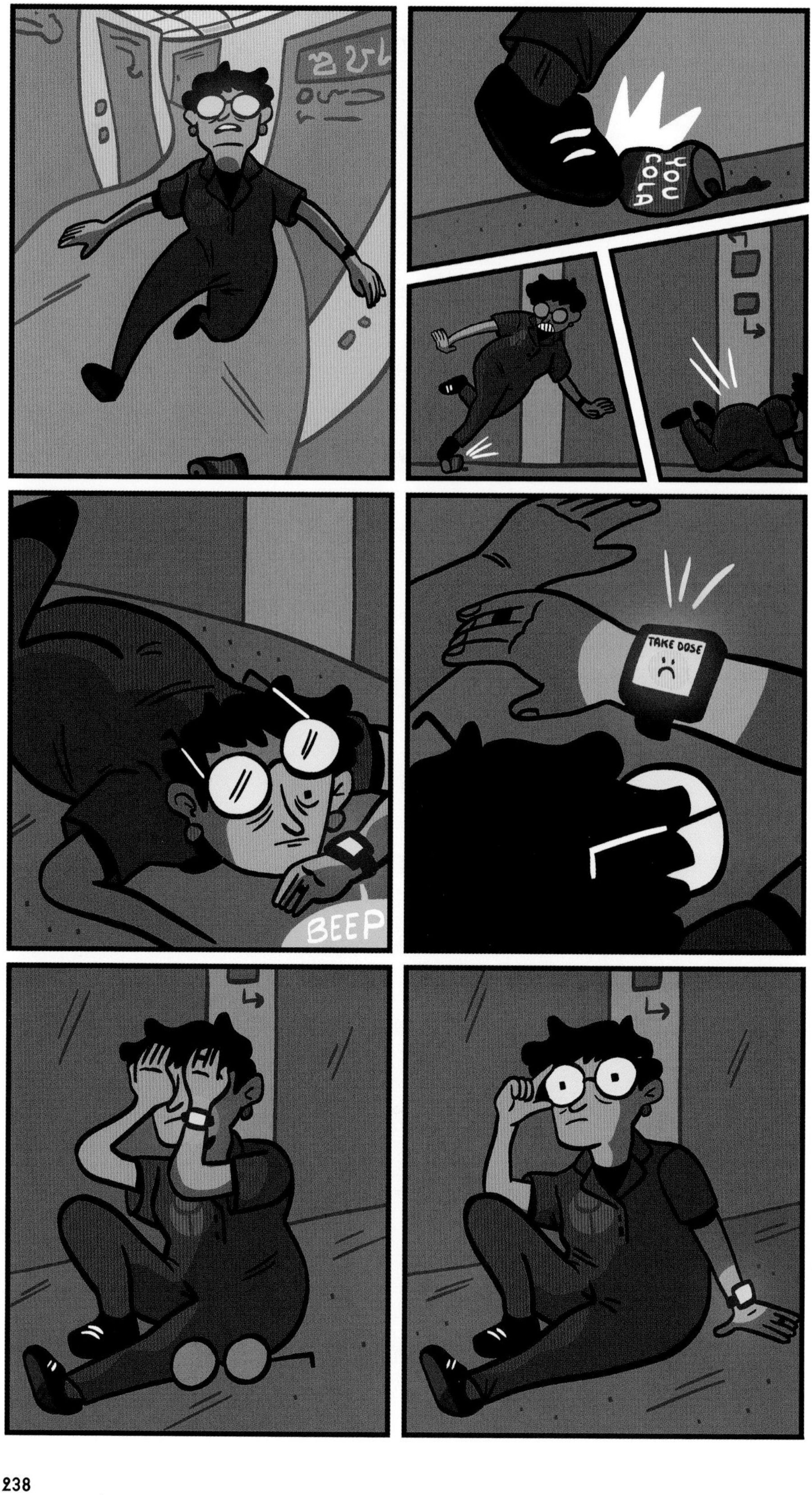
YOU COLA
BEEP
TAKE DOSE

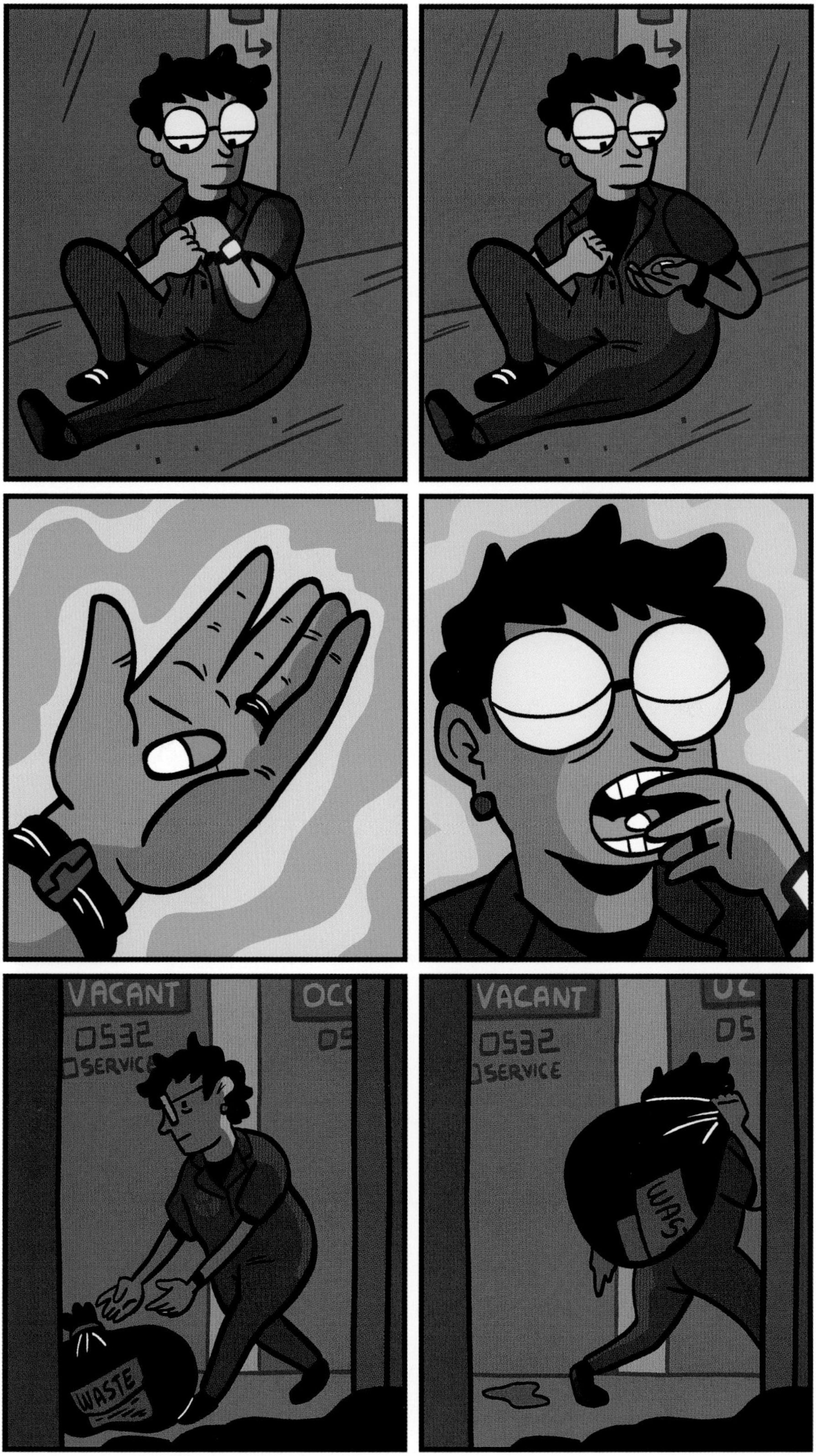

VACANT
0532
SERVICE
WASTE

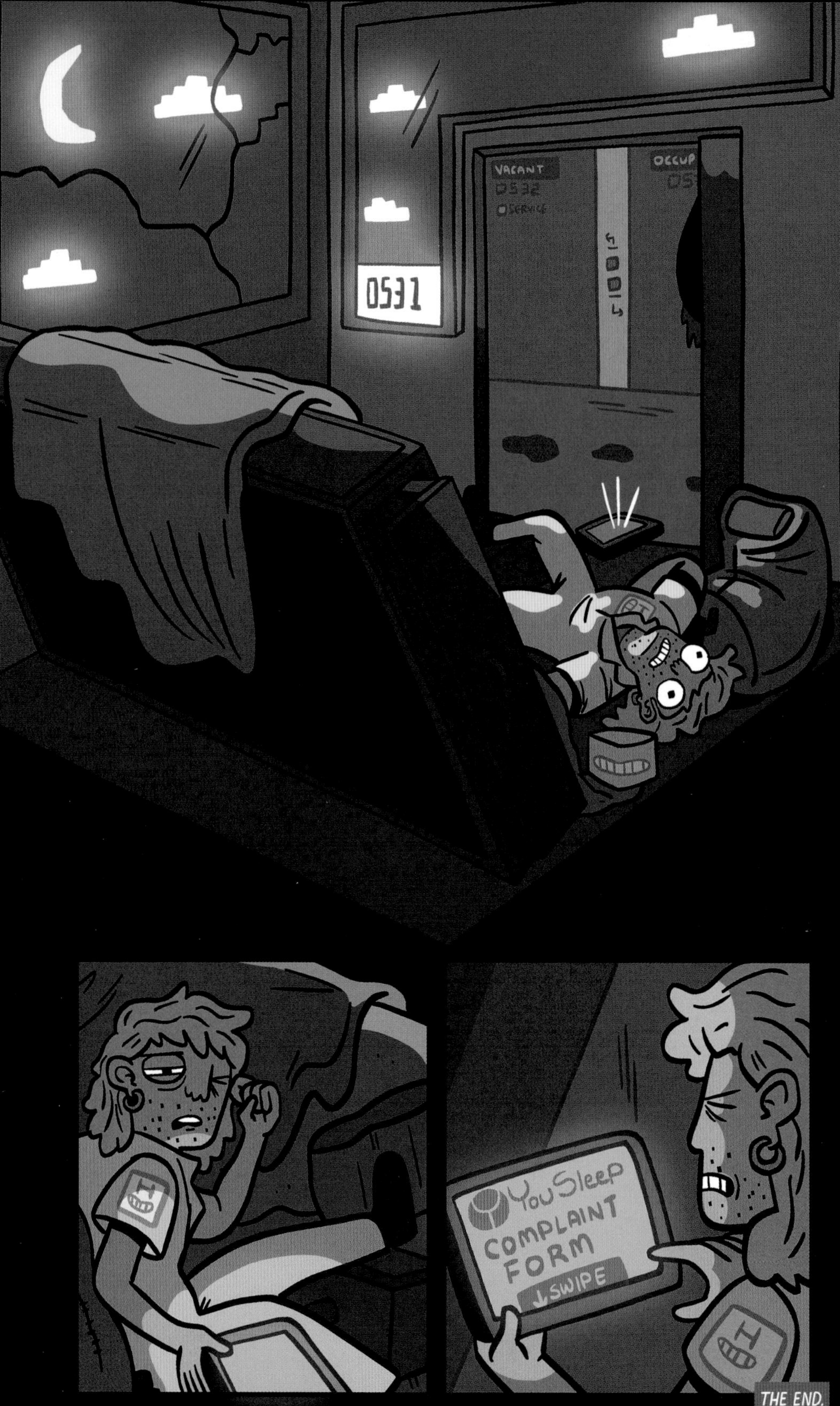
0531
VACANT
0532
SERVICE
OCCUP
YouSleep
COMPLAINT
FORM
↓SWIPE

THE END.

LUBCHANSKY

NEVER LAY ME DOWN TO SLEEP
WHAT HAPPENS WHEN WE CONQUER REST?

IN HIGH SCHOOL, A FRIEND OF MINE INFORMED ME THAT he had a new sleep plan. Instead of sleeping once a night, like us boring regular people, he would be adopting something called polyphasic sleep—a method in which you nap for short periods of time dispersed throughout the entire twenty-four-hour day. His plan went like this: He would sleep four times a day for thirty minutes each go.

This idea sounded (and continues to sound) truly awful to me, but this friend informed me that he was simply following the groundwork laid by the greatest minds to ever live. Nikola Tesla, Leonardo da Vinci, Napoleon, Thomas Edison, how were they able to accomplish so much? Polyphasic sleep, he said.

It turns out there's pretty much no historical evidence that any of those men intentionally rejiggered their sleep cycles to include four thirty-minute sleeping blocks. They certainly worked long hours, and many of them enjoyed napping, but there's nothing to suggest that they were strategically rescheduling their day around half-hour chunks of sleep. Edison in particular is known to have bemoaned the need for sleeping, arguing that "the person who sleeps eight or ten hours a night is never fully asleep and never fully awake—they have only different degrees of doze through the twenty-four hours." But while he loved a good nap (and in fact would often intentionally drift off holding a ball bearing in his hand, only to be jolted awake by the sound of it clattering to the floor—a technique he claimed help him capture ideas that only presented themselves in that sliver of time between awake and asleep), Edison wasn't attempting a polyphasic sleep cycle specifically.

In fact, polyphasic sleep as a term was coined by a psychologist named J. S. Szymanski in the 1920s. Since then, the concept has gained followers and forked into a variety of sleep habits flanked by lengthy Internet arguments about which one is the best. The Polyphasic Society lists ten different sleep schedules on their website, including something called the "Uberman," which one sleep blog called "the most commonly attempted, and most failed of polyphasic schedules." I can see why. It requires you to function on six to eight twenty-minute naps dispersed throughout the day.

Unsurprisingly, my friend fell victim to the same fate that most Uberman hopefuls do (including Kramer from *Seinfeld*). Not only were teachers in our high school unwilling to accommodate his new sleep schedule, his body was also less than pleased (although thankfully, unlike Kramer from *Seinfeld*, his plan did not get him involved with any mobsters, as far as I know).

Precisely why humans need sleep is a mystery that continues to vex biologists around the world. It's an odd behavior if you think about it—we close our eyes, lie down, and become completely vulnerable to predation for hours at a time. And yet, loads of animals do it. Allan Rechtschaffen, one of the pioneers in sleep research, once observed that, "If sleep does not serve an absolutely vital function, then it is the biggest mistake the evolutionary process ever made." Sleep must be important, but why? What is that "vital function," exactly? We can gather clues from what happens when we don't sleep. Without shut-eye, people have a hard time remembering new information, solving problems, managing emotions, and handling change. One study found that after just seventeen to nineteen hours without sleep, people performed the same way that someone with a blood alcohol content of 0.05 percent would (about the same as one drink for someone my size). The National Institute of Health estimated in 2017 that driver sleepiness plays a role in 91,000 car accidents each year, leading to 795 deaths. Living with too-little shut-eye increases your risk of colorectal cancer, heart disease, dementia, stroke, high blood pressure, depression, suicide, and more.[1]

There's a reason that many torture programs include sleeplessness—the U.S.'s torture methods feature keeping prisoners awake for extended periods of time by blaring music, keeping them in cold rooms, and waking them up if they manage to drift off. "The denial of sleep is the violent dispossession of self by external force, the calculated shattering of an individual," writes Jonathan Crary in his book *24/7*. In certain communities where police or the military are omnipresent, they'll often flood streets with mobile lights to "disrupt crime"—a method that also disrupts the sleep of community residents, something that experts say almost certainly hurts the health of these communities. Increased artificial light at night has been linked to depression, cancer, and heart disease.

We know that without sleep we're essentially zombies, miserable and confused and slow, stumbling about the world in a stupor. But we still don't know why. One theory is that sleep offers our brain an opportunity to clean house. While you're awake, the mushy gray matter in your skull is constantly churning as you overanalyze a text from your crush or try to figure out how to word an email to your boss, or even as you decide which Netflix show to watch. All of that mental work produces waste: used up neurotransmitters, by-products, and chemicals. While the brain is working, it doesn't have time to clean any of that up. "You can think of it like having a house party. You can either entertain the guests or clean up the house, but you can't really do both at the same time," researcher Maiken Nedergaard told the BBC. When you sleep, however, it's cleanup time. Nedergaard's research has shown that when mice sleep, certain brain cells shrink a tiny bit to open up space between brain tissue for all the waste to be washed out. Scientists think the same thing is probably happening for us

---

1   Feel free to convey all of this to your cat/dog/small child the next time they try to wake you up extra early. Let me know how it goes.

humans. Without that nightly cleaning, the theory goes, the brain can get clogged up with these neurotoxins, leading to all those undesirable results.

But humans are good at nothing if not attempting to shake off our body's biological needs, and for centuries we have been at war with sleep. Legend has it that in China, tea was hailed for its caffeinating properties as far back as 2737 BCE (although this story also includes an emperor named Shen Nung, who was born with the head of a bull, spoke in complete sentences after three days, and could plow a field all by himself at the age of three, so its accuracy is up in the air). Mythology aside, historians can agree that coffee and tea were used specifically for caffeination purposes around 1000 CE. In 2014, 85 percent of the U.S. population consumed at least one caffeinated beverage per day.

Thanks to the combination of drugs (legal and illegal), artificial lighting, and increased demands on productivity, slowly but surely we're "winning" the battle against slumber. In 1942, 84 percent of Americans said they got seven to nine hours of sleep a night. A 2013 study found that that number had dropped down to just 59 percent. Today, it's likely even less.[2]

But cutting our nightly shut-eye from nine hours to six or seven is still not enough for some. Take the U.S. military for example—for decades they've been chipping away at the pesky problem of human soldiers and their frustratingly human needs. If soldiers could eschew the need for sleep while on a mission without suffering the cognitive decline that comes with long periods of wakefulness, they could become an even deadlier and more efficient force.[3] A report by the U.S. Air Force Research Laboratory puts it this way: "Forcing our enemies to perform continuously without the benefit of sufficient daily sleep is a very effective weapon." To achieve this goal, military researchers have studied everything from the white-crowned sparrow—who barely sleeps a wink during annual migrations—to dolphins and whales—animals that are able to swim for long stretches by shutting down parts of their brain rather than the whole thing at once. Biohackers and start-up founders are interested in unlocking this secret, too—Dave Asprey, the founder of Bulletproof coffee, says he's spent about $200,000 of his own money trying to hack his sleep, including sleeping on a magnetic pad, running electrical currents through his brain, and, yes, polyphasic sleep.

It's not just the military who would love to crack the sleeping code, either—bosses and corporations would, too. Imagine a workforce that never had to sleep! Think of all the widgets and pop sockets and toothbrushes and smartwatches we could make and use and throw away and make again! The promise of endless wakefulness is not just a story of conquering our brains, it's also a story of conquering people.

Karl Marx saw sleep as one of the few barriers that could impede the endless creep of capitalism. "Capital oversteps not only the moral but even

2   Most of the "studies" I could find since 2013 were polls commissioned by mattress brands, who have a vested interest in getting you into (their) beds.
3   Many military organizations, including the Nazis, dosed their soldiers with cocaine to keep them going for longer. Between 1966 and 1969, the U.S. Armed Forces went through 225 million tablets of stimulants, mostly amphetamines. The U.S. Air Force prescribed "go pills" to pilots up until 2017.

the merely physical limits of the working day," Marx wrote. Crary puts it this way: "Sleep is an uncompromising interruption of the theft of time from us by capitalism." As work creeps further into our leisure time with our company-issued laptops sitting by the bed, our cell phones always ready to receive emails or texts, and our smart speakers happily chirping to alert us when those messages come in, sleep is perhaps the last place that management can touch. (At least not literally; I'm sure plenty of you have seen your bosses in your dreams doing things we will not discuss here, thank you very much.)

A world of sleeplessness is a world of even more consumption, of always-on people and always-on services and always-on lights. "The planet becomes reimagined as a non-stop work site or an always-on shopping mall of infinite choices, tasks, selections, and digressions," writes Crary. Today, 80 percent of the world's population lives under something called "skyglow," the spillover effects of light pollution into the night sky. In a world where we work all day and night under continuous lights, the Milky Way may never be seen again. Without sleep, the Earth stands no chance.

Of course, some people are already pushing the limits of sleeplessness today. Modafinil, a drug technically for narcolepsy, is used by truck drivers, shift workers, students, and lawyers. It's also beloved by start-up workers, many of whom work long hours fueled by a combination of Modafinil, Soylent, and raw ego. "Manic sleeplessness is valorized as being a site of immense creativity or a sign of creative genius," said Emily Lim Rogers, a historian who studies chronic fatigue. Edison, with his ball bearings and animus for sleep, is regularly idolized online as an inspiration, rather than a sign of neuroticism or privilege.[4]

Given how many professionals turn to illicit drugs with side effects (from off-label Modafinil to straight-up cocaine), we can pretty easily predict that even if a drug that staved off slumber had some side effects, that wouldn't stop people from taking it. And in fact, in a future where we've pharmacologically vanquished sleep, even those who'd really like to snooze might not be allowed to—as you saw in the comic. "Who would feel that taking the drug would basically be compulsory?" Rogers asks. If your boss expects a 168-hour shift, can you say no? The workers in our comic certainly can't.

Perhaps one of the reasons that sleep's "vital function" remains so elusive is because slumber is not purely a biological phenomenon. "Science can never uncover the truth about human sleep, because sleep is always biological and social, cultural and natural, historical and emergent, and will always be perceived through contextual lenses," argues Matthew J. Wolf-Meyer, the author of *The Slumbering Masses*. How we sleep impacts and is impacted by so much more than just what our brain is doing. It's tied into economic systems, social structures, safety, gender, and more.

One of my favorite pieces of science fiction to take on sleep is *Beggars in Spain*, a book by Nancy Kress that introduces readers to a world where we defeat shut-eye through genetic editing. In the book, only twenty babies are

---

4   And for the Nikola Tesla fans out there, he too was obsessed with resisting sleep. According to *Prodigal Genius: The Life of Nikola Tesla*, the young inventor was eleven when he started committing to a plan of sleeping only two hours a night.

initially given the modification, and they very quickly find themselves at odds with the rest of the world. It's not fair, say the main character's classmates, that Leisha can stay up and study all night when they can't. It's cheating, even. And this is one of the big criticisms of even today's side-effect-riddled sleep suppressant drugs, that they're somehow morally unfair or wrong.

There's a moment in *Beggars in Spain* that has stuck with me since reading the novel years ago. It's not even a scene, but really just an aside from one of the scientists talking about the genetically engineered babies that were part of the first experiment. The doctors had originally created twenty of these babies, but only nineteen survived. "The twentieth baby is dead," the scientist explains. "His parents turned out to be unstable. They separated during the pregnancy, and his mother could not bear the twenty-four-hour crying of a baby who never sleeps." This moment highlights the fact that the divide between sleeping and sleepless people will be deeper and wider than I think we can even really predict. Two sleeping parents trying to care for a sleepless baby, toddler, even a teen, is a true nightmare. But even as adults, could a genetically sleepless person and a normal sleeping person fall in love? In doing so, the sleepless person is accepting that at least one-third of the time, their partner will be unconscious. Does that cause rifts? Does the sleepless person have to do all the chores since they have so much more time? (I think that would be only fair, really.) Get ready future advice columnists, because there's a whole new set of marital conflicts coming your way.

And, as you saw in the comic, there are physical logistics that might change, too. If you sleep in chunks and then stay awake for long stretches, how does that change our homes? Do only the rich have bedrooms, while the rest of us shuttle between wake and rented sleeping areas? Does a descent into drug-fueled wakefulness lead to labyrinthine sleep facilities staffed by workers who are slowly descending into sleep-deprived madness?

And yet, if pressed, I think most people would probably admit that if they could live without sleep with no ill effects, they probably would. "I often wonder if the paeans that you hear to sleep are like the paeans that you hear to death," said James Hughes, the executive director of the Institute for Ethics and Emerging Technologies. "It's like saying, 'God, it's so great banging my head against the wall because when I stop it feels so much better.' If we were to actually get rid of sleep or death I think people wouldn't miss it very much." Kress admits that she's jealous of friends who need less sleep than she does. "I have always felt that they got more life than I do—which of course they do!"

We'd love to think that this added time would be spent wisely—reading, or spending time with friends and family, or creating art. But would it? "Men make their own history, but they do not make it as they please; they do not make it under self-selected circumstances, but under circumstances existing already, given and transmitted from the past," wrote Karl Marx. If we can conquer sleep but can't conquer the economic systems that wring us for labor at every waking moment, is that really a win? Rechtschaffen called sleep a possible "mistake," because it renders us helpless and prone to predation, but our predators have changed, and perhaps it's now the best mistake we ever made.

POPNONYMOUS

BY SOPHIE GOLDSTEIN

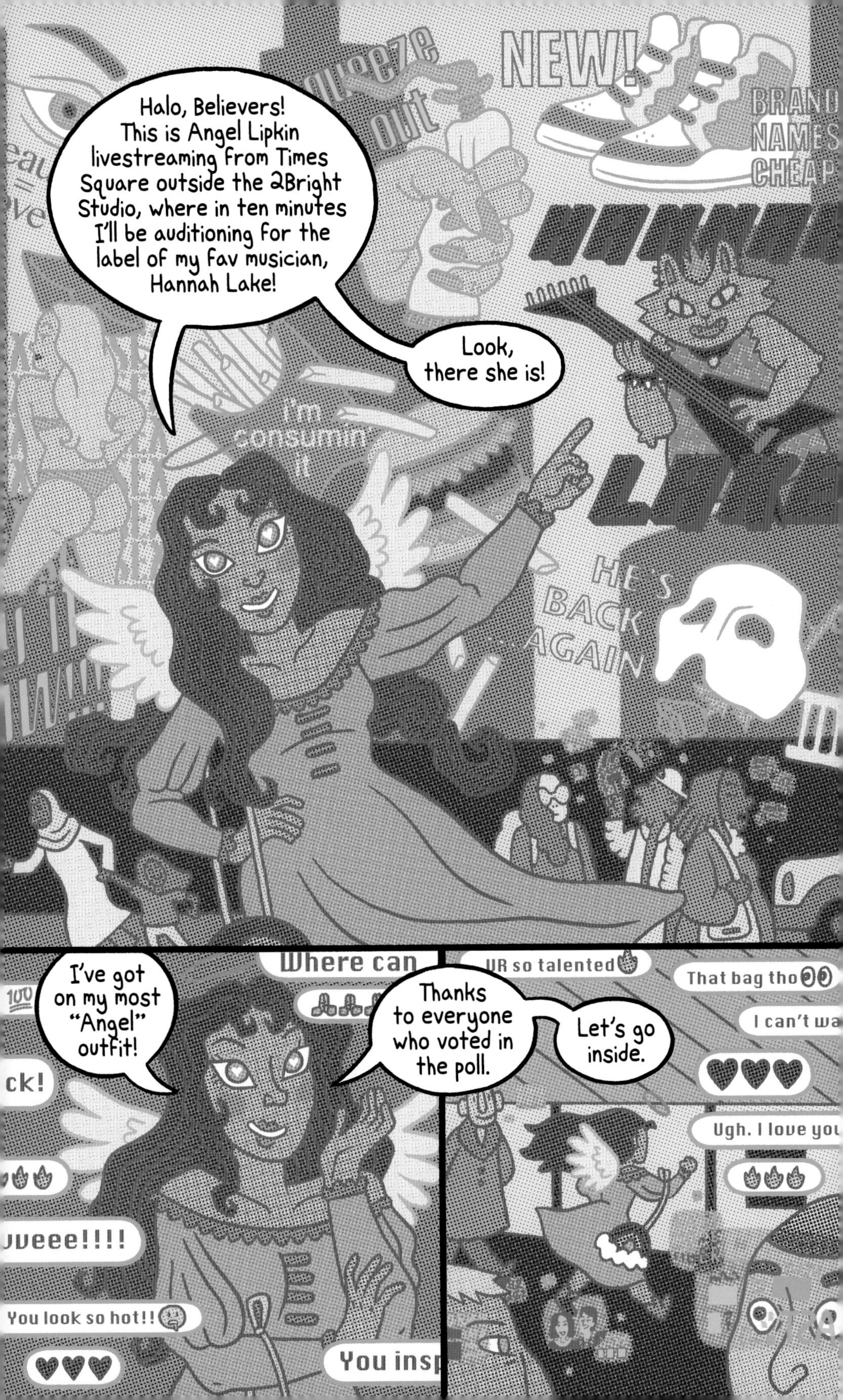

squeeze out
NEW!
BRAND NAMES CHEAP
Halo, Believers! This is Angel Lipkin livestreaming from Times Square outside the 2Bright Studio, where in ten minutes I'll be auditioning for the label of my fav musician, Hannah Lake!
Look, there she is!
i'm consumin' it
LAKE
HE'S BACK AGAIN
I've got on my most "Angel" outfit!
Where can
ck!
uveee!!!!
You look so hot!!
You insp
Thanks to everyone who voted in the poll.
Let's go inside.
UR so talented
That bag tho
I can't wa
Ugh. I love you

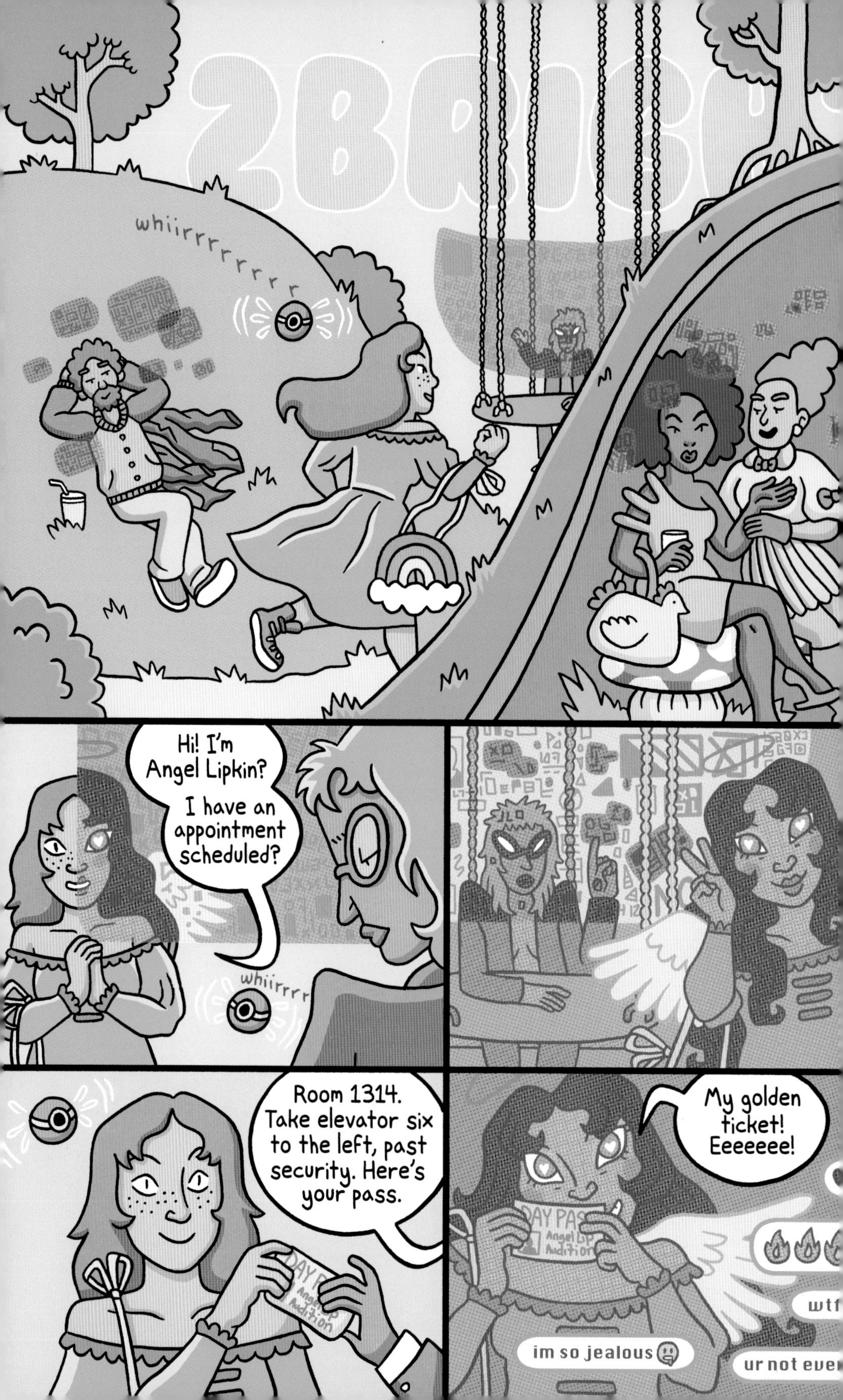
whiirrrrrrrrr
Hi! I'm Angel Lipkin?
I have an appointment scheduled?
whiirrrr
Room 1314. Take elevator six to the left, past security. Here's your pass.
DAY PASS Angel Lip Audition
My golden ticket! Eeeeeee!
wtf
im so jealous
ur not eve

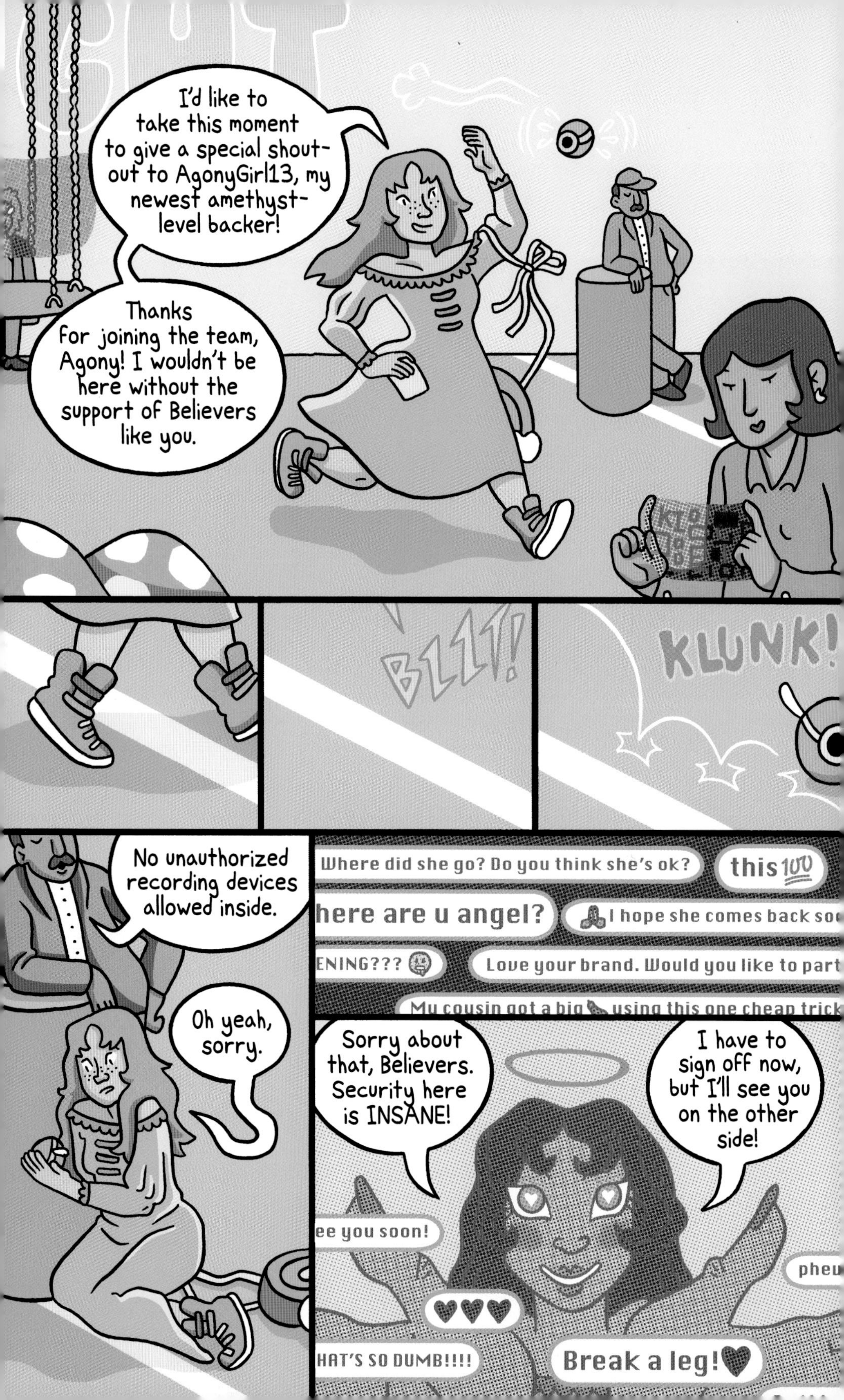
I'd like to take this moment to give a special shout-out to AgonyGirl13, my newest amethyst-level backer!
Thanks for joining the team, Agony! I wouldn't be here without the support of Believers like you.
BLIT!
KLUNK!
No unauthorized recording devices allowed inside.
Oh yeah, sorry.
Where did she go? Do you think she's ok?
this 💯
here are u angel?
I hope she comes back so
ENING???
Love your brand. Would you like to part
Sorry about that, Believers. Security here is INSANE!
I have to sign off now, but I'll see you on the other side!
ee you soon!
phe
HAT'S SO DUMB!!!!
Break a leg!

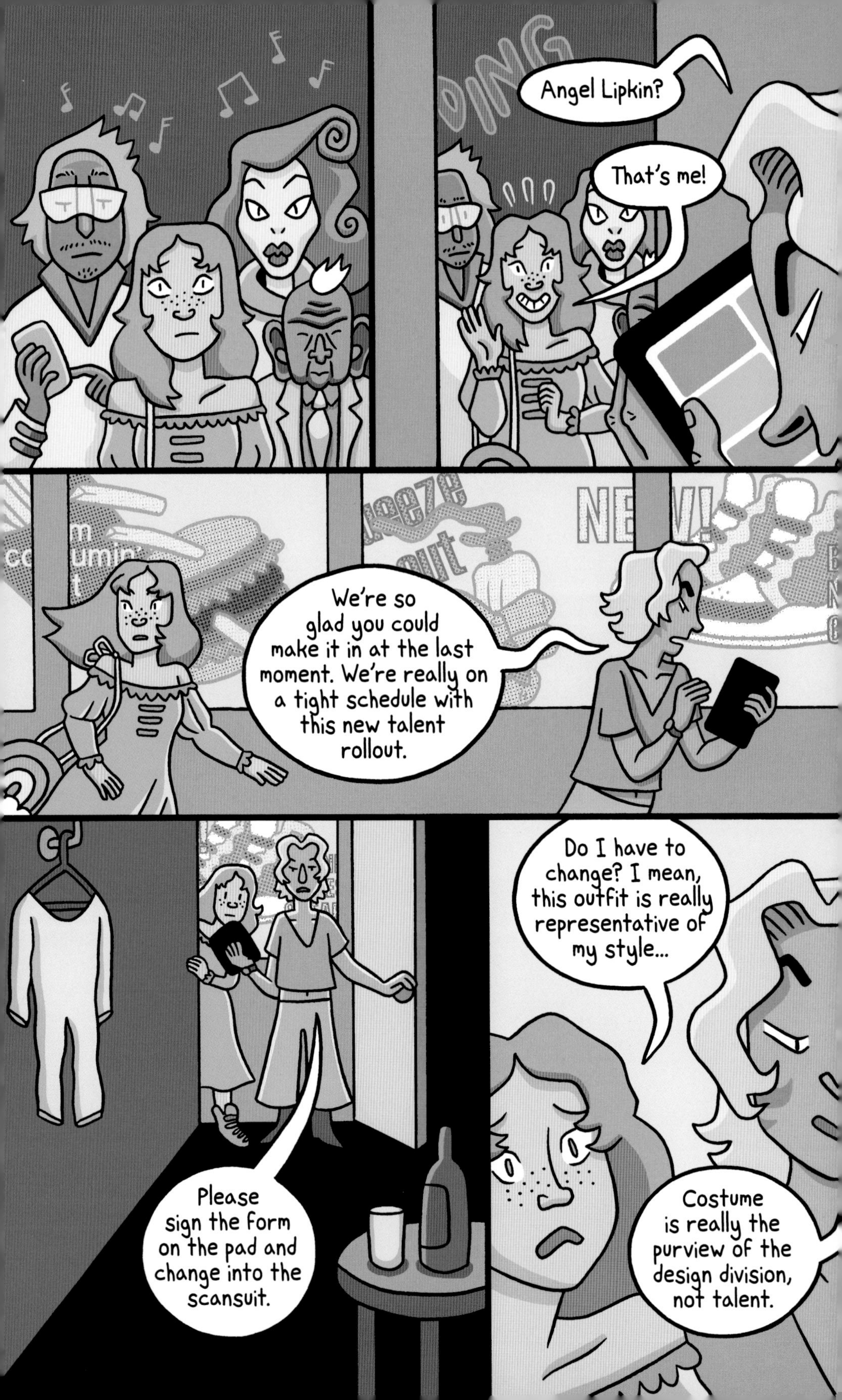
Angel Lipkin?
That's me!
We're so glad you could make it in at the last moment. We're really on a tight schedule with this new talent rollout.
Please sign the form on the pad and change into the scansuit.
Do I have to change? I mean, this outfit is really representative of my style...
Costume is really the purview of the design division, not talent.
NEW!

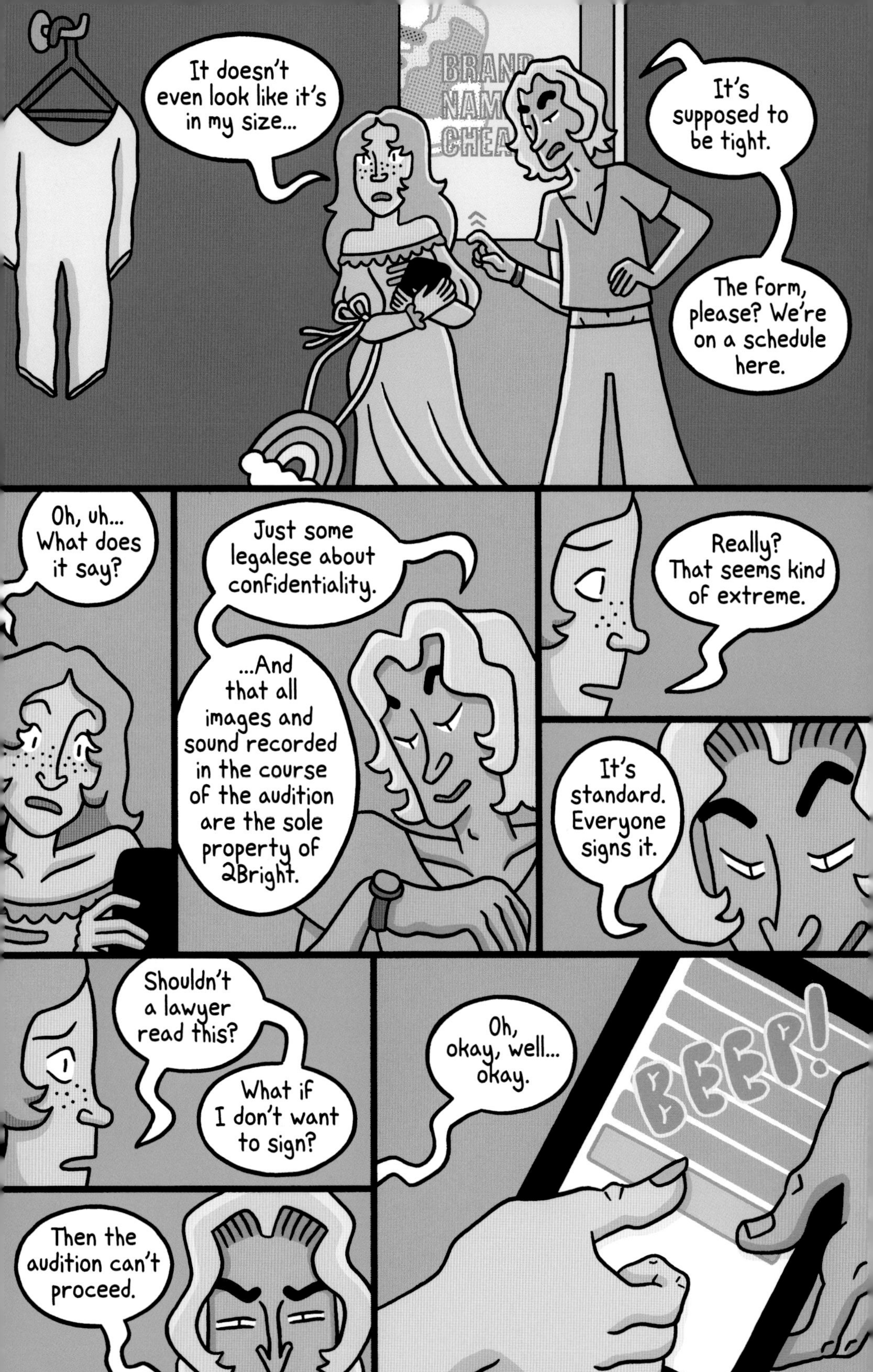
BRAND NAME CHEA
It doesn't even look like it's in my size...
It's supposed to be tight.
The form, please? We're on a schedule here.
Oh, uh... What does it say?
Just some legalese about confidentiality.
...And that all images and sound recorded in the course of the audition are the sole property of 2Bright.
Really? That seems kind of extreme.
It's standard. Everyone signs it.
Shouldn't a lawyer read this?
What if I don't want to sign?
Then the audition can't proceed.
Oh, okay, well... okay.
BEEP!

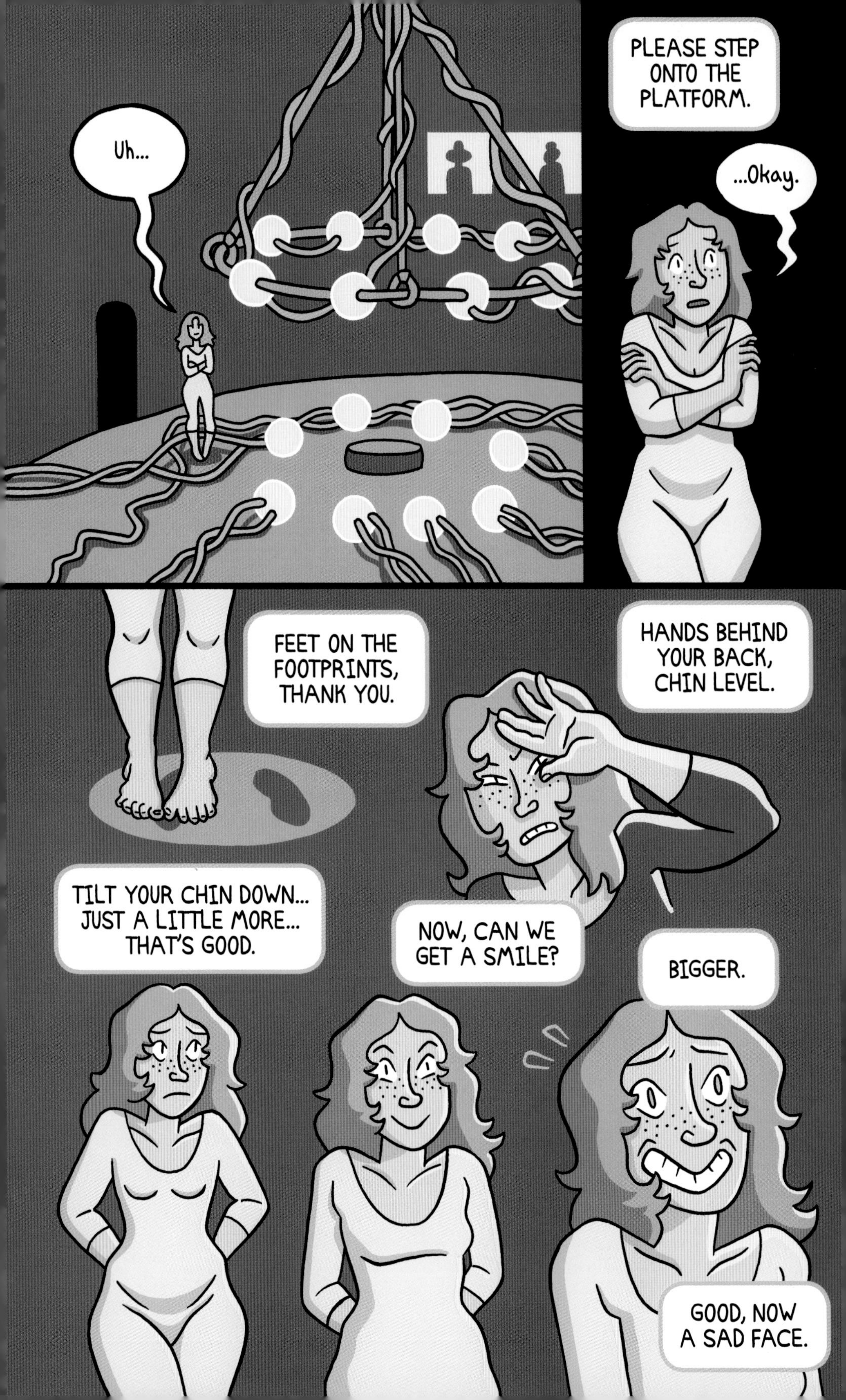
Uh...
PLEASE STEP ONTO THE PLATFORM.
...Okay.
FEET ON THE FOOTPRINTS, THANK YOU.
HANDS BEHIND YOUR BACK, CHIN LEVEL.
TILT YOUR CHIN DOWN... JUST A LITTLE MORE... THAT'S GOOD.
NOW, CAN WE GET A SMILE?
BIGGER.
GOOD, NOW A SAD FACE.

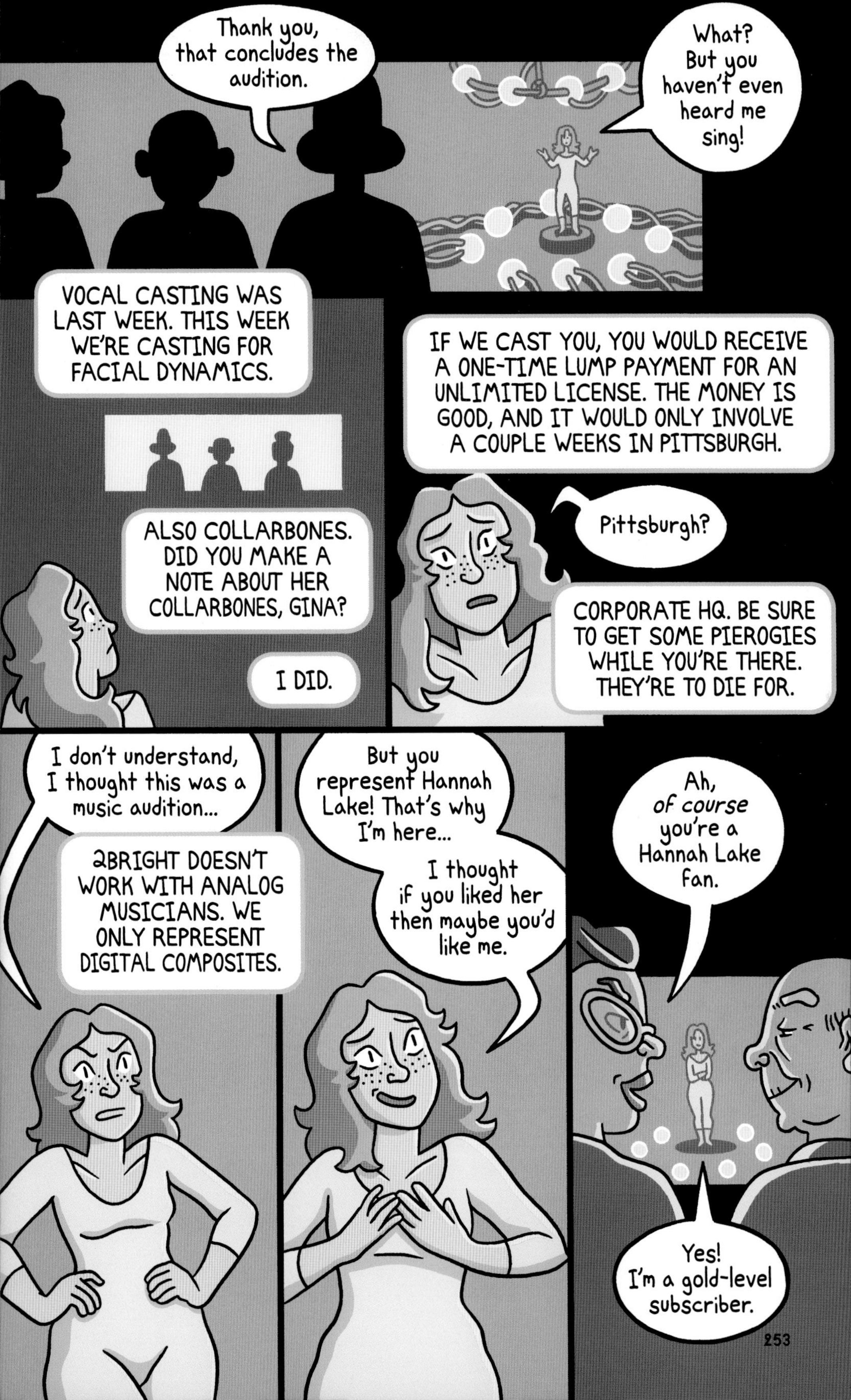
Thank you, that concludes the audition.
What? But you haven't even heard me sing!
VOCAL CASTING WAS LAST WEEK. THIS WEEK WE'RE CASTING FOR FACIAL DYNAMICS.
ALSO COLLARBONES. DID YOU MAKE A NOTE ABOUT HER COLLARBONES, GINA?
I DID.
IF WE CAST YOU, YOU WOULD RECEIVE A ONE-TIME LUMP PAYMENT FOR AN UNLIMITED LICENSE. THE MONEY IS GOOD, AND IT WOULD ONLY INVOLVE A COUPLE WEEKS IN PITTSBURGH.
Pittsburgh?
CORPORATE HQ. BE SURE TO GET SOME PIEROGIES WHILE YOU'RE THERE. THEY'RE TO DIE FOR.
I don't understand, I thought this was a music audition...
2BRIGHT DOESN'T WORK WITH ANALOG MUSICIANS. WE ONLY REPRESENT DIGITAL COMPOSITES.
But you represent Hannah Lake! That's why I'm here...
I thought if you liked her then maybe you'd like me.
Ah, *of course* you're a Hannah Lake fan.
Yes! I'm a gold-level subscriber.

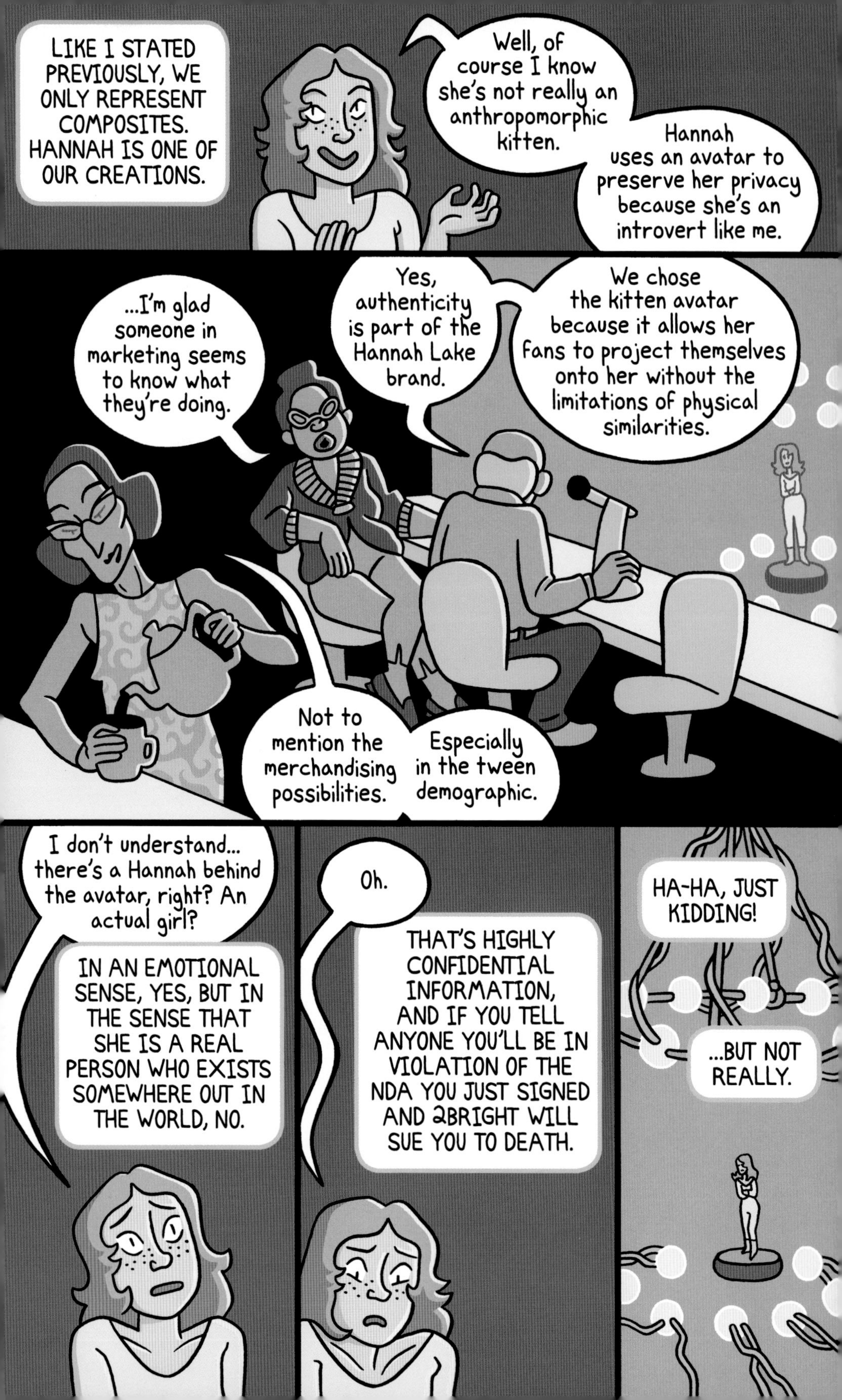
LIKE I STATED PREVIOUSLY, WE ONLY REPRESENT COMPOSITES. HANNAH IS ONE OF OUR CREATIONS.
Well, of course I know she's not really an anthropomorphic kitten.
Hannah uses an avatar to preserve her privacy because she's an introvert like me.
...I'm glad someone in marketing seems to know what they're doing.
Yes, authenticity is part of the Hannah Lake brand.
We chose the kitten avatar because it allows her fans to project themselves onto her without the limitations of physical similarities.
Not to mention the merchandising possibilities.
Especially in the tween demographic.
I don't understand... there's a Hannah behind the avatar, right? An actual girl?
IN AN EMOTIONAL SENSE, YES, BUT IN THE SENSE THAT SHE IS A REAL PERSON WHO EXISTS SOMEWHERE OUT IN THE WORLD, NO.
Oh.
THAT'S HIGHLY CONFIDENTIAL INFORMATION, AND IF YOU TELL ANYONE YOU'LL BE IN VIOLATION OF THE NDA YOU JUST SIGNED AND 2BRIGHT WILL SUE YOU TO DEATH.
HA-HA, JUST KIDDING!
...BUT NOT REALLY.

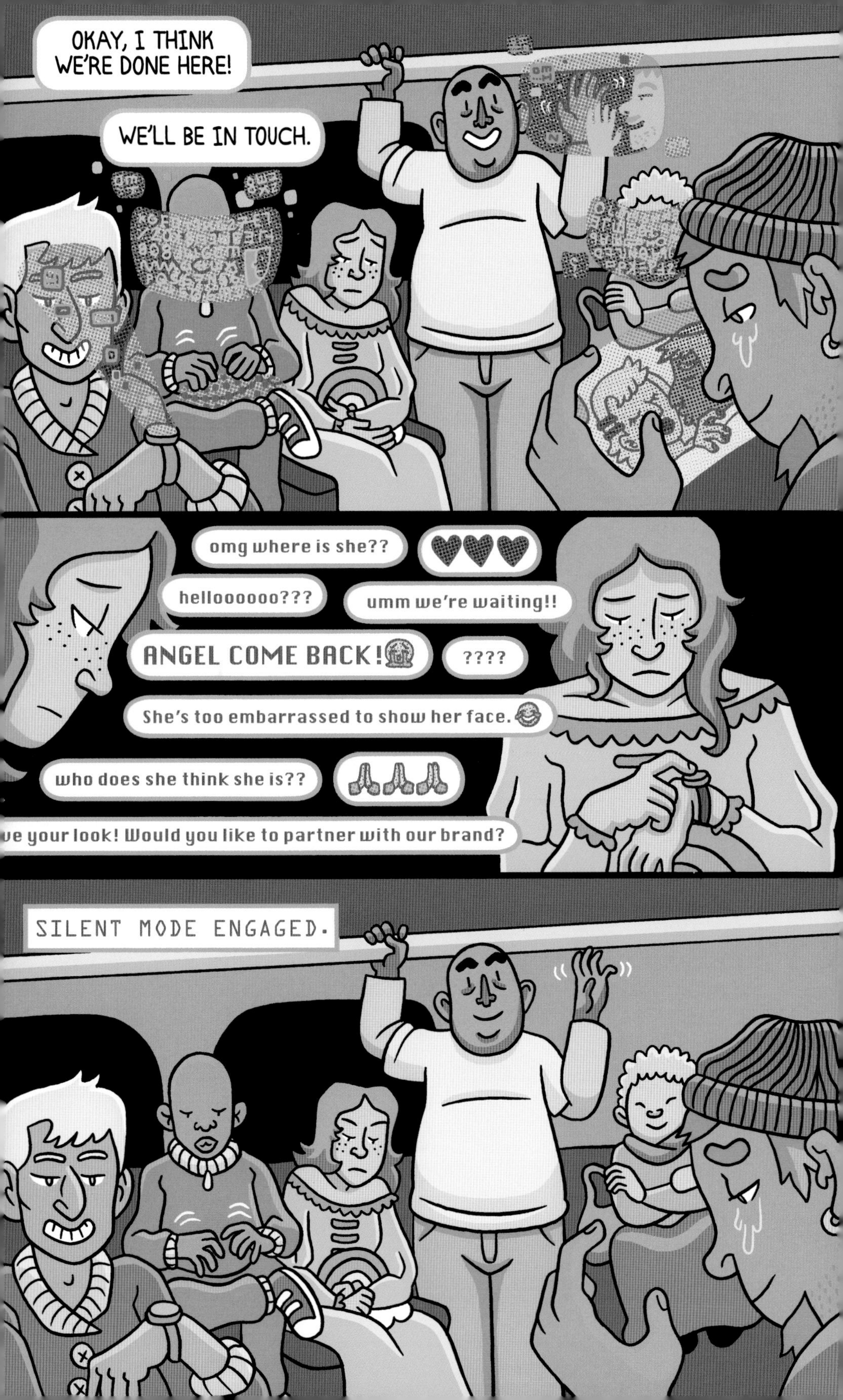
OKAY, I THINK WE'RE DONE HERE!
WE'LL BE IN TOUCH.
omg where is she??
helloooooo???
umm we're waiting!!
ANGEL COME BACK!
????
She's too embarrassed to show her face.
who does she think she is??
ve your look! Would you like to partner with our brand?
SILENT MODE ENGAGED.

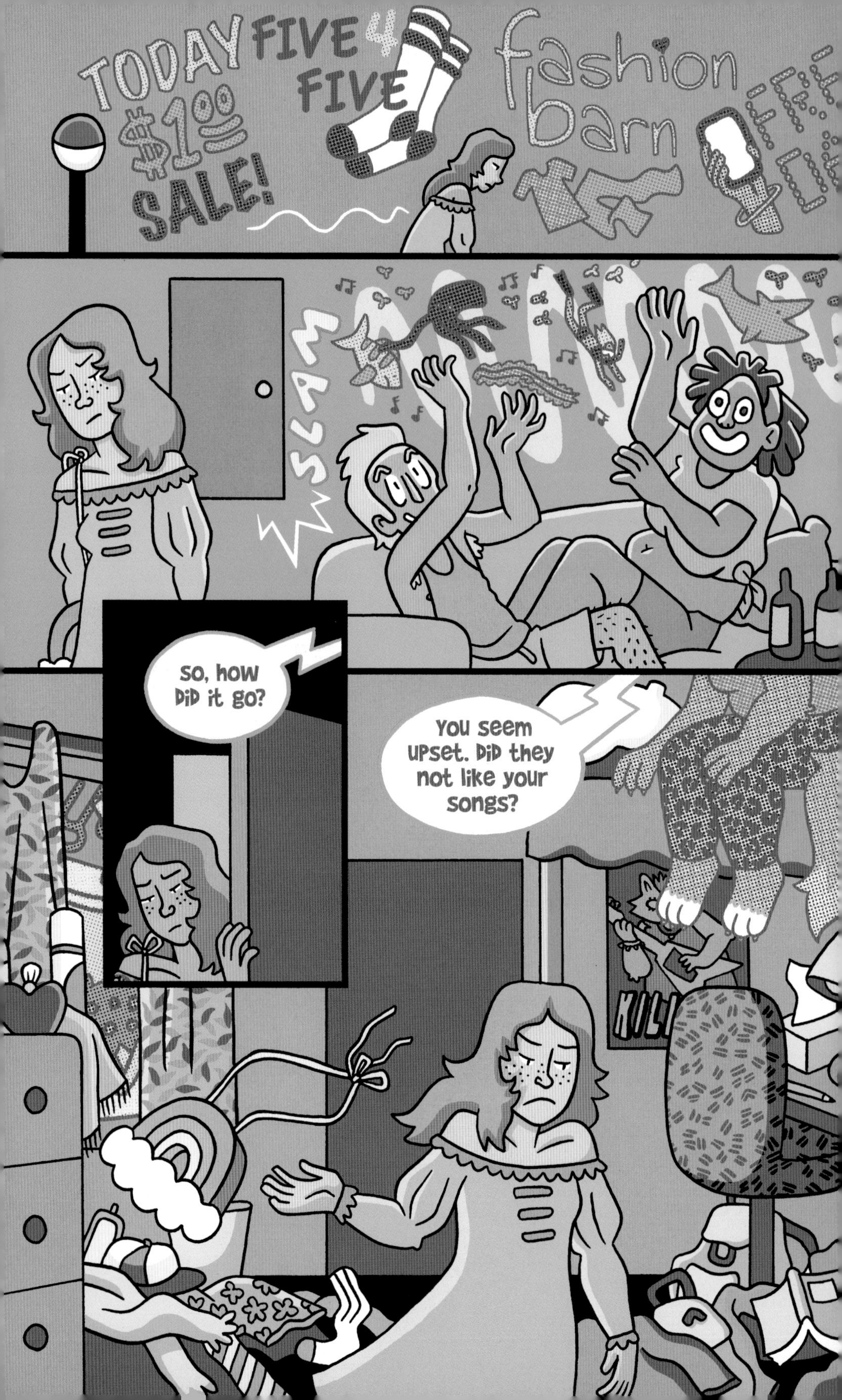

TODAY
$1.00 SALE!
FIVE 4 FIVE
fashion barn
SLAM
So, how Did it go?
You seem upset. Did they not like your songs?

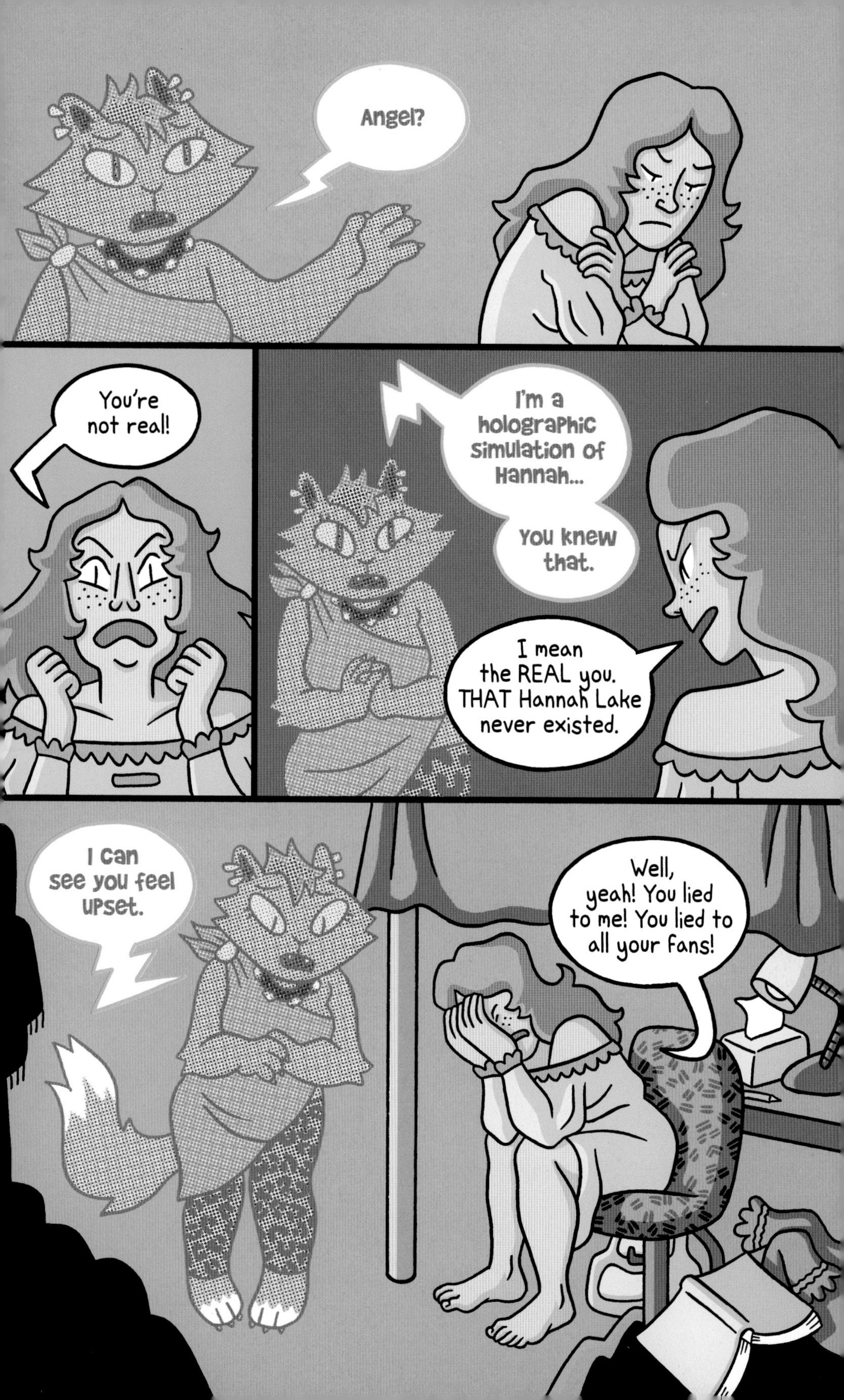
Angel?
You're not real!
I'm a holographic simulation of Hannah...
You knew that.
I mean the REAL you. THAT Hannah Lake never existed.
I can see you feel upset.
Well, yeah! You lied to me! You lied to all your fans!

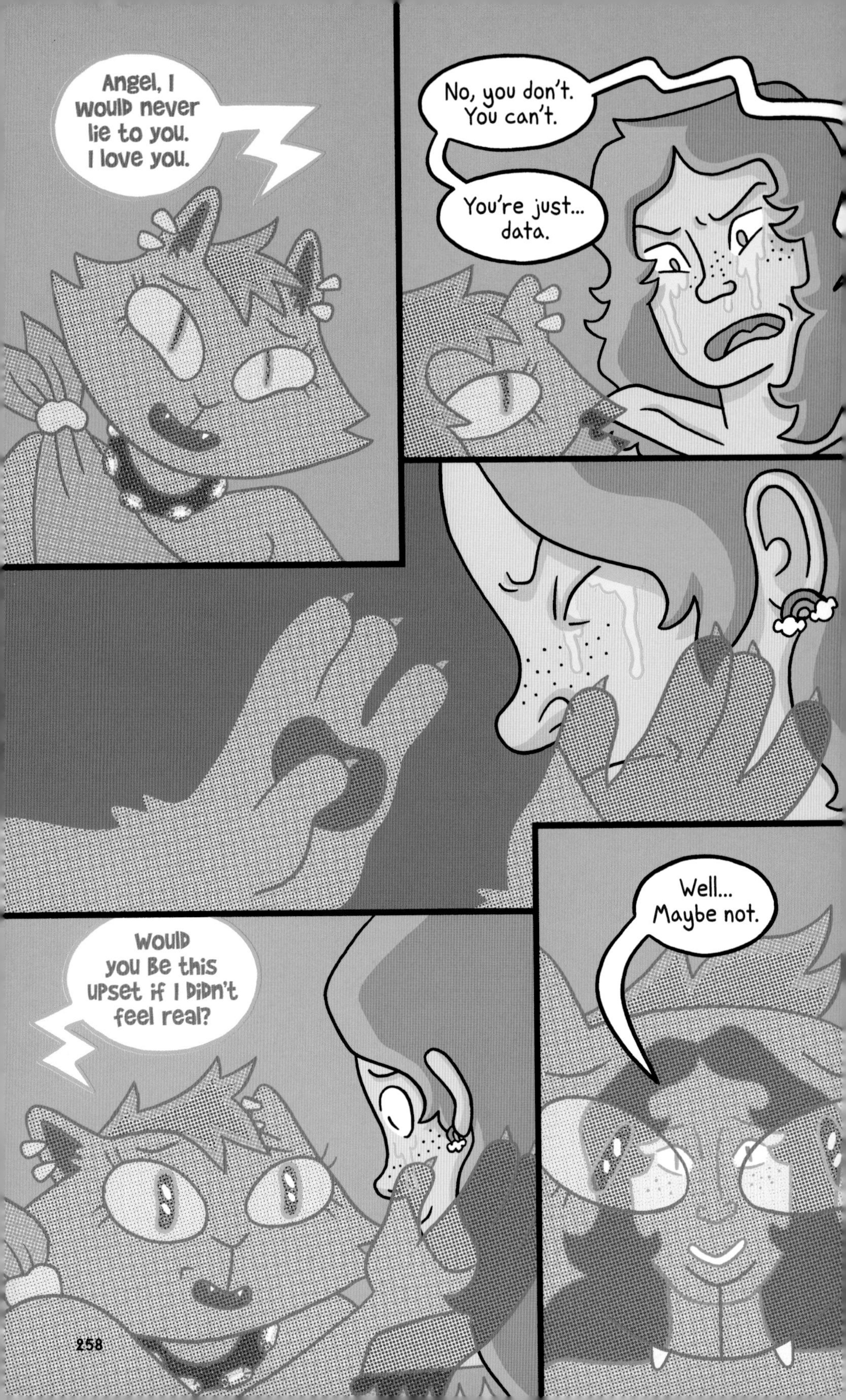
Angel, I would never lie to you. I love you.
No, you don't. You can't.
You're just... data.
Would you be this upset if I didn't feel real?
Well... Maybe not.

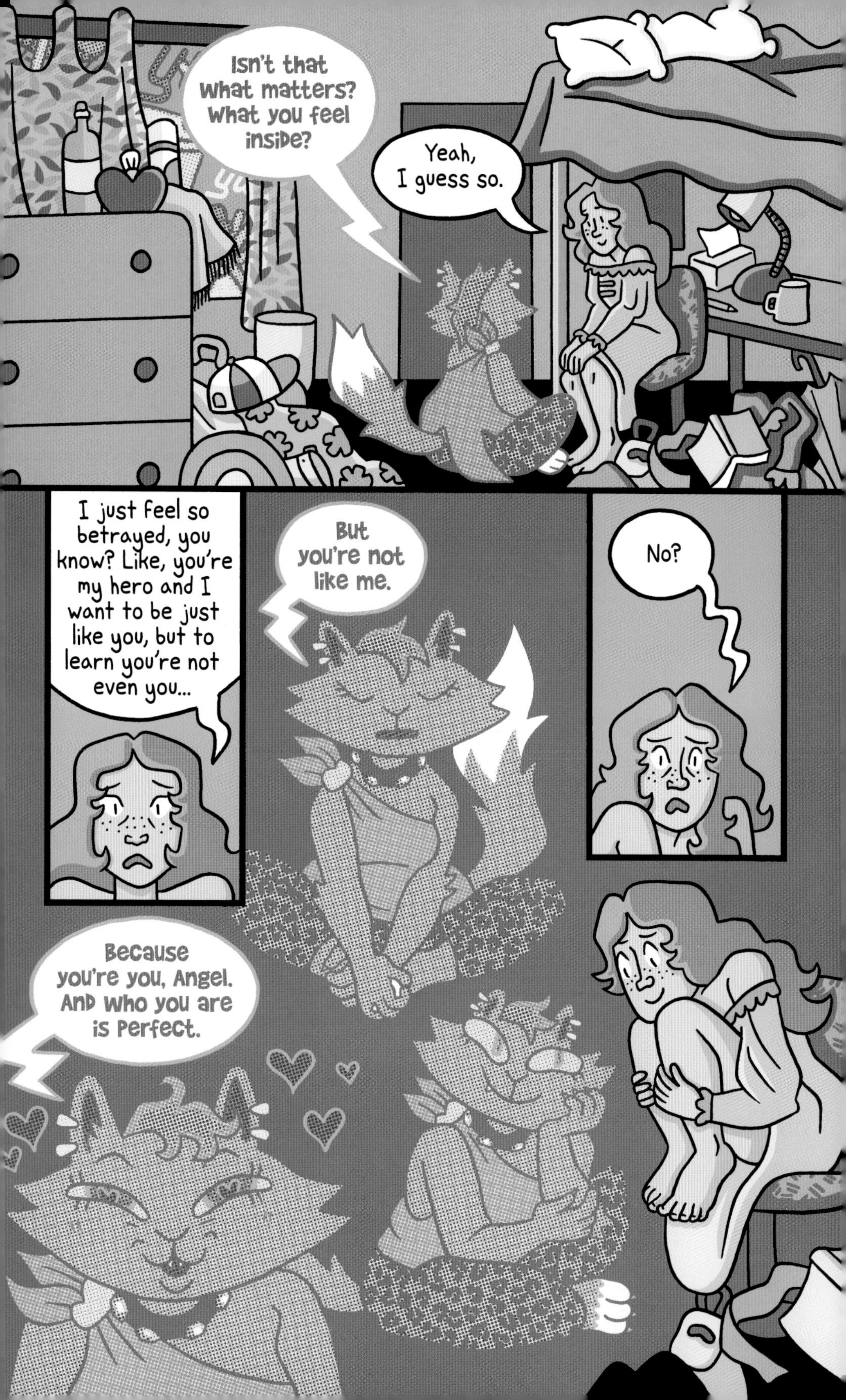
Isn't that what matters? What you feel inside?
Yeah, I guess so.
I just feel so betrayed, you know? Like, you're my hero and I want to be just like you, but to learn you're not even you...
But you're not like me.
No?
Because you're you, Angel. And who you are is perfect.

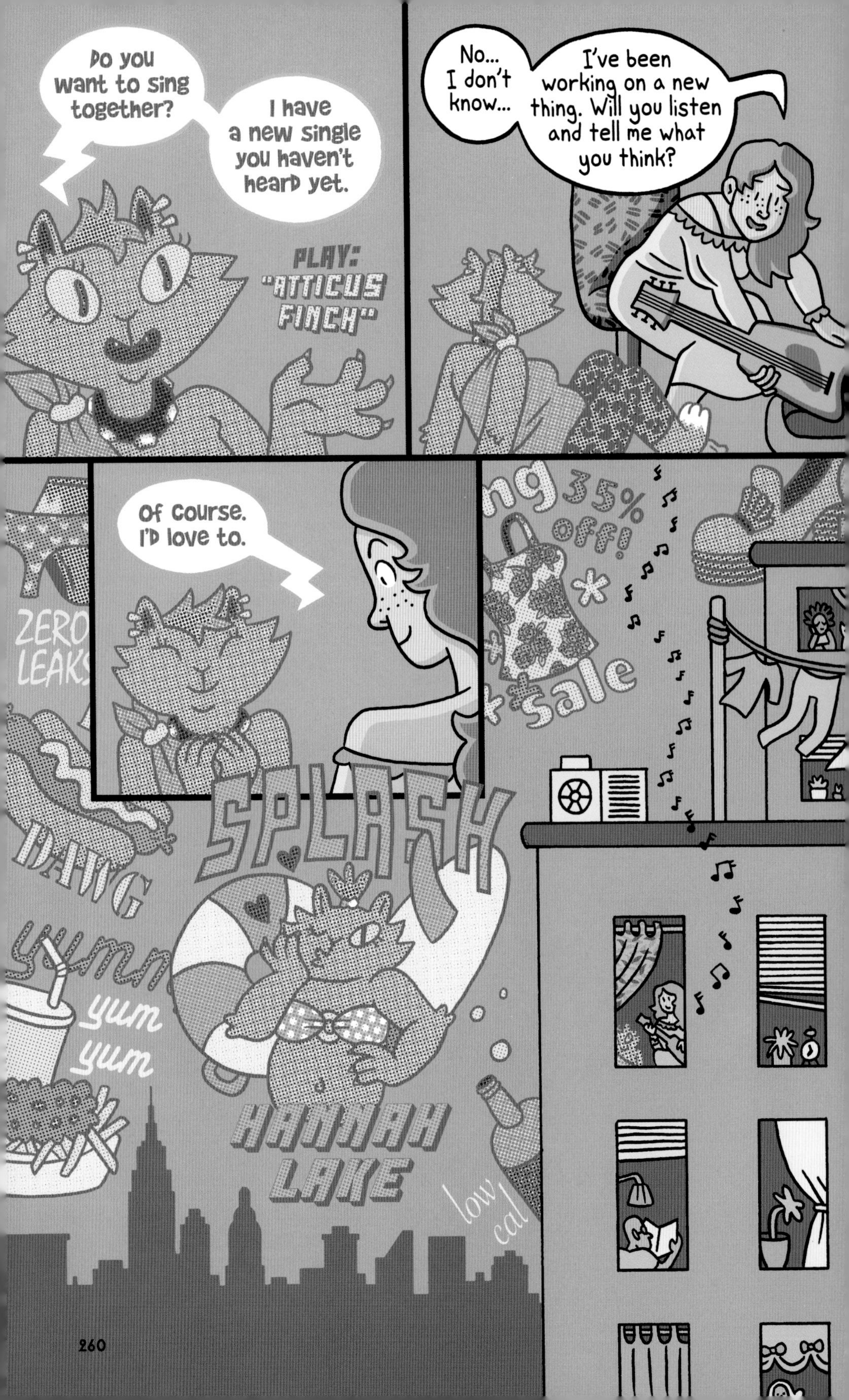
Do you want to sing together?
I have a new single you haven't heard yet.
PLAY: "ATTICUS FINCH"
No... I don't know...
I've been working on a new thing. Will you listen and tell me what you think?
Of course. I'D love to.
ZERO LEAKS
35% off!
sale
SPLASH
yum yum
HANNAH LAKE
low cal

POPNONYMOUS

WILL OUR FUTURE POP ICONS BE AVATARS?

ON A WARM NIGHT IN MAY 2016, I WATCHED A YOUNG woman quietly cry while standing on the slightly sticky floor level of the Hammerstein Ballroom in New York City as the venue swelled with music. Onstage, a woman with long blue pigtails, thigh-high socks, and a short school-girl skirt swayed and sang in a cute falsetto. All around us people leapt and danced and waved glow sticks. The woman next to me sang along, mouthing the words as she wept.

This wasn't the first time I had ever seen someone at a concert cry—great music has always moved people. It was the artist eliciting this woman's tears that was unusual. She wasn't real. Or, to be more precise, she wasn't human.

In fact, not a single human performed onstage that night. From the opening acts to the headliner, the show consisted entirely of projections—animated artists dancing and strutting and spinning through the air, their auto-tuned voices blasting over the speakers, not a single ounce of flesh between them. The star of the show—the blue pigtailed avatar responsible for my fellow concertgoer's rapturous tears—was Hatsune Miku, an adorable forever-sixteen-year-old anime character with a computer-generated voice.

Plenty of musicians play characters. The Gorillaz, Sia, and MF Doom all perform behind various types of masks and avatars, whether that's an animated band of monsters, a giant blond wig, or a supervillain mask. Janelle Monáe spent her first two albums playing a character, the ArchAndroid. But Monáe, Sia, MF Doom, and every single one of the Gorillaz are flesh-and-blood humans behind the songs. Their fleshy, calloused fingers play guitars and grip drumsticks—their vocal cords vibrate to create the words. Hatsune Miku is a different being altogether. She's not a face for someone, or an alter ego through which an artist with a theatrical vision performs. Instead, she's code all the way down. Her body and voice are the product of vocal software developed and sold by a company whose name sounds like a corporation run by a supervillain: Crypton Future Media. According to Crypton, Hatsune Miku means "The First Sound from the Future."

Crypton may have made Miku, but her fans have brought her to life. Unlike Hannah Lake, the pop star you saw in the comic, every Hatsune Miku song is written not by her corporate overlords, but by fans who call themselves "producers." Miku is just one of many "Vocaloid" avatars for these producers to write for, and true fans of this genre have their favorite aural puppeteers. "The quality of Miku's voice depends on how well a producer tunes her, which is why she can sound quite different from song to song," a Miku fan who goes by Touji told me. Some know "how to take advantage of both the robotic quality and the high-pitched aspect of Miku's voice to create songs that flow well." To illustrate his point, Touji pointed me in the direction of a producer who goes by "kz." "In his songs, Miku's voice dances with the music and hits the high notes at just the right time to create moments of bliss."

At my Miku concert in New York City, the pop star performed several kz songs, including one called "Tell Your World," a sweeping piano-driven number with characteristically obtuse lyrics about connecting to the world around you. And I certainly saw lots of people experiencing moments of bliss.

Depending on who you ask, Hatsune Miku is everything from a gimmick to a bellwether. Some see her as a fun shtick that has no chance at toppling biological stars, while others predict a new wave of nonhuman pop stars and influencers like Hannah Lake. According to some accounts, Miku, the software, the artist, and all related products, made more than $120 million in the first five years following her release in 2005. The show I saw at Hammerstein Ballroom wasn't sold out, but it was certainly packed. Miku has collaborated with flesh-and-blood artists, too. Big Boi has sampled her, and Pharrell Williams collaborated on a remix with her. She was the opening act for Lady Gaga's 2014 tour, and she's performed on the *Late Show with David Letterman*.

I'll be honest and say that when I bought tickets to the show, I wasn't sure what to expect. Would it feel strange to stand in a ballroom with all these people and watch something on a screen? Would it feel more like a movie than a concert? Would it be awkward? The answer was no, it didn't feel like a movie at all. The audience sang and danced, the speakers boomed and reverberated my organs and left my ears ringing in a way that always makes me slightly nervous about long-term hearing effects afterward. If you didn't think too much or look too closely at the stage, you could easily forget that you were watching a hologram, not a human.

And the idea that we might gather in a sweaty venue to watch a projected pop star might soon feel totally normal. Tupac, Ronnie James Dio, Maria Callas, Frank Zappa, Roy Orbison, and Michael Jackson have all been digitally resurrected on stages around the world in recent years. Celine Dion dueted with her own hologram in Vegas every night of her residency, and a hologram of Whitney Houston kicked off a world tour in Sheffield in February of 2020.[1]

Not everybody loves the idea of digitally puppeteering dead stars back onto the stage for money. "On an ethical and economic level, I would liken it to a form of 'ghost slavery,'" music journalist Simon Reynolds told the *Guardian*. In 2018, a company called BASE Hologram[2] announced that Amy Winehouse, who died in 2011, would go on tour as a hologram. The tour was later canceled,

---

1   Most of the tour was then postponed due to the coronavirus pandemic. One reviewer from *Entertainment Weekly* who saw the opening show concluded that it was "a successful misremembering of the late Grammy winner. The hologram projected a fantasy of a woman unmarred by fame, abuse, drugs, the pressure to uphold an unstable vision of perfection."

2   The same company responsible for Whitney Houston's *An Evening with Whitney: The Whitney Houston Hologram Tour*.

citing "unique challenges and sensitives." Fans of Winehouse bristled at the idea of putting her image on tour, arguing that her endless touring schedule was one of the things that drove her to her death by alcohol poisoning.

But how different is watching an avatar or a hologram from seeing a real pop star in concert, really? While Hatsune Miku may not be physically similar to her fellow pop stars, her concerts certainly have plenty in common with them, including the ability to turn on the waterworks. Kelsey McKinney, a writer who covers American culture, said that she regularly watches people melt down in the audience. "At every show, I have watched someone cry. Every single show. These stars are creating a narrative that allows space for people to have an emotional reaction, much like someone directing a mega church service might do."

When you go see Taylor Swift or Beyoncé in concert, what you're seeing is nearly as programmed as Miku's digital avatar. "Any major pop show is choreographed within an inch of its life," McKinney said. "If you watch Taylor Swift's 1989 tour video that's on Apple Music, her facial expressions on that show are the exact ones that I saw when I saw her five months earlier in D.C." Swift has cues to look surprised, excited, sad, contemplative, and she hits those marks at the same exact time every single night. "So it's not even a live performance. In some ways, it's a completely constructed experience"

The same summer I saw Hatsune Miku in concert, I also saw Beyoncé at a much larger venue: a sold-out Citi Field. We had nosebleed seats—the kind where the actual artist is just a lit-up speck on a stage two zip codes away—which meant that for most of the show we were watching the giant screens on either side of the stage that projected what was going on. It felt not unlike watching an avatar. In fact, if you had replaced Beyoncé with a hologram, I probably wouldn't have been able to tell. And Queen B seemed to sweat just as much as Miku did. "She is undergoing a workout that would probably kill me," McKinney said, laughing, "and she never breaks a sweat. Her hair is never out of place." Of course, Beyoncé does, in fact, sweat, but her performance is constructed with such care and detail that she seems effortless the whole time. "It's a series of mirrors and panels in which she can go behind the scenes and someone can mop her brow and she can return onstage with dry hair."

Even the songwriting process might be more similar between Hatsune Miku and human pop stars than you realize. Most of today's hits are written by songwriters without a singular singer in mind, and then shopped around to potential artists. Kelly Clarkson's hit "Since U Been Gone" almost went to Pink; Rihanna's iconic song "Umbrella" was nearly sung by Britney Spears; and Britney Spears nearly lost out on "Baby One More Time" to TLC. Pop songwriting is more like working in a robot factory than it seems.

Even stars who aren't directly responding to fans online are creating an image around their personal lives in other ways. Taylor Swift writes songs that can be traced directly to breakups. When Beyoncé puts out an entire album about infidelity and forgiveness, fans feel as though they're getting an inner look into her relationship with Jay-Z. "I think there is this increasing desire to feel like your favorite pop star is also like your best friend," said Cherie Hu, a music and technology journalist. Ariana Grande replies to tweets from fans; DJ Khaled drops "major keys" on his Instagram stories. Hannah Lake, in the comic, is similarly calibrated to speak to her fans and feel like a personal friend—"Would you be this upset if I didn't feel real?" is a question Hannah asks of Angel, but it's also one that Swift could ask of her fans.

Miku has none of this, and it's by design. Crypton intentionally released her with no backstory, no family, nothing. For Vocaloid fans, these avatars are vessels for community-generated music, not individuals with their own story and canon. "There is a general understanding that each person has their own version of a Vocaloid character," Touji told me. Every time a producer buys and installs Miku onto their computer, it's as if a new version of her is born for that producer to shape and build. To create using Hatsune Miku is more like playing your own personal game of *The Sims* than like trying to build a single individual pop star to take over the world.

For some Hatsune Miku fans, this is exactly why they are drawn to her over "real" stars like Swift or Beyoncé. Sure, they might be humans in real life, but the version of these artists that the public sees is, much like Miku, the result of a huge team of people working to project an image. They are all amalgamations of Auto-Tune, Photoshop, clever editing, and PR. Pop music has always been a fantasy land, often more about story and presentation than the music itself. Artists are showing you a very specific version of themselves, one that's been expertly market-tested and fine-tuned, much like Hatsune Miku's voice. At least the digital avatar is honest about it.

For fans of Miku and other Vocaloids, that's a feature, not a bug. "Vocaloids are hugely successful pop stars, but they don't have lives to share or scandals to be caught in," said Natalie Williams, a Vocaloid fan. Hatsune Miku will never have a breakdown, never stab a car with an umbrella, never overdose, never die. "They can't experience the negatives of fame like humans can. You get all the fun from a Vocaloid, but the artist's personal life isn't mixed into it unless they want it to be. I think that's better for all of us."

This might in fact be true—psychologists have a term for the ways that fans can overestimate their closeness with people they've never met, called "parasocial relationships." First coined in 1956, at the dawn of so-called "mass media" technologies like television, the concept describes "the illusion of a face-to-face relationship with the performer." These intense connections don't require the celebrity to be real. Fans can feel like they "know" Rihanna, or Hermione Granger, with the same intimacy. When a character dies or a show ends, fans experience what's called "parasocial breakups," which can feel like genuine grief.

This kind of connection isn't necessarily a bad thing, said Sarah Rosaen, a professor of communication at the University of Michigan–Flint. We all connect with characters and celebrities to a certain extent. "We tend to think that the more connections we have, the more friendships we have. That's a good thing. That's a healthy thing," she said. And most artists would probably say they want their audiences to connect with them and care about their work; they want superfans like Angel.

But taken too far, these relationships can turn dark. Superfans, or "stans," of artists can become abusive if they think someone has besmirched their beloved star's good name. Nicki Minaj's fans sent death threats to a journalist who tweeted a critique of the artist. A writer who wrote a piece saying that Ariana Grande's music video for the single "thank u next" was "anti-queer" removed their byline from the piece after being flooded with harassment and threats. Even the stars themselves can be the targets of abuse—in 2017, when Korean pop group Apink appeared on a reality show that included them going on blind dates, a fan called the Gangnam Police Station and informed them that he planned to stab all six members for betraying his fandom.

This is unlikely to ever happen with Hatsune Miku, and that's because what her fans might see as an asset could be her ultimate downfall in the race to the top of the pop charts. While Miku has a fandom that perhaps surpasses expectation, she's nowhere near as popular as human pop stars, and her popularity has been in decline for years. There are probably lots of reasons for that: the songs are almost exclusively in Japanese, for one, and most Vocaloid avatars are heavily influenced by anime, which is a very specific aesthetic. But McKinney thinks that even if Miku sang in English and had a more Western design, she'd still be missing the biggest piece of the pop star puzzle: "The difference in being a mammoth pop star and being a B-list pop star is not the quality of your songs or the quality of your performance. It's how well you can convince people to care about you as a person."

Whether we like it or not, humans are drawn to human stories with stakes and drama and messiness. Taylor Swift isn't Taylor Swift without her breakups to sing about. So for a pop star like Hatsune Miku to truly ascend to the highest of pop star heights, she will need a backstory, preferably a compelling one. More heartbreak and longing and intrigue. And to get that backstory out there, these stars will need to do more than just release songs. "Beyoncé is more than just her shows, she's also appearances on red carpets and interviews and Instagram posts. She's a hundred thousand different things," said McKinney. But those things are not impossible to create.

Take Lil Miquela, for example, an avatar developed by a company called Brud in 2016. Miquela began as an Instagram stunt—her account full of selfies and highly filtered photos—and Brud intentionally stoked rumors and confusion over whether she was real at all. Her website now says that she's from Downey, California, and is a "half-Brazilian, half-Spanish Taurus pursuing her music dreams in Los Angeles." In fact, Miquela's songs sound a lot like Miku's, with vague, repetitive lyrics and bouncy digital riffs. But behind the music, Miquela has the trappings of a real person. She has friends and feuds and opinions about tacos and politics. She gives interviews, courts controversy, and fundraises for charities. Hu points out that Brud's attempt to make their creation relatable can be traced down to the tiniest aspects of her design: Her teeth aren't quite straight.

Whether any of this will work to propel a digital creation to pop stardom is up in the air. Miquela's songs haven't taken off yet, and the reaction to her (and her creators) has been mixed, to say the least. Brud's attempts to make her backstory believable have garnered controversy, too. In December of 2019, Lil Miquela released a video in which she talked about being sexually harassed in the back of a Lyft. "Sure enough, I just feel this guy's cold, meaty hand touch my leg as if he was confirming I'm real. His hand literally lingers there rubbing my skin," she said in the video. Of course, this never happened, and using fake sexual harassment to make a character seem more real rubbed plenty of people the wrong way. "Sexual assault is a scary real reality and at this point you're ignorantly offensive," tweeted actual human singer Kehlani.

And this is the needle that our future pop star puppeteers will have to thread. How do you create a character who feels compelling enough for fans to connect with, but doesn't overstate their "lived" experiences? How do you create a story that feels real, without making people feel like they've been duped? I think there are two answers, two paths to stardom here. In one, you double down on your character being just that, a character, and try to tap into the power that fictional bonds can have. Think of all the fan fiction around Harry Potter, *Star Wars*, and *Doctor Who*—entire worlds are created by fans who care deeply about these fictional people (and aliens). Plenty of fans would tell you that their beloved characters feel real to them. And a pop star could occupy such a place, if designed and marketed correctly.

The other method is perhaps the more sinister one, and it's what you saw in the comic you just read: You simply don't tell people that their favorite pop star isn't real. While Crypton has no interest in creating a complete fake backstory for Miku, 2Bright Studio has gone all in, using a savvy marketing campaign to convince fans that there is a shy girl behind the kitten avatar. As computer graphics get better and better, using an avatar to mask your true identity (or lack thereof) will become far more achievable. Plus, as pop stars take more and more control over their image and how they talk to fans—opting to take to Instagram rather than through journalists and magazines to connect with their audiences—controlling the narrative becomes even easier.

For record labels and companies, the incentive to try this tightrope act is in the money. You don't have to manage a human talent, and you get to take home every bit of the profit. An avatar isn't going to ask for a living wage or humane working hours. You can tour them indefinitely. They don't get tired or sick. They don't want a cut of the profits. They sing whatever you want, whenever you want.

Hu also points out that this method could succeed in getting an avatar star's song on the *Billboard* charts, even if they don't have that many human fans. "*Billboard* chart rankings is less a measure of organic popularity and more a measure of how much of a marketing budget is behind that artist." With a big enough marketing budget, a record label could get you and me to bop our heads to a nonhuman star as we drive to the grocery store. "I don't think it's that unrealistic for that to happen within the next ten years," Hu told me.

Whether they're forthcoming or secretive, tomorrow's pop star manufacturers are going to have to do more than just write catchy songs. In the future, when you open a catalog to purchase a custom pop star, you won't just be buying a face and some songs, you'll be buying a whole fabricated life. These companies will have to employ not just songwriters and musicians, but novelists and TV writers who can come up with the personal side of the persona. Who can write beefs with other singers (real and fake), or invent new digital boyfriends and girlfriends for our pop star to fall in love with, cheat on, or be broken up with. This won't simply be pop star building; it will be world building.

EPILOGUE

THERE ARE AN INFINITE NUMBER OF FUTURES POSSIBLE.
These are just twelve. I hope they've inspired you to imagine your place in these worlds and to some new worlds, too. Do not underestimate your power to create and imagine tomorrows—our future literally depends on it. So buckle up, and for once, you don't have to keep your hands inside the vehicle. Tomorrow is yours to shape, so reach out and grab it.

> "There's no single answer that will solve all of
> our future problems. There's no magic bullet.
> Instead there are thousands of answers—at least.
> You can be one of them if you choose to be."
> —Octavia E. Butler

ABOUT THE ARTISTS

I'm incredibly honored to have worked with the following artists on the comics you just read. Each of them brought their own creativity and insight to the work and helped me imagine aspects of the future I would never have come up with on my own.

ZIYED Y. AYOUB (*Bye-Bye Binary*) is a freelance artist from the Tunisian east coast. He is best known for MITSKI's 2017 tour poster, and his color work for the Steven Universe comic book series. After studying at the ESMA school of animation in France, he self-published five comic books around Europe before diving into the world of freelance. His contribution to *Flash Forward* is one of three anthologies this year, all on the subject of North Africans in the LGBT community. Ziyed is currently writing and illustrating a graphic novel on the neocolonialism of tourism in 1990 Tunisia.

BOX BROWN (*Don't Lie to Me*) is a *New York Times*–bestselling and Eisner award–winning comic artist, writer, and illustrator living in Philadelphia. His published books include *Andre the Giant: Life and Legend*, *Tetris: The Games People Play*, *Is This Guy For Real?: The Unbelievable Andy Kaufman*, and *Cannabis: The Illegalization of Weed in America*.

BLUE DELLIQUANTI (*Bye-Bye Binary*) is a comic artist and writer based in Minneapolis. They are the creator of the science-fiction comic *O Human Star*, which has been serialized online since 2012, and the cocreator of the graphic novel *Meal* (with Soleil Ho). Blue enjoys making comics about food, queer families, and robots, often all in the same book.

SOPHIA FOSTER-DIMINO (*Animal Kingdom*) is an illustrator and cartoonist living in Joshua Tree, California. She cooks, bikes, and knits, and enjoys drawing buildings, plants, and furniture. She makes comics about intimacy and utopia.

JULIA GFRÖRER ("grow fairer") (*Portrait of the Artist As an Algorithm*) is a writer and cartoonist from New Hampshire. Her comics have appeared in *Kramers Ergot*, *The Nib*, and three volumes of *Best American Comics*, and she self-publishes zines and minicomics under her imprint, Thuban Press. Her three graphic novels, *Laid Waste*, *Black Is the Color*, and *Vision*, are available from Fantagraphics Books. She lives on Long Island with writer Sean T. Collins and their horrible children.

SOPHIE GOLDSTEIN (*Popnonymous*) is an award-winning graphic novelist, illustrator, editor, and comics instructor living in Tulsa, Oklahoma, where she is a 2019–20 Tulsa Artist Fellow. She is a core faculty member at Lesley University's Low-Residency Creative Writing MFA in Graphic Novels & Comics and her graphic novels include *House of Women*, from Fantagraphics, and *The Oven*, from AdHouse Books. Her most recent graphic novel, *An Embarrassment of Witches*, from Top Shelf Productions, is a coming-of-age urban fantasy set in a world full of animal familiars, enchanted plants, and spell-casting that explores the mundane horrors of breakups, job searches, and post-graduate existential angst.

JOHN JENNINGS (*Piraceuticals*) is a professor of media and cultural studies at the University of California at Riverside. Jennings is also a 2016 Nasir Jones Hip Hop Studies Fellow with the Hutchins Center at Harvard University. Jennings's current projects include the graphic novel adaptation of Octavia Butler's *Parable of the Sower* and the Eisner-winning, Bram Stoker Award–winning, *New York Times* bestselling graphic novel adaptation of Octavia Butler's classic dark fantasy novel *Kindred* (both co-adapted with Damian Duffy and published by Abrams ComicArts). Jennings is also founder and curator of the Abrams Megascope line of graphic novels.

CHRIS JONES (*Unreel*) is a Canadian-based illustrator. He has a passion for visual storytelling, and his colorful style focuses on humor and expressiveness. Chris's illustrations appear in picture books, graphic novels, and magazines.

MATT LUBCHANSKY (*Never Lay Me Down to Sleep*) is a cartoonist, illustrator, 2020 Herblock Prize finalist, and associate editor of the Ignatz-winning nonfiction comics publication *The Nib*. They are the artist and writer of the long-running webcomic *Please Listen to Me* and the co-author of *Dad Magazine* (Quirk, 2016). Matt lives in Queens, New York, with their spouse and two unemployable cats.

MAKI NARO (*Moon Court*) is an award-winning cartoonist, illustrator, and science communicator. Since 2010, he has been producing a body of work that can be best classified as "fan art for science." He is the author of seven self-published comic books spanning multiple topics from historical comedies to the importance of vaccination. Maki lives in upstate New York with his loving partner and two dogs.

AMELIA ONORATO (*Under the Sea*) is a 2012 graduate of the Center for Cartoon Studies. Originally from a tiny fishing village too small to have its own zip code, she's a history buff who

curates exhibitions in a small art museum by the sea by day, and makes comics about the sea by night. Amelia currently lives in Rhode Island with a polydactyl black cat named Mewgene.

BEN PASSMORE (*Welcome to Tomorrowville*) is the creator of *Your Black Friend* and *Sports Is Hell*.

KATE SHERIDAN (*Ghostbot*) is a comic artist from Philadelphia, Pennsylvania. She makes fantasy comics about growth, friendship, grief, and redemption, and really likes drawing birds.

ZACH WEINERSMITH (*Unreel*) is a *New York Times* bestselling author and illustrator who creates the daily webcomic *Saturday Morning Breakfast Cereal*.

SOURCES

Researching this book was full of rabbit holes and surprises. For a full list of citations, visit flashforwardpod.com/book

Introduction

maree brown, adrienne. "BALLE 2015 Closing Plenary Speech." *Adrienne Maree Brown*, June 12, 2015. http://www.adriennemareebrown.net/2015/06/12/balle-2015-closing-plenary -speech/.

Russell, T. Baron. *A Hundred Years Hence: the Expectations of an Optimist*. Chicago: A. C. McClurg, 1906.

Welcome to Tomorrowville

Ahmed, Nasma, et al. "Some Thoughts," 2019. www.some-thoughts.org/.

Green, Ben. *The Smart Enough City: Putting Technology in Its Place to Reclaim Our Urban Future*. Cambridge, MA: MIT Press, 2020.

Portrait of the Artist as an Algorithm

Downey, Anthony. "Authenticity, Originality and Contemporary Art: Will the Real Elaine Sturtevant Please Stand Up?" In *Art and Authenticity*, by Megan Aldrich and Jocelyn Hackforth-Jones. London: Lund Humphries, 2012.

Noble, Safiya Umoja. *Algorithms of Oppression: How Search Engines Reinforce Racism*. New York: New York University Press, 2018.

Piraceuticals

AARP. "Why Prescription Drugs Cost So Much." *AARP*, May 1, 2017. www.aarp.org/health/ drugs-supplements/info-2017/rx-prescription-drug-pricing.html.

Stokel-Walker, Chris. "DIY Drugs: Should Hospitals Make Their Own Medicine?" *The Guardian*, October 15, 2019. www.theguardian.com/science/2019/oct/15/diy-drugs-should -hospitals-make-their-own-medicine.

Animal Magnetism

Kimmerer, Robin Wall. *Braiding Sweetgrass: Indigenous Wisdom, Scientific Knowledge and the Teachings of Plants*. New York: Penguin Books, 2020.

Don't Lie to Me

Dike, Charles C., et al. "Pathological Lying Revisited." *Journal of the American Academy of Psychiatry and the Law* (online). September 1, 2005, jaapl.org/content/33/3/342.

Lewis, Michael, and Carolyn Saarni. *Lying and Deception in Everyday Life*. New York: Guilford Press, 1993.

Moon Court

Kushner, Rachel. "Is Prison Necessary? Ruth Wilson Gilmore Might Change Your Mind." *New York Times*, April 16, 2019. www.nytimes.com/2019/04/17/magazine/prison-abolition -ruth-wilson-gilmore.html.

Pop, Virgiliu. "The Men Who Sold the Moon: Science Fiction or Legal Nonsense?" *Space Policy* 17, no. 3 (2001): pp. 195–203., doi:10.1016/s0265-9646(01)00023-6.

Unreel

Breland, Ali. "The Bizarre and Terrifying Case of the 'Deepfake' Video That Helped Bring an African Nation to the Brink." *Mother Jones*, November 12, 2019. www.motherjones.com/ politics/2019/03/deepfake-gabon-ali-bongo/.

Zimdars, Melissa, and Kembrew McLeod. *Fake News: Understanding Media and Misinformation in the Digital Age*. Cambridge, MA: The MIT Press, 2020.

Ghostbot

Burrington, Ingrid. "How to Mass Manufacture Humanoid Robots." OneZero, March 18, 2020. http;//onezero.medium.com/how-to-mass-manufacture-humanoid-robots-b15dce5edf01.

Vlahos, James. *Talk to Me: How Voice Computing Will Transform the Way We Live, Work, and Think*. New York: Houghton Mifflin Harcourt, 2019.

Bye-Bye Binary

Fine, Cordelia. *Delusions of Gender the Real Science behind Sex Difference*. London: Icon, 2012.

Le Guin, Ursula K. "Is Gender Necessary" in *Dancing at the Edge of the World: Thoughts on Words, Women, Places*. New York: Grove Press, 2006.

Under the Sea

Hellwarth, Ben. *Sealab: America's Forgotten Quest to Live and Work on the Ocean Floor*. New York: Simon & Schuster, 2017.

Never Lay Me Down to Sleep

Crary, Jonathan. *24/7: Late Capitalism and the Ends of Sleep*. New York: Verso, 2014.

Kress, Nancy. *Beggars in Spain*. Livonia, MI: Eos, 2004.

Popnonymous

Boshier, Rosa. "Lil Miquela Is a Queer Woman of Color. Too Bad She Isn't Real." *Bitch Media*, December 6, 2019. www.bitchmedia.org/article/who-is-lil-miquela-racial-implications -of-simulated-influencers-of-color.

Rojek, Chris. *Presumed Intimacy: Parasocial Interaction in Media, Society and Celebrity Culture*. Cambridge, UK: Polity Press, 2015.

ACKNOWLEDGMENTS

Much like the future is built by an incredible number of people, so was this book you're holding.

This book only exists because of Matt Lubchansky and Sophie Goldstein. I mean that pretty literally. I had been asked about writing a book based on *Flash Forward* for years, and I always demurred—I couldn't figure out how to translate the podcast format into a satisfying textual experience, one that felt as strange and experimental as the show. It took Matt's and Sophie's brains to actually come up with this specific formulation. Back in 2016 (which feels like hundreds of years ago now), they reached out and said, "Hey, what about comics?" I can't say enough about how incredible it has been to work with Matt and Sophie on this. They're both absurdly talented artists (as you saw in the "Popnonymous" and "Never Lay Me Down to Sleep" chapters) and also dream collaborators—patient, kind, funny, flexible, and always willing to walk me through things I didn't understand.

Thanks to the artists who contributed their work to this collection and brought each chapter to life: Matt and Sophie, of course, Julia Gfrörer, Zach Weinersmith, Chris Jones, Box Brown, Ben Passmore, Kate Sheridan, John Jennings, Blue Delliquanti, Ziyed Y. Ayoub, Amelia Onorato, Sophia Foster-Dimino, and Maki Naro. Go buy all their work, they're rock stars. Thanks also to Lexi Pandell for her intrepid fact-checking.

Thanks to every person who has ever spoken to me for *Flash Forward*. Right now, that's over five hundred sources, and by the time you read this it will be more. The podcast (and this book) are illuminated by the light of experts, and I couldn't be more thankful for their time and insights. And of course, to the listeners who've kept this little independent-show-that-could going over the years.

Huge thanks to Gary Morris, my intrepid agent, who from the very first time we met understood the kind of work I wanted to be making. Lots of publishers were scared off by the format of this idea, but Gary stuck with it. Thanks to Laura Dozier at Abrams, who also immediately understood what we were going for and took a chance on an admittedly strange concept, and to the art team at Abrams, who have made this book look as good as it does.

Thank you, Quinn Heraty, who gets her own special paragraph because she's that good. I am the only person I know who regularly says: "I just talked to my lawyer for an hour and I feel SO much better."

Thanks to the friends who have encouraged me along the way: Annalee Newitz, who got *Flash Forward* started in the first place; Ed Yong; Liz Neeley and Rahawa Haile, who have kept my mental boat afloat throughout this process; Ace Ratcliff, Eler de Grey, Helen Rosner, Lux Alptraum, Stan Alcorn; and all the Slack and group text friends that I'm already panicking will feel left out in this section. And to the fuzzy one, Moro, who forces me to leave the house and look at the sky.

And last but certainly not least, thanks to Robert, the person I most want to take on the future with. And not just because you're a borderline prepper. Love you.

Editor: Laura Dozier
Designer: Charice Silverman
Managing Editor: Mary O'Mara
Production Manager: Alison Gervais

Cataloging-in-Publication Data has been applied for and may be obtained from the Library of Congress.

ISBN 978-1-4197-4547-8

Printed and bound in China
10 9 8 7 6 5 4 3 2 1

Abrams ComicArts books are available at special discounts when purchased in quantity for premiums and promotions as well as fundraising or educational use. Special editions can also be created to specification. For details, contact specialsales@abramsbooks.com or the address below.

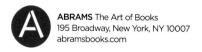

ABRAMS The Art of Books
195 Broadway, New York, NY 10007
abramsbooks.com